South Australia
a Lonely Planet Australia guide

Denis O'Byrne

D0067930

South Australia

1st edition

Published by
Lonely Planet Publications
Head Office: PO Box 617, Hawthorn, Vic 3122, Australia
Branches: 155 Filbert St, Suite 251, Oakland, CA 94607, USA
               10 Barley Mow Passage, Chiswick, London W4 4PH, UK
               71 bis rue du Cardinal Lemoine, 75005 Paris, France

Printed by
SNP Printing Pte Ltd, Singapore

Photographs by
Michelle Coxall
Greg Herriman
Richard I'Anson
Richard Nebesky
Denis O'Byrne

Front cover: Vineyard in the Clare Valley (Denis O'Byrne)
Title page: Ruins of Kanyaka Homestead, near Hawker (Michelle Coxall)

Published
September 1996

Although the authors and publisher have tried to make the information as accurate as possible, they accept no responsibility for any loss, injury or inconvenience sustained by any person using this book.

National Library of Australia Cataloguing in Publication Data

O'Byrne, Denis, 1947-
    South Australia

    1st ed.
    Includes index.
    ISBN 0 86442 383 7.

    1. South Australia – Guidebooks. I. Title. (Series :
    Lonely Planet Australia guide).

919.4230463

text & maps © Lonely Planet 1996
photos © photographers as indicated 1996

Denis O'Byrne

Denis was born in the Adelaide Hills and raised at Robe, in the state's south-east. He left South Australia when he was 17 and has since lived in various places, returning home often to visit family in Adelaide, or to go fishing on Eyre Peninsula. He describes his career as a zig-zag path leading nowhere, having worked as a surveyor, plant operator, national park ranger, builder's labourer, building consultant and freelance writer, among other things. Denis isn't sure whether Lonely Planet represents a zig or a zag or perhaps both; he worked on *Outback Australia* and *Vanuatu* before heading for South Australia to do this guide.

From the Author

Many people provided advice and assistance during the research phase of this book and I'm grateful to them all. In particular, Phil Brennan of the Department of Environment & Natural Resources gave enthusiastic support, while Adam Best of Recreation SA generously provided a pile of maps and other items.

A special mention to: Peter Caust of the Underground Bookshop in Coober Pedy; Peter Erxleben of the Pine Grove Motel in Ceduna; the Friends of the Heysen Trail; Jenny Genrich of the Ceduna Travel Centre; Rosemary Gower of the Barmera Travel Centre; Evelyn Gray of Bicycle SA; Sheree Hannam of Eyre Travel in Port Lincoln; Brett Knuckey of Birdwood; Barry and Jane Matthew of the Bunkhaus in Nuriootpa; Harvey Neal of Adelaide; Noel Saxby of the SA Police; Doug Sprigg of Arkaroola; Anne Weddle of the Clare Tourist Centre; and Rugby Wilson of the Blue Gum Café in Kingscote.

Thanks also go to members of my family for willingly lending a hand whenever I requested it, particularly my brother Peter and my niece, Kristy, who proved an expert on Adelaide's nightlife, among other things. My sister Jenny and her friend Dick did a good job steering me around the Barossa wineries, even if the final few were a trifle blurry.

Last, but by no means least, I'd like to thank Allan O'Keefe, my business partner, for holding the fort and retaining his sense of humour during my interminable absences on this project.

From the Publisher

This 1st edition of *South Australia* was edited by Suzi Petkovski and Jane Marks. Jacqui Saunders coordinated the mapping and illustration, assisted by Jenny Jones, Tamsin Wilson and Tony Fankhauser, while Ann Jeffree steered the book through the perils of layout. Illustrations were a joint effort by Jacqui and Ann, with help from Anthony Phelan. Thanks to the cast of thousands (well almost) who lent a hand – Kirsten John, Janet Austin and Lindsay Brown in editing, Brigitte Barta, Jane Fitzpatrick, Rowan McKinnon, Anne Mulvaney and Mary Neighbour in proofing, and Michelle Stamp and Tamsin Wilson in the final check. David Kemp designed the cover and, last but not least, Kerrie Williams whipped up the index.

Warning & Request

Things change – prices go up, schedules change, good places go bad and bad places go bankrupt. Nothing stays the same. So if you find things better or worse, recently opened or long since closed, please write and tell us and help make the next edition better.

Your letters will be used to help update future editions and, where possible, important changes will also be included in an Update section in reprints.

We greatly appreciate all information that is sent to us by travellers. Back at Lonely Planet, we employ a hard-working readers' letters team to sort through the many letters we receive. The best ones will be rewarded with a free copy of the next edition or another Lonely Planet guide if you prefer. We give away lots of books, but, unfortunately, not every letter/postcard receives one.

Contents

Map Legend

BOUNDARIES

·━·━·━·━·━·	International Boundary
━··━··━··━	Regional Boundary

ROUTES

━━━━━━	Freeway
━━━━━━	Highway
━━━━━━	Major Road
━ ━ ━ ━	Unsealed Road or Track
━━━━━━	City Road
━━━━━━	City Street
┼┼┼┼┼┼┼	Railway
━━━━━━	Underground Railway
━━━━━━	Tram
━ ━ ━ ━	Walking Track
• • • • • •	Walking Tour
- - - - - -	Ferry Route
┼┼┼┼┼┼┼┼	Cable Car or Chairlift

AREA FEATURES

	Parks
	Built-Up Area
	Pedestrian Mall
	Market
+ + + + + +	Cemetery
	Reef
	Aboriginal Land
⌒⌒ ⌒	Mountain Range

HYDROGRAPHIC FEATURES

	Coastline
	River, Creek
- - - -	Intermittent River or Creek
━≫━≫━	Rapids, Waterfalls
	Lake, Intermittent Lake
	Canal
⊥ ⊥ ⊥	Swamp, Salt Lake

SYMBOLS

✪	CAPITAL	National Capital	◔	⛽	Embassy, Petrol Station
◉	Capital	Regional Capital	✈	✝	Airport, Airfield
◍	CITY	Major City	▭	✿	Swimming Pool, Gardens
●	City	City	❖	🦘	Shopping Centre, Zoo
●	Town	Town	⚲	⚑	Winery or Vineyard, Golf Course
●	Village	Village	←	**A25**	One Way Street, Route Number
▪ ▼		Place to Stay, Place to Eat	🏛	⚱	Stately Home, Monument
☕ 🍺		Cafe, Pub or Bar	🏛	✗	Castle, Mine
✉ ☎		Post Office, Telephone	⌒	⌂	Cave, Hut or Chalet
❶ ⑤		Tourist Information, Bank	▲	※	Mountain or Hill, Lookout
◗ ℗		Transport, Parking	🔆	⌅	Lighthouse, Shipwreck
🏛 ⌂		Museum, Youth Hostel	)(	◎	Pass, Spring
⚏ ⚐		Caravan Park, Camping Ground	🦆	🏄	Beach, Surf Beach
✚ ⊞		Church, Cathedral		∴	Archaeological Site or Ruins
☪ ✡		Mosque, Synagogue			Ancient or City Wall
⌗ 卍		Buddhist Temple, Hindu Temple			Cliff or Escarpment, Tunnel
✚ ★		Hospital, Police Station			Railway Station

Note: not all symbols displayed above appear in this book

Introduction

South Australia epitomises the 'sunburnt country' and 'wide brown land' of the nation's literature and legend. It's by far the driest state, and as for space ... 80% of its vast area is home to only 1% of the population. If you want to experience the mystical outback there are few better places to do it.

There's a lot more to South Australia, however, than wide horizons. Its 3700-km coastline varies from sheltered bays to some of the country's finest surf beaches. Inland is the stunning scenery of the 800-km-long Mt Lofty and Flinders ranges made famous by local artist Hans Heysen. And meandering through the state on its final 650 km to the sea is the mighty Murray, which has all the romance and atmosphere of big rivers anywhere. Paddle-steamers still ply what was once the inland highway of Australia.

In terms of outdoor activity, you can do just about anything in South Australia (even ice-skating, snow-skiing and tobogganing, at a huge facility in Adelaide). You can bushwalk in forested hills, among arid ranges and along pristine coastline. You can climb soaring cliffs in the Flinders Ranges, cycle the 700-km Mawson Trail and go wilderness camping far (and I mean *far*) from the sight and sound of civilisation.

If you prefer the water, there's swimming, windsurfing, scuba diving, fishing, canoeing and sea kayaking; you can go cave-rafting under the Nullarbor Plain, or surfing at world-famous Cactus Beach. If it's wildlife you want to see, you can expect to find whales, seals, penguins, koalas and kangaroos, among others, all in their natural surrounds.

You can enjoy most of these activities in

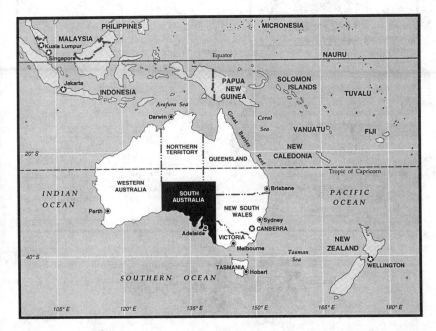

conservation areas; South Australia has 21% of its entire area under some form of official conservation management. The conservation areas range from national parks to game reserves, where you can go hunting in season. Best known of the parks is the Flinders Ranges National Park. It's a respectable size at 94,500 hectares, but small compared with the huge national parks and reserves in the state's far north.

Conveniently close to the capital city of Adelaide is the Barossa Valley, a world-class producer of shiraz and one of Australia's premier wine-producing districts. Other excellent wine districts in South Australia include Coonawarra and Padthaway, the Clare Valley, McLaren Vale and the Adelaide Hills. Complementing this is a wealth of fine restaurants, all selling fresh local tucker.

South Australia's rich cultural heritage includes ancient rock engravings (in fact, the oldest in the world) and the traditions of its early German and Cornish settlers. Thanks to the biennial Adelaide Festival of Arts, civilised Adelaide is recognised as one of Australia's cultural capitals. The city has many wonderful Victorian buildings that have escaped redevelopment, as well as a lively visual and performing arts scene.

Allow plenty of time to look around this big state with its many diverse attractions. South Australia is a great place. Enjoy it!

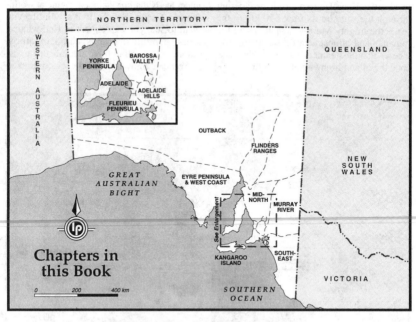

Facts about South Australia

HISTORY
Aboriginal Settlement

Australian Aboriginal (which literally means 'indigenous') society has the longest continuous cultural history in the world. Although mystery shrouds many aspects of Australian prehistory, it is almost certain that the ancestors of today's Aboriginal people came across the sea from South-East Asia at least 50,000 years ago.

Although much of Australia is now arid, those early migrants found a much wetter continent, with vast forests and lakes teeming with food resources. The fauna included giant flightless birds, three-metre-tall kangaroos and wombat-like mammals the size of beef cows. Apart from a few carnivorous predators and poisonous snakes, the environment was relatively non-threatening.

Because of these favourable conditions, archaeologists suggest that within a few thousand years the Aboriginal people had populated most of the continent except the drier central regions, which were occupied 25,000 years ago. The earliest known relics of the Aboriginal occupation of South Australia (SA) are rock carvings near Olary which have been dated at 43,000 years. This makes them 16,000 years older than the Neanderthal carvings of Europe.

Aboriginal Society

At the time of European settlement, SA was thought to have been populated by between 10,000 and 15,000 Aboriginal people living in 43 tribal groups. About half lived in the temperate, well-watered area between Gulf St Vincent and the Victorian border.

While the arid inland was sparsely populated, few parts were permanently uninhabited. Even the hostile Simpson Desert in the extreme north-east was occupied on a year-round basis. Here the people survived thanks to water obtained from scattered permanent wells, along with an encyclopaedic knowledge of the desert's resources.

The Aboriginal people lived in extended family groups, or clans, within defined areas of land. Contrary to popular belief they did not wander aimlessly in search of food and water. Rather, almost every facet of their lives was governed by millennia of ritual and tradition, with religious requirements being a powerful influence. In fact, the overwhelming force in Aboriginal life was the obligation to observe laws handed down by their spirit ancestors, who had created the landscape and all life during the so-called Dreamtime.

The traditional role of the men was that of hunter, tool-maker and custodian of male law; the women gathered and prepared food, and reared the children. There was also female law and ritual for which the women were responsible. Ultimately, the shared effort of men and women ensured the continuation of their social system.

Knowledge and skills developed over thousands of years enabled the Aboriginal people to utilise their environment to the

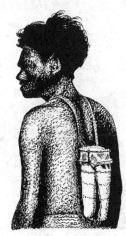

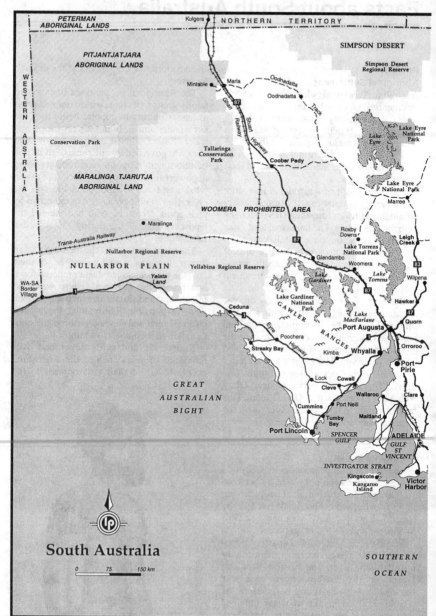

South Australia

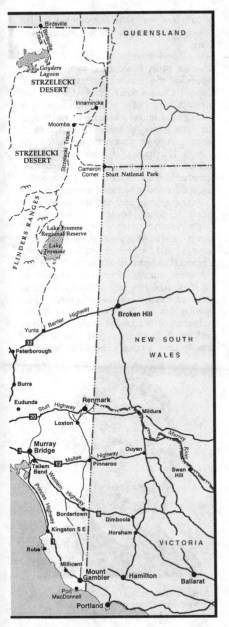

fullest. An intimate understanding of animal behaviour and plant ecology ensured that serious food shortages were rare. On the Murray River and associated wetlands, food sources were harvested using canoes made from the bark of river red gums; so-called 'canoe trees' (those showing the huge scars of bark removal) are still common in these areas.

The only major modification of the landscape practised by Aboriginal people was the seasonal and selective burning of undergrowth in the forests, dead grass on the plains and perennial tussock grasses of desert areas. This promoted the growth of fire-dependent food plants, while new shoots attracted game animals such as kangaroos. It also reduced the likelihood of large-scale fires and made the country easier to travel over.

The boomerang and spear were used throughout the continent; different techniques were adapted to the environment and the species being hunted. On the Coorong, long crescent-shaped lines of rock were built from the shore to catch fish as the water level receded. On Eyre Peninsula, the men went spear fishing at night in shallow water using burning brands as torches. Bird snaring was carried out from wickerwork hides in the South-East.

The Aboriginal people also traded goods across Australia. The trade routes followed the paths of Dreamtime ancestors; one ran from Lake Alexandrina through the Flinders Ranges and south-west Queensland to the Gulf of Carpentaria. Many of the items traded had great spiritual significance. Others were practical commodities such as *pituri* (a drug), and certain types of stone and wood for making tools or weapons. The longer trade routes passed through 'exchange centres', where not only goods but songs and dances were traded.

The Europeans

As far as is known, the first non-Aborigine to see SA's coast was the Dutch navigator Francois Thijssen aboard *Gulden Zeepaard*, in 1627. While on his way from Holland to Batavia (present-day Jakarta), he detoured to explore the coast as far east as Nuyts Archipelago, south of Ceduna.

Next, in 1792, came the French ships *Recherche* and *L'Esperance*, under Rear-Admiral Bruni d'Entrecasteaux. He likewise confined himself to the far west coast, describing it as so sterile and uniform 'that the most fertile imagination could find nothing to say about it'.

The first British explorer on the scene was Lieutenant James Grant, in 1800. He sailed along the far south-east coast and named several key features, including Mt Gambier and Mt Schank. This still left most of the SA coast as an unknown quantity as far as Europeans were concerned.

Matthew Flinders The English were very keen to beat the French in being the first to chart the huge unknown chunks of Australian coastline. They chose a young Royal Navy lieutenant, Matthew Flinders, to undertake the daunting task.

Flinders left England in mid-1801 in command of the *Investigator* and reached Fowlers Bay, 125 km west of Ceduna, the following January. From there he sailed east and charted and named Spencer Gulf, Gulf St Vincent and Kangaroo Island, but failed to recognise the mouth of the Murray River, which was disguised by sandbars and surf. Generally, his surveying work proved to be so accurate that much of the data he collected is still in use today.

On 8 April 1802, Flinders unexpectedly met the French ship *Le Géographe* anchored in a bay – which he called Encounter Bay – just west of the Murray mouth. The French, under Captain Nicholas Baudin, had sailed from the east, examining the coast as they went. They likewise unknowingly passed the Murray's outlet, which was to remain a mystery until Charles Sturt revealed it 28 years later.

Flinders informed sealers of the abundant wildlife he'd seen on Kangaroo Island, and in 1803 the hunting of kangaroos, wallabies and seals for their skins commenced there. He had ended speculation of a north-south channel through Australia, but the prospect of an inland sea in the vast outback fuelled debate and lured expeditions for decades to come.

Charles Sturt Determined to unravel the riddle of the westward flowing rivers, Captain Charles Sturt left Sydney for the inland late in 1829. At the Murrumbidgee River he assembled a whale-boat and took to the water, rowing downstream until he met a large, unknown waterway he called the Murray. Continuing for a further 26 days, he arrived on the shores of Lake Alexandrina. Here he landed to make a survey, rhapsodising at the country he found around him.

Referring to the area near the future site of Adelaide, Sturt wrote: '... the colonist might venture with every prospect of success, and in whose valleys the exile might hope to build for himself and for his family a peaceful and prosperous home.'

Such comments attracted the attention of the National Colonisation Society, a radical group of English colonial reformers. Their opinion was that previous British colonies had been poorly founded, mainly because of problems with convicts and land distribution. Instead, a colony should be based on

Explorer Charles Sturt solved the mystery of the westward flowing rivers by following the Murray (which he named) to the sea

planned free emigration and land sales rather than free grants.

The theorists believed that by controlling the sale of land – it would be surveyed before being sold – they could balance the flow of labour and capital, thus avoiding an unproductive and unseemly free-for-all. Money from land sales would be used for public works and to pay for the passage of poor but energetic young emigrants, who would be supported by the fund until they found employment. In this way, such a colony would be self-supporting, with no need for subsidy from the British Government. From the reports of Flinders and Sturt, it seemed SA was an ideal place to put their theories into practice.

Colonisation

In 1834 the British Parliament passed the SA Colonisation Act, which was inspired by the ideas of the reformers. It allowed the settlement of around 800,000 sq km, but no convicts would be admitted under any circumstances. This made SA the only Australian colony to be established entirely by free settlers.

The British Government refused to take any responsibility for the new colony in terms of financial backing or carrying out its reformist charter. A Board of Commissioners was set up to control emigration and land sales, and to undertake planning. In its first six years SA had a hybrid government made up of representatives of the Board and the British Government.

The first official settlement was established in 1836 at Kingscote on Kangaroo Island. However, the colonial surveyor-general, Colonel William Light, rejected Kingscote and several mainland sites for the capital, selecting Adelaide instead. The first governor, Captain John Hindmarsh, landed at present-day Glenelg (a suburb of Adelaide) on 28 December 1836, and proclaimed the Province of SA later that day.

Despite its optimistic birth, the colony was on the verge of collapse two years later. Emigrants were unemployed and farming had barely started owing to the lack of surveyed land.

The second governor, Lieutenant George Gawler, arrived in 1838 and, being more energetic than his predecessor, instigated a vigorous programme of land surveys.

By 1841 about 1000 sq km had been made available for settlement and Adelaide had grown from a collection of huts into something approximating a town. However, the construction of numerous public buildings and other works had a disastrous effect on the colonial coffers.

Gawler was recalled in 1841 and replaced by the third governor, George Grey, who immediately made himself unpopular by tightening purse strings and reducing the salaries of public servants. Supported migration ceased, employment was hard to come by and SA plunged into its first recession.

But Grey's parsimonious ways had the desired effect – economic life was improving by 1843. Some wool was being exported and wheat farms were producing a surplus, although labour for harvesting was in short supply. Migration recommenced and the population rapidly increased; the 1844 census showed that SA had a European population of 17,366. Also, discoveries of rich copper lodes at Kapunda and Burra were a tremendous boost to confidence as well as the economy.

By the time Grey departed in 1845 the infant colony was at last on its feet. Because the land was largely owned by South Australians, the profits stayed in the colony and contributed to community wealth.

A decade later things were looking good and getting better. The colony was one of the world's major producers of copper, and pastoral leases had reached the northern Flinders Ranges. In 1850, SA produced 18,200 tonnes of wheat and 4700 tonnes of copper metal; 26,000 hectares were under cultivation and there were one million sheep and 100,000 cattle. A year later, the human population excluding Aboriginal people was 63,700, a quarter of whom lived in Adelaide.

Early Emigrants

The first emigrants to arrive in SA were mainly poor English, Scottish and Irish people with agricultural or trade experience. About 12,000 emigrated from these areas in the first four years of settlement. There was a deliberate policy of selecting young married persons so as to encourage natural increase and foster interest in the future of the colony. Throughout the history of SA, most of its emigrants have come from the UK and Ireland.

Another important group were the 800 German farmers and artisans who emigrated between 1838 and 1841. This group was largely composed of Lutherans who disapproved of what was happening to their church in Prussia, and who'd decided to come to SA to escape persecution. One of the first villages they established was Hahndorf, in the Adelaide Hills.

A second group of 5400 hard-working Germans arrived by 1850, with many more to follow throughout the '50s. They settled mainly in the Adelaide Hills and the Barossa Valley, where some noticed the similarity of the soils and climates to wine-growing areas of their homeland. Vineyards were established and so the SA wine industry was born.

Following the discovery of copper at Kapunda and Burra, then at Moonta and Kadina, a new wave of emigrants came from Cornwall. They were skilled miners and builders, and developed a strong subculture in the areas they settled.

The Explorers

SA's first 30 years saw a number of important exploring achievements. Between 1839 and 1841, Edward John Eyre made the first traverses of the Flinders Ranges; his enthusiastic reports of potential agricultural land in the Mid-North gave impetus to the settlement of that region. In 1840 he set out from Port Augusta to explore the west coast, suffering appalling hardship in the five months it took him to reach Albany in Western Australia.

In 1839, Charles Bonney drove the first herd of cattle from Melbourne to Adelaide via Mt Gambier. His route proved a good alternative to the Murray River stock route from NSW, where bloody clashes between drovers and Aborigines were common. It also opened up the Lower South-East, which became one of the colony's finest agricultural areas.

Five years later, Charles Sturt set off to look for the inland sea. With the courage of his convictions he took a whale-boat with him, but after 18 months of terrible privation he was forced to abandon it in a waterless red sea of stones and sandhills. If nothing else he had discovered the Simpson Desert, one of Australia's most inhospitable regions.

Perhaps SA's greatest explorer was John MacDouall Stuart, who made several epic forays into the arid interior between 1858 and 1862. His most famous feat took place in 1862 when, on the third attempt, he succeeded in crossing the continent from south to north. Stuart's heroic efforts opened up a route for a telegraph line between Adelaide and Darwin, and led to SA taking control of the Northern Territory (NT).

The Copper Rush

Copper has been mined in about 300 places in SA, but only a handful of these have had any economic significance. The four major exceptions helped save SA from bankruptcy on more than one occasion.

Mines were developed on rich deposits at Kapunda (1844), Burra (1845), Moonta (1859) and Kadina (1861), all of which contained oxidised ore assaying up to 30% copper. Other ore bodies were worked in the Flinders Ranges (the Blinman mine was significant) but the lack of water, isolation and distance from the sea made them generally marginal propositions.

By the 1870s, SA had replaced Cornwall as the major copper producer in the British Empire – a major reason why so many Cornish miners emigrated to the colony. Although Kapunda and Burra both closed down in the late '70s, Moonta and Kadina were worked until 1923. The latter were big mines by world standards of the day and supported the largest towns in the colony outside Adelaide. The thousands of Cornish families who lived there gave the area the nickname 'Little Cornwall', which has stuck to this day. The smelters at nearby Wallaroo were on a vast scale; they contained 30 furnaces and produced 40 tonnes of copper each day.

Copper made many people in SA rich. It also left a legacy of fine public buildings in the mining towns and Adelaide. Another beneficiary was the University of Adelaide, founded in 1874 with grants made from mine profits. It was the first in Australia to admit women to degree courses.

Wheat & Wool

In 1865, SA had half of all the land under wheat in Australia, however, overcropping had already begun to exhaust the soils in the Adelaide Hills and Fleurieu Peninsula. When more land was opened up in the north in the '70s, there was a mass exodus from these areas. It wasn't until 1897 that another colony (Victoria) sowed more wheat than SA.

Although wheat growing was perceived as a solid foundation for the colony's prosperity, there was much public debate on the wisdom of allowing large estates to outbid and thus limit settlement by small farmers. The Strangways Act of 1869 eased this situation by allowing credit terms, whereas previously land could only be bought with cash.

The Strangways Act ushered in a wheat boom which resulted in the creation of many towns, particularly in the Mid-North and southern Flinders Ranges. It also fostered the development of new railways and port facilities. By 1880 the Willochra Plains in the central Flinders Ranges were under the plough, and there was enthusiastic trumpeting of 'a rich golden harvest' extending all the way to the NT. However, sanity returned with the onset of drought in the mid-1880s.

If wheat was SA's foundation, wool was its wealth, at least for a large number of colonists. Generally it was sheep farmers who opened up the country for settlement, particularly in areas distant from Adelaide.

As with wheat growers, the first pastoralists had little if any understanding of the natural environment. They had a tendency to overestimate carrying capacity, which led to gross overstocking. The fact that no pasture was kept in reserve brought ruin to many in the 1865 drought.

The wool industry, then as now, was based on merinos; starting in the 1840s, South Australian breeders have developed a strain that is better suited to semi-arid conditions, while retaining the fineness of fleece for which merinos are famous.

South Australia has 18 times more sheep than people. Wool remains the second biggest agricultural earner, after grain.

Goyder's Line As silly as it now seems, the early wheat farmers were convinced that 'rain follows the plough'; all they had to do was clear the native vegetation, till the soil, and rainfall would increase. Talk about wishful thinking! Still, a run of good seasons in the 1850s and early '60s confirmed their belief as the farming frontier pushed northwards.

Unfortunately, reality was about to rear its ugly head in the form of the 1864-65 drought, which devastated pastoralists and wheat growers alike. Sent to report on the disaster, the colonial surveyor-general George Goyder drew a line on the map which showed the northern limit of rainfall in 1865. Fortuitously, this approximated the 250 mm isohyet, which roughly coincides with the southern limit of the saltbush country.

After further droughts, particularly in the 1880s, 'Goyder's Line' was accepted as the true demarcation between cereal farming and pastoralism. In recent times, however, new hardier varieties of wheat have allowed farms to push closer to the 200 mm isohyet.

Devastation of the Aboriginal People

South Australia's Aboriginal population had suffered the first ill-effects of European settlement long before 1836. Starting with smallpox soon after the arrival of the First Fleet in 1788, epidemics originating in Sydney moved west and swept like bushfires down the Murray. In 1830, Sturt noticed great gaps in the age structure of the Aborigines he met, remarking how obvious it was that death had been busy among them. Also, sealers based on Kangaroo Island had been raiding the Encounter Bay area for women as early as 1803.

British colonies had a poor record in their relationships with indigenous people, who invariably suffered greatly as a result of settlement. The British Colonial Secretary had made it clear to SA's Board of Commissioners that this new colony was to be different – as in all other things, it would provide a model for others to follow. It was hoped that, in comparison with what was happening in neighbouring colonies, '… the colonisation of South Australia will be an advent of mercy to the native tribes'.

One of the Commissioners' humanitarian principles was to appoint 'Protectors of Aborigines' (the explorer Edward John Eyre was an early one) to ensure the welfare of Aboriginal people. They recognised that the indigenous inhabitants had rights over the land, which would only be occupied with their permission. Various other high-minded ideals were espoused by the commissioners, but in practice these were generally ignored.

The Aboriginal people often violently objected to the takeover of their land, and there were frequent bloody clashes in several areas, notably around the Murray River and Eyre Peninsula. Although the Aborigines landed some telling blows, in the end their boomerangs and spears couldn't compete with bullets and poisoned flour. There are several recorded massacres. One occurred on the Birdsville Track when a large group of men, women and children were shot in retaliation for the spearing of a bullock.

In the early 1840s Governor Gawler opened ration distribution depots in an attempt to pacify the Aboriginal people – he hoped that handouts of food would compensate for their loss of land and resources. Generally, the depots were at remote police stations set up to protect settlers and overlanders from Aboriginal attack.

Twenty years later the emphasis of most ration depots shifted from appeasement to providing succour for a people devastated by disease and deprivation. Aboriginal populations in settled areas declined dramatically, although those in remoter parts were probably still largely unaffected. Only 40 years after settlement it was estimated that the colony's Aboriginal population had fallen by 50%. By this time entire groups had become extinct, particularly in the areas closest to Adelaide.

While the north and north-east were eventually taken up by pastoralists, with the usual appalling consequences for the Aboriginal people, the north-west was never settled. Apart from the atomic bomb tests at Maralinga, the Aborigines were left to continue their traditional lives relatively undisturbed.

Self-Government to Federation

SA was initially governed by a body made up of representatives of the Board of Commissioners and the British Government. However, the financial problems of the early 1840s upset the British Government, which had to pay off the debts. As a punitive measure, it abolished the Board in 1842 and made SA an ordinary Crown colony.

In 1856, a new bill created the SA Parliament (with executive ministers responsible to the elected representatives) and gave SA the most democratic constitution of any Australian colony.

Recession came again in the mid-1860s and once again copper helped stave off bankruptcy. Apart from this hiccup, prosperity continued right through the 1850s until the 1880s. This was reflected in the growth of the transport system.

By 1860 a steam railway had opened to Kapunda; 30 years later, SA had 2700 km of railway connecting Adelaide to places such as Oodnadatta in the north, Melbourne (the first Adelaide to Melbourne train ran in 1887), and Cockburn near the New South Wales (NSW) border on the Broken Hill route. There were also 3200 km of macadamised roads.

Steam navigation commenced on the Murray River in 1853, with at least 100 boats engaged in the river trade by 1878.

Following the exploration feats of John MacDouall Stuart, SA gained control of the NT (previously part of NSW) and, in 1870, commenced work on an overland telegraph line to Darwin. This ambitious undertaking was completed in a mere two years (there were no unions then) and linked SA to the world telegraph network.

The drought of the early 1880s heralded a general recession that was to last until 1900. Public debt mounted, and in desperation the government became the first in Australia to introduce a tax on income. However, as the taxes proved inadequate, the government decided to pin its hopes on new agricultural developments. These offered new farmers blocks of land and government loans, and resulted in major irrigation schemes on the Murray and the draining of vast seasonal swamps in the South-East. Also, the use of superphosphate fertiliser meant that crops could be grown on previously exhausted soils.

A number of reforms were passed by the SA Parliament during this period. They included the establishment of Australia's first Juvenile Court in 1890 and the granting of free education in 1891. In 1895, SA became the first Australian colony to recognise women's right to vote in parliamentary elections, and the first place in the world to allow women to stand for parliament.

Early 20th Century

South Australia experienced slow but steady growth following amalgamation of the colonies into the Commonwealth of Australia in 1901.

Manufacturing became increasingly important, particularly in the field of heavy engineering. The Port Pirie smelter, built to treat the lead-zinc ore of Broken Hill, was enlarged during WWI. It was soon producing 10% of the world's lead, as well as silver and zinc.

The war was a time of division in SA, with patriotic fervour on the one hand and shameful persecution of German emigrants on the other. Before 1914 the state had numerous German (or German-sounding) place-names, but in a fit of zeal these were either anglicised or replaced. Many were changed back during the centennial celebrations in 1936, when the huge contribution of German settlers to the development of SA was officially recognised.

After WWI, returned soldiers were offered blocks of undeveloped land on the Murray River and in marginal areas, but the scheme wasn't a great success.

The early 1920s brought brief prosperity before a four-year drought led into the Great Depression, which hit with a crunch in 1929 and didn't really end until WWII. All the states suffered during this period, but SA suffered worst of all: in 1931 over 70,000 unemployed out of a total population of 575,000 were dependent on welfare. South Australians fled across the border in droves. Despite this, 24% of wage-earners were still out of work in 1933.

What's in a Name?
South Australians are often referred to as 'Crow-eaters' by people of other states. The reason is lost in time, but it may have had something to do with SA's dry climate and infertile soil. Perhaps a South Australian with a crow to eat was considered more fortunate than most! ■

Australia's longest-serving state premier, Tom Playford, took office in 1938 and presided over 26 years of growth. During WWII the first pipeline was built from Morgan to Whyalla, ship building commenced at Whyalla, and the Leigh Creek coalfields were opened up for electricity production. In 1948 the 40-hour working week became a reality, and work started on the Woomera rocket range, in the outback north-west of Port Augusta.

Late 20th Century

Industrial development quickened during WWII and the momentum continued into the 1950s. Encouraged by a booming market and protective tariffs on imported goods, the number of factories increased dramatically. The state was now changing from a rural economy to a predominantly industrial one.

Under the shrewd guidance of Tom Playford, SA captured a relatively large share of the national growth in industry and overseas migration. There were so many new arrivals that in 1955 Adelaide gained the satellite city of Elizabeth, which mainly housed migrants from the UK.

After WWII there was yet another rural revolution involving 'soldier settlers', this time on the infertile soils of higher rainfall areas. Previously these had been considered unsuitable for farming, but it was found that they could be turned into productive pastures with the addition of trace elements such as zinc and potassium. In this way a further 500,000 hectares were added to the state's agricultural land.

In 1965 the Playford Government lost office to the Labor Party, ushering in an era of rapid change. One of the first reforms was an act prohibiting racial discrimination, the first in Australia.

By this time the state's economy and population growth were stagnating, which showed up the shortcomings of an economic base dependent on the manufacture of motor vehicles and household appliances.

Fuelled by overseas competition, the deepening industrial recession saw the last ship to be built at Whyalla roll down the slipway in 1978. At about the same time, plans for a second satellite city, Monarto, were shelved.

Although the '70s were a difficult time for SA, the Labor Government under controversial premier Don Dunstan could claim several important achievements, particularly in the arts. These included the creation of the SA Film Corporation (1972) and the State Opera of SA (1976), and the opening of the Adelaide Festival Theatre (1973).

Dunstan also presided over several major reforms, such as the Sexual Discrimination Act of 1975. Other reforms improved legislation dealing with women's issues, capital punishment (it was banned) and Aboriginal land rights.

Hope for an economic recovery came with the discovery of a huge deposit of uranium, copper, silver and gold at Roxby Downs in 1976, coupled with continued discoveries of oil and gas in the Cooper Basin throughout the '70s. Employment growth through industrial development was a major goal of the Liberal Government, which took over from Labor at the 1979 election.

The mining industry generally prospered throughout the 1980s, although it was coming under increasing fire from environmentalists. However, older industries such as the manufacture of motor vehicles and household appliances, and steelmaking at Whyalla, were faring poorly. By 1989 the rural sector too was in crisis, through a combination of drought, soaring interest rates and tumbling commodity prices.

Australia slipped into a general recession following a development and investment boom in the late 1980s; as in the Great Depression of the '30s, its effects were felt worst in SA. In 1995 the state was still in recession, although agriculture was looking bright thanks to a bumper cereal harvest, burgeoning wine sales (everyone was drowning their sorrows) and improving wool prices. The other major bright spots were aquaculture, seafood processing, mining and the development of high-tech industries.

Aboriginal Land Rights

In 1966 the South Australian Government made the first move of any state this century to give Aboriginal people title to their land. This involved the creation of the Aboriginal Lands Trust, in which was vested title to the missions and reserves still operating in SA. These lands were then leased back to their Aboriginal occupants, with repeated rights of renewal.

The Pitjantjatjara Land Rights Act came into effect in 1981, and gave freehold title over a vast area in the far north-west to the Anungu Pitjantjatjaraku (Pitjantjatjara people). A further 76,000 sq km, which had been taken over by the Federal Government as part of the Maralinga project, was returned to its traditional owners in 1984.

Land held under Aboriginal freehold title cannot be sold or resumed. Entry by 'outsiders' is restricted – you need a permit from the appropriate council – and no development of any kind can take place without permission from the traditional owners.

GEOGRAPHY

South Australia covers 984,400 sq km, or 12.8% of the area of Australia. The fourth largest state, it extends 720 km eastwards from the West Australian border to the Victoria, New South Wales and Queensland borders, and between 240 and 910 km northwards from the Southern Ocean to the NT border.

The state's coastline stretches for 3700 km and includes two major indentations: Gulf St Vincent and Spencer Gulf, both of which are shallow and support important fisheries. There are around 100 islands, the largest by far being Australia's third largest island, Kangaroo Island.

The topography of SA mainly consists of vast plains and low relief. More than 80% of

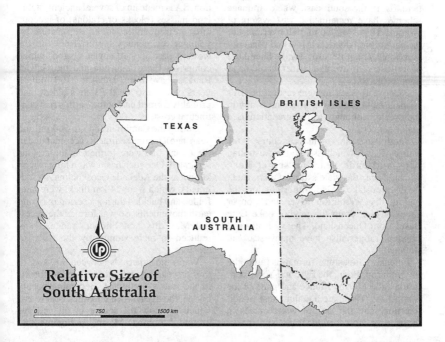

Relative Size of South Australia

the state is less than 300 metres above sea level and few points rise above 700 metres. The only hills of any significance are the Mt Lofty and Flinders ranges, which form a continuous north-south spine stretching 800 km from the coast into the far interior. There's also the Musgrave Ranges in the extreme north-west. The latter include Mt Woodroffe (1435 metres), the state's highest point.

About 80% of SA is classed as arid. Known as the outback, this inland region is mainly covered by stunted saltbush and acacia scrub, with mining and low-intensity sheep and cattle grazing the main economic activities. It has extensive sandy and stony semi-deserts in the east and west; the Tirari, near Lake Eyre, is the closest thing to real desert in Australia. Huge, mainly dry salt lakes such as Lake Eyre and Lake Torrens are a feature of the outback's eastern half.

The more temperate south is one of Australia's major agricultural regions, particularly in the south-east, where drainage schemes have reclaimed a vast system of swamps. However, the rainfall over most of the agricultural districts is low and generally unreliable, and if it wasn't for the liberal use of fertilisers the average farmer would be as poor as the soils.

Faced with such meagre resources, SA's farmers have become as efficient as any in the world, although soil degradation is a major concern.

South Australia's main watercourse is the Murray River, which rises in the Australian Alps and ends near the sea at Lake Alexandrina, the state's largest permanent freshwater lake. Also important are the mainly dry Warburton River and Cooper Creek, which drain the mighty Lake Eyre Basin from Queensland. The Mt Lofty and Flinders ranges also have many seasonal streams.

Extensive limestone formations underlie the Nullarbor Plain, the Eyre and Yorke peninsulas, the Murray Mallee and parts of the South-East. These are a major cause of soil infertility and the lack of watercourses in those areas. However, the use of superphos-

phate and trace elements have enabled all but the dry Nullarbor Plain to be developed for cereal crops.

Water Supply

South Australia's low rainfall and lack of surface run-off have created a huge challenge in developing the state. Many towns in the South-East and on Eyre Peninsula rely on underground basins for their survival. In some areas, these resources are being exploited beyond the recharge rate.

For the rest of the state, the solution to unreliable rainfall has been to supply communities, including Adelaide, with water piped over long distances. In fact, about 90% of the entire population is now either wholly or partly dependent on water from the Murray River.

GEOLOGY

Largely levelled by erosion and sedimentation, SA is made up of several ancient, stable land masses (blocks or cratons) of igneous and metamorphic rocks separated by younger sedimentary basins. Rocks in the western part of the Gawler Craton, which comprises Eyre Peninsula and the Gawler Ranges, have been dated at 2700 million years old. These are the state's oldest, and probably formed part of the Earth's first continental crust.

During the Cambrian (545 to 500 million years ago), marine sediments accumulated in the basins that were formed as the cratons separated. One such basin was a long trough known as the Adelaide Geosyncline; its sediments, which were 24 km thick, were later folded and buckled during a period of strong earth movements. So was formed the ancestral Mt Lofty and Flinders ranges, now reduced to mere stumps by the force of erosion.

Warm moist periods between 300 and 70 million years ago produced extensive forests in the state's north-east. Becoming deeply buried, the trees turned into thick coal seams which are now the source of oil and gas around Moomba. Marine sediments laid down during this period are a source of precious opal at Coober Pedy.

More recently, the sea invaded the Murraylands region, leaving rich fossil deposits that can be seen in the cliffs along the Murray River. Lakebed deposits contain fossil remains of diprotodons and other megafauna such as giant kangaroos – the precursors of today's marsupials.

Over the past two million years the sea level has risen and fallen many times, leaving parallel lines of coastal sand dunes now stranded well inland in the South-East. There have also been great fluctuations in climate, with periods of aridity much more extreme than today – the long parallel dunes of the Simpson and Great Victoria deserts were formed about 10,000 years ago in a time of peak aridity.

CLIMATE

South Australia has a Mediterranean climate of hot, dry summers and cool winters, with most rain falling between May and August. Although the winters are classed as 'mild', snow does fall from time to time along the higher points of the Mt Lofty and Flinders ranges.

Heat is the major climatic extreme, with daily maximums around 35°C being common in the outback from late spring to early autumn. The highest temperature recorded so far is 50.7°C at Oodnadatta in January 1960; the lowest is -8.2°C at Yongala, near Peterborough, in July 1976.

Over 80% of the state normally receives less than 250 mm of rain annually, while nearly half has an annual evaporation rate exceeding 3000 mm. This combination makes SA by far the driest Australian state. The only areas to exceed 750 mm of rainfall are parts of Kangaroo Island, the Mt Lofty Ranges and the state's extreme south-east corner. The wettest area is around Mt Lofty, just east of Adelaide, which receives an annual average of 1200 mm.

Generally, the further north you go in SA, the hotter and drier it gets. Australia's most arid region is in the state's north-east around

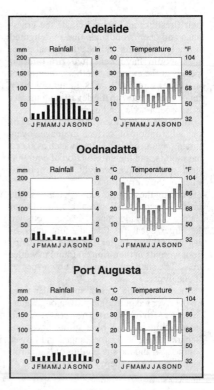

Lake Eyre, where the average – and extremely erratic – annual rainfall is less than 150 mm. This may not seem so bad until you compare it with the annual evaporation rate: a whopping 3500 mm or more. Not surprisingly, light showers over the outback often evaporate before they hit the ground.

FLORA

Over the ages SA's native vegetation has experienced several massive changes. Millions of years ago the state was covered by temperate rainforest. However, increasing aridity and bushfires brought about the present dominance of fire and drought tolerant plants such as acacias, eucalypts and saltbush.

Then the Aboriginal people arrived with

their firesticks and helped create the grass-lands and open woodlands that so delighted the early explorers. While Aboriginal prac-tices would have benefited fire-tolerant species at the expense of others, their effect on the environment was generally very minor compared with the devastating impact of European-style land use.

Since the 1840s, the wholesale clearing of land, disruption of surface drainage, over-grazing by introduced animals such as sheep and rabbits, and the introduction of over 900 plant species have brought catastrophe to much of the native flora.

Despite these unfortunate changes, the native flora is still often a magnificent feature of the landscape. Most obvious are the larger eucalypts (called 'gum trees' or just plain 'gums' after the resin that drips from wounds in their trunks) found in wetter areas. The state has about 60 known species of eucalypt.

South Australia's most spectacular trees are the river red gums that grow along water-courses throughout the state. Also outstanding are the blue gums and can-dlebarks of the Mt Lofty Ranges and Lower South-East, and the sugar gums of Kangaroo Island and the southern Flinders Ranges. At their best, these species can exceed 30 metres in height. The coolibah – another eucalypt species – is the dominant tree on floodplains throughout the outback.

Various species of shorter, multi-stemmed eucalypts called 'mallees' dominate the drier, more infertile areas in the south. These plants are superbly adapted to fire and drought owing to the numerous buds in their tuberous roots; these allow quick recovery should disaster befall the surface growth. Unfortunately, mallee woodlands and scrublands have suffered particularly badly from agriculture, with the majority south of the 200-mm isohyet having been cleared for cereal crops.

There's a distinct boundary between the eucalypt-dominated communities of the south and the acacia communities further north; keep your eyes open and you'll see it as you drive along Highway 1 south and west of Port Augusta. Acacias are usually called 'wattles' because plants of the species were popular with pioneers for making 'wattle-and-daub' huts.

Arguably the state's most attractive flow-ering acacia is the golden wattle, a small tree found in wetter areas – it's Australia's floral emblem. In the Mt Lofty Ranges and down

---

The 'Lungs of the Sea'

Mangrove forests cluster around many sheltered bays and inlets along the South Australian coast, from Port Adelaide to the far west near Ceduna. There is only one species, the grey mangrove *Avicennia marina*, which is found in all mainland states and grows to 10 metres tall.

Mangroves grow only in the intertidal zone, where survival means coping with a harsh, constantly changing environment. The forest floor can be under two or three metres of water at high tide, then lie completely exposed as the water drains away.

The mud on the forest floor is so fine that oxygen cannot penetrate more than a mm or two below the surface. In response, mangroves have developed delicate aerial roots to enable them to breath – you'll see them sticking up like spikes from the mud. The roots also take in salt water. They filter out most of the salt, and any that remains is excreted from tiny glands on the underside of the leaves.

Sediments and vegetable material (such as leaves) fall off as the water slows down through the trees, creating rich organic deposits which are broken down by bacteria, crustaceans and other invertebrates. In turn, the waste products generated by these organisms are a major food source for plankton and small fish. Mangroves also attract insects, which are eaten by fish and birds. Apart from providing a nursery environment for many fish, mangroves are breeding sites for water birds.

Despite the fact that mangroves are unique and fill an important role in the natural environment, they have generally been used as sites for either rubbish dumps or for marinas and housing. A visit to the St Kilda Mangrove Trail (see the Mid-North chapter) or a guided canoe trip on the Port River (see the Activities chapter) will convince you that mangroves are a lot more than just smelly, mosquito-infested places. An ecology that's often called 'the lungs of the sea' deserves to be treated with respect. ∎

in the South-East you'll see blackwood, a tall wattle (to 30 metres). Blackwood is a prized furniture hardwood.

Distinctive and widespread outback acacias include myall (the dark, gnarled trees you see around Port Augusta) and mulga. The latter, which is the most common of all arid-zone wattles, is particularly favoured by Aboriginal people for making boomerangs, spears, shields, digging sticks and the like. Another common wattle with hard, narrow leaves is called 'dead finish', so called because when these tough plants start to die in a drought you know the country's finished!

Saltbush also forms major plant communities in the outback, often in association with acacias. Although saltbush looks unpromising, it makes nutritious food for grazing animals such as kangaroos, sheep and cattle.

Also of interest are SA's mangrove swamps, particularly along the shores of Gulf St Vincent and Spencer Gulf. Although often considered insignificant, they are of enormous ecological importance. Mangroves are major breeding areas for a number of species of waterbirds as well as fish, including the King George whiting, SA's most popular table fish.

Last but by no means least is the bewildering variety and number of wildflowers, which range from delicate orchids to hardy paper daisies. The state's floral emblem is Sturt's desert pea, an annual ground creeper with large, vivid crimson blooms; in winter and early spring you often see great mats of these plants in the north.

Equally famous is an introduced weed known as either Salvation Jane or Patterson's curse, depending on your point of view – apiarists love them, but they can be poisonous to stock. Their massed, rich-purple flowers are a stunning feature of the Mid-North and Flinders Ranges in early spring. Wild hops, another weed of the Flinders, puts on a good springtime show with its red, papery flowers.

Also magnificent are the heaths of coastal SA and the white sands of the mallee belt. In winter and spring these normally drab,

unexciting communities are transformed by flowers of every hue.

The same applies in the outback; after good autumn and winter rains, the harsh semi-desert plains explode with colour, as daisies and other annuals hurry to set seed before the soil dries out again.

The arid zone botanical park at Port Augusta, which opened in September 1996, is an excellent place to learn about the plants of SA's dry country. Adelaide's Botanic Gardens on North Terrace boast a large collection of temperate-zone flora including a mallee section; the Wittunga Botanic Garden at Blackwood (a southern suburb of Adelaide) is also good for natives.

FAUNA

South Australia has a rich diversity of wildlife despite the often devastating effects (habitat loss, competition and predation) of introduced animals. All up, the state has about 70 species of native land mammals (including 16 bats and two monotremes), 27 marine mammals, around 380 birds, 210 reptiles and 12 frogs.

At least 30 species of land mammals (including one bat) have become extinct in SA since European settlement and a number of others are rare or endangered. Some species that were once found over vast areas of the South Australian mainland now survive only on islands.

Almost all the marine mammals suffered greatly from overhunting last century, and many are still vulnerable. No birds have become extinct, apart from the dwarf emu of Kangaroo Island, although several are under threat.

Land Mammals

The native land mammals range in size from the red kangaroo, which stands up to two metres tall, to the silky mouse, which is about the same size as the common house mouse. They include koalas, platypuses, kangaroos, potoroos, bandicoots, water rats, marsupial moles, gliding possums, pygmy possums and various rats and mice.

South Australia has four species of kangaroo: the red kangaroo; western and eastern grey kangaroos; and the euro. The eastern grey is restricted to the eastern margin of the state, but the others are widely distributed and extremely common. Euros are generally found in hilly country in the drier areas.

Kangaroos have actually benefited from European settlement thanks to improved pastures and watering points, and the reduction in hunting by Aboriginal people and dingoes. Good seasons lead to population explosions which (to the outrage of many) are reduced by culling under a quota system. A total of 284,300 reds, 55,600 western greys and 30,500 euros were killed for meat and skins in SA in 1994.

Rock-wallabies are smallish, extremely agile relatives of kangaroos that live in colonies in the rocky ranges. SA has two species, including the endangered yellow-footed rock-wallaby of the Flinders and Gawler ranges. This is one of Australia's most attractive marsupials, a fact which almost brought about its downfall: last century it was nearly hunted to extinction for its skins. Now fully protected, the species may recover provided foxes and feral goats are controlled.

Camped in sandy areas of the outback, you'll often see tracks like those of tiny kangaroos around your swag in the morning. They were probably left by the spinifex hopping-mouse, which spends the daylight hours in deep burrows under vegetation. Similar tracks are left by Mitchell's hopping-mouse in southern mallee areas. Both species are common.

South Australia doesn't have many koalas, but you may see them in the Adelaide Hills, along the Murray River and on Kangaroo Island. They feed only on the leaves of certain species of eucalypt and are vulnerable to fox predation; they're also prone to eating themselves out of house and home if their numbers aren't regulated. Like almost all native mammals they're active mainly at night, so if you see one during the day it's likely to be dozing way up in a tree.

Wombats are much more common than koalas, to which they're related, but you're only likely to see them at night as they cross the roads. These slow, heavy (up to 30 kg) marsupials are quite common along Highway 1 west of Ceduna, and if you keep an eye out you'll see their burrows beside the road.

Australia's two primitive monotremes (egg-laying mammals) are both found in SA. While the amazing duck-billed platypus is restricted to Kangaroo Island, where it was introduced, the short-beaked echidna (or spiny anteater) is found throughout the state. Feeding on ants and termites, the echidna is active on cool days in the temperate south.

Birds

Around 380 species of birds have been recorded in SA, including 35 migrants, eight introduced species, and a number of occasional visitors such as the albatross.

The most numerous group is the waders with around 70 species, almost half of which are annual migrants from breeding grounds in the northern hemisphere. They range from tiny dotterels to herons; many, particularly the migrants, are confined to the coast while others are found wherever there's surface water. Largest of all is the brolga, which has a wingspan of two metres. You're most likely to see them stalking through the lignum on dried-up outback floodplains.

There are 11 native ducks, including the endangered freckled duck, plus a number of other widespread waterbirds such as terns and cormorants. Swans and pelicans range from outback waterholes to coastal shallows.

The largest and most common family of SA birds comprises the honeyeaters, of which there are 30 species. You'll find them wherever there are insect-attracting flowering plants; despite their common name they also eat insects, fruits and berries. Honeyeaters occupy every vegetation zone, with the singing and spiny-cheeked honeyeaters and the yellow-cheeked miner occurring throughout the state. Rarest of all is the endangered black-eared miner, which is restricted to mallee scrub on the Victorian border.

Many of the state's 25 species of parrots

and nine species of cockatoos are very attractive. Several of these birds, including the glossy black cockatoo and orange-bellied parrot, have suffered dramatically from loss of habitat and are now endangered. You'll be famous if you can get a clear photograph of the night parrot. This secretive nocturnal species of inland Australia has been sighted only a few times this century.

Others, such as the galah and little corella, have benefited from European farming practices. Great flocks of these two species of cockatoo are common in parts of the northern wheat belt.

Flocks of thousands of bright yellow-and-green budgerigars are a magnificent feature of the outback in good seasons. It's difficult to know why anyone would want to breed out the natural colour of these delightful little birds.

Also colourful are the fairy wrens (five species), chats (three), robins (seven) and finches (five). These families have representatives in most habitat types.

South Australia has 21 species of raptors (birds of prey), including the endangered peregrine falcon. There are six species of owls and nightjars. While you'll see falcons, kites, hawks or eagles in (or above) all habitats, the only owl you're likely to come in contact with is the boobook owl. Found in a wide range of habitats, its mournful 'boobook' is a common nightly sound throughout rural SA.

For more on birds, see Birdwatching in the Activities chapter.

Reptiles
Of Australia's 750 known species of reptiles, 210 are found in SA. Unexpectedly, the richest habitats in terms of species are the arid spinifex grasslands, particularly the Simpson Desert in the north-east and the Great Victoria Desert in the west.

Included are four species of side-necked tortoises and three marine turtles. The side-necked tortoises are not true tortoises, which are land-dwelling – they're really freshwater turtles, but are called tortoises to conveniently separate them from their saltwater cousins. Marine turtles that have strayed from northern breeding grounds are often sighted off the western and southern coasts of Eyre Peninsula.

Snakes All SA's 42 species of snakes are protected, even the fierce inland taipan of the far north-east. This large and aggressive species is the world's most venomous snake. Fortunately, it's quite rare.

There are several other dangerous snakes to stay away from, including the common death adder, the desert death adder, the common tiger snake and the black tiger snake. You'll know the death adders by their broad triangular heads, short thick bodies and thin tails. Tiger snakes grow to 1.5 metres and have broad crossbands, although these are not so obvious in the black variety, which is found on many islands.

Although a number of SA's snakes are dangerous to humans, many more are harmless. They include its eight species of blind snake – they're mainly active at night, so are rarely seen. Its four species of python are also mainly nocturnal; the largest of these generally slow-moving snakes is the carpet (or diamond) python, which grows up to 3.5 metres long.

Nankeen kestrels hover for long spells, before suddenly swooping to collect their prey.

The Dog Fence
A barrier against sheep-killing dingoes, the Dog Fence stretches for thousands of km across south-eastern Australia, from the Nullarbor cliffs on the Great Australian Bight to Jimbour, in south-east Queensland. Originally a whopping 8614 km long, it was shortened to around 5500 km in 1980.

Made of wire-netting and reaching 1.8 metres high, the fence meanders for 2250 km across SA – you pass through it on the Eyre Highway near Yalata, the Stuart Highway north of Coober Pedy and on the Oodnadatta and Birdsville tracks.

Maintenance is an on-going headache. The job is shared by individual landholders and the state government, which spends $500,000 on upkeep each year. Parts of the fence are over 100 years old and in need of replacement, while even the newest sections are under constant assault from emus, kangaroos, livestock, floods and shifting sand.

Funding shortages have meant the Dog Fence has been left to deteriorate in some areas, and dingo attacks on sheep inside the fence are on the increase. In 1995 a dingo was shot on a station near Port Augusta – about 300 km inside the fence – after it killed 100 sheep! ∎

Lizards The 161 species of lizard in SA include the pygmy blue-tongue, which was thought to be extinct until its recent rediscovery.

A couple of the strangest lizards are found in the arid north. These are the Lake Eyre dragon, which lives on the lake's dry salt crust, and the thorny devil, with its deceptively ferocious appearance. Both survive entirely on a diet of small black ants.

Largest of all is the perentie, which grows to over two metres. The perentie belongs to the goanna family, of which there are seven species in SA, and is easily identified by the regular pattern of large yellow spots on its back. Unlike other lizards, goannas have forked tongues.

Skinks and geckos make up the bulk of the lizard population, but as they're mainly very small and secretive, and often only active at night, you're unlikely to see them. Always check fallen branches for geckos – which may be hiding under bark or in hollows – before you throw them on the campfire. Shingle backs and blue tongues are the largest of the skinks; they're slow and sleepy, and will try to frighten you with gaping mouths if you get too close.

The most commonly seen lizards belong to the dragon family, of which SA has 63 species. They tend to hibernate in the coldest months, but as the weather starts to warm up you'll often find them sunning themselves on the road or perched on rocks or posts. Generally they'll speed off when disturbed, although the larger ones might stand their ground.

Amphibians
Australia's only amphibians are frogs. With 12 species, SA isn't particularly rich in frogs compared with other states, which isn't so surprising considering its dry climate. One of the best adapted is a unique water-holding frog. This species grows to eight cm in length and can live underground for years during drought, surviving on its last big drink until the next rains.

Introduced Feral Species
The dingo, or native dog, which arrived in northern Australia about 5000 years ago, has been linked with the extinction of a number of species on the mainland. Other introduced species such as rabbits, foxes and starlings have also been an environmental as well as economic disasters.

A number of other feral animals in SA originated from livestock or pets that 'went bush'. Goats are a real problem in the Flinders Ranges, where thousands are shot or trapped each year. The camels that roam the far north are now being trapped and (ironically) sold back to Arabia. The major environmental problems that stem from these animals are changes in plant cover and soil degradation.

NATIONAL PARKS & RESERVES
South Australia has an impressive 300

national parks, conservation parks, recreation parks, game reserves, wilderness protection areas and regional reserves. About 209,500 sq km (or 21.3% of the state) is under some form of official conservation management. All public conservation areas in SA are under the control of the Department of Environment & Natural Resources, with day-to-day management being carried out by the department's National Parks & Wildlife Service Division (NPWS).

By far the largest category in terms of size are the seven regional reserves, which make up half the total area. These vast tracts of land provide protection for important habitats and natural features, while allowing other land uses such as mining and pastoralism to take place. They're restricted to the remote arid regions of the state.

There are 17 national parks covering a total of 42,263 sq km and ranging in size from 8.4 sq km (Belair) to 13,492 sq km (Lake Eyre). All the large national parks are in semi-desert areas, with the vast Lake Torrens and Lake Gairdner parks consisting entirely of the beds of mainly dry salt lakes – likewise about two-thirds of Lake Eyre National Park is saltpan. Inevitably, and mainly because there's not much left of it, the natural environment in major agricultural areas is poorly represented in national parks.

Many of the state's scenic and ecological highlights are protected in national parks. On Kangaroo Island, Flinders Chase is famous for its wildlife, including rare species of birds and mammals. The Flinders Ranges, Mt Remarkable and Gammon Ranges national parks in the Flinders Ranges have stunning scenery, great bushwalks and colonies of the endangered yellow-footed rock-wallaby. Canunda, Coffin Bay, Innes and Lincoln are popular coastal parks; Nullarbor National Park, on the far-west coast, has most of its major features underground. Witjira in the far north has the fascinating Dalhousie Springs, a unique wetland habitat on the edge of the Simpson Desert.

The state's 10 game reserves cover 250 sq km and give some protection to native game species such as duck and quail. However, the safety factor disappears during annual open seasons, when licensed shooters are allowed in to hunt them.

Allan Fox's *Centenary Field Guide of Major Parks & Reserves of SA* ($17.95) gives descriptions and limited coverage of highlights and activities at 49 parks.

National Parks Offices

The Department of Environment & Natural Resources (☎ 8226 4000) has its head office at 91-97 Grenfell St (GPO Box 667, Adelaide, SA 5001). Regional and district offices of the NPWS, which are responsible for the day-to-day management of conservation areas, are at:

Mt Lofty Ranges
    Belair National Park, Belair (☎ 8278 5477) – includes the southern Mt Lofty Ranges and northern Fleurieu Peninsula
    Smith Rd, Cobblers Creek, Salisbury East (☎ 8281 4022) – includes the central and northern Mt Lofty Ranges
Fleurieu Peninsula
    57 Ocean St, Victor Harbor (☎ 8552 3677) – mainly parks of the peninsula's southern half
Kangaroo Island
    37 Dauncey St, Kingscote (☎ 8553 2381)
South-East
    11 Helen St, Mt Gambier (☎ 8735 1177)
    Princes Highway, Meningie (☎ 8575 1200) – parks between Meningie and the Dukes Highway, including the Coorong National Park
Murray Lands
    28 Vaughan Terrace, Berri (☎ 8595 2172) – includes the Murray River and Murray Mallee
Yorke Peninsula
    Stenhouse Bay, Innes National Park (☎ 8854 4040)
Northern
    9 Mackay St, Port Augusta (☎ 8648 5301) – includes the southern Flinders Ranges and far northern Eyre Peninsula
Eyre Peninsula
    75 Liverpool St, Port Lincoln (☎ 8688 3111) – parks in the southern half of Eyre Peninsula
Far West
    11 MacKenzie St, Ceduna (☎ 8625 3144) – parks west from Elliston to the WA border
Far North
    60 Elder St, Hawker (☎ 8648 0048) – includes the northern Flinders Ranges and entire outback

Contact the Natural Resources Information Office (☎ 8204 1910) at 77 Grenfell St in Adelaide for general information on parks and reserves throughout the state. For anything of a 'hands-on' nature contact the offices listed above. They can tell you about such things as camping, walking track and road conditions on their parks; if they can't, they'll put you onto the appropriate ranger in the field.

GOVERNMENT & POLITICS

South Australia is one of the six states and two territories that make up the Commonwealth of Australia.

The British monarch, who is also Australia's head of state, is represented in SA by a Governor, who has a responsibility to maintain lawful government in the state. However, while Governors retain important powers, they seldom become involved in political debate.

Australia's Federal Government, which is based on the British system, has a lower house (the House of Representatives) and an upper house of review (the Senate). South Australia contributes 12 senators and 12 members of parliament, with the Liberal Party holding a clear majority in both cases at the last election (1996). Voting is compulsory above 18 years of age in both federal and state elections.

The South Australian State Government consists of a House of Assembly (47 members) and a Legislative Council (22 members), with the leader of the majority party being called the Premier. Each Parliament has a life of four years. It is Labor policy to abolish the council, and recently some Liberals have been making supportive noises.

ECONOMY

South Australia's economy was based on copper, cereal crops and wool from the earliest days of settlement until after WWI. The latter two are still mainstays, but agriculture has now taken a back seat to manufacturing in terms of employment and income. Tourism is another major earner – in fact, in terms of gross income it exceeds mining.

South Australian exports in 1993-94 were worth $3873 million, which represented 6.3% of the national figure; imports from overseas during the same period totalled $2803 million. The major commodities exported were food (29.8%) and machinery and transport equipment (15%), while motor vehicle parts and accessories were by far the major imports. Wheat, the most valuable export commodity, accounted for 17% of all wheat exported from Australia.

In 1993-94, Japan was SA's largest export market, accounting for 16% of all exports; all up, the countries of east Asia purchased 49%. Other major export markets were the EEC and the USA.

Tourism

Tourism was worth an estimated $1800 million in 1994-95. During that time there were an estimated 858,000 visitors from interstate (52% from Victoria) and 260,000 from overseas. Most international visitors came from the UK and Ireland (20%), USA and Asia (both 13%) and Germany (12.5%). The most popular destination by far with both domestic and overseas visitors was Adelaide; the South-East was second with interstaters, while the Barossa was runner-up with international visitors.

POPULATION & PEOPLE

The 1991 census revealed that SA's population was 1,400,622.

Most South Australians (76%) were born in Australia. Of the remainder, 10.4% were born in the UK and Ireland, 2% in Italy, 1% in Greece and 1% in Germany. Nearly 2.5% of the population was Asian-born, with Vietnamese being the largest group (0.6%).

The census put the population of Aboriginal people at 16,250, which is probably a little higher than it was at the time of European settlement. Most of the state's Aborigines (41%) live in Adelaide.

Population Distribution

Among Australian states and territories, SA has the highest concentration of its people living in its capital city. Only 17% of the state's population lives in towns outside Adelaide. The largest country town is Whyalla with 25,500 people, followed by Mt Gambier with 20,813 and Port Augusta with 15,200 – these are the only country centres with populations exceeding 15,000. Many of the smaller country centres are declining due to government 'rationalisation' of services and a population shift, particularly of younger people, to Adelaide and larger country centres.

Only around 1% of the entire state population lives in the driest 80%. This amounts to a population density in that area of 0.02 persons per sq km. However, the spread is by no means even, as over 50% of the region's population lives in its four main towns: Coober Pedy, Leigh Creek, Roxby Downs and Woomera.

EDUCATION

Education is available to all South Australians, and attendance at school is free and compulsory between the ages of six and 15 years. Primary and secondary education is available within the state school system or the private system.

There are three universities, all in Adelaide. The oldest is the University of Adelaide, established in 1874. A total of 44,450 students were attending university in SA in 1993, when 6.4% of the total population claimed to hold a bachelor degree or higher.

ARTS & CULTURE

For a time SA called itself 'The Festival State', but 'State of the Arts' might have been more appropriate. The visual arts scene in SA includes a marvellous state gallery, while the performing arts boast an opera company, several good theatre companies, a dance company and a symphony orchestra.

To find out what's happening on the arts scene, get hold of the free newspaper *Arts Monthly* – it comes with *The Advertiser* on the first Tuesday in the month. Look under Weekend Watch in Friday's *Advertiser* for a listing of weekend events.

Numerous museums throughout the state preserve examples of Aboriginal and European cultural heritage. Generally, the best in country areas are owned or managed by the National Trust.

Aboriginal Culture

The SA Museum in Adelaide has a comprehensive collection of Aboriginal art and cultural artefacts. Also in Adelaide, the Tandanya Centre has a gallery featuring exhibitions of Aboriginal art from around Australia.

Cultural sites featuring cave paintings and petroglyphs (rock carvings) are scattered through the northern Flinders Ranges, and several of them can be visited. Other well-known petroglyph sites are near Innamincka on Cooper Creek. In 1992 the world's oldest rock carvings were found in the Olary region, 350 km north of Adelaide. If you want to visit them, Gecko Tours (☎ 8339 3800) of Adelaide are the people to speak to. They have an excellent three-day tour ($390) exploring the Aboriginal heritage of the Olary area.

You can visit the Pitjantjatjara people in the far north-west on a guided tour and experience something of their culture (see Organised Tours early in the Outback chapter). There are Aboriginal heritage centres on the Coorong and in Marree.

Painting

South Australia's first professional artists were the Chauncy sisters, Martha and Theresa, who arrived in the colony just six weeks after its proclamation. They were serious artists who had trained as miniature portraitists, with Martha using oils and watercolours and Theresa wax; Martha also painted landscapes and flower studies. Both exhibited at the Royal Academy in London, then the most prestigious exhibition venue in the British Empire. Despite this, and the fact that Martha was Australia's second professional female painter and Theresa its first female sculptor, they are still little-known even in SA.

Women dominated SA's visual arts scene

from the 1890s to the 1940s, when they were the most influential art teachers and the chief supporters of modernism. Significant SA female painters during this evolutionary period were Dorrit Black, Stella Bowen, the Hambidge sisters (Alice, Helen and Millicent), Nora Heysen and Margaret Preston. Heysen, a daughter of Hans Heysen, won the Archibald Prize, Australia's major award for portraiture, in 1938.

In contrast, the only really notable male painters of the period were Hans Heysen and Horace Trenerry. Heysen became SA's best-known artist and one of Australia's most famous landscape artists. Unlike many, he became a popular figure in his own lifetime; working in oil and watercolours, he captured the atmosphere and beauty of SA's rural landscapes very successfully.

There's a large collection of Heysen's work in the Art Gallery of SA, which purchased its first Heysen in 1904; it also has his last documented painting, executed in 1966 two years before his death. Established in 1880, the gallery contains a comprehensive collection of Australian, Asian and European art.

Other major art galleries in Adelaide include the Adelaide Festival Centre, the Royal SA Society of Arts and the Contemporary Arts Centre. There's also the Jam Factory Craft & Design Centre, which houses craft workshops and galleries.

The *Arts & Crafts Guide* ($4) gives a run-down on galleries and craft shops within a two-hour drive of Adelaide.

Architecture

Despite development, central Adelaide retains many fine stone buildings from the early days of settlement. The conservation of important heritage buildings became a major public issue after several historic landmarks were demolished in the 1970s. Today, many of the state's most significant heritage buildings are protected by National Trust and state heritage legislation.

Adelaide has numerous gracious mansions and stately homes from the Victorian era that were built for the colonial gentry who had profited from wool, copper or in business. There's also an abundance of solid, 19th century middle-class villas and working-class cottages in the older suburbs. Most are concentrated in the city and nearby suburbs such as North Adelaide and Glen Osmond.

Many towns sprang from the copper and wheat booms of the 1840s to 1870s. Buoyed by wealth and optimism, their founders tended to build solidly and grandly in stone, particularly when it came to churches, hotels and public buildings. Since then, the lack of major development in such towns has generally preserved their historic streetscapes.

Hans Heysen

Born in Hamburg, Germany, in 1877, Wilhelm Ernst Hans Heysen emigrated to Adelaide with his family at the age of seven. He started painting as a boy and sold his first watercolour, *The Wet Road*, at 16.

Recognising his talent, a group of Adelaide businessmen financed Heysen to study and paint in Europe between 1899 and 1903. He returned to Adelaide and became a private art teacher, winning the Wynne Prize in 1904 with *Mystic Morn*. It was the first of nine times he was to win this prestigious national landscape award.

Heysen's first major exhibition was held in 1908, and within 20 years he was extremely successful – sales of his work at a 1927 exhibition set an Australian record. A prolific artist, he had thousands of paintings and drawings to his credit over a career that spanned 73 years. His work hangs in all Australian state galleries, numerous provincial galleries and the British Museum.

Painting mainly in watercolours, Heysen focused on the majesty of the Australian gum tree and the rural landscape of the Mt Lofty and Flinders ranges. His paintings, especially *Grey Morning* and *Into the Light*, skilfully highlight the interplay of light and nature, and reveal his great love of the Australian countryside. One of Heysen's favourite areas was the Adelaide Hills, where he lived for 50 years near the small German town of Hahndorf.

Heysen was knighted in 1950 and died in 1968. ■

You'll find some of the best examples at Burra, Kapunda, Mintaro, Moonta, Quorn and Robe.

Architectural styles in several country areas reflect the culture of their first settlers. Examples are the distinctive Lutheran churches and German farmhouses of the Barossa Valley, the English country homes of the Adelaide Hills, the 'Englishness' of Mintaro, and the Cornish cottages and sombre Methodist chapels of the copper towns.

Also of interest are the many buildings (historic and otherwise) that show clever adaptation to the local climate and, in many cases, the lack of readily available manufactured building materials. They include the miner's dugouts at Burra and Coober Pedy, the thatched farm sheds of the Mid-North and Barossa Valley, the pine-and-pug settler's cottages in the Flinders Ranges, and the broad-verandahed homesteads throughout the pastoral districts.

The informative monthly *State Heritage Newsletter* is published by the State Heritage Branch of the Department of Environment and Natural Resources – you can pick one up at the State Information Centre, 77 Grenfell St.

National Trust The National Trust is dedicated to preserving historic buildings and artefacts as well as significant natural features in all parts of Australia. The Trust manages 138 sites in SA alone and these are generally open to the public.

Membership entitles you to free entry to many National Trust properties for your year of membership. Annual membership costs $44 for individuals ($31 concession) and $62 for families ($44 concession), and includes a monthly or quarterly magazine.

In SA, the Trust's head office (☎ 8223 1655) is at Ayers Historic House, 288 North Terrace, Adelaide. There's another Trust office at 452 Pulteney St.

Performing Arts
The focal point for performing arts in SA is the Adelaide Festival Centre. It's the major venue for the biennial Adelaide Festival of Arts, regarded as the nation's foremost performing arts and cultural event. There are several other important arts events, including the biennial Come Out Festival, which celebrates art by and for young people.

The State Opera of SA was established in 1976 and is a major employer of local artists. It has premiered many major works in Australia.

Adelaide has a number of theatre companies including the State Theatre Company, which is based at the Adelaide Festival Centre. Other local drama companies to watch out for include the Red Shed and the SA Theatre Company.

There's also the Adelaide-based Meryl Tankard Australian Dance Theatre, one of the nation's most highly respected performing arts companies. Under the guidance of Meryl Tankard it presents its own unique and exciting form of modern dance.

The SA Country Arts Trust has theatre complexes at Mt Gambier, Port Pirie, Renmark and Whyalla. As well as providing a touring programme, it employs a number of arts development officers who support and promote cultural activities in country areas.

Music
Adelaide offers a wide choice of music. You can foot-tap to an Irish band at the Irish Club, hear rock belted out by a pub band, or relax to the strains of the Adelaide Symphony Orchestra (ASO). There's also a healthy jazz scene.

Some of the most enjoyable opportunities for listening to jazz and classical music are the wine festivals held annually in the Barossa and Clare Valleys and at McLaren Vale (see Cultural Events in the Facts for the Visitor chapter).

The ASO, which is supported by the Australian Broadcasting Commission, holds around 100 concerts throughout the state each year, including several free family concerts. Contact them on ☎ 8343 4834 for details of forthcoming performances.

There's also the Adelaide Chamber Orchestra for lovers of chamber music.

Rock Adelaide has plenty of rock venues where you can listen to anything from grunge to cover bands. Although things aren't so wonderful in the country, you can usually find a good band or two on a Friday and Saturday night in the larger towns.

Several Adelaide rock acts, such as Paul Kelly and Cold Chisel, have done well on the national and international stage.

Folk Lovers of folk and bluegrass music won't be disappointed as there are annual festivals and regular session venues throughout the settled areas. The major event is the SA Folk & Music Festival, held at Victor Harbor over the October long weekend; others occur on Kangaroo Island (January) and at Kapunda (the weekend before Easter), Birdwood (the Medieval Festival is held in March) and Laura (April).

You'll find folk music and folk dancing clubs in Adelaide and many country areas, including the Barossa Valley, Mount Gambier, Port Lincoln and Victor Harbor.

For information on folk happenings throughout the state, contact the Folk Federation of SA (☎ 8340 1069) at the Governor Hindmarsh Hotel, 59 Port Rd, Hindmarsh. Alternatively, get hold of the federation's free and very informative newspaper *Infolkus*.

Literature
SA has produced a number of notable writers. CJ Dennis (of *The Songs of a Sentimental Bloke* fame) and Adam Lindsay Gordon were famous colonial poets; novelist and feminist Catherine Helen Spence created an Australian literary milestone when she wrote *Clara Morison* in the 1850s.

Well-known contemporary writers include Colin Thiele *(Sun on the Stubble, Blue Fin* and *Storm Boy)*, Peter Goldsworthy *Honk if you're Jesus*, Gillian Rubinstein *(Space Demons)*, Mem Fox (author of top-selling children's book *Possum Magic)*, award-winning crime writer Geraldine Halls

(under the pen name Charlotte Jay) and the late poet John Bray (the John Bray Award is the Adelaide Festival of Arts' literary poetry prize). See Books in the Facts for the Visitor chapter for some titles by local writers and poets.

Creative writing in SA is encouraged by the Writers' Centre (☎ 8223 7662) at 187 Rundle St in Adelaide, an information and resource centre for writers.

There's also the Friendly Street Poets, which meets for readings on the first Tuesday of every month at the Box Factory, 59 Regent St South, Adelaide.

Cinema
The SA Film Corporation was established in 1972 as a means of kick-starting a local film industry. It did this with commendable success, creating acclaimed productions such as *Picnic at Hanging Rock, Sunday Too Far Away, Storm Boy* and *Breaker Morant* in the '70s. The corporation's major role these days is to encourage Australian and overseas producers to use SA as a base for low-budget features.

RELIGION
By far the most common religion in SA is Christianity, with 70% of the population claiming affiliation in the 1991 census – the number had dropped by 4% over the past decade. Of these, the largest denomination is Roman Catholicism with 21% of the population, followed by the Anglican Church (18%), the Uniting Church (14.3%) and Lutheranism (5%). By far the fastest growing denomination is the Pentecostal church (1.4% of the population). Non-Christian religions claim 1.3% of the population, with almost half being Buddhists.

About 17% of the population describe themselves as having no religion at all.

LANGUAGE
Any visitor from abroad who thinks Australian (that's 'strine') is simply a weird variant of English will soon have a few surprises. For a start many Australians don't even speak

Australian – they speak Italian, Lebanese, Vietnamese, Turkish or Greek.

Those who do speak the native tongue are liable to lose you in a strange collection of Australian words. Some have entirely different meanings here than in English-speaking countries north of the equator; some commonly used words have been shortened almost beyond recognition. Others are derived from Aboriginal or foreign languages, from the slang used by early convict settlers or (shudder) from TV.

If you want to pass for a native, first try speaking quickly and slightly nasally. When you've mastered that, shorten any word of more than two syllables and then add a vowel to the end of it, making anything you can into a diminutive (biscuits become bikkies, and even the Hell's Angels are reduced to mere 'bikies'). Finally – if you want to get thrown out of the pikkies (the movies) – pepper your speech with as many expletives as possible.

Lonely Planet publishes *Australia – a language survival kit*, an introduction to both Australian English and Aboriginal languages.

Facts for the Visitor

VISAS & EMBASSIES

All visitors to Australia need a visa. Only New Zealand nationals are exempt, and even they receive a 'special category' visa on arrival.

Visa application forms are available from either Australian diplomatic missions overseas or travel agents, and you can apply by mail or in person. There are several different types of visas, depending on the reason for your visit.

Australian Embassies

Australian consular offices overseas include:

Canada
>Suite 710, 50 O'Connor St, Ottawa (☎ (613) 236 0841; fax 236 4376)
>Also in Toronto and Vancouver

France
>4 Rue Jean Rey, 75724 Paris Cedex 15 Paris (☎ (01) 4059 3300; fax 4059 3310)

Germany
>Godesberger Allee 107, 53175 Bonn (☎ (0228) 81 030; fax 810 3130)
>Also in Frankfurt and Berlin

Hong Kong
>23/F Harbour Centre, 25 Harbour Rd, Wanchai, Hong Kong Island (☎ 2827 8881; fax 2827 6583)

Indonesia
>Jalan HR Rasuna Said Kav C 15-16, Jakarta Selatan 12940 (☎ (021) 522 7111; fax 522 7101)
>Jalan Prof Moh Yamin 51, Renon, Denpasar, Bali (☎ (0361) 23 5092; fax 23 1990)

Italy
>Via Alessandria 215, Rome 00198 (☎ (06) 852 721; fax 8527 2300)
>Also in Milan

Japan
>2-1-14 Mita, Minato-ku, Tokyo 108 (☎ (03) 5232 4111; fax 5232 4149)
>Twin 21 MID Tower, 29th floor, 2-1-61 Shiromi, Chuo-ku, Osaka 540 (☎ (06) 941 9271; fax 920 4543)
>7th floor, Tsuruta Keyaki Bldg, 1-1-5 Akasaka Chuo-ku, Fukuoka City 810, Kyushu (☎ (092) 734 5055; fax 724 2304)
>8th floor, Ikko Fushimi Bldg, 1-20-10 Nishiki, Naka-ku, Nagoya 460 (☎ (052) 211 0630; fax 211 0632)
>Also in Sapporo and Sendai

Malaysia
>6 Jalan Yap Kwan Seng, Kuala Lumpur 50450 (☎ (03) 242 3122; fax 241 5773)
>Also in Kuching and Penang

Netherlands
>Carnegielaan 4, 2517 KH, The Hague (☎ (070) 310 8200; fax 310 7863)

New Zealand
>72-78 Hobson St, Thorndon, Wellington (☎ (04) 473 6411; fax 498 7118)
>Union House, 32-38 Quay St, Auckland 1 (☎ (09) 303 2429; fax 377 0798)

Singapore
>25 Napier Rd, Singapore 1025 (☎ 737 9311; fax 733 7134)

South Africa
>292 Orient St, Arcadia, Pretoria 0083 (☎ (012) 342 3740; fax 342 4222)
>Also in Cape Town

Sweden
>Sergels Torg 12, Stockholm (☎ (08) 613 2900; fax 24 7414)

Thailand
>37 South Sathorn Rd, Bangkok 10120 (☎ (02) 287 2680; fax 287 2029)

UK
>Australia House, The Strand, London WC2B 4LA (☎ (0171) 379 4334; fax 465 8210)
>Also in Edinburgh and Manchester

USA
>1601 Massachusetts Ave NW, Washington DC 20036 (☎ (202) 797 3000; fax 797 3168)
>Also in Atlanta, Boston, Chicago, Denver, Honolulu, Houston, Los Angeles, New York and San Francisco

Tourist Visas

Tourist visas are issued by Australian consular offices abroad; they are the most common form of visa and are generally valid for a stay of up to six months within a 12-month period. If you intend staying less than three months, the visa is free; otherwise there is a $30 processing fee.

When you apply for a visa, you need to present your passport and a passport photo, as well as sign an undertaking that you have an onward or return ticket and 'sufficient funds' – the latter is obviously open to interpretation.

Working Visas

Young visitors from Britain, Ireland, Canada, Holland and Japan may be eligible for a 'working holiday' visa. 'Young' is fairly loosely interpreted as around 18 to 26, and working holiday means up to 12 months. However, the emphasis is supposed to be on casual employment rather than a full-time job, so you are only meant to work for a total of three months. Officially this visa can only be applied for in your home country, but some travellers report that the rule can be bent.

See the section on Work later in this chapter for details of what sort of employment is available in SA and where.

Visa Extensions

The maximum stay allowed to visitors in Australia is one year, including extensions.

Visa extensions are made through Department of Immigration & Ethnic Affairs offices in Australia and, as the process takes some time, it's best to apply about a month before your visa expires. There is an application fee of $200, but beware – even if they turn down your application they can still keep your money!

To qualify for an extension you must take out private medical insurance to cover the period of the extension, and have a ticket out of the country. Some offices are more strict in enforcing these conditions than others.

Foreign Embassies & Consulates

The principal diplomatic representations to Australia are in Canberra. The state capitals also have representatives of other countries, and you'll find them listed in the various Yellow Pages phone books under 'Consulates & Legations'. The important ones in Adelaide include:

Germany
    Consul, 23 Peel St, Adelaide (☎ 8231 6320)
Japan
    Honorary Consul-General, 29 Winham Ave, Reynella (☎ 8381 6047)
Netherlands
    Consul, 151 South Terrace, Adelaide (☎ 8231 9000)

UK
    British Consulate, Level 22, 25 Grenfell Street, Adelaide (☎ 8212 7280)

CUSTOMS

When entering Australia you can bring most articles in free of duty provided that Customs is satisfied they are for personal use and that you'll be taking them with you when you leave. There's also the usual duty-free per person quota of one litre of alcohol, 250 cigarettes and dutiable goods up to the value of A$400.

With regard to prohibited goods, there are two areas you need to pay particular attention to. Number one is, of course, dope – Australian Customs have a positive mania about the stuff and can be extremely efficient when it comes to finding it. Unless you want to make first-hand investigations of conditions in Australian jails, don't bring any with you. This particularly applies if you are arriving from South-East Asia or the Indian subcontinent.

Number two is animal and plant quarantine. Australia has so far managed to escape many of the nasties so prevalent in other parts of the world, so the authorities are naturally keen to prevent weeds, pests or diseases getting into the country. Thus you will be asked to declare all goods of animal or vegetable origin – wooden spoons, straw hats, the lot – and show them to an official. Obviously, any attempt to bring fresh food and live animals into the country will be frowned upon. (Even within Australia there are restrictions on taking fruit, vegetables, plant cuttings, cut flowers and so on between states.)

Weapons and firearms are either prohibited or require a permit and safety testing. Other restricted goods include non-approved telecommunications devices and products (such as ivory) made from protected wildlife species.

MONEY
Currency

Australia's currency is the Australian dollar, which comprises 100 cents. There are coins for 5c, 10c, 20c, 50c, $1 and $2, paper notes for $100 only, and plastic notes for $5, $10, $20 and $50.

There are no notable restrictions on importing or exporting currency or travellers' cheques except that you may not take out more than A$5000 in cash without prior approval.

Exchange Rates
In recent years the Australian dollar has fluctuated quite markedly against the US dollar, but it now seems to hover around the 70c to 75c mark – a disaster for Australians travelling overseas but a real bonus for inbound visitors.

Canada	C$1	=	A$0.94
France	FF1	=	A$0.25
Germany	DM 1	=	A$0.86
Hong Kong	HK$10	=	A$1.66
Japan	¥100	=	A$1.19
New Zealand	NZ$1	=	A$0.87
United Kingdom	UK£1	=	A$1.96
United States	US$1	=	A$1.28

Changing Money
Changing foreign currency or travellers' cheques is no problem at almost any bank, and is normally done quickly and efficiently.

Outside banking hours you may be able to change foreign currency at your hotel or motel, although they'll usually give you less than what you'd receive at a bank. Other out-of-hour's alternatives in the city include the American Express office at 13 Grenfell St, and the 'Payment of Accounts' office on the fifth floor of the Myer Centre on Rundle Mall. The latter has the best hours; it opens at 9.30 am from Monday to Saturday and closes at 5.30 pm from Monday to Thursday, 9 pm on Friday and 5 pm on Saturday – on Sunday it's open from 11 am to 5 pm.

Travellers' Cheques
There are a variety of ways to carry your money around Australia. If your stay is limited then travellers' cheques are the most straightforward; they generally enjoy a better exchange rate than foreign cash in Australia.

American Express, Thomas Cook and other well-known international brands of travellers' cheques are all widely used in Australia. A passport will usually be adequate for identification; it would be sensible to carry a driver's licence, credit cards or a plane ticket in case of problems.

Buying Australian dollar travellers' cheques is a recommended option. These can be exchanged immediately at the bank cashier's window without being converted from a foreign currency and incurring commissions, fees and exchange rate fluctuations. Not only that, but you may get caught short of cash outside banking hours; in country areas you'll generally find it much easier to change a travellers' cheque in Australian dollars than one in an overseas currency.

Credit Cards
Except in some remote areas, credit cards are widely accepted in SA and are a convenient alternative to carrying a wad of travellers' cheques. The most common credit card, however, is the purely Australian Bankcard system. Visa, MasterCard, Diners Club and American Express are also widely accepted.

Cash advances from credit cards are available over the counter and from many automatic teller machines (ATMs), depending on the card.

Local Bank Accounts
If you're planning to stay longer than just a month or so, it's worth considering other ways of handling money that give you more flexibility and are more economical. This applies equally to Australians setting off to travel around the country.

Most travellers these days opt for an account which includes a cash card, which you can use to access your cash from ATMs found all over Australia. Westpac, ANZ, National and Commonwealth bank branches are found nationwide; in the larger country towns there'll be at least one place where you can use your card.

ATM machines can be used day or night,

and it is possible to use the machines of some other banks: Westpac ATMs accept Commonwealth Bank cards and vice versa; National Bank ATMs accept ANZ cards and vice versa. There is a limit on how much you can withdraw from your account. This varies from bank to bank but is usually around $800 per day.

Even in the outback – although you'd be crazy to count on it – many businesses, such as service stations, supermarkets and convenience stores, are linked into the EFTPOS system (Electronic Funds Transfer at Point Of Sale); at places with this facility you can use your bank cash card to pay for services or purchases direct, and sometimes withdraw cash as well. Bank cash cards and credit cards can also be used to make local, STD and international phone calls in special public telephones, found in many towns throughout the country.

Opening an account at an Australian bank is not all that easy these days, especially for overseas visitors. A points system operates and you need to score a minimum of 100 points before you can have the privilege of letting the bank take your money. Passports, driver's licences, birth certificates and other 'major' IDs earn you at least 40 points; minor ones such as credit cards get you around 20 points. Just like a game show really! However, if visitors apply to open an account during the first six weeks of their visit, then just showing their passport will suffice.

A Commonwealth savings account is the most useful one to have if you're going to be travelling in the more sparsely settled areas of SA. This is simply because in the bush, where banks are often scarce, just about every post office has a Commonwealth agency. However, the amount of cash you can withdraw at such places is often restricted, particularly in small remote centres.

If you don't have an Australian Tax File Number, interest earned from your funds will be taxed at the rate of 48% and this money goes straight to everybody's friend, the Deputy Commissioner of Taxation. You may be able to reclaim this by filing a tax return when leaving the country if the total you have officially earned falls below the tax-free threshold – currently around $6000.

Costs

Compared with the USA, Canada and European countries, South Australia is cheaper in some ways and more expensive in others. Manufactured goods tend to be more expensive: if they are imported they have all the additional costs of transport and duties, and if they're locally manufactured they suffer from the extra costs entailed in making things in comparatively small quantities. Thus you pay more for clothes, cars and other manufactured items.

On the other hand, food is both high in quality and low in cost. Accommodation is generally very reasonably priced. There aren't many backpackers' hostels outside Adelaide, but most towns where tourists go have a caravan park with on-site vans for around $25 for two people.

The biggest cost in any extensive tour of SA is going to be transport, simply because the state is so vast. If there's a group of you, buying a second-hand car may be the most economical way to go. Provided you look after it – and you don't pay too much in the first place – you should get most of the purchase price back when you sell it. See the Getting Around chapter for information on buying a car.

Tipping

It isn't customary to tip in Australia. If the service has been especially good and you want to leave a small tip, there is no set amount – just leave what you think is a fair thing. Taxi drivers don't expect tips, but of course they won't hurl one back at you either. In contrast, try getting out of a New York or London cab without leaving your 10 to 15%.

WHEN TO GO

Any time is a good time to be in SA, but as you'd expect in a state this large, different parts of it are at their best at different times. Generally, spring and autumn give the greatest flexibility for a short visit as you can combine highlights of the whole state while avoiding extremes of weather.

Summer sees Crow-eaters (the local vernacular for South Australians) flock like migrating birds to the coast, where most days are warm enough for swimming and lazing around outdoors. In the north it's generally too hot to do anything much except slump under an air-conditioner with a cold drink.

In winter, when the south is cold and wet, the outback beckons with its generally mild to warm days and clear skies. It's cool – often freezing – at nights, and this kills off the bushflies, which in the warmer months can be an absolute nightmare.

Late winter and spring usually brings out magnificent wildflowers all the way from the coastal heath up through the mallee and into the Flinders Ranges and outback. Some years these can be worth a trip in themselves.

The other major consideration when travelling in SA is school holidays. The main holiday period is from mid-December to late January; there's a week in early to mid-April, a fortnight in late June to mid-July, and another week in late September to early October. South Australian families take to the road (and air) en masse at these times. As a result, many places are booked out, prices rise and things generally go a bit crazy, particularly over the Christmas break.

TOURIST OFFICES
Local Tourist Offices

Tourism in the state is overseen by the South Australian Tourism Commission. Their main tourist information and booking office is the South Australian Tourism Commission (SATC) (☎ 8212 1505; toll-free 1800 882 092), at 1 King William St in Adelaide. It's open from 8.45 am to 5 pm on weekdays and from 9 am to 2 pm on weekends and public holidays.

As well as supplying a bewildering array of brochures, price lists, maps and other information, the SATC (and its interstate and overseas offices) can book transport, tours and accommodation for you.

A step down from the SATC are the local or regional tourist offices. Every major town

in SA has a professional tourist office or information outlet of some type or other and in most cases these are excellent. They also give you the benefit of local knowledge, which is something you don't really get from the SATC. Even the smallest town will have a place – usually the pub, caravan park or general store – where you can get information on the local area.

Other good places to ask are accommodation venues, particularly hostels and caravan parks – they know what's worthwhile locally as they get constant updates from their guests.

Interstate Tourist Offices

Addresses of the SATC interstate are:

New South Wales
247 Pitt St, Sydney 2000 (☎ (02) 264 3375)
Queensland
25 Lavarack Ave, Eagle Farm 4007 (☎ (07) 868 3147
Victoria
455 Bourke St, Melbourne 3000 (☎ (03) 9606 0222)
Western Australia
13/14 Mezzanine floor, Wesley Centre, 93 William St, Perth 6000 (☎ (09) 481 1268)

Tourist Offices Abroad

SATC offices or representatives overseas are:

Japan
28F The New Otani Garden Court, 4-1 Kioicho, Chiyoda-Ku, Tokyo 102 (☎ (03) 326 28981)
New Zealand
1st Floor, CML Building, 157 Queens St, Auckland (☎ (09) 307 6600)
Singapore
c/- MDK Consultants, 100 Amoy St, Singapore 0106 (☎ 222 3660)
UK
c/- Robert Hardless & Associates, 612 Kingston Rd, London SW20 8DN (☎ (181) 545 0450)
USA
c/- Australian Travel Headquarters Inc, Suite 160, 1700E Dyer Rd, Santa Anna, California (☎ (714) 852 2270).

USEFUL ORGANISATIONS

SA has a swag of organisations formed for just about every conceivable purpose, and a handful are included here. To find the rest,

Disabled Access in South Australia

Most of South Australia's main tourist areas have wheelchair accessible features. Adelaide is regarded as Australia's most accessible city – it is compact with few gradients and good crossovers at most intersections. There is plenty of accessible accommodation at the five-star end of the market: the Hilton has 25 rooms, the Hyatt 20 rooms and the Park Royal seven rooms. At Glenelg, the Ramada has nine rooms. Further information about accommodation is available from the Royal Automobile Association (RAA) of South Australia, 41 Hindmarsh Square, Adelaide, ☎ 8202 4500.

Other information sources include:

NICAN, PO Box 407, Curtain, ACT 2605 (☎(06) 285 3713 fax (06) 285 3714) is an Australia-wide directory providing information on accessible accommodation, sporting and recreational activities.

The Australian Council for the Rehabilitation of the Disabled (ACROD), 262 South Terrace, Adelaide (☎ 8232 2366) has published *Access Adelaide 1992*, including information on accessible public toilets, buildings and services.

The Disability Information & Resource Centre (DIRC), 195 Gillies St (☎ (08) 8223 7522/TTY 8223 7579) has accessible toilets and shower and is probably the main information service in South Australia. It can direct you to travel agencies experienced and knowledgeable about mobility restricted travel. DIRC also has an electronic bulletin board service called Common Ground (☎ 8223 2131, via computer and modem).

Golden Roo Tours (☎ (08) 8536 3542 or 018 803452) conducts daily and longer tours in hydraulic lift-equipped vehicles for two wheelchairs. Independent Travellers, 167 Gillies St, Adelaide SA 5000, (☎ 8232 2555/fax 8232 6877/freecall 008 811355) is a licensed travel agency specialising in organising holidays for people with special needs, and can arrange care.

Easy Access Australia – A Travel Guide to Australia includes a chapter covering South Australia. It costs $24.85, including postage and handling, from PO Box 218 Kew 3101.

Accessible parking and toilets are available at Adelaide airport but passengers board their flights via stairs from the tarmac. Wheelchair passengers are boarded via a modified fork-lift arrangement which conveys you to the plane door. Both Ansett and Qantas provide the service to get you on board safely.

From Melbourne you can take the V/Line train to Ballarat then change to an accessible V/Line bus for the journey to Adelaide (Melbourne ☎ (03) 9619 2354/5 or freecall 008 131716). The Indian Pacific train runs from Sydney to Perth via Adelaide twice weekly with an accessible carriage (but not suitable for all people); Sydney ☎ (02) 255 7833, Adelaide ☎ 8217 4240.

The Adelaide city council recognises disabled parking stickers issued in other states and there is an excellent supply of off-street car parking off North Terrace and Hindley St. The *City of Adelaide Access Map and Directory* showing accessible buildings and toilets is available from the South Australian Tourism Commission, ☎ 8212 1505, 1 King William St, and an information booth in Rundle Mall.

Access Cabs on ☎ 8234 6444 provides wheelchair accessible taxis while Avis and Hertz provide hand-controlled hire vehicles.

Bruce Cameron

check under 'Organisations' in the Yellow Pages telephone book.

Conservation Groups

The Conservation Council of SA (CCSA) (☎ 8223 5155) is at 120 Wakefield St in Adelaide. It's the major umbrella organisation for conservation groups in the state, with around 60 members. Major conservation issues in SA include water issues (such as overuse of ground water resources and increasing salinity in the Murray River), clearance of native vegetation and the problems of land degradation.

The Australian Conservation Foundation (☎ 8232 2566) and the Nature Conservation Society of SA (☎ 8223 6301) have their offices in the same building.

Australian Trust for Conservation Volunteers

This nonpolitical, nonprofit group organises practical conservation projects (such as tree planting, walking track construction and flora and fauna surveys) for volunteers to take part in. Travellers are welcome. It's an excellent way to get involved with the conservation movement and, at the same time, visit some of the more interesting areas of the state. Volunteers could find themselves working anywhere from the Nullarbor to Lake Eyre to Naracoorte to Kangaroo Island.

ATCV projects are generally undertaken over a weekend or a week; all food, transport and accommodation is supplied in return for a small contribution to help cover costs. There are three packages available: the Conservator Package (one to 20 days) costs $20 per day plus a $25 membership fee; the Banksia Package, which lasts four weeks for $560 (membership included); and the six-week Echidna Package, which costs $840 including membership. For information, contact the SA office (☎ 8207 8747) at the TAFE College, Brookway Drive, Campbelltown in Adelaide.

BUSINESS HOURS & HOLIDAYS
Business Hours
Most shops open at 9 am and close at 5 or 5.30 pm weekdays, and either noon or 5 pm on Saturday. In most larger towns there is one late shopping night each week, when the doors stay open until 9 or 9.30 pm. Sunday trading is catching on in Adelaide, but elsewhere the doors remain closed on the Sabbath. Of course there are many exceptions, and all sorts of places stay open late and all weekend – particularly milk bars, convenience stores, supermarkets and road-houses.

Banks are open from 9.30 am to 4 pm Monday to Thursday, and until 5 pm on Friday; the notable exception is the Adelaide Bank, where most branches stay open until 6 pm on Wednesday and from 9 am to 12 noon on Saturday. Credit unions and building societies have the same hours as the Adelaide Bank.

Post offices are open from 9 am to 5 pm on weekdays.

Holidays
The Christmas holiday season is part of the long summer school vacation. This, and Easter, are the times you are most likely to find long queues and accommodation booked out. There are three other shorter school holiday periods during the year (see When to Go earlier in this chapter).

The following is a list of public holidays in SA:

New Year's Day – 1 January
Australia Day – 26 January
Easter – Good Friday, Easter Saturday to Monday
Anzac Day – 25 April
Adelaide Cup Day – third Monday in May
Labour Day – first Monday in October
Christmas Day – 25 December
Boxing Day – 26 December

CULTURAL EVENTS
The biennial three-week Adelaide Festival of Arts is Australia's premier cultural celebration. Writers' Week is run as part of the Festival and is one of only three or four top international literary festivals. Over 20 international and 50 interstate writers of note are invited for a week of panel and meet-the-author sessions. Other notable events include several music, food and wine festivals in the state's major wine-growing areas.

Migrants from many countries have added an international flavour to the SA cultural scene, with popular festivals such as the Hahndorf German Festival and the Kernewek Lowender (literally Cornish Festival). There are also typically Australian events – like surf-lifesaving competitions on beaches during summer; or the outback race meetings, which draw together isolated town and station folk, and more than a few eccentric bush characters.

There are happenings in SA all year round and the following is just a brief overview. Check the SATC for dates and details of others.

January
> This must be German month, what with the Schutzenfest (a shooting festival with lots of feasting and fun) in Adelaide, the Hahndorf German Festival at Hahndorf and the Oom-Pah-Fest (a brass band festival) at Tanunda in the Barossa. At Port Lincoln there's Tunarama, a mad-cap celebration of the tuna industry.

February
> There are no major events, but you can go to rodeos at Berri, Bordertown, Freeling and Peterborough. There's also the Compass Cup, at Mt Compass on the Fleurieu Peninsula, where you

can watch cow-racing and throw cow turds – dry ones, fortunately.

March

There's the *Multicultural Carnival* in Adelaide, the *Essenfest* (another eating festival) at Tanunda and the *Adelaide Hills Harvest Festival*. You could also try the *Medieval Fair* at Birdwood, in the Adelaide Hills, with jousting and other knightly spectacles, and the *Strzelecki Stomp* at Lyndhurst.

Held on even-dated years, the acclaimed *Adelaide Festival of Arts* is three weeks of music, theatre, opera, ballet, art exhibitions, light relief and plenty of parties. The *Fringe Festival* holds 'alternative' cultural activities – ranging from bizarre to serious to experimental – over the same period.

April

Anzac Day, the national public holiday on 25 April, commemorates the landing of Anzac troops at Gallipoli in 1915. Memorial marches by the returned soldiers of both world wars and the veterans of Korea and Vietnam are held all over the state.

Good things this month include the *Celtic Folk Festival* at Kapunda and the *Barossa Valley Vintage Festival*, which is held on odd-numbered years.

May

The four-day *Kernewek Lowender Cornish Festival* at Kadina, Moonta and Wallaroo celebrates the Cornish heritage of Yorke Peninsula's 'Copper Triangle'. There's plenty of Celtic fun and games, and you can try traditional Cornish pasties and beer.

Other good ones this month include the *Autumn Leaves Festival* at Aldgate, in the Adelaide Hills, and the *Clare Valley Gourmet Weekend*. At McLaren Vale, on the Fleurieu Peninsula, the *From the Sea to the Vines Festival* features seafood and fine wine.

June

Country music freaks will enjoy the *Riverland Country Music Festival* and the *Country Music Awards* at Barmera.

July

July is a cold and wet month for festival freaks. Still, there's the *Marananga Night of Music* with brass bands in the Barossa, and the *Willunga Almond Blossom Festival*, a high time for almond lovers on the Fleurieu Peninsula. For something entirely different, try the *Australian Camel Cup* at Marree.

August

The highlight is the *Barossa Classic Gourmet Weekend*, during which lovers of good food and wine may think they've found paradise.

September

This is another good month for music, with the *State Folk & Music Festival* at Victor Harbor, the *Festival of Country Music* at Port Pirie, and the very popular *International Barossa Music Festival* – this one has at least a week (it may be increased to a fortnight in future) of picnics, wine and big-name bands playing jazz, rock and classical music. There's also an *Oysterfest* at Ceduna, on the west coast.

October

There's even more eating and drinking, this time at the *McLaren Vale Wine Bushing Festival* and the *Continuous Picnic*, both in the wine-growing area around McLaren Vale south of Adelaide.

November

The annual *Christmas Pageant* is a fun time for kids, with a huge procession through Adelaide's streets of floats featuring fairy tale characters and the like.

December

In December everyone is too busy packing for the holidays to be concerned with festivals.

POST & COMMUNICATIONS

Postal Rates

Australia's postal services are relatively efficient but not too cheap. It costs 45c to send a standard letter or postcard within Australia, while aerogrammes cost 70c.

Air-mail letters/postcards cost 75/70c to New Zealand, 85/80c to Singapore and Malaysia, 95/90c to Hong Kong and India, $1.05/95c to the USA and Canada, and $1.20/1 to Europe and the UK – letters over 20 grams will cost more to send.

Sending Mail

Post offices are open from 9 am to 5 pm Monday to Friday. However, you can often get stamps from local post offices operated from newsagencies or from Australia Post shops (mainly in Adelaide), on Saturday morning.

Receiving Mail

All post offices will hold mail for visitors. You can also have mail sent to you at the American Express office in ANZ house at 13 Grenfell St, Adelaide provided you have an Amex card or carry Amex travellers' cheques – you'll need an acceptable ID if you don't have a card.

Telephone

Local Calls Local calls from public phones cost 40c for an unlimited amount of time. You can make local calls from gold or blue phones – often found in shops, hotels, bars, etc – and from payphone booths.

Long Distance Calls It's also possible to make long-distance (STD – Subscriber Trunk Dialling) calls from virtually any public phone. Many public phones accept the Telstra Phonecards, which come in $2, $5, $10 and $20 denominations, and are available from retail outlets such as post offices and delis and newsagents which display the Phonecard logo. You keep using the card until the value has been used in calls. Otherwise, have plenty of 20c, 50c and $1 coins, and be prepared to feed them through at a fair old rate. STD calls are cheaper in off-peak hours – see the front of a local telephone book for the different distance rates.

STD calls are cheaper at night. In ascending order of cost:

Economy – from 6 pm Saturday to 8 am Monday; 10 pm to 8 am every night
Night – from 6 to 10 pm Monday to Friday
Day – from 8 am to 6 pm Monday to Saturday

International Calls From most STD phones you can also make ISD (International Subscriber Dialling) calls. Dialling ISD you can get through to overseas numbers almost as quickly as you can access local numbers and if your call is brief it needn't cost very much.

All you do is dial 0011 for overseas, the country code (44 for Britain, 1 for the USA or Canada, 64 for New Zealand), the city code (171 or 181 for London, 212 for New York, etc), and then the telephone number. And have a Phonecard, credit card or plenty of coins to hand.

To use Optus rather than Telstra (which may or may not be cheaper – the two are constantly trying to undercut one another), dial 1 or 1456 before the ISD country code or STD area code. The prefix differs according to preferential dialling: you dial 1456 to access Optus from a Telstra phone; those who have not yet subscribed through a ballot dial 1; and Optus subscribers dial normally (0011 etc). Optus is only available from private phones in certain areas.

Using a public phone, a standard Telstra call to the USA or Britain costs 40 cents on connection and $2.40 a minute ($1.60 off peak); New Zealand is 40 cents on connection and $2 a minute ($1.20 off peak). Off-peak times are available for all countries, but varies depending on the destination – ring ☎ 0102 for details. The weekend is the cheapest time to ring.

With the competition offered by Optus, Telstra often has discount specials to various destinations, although many of these are only available from private phones.

Country Direct is a service that gives travellers in Australia direct access to operators

---

Phone Changes

Australia is running out of telephone numbers! In response, Austel (the Australian Telecommunications Authority) is giving every phone and fax number an additional one or two digits to bring the total to eight. This process began in 1994 and is scheduled to be completed in March 1999.

When the changes are complete, Australia will have only four area codes instead of the 54 it had in 1994. The area code for SA will be 08 in company with Western Australia and the Northern Territory.

In SA the first numbers were changed in February 1995 and the process will be completed in February 1997. The changes are straightforward, except for Kangaroo Island, where they become a little tricky. Adelaide's new numbers came into effect in August 1996 and are given in this book.

After each change there is a six-month period when both the old and new numbers are accessible. This is followed by a further three-month period when a recorded message will refer the caller to the White Pages information section.

For details of changes to each region see the Information section at the start of each chapter. ■

in numerous countries, to make collect or credit card calls. For a list of the most-often called countries hooked into this system, check under Operator Assisted Services in the telephone book; for details of other countries ring ☎ 0103.

Some public phones are set up to take only bank cash cards or credit cards, and these too are convenient, although you need to keep an eye on how much the call is costing as it can quickly mount up. The minimum charge for a call on one of these phones is $1.60, which includes 40c for Telstra.

Toll-Free Calls Many businesses and some government departments operate a toll-free service, so provided you're ringing from outside the Adelaide metropolitan area, it's a free call. Toll-free numbers have the prefix 1800 (or the old toll-free prefix 008). Phone numbers with the prefixes 018, 015 or 041 are mobile or car phones.

Nine-digit numbers starting with 0055 are for recorded information services. These calls cost from 35c to 70c per minute.

TIME
Australia is divided into three time zones: Western Standard Time is plus eight hours from GMT/UTC (WA only), Central Standard Time is plus 9½ hours (NT, SA) and Eastern Standard Time is plus 10 (Tasmania, Victoria, NSW, Queensland). When it's noon in SA it's 10.30 am in the west and 12.30 pm in the east.

During summer things get slightly confused as daylight saving time (when clocks are put forward an hour) does not operate in WA, Queensland or the NT, while in Tasmania it lasts for two months longer than in the other states.

In SA, daylight saving starts at the end of October and finishes at the end of March.

ELECTRICITY
Voltage is 220-240 V and the plugs are three-pin, but not the same as British three-pin plugs. Users of electric shavers or hairdryers should note that, apart from in fancy hotels, it's difficult to find converters to take either

US flat two-pin plugs or the European round two-pin plugs. Adaptors for British plugs can be found in good hardware shops, chemists and travel agents.

WEIGHTS & MEASURES
Australia uses the metric system. Petrol and milk are sold by the litre, apples and potatoes by the kg, distance is measured by the metre or km, and speed limits are in km per hour (km/h).

For those who need help with metric there's a conversion table at the back of this book.

BOOKS
Adelaide has a large number of new and secondhand bookshops; look under Books in the Yellow Pages telephone book. Most general bookshops in the state have a section devoted to Australiana, with books on almost every subject you care to mention.

Aboriginal History
The award-winning *Triumph of the Nomads*, by Geoffrey Blainey, chronicles the life of Australia's original inhabitants, and convincingly demolishes the myth that the Aborigines were 'primitive' people trapped on a hostile continent. They were in fact extremely successful in adapting to and overcoming the difficulties presented by the climate and resources (or seeming lack of them) – the book's an excellent read.

Another very good book on this subject is Josephine Flood's *Archaeology of the Dreamtime*, which has quite a bit on SA.

For a sympathetic historical account of what's happened to the original Australians since whites arrived, read *Aboriginal Australians* by Richard Broome.

A Change of Ownership, by Mildred Kirk, covers similar ground to Broome's book, but does so more concisely, focusing on the land rights movement and its historical background. For something specific to SA, try *Survival in Our Own Land*, edited by Christobel Mattingley & Ken Hampton, which has present-day and historical accounts by Nungas (South Australian Aborigines).

The excellent *Flinders Ranges Dreaming* by Dorothy Tunbridge is a collection of 50 Dreamtime stories from the Adnyamathanha people of the northern Flinders Ranges. It has many maps and beautiful photographs and makes a great guide to important non-secret Aboriginal cultural sites in the region. The book was an initiative of young Adnyamathanha who were afraid of losing their heritage.

European History

For a good introduction read *A Short History of Australia*, a most accessible and informative general history by the late Manning Clark, a highly regarded Aussie historian. *The Exploration of Australia*, by Michael Cannon, is coffee-table book in size, presentation and price, but it's a fascinating reference book about the gradual European uncovering of the continent.

For serious students, the *Flinders History of SA* (Wakefield Press, 1986), in three hefty volumes, is extremely comprehensive and takes you from the genesis of the colony in London to the 1980s. Each volume covers a different aspect: social history, political history and economic history.

Much more concise, and correspondingly cheaper, is *A History of SA – From Colonial Days to the Present*, by RM Gibbs.

Cooper's Creek, by Alan Moorehead, is a classic account of the ill-fated Burke and Wills expedition which dramatises the horrors and hardships faced by the early explorers. Charles Sturt, Edward John Eyre and John MacDouall Stuart were famous South Australian explorers and all kept detailed journals; these have been published and can be read at the State Library, if no longer in print.

For something more light-hearted try *Maisie: Her Life, Her Loves, Her Letters 1898-1902*, edited by Joan Willington (Wakefield Press). This collection of letters gives a fascinating look at the social life of colonial SA as seen through the eyes of an enthusiastic young lady, Maisie Smith.

Fiction

You don't need to worry about being starved of good reading matter during your trip to South Australia; there's plenty of excellent recent local literature, including the works of novelists such as Peter Goldsworthy, Geraldine Halls, Ben Winch and Barbara Hanrahan, and prize-winning poet Nan Whitcombe.

Goldsworthy's novels *Maestro* and *Honk if you're Jesus* have received critical acclaim. His most recent novel is *Wish*, a biologically engineered love story involving a gorilla and a man.

The colonial SA writer Catherine Helen Spence was a controversial figure 140 years ago when she wrote *Clara Morison*. This novel details the struggles of a young, educated Scottish woman who, after being jilted on arrival in SA in the 1850s, finds she must make a new life for herself among the working class. It's considered a milestone in Australian literature.

Originally from Tumby Bay, the popular travel writer and poet Kate Llewellyn's most recent work is *Floral Mother*, a collection of thinking essays on the themes of nature, food and family.

Emerging young local writer Ben Winch has set *My Boyfriend's Father*, a rites-of-passage novel for the '90s, in Adelaide, while Garry Disher has charted one family's fortunes in the wheat and wool country of SA's mid-north in his latest book, *The Sunken Road*.

Also worth reading is *Bringing the Water*, an anthology on the theme of clean water, which is an appropriate subject in a dry state like SA. This collection of 35 stories from local writers was inspired by the fact that Port Adelaide was the only major port in Australia where ships refused to take on drinking water.

Geraldine Halls is a local thriller writer (using the pen name Charlotte Jay) of international fame. Halls' acclaimed and popular novel *This is my Friend's Chair* is a beautifully paced saga of the disintegration of an Adelaide family over 50 years from the 1920s.

Travel Guides

This is the only comprehensive travel guide to SA, although there is superficial coverage of the state in national guides such as Lonely Planet's *Australia – a travel survival kit* and Rough Guides *Australia*.

There are some good regional books such as the RAA's *Adelaide Hills*, the *Mid-North &Yorke Peninsula*, the *South East* and the *Flinders Ranges* – these cost $4 to members and $8 to nonmembers. The Royal Geographical Society of Australasia (South Australian Branch) (RGSA (SA)) has the truly excellent *Explore the Barossa* and *Guide to the Flinders Ranges*. They're great value for anyone wanting a more in-depth look at these fascinating areas.

There are a number of outback guides including Lonely Planet's *Outback Australia*, which covers remote tracks and highways in SA. It includes lots of practical advice, as does Brian Sheedy's *Outback on a Budget*. There are a number of other books about vehicle preparation and driving in the outback, including the hefty *Explore Australia by Four-Wheel Drive* by Peter & Kim Wherrett (Viking O'Neil). *Sean & David's Long Drive*, a hilarious, offbeat road book by young Australian author Sean Condon, is one of the titles in Lonely Planet's new 'Journeys' travel literature series.

MAPS

One of the best places to go for touring maps is the RAA headquarters (☎ 8202 4500), at 41 Hindmarsh Square in Adelaide. Here you'll find state, regional, local, town and souvenir maps; the RAA's own regional maps, which are free to members ($1.50 to nonmembers) give a complete coverage of the state and are generally the best available.

Also excellent are Bicycle SA's cycle route maps ($7.50) – ideal for motoring as well – which are available from major cycle shops and the State Information Centre. The RAA stocks Westprint's well-regarded maps ($6.95) of the Simpson Desert region, the Flinders Ranges and Yorke Peninsula.

Other touring maps are published by the oil companies and you can buy them up at most service stations.

The Department of Environment & Natural Resources publishes illustrated maps with text ($6.95) of the Adelaide Hills, Kangaroo Island, the Barossa and the outback – these are ideal for laminating as mementos. Carto Graphics does similar maps for similar prices of the Fleurieu Peninsula, the South-East and the Nullarbor Plain.

Universal Business Directories (UBD) street directories *Adelaide* ($20.95/26.95 for RAA members/nonmembers) and *SA Cities & Towns* ($17.95/23.95) are both excellent; Gregory's Adelaide directory ($18.95/23.95) is just as comprehensive, and is a handier size for the glovebox.

For bushwalking and other activities requiring large-scale maps, the 1:100,000 topographic sheets put out by the Australian Surveying & Land Information Group (AUSLIG) are the ones to get. Two of the main outlets in Adelaide are run by the Department of Environment & Natural Resources: Mapland, at 282 Richmond Rd, Netley, and the Land Information Centre in the Colonel Light Centre, at 25 Pirie St in the city. The Map Shop at 16 Peel St also has a comprehensive range. The more popular sheets are generally available over the counter at shops that sell specialist bushwalking gear and outdoor equipment.

MEDIA
Newspapers & Magazines

Adelaide's lone daily newspaper, *The Advertiser*, is published from Monday to Saturday, while the *Sunday Mail* appears on Sunday; the free literary newspaper, *Adelaide Review*, appears monthly. There are around 30 suburban and country newspapers, which naturally focus on local issues. They're a good guide to what's going on in their particular area.

You can buy the major interstate newspapers and magazines at any good newsagent. The State Library on North Terrace has a number of international newspapers in its reading area.

Radio & TV

SA has over 20 commercial and noncommercial amplitude-modulated (AM) services, with eight of these in Adelaide, and nearly 50 VHF frequency-modulated (FM) services, of which 11 are in Adelaide. They include the Australian Broadcasting Corporation (ABC), which broadcasts on both bands.

Services operating in the FM sub-band 87.5 to 88 Hz provide information services in such formats as tourist attractions, foreign language and religion. They are found at Glenelg (an Adelaide suburb), Hahndorf in the Adelaide Hills, Lyndoch in the Barossa Valley, and Bordertown in the South-East.

Sadly, there are no radio stations in the sparsely populated outback. If you've fitted a good, long-range aerial you should be able to pick up the ABC just about all the way from Port Augusta to Alice Springs. If you haven't, buy a tape deck and some tapes.

There are five TV stations in Adelaide, including the ABC (Channel 2). Affectionately known as 'Auntie', the ABC has a good reputation for news and current affairs, but has been accused of staidness. The same can't be said about the Special Broadcasting Service (SBS) on Channel 0, which has foreign language news and movies, including alternative films. For weekly programmes check *The Guide* in Thursday's *Advertiser*.

Country SA receives five commercial TV services including Imparja, an Aboriginal-run station operating out of Alice Springs which has a 'footprint' covering much of rural SA. It broadcasts a variety of commercial programmes and Aboriginal-oriented features.

FILM & PHOTOGRAPHY

Including developing costs, 36-exposure Kodachrome 64 and Fujichrome 100 slide film costs around $22 for a single roll.

There are a number of camera shops in Adelaide and the major towns, and the standard of camera service is generally high. The standard of developing is also high, with many places offering one-hour developing

of print film. Unfortunately, you have to send your Kodachrome slide film to Melbourne for developing.

SA conditions present no special problems to photographers, provided you have a modicum of ability, although in the outback you have to allow for the intensity of the light. Best results in northern regions are obtained early in the morning and late in the afternoon, when the light (hence contrast) is much softer. As the sun gets higher, colours appear washed out and contrasts are much harsher. You must also allow for the intensity of reflected light when taking shots on the beach.

In the north, especially in summer, allow for temperature extremes and do your best to keep film as cool as possible, particularly after exposure; *never* leave your camera or film in the glovebox or on the dash when the vehicle's in the sun. The only other likely hazards are getting dust in the camera (keep it in a dustproof container) and running out of film.

As in any country, politeness goes a long way when taking photographs; always ask before taking pictures of people. Note that many Aboriginal people do not like to have their photographs taken, even from a distance.

LAUNDRY

Most accommodation houses in SA either have modern, coin-operated laundry facilities, or they'll arrange to have your washing done.

Otherwise there are plenty of self-service laundromats (usually open 12 hours daily, seven days) and drycleaning outlets. The larger country towns will generally have one of each.

In Adelaide, look under 'Drycleaners' and 'Laundries-Self Service' in the Yellow Pages telephone book to locate services near you.

Most coin-operated washing machines will only take $1 and 20c coins. Expect to pay at least $2 for a load of washing and $2 for the dryer.

It usually costs around $12 to dryclean three garments, provided none are pleated.

HEALTH

So long as you have not visited an infected country in the past 14 days (aircraft refuelling stops do not count) no vaccinations are required for entry. Naturally, if you're going to be travelling around in places apart from Australia, appropriate immunisations are highly advisable.

Medical care in SA is first-class and only moderately expensive. Health insurance cover is available in Australia, but there is usually a waiting period after you sign up before any claims can be made.

If you have an immediate health problem, phone or visit the casualty section at the nearest public hospital; there are 81 of them (including 68 outside Adelaide) with a total of 5100 beds. Visits to public hospitals are free, but if you want to see a private doctor the consultation fee will be around $30.

Visitors from the UK, New Zealand, Malta, Italy, Sweden and the Netherlands have reciprocal health rights in Australia and can register at any Medicare office. This entitles them to free or heavily subsidised medical treatment at public hospitals and from clinics which 'bulk bill' (ie the bill for the treatment is sent direct to Medicare).

Travel Insurance

Even if you normally carry health or hospitalisation insurance, or live in a country where health care is provided by the government, it's still a good idea to buy some travellers' insurance that covers both health and loss of baggage.

Make sure the policy includes health care and medication in the countries you plan to visit and includes a flight home for you and anyone you're travelling with, should your condition warrant it. It's not a bad idea to have ambulance cover as well, because a ride in one may ruin the holiday budget.

Medical Kit

It's always a good idea to travel with a basic medical kit even in areas where first-aid supplies are generally readily available. Obviously, a first-aid kit is essential in the outback, which is one of the last places you'd want to be caught unprepared.

Some of the items that should be included in any kit are: band-aids, a sterilised gauze bandage, elastoplast, cotton wool, a thermometer, tweezers, scissors, antibiotic cream and ointment, contraceptives (if required), paracetamol or aspirin (for pain and fever), an antiseptic agent, a broad-spectrum, water-resistant sunscreen lotion (graded at least 15+) and insect repellent. Calamine lotion, antihistamine cream and old-fashioned Tiger Balm are all useful for insect bites. Unless you're an expert, it's commonsense to have a good first-aid book as well, and *don't* forget any medication you're already taking.

For sound advice on anything more comprehensive, ask at any of the numerous St John Ambulance centres scattered around the state; they also sell kits and first-aid books.

Health Precautions

Travellers from the northern hemisphere need to be aware of the intensity of the sun in SA, particularly in summer. The situation is even worse now that there's a hole in the protective ozone layer, and those ultraviolet rays can have you burnt to a crisp even on an overcast day; if in doubt wear protective lotion, a wide-brimmed hat and a long-sleeved shirt with a collar. Australia has a high incidence of skin cancer, a fact directly connected to exposure to the sun. Be careful.

Dehydration and heat-related illnesses are real dangers in warm weather, particularly if you're not used to the heat. At such times it's important to drink plenty of water (*not* alcohol or soft drinks, which increase dehydration) and to take it easy – rest in the shade rather than run around in the sun.

SA's most important insect-borne diseases are Ross River fever and Murray Valley encephalitis, both of which are carried by mosquitoes. Certain charming flies have a habit of wallowing in horrible things, like human excrement, then transferring the bacteria to you by walking and vomiting on your food. Bury your waste if there are no toilet facilities where you're camping.

The contraceptive pill is available on prescription only, so a visit to a doctor is necessary. Doctors are listed in the Yellow Pages phone book or you can visit the outpatients section of a public hospital. Condoms are available from chemists, many convenience stores, and vending machines in public toilets.

HIV/AIDS The Human Immunodeficiency Virus (HIV) may develop into Acquired Immune Deficiency Syndrome (AIDS). HIV is a major health problem in many countries, and any exposure to human blood, blood products, or body fluids may put you at risk.

In many developing countries, transmission is predominantly through heterosexual sexual activity. This is quite different to industrialised countries like Australia, where transmission is mainly through sexual contact between males, or contact with contaminated needles used by IV drug users.

Apart from abstinence, the most effective prevention is always to practise safe sex using condoms. It is impossible to detect the HIV-positive status of a person without a blood test.

HIV/AIDS can also be spread through infected blood transfusions; fortunately, all donor blood in SA is screened for HIV and hepatitis, but be careful if you're travelling here through Asia or Africa. It can also be spread by dirty needles – vaccinations, acupuncture, tattooing, and ear, nose and body piercing are potentially lethal if the equipment has not been sterilised.

For confidential advice and information on HIV/AIDS, contact the Aids Council of SA (☎ 8362 1611; toll-free 1800 888 559) between 9 am and 5.30 pm weekdays. If you require urgent help with an AIDS-related illness outside these times, call the 24-hour counselling service Lifeline (☎ 8212 3444).

WOMEN TRAVELLERS

SA is generally a safe place for women travellers, although as a rule of thumb it's best to avoid walking alone late at night in any of the larger towns – particularly near clubs and pubs. Sexual harassment is unfortunately still second nature to many Aussie males, and it's generally true to say that the further you get from 'civilisation' (ie Adelaide), the less enlightened your average Aussie male is going to be.

Female hitchers should exercise caution at all times (see the section on hitching in the Getting Around chapter.) In fact, females intending to hitch alone should definitely think again.

The Women's Information Switchboard (☎ 8223 1244; toll-free 1800 188 158) in Adelaide operates from 9 am to 9 pm daily except public holidays. It can give you information, advice or referrals on just about anything of specific interest to women, including current issues, health, social venues, recreation and activities.

For health matters between 9 am and 5 pm weekdays, call the Women's Health Information & Counselling Line on ☎ 8267 5366.

You can also check under 'Women's Organisations & Activities' in the Yellow Pages telephone book.

GAY & LESBIAN TRAVELLERS

Gayline (☎ 8362 3223) in Adelaide operates between 7 and 10 pm every night and during the day (weekends only) from 2 to 5 pm. It offers a counselling and referrals service and can also give information on social activities, accommodation and other matters. They'll also give you up-to-date information on gay-friendly doctors and other service providers.

The fortnightly newspaper *Adelaide gt*, published by Adelaide Gay Times (☎ 8232 1544) at 55 Halifax St, Adelaide, is an excellent reference for visiting gays and lesbians; apart from general articles, there's social news, reviews, venues, classifieds and community listings. Call them for details of outlets.

Also published by Adelaide Gay Times, the *Lesbian & Gay Adelaide Map* shows venues and services of interest in the city area.

EMERGENCY

In the case of a life-threatening situation dial 000. This call is free from any phone and the operator will connect you with either the police, ambulance or fire brigade. To dial any of these services direct, check the inside front cover of any local telephone book.

Crisis Care (☎ 13 16 11; toll-free 008 131 611) offers an after-hour's counselling and referral service for anyone experiencing a crisis of a personal nature, whether it be accommodation or a problem with your partner. It operates weekdays from 4 pm to 9 am and 24 hours on weekends and public holidays.

For other telephone crisis and personal counselling services (such as sexual assault, poisons information or alcohol and drug problems), check 'Community Help Reference' near the front of the White Pages telephone book.

DANGERS & ANNOYANCES
Animal Hazards
Snakes & Spiders There are a few unique and sometimes dangerous creatures, although it's unlikely that you'll come across any of them, particularly if you stick to the cities. Here's a run down just in case.

The best-known danger in the bush, and the one that captures visitors' imaginations, is snakes. Although there are many venomous snakes there are few that are aggressive, and unless you have the misfortune to stand on one it's unlikely that you'll be bitten. Some, such as tiger snakes, will attack if alarmed; all will try to bite if they're provoked!

To minimise your chances of being bitten always wear boots, socks and long trousers when walking through undergrowth where snakes may be present. Don't put your hands into holes and crevices, and be careful when collecting firewood. As most people are bitten while trying to catch or kill snakes, the best approach is to leave them alone. If you do see one, give it a wide berth so it can get on with its business. It'll probably be more worried about you than you are of it.

Snake bites do not cause instantaneous death and antivenenes are usually available, although in remote areas this may be some distance away. Keep the victim calm and still, wrap the bitten limb tightly, as you would for a sprained ankle, and attach a splint to immobilise it. Then seek medical

help, if possible with the dead snake for identification; don't attempt to catch the snake if there is even a remote possibility of being bitten again. Tourniquets, slashing the puncture wounds with razor blades, and sucking the poison out are now comprehensively discredited.

The female common redback spider is particularly lethal, and it's generally best not to play with any spider. Be careful around buildings, where redbacks tend to congregate, and check outdoor furniture before using it. You should also look under the seat for spiders before sitting down in bush dunnies, particularly the long-drop variety. For redback bites apply ice and seek medical attention.

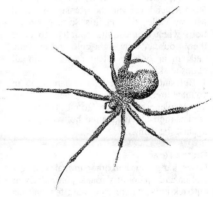

The feared redback spider is only about half this size, but check under the toilet seat anyway, *before* you sit down...

Insects For four to six months of the year – and even longer in the hotter outback areas – you'll have to cope with two banes of the Australian outdoors: the fly and the mosquito.

In Adelaide the flies are not too bad, despite what city folk might tell you; it's in the country that they start getting out of hand, and the further 'out' you get the worse the flies seem to be. In the north, where they can be particularly troublesome, they emerge with the warmer spring weather (late

August) and last until winter. They love to crawl on your face and drink from your eyes (tears are a valuable source of protein) and in bad times they don't just come in twos and threes; they swarm!

If you're not used to flies (and who could be?) buy yourself a fly veil to cover your head before heading north – you can get them at the larger camping and outdoor shops in Adelaide. Failing that, you'll have to rely on either the 'Great Australian Wave' (ineffective and tiring) or repellents such as Aerogard and Rid to deter the little bastards.

Mossies too can be a problem in the warmer months, particularly near water that's been laying about for a few days – it doesn't take long for them to breed up. They can carry viruses such as the debilitating Ross River fever and the occasionally fatal Murray Valley encephalitis, so take precautions when in mosquito country. To deter them you can wear light-coloured clothing and smear or spray Rid repellent on all exposed skin.

Bull-ants can give you a hard time in country areas – you'll know them by their aggressiveness and size (about 20 mm), as well as their bite (like a red-hot wire jabbed against the skin).

On the Road

Cows, kangaroos and other animals can be a real hazard on country roads, particularly in outback areas where fences are few and far between. A high-speed collision with one will badly damage if not wreck the car, kill the animal and maybe even the vehicle's occupants. Animals lack road-sense, as do drivers who've been drinking alcohol. If you're going to get on the booze, give someone else the car keys.

See the Getting Around chapter for more on driving hazards.

Bushfires

Bushfires happen every year in SA. Sometimes they can be catastrophic, with many human deaths and the loss of millions of dollars worth of property and livestock. Don't be the mug who starts one! Always site your campfire in a large open space at least three metres from any flammable vegetation, and make sure it's out before you leave. Keep the fire small and provide a windbreak if necessary. Campfires are banned during the fire danger period, which varies from region to region but is usually from 1 November to 31 March; check with the Country Fire Service on ☎ 8204 3333.

In hot, dry, windy weather, be extremely careful with any naked flame – no cigarette butts out of car windows, please. On a Total Fire Ban day (listen to the radio or watch the billboards on country roads), it is forbidden to use even a camping stove in the open, let alone light a campfire. The locals will not be amused if they catch you breaking this particular law, which carries severe penalties, and they'll happily dob you in.

If you're unfortunate enough to find yourself driving through a bushfire, don't make the mistake of trying to run for safety, because you may not get there. Try to park in an open space away from trees and tall dry grass, and stay inside your car with the windows wound up until the danger is past. Lie on the floor under the dashboard, covering yourself with a wool blanket if possible. The front of the fire should pass quickly, and you'll be much safer in the car than out in the open. It's very important to cover up with a wool blanket or protective clothing, as heat radiation is the big killer in bushfire situations.

Bushwalkers should take local advice before setting out, particularly in forested areas such as the Adelaide Hills and southern Flinders Ranges. On a day of Total Fire Ban, don't go – delay your trip until the weather has changed. Chances are that it will be so unpleasantly hot and windy, you'll be better off in an air-conditioned pub sipping a cool beer.

If you're out in the bush and you see smoke, even at a distance, take it seriously. Go to the nearest open space, downhill if possible. A forested ridge is the most dangerous place to be as fire moves very quickly uphill.

Having said all that, far more bushwalkers in SA die of thirst and exposure than in bushfires!

WORK

If you come to Australia on a 12-month 'working holiday' visa you can officially only work for three out of those 12 months; working on a regular tourist visa is strictly *verboten*. Many travellers on tourist visas do find casual work, but in SA, which has an unemployment rate hovering around 10%, and youth unemployment as high as 50% in some areas, it is becoming more difficult to find a job – legal or otherwise.

To receive wages in Australia you must be in possession of a Tax File Number, issued by the Taxation Department. Forms are available from post offices and you'll need to show your passport and visa.

The best prospects for casual work include factories, bar work, waiting on tables or washing dishes, other domestic chores at outback roadhouses, nanny work and fruit picking.

If you're coming to SA with the intention of working, it's commonsense to make sure you have enough funds to cover your stay, or have a contingency plan if the work is not forthcoming. Having said that, it *is* still possible to find short-term work, it's just that the opportunities are far fewer than in the past.

The Commonwealth Employment Service (CES) has offices throughout the state, and the staff usually have a good idea of what's available where – even if they have nothing on their books they should be able to advise you on who to contact locally. Country CES offices worth checking include:

Barossa & Clare Valleys
   Cnr Cowan and Murray Sts, Gawler
   (☎ 08) 8522 0400)
Eyre Peninsula
   85 Tasman Terrace, Port Lincoln
   (☎ (08) 8621 1100)
Fleurieu Peninsula
   Shop 27, Central Shopping Centre, Victor Harbor
   (☎ (08) 8552 4388)
Flinders Ranges & Outback
   99 Commercial Rd, Port Augusta
   (☎ (08) 8647 3600)
Murray River
   3 Riverview Dve, Berri (☎ 08 8580 1111)
   8 Bridge St, Murray Bridge (☎ (08) 8532 4888)

Apart from the CES, you should check hostel notice boards, ask at the local pub and try the classified section of the daily papers under Situations Vacant, especially on Saturday. Otherwise try the agencies listed in the Yellow Pages telephone book under 'Employment Agencies', 'Employment – Labour Hire Contractors' and 'Personnel Consultants'.

The main opportunities for casual work are in the fruit-growing and wine industries; it will help if you have experience in the tourism and hospitality industries. Listed are the main harvest times and crops in SA, and seasons and regions for other work.

Activity	Time	Region/s
Citrus	Jan-Dec	Riverland
Tourism/hospitality	Jan-Feb	Coast
Fish processing	Jan-Sep	Port Lincoln, Ceduna
Grape picking	Jan-Apr	Riverland, Barossa, Clare, South-East
Peaches	Feb-Mar	Riverland
Apples/pears	Feb-Apr	Adelaide Hills
Grapevine pruning	Jun-Aug	Riverland, Barossa, Clare, South-East
Strawberries	Oct-Feb	Adelaide Hills
Stone fruits	Nov-Mar	Riverland

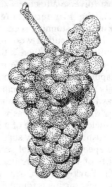

WWOOF

Willing Workers on Organic Farms (WWOOF) is a relatively new organisation in Australia, although it is well established in other countries. The idea is that you do a few hours work each day on a farm in return for bed and board. Some places have a minimum stay of a couple of days but many will take you for just a night. Some will let you stay for months.

Becoming a WWOOFer is a great way to meet interesting people and to travel cheaply. There are about 400 WWOOF associates in Australia, including over 30 in SA, and most participants are concerned to some extent with alternative lifestyles. In SA you'll find them scattered from Kingscote on Kangaroo Island, to Mannum on the Murray, to Marree in the outback, to Elliston on Eyre Peninsula.

To join WWOOF send $25 ($30 if you're two people travelling together) to WWOOF, Buchan, Vic 3885 (☎ (03) 5155 0218); they'll send you a membership number and a booklet which describes participating places all over Australia. The best time to phone the office is between 5 pm and 8 pm.

HIGHLIGHTS

The state's major attractions include Adelaide (a relaxed, attractive city with a vibrant cultural scene), the Barossa Valley (outstanding wines and German heritage), the South-East (diverse attractions and close to Victoria), the Flinders Ranges (great bushwalking and stunning scenery) and the Adelaide Hills (beautiful wooded hills and historic villages). Then there's the Cornish heritage of SA's copper-mining towns: Burra, Kapunda, Kadina and Moonta.

The only significant permanent waterway, the Murray River, has houseboating along its 650 km while in SA, as well as water sports and the timeless atmosphere of a big river.

South Australia has many superb beaches and some spectacular coastal scenery, such as the cliffs of western Eyre Peninsula and southern Yorke Peninsula. Some of Australia's best surfing is found in these two areas. If you like fishing, there are countless places along the coast where there are far more fish than people trying to catch them, even in summer.

Kangaroo Island, with its seal colonies and koalas, has really caught on as an 'ecotourism' experience, as has whale-watching at places like Victor Harbor and Head of Bight. There's also the opportunity to see a great white shark at close quarters on a tour off Port Lincoln, although the experience may put you off swimming in the sea for life.

In the vast outback you can experience some of Australia's loneliest yet most compelling country along the famous Strzelecki, Oodnadatta and Birdsville tracks. The opalmining town of Coober Pedy, where many people not only work but live underground, is totally unique. Andamooka, another outback opal town, is without doubt the closest thing in SA to frontiersville – it's like the moon with houses or, as the locals say, like Coober Pedy before it got civilised.

ACCOMMODATION

Unless stated otherwise, all rates given in this book are low season.

South Australia has plenty of accommodation, particularly in Adelaide, in popular holiday areas such as Yorke Peninsula and Kangaroo Island, and along the major highways. Except in remote areas, where you'll probably have to rely on your own resources, you'll rarely have much trouble finding somewhere to lay your head – unless, of course, it's a peak holiday period and you haven't booked.

For the budget conscious there are youth hostels, backpackers' hostels and caravan parks, while many hotels and holiday flats are also good – although the latter may not be so appealing pricewise in peak periods. There's a swag of motels right around the state, and B&B places are becoming very common in some areas. However, neither of these categories are what you'd call cheap.

A typical town with 1000 people will have a basic motel at around $40/45 for singles/doubles and a hotel or two with rooms (shared facilities) at $20/30 or better. There'll be a caravan park with tent/caravan sites for around $10/14, on-site vans for $25 or so for two, and self-contained cabins for $35, also for two. There might also be a B&B place for around $60 for two with a cooked breakfast. If the town is on a highway, or is a holiday destination, it'll probably have a number of accommodation places.

The rates for four or five people in a room are always worth checking, as most hotels and motels have at least one 'family' room with four or five beds. On-site cabins and caravans have up to six beds and are very competitive for small groups.

There are a couple of free backpackers' newspapers and booklets available at hostels around the country, and these have fairly up-to-date listings of hostels.

For a more comprehensive reference, the RAA publishes the *Accommodation Guide* ($5 members, $10 nonmembers), which lists most hotels, motels, B&B, holiday flats, farm stays, houseboats and backpackers' hostels in almost every city and town in the country. They also put out *Tourist Park Accommodation* (members $4, nonmembers $8), which lists caravan parks, cabins and camping grounds Australia-wide. These references are updated every year so the prices are generally fairly accurate.

Camping & Caravanning
South Australia has a large number of caravan parks and most times you'll find space available. If you want to get around on the cheap, camping is the way to go as nightly costs for two are around $8 to $13. Even cheaper are the basic camp grounds you find in national parks. Sites here are usually around $5 per vehicle.

In general, SA's caravan parks are well kept, conveniently located and excellent value. Many have on-site vans that you can rent for the night. These give you the comfort of a caravan without the inconvenience of actually towing one of the confounded things.

On-site cabins are also widely available. These have at least one bedroom, or at least an area which can be screened off from the rest of the unit, and usually their own kitchen, bathroom and toilet. Although small they are much less cramped than a caravan, and the price difference is generally not that great – for two people, say $25 to $30 for an

on-site van, $30 to $40 for a self-contained cabin.

In winter, if you're going to be using on-site vans and cabins on a regular basis, it's worth investing in a small heater of some sort as they're often unheated. As a rule you will also have to provide your own sheets, blankets and (usually) cooking utensils and so forth.

Camping in the bush is for many people one of the highlights of a visit to SA. In the outback you won't even need a tent most of the time as it hardly ever rains. Swags are the way to go. A night spent around a campfire under the Southern Cross is unforgettable; the silence is immense, the stars magnificent.

Bush camping has a long tradition in South Australia

Youth Hostels
There's a very active Youth Hostel Association (YHA), with 11 hostels scattered around the state. Youth hostels are part of the International Youth Hostel Federation (IYHF, also known as HI, Hostelling International), so if you're a member of the YHA in your own country, your membership entitles you to use Australian hostels as well.

YHA hostels in SA provide basic accommodation, usually in small dormitories or bunk rooms. All have cooking facilities, toilet and bathroom facilities – these are very basic in some – and there's usually a communal area where you can sit and talk. Most have a maximum-stay period – because some are often full it would hardly be fair for people to stay too long while others are being turned away. Nightly charges in SA are rock bottom – between $6 and $10 a night, plus a $2 surcharge for nonmembers and a $10 key deposit where applicable. Only the Adelaide hostel has a full-time warden.

With increased competition from the proliferation of backpackers' hostels, YHA hostels have done away with the old fetishes for curfews and doing chores, but still retain segregated dorms.

However, you must have a regulation sheet sleeping bag or bed linen – for hygiene reasons a regular sleeping bag will not do. If you haven't got sheets they can be rented at many hostels ($1.50), but it's cheaper, after a few nights' stay, to have your own. YHA offices and some larger hostels sell the official YHA sheet bag.

The annual *YHA Accommodation Guide*, which is available from all Australian and some overseas YHA offices, describes 130 YHA hostels around Australia. YHA members are eligible for discounts on 800 products and these are listed in the *YHA Discount Book*.

The Youth Hostels Association of Australia office (☎ 8231 5583) is at 38 Sturt St in Adelaide. You'll find information here on YHA hostels throughout the country and there's also a travel agency specialising in all aspects of budget travel. The office is open between 9.30 am and 5.30 pm on weekdays.

If you're not a member, think about joining. A senior membership costs $42 for the first year and $26 renewal, and entitles you to discounts (usually 10%) on such things as accommodation, travel insurance, bus passes and holiday packages. If you're an overseas resident joining in Australia, membership will cost $26.

Backpackers' Hostels

In recent years the number of backpackers' hostels has increased dramatically, particularly in Adelaide. Their standard varies enormously: some are shabby, gloomy and depressing, with cramped facilities, while others (a minority) are bright and cheerful. You'll find old houses, hotels and mansions that have been converted to backpackers' hostels, while a few have been purpose-built.

The managers sometimes have backpackers running these places, in which case it's usually not too long before standards start to slip. If you hear of any that promote themselves as 'party' hostels, don't go there if you want a quiet time. Probably the best places are the smaller, more intimate hostels where the owner is also the manager. These are usually the older hostels which were around long before the 'backpacker boom'.

The proliferation of hostels has also brought about intense competition, and you'll usually find hostel staff touting for custom at Adelaide's central bus station. To this end many have introduced inducements, such as the first night free or free breakfasts, and virtually all have courtesy transport.

Prices at backpackers' hostels are generally in line with YHA hostels – typically $10 to $12, although the $8 bed is still alive and well in some places.

There's at least one organisation (VIP) which you can join where, for a modest fee (typically $15), you'll receive a discount card (valid for 12 months) and a list of participating hostels – you get a typical discount of $1 on a night's accommodation. This is hardly a great inducement to join, but you do also receive useful discounts on other services, such as bus passes, so they're worth considering.

One practice that many people find objectionable – in independent hostels only, since it never happens in YHAs – is the 'vetting' of Australians and sometimes New Zealanders, who may be asked to provide a passport or double ID which they may not carry. Virtually all city hostels ask everyone for some ID – usually a passport – but this can also be used as a way of keeping unwanted customers out.

If you're an Aussie and encounter this kind of reception, the best you can do is persuade the desk people that you're genuinely travelling the country, and aren't just looking for a cheap place to crash for a while.

It will help if you produce a YHA or VIP card.

These cards also come in handy at the few hotels and motels that offer backpacker accommodation; in lieu of a passport, the managers will usually accept them as evidence that you really are a backpacker.

B&Bs

This is the fastest growing segment of the accommodation market, with new places opening all the time. The network of B&Bs throughout the state includes restored miners' cottages, converted stables, renovated and rambling old guesthouses, up-market country homes, shearer's quarters, romantic escapes and simple bedrooms in family homes. Many of these places are listed throughout the book.

B&B tariffs cover a wide range, but are typically in the $50 to $100 (per double) bracket. However, it's becoming difficult to find places under $70 in popular areas close to Adelaide. These days most B&B places are 'self-catered' – that is, the breakfast ingredients are provided, and you cook them yourself.

The SATC puts out the free booklet *Bed & Breakfast – Town & Country*, which covers around 160 B&Bs and host farms throughout SA.

Hotels & Pubs

Most of SA's numerous hotels – even the smallest towns seem to have one – are older places dating from at least early this century. Some go way back to the 1840s.

Originally pubs had to provide accommodation for weary travellers but this practice has long faded into history. Today, every place called a hotel does not necessarily have rooms to rent, although many still do – there's usually a sign out the front stating the fact. A 'private hotel', as opposed to a 'licensed hotel', really is a hotel and does not serve alcohol. A 'guesthouse' is much the same as a 'private hotel', although it may be licensed!

The older hotels are generally very photogenic places with great character; they're typically double-storey, with solid bluestone walls and big, wrap-around verandahs with lots of iron lacework. Many were built during 'boom' economic times, when no expense was spared to make optimistic statements. As a result they're often among the largest and most extravagant buildings in town.

Unfortunately, however, these older pubs can sometimes be on the weary side, with sagging mattresses, smelly carpets and peeling wallpaper – although many are now being renovated with the profits generated by poker machines. In summer you should ask whether or not the rooms have ceiling fans or air-con (these are a must in hotter parts), and in winter if there's wall heating or electric blankets. If there isn't, check there are enough blankets. If you're desperate for sleep, and the pub is busy, request a room that's not above the bar or facing the street.

If you don't mind the share facilities, most hotels are great value. Apart from their atmosphere, you get a plain but substantial meal for a good price, and there's usually a few local characters to meet in the bar. The rooms generally cost around $25/35 (more with private facilities) but you can often find a single room for $20; when comparing prices, remember to ask if breakfast is included.

Motels, Serviced Apartments & Holiday Flats

If you've got transport and want a more modern place with your own bathroom and other facilities, then you're moving into the motel bracket. There are stacks of motels in SA, but they're usually away from town centres unless a pub has decided to tack units on. Prices vary and with the motels, unlike hotels, singles are generally not much cheaper than doubles. If you're by yourself you'll seldom find a motel room for less than $35; in many places finding anything much cheaper than $45/50 for singles/doubles is a challenge.

Serviced apartments and holiday flats are much the same thing and bear some resemblance to motels. Basically holiday flats are found in holiday areas, serviced apartments in cities. A holiday flat is much like a motel room but usually has a kitchen or cooking facilities so you can fix your own food. Usually holiday flats are not serviced like motels – you don't get your bed made up and the cups washed out. In some holiday flats you have to provide your own sheets and bedding but others are operated just like motel rooms with a kitchen. Most motels in SA provide at least tea and coffee-making facilities and a small fridge; a holiday flat will have cooking utensils, cutlery, crockery and so on.

Holiday flats are often rented on a weekly basis but even in these cases it's worth asking if daily rates are available – this is often the case in quiet times. Paying for a week, even if you stay only for a few days, can still be cheaper than having those days at a higher daily rate. If there are more than two of you, another advantage of holiday flats is that you can often find them with two or more bedrooms. A two-bedroom holiday flat is typically priced at about 1½ times the cost of a comparable single-bedroom unit.

In holiday areas like Kangaroo Island, motels and holiday flats can be virtually interchangeable terms – there's nothing really to distinguish one from the other. In Adelaide, on the other hand, serviced apartments are often a little more obscure, although they may be advertised in the newspaper's classified ads. In the country, the best way to find out about holiday flats is to ring around the local real estate agents.

University Colleges

Although it is students who get first chance at these, nonstudents can also stay at a couple of Adelaide's university colleges during the uni vacations. These places are reasonably cheap and comfortable and provide an opportunity for you to meet people. For details, see under Places to Stay in the Adelaide chapter.

Farm Stays

For something really different you can stay on a farm (known as 'stations' in the outback) and get some first-hand experience of country living. With commodity prices the way they are, mountainous wool stockpiles and a general rural crisis, tourism offers the hope of at least some income for farmers, at a time when many are being forced off the land.

Farm accommodation varies from renovated shearer's quarters to old homesteads to modern cabins; you'll often eat with the owners, who may have activities arranged for you, or you may be left entirely to your own devices. You can usually stay in shearer's quarters for around $15 per person, although a minimum charge of $50 or more may apply. Many of these places are described throughout the book; otherwise contact SATC for details.

You can also try SA Homestead Hosted Farm Stays (☎ (08) 8576 5215), which has a number of member properties of 400 hectares or larger scattered around the state. You stay with the family and they entertain you or organise activities from around $60 to $90 per person for full board (bed and all meals).

Other Accommodation

There are plenty of places where you can camp for free, such as roadside rest areas where overnight camping is permitted. In the outback there are tens of thousands of square km where nobody is going to complain if you decide to put up the tent.

If you want to stay longer in Adelaide, the first place to look for a shared flat or a room is the classified ad section of *The Advertiser*. Also check notice boards in universities and hostels.

Finally, you can cruise the Murray River on a fully self-contained houseboat, although they're not for the budget-minded. For example, the weekly hire of a two-berth/four-berth houseboat will set you back around $485/540 in winter and $580/650 in peak periods. The houseboat scene is constantly changing, but the comprehensive booklet *SA Hire Houseboats*, put out by the Houseboat Hirers Association and available from SATC, has many listings and will give you the drum on what to expect.

FOOD

Tucker can be one of the real highlights of SA; Adelaide alone has around 700 restaurants, and even in the outback you'll find eateries serving up a style of gourmet food that was unthinkable just a few years ago.

Immigration has resulted in a very exciting food scene in SA. The Greeks, Yugoslavs, Italians, Lebanese and many others who flooded into Australia in the '50s and '60s brought, thank God, their food with them. More recent arrivals include the Vietnamese, who have added another facet to Adelaide's food scene.

Today you can have excellent Greek moussaka (and a bottle of retsina to wash it down), delicious Italian saltimbocca and pasta, or good, heavy German dumplings; you can perfume the air with garlic after stumbling out of a French bistro, or try all sorts of Middle Eastern and Arab treats. The Chinese have been sweet & souring since the gold-rush days, while more recently Indian, Thai and Malaysian restaurants have been all the rage. And for cheap eats, you can't beat some of the Vietnamese places.

Australian Food

Although there is no real definition of what constitutes Australian cuisine, there is certainly some excellent local food to try. For a start there's the great Australian meat pie – every bit as sacred an institution as the hot dog is to a New Yorker. There are a number of small bakeries that do a really good job on this classic dish, but the standard, factory-produced item is an awful concoction of anonymous meat and dark gravy in a soggy pastry case. Avoid them! In Adelaide and a few country places you can really delve into local culture with a 'pie floater' (a meat pie and tomato sauce floating in thick, green pea soup). It sounds horrible, doesn't look so hot either, but tastes great.

The really good news about South Australian tucker is the fine ingredients. Nearly everything is grown or caught right here, so you're not eating food that's been shipped halfway around the world. Everybody knows about our wonderful steaks ('This is

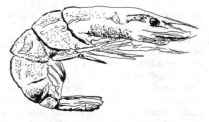

King prawns are a fresh and delicious delicacy of SA. Other sought-after seafood includes rock lobsters (crayfish), oysters and King George whiting.

cattle country, so eat beef you bastards', announce the farmers' bumper stickers), but there are lots of other things to try.

South Australia has a superb range of seafood: fish like tommy ruffs, groper and the esteemed King George whiting, or succulent lobsters and home-grown oysters. Fish & chips is very popular as a takeaway meal, although many cooks are heavy-handed with the salt and grease; check out the shops around dinnertime to discover the good ones (they'll be busy), and if you don't want salt, say so.

Vegetarians get a fair go these days; there are some excellent vegetarian restaurants in Adelaide, while in the country you'll find that the better lunch shops usually have vegetarian dishes.

Places to Eat

If you want something familiar and utterly predictable there are McDonald's, Kentucky Frieds, Pizza Huts and all the other well-known names looking no different than they do anywhere else in the world. There are also exceptionally fine restaurants of most cuisines, and Adelaide has more restaurants per head of population than any other city in Australia.

For real value for money there are a couple of dinky-di Australian eating places you should certainly try. For a start, Australian delis are terrific and they'll put together a superb sandwich. Hunt out the authentic-looking ones in any big town and you'll get a sandwich any New York deli would have trouble matching, and it's a safe bet it'll be half the price.

In the evening the best value is to be found in the pubs, particularly now that most have poker machines – there is often cut-throat competition to get customers through the door. Look for 'counter meals', so called because they used to be eaten at the counter in the front bar; they still are, but now you can get them in the lounge bars as well. Many pubs have fancy, almost restaurant-like dining rooms, where meals are a little more expensive than in the front bar – you pay more for the atmosphere, as the food comes out of the same kitchen.

Pub meals are usually simple (schnitzels, chicken and grills are perennial) but well-prepared and substantial. You'll normally pay $6 to $10 for a hearty feed, although you can see them advertised for as little as $3 where competition is particularly fierce.

For even better value, some pub dining rooms have serve-yourself salad bars where you can eat as much salad, French bread and so on as you like. If your conscience gets the better of you, you can always donate a few extra dollars through the pokies.

Counter meals are usually served as counter lunches or counter teas, the latter a hangover from the old northern English terminology where 'tea' meant the evening meal. In fact, Crow-eaters tend to say 'dinner' for lunch and 'tea' for dinner. One catch with pub meals is that they usually operate fairly strict hours, and tea time is typically just 6 to 7.30 or 8 pm.

DRINKS
Beer

South Australians are rightly proud of their excellent beers; as enthusiasts will tell you, they make the stuff that comes out of Sydney and Melbourne taste like by-product. Mind you, any Australian beer tastes awful at room temperature on a warm day –

drink it chilled. Beer is commonly called 'piss', and if you've had too much of it then you're 'pissed'.

Adelaide has two excellent large breweries: Coopers and SA Brewing. Coopers is the only Australian brewery still wholly owned by Australians – the Cooper family established the business in 1862 and has owned it ever since. It has a range of light and full-strength ales and beers for the connoisseur and these have won many awards.

Coopers also produces an excellent stout; don't despair if you're desperate for a Guinness, as several pubs in Adelaide have it on tap. Some locals drink a mixture of stout and lemonade (called portagaff), or stout and beer (called black-and-tan).

A word of warning to visitors: SA beer has a higher alcohol content than British or American beers. Standard beers contain around 5% alcohol, while 'light' beers have between 2% and 3.5%.

And another warning: people who drive under the influence of alcohol and get caught lose their licences. The maximum permissible blood-alcohol concentration level for drivers in most parts of Australia, including SA, is 0.05%.

All around Australia, the containers beer comes in, and the receptacles you drink it from, are called by different names. In SA, you usually buy it from the bottle shop in 'echoes' (375-ml bottles); beer is served across the counter in glasses of various sizes – you ask for a 'butcher' (a 200-ml glass), 'schooner' (285-ml), 'pint' (425-ml) or 'mug' (570-ml). As well, you might be asked if you want 'super', 'heavy' or 'draught' (all names for full-strength beer) or 'light' (low-alcohol beer).

While Australians are generally considered to be heavy beer drinkers, per capita beer consumption has been falling faster than in any other developed country. In the past decade per capita consumption has decreased by 20%.

Wine

If you don't fancy the local beer, try the wines. SA has some superb wine-producing areas. Best known is the famous Barossa Valley, while the Clare Valley and Coonawarra are also excellent. Then there's the Riverland, the Adelaide Hills and McLaren Vale – not quite so popular, but still with hidden treasures.

Overseas experts now realise just how good SA wines can be, and exporting them has grown into a multimillion dollar industry. In fact, it's one of the few really bright lights in a generally gloomy economic climate. Furthermore, local wines are relatively cheap. You can pick up a decent bottle of red or white from a liquor outlet for around $8 to $10, and if you aren't fussy you can do a fair bit better than that.

All over SA you'll find restaurants advertising that they're BYO. The initials stand for 'Bring Your Own' – it means that they're not licensed to serve alcohol, but you are permitted to bring your own with you. This is a real boon to budget-minded travellers because you don't have to pay the generally hefty mark-up. On the other hand, most BYO restaurants do charge a small 'corkage' fee if you do take your own.

An even more economical way of wine drinking is to do it free at the wineries; most have tasting rooms where you walk straight in and say what you'd like to try. However, free tastings don't mean you can guzzle it down like it's going out of fashion. The servings are generally tiny (particularly if it's a boutique winery) and it's expected that you will buy something if, for example, you ask to taste every chardonnay the vineyard has ever produced.

ENTERTAINMENT
Cinema

Adelaide has the commercial cinema chains, such as Hoyts and Greater Union. Their cinema centres have anything from two to six screens in the one complex. Seeing a new-release mainstream film usually costs around $12 ($7.50 for children under 15) –

less on special nights. There's also the odd drive-in cinema that refuses to go out of business.

Adelaide also has art-house and independent cinemas which generally screen either films that aren't made for mass consumption or re-runs of classic and cult movies. The main one is the Mercury Cinema.

Discos & Nightclubs

There's no shortage of these either, although almost all are confined to Adelaide and the larger towns. Clubs range from the exclusive 'members only' variety to barn-sized discos where anyone who wants to spend the money is welcomed with open arms. Admission charges are usually between $10 and $16.

Some places have certain dress standards, but it is generally left to the discretion of the people at the door – if they don't like the look of you, bad luck. The more 'up-market' nightclubs attract an older, more sophisticated and affluent crowd, and generally have stricter dress codes, smarter decor and higher prices.

Many city and suburban pubs have discos and/or live music. These are often great places for catching live bands, which can be either nationally well-known names or upcoming performers trying to make a name for themselves. Most of Australia's popular bands started out on the pub circuit in one city or another.

Spectator Sports

Australian Rules Football SA has plenty to offer the sports fan. The most popular spectator sport by far is Australian rules football, which is played from April to October.

A fast, tactical and physical game featuring spectacular high marking and bone-crushing tackles, Aussie rules is unique – only Gaelic football is anything like it. Although there are some enthusiastic punch-ups on the field, the crowds, in contrast, are noisy but lawabiding (a pleasant surprise for visiting British soccer fans).

SA is a stronghold of Aussie rules, although there's only one local team – the

Adelaide Crows – in the national Australian Football League (the AFL); another, Port Adelaide, may enter in 1997.

If you want to see Crow-eaters at their most parochial, go along to an Aussie Rules football match featuring the Adelaide Crows.

Soccer Soccer is very much a poor cousin: it's widely played on an amateur basis but the national league is only semiprofessional and attracts only a relatively small following. However, it's slowly gaining in popularity thanks in part to the success of the national team. At the local level in Adelaide, there are ethnically based teams representing a range of national origins.

Cricket During the other (non-football) half of the year there's cricket and tennis. Interstate and international cricket games are played on the historic Adelaide Oval – it was established in the 1870s and has a famous scoreboard. International Test and one-day matches are played there virtually every summer. As you can imagine, it's a great day in SA if the state side beats the Poms at the Adelaide Oval.

Tennis Tennis is very popular; most towns have tennis courts and there are active clubs all over the place. Every summer the Memorial Drive Tennis Club in Adelaide hosts the SA Men's Open and the SA Country Carnival.

Basketball Basketball is growing in popularity, particularly since SA has both men's and women's teams in the national league (the NBL). The importation of talent from the USA has helped lift the standard, and this has done wonders for the game.

Other Sports There are many more sports you can watch, such as surfing, netball, tennis, rugby (both codes), judo, athletics and hockey. If you have a special interest in any sport, contact the organising body and they'll tell you all you want to know – there's a long list of them under 'Organizations – Sporting' in the Yellow Pages telephone book.

Gambling

South Australians love a bet – hardly any town is without a horse-racing track, a Totalisator Agency Board (TAB) betting office or a licensed bookmaker. In fact, Adelaide must be one of the few cities in the world to have a public holiday for horse racing (Adelaide Cup Day). The whole state also more-or-less grinds to a standstill while the Melbourne Cup is being run.

Legal on- and off-course betting is available for horse racing, harness racing (the trots), greyhound racing, foot racing and various sporting events. Gambling in the country is usually centred on the pubs; PubTabs (pubs acting as TAB betting offices) have big-screen Sky-TV facilities, which allows you to watch your cash go down the drain and drown your sorrows at the same time.

Adelaide has a large casino, while poker machines are just about everywhere in pubs and clubs throughout the state. As well, there are always lotteries and 'instant money games' on the go – you can buy tickets at most newsagents as well as many shops and hotels.

THINGS TO BUY

There are lots of things *not* to buy – like plastic boomerangs, fake Aboriginal ashtrays and T-shirts, and all the other terrible things that fill the tackier souvenir shops. Most of these 'goods' come from Taiwan or Korea anyway! Before buying an Australian souvenir, turn it over to check that it was actually made here.

Aboriginal Art

Top of the list for any real Australian purchase would have to be Aboriginal art.

Thanks largely to tourism, Aboriginal artists have turned their attention to more portable media, and now use acrylic paints to record their ancient symbols and stories on canvas and linen, rather than ochre on rock overhangs. Other items being produced for sale include traditional wooden tools and weapons, carved wooden animals and necklaces. Didgeridoos (tubular wooden wind instruments from one to two metres long) come from the Top End of the NT, but you can find them for sale at many places around SA.

The prices being asked for the best paintings – which are mainly from the NT – are way out of reach for the average traveller. However, there are plenty of cheaper but still excellent mementos such as prints, small carvings and beautiful screen-printed T-shirts produced by Aboriginal craft co-operatives – there are copies, so it's worth shopping around and paying a few dollars more for the real thing.

One of the best places in the state to buy Aboriginal arts and crafts is Tandanya, in Adelaide. You'll also find local outlets in a few remote places such as Coober Pedy and Marree, in the north, and Yalata, on the Eyre Highway to Western Australia (WA).

Australiana

The term 'Australiana' is a euphemism for souvenirs – the things visitors typically buy as gifts for all the folk back home. They are supposedly representative of Australia and its culture, although many are extremely dubious. Some of the more popular items include: stuffed toy animals, especially koalas and kangaroos; wool products such as hand-knitted jumpers; sheepskin products; bush hats, with Akubra being the most famous and also the most expensive; and T-shirts and other clothing, usually with Australian symbols or tacky slogans such as 'No flies on me, mate!'

The seeds of many SA native plants are for sale, but check that you'll be allowed to take them home. Sturt's desert pea (the state's floral emblem) makes a great souvenir in the garden – provided you live somewhere hot and dry.

Another favourite is quandong jam, or tinned witchetty grubs, honey ants and other bush tucker. They're even experimenting with putting emus and kangaroos into tins.

Aussie Clothing

While you're in SA, fit yourself out in some local clobber – made in Australia for Australian conditions.

Start off with a foundation of Bonds cotton undies and a singlet, a pair of Holeproof Explorer socks and Blundstone elastic-sided boots. Slip on a pair of Stubbie shorts and a Yakka shirt, or overalls, and you've got the complete Aussie outdoors working uniform.

Then there's the bush gear made by RM Williams – riding boots, moleskin trousers, shearer's shirt, a greasy-wool jumper, a Bluey (a coarse woollen worker's coat) or a Driza-bone (an oilskin riding coat). You can top it all off with an Akubra hat, made from the fur of rabbits that might have lived in the SA outback.

Opals

The opal is Australia's national gemstone, and opal jewellery is a popular souvenir. Most of the state's production comes from

---

Buying an Opal

Precious opal exhibits a play of colour. It comes in several varieties, including jelly (colourless-transparent opal with little colour), crystal (jelly with more colour), white, milky (somewhere between crystal and white) and black (transparent to opaque opal with a dark background colour). Potch is opal without a play of colour and hence has no value.

Cut opal comes in various forms: solids are natural stones that have been cut and polished but otherwise not interfered with; doublets are thin slices of precious opal glued to backs of dark potch or synthetic material; and triplets are doublets with a layer of clear glass, potch or quartz cemented to the face. Domed opals are generally more attractive than flat ones because of their greater depth of pattern and play of colour.

Whichever type you decide to buy, there are several characteristics that determine the stone's value. Number one is brilliance – a brilliant stone is far more attractive than a dull stone, hence is more valuable.

Second is pattern. Large patterns are better than small ones, and if it is an interesting one or has some definable shape (such as a flower, bird or cross) so much the better.

Third is colour. A stone with a dominance of strong red is most valuable, followed by orange, green and blue.

The best opals are beautiful when seen from any angle and in any light, whether it be direct sunlight, semishade, shade or artificial light. Some look best in particular types of light – an opal may show brilliant colour in shade, but not in direct sunlight.

Another consideration is shape. Unless the opal is valuable, choose a standard shape so that it won't need a special (and costly) mounting.

Finally, faults or flaws such as sand, cracks or areas of potch all reduce the value of a stone. The easiest way to detect sand and cracks is to hold the opal up to the light. ■

Coober Pedy, and this is a good place to buy it, although it's reported that you can get better deals in Andamooka, which doesn't have so many tourists. Don't despair if you're not going to visit either of these places, as there are several good outlets in Adelaide.

When selecting an opal it's very much a case of beauty being in the eye of the beholder. A flawless opal with brilliant colour in an interesting pattern may be out of your price range, but if you shop around you should be able to pick up something that's affordable as well as appealing. Always ask the shop assistant for advice and get them to explain anything you're not sure of. A reputable shop will give you a written guarantee on more expensive purchases.

Finally, overseas visitors don't have to pay the 30% sales tax on opal. If anyone is offering discounts of, say, 50%, it's a good sign that their prices are way too high.

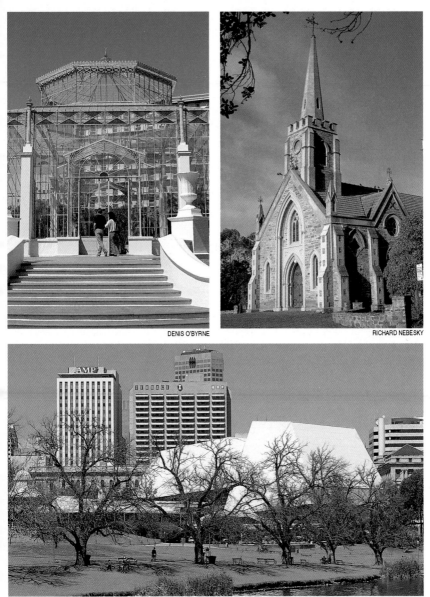

DENIS O'BYRNE

RICHARD NEBESKY

DENIS O'BYRNE

Top Left: Historic Palm House in Adelaide Botanic Garden
Top Right: St Andrews Church, Strathalbyn
Bottom: Looking across the Torrens River to the Festival Centre, Adelaide

DENIS O'BYRNE

MICHELLE COXALL

DENIS O'BYRNE

DENIS O'BYRNE

Top: Glenelg, Adelaide's most popular beach
Middle Left: Clarendon Police Station, Adelaide Hills
Bottom Left: PS Mundoo paddling out of Goolwa
Bottom Right: Adelaide Hills near Norton Summit

Outdoor Activities

With its dry temperate climate, 3700-km coastline, rugged hills and wide open spaces, SA is a great place to indulge in outdoor activities. If you want to do things like horse or camel riding, abseiling, caving, bushwalking, cycle touring, surfing, fishing, scuba diving, canoeing, windsurfing and skydiving, there are many opportunities available.

There is no comprehensive guide to outdoor activities in the state, but some research at SATC and the Department of Recreation & Sport (☎ (08) 8226 7301), and a check of the Yellow Pages telephone book, will point you in the right direction.

The booklet *South Australian Outdoors* ($2), put out by Bushwalking Leadership SA and Canoe SA – both at State Association House, 1 Sturt St, Adelaide – contains useful information and addresses for visiting bushwalkers, canoeists, cavers and climbers.

Most of the appropriate state organisations or major clubs have been listed here; otherwise ask any specialty equipment supplier.

Bushwalking

In SA, tramping, trekking and hiking are called bushwalking. Throughout the state there are over 2000 km of designated walking trails, of which the Heysen Trail is the longest and most well known. There are also 4WD tracks, and plenty of places where there are no tracks at all apart from cattle, sheep and kangaroo pads. You don't have to be an expert, or incredibly fit, as there's a swag of opportunities for the inexperienced or those with only moderate fitness.

Note that many tracks, particularly in forested areas, are closed during the Fire Danger Period and Total Fire Ban days.

Information

Every national park, conservation park and state forest in SA has an office somewhere where you can seek information on marked and unmarked routes in that area. The rangers or foresters will be able to advise you on what's available. For the telephone numbers of regional NPWS offices see National Parks Offices in the Facts about South Australia chapter.

The following organisations can also help with information:

Federation of SA Walking Clubs, State Association House, 1 Sturt St, Adelaide (☎ (08) 8213 0624)
Friends of the Heysen Trail & Other Walking Trails, 10 Pitt St, Adelaide (☎ (08) 8212 6299)
Royal Geographical Society of Australasia (SA Branch), GPO Box 419, Adelaide 5001; its office hours are Tuesdays only from 9.30 am to 1 pm (☎ (08) 8207 7265)

Books & Brochures A reasonable general state guide is Tyrone T Thomas's *Fifty Walks in South Australia* (Hill of Content Publishing Company, 1992). Like most of the following guides, you should use it in conjunction with a large-scale topographical map. Lonely Planet's *Bushwalking in Australia*, which includes the Mt Remarkable and Wilpena areas of the Flinders Ranges, also has good maps.

Regional guides include the excellent *Explore the Barossa* and *Guide to the Flinders Ranges*, both by the RGSA (SA), which describe a number of walks in those areas. Another good one is *Walks with Nature (20 Nature Walks in the Mount Lofty Ranges)* by the Nature Conservation Society of SA.

Twenty Bushwalks in the Adelaide Hills by Thelma Anderson; Adrian Heard's *Walking Guide to the North Flinders Ranges* and *Flinders Ranges Walks* by the Conservation Council of South Australia are useful but limited.

Books specifically on the Heysen Trail are *The Heysen Trail – Encounter Bay to the Barossa Valley* and *The Heysen Trail – Parachilna to Hawker*, both edited by Terry Lavender and others.

The Natural Resources and State Information Centres at 77 Grenfell St in Adelaide have a large number of brochures describing walks of various kinds throughout the state. These include a comprehensive coverage of the Heysen Trail in a series of map-guides (see the section on the Heysen Trail, below).

Maps With the exception of the northern Flinders Ranges, the more popular bushwalking areas have been mapped at 1:100,000 or greater. Although the maps are generally good, they were all out of date before they were printed. This means you should never take them too literally when it comes to water supplies outside settlements – the waterhole may have silted up, or the tank rusted away.

Friends of the Heysen Trail, Flinders Camping, the Scout Outdoor Centre and Paddy Pallin all sell large-scale maps as well as guides to the Heysen Trail, and have a range of free brochures. Outside Adelaide, ask at NPWS offices: if they don't sell them, they should know who does, although it may be a bit late if you haven't organised yourself by then.

Volunteer Programmes

Friends of the Heysen Trail can help if you want to spend some time doing volunteer work, such as walking track maintenance and development.

Guided Walks

A number of operators in Adelaide offer guided walks. They include the YWCA (☎ (08) 8340 2422), which runs courses in outdoor skills for women. In the recent past it conducted women-only bushwalks in various parts of SA; they may be doing this again, so give them a ring.

Ecotrek (☎ (08) 8383 7198) has been around a long time and does walks into the northern Flinders Ranges, Kangaroo Island and other areas.

Adventure SA (☎ (08) 8223 5544 or 014 098 372) visits the Flinders Ranges near Quorn on a weekly basis from May to early October. Osprey Wildlife Expeditions (☎ (08) 8388 2552) offers a guiding service to anywhere in SA, but specialises in the Flinders Ranges, Gawler Ranges and Coorong.

The Scout Outdoor Centre (☎ (08) 8223 5544) has a yearly programme of weekend and extended walks throughout the state, while Friends of the Heysen Trail often do guided weekend walks. Flinders Camping (☎ (08) 8223 1913) sponsors the Keep Fit SA bushwalk programme of day walks in the Adelaide Hills – the cost for casual walkers is around $6.

Several operators offer guided walks on Kangaroo Island (see the chapter on Kangaroo Island).

Preparation

Generally speaking, if you want to go on longer walks by yourself in SA you'll have to rely on your own resources. Many areas are sparsely populated and the general lack of facilities away from settled areas makes preparation the key to an enjoyable walk.

Winter is the best time for walking in the north, although you can never count on the weather being fine; a few years back it snowed on St Mary Peak, while maximums around 10°C, with light rain and a bitter wind, are sometimes experienced. In the south, autumn and spring are more popular because weather conditions are usually less extreme.

Don't forget that spring is very changeable; the day can easily start off sunny and end with rain and frigid blasts from the South Pole.

Always carry windproof clothing in the cooler months as many southern ridges have no vegetation other than low grass. In fact, hypothermia (overcooling of the body) can be a real health risk in winter, particularly if you're poorly prepared and happen to get lost.

For advice on safety and preparation, get hold of the informative brochure *A Guide to Safe Walking*, which is specific to SA.

THE HEYSEN TRAIL

Completed in 1992, the 1000-km Heysen Trail starts at Cape Jervis, south of Adelaide, and winds along the ridgetops of the Mt Lofty and Flinders Ranges to finish in Parachilna Gorge north of Wilpena Pound. It was named after the famous South Australian landscape artist Sir Hans Heysen.

The trail features some of the state's major scenic and historical highlights, and traverses two of its finest conservation areas: the Mt Remarkable and Flinders Ranges national parks.

From Cape Jervis you head east along the coast, with lookouts en route for sightings of southern right whales in season. The trail then winds north through the often steep and forested Mt Lofty Ranges. In the Barossa Valley you can relax at a winery or two before setting off for the old copper-heritage

---

Bushwalking Safety

Bushwalking safety is basically commonsense and includes the following rules:

- Know what to expect and don't do the walk if you think it might be outside your limitations; always get expert advice if you're not sure.
- *Always* let someone responsible know your plans (times, route and so on); this should be a person (your mother, for example) who's sure to raise the alarm if you don't show up on time. Never simply drive off after your walk without telling the person looking out for you that you've returned.
- Walk with at least one other person, preferably two. It's nice to have company, and if there's a problem someone can go for help.
- To be on the safe side, carry extra water in army canteens (not flimsy plastic bottles) even on short walks. Allow four litres per person per day in warm weather.
- To avoid dehydration, drink constantly in warm weather. Soft drinks may taste good, but they won't quench your thirst and are potentially dangerous because they contribute to water loss from the body. Have a couple of big drinks before setting out, then have more at regular intervals – don't wait until you start feeling thirsty.
- Always cover up against the sun. Wear a wide-brimmed hat and loose-fitting, close-weave cotton clothing that gives maximum skin protection; smear 15+ broad-spectrum sunscreen on exposed skin. The more comfortable you are, the less fluids you'll lose through sweating and the less likely you'll be to suffer heat exhaustion or worse. That's not to say you can't enjoy bushwalking in summer; you can, but you have to be sensible. Confine your walking to early in the morning and late in the day, when it's relatively cool, and rest up in the swimming pool (or shade) while it's hot.
- Wear long trousers and closed footwear in warm weather – poisonous snakes are common in some places.
- Be prepared for unseasonable cold weather.
- Never light wood fires in the open during the Fire Danger Period; if you light one at other times (assuming you're allowed to) keep it small to conserve firewood for others.
- *Never* wander away from tracks or other obvious features unless you know you can find your way back. If you find yourself geographically challenged (ie lost), don't panic. If you can't retrace your steps, sit quietly and wait for someone to come – which will happen when you're reported missing. It may help if you're carrying a mirror so you can signal any aerial searchers.
- Carry a first-aid kit and know how to use it. ∎

towns of Kapunda and Burra. Next come rugged Mt Remarkable and Mt Brown, with the ramparts of Wilpena Pound now in sight. You actually pass through the pound en route to the beautiful Aroona Valley, after which you're only a day or two from a celebratory beer in the Blinman or Parachilna pubs.

Although the Heysen Trail is designed as a long-distance track, the many access points along the way make it ideal for half-day and day walks. You'll find details of transport services en route in later chapters.

The trail varies from narrow pads to formed roads and is generally clearly marked with orange direction arrows and red markers. Except for a handful of very steep or rough areas the going is seldom really difficult for fit and experienced walkers.

As much of the trail crosses private property, the following 'country code' has been devised to keep walkers on-side with the landholders (obviously these apply to all other walks, too):

- Leave gates as you find them (either shut or open).
- Be careful not to waste, pollute or otherwise abuse water supplies; bury toilet waste at least 50 metres from watercourses.
- Don't disturb livestock or set up camp near stock-watering points – keep dogs on a lead at all times.
- Protect fences by climbing the stiles provided.
- Take your rubbish home or dispose of it at an authorised dumping place.
- Observe fire restrictions.
- Regularly check your clothing for the seeds of noxious plants; if you find any, put them in a plastic bag and hand them in to a NPWS or district council office.
- Stay on the track when crossing private property.

There are quite a few places to stay along the trail, including camping grounds, YHA hostels, huts and shearer's quarters, although they become fewer past Hawker. Most of these will be covered later in the book. While there are plenty of bush camp sites, a permit is required to camp in conservation areas and some state forests, and you must have the landholder's permission to camp on private property.

Each of the trail's 15 sections is described by its own fold-out map-guide ($5.50), which includes an excellent 1:50,000 topographic strip map. However, most of the information is repetitive and there's a general deficiency in terms of giving distances and conditions. The various sections have been summarised below to give a rough idea of what to expect; all distances are indicative only – they don't take slope into account.

The trail is closed during the Fire Danger Period, which varies from north to south.

Cape Jervis to Newland Hill (60 km)

Starting at Cape Jervis (from where you can catch the ferry to Kangaroo Island), the trail follows the rugged coastline eastwards around to Newland Head, at about 50 km, where you turn inland.

Although conditions are often far from easy, there are some great highlights including superb coastal views, sandy beaches and beautiful forest – a spectacular waterfall on Deep Creek, in Deep Creek Conservation Reserve, runs all year round (it's the only reliable water in this section). There's also a good chance of seeing southern right whales in winter and early spring.

Newland Hill is beside a sealed road about six km south-west of Victor Harbor.

Conditions There are many tough stretches of dense forest, spiky scrub, long steep slopes and soft beaches; you need to be fit, experienced, well-equipped and have tough clothing (including gardening gloves) that'll protect you against thorns.

Places to Stay & Eat There's a motel and shearer's quarters in Cape Jervis, and four camping grounds with basic facilities in the Deep Creek and Newland Head conservation parks.

You can buy meals and supplies in Cape Jervis and Victor Harbor.

Getting There & Away A daily bus service runs from Adelaide to Cape Jervis. Good roads lead in to Deep Creek Conservation Park and Waitpinga Beach, and you can get a taxi ($10) from Victor Harbor to Newland Hill. Apart from that, access points are limited.

Newland Hill to Mt Magnificent (65 km)
This section meanders through a mix of native forest and farmland, with stunning views from high points such as Mt Cone and Mt Magnificent. In places near the former (a bald and barren place) you get a panorama that includes The Bluff at Victor Harbor and Mt Lofty near Adelaide. En route you pass through the little towns of Inman Valley and Mt Compass.

Mt Magnificent is 25 km north north-east from Victor Harbor.

Conditions The whole of this section is hilly, with parts of it being particularly steep and rugged. There are several wet creek crossings in spring – don't try to cross the Finniss River if it's in flood. Windproof clothing is a must as many ridgetops are exposed.

Places to Stay & Eat There are plenty of places to stay in Victor Harbor, including a hostel and caravan parks. Inman Valley has a *YHA hostel*.

You can also camp (no facilities) in the Finniss Conservation Park (ranger ☎ (085) 36 2881) and the Myponga and Yulte conservation parks (ranger ☎ (085) 59 2263).

Meals and supplies are available in Victor Harbor, Inman Valley and Mt Compass. *Mt Magnificent Farm*, which is just a short walk from the summit of Mt Magnificent, sells teas and light lunches.

Getting There & Away There are a number of access points where roads cross the trail. Daily buses go from Adelaide to Victor Harbor, where you can get a taxi to Newland Hill ($10) and Inman Valley ($15). The main road from Adelaide to Victor Harbor passes through Mt Compass; on a weekend you may be able to hitch from Mt Magnificent Farm to Mt Compass, but don't count on it.

Mt Magnificent to Mt Lofty (50 km)
There's plenty of variety on this section, which crosses an attractive, hilly mosaic of farmland, native bush, pine forest and the townships of Mylor, Bridgewater and Picca-dilly.

Past Piccadilly you can walk through the 97-hectare Mt Lofty Botanic Gardens. From the garden you make the final ascent to Mt Lofty, where there's a beautiful view over Adelaide, then it's a short downhill walk to the Cleland Conservation Park.

Other highlights along the trail include the abandoned Echunga goldfield (near Mylor), the old Bridgewater Mill (now an up-market winery restaurant) and Engelbrook (a National Trust property near Bridgewater).

Mt Lofty is 10 km south-east of the city centre.

Conditions The walk is hilly throughout, but not particularly arduous except in the steeper areas between Mt Magnificent and Kuitpo. Parts of the Kuitpo Forest are boggy when wet. Crossing the Onkaparinga River near Mylor when it's in flood is definitely not recommended.

Places to Stay & Eat You'll find YHA hostels scattered along the trail at Kuitpo, Mylor and Mt Lofty. As well, there are two very basic camping grounds in the Kuitpo Forest – a rough hut at the *Rocky Creek Hut* camping ground is handy if it's raining.

You can purchase meals and supplies in Mylor, Bridgewater and Picadilly.

Getting There & Away There are numerous access points where the trail crosses sealed and unsealed roads.

Public buses run from Adelaide to the Cleland Conservation Park and Aldgate, near Bridgewater.

Mt Lofty to the Barossa Range (80 km)
On this section you're often up on the high ridgetops as you walk through native bush, pine forests and farmland close to Adelaide. The trail passes through the townships of Norton Summit and Cudlee Creek, and you

can do short detours to Gumeracha and Kersbrook. The section finishes in beautiful hills on the edge of the Barossa Valley, where huge gum trees are a feature.

The Mt Lofty Ranges are extremely steep at first, which will give you plenty of excuses to stop and admire the views. These are often nothing short of magnificent, particularly around Montacute Heights. A couple of detours near Norton Summit take you to the National Trust property of Marble Hill, and down to the waterfalls in Morialta Conservation Park (best in winter and early spring).

Conditions There's some very steep, hard going between Mt Lofty and the Warren Conservation Park; the slopes are particularly difficult around Montacute Heights and the Montacute Conservation Reserve, so don't attempt this part unless you're really fit. Fortunately, the trail generally follows the ridge tops.

Past Warren Conservation Park the going is much easier, apart from some testing little climbs such as Mt Crawford.

Places to Stay & Eat There are YHA hostels at Mt Lofty and near Norton Summit and Kersbrook; *Fuzzies Farm* is also near Norton Summit. You can camp in the Mount Crawford Forest with a permit from the forester, and there's a caravan park at Cudlee Creek at the eastern end of the Torrens Gorge.

You can buy meals and supplies in Norton Summit, Cudlee Creek, Gumeracha and Kersbrook.

Getting There & Away There are numerous access points off sealed and unsealed roads, including the Gorge Rd and Main North-East Rd from Adelaide to Birdwood.

Daily buses run from Adelaide to the Cleland Conservation Park near Mt Lofty. Another bus service runs up Gorge Rd from Adelaide to Birdwood on weekdays only and can drop you off on the way through.

Barossa Range to Hamilton (85 km)
After crossing the scenic Barossa Range, with its magnificent gums and the Kaiser Stuhl Conservation Park, you're in wine country at Tanunda in the Barossa Valley. From here the trail wends its way through farmland and vineyards, just bypassing Nuriootpa before leaving the valley past the little town of Greenock. Short detours take you to some good wineries along the way.

You basically follow fences from Greenock to the tiny town of Hamilton, about 15 km north-west of the old copper-mining town of Kapunda. The country is mainly open rolling farmland and there are some great rural views – Mt Belvidere, near Greenock, is well worth the climb.

Conditions There are steep slopes in the Barossa Range, but nothing too daunting for those who survived the previous section. Past the ranges the country is undulating and open; make sure you take windproof clothing.

Places to Stay & Eat There are a number of places to stay and eat in Tanunda, Nuriootpa and, to a much lesser extent, Kapunda. Nuriootpa has an excellent backpackers hostel – it's on Nuraip Rd, a 3.5-km walk from the trail – and there are places to camp at Tanunda and Kapunda.

You can stop for supplies and meals in Greenock.

Getting There & Away Access points are limited in the Barossa Range, but from Tanunda on you can join the trail at numerous road crossings. There's a daily bus to the Barossa from Adelaide, and a taxi service once you get there; Kapunda has a daily bus (weekdays only) from Gawler – to get to Gawler you can catch the bus or train from Adelaide.

Hamilton to Logans Gap (75 km)
From Hamilton the trail closely follows a timbered ridge before climbing Peters Hill, which gives you a great view of the saw-toothed Tothill Range to the north-east. After crossing the intervening farmland, you follow the range for the final 43 km to Logans Gap. Tothill Range is very scenic in

places and has plenty of trees and wildlife, plus a number of ruined farmhouses along its foot. Logans Gap is 15 km south of Burra.

Conditions Apart from some steep rugged sections, the going is fairly easy.

Places to Stay The entire section is on private property, with no facilities for walkers apart from a hut with bunks and drinking water just north of Peters Hill.

Getting There & Away There are a number of access points from minor roads in the area, including access to Logans Gap.

Logans Gap to Newickie Creek (55 km)

This section encompasses hilly, mainly open country, with many magnificent views from the highest points. The sense of open space is amazing as you follow the top of the ridge into Burra, the old copper-mining town.

Past Burra, which is about 23 km from Logans Gap, the trail enters a wide belt of jumbled, rounded hills – they're scenic, if barren, and there's very little water for the next 20 km or so. In dramatic contrast, the final stretch is well-watered and has plenty of attractive bushland.

Newickie Creek is about 23 km north-east of Burra.

Conditions There are many steep slopes, including some long ones, but overall the going is easy to moderately difficult, if stony in parts. The ford over Burra Creek, in the hills south-east of Burra, requires care if it's been raining.

Places to Stay & Eat The only commercial facilities are in Burra, where there are plenty of beds and eateries.

Getting There & Away Daily bus services pass through Burra from Adelaide. Elsewhere, access points on this section are limited to a few minor road crossings, including the section ends.

Newickie Creek to Spalding (85 km)

This area is sparsely populated – apart from scattered farms there are only the townships of Hallett and Spalding. This section has varied landscapes, with rugged hills and gorges in the east and more gentle topography in the west. There are fantastic sweeping panoramas from the higher points – arguably the best view is from Mt Bryan (936 metres), the highest point in the Mt Lofty Ranges. Other highlights include Tourillie Gorge (once the wagon road between Hallett and the Murray Plains) and abundant wildlife, particularly near the abandoned settlement of Mt Bryan East.

Conditions There are a couple of ranges with steep rugged slopes in the 40 km between Newickie Creek and Hallett, but other than that the going is generally easy. A general lack of trees on the higher points means there's very little protection from bitter winter winds.

Places to Stay & Eat You can stay in the old *Mt Bryan East Schoolhouse*, the *Hallett Railway Station*, the *Willalo Hall* between Hallett and Spalding, and the Spalding pub and camping ground. Meals and supplies are available in Hallett and Spalding.

Getting There & Away There are buses most days from Adelaide to Hallett and Spalding. The only access points between Newickie Creek and Hallett are a couple of minor roads near Mt Bryan East. Between there and Spalding the trail crosses a good network of minor roads.

Spalding to Hughes Gap (85 km)

The trail crosses sparsely populated hills of the Northern Mt Lofty Ranges, then enters the Flinders Ranges at the township of Crystal Brook; Hughes Gap is about 10 km further on. There's some beautiful walking en route, particularly along Never Never Creek (between Bundaleer Reservoir and the Bundaleer Forest) and Crystal Brook, where the river red gums are superb. Great views are common; the best are from high points in the Campbell Range and the hills east of Crystal Brook.

There's a reptile house and fauna park at historic Bowman Park, between Crystal Brook township and Hughes Gap. The gap is about seven km north of Crystal Brook.

Conditions Apart from some long steep sections, the walking is generally very easy. The crossing over Rocky River is a wet one (don't attempt it in a flood), and there's always boggy ground just past Bowman Park.

Places to Stay & Eat There are pubs with rooms and meals at Spalding, Georgetown and Crystal Brook and caravan parks at Spalding, Crystal Brook and Bowman Park. You can also stay in shearer's quarters at Bowman Park and 11 km east of Georgetown at *Wirrilla Homestead* (☎ (08) 8842 3762).

Check with the forester (☎ (086) 65 4044) before camping in the Bundaleer Forest Reserve.

Getting There & Away There are bus services most days from Adelaide to Spalding and Crystal Brook, but otherwise access points are extremely limited. They include the Bundaleer Reservoir and Bundaleer Forest, both off the main road between Spalding and Jamestown.

Hughes Gap to Melrose (75 km)
The trail leaves Crystal Brook just past Hughes Gap and climbs onto the main spine of the southern Flinders Ranges. For most of the next 35 km – there's a detour to the Wirrabara Forest headquarters – you follow fire tracks on the remote, timbered ridgetop. The ridge varies from 350 to 700 metres in height, and almost all the way along there are marvellous views over Spencer Gulf to the west. You should see euros, and there are plenty of birds.

In the northern half the trail descends off the range and crosses rolling farmland with big gums to picturesque Melrose, under Mt Remarkable. En route it passes within a km of Murraytown, a tiny village with a good pub.

Conditions Apart from some rough and steep sections the going is generally easy.

Places to Stay & Eat In the Wirrabara Forest there's a *YHA hostel* and a basic camping ground, and you can camp at the sportsground at nearby Wirrabara township. Otherwise there's a caravan park in Melrose, as well as the *Mt Remarkable Hotel*, which has beds and meals. You can also buy meals in Wirrabara and Murraytown, and supplies in all three towns.

Getting There & Away In the southern half, access points are limited to Hughes Gap (reached from Crystal Brook township) and the Wirrabara Forest (seven km from Wirrabara, on Main North Rd). For the final 20 km the trail is within a km of Main North Rd, which links Adelaide with Wirrabara and Melrose.

There's a bus service from Adelaide through Wirrabara, Murraytown and Melrose.

Melrose to Woolshed Flat (70 km)
This spectacular section takes you from Melrose to Woolshed Flat, in the Pichi Richi Pass about 16 km south of Quorn. Its numerous highlights include wildlife, views, magnificent gums and a strong sense of solitude; the pubs in Melrose and Wilmington are pretty good too.

You start off by toiling up through the trees to the summit of Mt Remarkable, in Mt Remarkable National Park. From here the trail slowly descends along steep, rugged ridges to Wilmington, near the halfway point. En route you can visit the old Spring Creek copper mine and detour to Alligator Gorge in the national park.

From Wilmington you walk up the Port Augusta road to Horrocks Memorial, after which it's 30 km of rough, timbered ridges to Woolshed Flat. There are plenty of outstanding views, particularly from Mt Brown and the hilltops just east of the memorial.

Conditions Fitness and solid preparation are required for the entire section, which is remote and often steep and rocky. Wear boots that are suitable for boulder-hopping along creeks, and tough clothes for protection against dense scrub.

Places to Stay & Eat There are caravan parks and pubs to stay at in Melrose and Wilmington, plus basic bush camping grounds on Mt Remarkable and near Wilmington and Woolshed Flat. You can also stay at Gunyah and Broadview homesteads north of Wilmington.

Getting There & Away The main access points are at Melrose, Wilmington and Woolshed Flat, all of which are serviced by buses.

Woolshed Flat to Buckaringa Gorge
(65 km)
There are plenty of attractions in this generally rugged, remote section, which passes through Quorn and the Dutchmans Stern Conservation Park. They include spectacular scenery, sweeping panoramas, the Pichi Richi historic railway and a chance to see rare yellow-footed rock-wallabies.

From Woolshed Flat you can follow the main road to Quorn or take the longer (by nine km) route via the steep and scrubby Emeroo Range – it's tough going but the views are worth it.

At Quorn you're faced with 40 km of mainly hard, isolated country with excellent views, attractive gums and rock formations to admire along the way. Dutchmans Stern has nice scenery and plenty of wildlife, and you can literally see to the edge of the world from Mt Arden, near the northern end. En route you pass one of Edward John Eyre's 1839 camps.

Buckaringa Gorge is about 27 km north of Quorn.

Conditions You shouldn't attempt this section unless you know what you are doing. There's limited water on the trail and there are many difficult sections.

Places to Stay & Eat There are four pubs, a motel and a caravan park in Quorn, and

shearer's quarters at the ranger station in Dutchmans Stern Conservation Park.

Getting There & Away A bus runs most days from Port Augusta to Quorn. Access points on this section are limited and include Woolshed Flat, Quorn, Dutchmans Stern and Buckaringa Gorge.

Buckaringa Gorge to Hawker (62 km)
More wildlife, views, gum-lined creeks and scenic rocky ridges are the main attractions; although rugged and spectacular in parts, the country is much more subdued and open than before – there are even a few isolated homesteads en route.

Near its northern end the trail climbs Jarvis Hill, from where you can see the distant purple wall of Wilpena Pound. This section ends just past the ruins of Old Wonoka, about seven km from Hawker on the Leigh Creek road.

Conditions The going varies from easy to difficult throughout, with careful navigation required in the rougher areas.

Places to Stay & Eat Hawker has supermarkets and a good range of accommodation including a pub, motel and two caravan parks. You can also stay at *Yappala Homestead* (☎ (086) 48 4164) near Old Wonoka.

Getting There & Away There's a bus service most days to Hawker. The limited access points include Buckaringa Gorge, Simmonston and Old Wonoka.

Hawker to Wilpena (50 km)
There are some stunning scenic highlights on this section, which takes you through semiarid station country dominated by the spectacular Elder Range and Wilpena Pound's south wall. Apart from the Elder Range, which towers 700 metres above the trail as you skirt its rugged eastern flank, there's abundant wildlife, beautiful gumlined creeks and native pine forest.

About nine km before the tourist village at Wilpena you cross the Wilpena Pound

Range at Bridle Gap (the view from here is magnificent) and enter the pound. The range marks the southern boundary of the Flinders Ranges National Park.

Conditions The remoteness and often tough conditions make this section one for the experienced, well-prepared walker. Water supplies are extremely limited.

Places to Stay & Eat You can stay at *Wonoka Homestead* (☎ (086) 48 4035), *Mt Little Homestead* and *Henschke Cottage* (both ☎ (086) 48 4206), all of which are in the first 18 km from Hawker. Other than that, there's a motel and camping ground at Wilpena.

Meals and supplies are available at the Wilpena store.

Getting There & Away The main access points are at Hawker and Wilpena, and on the Moralana scenic drive which links the Wilpena and Leigh Creek roads. A bus service goes from Port Augusta to Hawker and Wilpena most days.

Wilpena to Parachilna Gorge (65 km)
This section features the rugged landscapes for which the Flinders Ranges are famous; other highlights include historic ruins and wildlife: the birdlife is prolific, and you may see yellow-footed rock-wallabies as well as euros and red kangaroos.

Leaving Wilpena you head north-west along the foot of the towering Wilpena Range, then north along scenic valleys in the equally inspiring ABC Range. You leave the Flinders Ranges National Park at the old Aroona homestead, about 46 km from Wilpena; from here the trail follows a deep, narrow valley between the ABC and Heysen Ranges to beautiful Parachilna Gorge.

The gorge, which marks the Heysen Trail's northern end, is on the main road between Blinman (15 km) and Parachilna (17 km). Both these places have good pubs where you can down a celebratory drink or two.

Conditions The trail crosses extremely

rugged country, but generally isn't as difficult as you might think. Even so, you have to be experienced, fit and well prepared to do the entire section. There's good potential for short walks at the various access points.

Places to Stay & Eat Supplies, meals and beds are available at Wilpena and Blinman, both of which have a pub and a camping ground. You can also stay in Parachilna (there's a pub, backpacker beds and a camping ground) and at the *Angorichina Tourist Village*, which is only a short walk from the trail's northern end.

There are a couple of basic camping grounds in the national park; contact the ranger for permission to camp elsewhere.

Getting There & Away There's a bus service from Port Augusta to Wilpena and Blinman (they'll drop you off at Angorichina if you ask). Other than the section ends, access points are limited to a handful of spots in the national park.

OTHER WALKS
There are networks of tracks in the Flinders Ranges and Mt Remarkable national parks, and the Arkaroola Wildlife Sanctuary. The Gammon Ranges National Park has stacks of potential for walkers who don't need a track to follow.

In the Mid-North, the 55-km Riesling Trail follows the dismantled railway through the Clare Valley between Riverton and Hilltown, with the odd winery along the way.

The Barossa has good walks, too, even though it is relatively closely settled. You can wander between the wineries and historic Lutheran churches, or check the timbered hills all around. The Para Wirra Recreation Park and Kaiser Stuhl Conservation Park, both in the Barossa Range, are worth visiting for their walks, native bushland and wildlife.

You'll find plenty of opportunity in the conservation parks and state forests in the Mt Lofty Ranges near Adelaide. Belair National Park, Morialta Conservation Park and Cleland Conservation Park, all on Adelaide's outskirts, have some excellent walks.

Further south, on Fleurieu Peninsula, Deep Creek Conservation Park near Cape Jervis is very scenic but walking conditions can present a challenge.

On Kangaroo Island, the Flinders Chase National Park and Cape Gantheaume Conservation Park are also good; the two day coastal walk around Cape Gantheaume to Seal Bay is for experienced walkers only.

In the Lower South-East, the Coorong and Canunda National Parks have plenty of walks including huge dunes and long, empty beaches. Ngarkat Conservation Park in the upper South-East has magnificent wildflowers in late winter and early spring, as do others in the mallee belt. There are several mallee parks on Eyre Peninsula.

Although many visitors feel a little awed by – and uncomfortable in – the outback's vast and unpopulated spaces, there are countless good walks in its various environments. Cooper Creek in the Innamincka Regional Reserve is outstanding, as is Lake Eyre when there's water in it.

Cycle Touring

There are some great cycling areas in SA and touring cyclists are a common sight. Cycling through the outback wouldn't be everyone's cup of tea – it's often very monotonous, as is the Murray Mallee. However, regions like the Fleurieu Peninsula, Mt Lofty Ranges, Barossa Valley and Flinders Ranges offer plenty of variety, as well as challenges if you want them.

In Adelaide there's a good network of cycle routes. They include the path through the River Torrens Linear Park, which takes you for about 40 km along the River Torrens from the sea into the foothills of the Mt Lofty Ranges.

The most popular bike for serious touring cyclists is a mountain bike, followed by a wide-tyred touring bike. These give you the flexibility to ride on dirt roads and tracks, which are usually bad news for narrow-tyred racers. Be warned that cycling on walking tracks and management tracks in national parks and conservation parks is strictly forbidden at present, although the policy is under review. In the meantime, you can only use public roads and designated cycle paths in these areas.

There are a couple of places in Adelaide and Glenelg where you can hire good bikes (see the Getting Around sections in the Adelaide chapter), but generally the hire bikes in country areas are pretty ordinary. If you don't have your own, you can hire one by the hour, day, week or month, or take a guided tour; for details of tour operators see Bicycle in the Getting Around chapter.

Information
Bicycle SA (☎ (08) 8213 0637) at State Association House, 1 Sturt St, Adelaide, is the state umbrella organisation for touring cyclists. They're very friendly and helpful and can provide expert advice on such matters as touring routes, conditions, preparation and suppliers. Visitors are welcome to join them on their various activities, which include supported rides, camping weekends and guided tours – ask them for a calendar.

Guide to Cycling in SA ($7.50), published by Bicycle SA, is a useful general reference containing a wealth of information as well as some route details.

Maps All of SA where you're likely to go cycling is mapped at 1:250,000, while the more settled areas have 1:100,000 coverage or larger.

The Department of Recreation & Sport is producing a state-wide cycle touring atlas made up of individual folding map-guides. These are very informative, and the map part, which may highlight several worthwhile routes, is a useful 1:250,000 or larger. (Use them in conjunction with an RAA touring map so you can see where you are in relation to nearby towns.) The maps cost $7.30 each from Bicycle SA, map shops (see under Books & Maps in the Facts for the Visitor chapter) or any good touring-cycle shop.

Guides produced so far cover the Fleurieu Peninsula, Kangaroo Island, the Barossa

Valley, the lower Mid-North, the lower Murray River, the Riverland, Yorke Peninsula and the South-East; more are planned, so check with Bicycle SA for an update.

THE MAWSON TRAIL

Like bushwalkers, SA cyclists have their own long-distance challenge route: the Mawson Trail. When completed in 1997, it'll take you 800 km from the Festival Centre, in the heart of Adelaide, to Blinman in the northern Flinders Ranges. Until then it's been determined as far as Hawker, at the 700-km mark.

The trail is named after Sir Douglas Mawson, a great Australian explorer and geologist who, like Sir Hans Heysen, found inspiration in the Flinders Ranges. It's been designed to make use of a series of mainly dirt roads and 4WD tracks that takes cyclists into the scenic back country away from main roads. Much of the route is remote from people and facilities, and there's quite a bit of difficult cycling – all qualities which help make it an unforgettable experience.

Obviously your bike and associated equipment (like panniers and pumps) will need to be in tip-top condition, particularly for the more rugged sections of the Mawson Trail. If you're not sure, have it checked by an expert and then go for a fully loaded test ride *before* you leave home. John Harland's *The Australian Bicycle Book – Maintenance & Road Skills* is recommended as a general reference.

For convenience, the trail is broken into four sections, each with its own brochure complete with strip maps. The maps are excellent, but they're reductions of 1:50,000 topographical maps, so you'll need a low-power magnifying glass to read them comfortably. The trail has been marked throughout at intersections and at one-km intervals.

Apart from the section north of Wilmington, where you should allow for at least one bush camp, the entire Mawson Trail can be planned as day rides between towns. You'll find details on accommodation and bus services in later chapters.

Adelaide to Marrabel (170 km)

Starting at the Festival Centre, you safely and easily get through the suburbs along the River Torrens Linear Park cycle path to Athelstone, on Gorge Rd. From here you head north – with several steep climbs en route – through the scenic Adelaide Hills via Lobethal and Birdwood to the Barossa Valley wineries. The trail continues to the copper heritage town of Kapunda, and this section ends near the town of Marrabel, about 23 km further on.

Marrabel to Spalding (220 km)

The trail passes through the bald hills around Burra en route to Spalding, doing a major switch back along the way. Apart from these towns there's not much sign of civilisation except for scattered farmhouses; between Burra and Spalding you pass close to tiny Hallett, which has a pub and store. There are challenging hills almost all the way along this section.

Spalding to Wilmington (170 km)

You cycle through the townships of Spalding, Laura, Melrose and Wilmington, and pass close to Gladstone, Jamestown and Wirrabara. The country is mainly rolling farmland, but near the latter you push (or stagger!) right up onto the southern Flinders Ranges in the Wirrabara Forest. This is a great, if testing, introduction to the stunning views you'll find further north.

Wilmington to Hawker (140 km)

This section is extremely scenic, particularly between Wilmington and Quorn where you pass Mt Brown – your leg muscles will be screaming if you try and do this bit in one go. There are more testing ridges and hills, separated by plains and gum-lined creeks, between Quorn and Hawker, with marvellous landscapes all around. En route you pass picturesque Warren Gorge, where there's a camping area.

For more details on cycling see the Bicycle section in the Getting Around chapter.

Other Land Activities

ROCK CLIMBING

Popular rock-climbing areas near Adelaide are the Morialta Conservation Park and Onkaparinga Gorge in the Onkaparinga River Recreation Park. These have cliffs 10 to 15 metres high with routes suitable for beginners to advanced grades.

At Moonarie, on the south-eastern side of Wilpena Pound in the Flinders Ranges National Park, cliffs to 120 metres have plenty of potential for skilled climbers – this is definitely not a place for beginners.

Ecotrek (☎ (08) 8383 7198) in Adelaide offers instruction in abseiling and rock climbing on scheduled outings near Adelaide. Paddy Pallin and the Scout Outdoor Centre, both on Rundle St, specialise in rock climbing and can give you information about the local scene.

There are several pocket-sized guides to climbing in SA. *A Rock Climber's Guide to the Flinders Ranges* by Nick Nagle describes 400 routes. *Rock Climbs Around Adelaide*, edited by Nyrie Dodd, has details on a large number of mainly short climbs. *Moonarie – A Rockclimber's Guide*, edited by Tony Barker, describes numerous climbs in that area.

CAVING

South Australia has extensive cave systems around Mt Gambier in the South-East, and in the far west under the Nullarbor Plain. However, the majority are off-limits to casual cavers. You can visit 'show' caves on guided tours at Tantanoola and Naracoorte, both near Mt Gambier in the South-East, and at Kelly Hill on Kangaroo Island; Naracoorte and Kelly Hill also have guided adventure caving. For details see the chapters on these regions.

The only way for most people to see the Nullarbor caves, which are all in the Nullarbor National Park and adjoining Nullarbor Regional Reserve, is with an accredited tour company such as Nullarbor Adventure Tours (☎ (086) 25 3447) of Ceduna. They have a four day trip for $595, including Abrakurrie Cave (largest in the southern hemisphere) and rafting in Weebubbie Cave. Another good operator, Osprey Wildlife Expeditions (☎ (08) 8388 2552) does six/nine-day caving trips for $995/1250 all-inclusive ex-Adelaide, also with rafting.

If you're a skilled caver travelling independently and wishing to visit the Nullarbor caves, contact the ranger at the Ceduna NPWS regional office (☎ (086) 25 3144) and you may be able to work something out.

BIRDWATCHING

South Australia is a big place with many different habitats ranging from wetlands to arid gibber plains and eucalypt forests to mulga scrub. If you go to the right places you can expect to see lots of the 380 or so species that have been recorded throughout the state. SA birds range from the tiny (80-mm long) weebill to the flightless emu, which can look the average adult human in the eye. There are even said to be feral ostriches north of Port Augusta. There's also the mighty wedge-tailed eagle – Australia's largest raptor with a wingspan up to three metres or more. You'll see plenty of these noble birds feasting on dead animals along the Stuart Highway and other outback roads.

Generally, the most species are found where there's a diversity of habitats in close proximity. Parts of the Flinders Ranges, such as the Mt Remarkable, Flinders Ranges and Gammon Ranges national parks, have large trees, dense scrub, massive rocky outcrops, open grassy areas, reedbeds and waterholes virtually side by side. Many coastal areas, such as St Kilda and the Coorong National Park, have shallows backed by scrub or mangroves. The Murray River has billabongs, lakes, grassy flats, large trees and extensive cane-grass thickets.

The most productive areas for seeing parrots and cockatoos are along the Murray and in timbered areas of the South-East and the southern Mt Lofty Ranges.

In the arid outback, any isolated source of permanent water, whether it be a tank or a waterhole, becomes a focus for birds which must drink regularly to survive. Prime spots include Cooper Creek near Innamincka and Purnie Bore, in Witjira National Park. Flocks of cockatoos and pigeons come in to drink at such places, which also provide stepping stones for migratory water birds on their long journeys across Australia. The inland salt lakes are mainly dry, but when they fill after rare, prolonged heavy rain they can become major nesting areas.

Although much of SA below the 250-mm isohyet has been cleared for agriculture, there are still large areas of native bush in conservation parks in the Murraylands, the Upper South-East and Eyre Peninsula. These are fantastic for honeyeaters and insect-eaters when the mallee gums and banksia are in flower (July to October is the best period). Here you'll also find the elusive mallee fowl, which incubates its eggs in a huge pile of rotting vegetation.

On Kangaroo Island, where 243 bird species have been recorded, the native vegetation has suffered rather less from agriculture. You may see several species considered uncommon elsewhere, including the glossy black cockatoo and the Cape Barren goose. The island's northern coastal shallows are excellent places to observe water birds such as gulls, ducks, pelicans, swans and waders. Elsewhere, you might spot an osprey or white-bellied sea-eagle patrolling the coastal cliffs.

The South-East has major wetlands at the Coorong and Bool Lagoon, where water birds reign supreme. The Coorong is noted for its large flocks of ducks and pelicans, while Bool Lagoon has a huge ibis rookery. Other good spots to see nesting waders and other water birds include the mangrove swamps around both gulfs.

Rangers conduct penguin-watching tours on Granite Island (off Victor Harbor) and Kangaroo Island. The little (or fairy) penguin is the only species to breed on the Australian mainland and nearby islands. Several islands off the far west coast are breeding grounds for millions of short-tailed shearwaters.

There are several reference books on Aus-

tralian birds. A good one is Graham Pizzey's *A Field Guide to the Birds of Australia*. Osprey Wildlife Expeditions (☎ (08) 8388 2552) offer a birdwatchers' guiding service anywhere in SA for $650 per day for two persons (additional persons $65).

Juvenile Pacific gull

FOSSICKING

In SA, fossicking is officially defined as 'the gathering of minerals for recreation, providing this is done without disturbing the land or water by machinery or explosives'. There's reasonable fossicking potential in SA, with precious and semiprecious gemstones occurring in a number of areas. At present the only gems being mined commercially are jade near Cowell on Eyre Peninsula – the mines here are temporarily closed – and precious opal at Andamooka, Coober Pedy and Mintabie. Gold and copper were mined from many places in the past. The Mt Lofty Ranges (including the Adelaide Hills) and an arc of country between Burra and Olary have a number of old goldfields.

Diamonds, emeralds, sapphires and rubies have been found, but not in commercial quantities. In terms of numbers of minerals, the most interesting places to look are in the far northern Flinders Ranges, the eastern Flinders Ranges between the Barrier

Highway and Lake Frome, and the Middleback Ranges on Eyre Peninsula.

The minimum equipment required for fossicking is sharp eyes and a basic knowledge of where to look. Most fair dinkum fossickers will also have at least a geological pick, a couple of small sieves and a small shovel. Because water is usually in short supply, a drum for washing sieved material may also be required.

You don't need a permit to fossick, but you must have the landholder's permission. The only exception to this rule is in a declared fossicking area, which you'll find on the three opal fields and the old gold diggings at Jupiter Creek, Chapel Hill (both near Echunga in the Adelaide Hills) and Watts Gully (in the Mt Crawford Forest, also in the Adelaide Hills).

The best place to start is the Department of Mines & Energy (☎ (08) 8274 7500) at 191 Greenhill Rd in Parkside, Adelaide. They have a series of useful brochures on fossicking, and others that take you on self-guided tours of historic mines. You can also get geological maps here.

HORSE & CAMEL RIDING

There are plenty of chances to see the countryside on a horse, but rather less on a camel. You can do rides lasting from 30 minutes to seven days, but most trail-ride operators will only take you out for a day at the most.

The Flinders Ranges is one of the most popular regions; horse rides are offered at a number of places including Balcanoona, Burra, Germein Gorge, Pichi Richi Pass, Wilmington and Wilpena. At Balcanoona and Wilpena you can learn about the country from local Aboriginal guides. Seven-day camel treks through station country are on offer at Blinman.

You can do camel treks along the Murray and coastal rides on Yorke Peninsula; alternatively, take a camel out for dinner to a winery at McLaren Vale.

There are many more options for horse rides throughout the state. This book mentions a number of them (look under Organised Tours in the chapters on each region), and

you should also check with SATC and local tourist offices.

Water Activities

CANOEING & KAYAKING

Canoeing opportunities are generally limited to the Murray River and its associated lakes and wetlands. However, the fact that the Murray winds through SA for 650 km helps make canoeing a major form of recreation.

Other minor areas of interest include the mangrove inlets between Port Adelaide and St Kilda (these are good for dolphins and birdlife), the Onkaparinga River south of Adelaide and, although most of it is in Victoria, the Glenelg River in the state's extreme south-east corner.

For an adventure, there'd be nothing like a trip along Cooper Creek when it comes down in flood through the dry outback. However, this is only for experts. The main danger here is getting lost, as the creek spreads out over a vast floodplain covered in coolibahs.

While the Murray lacks white-water excitement, there's plenty of wildlife, good fishing, magnificent river scenery, and quiet places to camp. For most of the year conditions are suitable for beginners in company with a skilled guide or instructor. Novices should stay on dry land during periods of maximum flow, which usually occur in November and December. At such times you have to be extremely careful of trees and snags, as in a strong current you can easily end up capsizing and becoming trapped under the canoe. Weirs must be avoided at all times because of their potentially lethal backpull.

You may be tempted to canoe across Lake Alexandrina, but don't do it. Being shallow, it becomes extremely choppy in windy conditions. If the wind comes up you may find it difficult to make it back to shore, in which case you'll be at severe risk of fatal hypothermia (not to mention drowning).

The free brochure *A Guide to Safe Canoeing*, by the Department of Recreation & Sport, has good information on canoes and safety. In general, the following rules should always be observed:

- Wear a buoyancy vest and be able to swim at least 100 metres in canoe clothing.
- Be skilled in handling capsizes and rescue situations, and know resuscitation procedures.
- Know how to treat hypothermia.
- Avoid weirs and snags.
- Don't drink the river water without boiling it and don't make it any more polluted than it already is.
- Pack belongings in waterproof containers (an obvious one, but you'd be amazed how many don't).
- Kayakers must be able to do the Eskimo roll.

Many of the safety rules and 'country code' for bushwalking are applicable to canoeing.

Sea kayaking is not a big sport in SA, but there are still some good spots to do it in. These include the Rapid Bay area south of Adelaide, the northern coast of Kangaroo Island, Boston Bay at Port Lincoln, the bays of Spencer Gulf and Gulf St Vincent, and the islands off Victor Harbor.

Information

The first stop for information on everything to do with canoeing and kayaking is Canoe SA (☎ (08) 8213 0629), at State Association House, 1 Sturt St, Adelaide. Although their emphasis is on education, they have lists of club and tour operators, hire availability, details of events and route guides.

The Department of Recreation & Sport has published a series of five canoe guides ($7.30) to the Murray and associated wetlands. These are very informative and include excellent topographical maps at a scale of 1:50,000. One map covers the 65 km from Morgan to Swan Reach, which features high cliffs rich in fossils. The other four help you explore most of the river and its lakes, billabongs and anabranches as it meanders between Overland Corner and the Victorian border. There are gaps between Barmera and Loxton, and Berri and Renmark, but the Katarapko and Bulyong Island sections of the Murray River National Park are included.

For general information and touring notes, get hold of the free brochure *River Murray Canoe Guide* produced by the Department of Recreation & Sport.

Hire & Tours

Hire canoes and kayaks are available on a daily, weekly or longer basis in Adelaide and several places on the Murray, including Barmera, Loxton and north of Mannum.

Guided canoe tours operate on such waterways as the Murray River, the Port Adelaide mangrove inlets, the Coorong and the Cooper Creek system. You can also do kayak trips of up to a day along the coast between Second Valley and Cape Jervis. The following operators in and near Adelaide do canoe and/or kayak tours:

Canoeing
    Ecotrek (☎ (08) 8383 7198): from two days on the Murray and longer on Cooper Creek and the Coongie Lakes
    Adventure SA (☎ (08) 8223 5544 or 014 098 372): has a flexible programme of trips including the Murray River (three days for $175) and Port Adelaide mangrove inlets (one day for $65)
    Mangrove Fun Paddles (☎ (08) 8449 7252): day trips to the mangrove inlets
Sea Kayaking
    Blue Water Sea Kayaking (☎ (08) 8598 4001): day trips along the coast south of Adelaide

SWIMMING & SURFING

There are fine swimming beaches right along the South Australian coast, with the safest generally being on Gulf St Vincent and Spencer Gulf. You have to be very wary of rips and undertows anywhere that's exposed to the Southern Ocean and Investigator Strait, which lies between Kangaroo Island and the mainland.

Adelaide has a number of good beaches stretching from Seacliff to Grange; northwards from Grange they're a bit too 'weedy' for real enjoyment. Further south there are several beaches with reasonable surf in the right conditions – Seaford and Southport have reliable if small waves. Skinny dipping is permitted at Maslins Beach, 40 km south of the city.

You'll find potential for surfing in any

area that's exposed to the Southern Ocean's rolling swells. The closest surf of any real consequence to Adelaide is near Victor Harbor at Waitpinga Beach, Middleton and Port Elliot. Kangaroo Island's southern coast also has some worthwhile spots, with Pennington Bay being the most consistent. Pondalowie, on the 'foot' of Yorke Peninsula, has the state's most reliable strong breaks, although when conditions are right there are more powerful ones nearby. There are other notable surfing spots scattered along the western coastline of Eyre Peninsula; Elliston is a good one while Cactus Beach, on remote Point Sinclair, is world-famous for its surf.

Aussie surf star Nat Young has written the *Surfing & Sailboard Guide to Australia* which includes a number of places in SA. Although hardly suitable for carrying around, the expensive coffee-table book *Atlas of Australian Surfing*, by Mark Warren, does contain useful information.

Ring ☎ 0055 31543 or (08) 8271 1277 for surf reports along the coast between Adelaide and Goolwa.

WINDSURFING

There's endless potential for windsurfing (also known as wave-sailing, sailboarding and board-sailing) along the South Australian coast and on many lakes.

Adelaide beaches present conditions as extreme as anywhere, and in summer you get strong sea breezes that are ideal for slalom surfers. The windiest beaches (from north to south) are Semaphore, Henley Beach, North Glenelg, Somerton and Seacliff. Each has its own set of hazards, so check with locals before plunging in. Sellicks Beach, 50 km or so south of the city, is another good spot in the right conditions.

The most popular place in the state for both advanced and novice windsurfers is Goolwa, on the Fleurieu Peninsula, where you get a range of conditions in a reasonably small area. Other hot spots include Barmera (Lake Bonney), Beachport (Lake George), Meningie (Lake Albert) and Milang (Lake Alexandrina). Kingston SE, Port Lincoln

and the beaches around Yorke Peninsula are good coastal spots.

If you're interested in entering competitions, get hold of a copy of *Boardsailing News* from any windsurfing shop. Glascraft Marine (Sailboards) (☎ (08) 8232 0203), at 243 Pirie St in Adelaide, is a good source of general information on what's happening around the state.

SCUBA DIVING

There are plenty of good dive spots along the coast, including jetties, wrecks, drop-offs, caves, reefs and sponge beds.

While shore-diving off Adelaide's metropolitan beaches is limited, there are numerous worthwhile boat sites. These include the 40-metre sunken dredge *South Australian*, which lies at 20 metres about six km off Glenelg. Built in Holland in 1911, it was sunk in 1985 to form a sunken reef and is now home for a staggering variety of marine life. It's generally regarded as the best of Adelaide's dive sites.

At Port Noarlunga, 18 km south of Adelaide, you can shore dive or snorkel in the Marine Reserve – it's accessible from the end of the jetty – or boat dive on the *HA Lumb*, a sunken fishing vessel. The reef has a sign-posted underwater trail suitable for snorkellers. Port Noarlunga is the state's most popular diving area thanks to its accessibility.

Further south, the reefs off Snapper Point (42 km) and Aldinga (43 km) are still good for fish and other creatures despite the effects of stormwater run-off from nearby housing developments. You can snorkel off the shore at Snapper Point, but the Aldinga Reef, with its drop-off (to 22 metres) and swim throughs, is more suited to boat diving.

At 88 km from Adelaide, the Rapid Bay jetty has a wonderful abundance of marine life. Unfortunately, the jetty is very long and the best diving is (you guessed it) off the end – but everyone says the walk is worth it. Take a rope for hauling your gear out of the water at low tide.

Further afield, Yorke Peninsula has great potential under almost any wind conditions – if one side is too rough, the other will usually be diveable. Attractions here include several jetty dives (fish, starfish, colourful sponges, nudibranches and soft corals), the wrecks around Wardang Island and Edithburgh, and spectacular underwater topography off the south coast.

Other good areas around the state include the reefs off Robe and nearby Cape Jaffa in the South-East, the marine life at Point Sir Isaac near Port Lincoln, and the reefs, wrecks and drop-offs around Kangaroo Island. At Dangerous Reef off Port Lincoln you can watch white pointer sharks from the safety of a suspended cage (see the section on Port Lincoln in the Eyre Peninsula chapter for details).

Although out of date, Peter Christopher's slim but informative *Divers' Guide to South Australia* covers numerous accessible sites around the state, so is definitely worth getting. The *Australian Divers' Guide*, by Peter Stone, has a section on SA. As well, the Adelaide Skin Diving Centre, at 7 Compton St, Adelaide, publishes *A Listing of Adelaide Dive Sites*, which describes 15 sites.

Dive charter operators in and near Adelaide include:

Adelaide
  Adelaide Skin Diving Centre (☎ (08) 8231 6144): visits sites off Adelaide and Kangaroo Island
  Glenelg Scuba Diving Centre (☎ (08) 8294 7744): visits sites off Adelaide and the near coast; publishes a programme of dives in its monthly newsletter
  Great Bight Tours (☎ (08) 8369 2773: does charters to Port Lincoln
  Smuggler Charter (☎ 015 973 329): relatively inexpensive dives, can leave from any boat ramp in SA
  Super Elliotts Dive Centre (☎ (08) 8223 2522): mainly weekend dives off Adelaide, leaving Saturday from Glenelg and Sunday from O'Sullivans Beach
Fleurieu Peninsula
  Victor Harbor Boat Charters (mobile ☎ 0414 52 7474 and 0414 52 7474): dives on the south coast near Victor Harbor
Kangaroo Island
  Adventureland Diving (☎ (0848) 31 072): based near Penneshaw
  Kangaroo Island Diving Safaris (☎ (0848) 93 225): specialises in the north coast

The Scuba Divers Federation of SA, at the Adelaide Skin Diving Centre (ask for Helena), is happy to provide advice to visiting divers.

CAVE DIVING

There is some world-class cave diving around Mt Gambier, in the South-East, where you'll find dozens of sites including huge caverns and deep sink holes. The area holds excellent potential for suitably trained divers, as the formations and water clarity are said to be legendary.

As a result of several tragedies in the early 1970s, however, the only chance you have of getting permission to scuba dive in most caves in this area is to join the Cave Divers Association of Australia (CDAA) and be trained to their requirements. Information on the different categories of membership can be obtained by writing to CDAA at PO Box 290, North Adelaide, SA 5006.

With a permit from the NPWS office in Mt Gambier, you can dive and snorkel in crystal-clear water at the Piccaninnie Ponds and Ewens Ponds conservation parks south of that town. Only certified divers will be granted permission to scuba dive.

FISHING

There is fantastic potential for fishing in many parts of SA. Apart from the coast, where conditions range from pounding surf to millpond calm, there's the Murray River and numerous lakes and freshwater streams. You can even catch fish in many outback waterholes.

Surf beaches all the way along the coast are good for large species such as Australian salmon (actually a perch), mulloway, and shark, and smaller ones like tommy ruff (usually known as tommies), trevally, bream, tailor and flathead. Popular spots include the ocean beaches between Port Lincoln and Ceduna on the west coast, Browns Beach on the southern tip of Yorke Peninsula, Waitpinga Beach near Victor Harbor, Pennington Bay on Kangaroo Island, and the Ninety Mile Beach near Kingston.

Generally the best sea fishing is from a boat, particularly where the bottom shelves gently away as in the gulfs. Fortunately, SA has plenty of jetties (about 80 of them) that allow you to fish in deeper water. There are some beauties on Yorke Peninsula and Eyre Peninsula, where large cargo vessels come in to load wheat; Port Giles, Wallaroo and Ceduna have outstanding deep-water jetties where you can catch a wide range of species.

Many jetties are also good for squid and blue-swimmer crabs. The latter can be caught in shallow sheltered water in the northern coastal areas of the two gulfs and in suitable habitats along the west coast.

Fishing off the rocks yields species such as sweep, groper, snapper, salmon trout and trevally; you can also catch salmon and mulloway where the rocks are exposed to the Southern Ocean. However, you've got to watch out for the huge killer waves (known as king waves) that occasionally roll in from the ocean.

Rock fishing is one of the most dangerous recreational sports; there are several drownings every year thanks to king waves and recklessness. It's smart to wear light clothing and a buoyancy vest if you're fishing close to the water, particularly where the rocks are exposed to swells.

Apart from deteriorating water quality and interference with its natural flow regimes, the poor old Murray has also suffered through the introduction of European carp. These things have had a devastating effect on native aquatic species through both competition and their feeding habits, which muddy the water. Catch as many carp as you like, then chop them up and feed the pelicans – it's illegal to throw them back alive.

The most popular eating fish in SA is the succulent King George whiting – they even taste wonderful after being frozen. You can catch them right along the coast, but the best spots are in sheltered waters with sandy bottoms. Most whiting are caught in the gulfs, Investigator Strait and bays along the west coast.

Any town where tourists go to catch fish will have somewhere – either a gear shop, service station or seafood wholesaler – where you can buy bait and at least basic equipment.

Information

Where to Fish in South Australia by SA Fishing Tackle Agencies mentions a large number of spots and has 88 maps. David Capel's *Diary of Fishing & Boating for SA* is less detailed, but also worth getting.

Then there's the *South Australian Angler*, an informative bimonthly magazine with feature articles on fishing around the state. *Southern Fisheries*, the free quarterly magazine published by the Department of Primary Industries, has fascinating articles on all sorts of topics to do with fresh and saltwater fisheries, as well as short pieces on everything from seafood recipes to fishing tips. *South Australian Waters*, another useful quarterly, gives a broader coverage of aquatic sports and issues, with a strong fishing content.

To find out what's currently hot, and what's not, check Saturday's *Advertiser* and the *Sunday Mail*. Alternatively, any fishing equipment supplier will give you pointers for their particular area.

Regulations

Fishing restrictions in SA include bag limits, legal sizes, seasonal closures, restricted areas and protected species. To find out about them, read *Recreational Fishing in South Australia*, a free booklet put out by the Department of Primary Production's Fisheries Division (☎ (08) 8226 2314). It's available at most fishing suppliers.

And no, you don't need a licence to fish in SA, provided you're a recreational angler using a hook and line.

Charters

There are numerous fishing charter operators around the coast and these are mentioned later in the book. Costs are typically between $30 and $50 per person for a half-day trip including gear but not meals; minimum numbers invariably apply.

Provided you have a South Australian or

Marine Mammals of South Australia

One of the great thrills of any visit to SA is observing marine mammals at close quarters. The state's waters are home to 25 species of cetaceans (dolphins and whales), almost a third of all those on the globe. As well, one species of fur seal and one of sea lion live in permanent colonies along the coast. Other seals, such as the leopard seal, are occasional visitors from Antarctic waters.

Whaling and sealing were SA's first industries. Seals were killed for their skins on Kangaroo Island from 1803, while the first two whaling stations were established in 1837 at Victor Harbor. Others were at Port Lincoln and sites further west near Smoky Bay and Ceduna. The industry was based on the southern right whale, called 'right' by whalers because it had large quantities of valuable oil and baleen and was easy to kill. The southern right existed in large numbers, but over-exploitation soon reduced the population to uneconomic levels. All whaling operations in the state ceased by the early 1870s.

The southern right whale comes close to shore on its annual breeding migration, and so is often seen from clifftops and other vantage points. The state's two dolphin species are also a common sight, but the remaining 22 species of cetaceans are rarely seen even from boats as they all live out near the edge of the continental shelf. They include the blue whale, fin whale, sperm whale, humpback whale and killer whale. Every year there are several strandings along the coast, usually of one to three animals at a time.

Mysticeti – Baleen Whales

Southern Right Whale *Eubalaena australis*
Once numbering an estimated 100,000 worldwide, only a few hundred southern right whales remained by 1935, when they became fully protected. For decades the whales were rarely sighted along the SA coast and the outlook was gloomy. Now the population appears to be recovering and they're returning to breed each year in increasing numbers. Today there are an estimated 1500 to 3000 southern right whales worldwide, with about 500 living in the Southern Ocean off Australia.

Every year between June and October 100 or so mostly adult whales are seen on their annual breeding migration to warmer waters along the South Australian coast. At least half make for the head of the Great Australian Bight, where around 20 calves are born along a 20-km stretch of coastline. This nursery area is to be included in an 8600 sq km marine park now being proposed for the coast between Cape Adieu and the Western Australian border.

Southern right whales sieve their food through fine baleen known as baleen, hence their classification. They can easily be identified by the large white lumps (or callosity) on the head and their lack of a dorsal fin. Adults reach 18 metres in length, four metres in diameter, and weigh up to 90 tonnes. Calves measure around five metres at birth. The peak of the southern right whale season along the coast is August and September.

interstate boat licence, you can hire dinghies with outboards at several places.

WATCHING MARINE MAMMALS

For nature enthusiasts, the icon of SA's 27 species of marine mammals is the southern right whale, which is often seen along the ocean coast during its annual breeding migration. Unlike the state's other whales, it often comes in to within a few hundred metres of shore. Hot spots for whale-watching include Victor Harbor, the south coast of Kangaroo Island, Port Lincoln, Elliston and (the hottest and most reliable of them all) Head of Bight on the far west coast.

Generally, the best place to watch for southern right whales is from a high point through low to medium-power binoculars.

The glossy black animals have bus-like dimensions, and when feeling frisky they can put on spectacular displays of breaching (leaping out of the water), tail-splashing, courting and mating. Watching these magnificent creatures in action is an unforgettable experience.

The only other cetaceans you're likely to see are common and bottlenose dolphins. These playful animals often frolic amongst human surfers at places such as Middleton (near Victor Harbor) and Blackfellows (near Elliston). Dolphins are a common sight in the mangrove inlets near Adelaide.

New Zealand fur seals and Australian sea lions breed on a number of islands including Kangaroo Island; you'll also find sea lion colonies on the mainland at Cape Labbatt

Odontoceti – Toothed Whales & Dolphins

Bottlenose Dolphin *Tursiops truncatus*
This dark-grey species is found right along the coast. It normally grows to three metres and has a relatively short beak compared to its cousin, the common dolphin. Bottlenose dolphins are extremely powerful swimmers and will sometimes leap several metres out of the water. They'll also act cooperatively in such matters as rounding up a school of fish and taking turns to feed. Several bottlenose dolphins live in the Port River near Adelaide.

Common Dolphin *Delphinus delphis*
These, the most common of dolphins (hence the name), are found throughout the world. In SA they grow to two metres and are often seen playing in the waves – they'll also surf with humans if given half a chance. You'll recognise them by their relatively long beak and the yellow-and-black pattern along their sides. Like the bottlenose dolphin its favourite foods include squid.

False Killer Whales *Pseudorca crassidens*
Growing to six metres, these black to dark-grey whales have been recorded numerous times along the SA coast. They're difficult to tell apart from pilot whales, which are also often reported. Both have the same colour and protruding foreheads, or melons, used in echolocation.

Seals

New Zealand Fur Seal *Arctocephalus forsteri*
Once slaughtered in their thousands for their luxuriant skins, fur seals are now thriving around New Zealand, parts of southern Australia and on sub-Antarctic islands. They're usually seen basking on rocks, particularly on Kangaroo Island where there are several colonies. Males grow to 2.5 metres, females to 1.5 metres; they have grey-brown fur and a more pointed nose than the Australian sea lion.

Australian Sea Lion *Neophoca cinerea*
This is the only pinniped (seal) that's endemic to Australia. Sea lions are about the same size as the New Zealand fur seal, but you can easily identify the males by their black to dark-brown back and sides, and white crown and nape; the females are silvery grey above and cream below. Both sexes are extremely territorial during the variable breeding season.

The total population of Australian sea lions is around 12,000, making it one of the rarest seal species. The largest populations are on the Pages Islands east of Kangaroo Island (2250), Dangerous Reef off Port Lincoln (1000) and Seal Bay on Kangaroo Island (500). Other colonies are found along the west coast of SA and on islands off the WA coast as far around as Geraldton. ∎

(near Streaky Bay) and along the mighty Nullarbor Cliffs. The easiest way to tell colonies of the two species apart is the fact that sea lions prefer sandy beaches, while fur seals like rocky platforms.

Information

The SA Whale Centre in Victor Harbor operates the 'whale information network' from its interesting interpretive centre on Railway Terrace. To report a sighting, call them on ☎ (085) 52 5644; for current information on where the whales are, call ☎ 0055 31 223. If you're not going there, write to them at PO Box 950, Victor Harbor, SA 5211, for a copy of their very informative *SA Whale Watching Information Booklet*.

Essential reading for whale lovers includes *The Australian Guide to Whale Watching* by Tina Dalton and Ross Isaacs. It includes information on identification, behaviour, biology and conservation, as well as giving popular whale-watching spots.

Another is the SA Museum's *A Guide to Whales & Whale Watching in SA*, a much slimmer volume but still with plenty of good information and illustrations.

Organised Tours

Whale-watching tours to the Head of Bight are offered by Whales & Wildlife Eco Tours (☎ (08) 8379 0203), which combines aerial survey work and clifftop observations as part of an ongoing scientific research project.

In Ceduna, Nullarbor Adventure Tours (☎ (085) 25 3447) has a two-day trip with whale-watching and cave visits for $400. The Port Lincoln-based Great Australian Bight Safaris (☎ (086) 82 2750) does a five-day trip to Head of Bight via the scenic west coast for $650. Osprey Wildlife Expeditions (☎ (08) 8388 2552) have a six day tour ex-Adelaide which includes cave visits for $995.

Rangers will take you to visit the sea lion colony at Seal Bay, on Kangaroo Island.

Aerial Activities

SCENIC FLIGHTS

A number of operators around the state offer scenic flights in helicopters and light planes, usually from the local aerodrome or private landing areas. Arguably the most spectacular area to see from the air is the Flinders Ranges, where you fly over bold bluffs and stark ridges with views to large salt lakes and arid plains on either side. In the warmer months they're at their best for colour and smooth flying in early morning and late afternoon.

Also worthwhile is the coastline, particularly the more rugged areas fronting the Southern Ocean. You can admire soaring cliffs west of Investigator Strait, and between June and October there's always a good chance of seeing southern right whales.

Any flight over the outback is fascinating simply because of its vast expanse of unbelievably empty space. Actually it's not that empty, it just seems that way! Depending on where you are, you fly over scattered homesteads, station bores, salt lakes, gum creeks, desert sand ridges and endless gibber plains. You might even see ringers (Australian cowboys) on horses or motorbikes pushing a mob of sheep or cattle along. Lake Eyre is impressive enough when dry and definitely shouldn't be missed when it has plenty of water in it.

A word of warning here! Don't go flying over the outback or the Flinders Ranges in the middle of a hot day, particularly if you're prone to airsickness. The bumpy conditions may cause nausea.

Most scenic flight operators are mentioned in this book; look under Organised Tours at the start of each chapter. Otherwise check with SATC and local tourist offices.

BALLOONING

There's nothing quite like drifting silently over the countryside in a hot-air balloon, but the sport hasn't taken off at all in SA. In fact, you can only do it in the Barossa Valley – the people to talk to are Balloon Adventures (☎ (08) 8389 3195).

SKYDIVING

The state's only skydiving clubs are the SA Sport Parachute Club (☎ (08) 8341 6288), at Lower Light on the Port Wakefield Rd (about 45 minutes north of Adelaide city), and Sky Dive Adelaide (☎ (08) 8371 2766), at Strathalbyn on the southern end of the Adelaide Hills. Both are professional training organisations, so if you've never tried the adrenalin rush of skydiving, now's your chance.

First timers must do about 10 hours of theory and practise before being allowed to launch themselves into space – accompanied by instructors, of course. The all-inclusive cost for training and a first jump from 12,000 feet is $390 (video $60 extra).

Licensed skydivers can jump from 12,000 feet for $22 a time.

HANG GLIDING

Popular spots for hill jumps near Adelaide include Seaford, Maslins Beach, Normanville, Cape Jervis and Victor Harbor around the Fleurieu Peninsula coast, and the Barunga Ranges in the Mid-North.

The Hang Gliding Association of SA can be contacted through State Association House (☎ (08) 8213 0666), who'll give you their current telephone number. The association controls all hang-gliding and paragliding operations in the state and can advise you on opportunities best suited to your ability.

BUNGEE JUMPING

If you're a bungee-jumping junky then SA will disappoint you. The only operator is the Greenhills Adventure Park (☎ (085) 52 1222) at Victor Harbor, and then only during the summer school holidays. A jump costs around $70. Check first to make sure they're still doing them.

Getting There & Away

AIR

The Adelaide airport has domestic and international terminals seven km west of the city centre. See Getting Around in the Adelaide chapter for details on getting to and from the airport.

There are plenty of travel agents in Adelaide. Probably the best to try for discounted fares are the Flight Centre (☎ (08) 8231 0044) at 136 North Terrace, STA Travel (☎ (08) 8223 2426) at 235 Rundle St, and the YHA travel office (☎ (08) 8231 5583) at 38 Sturt St. Both the Flight Centre and STA have several offices around town.

Due to fierce competition, airfares from Adelaide to Europe are generally cheaper than from eastern capitals, while fares to Asia and the USA are generally a little dearer. The international airlines currently flying into Adelaide are: Cathay Pacific, 45 Grenfell St (☎ 13 17 47); Garuda Indonesia, 76 Waymouth St (☎ 8231 2636); Malaysian Airlines, Level 5, 144 North Tce (☎ 8231 6171); Qantas Airways, 144 North Tce (booking enquiries ☎ 8237 8541); and Singapore Airlines, 50 King William St (☎ 8238 2747).

Round-the-World Tickets

Round-the-World tickets are very popular and many of these will take you through Australia. The airline RTW tickets are often real bargains. Since Australia is pretty much at the other side of the world from Europe or North America it can work out no more expensive, or even cheaper, to keep going in the same direction right round the world rather than U-turn to return.

The official airline RTW tickets are usually put together by a combination of two airlines, and permit you to fly anywhere you want on their route systems so long as you do not backtrack. Other restrictions are that you (usually) must book the first sector in advance and cancellation penalties then apply. There may be restrictions on how many stops you are permitted and usually the tickets are valid from 90 days up to a year. A typical price for a South Pacific RTW ticket is around £760/US$1170.

An alternative type of RTW ticket is one put together by a travel agent using a combination of discounted tickets from a number of airlines. A UK agent like Trailfinders can put together interesting London-to-London RTW combinations including Australia for between £690 and £800.

Circle Pacific Tickets

Circle Pacific fares are a similar idea to RTW tickets and use a combination of airlines to circle the Pacific, combining Australia, New Zealand, North America and Asia. Examples would be Qantas-Northwest Orient, Canadian Airlines International-Cathay Pacific and so on. As with RTW tickets there are advance purchase restrictions and limits to how many stopovers you can make. Typically fares range between US$1760 and US$2240. Possible Circle Pacific routes are Los Angeles-Bangkok-Sydney-Auckland-Honolulu-Los Angeles or Los Angeles-Tokyo-Kuala Lumpur-Sydney-Auckland-Honolulu-Los Angeles.

The UK

The cheapest tickets in London are from the numerous 'bucket shops' (discount ticket agencies) which advertise in magazines and papers like *Time Out*, *City Limits*, *Southern Cross* and *TNT*. Pick up one or two of these publications and ring round a few bucket shops to find the best deal. Most bucket shops are trustworthy and reliable but the occasional sharp operator appears – *Time Out* and *Business Traveller* give some useful advice on precautions to take.

The cheapest London to Adelaide bucket-shop (not direct) tickets are about £385 one way or £638 return. Such prices are usually only available if you leave London in the low season – March to June. In September and mid-December fares go up by about 30%, while the rest of the year they're somewhere in between.

Many cheap tickets allow stopovers on the way to or from Australia. Rules vary, but recently most return tickets have allowed you to stay away for any period between 14 days and one year, with stopovers permitted anywhere along your route. As usual with heavily discounted tickets the less you pay the less you get. Nice direct flights, leaving at convenient times and flying with popular airlines, are obviously going to be more expensive.

From Adelaide in the low season you can expect to pay around A$1200 one way, and A$1800 return to London and other European capitals, with stops in Asia on the way. Again, all fares increase by up to 30% in the European summer and at Christmas.

North America

There are a variety of connections across the Pacific from Los Angeles, San Francisco and Vancouver to Australia, including direct flights, flights via New Zealand, island-hopping routes and more circuitous Pacific rim routes via nations in Asia. Qantas, Air New Zealand and United all fly USA-Australia; Qantas, Air New Zealand and Canadian Airlines International fly Canada-Australia. An interesting option from the east coast is Northwest's flight via Japan.

One advantage of flying Qantas or Air New Zealand is that on the US airlines, if your flight goes via Hawaii, the west coast to Hawaii sector is treated as a domestic flight. This means that you have to pay for drinks and headsets – goodies that are free on international sectors.

To find good fares to Australia check the travel ads in the Sunday travel sections of papers like the *Los Angeles Times*, *San Francisco Chronicle-Examiner*, *New York Times* or *Toronto Globe & Mail*. You can typically get a one-way/return ticket from the west coast for US$830/1000, or US$1000/1400 from the east coast.

At peak seasons – particularly the Australian summer/Christmas time – seats will be harder to get and the price will probably be higher. In the USA good agents for discounted tickets are the two student travel operators, Council Travel and STA Travel, both of which have lots of offices around the country. Canadian west-coast fares out of Vancouver will be similar to those from the US west coast. From Toronto fares go from around C$2230 return, from Vancouver C$1700.

If Pacific island-hopping is your aim, check out the airlines of Pacific Island nations, some of which have good deals on indirect routings. Qantas can give you Fiji or Tahiti along the way, while Air New Zealand can offer both and the Cook Islands as well. See the Circle Pacific section for more details.

One-way/return fares available from Australia include: San Francisco A$1000/1360, New York A$1150/1660 and Vancouver $1000/1360.

New Zealand

Air New Zealand and Qantas operate a network of trans-Tasman flights linking Auckland, Wellington and Christchurch in New Zealand with most major Australian gateway cities. You can fly directly between a lot of places in New Zealand and a lot of places in Australia. From New Zealand to Adelaide you're looking at around A$515 one way and A$689 return.

Asia

Ticket discounting is widespread in Asia, particularly in Singapore, Hong Kong, Bangkok and Penang. There are a lot of fly-by-nights in the Asian ticketing scene so a little care is required. Also the Asian routes have been particularly caught up in the capacity shortages on flights to Australia. Flights between Hong Kong and Australia are notoriously heavily booked while flights to or from Bangkok and Singapore are often part of the longer Europe-Australia route so they are also sometimes very full. Plan ahead. For much more information on South-East Asian travel and on to Australia see Lonely Planet's *South-East Asia on a shoestring*.

Typical fares from Adelaide to Singapore are A$729/989 one way/return. You can also pick up some interesting tickets in Asia to include Australia on the way across the Pacific. Qantas and Air New Zealand offer discounted trans-Pacific tickets.

From Adelaide return fares from the east coast to Kuala Lumpur and Bangkok are A$850 and A$1040, respectively.

Africa

The flight possibilities between Africa and Australia have increased markedly in the last few years. There is a number of direct flights each week between Africa and Australia, but only between Perth and Harare (Zimbabwe) or Johannesburg (South Africa). Qantas, South African Airways and Air Zimbabwe all fly this route.

Other airlines that connect southern Africa and Australia include Malaysia Airlines (via Kuala Lumpur) and Air Mauritius (via Mauritius), both of which have special deals from time to time.

From East Africa the options are to fly via Mauritius, or via the Indian subcontinent and on to South-East Asia, then connect from there to Australia.

South America

Two routes operate between South America and Australia. The Chile connection involves Lan Chile's twice-weekly Santiago-Easter Island-Tahiti flight, from where you fly Qantas or another airline to Australia. Alternatively there is the route that skirts the Antarctic circle, flying from Buenos Aires to Auckland and Sydney, operated twice-weekly by Aerolineas Argentinas.

Domestic Flights

Adelaide is a long way from other capitals (the closest, Melbourne, is 729 km by the shortest road route), so if your time is limited you may have to think about flying there.

There are only two main domestic carriers within Australia – Qantas (which merged with Australian Airlines) and Ansett –

despite the fact that the airline industry is deregulated. Kendell Airlines is the third carrier offering flights into SA, but it is only a very minor player on the interstate scene. This lack of competition means relatively high prices, although discounting is now a regular feature of the domestic flights scene.

Random Discounting One of the major features of the deregulated air travel industry is random discounting. As the airlines try harder to fill planes, they often offer substantial discounts on selected routes. Although this seems to apply mainly to the heavy volume routes, that's not always the case.

To make the most of the discounted fares, you need to keep in touch with what's currently on offer, mainly because there are usually conditions attached to cheap fares – such as booking 14 or so days in advance, only flying on weekends or between certain dates and so on. Also the number of seats available is usually fairly limited. The further ahead you can plan the better.

The places to which this sort of discounting generally applies are the main centres – Melbourne, Sydney, Brisbane, Cairns, Adelaide and Perth – but deals come and go all the time.

It is fair to say that on virtually any route in the country covered by Qantas or Ansett the full economy fare will not be the cheapest way to go. Because the situation is so fluid, the special fares will more than likely have changed by the time you read this. For that reason we list the full one-way economy fares throughout the book, although you can safely assume that there will be a cheaper fare available.

Discounts are generally greater for return rather than one-way travel.

If you're planning a return trip and you have 14 days up your sleeve then you can save 45% to 50% by travelling Apex. You have to book and pay for your tickets 14 days in advance and you must stay away at least one Saturday night. Flight details can be changed at any time, but the tickets are non-refundable. If you book seven days in advance the saving is 35% to 40% off the full fare.

For one-way travel, if you can book three days in advance a saving of around 10% is offered; for seven-day advance booking the discount is around 20%.

University or other higher education students under the age of 26 can get a 25% discount off the regular economy fare. An airline tertiary concession card (available from the airlines) is required for Australian students. Overseas students can use their International Student Identity Card.

All nonresident international travellers can get up to a 40% discount on internal Qantas flights and 25% on Ansett flights simply by presenting their international ticket when booking. It seems there is no limit to the number of domestic flights you can take, it doesn't matter which airline you fly into Australia with, and it doesn't have to be on a return ticket. Note that the discount applies only to the full economy fare, and so in many cases it will be cheaper to take advantage of other discounts offered. The best advice is to ring around and explore the options before you buy.

Another thing to keep your eyes open for is special deals at certain times of the year. For example, when the Melbourne Cup horse race is on in early November lots of extra flights are put on. These would normally be going in the opposite direction nearly empty so special fares are offered to people wanting to leave Melbourne when everybody else wants to go there. The Australian Formula One Grand Prix in Melbourne in March is a similar one-way-traffic event.

Air Passes With discounting being the norm these days, air passes do not represent the value they did in pre-deregulation days. However, there are a few worth checking out.

Qantas offers two passes. The Australia Explorer Pass can only be purchased overseas and involves purchasing coupons for either short-haul flights (for example, Hobart to Melbourne) at $170 one way, or for long-haul sectors (such as just about anywhere to Uluru) for $220. You must purchase a minimum of four coupons before you arrive in Australia, and once in the country you can buy up to four more.

There is also the Qantas Backpackers Pass, which can only be bought in Australia on production of identification such as a YHA membership or a VIP Backpackers or Independent Backpackers Card, or a Bus Australia card. You must purchase a minimum of three connecting sectors (such as Adelaide-Melbourne, Melbourne-Sydney and Sydney-Brisbane), and stay a minimum of two nights at each stop. The discount is quite substantial; a sample fare using this pass is Adelaide to Melbourne for $115 one way, as against the full economy return fare of $345.

Ansett has its Kangaroo Airpass, which gives you two options – 6000 km with two or three stopovers for $949 ($729 for children) and 10,000 km with three to seven stopovers for $1499 ($1149 for children). A number of restrictions apply to these tickets, although they can be a good deal if you want to see a lot of country in a short period of time. Fortunately, you don't need to start and finish at the same place. Restrictions include a minimum travel time (10 nights) and a maximum (45 nights). One of the stops must be at a non-capital city destination and be for at least four nights, and you can only stay at each destination once. All sectors must be booked when you purchase the ticket, although these can be changed without penalty unless the ticket needs rewriting, in which case there's a $50 charge. Refunds are available in full before travel commences and not at all once you start using the ticket.

On a 6000-km air pass you could, for example, fly Sydney-Alice Springs-Cairns-Brisbane-Sydney. That gives you three stops and two of them are in non-capital cities. T~~ regular fare for that circuit would be $1~~ but with current discounts (sev~~ advance purchase) it's $1217, so ~~ $368. A one-way route might b~ Melbourne-Sydney-Alice S~ Regular cost for that route ~ but with discounts it's $~ is $238.

Economy Fares If for some reason you can't take advantage of discounts, the typical one-way economy fares from Adelaide are $372 to Alice Springs, $494 to Brisbane, $536 to Darwin, $345 to Hobart, $240 to Melbourne and $346 to Sydney.

Note that all domestic flights in Australia are nonsmoking. Because Qantas flies international and domestic routes, flights leave from both the international and domestic terminals at Australian airports. Flights with flight numbers from QF001 to QF399 operate from international terminals; flight numbers QF400 and above from domestic terminals.

In Adelaide, Qantas (☎ 13 13 13) is at 144 North Terrace and Ansett (☎ 13 13 00) is at 142 North Terrace. Both have several travel centres around town.

Leaving Australia

There is a $27 departure tax when leaving Australia, but this is incorporated into the price of your air ticket and so is not paid as a separate tax.

Warning

The information in this chapter is vulnerable to change – prices for international travel are volatile, routes are introduced and cancelled, schedules change, rules are amended and special deals come and go.

Airlines and governments seem to take a perverse pleasure in making price structures and regulations as complicated as possible and you should check directly with the airline or travel agent to make sure you understand how a fare (and ticket you may buy) works.

In addition, the travel industry is highly competitive and there are many lurks and perks. The upshot of this is that you should get quotes and advice from as many airlines and travel agents as possible before you part with your hard-earned cash.

The details given in this chapter should be garded only as pointers and cannot be any titute for your own careful, up-to-date rch.

LAND
Bus

Bus travel is generally the cheapest way of getting from A to B, other than hitching of course, but the main problem is to find the best deal. A great many travellers see Australia by bus because it's one of the best ways to come to grips with the country's size and variety of terrain, and because the bus companies have such comprehensive route networks – far more comprehensive than the railway system.

There is only one truly national bus network – Greyhound Pioneer Australia (☎ toll-free 13 20 30), which has services between Adelaide and all major mainland cities. McCafferty's (☎ 8212 5066) is certainly the next biggest, with services virtually right around Australia except for the long haul across the Nullarbor between Perth and Port Augusta, but here you can take the Indian Pacific train using a McCafferty's bus pass. Their buses look much the same as Greyhound Pioneer and are similarly equipped with air-conditioning, toilets and videos.

The third option is Firefly Express (☎ 8231 1488), which runs to Melbourne every evening at 8.30 pm ($40) and on to Sydney for $50 (day service) and $45 (overnight service).

Thanks to competition the major companies frequently change their fares, but the following samples of standard prices will give you an idea. Greyhound Pioneer charges $53 to Melbourne (10 hours), $95 to Sydney (22 hours) via Melbourne, $189 to Perth (34 hours), and $142 to Alice Springs (20 hours). There's a 10% discount for backpackers. McCafferty's offers a similar discount and is generally a few dollars cheaper.

Greyhound Pioneer and McCafferty's depart from Adelaide's central bus station at 101-111 Franklin St near the city centre. Both have their offices there. The Firefly Express leaves opposite, at 110 Franklin St.

Both Greyhound Pioneer and McCafferty's have a variety of passes available, so it's a matter of deciding which suits your needs best.

Greyhound Pioneer Bus Passes The Unlimited Travel Pass gives you a set number of days bus travel within a specified period, the shortest being seven days travel in 30 days ($450), the longest 90 days travel in six months ($2225). The advantages of these passes is that you can travel one route as many times as you like, and have unlimited km. The disadvantages are that you may feel obliged to travel further than you might otherwise like to, simply because you have the days free to do so.

More popular are the set-route passes. These give you six or 12 months to cover a set route. You haven't got the go-anywhere flexibility of the unlimited travel bus pass but if you can find a set route which suits you – and there are 33 to choose from – then it generally works out cheaper than the unlimited travel pass. When a pass follows a circular route, you can start anywhere along the loop, and finish at the same spot.

The main limitation with this kind of pass is that you can't backtrack, except on 'dead-end' short sectors such as Darwin to Kakadu, Townsville to Cairns and from the Stuart Highway to Uluru (Ayers Rock).

Aussie Highlights allows you to loop around the eastern half of Australia from Sydney taking in Melbourne, Adelaide, Coober Pedy, Uluru, Alice Springs, Darwin (and Kakadu), Cairns, Townsville, the Whitsundays, Brisbane and Surfers Paradise for $690. There are one-way passes, such as the Go West pass from Sydney to Cairns via Melbourne, Adelaide, Uluru, Alice Springs, Katherine, Darwin (and Kakadu), and Townsville for $550. There's even an All Australia Pass which takes you right around the country, including up or down through the Centre, for $1200.

McCafferty's Passes McCafferty's have 15 set-route passes to choose from. On the routes which cross the Nullarbor, the pass includes travel on the Indian Pacific train service between Perth and Adelaide.

The Travel Australia Pass is the equivalent of Greyhound Pioneer's All Australia Pass, and costs $1160. The Point to Point Pass

takes in a loop from Cairns via Sydney, Melbourne, Adelaide, Uluru, Alice Springs and Tennant Creek for $600, while the Best of the East & Centre is the same but with the addition of travel to Darwin and Kakadu, for $700.

Other Bus Options There are a few smaller companies around Australia that offer flexible transport options. The trips, which are generally aimed at budget travellers, are a combination of straightforward bus travel and an organised tour. The buses are generally smaller and so not necessarily as comfortable as those of the big bus companies, but it's a much more interesting way to travel.

Companies that include Adelaide in their itineraries are:

Oz Experience (☎ (02) 9368 1766). This company is basically a backpackers' bus line, and offers frequent services in a big loop around the eastern half of Australia including Darwin, Adelaide and the east coast. It has several options as far as routes go and visits most of the major destinations, with off-the-beaten-track detours to cattle stations and national parks. You buy one of their 18 passes, which range from $110 to $833 depending on the distance, and are valid for six to 12 months. Your pass entitles you to unlimited stops, which means you can get on and off whenever and wherever you like. The drivers act as your guides, providing commentaries and advice; they can also pre-book your hostels, stop at supermarkets so you can do your shopping, and arrange discounts on most tours and activities along the way.

The Wayward Bus (☎ toll-free 1800 882 823). The Wayward bus offers transport between Adelaide and Melbourne via the Coorong and Great Ocean Road (three days, $150), Alice Springs via such places as the Flinders Ranges, Oodnadatta Track, Coober Pedy and Uluru (eight days, $560) and Perth (12 days, $770). Unlike the Oz Experience runs, these trips include sight-seeing and may include meals and accommodation. Check before booking.

Train

Rail travel in Australia is something you do because you really want to – not because it's cheaper, and certainly not because it's fast – apart from hitching it's generally the slowest way to get from anywhere to anywhere in Australia. On the other hand the trains are comfortable and you certainly see Australia at ground level.

Adelaide is connected by rail with Sydney, Melbourne, Perth, Broken Hill, Alice Springs and other centres. To Melbourne the daily overnight Overland takes about 12 hours and costs $50 in economy, $104 in 1st class and $170 with sleeper.

You can travel daily between Sydney and Adelaide via Melbourne on the Melbourne Express (Sydney to Melbourne) and Overlander (Melbourne to Adelaide), and twice weekly via Broken Hill on the Indian Pacific (Sydney to Perth). Via Melbourne it's $146/239/391 for an economy seat/1st-class seat/1st-class sleeper. The connection is poor in Melbourne – you will need to spend the day there. Via Broken Hill it's $120/241/376 economy seat/holiday-class sleeper (no meals)/1st-class sleeper (meals).

There's also the Speedlink – a daily bus and train connection which is not only cheaper but five or six hours faster. You travel from Sydney to Albury on the XPT train, and from Albury to Adelaide on a V/Line bus. Travel time is under 20 hours, and an economy/1st-class seat is $99/141.

Between Adelaide and Perth there is the Indian Pacific which runs twice weekly (Tuesday and Friday). The trip takes about 36 hours. Fares are $200/438/672 for an economy seat/holiday-class sleeper (no meals)/1st-class sleeping berth (meals).

The Ghan between Adelaide and Alice Springs runs weekly throughout the year (departing Thursday) and twice weekly from April to October (Monday and Thursday) for $140/309/500.

Interstate train services from Adelaide leave from the interstate terminal (information ☎ (08) 8231 7699; bookings 13 22 32) on Railway Terrace, Keswick, just south-west of the city centre.

Rail Passes There are a number of passes available that allow unlimited rail travel either across the country or just in one state. With the Austrail Pass you can travel anywhere on the Australian rail network, in either 1st class or economy. The cost is $780/460 in 1st/economy class for 14 days, $985/595 for 21 days, $1210/720 for 30 days, $1700/1030 for 60 days and $1950/1180 for 90 days.

The Austrail Flexipass differs in that it allows a set number of travelling days within a six-month period. The cost is $620/360 in 1st class/economy for eight days of travel, $870/520 for 15 days, $1210/735 for 22 days and $1540/945 for 29 days. The eight-day pass cannot be used for travel between Adelaide and Perth or Alice Springs.

As the railway booking system is computerised, any station (other than those on metropolitan lines) can make a booking for any journey throughout the country. For reservations telephone ☎ 13 22 32 during office hours; this will connect you to the nearest mainline station.

Getting Around

AIR

Kendell Airlines (☎ 13 13 00) is by far the main regional operator, with flights from Adelaide to such places as Ceduna ($194), Coober Pedy ($250), Kangaroo Island ($78), Mt Gambier ($147), Port Lincoln ($116) and Woomera ($184). They also fly to Uluru (NT), Broken Hill (NSW) and Portland (Victoria). For details of domestic flights and air passes to other cities within Australia see Domestic Flights in the Getting There & Away chapter.

There are also a number of smaller airlines flying to selected destinations – see the Getting There & Away sections at the start of the various chapters.

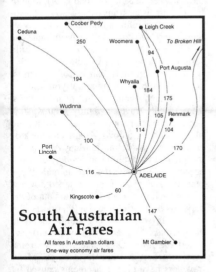

South Australian Air Fares

All fares in Australian dollars
One-way economy air fares

BUS & TRAIN

Country services within SA are provided by a number of mainly small companies of which Stateliner (☎ 8415 5555) is by far the largest. It runs mostly daily buses on main routes to places such as Ceduna ($64), Clare ($14.30), Coober Pedy ($82), Port Augusta ($27.20), Port Lincoln ($54.70), Renmark ($26.50) and Wilpena Pound ($49). The second-largest operator, Premier Roadlines (☎ 8415 5555), runs to places closer to Adelaide such as Moonta ($14.50) and Victor Harbor ($11). For details on other operators refer to the Getting There & Away sections at the start of the various chapters.

All intrastate bus services from Adelaide depart from the central bus station (☎ 8415 5533) at 101-111 Franklin St, near the city centre. Stateliner and Premier both have offices there.

Other than Adelaide suburban trains and a handful of tourist steam trains, there are no intrastate train services in SA. You can, however, get on and off the interstate trains as they travel through the state. SteamRanger (☎ 8231 1707) can give you the latest on steam trains running near Adelaide.

CAR

South Australia is a large, sprawling state, with public transport nonexistent in many regions. The car is the accepted means of getting from A to B, and more and more travellers are also finding it the best way to see the country.

Road Rules

Driving in SA holds few real surprises. Australians drive on the left-hand side of the road. There are a few local variations on road rules as applied elsewhere in the West. The main one is the 'give way to the right' rule – if an intersection is unmarked (unusual), you *must* give way to vehicles entering the intersection from your right.

Unless the signs say otherwise, the speed limit in built-up areas is 60 km/h and out on the open highway it's 110 km/h. The police have speed radar gun cameras and are very fond of using them in hidden locations in order to raise easy revenue. On the other hand, when you get far from the cities and traffic is light, you'll see a lot of vehicles moving a lot faster than 110 km/h. Oncoming drivers who flash their lights at you may be giving you a friendly indication of a speed camera ahead; they may also be telling you that you've left your headlights on, or they may just be flashing a greeting. The right thing to do is flash back – and slow down if you're speeding.

All new cars in Australia have seat belts back and front; if your seat has a belt you're required to wear it. You're liable to be fined if you don't. Small children must be belted into an approved safety seat.

Although overseas licences are acceptable in SA, an International Driving Permit is preferred.

On the Road
Road Conditions South Australia is not crisscrossed by multi-lane highways; there simply is not enough traffic and the distances are too great to justify them. Generally, the state's main roads are bitumen-surfaced and two laned. However, you don't have to go very far off the beaten track to find yourself on dirt roads. In the outback, most of the beaten tracks *are* dirt!

Drink Driving Driving under the influence of alcohol is a real problem, especially in country areas. Serious attempts have been made in recent years to reduce the road toll, and random breath tests are not uncommon in built-up areas. If you're caught with a blood-alcohol level of more than 0.05% then be prepared for a hefty fine and the loss of your licence.

Fuel Diesel, super and unleaded petrol are available from service stations sporting the well-known international brand names. Prices vary from place to place and from price war to price war, but in and around Adelaide it's generally in the 65 to 75c a litre range. In the outback the price soars towards a dollar; distances between fill-ups can be 200 km or more even on main roads, so check your car's consumption and carry spare fuel for emergencies.

Signposting Signposting on the main country roads is generally quite OK, but around Adelaide and other large towns it's often abysmal. You can spend a lot of time trying to find street name signs, and as for indicating which way to go to leave the city ... the best thing to do is buy a street directory and try not to get too frustrated.

Animals Cows, horses, sheep and kangaroos are common hazards in many country areas, particularly in the outback where roads tend to be unfenced – even if there are fences, kangaroos have no trouble either bounding over them or crawling underneath. You'll often notice that the only green grass in sight is along road shoulders and the drains alongside, so grazing animals tend to congregate there. Also, wedge-tailed eagles will often fly up directly in front of you from where they've been feasting on road kills. None of these animals has any road-sense whatsoever, so be careful; a collision with any of them is likely to kill or injure the animal (you may have to put it out of its misery) and could seriously damage your vehicle.

Being nocturnal, kangaroos are most active from dusk to dawn, but you also see them out and about on dull overcast days. They usually travel in family groups, so if you see one hopping across the road in front of you, slow right down – mum and the kids are probably just behind it. Many Australians try to avoid travelling altogether at night because of the hazards posed by animals. If you must travel at night, keep the speed down.

Finally, if a 'roo or cow appears out of the darkness in front of you, hit the brakes, dip your lights (so you won't continue to dazzle it and make it even more confused) and sound the horn. Only take more extreme evasive action if it is safe to do so. Many travellers have died in accidents caused by swerving to miss an animal on the road – it's better to damage your car than kill yourself and others with you.

Outback Travel The South Australian outback offers some great experiences in remote touring on dirt roads and sandy tracks. In fact

DENIS O'BYRNE

RICHARD NEBESKY

DENIS O'BYRNE

Top Left: Enginehouse, Burra Mine Museum
Top Right: Windmill and water tank, McLaren Vale
Bottom: The rugged coast of Flinders Chase National Park, Kangaroo Island

DENIS O'BYRNE

DENIS O'BYRNE

DENIS O'BYRNE

DENIS O'BYRNE

Top Left: Feeding the 'mob' at Rocky River, Flinders Chase National Park
Top Right: Looking across Kangaroo Island from Western River
Bottom Left: Replica of Frenchman's Rock, carved in 1802, Kangaroo Island
Bottom Right: View of the Murray from the Heading Cliffs lookout near Paringa

the Stuart Highway and the main routes to Lyndhurst, Roxby Downs and Wilpena are the only bitumen roads in the entire outback and northern Flinders Ranges. All other routes are either dirt or gravel surfaced; their condition varies depending on factors such as when it last rained and when the last grader went through.

It's commonsense to make sure your vehicle is in first-class mechanical shape before attempting any remote roads or tracks. Garages (and fuel supplies) are few and far between in these places; if you break down and become stranded in some small town waiting for parts, the experience could wreck your holiday budget. The RAA can advise on essential spares and tools to carry. Always pack extra water for the radiator – you may need it if you blow a hose, and it's best not to use up your drinking ration.

Most vehicle accidents on outback roads are due to speed and inexperience. Try to avoid the temptation to get the journey over with as quickly as possible, no matter how boring you may find it. Common hazards on dirt roads include loose surfaces, tight bends, blind crests, cattle grids, potholes and gutters; never drive through a dust cloud thrown up by another vehicle unless you can see what's coming.

Many unsealed roads are closed by heavy rain; some can become impassable for weeks if there's been extensive flooding. If the weather looks like closing in where you are, either get out fast or find somewhere high and dry to camp for a few days. Hopefully you'll have packed enough supplies for such emergencies.

Finally, if you do run into trouble in the back of beyond, stay with your car. It's easier to spot a car than a human being from the air, and you won't be able to carry your jerrycans of drinking water very far anyway.

For recorded information on road conditions in the outback and Flinders Ranges phone ☎ (08) 11633. Otherwise, contact police or roadhouses/hotels for local updates.

For the full story on safe outback travel, get hold of Lonely Planet's *Outback Australia*.

Car Rental

Adelaide has plenty of car-rental companies, but outlets are thin on the ground in country areas, except for a few centres like Kingscote, Port Lincoln and Whyalla. Competition among the city outlets is pretty fierce, so rates tend to be variable and lots of special deals pop up. and disappear again. For a group, care hire can be reasonably economical. And there are many places – like the Flinders Ranges – where if you haven't got your own transport the only realistic options are either to take a tour or hire a vehicle.

The three major companies are Budget, Hertz and Avis, with Thrifty coming along in fourth. Adelaide also has a large number of local firms. You can take it as read that the big operators will generally – but by no means always – have higher rates than the local firms.

The big firms have a number of big advantages, however. First of all they're the ones at Adelaide airport and most of SA's larger country towns. If you want to pick up a car or leave one at the airport then they're the best ones to deal with. However, you should keep in mind that many country outlets only have one or two cars – always book ahead.

Their second advantage is one-way rental – pick up a car in Adelaide and leave it in Sydney or Port Lincoln, for example. However, a variety of restrictions apply. Usually it's a minimum-hire period rather than repositioning charges. Only certain cars may be eligible for one-ways. Check the small print on one-way charges before deciding on one company rather than another.

The major companies offer a choice of deals, either unlimited km or a flat charge plus so many cents per km. On straightforward off-the-card city rentals they're all pretty much the same price. It's on special deals, odd rentals or longer periods that you find the differences. Weekend specials – usually three days for the price of two – are usually good value. If you just need a car for three days around Adelaide make it the weekend rather than midweek. Budget offer 'stand-by' rates and you may see other special deals available.

Daily rates are typically about $50 for a small car (Holden Barina, Ford Festiva, Daihatsu Charade, Suzuki Swift), about $75 for a medium car (Mitsubishi Magna, Toyota Camry, Nissan Pulsar) and about $100 a day for a big car (Holden Commodore, Ford Falcon), all including insurance. Most firms require that drivers be at least 21.

There are other factors to bear in mind about this rent-a-car business. If you want a car for a week, a month, or longer, you will be offered lower rates.

Don't forget the 'rent-a-wreck' companies. They specialise in renting older cars and have a variety of rates, typically around $35 a day. If you just want to travel around the city, or not too far out, they can be worth considering.

One thing to be aware of when renting a car in SA is that if you're travelling on dirt roads you are generally not covered by insurance. If there is no cover, and you have an accident, you'll be liable for all the costs involved. This applies to all companies, although they don't always point this out – as always, read the fine print and make sure you understand the conditions before renting.

4WD Rental Having 4WD enables you to get right off the beaten track into wilderness and outback areas and see and experience some wonderful things that are out of the reach of most travellers. Several companies in Adelaide rent 4WDs; with Hertz and Avis you can get one-way rentals between Adelaide and the NT.

Renting a 4WD vehicle is within the budget range if a few people get together. Something small like a Suzuki or similar costs around $100 per day; for a Toyota Landcruiser you're looking at around $150, which should include insurance and some free km (typically 100 km per day). Check the insurance conditions, especially the excess, as they can be onerous. Even in a 4WD the insurance cover of most companies does not cover damage caused when travelling 'off-road', which basically means anything that is not a maintained bitumen or dirt road.

Brits: Australia (☎ toll-free 1800 331 454) hires fully equipped 4WD vehicles fitted out as campervans – just the thing if you're going to 'do' the outback and the Flinders Ranges. These have proved extremely popular in recent years, although they are not cheap at $120 per day for unlimited km, plus collision damage waiver ($15 per day). Brits have offices in all the mainland capitals, as well as in Cairns and Alice Springs, so one-way rentals are possible.

Buying a Car

Local cars are not cheap – another product of the small population. If you're buying a second-hand vehicle reliability is all-important. Mechanical breakdowns in the outback can be very inconvenient (not to mention dangerous).

Shopping around for a used car involves much the same rules as anywhere in the Western world but with a few local variations. First of all, many used-car dealers in SA are just like used-car dealers from Los Angeles to London – they'd sell their mother into slavery if it turned a dollar. You'll probably get any car cheaper by buying privately through newspaper small ads rather than through a car dealer. However, buying from a dealer does give the advantage of some sort of guarantee, provided the car is less than 15 years, has less than 200,000 km on the clock and costs $3000 or more. Mind you, a guarantee isn't going to be much use if you're buying a car in Adelaide one week and setting off for Perth the next.

The only certainty is that the further you get from civilisation, the better it is to be in a Holden or a Ford. When your fancy Japanese car goes kaput on the Birdsville Track it's likely to be a one- or two-week wait while the new bit gets there. On the other hand, when your old Holden goes bang there's probably another old Holden sitting at the nearest roadhouse or garage with just the part you're looking for. Every scrap yard in SA is full of good old Holdens.

Note that in SA third-party personal injury insurance is always included in the vehicle registration cost. This ensures that every vehicle (as long as it's currently registered) carries at least minimum insurance. You're wise to extend that minimum to at least third-party property insurance as well – minor collisions with Rolls-Royces can be disastrously expensive.

In SA there are no compulsory safety checks prior to the registration of a vehicle in a new name. However, an inspection may be ordered by the Road Traffic Board in the case of an aged or interstate-registered vehicle.

Finally, make use of the Royal Automobile Association (RAA) – see Automobile Associations below for more details about them. If you're a member they'll advise you on any local regulations to be aware of, give general guidelines about buying a car and, most importantly, for a fee (around $85 for an on-site mechanical inspection) will check over a used car before you agree to purchase it. They also offer car insurance.

Automobile Associations
The Royal Automobile Association of SA (RAA) (☎ 8202 4500) provides a range of travel literature, excellent maps, detailed accommodation guides, a vehicle inspection service and an emergency breakdown service. Its headquarters, including bookshop and information centre, is on Grenfell St at 41 Hindmarsh Square in Adelaide.

The RAA has reciprocal arrangements with other state automobile associations and with similar organisations overseas. So, if you're a member of the NRMA in NSW, the AAA in the USA or the RAC or AA in the UK, you can enjoy all the benefits of membership of the RAA. The addresses of automobile associations in neighbouring states and territories are:

New South Wales
   National Roads & Motorists Association
   151 Clarence St, Sydney, NSW 2000
   (☎ (02) 9260 9222)
Northern Territory
   Automobile Association of the NT
   79-81 Smith St, Darwin, NT 0800
   (☎ (089) 81 3837)
Queensland
   Royal Automobile Club of Queensland
   300 St Pauls Terrace, Fortitude Valley, Qld 4006
   (☎ (07) 3361 2444)
Victoria
   Royal Automobile Club of Victoria
   422 Little Collins St, Melbourne, Vic 3000
   (☎ (03) 9607 2137)
Western Australia
   Royal Automobile Club of WA
   228 Adelaide Terrace, Perth, WA 6000
   (☎ (09) 421 4444)

The little yellow RAA sign you'll see on vehicle workshops as you're travelling around means the establishment is an authorised agent and provider of services to members. It's also a good guarantee that you won't be ripped off by an unscrupulous mechanic.

MOTORCYCLE
Motorcycles are a very popular way of getting around. The climate is just about ideal for biking much of the year, and the many small trails from the road into the bush often lead to perfect spots to spend the night in the world's largest camping ground.

The state's long, open roads are made for large-capacity machines above 750 cc, which crow-eating bikers prefer once they outgrow their 250 cc learner restrictions. But that doesn't stop enterprising individuals – many of them Japanese – from tackling the length and breadth of the continent on 250 cc trail bikes. Doing it on a small bike is not impossible, just tedious at times.

If you want to bring your own motorcycle into Australia you'll need a *carnet de passages*. When you try to sell it you'll get less than the market price because of restrictive registration requirements (not so severe in WA, SA and the NT). Shipping from just about anywhere is expensive.

However, with a little bit of time up your sleeve, getting mobile on two wheels in SA is quite feasible, thanks largely to the chronically depressed motorcycle market. The beginning of the southern winter is a good time to strike. Adelaide's daily newspaper has an extensive classified advertisement section where $2500 gets you something that will easily take you around the country, provided you know a bit about bikes. The main drawback is that you'll have to sell it again afterwards.

An easier option is a buy-back arrangement with a large motorcycle dealer in Adelaide (look in the Yellow Pages telephone book under Motor Cycles &/or Accessories). They're keen to do business, and basic negotiating skills allied with a wad of cash (say, $4000) should secure an excellent second-hand bike with a written guarantee that they'll buy it back in good condition minus $1500 or $2000 after your four-month, round-Australia trip. Popular brands for this sort of thing are BMWs, large-capacity, shaft-driven Japanese bikes and possibly Harley-Davidsons (very popular in Australia) – although you'll need a lot more than $4000 to buy a Harley. The percentage drop on a trail bike will be much greater (though the actual amount you lose should be similar), but very few dealers are interested in buy-back schemes on trail bikes. They get too knocked around!

You'll need a rider's licence, helmet and basic spare parts (motorcycle repair shops and parts are like hen's teeth in much of SA and interstate). A fuel range of 350 km will cover fuel stops up the Centre and on Highway 1 around the continent.

The 'roo bars' (outsize bumpers) seen on interstate trucks and many outback cars tell you one thing: never ride on the open road from early evening until after dawn (for details see the Car section earlier this chapter).

Beware of dehydration in the dry, hot air – force yourself to drink plenty of water, even if you don't feel thirsty. To this end, carry at least four litres per day in warm weather on remote roads, more off the beaten track. And finally, if something does go hopelessly wrong in the back of beyond, park your bike where it's clearly visible and observe the cardinal rule: *don't leave your vehicle.*

BICYCLE

Whether you're hiring a bike to ride around the city or wearing out your Bio-Ace chainwheels on a Mt Gambier-Marla marathon, you'll find that SA is a great place for cycling. There are some excellent bike tracks in Adelaide, and in the country you'll find thousands of km of roads which carry so little traffic that the biggest hassle is waving back to the drivers. The state's major cycling route, the Mawson Trail, takes you 700 km from Adelaide to Hawker, mainly on back roads. Especially appealing is that in most areas – with the Mawson Trail a notable exception – you'll ride a long way between hills of any consequence.

Bicycle helmets are compulsory in SA and throughout the rest of Australia. It's best to make yourself as visible as possible to other road-users by wearing light-coloured and (at night) reflective gear.

If you're coming specifically to cycle, it makes sense to bring your own bike. Check your airline for costs and the degree of dismantling/packing required. Within SA you can load your bike onto a bus to skip the boring bits. Note that bus companies require you to dismantle your bike, and some don't guarantee that it will travel on the same bus as you. Adelaide buses do not carry bikes, although they were planning to do trials – check with TransAdelaide for details.

You can buy a good steel-framed touring bike in Adelaide, where there are a number of good cycling shops, for about $500 (plus panniers). It is also possible to rent touring bikes and equipment from a few of the commercial touring organisations.

Until you get fit you should be careful to eat enough to keep you going – remember that exercise is an appetite suppressant. It's surprisingly easy to be so depleted of energy that you end up camping under a gum tree just 10 km short of a shower and a steak. No matter how fit you are, water is still vital. Dehydration is no joke and can be life-threatening.

It often gets very hot in summer, and you should take things slowly until you're used to the heat. South Australian heat is usually dry, so cycling in 35°C-plus temperatures isn't too bad if you wear a hat and plenty of sunscreen, and drink *lots* of water. Be aware of the blistering 'northerlies' that make north-bound cycling a nightmare in summer. In April, when the clear autumn weather begins, the Southerly Trades prevail, and you can have (theoretically at least) tailwinds all the way to Darwin.

Of course, you don't have to follow the main roads and visit towns. It's possible to fill your mountain bike's panniers with muesli, head out into the mulga, and not see anyone for weeks – or ever again (outback travel is very risky if not properly planned). Water is the main problem in SA's 'dead heart'. That tank marked on your map may be dry or the water from it unfit for humans, and those station buildings may have blown away years ago. That little creek marked with a dotted blue line? Forget it – the only time it has water is when there's a big rain.

Always check with locals if you're heading into remote areas, and notify a responsible person (like your mother) if you're about to do something particularly adventurous. That said, you can't rely too much on local knowledge of road conditions – most people have no idea of what a heavily loaded touring bike needs. What they think of as a great road may be pedal-deep in sand or bull dust, and cyclists have happily ridden along roads that were officially flooded.

There are a number of organised tours of varying lengths; if you get tired of talking to sheep as you ride along, it might be a good idea to include one or more tours in your itinerary. Most provide a support vehicle and take care of accommodation and cooking, so they can be a nice break from solo chores. Tours are offered by:

Bicycle SA (☎ 8213 0637) at State Association House, 1 Sturt St, Adelaide, has a programme of activities throughout the year including half-day to nine-day tours, camping weekends and endurance rides (200 to 1200 km).
Freewheelin' (☎ 8232 6860), at 237 Hutt St, Adelaide, has tours from one day to three weeks. They also hire complete cycling outfits.

For more details on cycle touring refer to the Cycle Touring section in the Outdoor Activities chapter.

HITCHING

Hitching is never entirely safe in any country; travellers who decide to hitch should understand that they are taking a small but potentially serious risk. Before making a decision, talk to local people about the dangers. Then, if you decide to go ahead, let someone who cares about you know the details of your proposed trip. The advice that follows should help to make your journey as fast and safe as possible.

Factor one is safety. More than two people hitching together will make things very difficult, and solo hitching is unwise for men as well as women. Two women hitching together may be vulnerable, and two men hitching together can expect long waits. The best option is for a woman and a man to hitch together.

Factor two is position – look for a place where vehicles will be going slowly and where they can stop easily. A junction or freeway slip road is a good place if there is stopping room. The ideal location is on the outskirts of a town – hitching from way out in the country can be as hopeless as from the centre of a city. Take a bus out to the edge of town.

Factor three is appearance. The ideal look for hitching is a sort of genteel poverty – threadbare but clean. Don't carry too much gear – if it looks like it's going to take half an hour to pack your bags aboard you'll be left on the roadside. You'll get the same result if you look like you haven't washed for a week.

Factor four is knowing when to say no. Saying no to a car-load of drunks is pretty obvious, but you should also be prepared to abandon a ride if you begin to feel uneasy for any reason. Don't sit there hoping for the best; make an excuse and get out at the first opportunity.

It can be time-saving to say no to a short ride that might take you from a good hitching point to a lousy one. Wait for the right, long ride to come along. On a long haul, it's pointless to start walking as it's not likely to increase the likelihood of your getting a lift.

Of course people do get stuck in outlandish places but that is the name of the game – in remote areas it's not wise to get dropped off at lonely turn-offs far from water.

If you're visiting from abroad, a nice prominent flag on your pack will help, and a sign announcing your destination can also be useful. Uni and hostel notice boards are good places to look for hitching partners. The main law against hitching is 'thou shalt not stand in the road' – so when you see the law coming, step back.

Just as hitchers should be wary when accepting lifts, drivers who pick up fellow travellers to share the costs should also be aware of the possible risks involved.

BOAT

The only passenger services in SA are the ferries that operate from Cape Jervis and Glenelg to Kangaroo Island; for details see the Getting There & Away section of the Kangaroo Island chapter.

TOURS

Taking a tour is a useful way to get around if you don't have your own transport, have only limited time, or would like the commentary. If you're a backpacker, some buses combine a tour with getting from A to B – see the Bus section in the Getting There & Away chapter for details. Otherwise there are plenty of conventional tours. Adventure Tours & Holidays in the Yellow Pages telephone book gives a good cross-section of what's available.

For budget tours in luxury coaches Stateliner and Premier Roadlines between them have a good range of services to areas near Adelaide and further out, including the Riverland and Flinders Ranges. Intrepid and Trekabout are among many smaller operators running 4WD tours. If you're into eco-tourism, there are some interesting companies in Adelaide with a variety of experiences to offer. These include Adventure SA, Ecotrek and Osprey Wildlife Expeditions. Desert Tracks and Gecko Tours specialise in Aboriginal culture and heritage.

Adelaide has many travel agents (see Travel Agents &/or Consultants in the Yellow Pages). Probably the best ones for bargain hunters are STA Travel (☎ (08) 8223 2426) at 235 Rundle St and the YHA travel office (☎ (08) 8231 5583) at 38 Sturt St. Most of the backpacker hostels have travel agencies or tour offices that specialise in the cheaper end of the market.

Adelaide

Adelaide (population 1,070,000) is a solid and gracious city; when the early colonists built they generally used stone and plenty of style. Although sterile office towers now dominate the central business district, there are still many fine public and commercial buildings and stately homes dating from the Victorian era.

The solidity goes further than architecture. Despite the liberalism of the Don Dunstan years (Dunstan was a flamboyant former premier), Adelaide has not lost its conservatism: it's still an 'old money' place.

Adelaide is dignified and calm in a way no other Australian capital city can match. It also enjoys a superb setting. The city centre is surrounded by grassy parklands, gardens and trees, while the metropolitan area is bounded by the picturesque Adelaide Hills on one side and the sandy swimming beaches of Gulf St Vincent on the other.

Adelaide once had a reputation for wowserism and is still referred to rather patronisingly as 'the city of churches'. It's true there are plenty of churches, including magnificent cathedrals. However, these are far outnumbered by pubs, nightclubs and licensed restaurants, as well as Australia's first nudist beach (Maslins Beach). It also has an arts and cultural scene which is second to none in Australia.

Adelaide is also an exceptionally easy place to get away from. The mighty Murray River, the historic towns and gardens of the Adelaide Hills, and the wineries of the Barossa Valley and McLaren Vale are all less than an hour's drive from the city centre. Even closer are some wonderful bushwalks in the conservation areas that fringe the metropolitan area.

History

At the time of European settlement, the area that is now Adelaide was occupied by the Kaurna people, a peaceful group numbering around 300. Their territory extended south

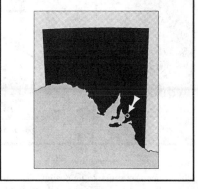

towards Cape Jervis and north towards Port Wakefield, and they had close ties with the Narungga of Yorke Peninsula. Little is known of their social life. However, they were skilled at working with skins and fibres; the skins were tanned and used for a variety of purposes, such as waterbags, and they made baskets and nets from reeds.

The site for Adelaide was chosen in December 1836 by the colony's far-sighted Surveyor-General, Colonel William Light,

GULF
ST
VINCENT

Adelaide

0   1.5   3 km

who created its remarkable design. The site was well-drained, had fertile soil and straddled the Torrens River, which guaranteed a ready water supply. However, the fact that it was 10 km from the coast caused anxiety to some, including Governor Hindmarsh, who tried to have it moved. Hindmarsh named the new capital after the wife of the British monarch, William IV.

Adelaide had a European population of 6557 in 1840 and 14,577 in 1851. By the early 1840s it had about 30 satellite villages, including the German settlements of Hahndorf, Klemzig and Lobethal. The capital's growth has reflected the state's cycle of boom and bust. A building boom in the 1870s and '80s coincided with the wheat boom, and was the time when much of today's fine architectural heritage was created. Rapid expansion also took place during WWI, the 1920s and the busy post-WWII years.

More recently, as the suburbs race towards Maslins Beach in the south and Gawler in the north, Adelaide has become a linear city squeezed between the Mt Lofty Ranges and the sea. Nearby towns such as Victor Harbor, Gawler and several Adelaide Hills centres are becoming dormitories for city workers. Fortunately, town-planning restrictions prevent the Barossa Valley, Adelaide Hills and Southern Vales from being gobbled up by houses.

Orientation

The city centre is laid out in a grid pattern bounded by broad terraces, with several park-like squares. The main street is King William St, which has Victoria Square at the city's geographical centre; most cross streets change their name at King William St. Walk north up King William St and you'll come to the South Australian Tourism Commission (SATC) on the corner of North Terrace.

Rundle Mall is colourful, with flower and fruit stalls; it's always a hive of activity (even on Sunday) and most of the big department stores are here. There are several busy arcades and food halls linking the mall with North Terrace to the north and Grenfell St to the south. The Royal Automobile Association of SA (RAA), Natural Resources Information Centre and State Information Centre are on Grenfell St.

Cross King William St at Rundle Mall and you're in Hindley St, which has plenty of reasonably priced restaurants as well as glitzy bars and nightclubs. These days, however, Hindley St looks decidedly weary, and Rundle St (the eastern extension of Rundle Mall) has become Adelaide's cosmopolitan heart. In Rundle St are the big East End Markets, a couple of good pubs and bars, and some of the city's best in alfresco dining, camping and outdoor gear, boutiques and *haute grunge*.

The next street north of Hindley and Rundle Sts is North Terrace. This is one of Australia's heritage jewels: a 1.6-km-long grand boulevard lined on the north side with a string of magnificent public buildings. They include the state art gallery, museums, state library and universities to the east, and the old parliament house and suburban railway station to the west.

Keep walking across North Terrace and you pass the Festival Centre on your left. Then you're at the Torrens River, where you can either walk east through the parklands to the Zoo and Botanic Garden, or continue straight ahead across the bridge into North Adelaide.

Maps Mapland (☎ 8226 4946), at the Department of Environment & Natural Resources, 282 Richmond Rd, Netley, has an excellent range of topographic and special interest maps as well as guides for cyclists and bushwalkers. These products are also sold at the department's Land Information Centre, in the Colonel Light Centre at 25 Pirie St. The Map Shop at 16 Peel St (between Currie and Hindley Streets) is another good one.

Information

Tourist Offices The South Australian Tourism Commission's travel centre (☎ 8212 1505; toll-free 1800 882 092) is at 1 King William St. It's open from 8.45 am to 5 pm on weekdays and from 9 am to 2 pm on weekends and public holidays.

Community Information SA-FM, a local radio station, has a 'community switchboard' which provides current information on everything from forthcoming concerts, art shows and festivals, to fire ban days, surfing conditions and beach reports; phone ☎ 8271 1277 between 9 am and 5 pm daily.

The Women's Information Switchboard (☎ 8223 1244) is open from 9 am to 9 pm daily except public holidays. It can give advice on just about anything of interest to women, and if they can't help, they'll direct you to someone who can.

Gayline (☎ 8362 3223) operates between 7 and 10 pm every night and during the day from 2 to 5 pm on weekends only. It offers a counselling service and can also give information on social activities and anything else of interest to gays and lesbians.

Post & Communications The GPO is in the city centre at 141 King William St. The poste restante, on the ground floor off King William St, is open from 7 am to 5.30 pm weekdays and 9 am to 1 pm Sunday; normal hours of business for the post office section are 8 am to 6 pm weekdays and 8.30 am to 12 noon Saturday. The GPO has a philatelic section and an Australiana gift shop selling Aboriginal artefacts, coffee-table books, videos, greeting cards and other souvenirs.

Adelaide's STD telephone code is 08 until February 1997, when 08 will be the code for the entire state.

Useful Organisations The RAA (☎ 8202 4500), which is at 41 Hindmarsh Square, has a good bookshop and you can get regional touring maps here also.

For details on national parks and natural history contact the Natural Resources Information Centre (☎ 8204 1910) at 77 Grenfell St. Also at 77, the State Information Centre (☎ 8204 1900) covers many other areas including outdoor activities, legislation, industries and environmental issues.

The place to go for advice on all matters affecting disabled travellers is the Disability Information Centre (☎ 8223 7522) at 195 Gilles St.

State Association House (☎ 8213 0666) at 1 Sturt St houses a number of sporting and outdoor organisations including Bicycle SA, Bushwalking Leadership and Canoe SA, and is a contact point for other organisations.

Bookshops Adelaide has numerous new, second-hand and antiquarian bookshops, and you'll find them listed in the Yellow Pages telephone book.

The RAA has an excellent traveller's bookshop with a good selection of titles including travel within and outside the state, bushwalking, natural and social history, and Aboriginal culture. All the larger general bookshops have a wide range of titles and include Mary Martin's at 12 Pirie St, Angus & Robertson at 112 Rundle Mall and Dymocks at 136 Rundle Mall. Dymocks has a particularly large travel section.

Smaller, more specialised outlets include Europa Bookshop at 238 Rundle St, which has a good selection of foreign-language and travel books; Imprints Booksellers, at 80 Hindley St, is open seven days a week (a rarity) and has quality literature, biographies and a gay and lesbian section. Murphy Sisters Bookshop, at 240 The Parade, Norwood, specialises in feminist and lesbian works, and has an excellent section on Aboriginal studies. The sisters own another shop at Semaphore: Sisters by the Sea, Shop 1, 14 Semaphore Rd.

The Conservation Council of SA, at 120 Wakefield St, sells a range of books on conservation and the environment. It also has quite a decent library.

For cheap second-hand books, try the Central and Orange Lane markets (see the Markets section for details).

Dangers & Annoyances You'll hardly ever meet a beggar in Adelaide but, like most places in the world, if you go looking for trouble you'll find it, particularly at night. Prime spots to avoid are the side streets off Hindley St and in the vicinity of the casino and the suburban railway station. Don't go wandering at night through the parklands along the Torrens – or anywhere else for that matter.

Rundle Mall was an after-dark trouble spot with many muggings and bashings until surveillance cameras were installed. Even so, it still helps to have eyes in the back of your head when getting money from ATMs here and elsewhere in Adelaide, even in broad daylight.

Always try to park your car in a well-lit area. If you must park in a dark spot, remove the rotor button or use an anti-theft device. *Never* leave valuables or important documents like your passport in the car. A camera or bag left in full view on the seat is an invitation for some idiot to relieve you of it.

South Australian car thieves stole 13,173 cars statewide in 1994 (a big decrease on 1992 when 18,270 vehicles were taken). Their favourite place is the city centre, where the worst areas in order are North Terrace, Rundle Mall, the Adelaide Parklands, the Casino and Hindley St.

Central Adelaide

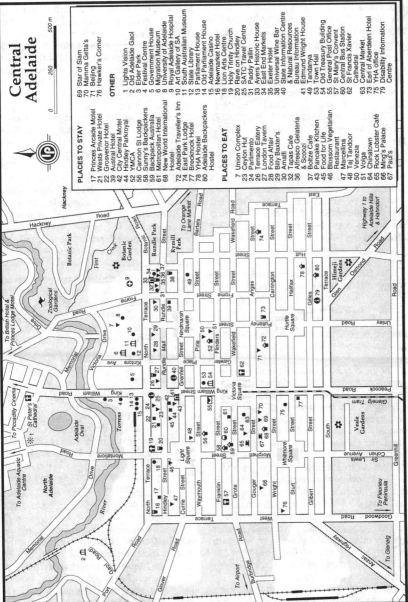

0   250   500 m

PLACES TO STAY

17 Princes Arcade Motel
21 Wests Private Hotel
22 Grosvenor Hotel
39 Austral Hotel
42 City Central Motel
43 Hindley Parkroyal
52 YMCA
56 Cannon St Lodge
58 Sunny's Backpackers
59 Backpack Australia
61 Metropolitan Hotel
68 New World International Hostel
72 Adelaide Traveller's Inn
74 East Park Lodge
77 Brecknock Hotel
78 YHA Hostel
80 Adelaide Backpackers Hostel

PLACES TO EAT

7   Union Complex
23 Ceylon Hut
24 Parlimento
26 Terrace Eatery
27 London Tavern
28 Food Affair
29 Billy Baxter's
30 Amalfi
32 Tapas Cafe
36 Alfresco Gelateria & Scoozi
37 Boltze Cafe
43 Pancake Kitchen
45 Food for Life
46 Bison Vegetarian Restaurant
47 Marcellina
48 Taj Tandoor
50 Venezia
51 Volga
64 Chinatown
65 Rock Lobster Café
66 Ming's Palace
67 Paul's
69 Star of Siam
70 Mamma Getta's
71 Beijing
76 Hawker's Corner

OTHER

1   Lights Vision
2   Old Adelaide Gaol
3   Elder Park
4   Festival Centre
5   Government House
6   Migration Museum
8   University of Adelaide
9   Royal Adelaide Hospital
10 Art Gallery of SA
11 South Australian Museum
12 State Library
13 Parliament House
14 Old Parliament House
15 Adelaide Casino
16 Newmarket Hotel
18 Lion Arts Centre
19 Holy Trinity Church
20 Rave on Hindley
25 SATC Travel Centre
31 Paddy Pallin
33 Ayers Historic House
34 East End Markets
35 Exeter Hotel
38 Universal Wine Bar
40 State Information Centre & Natural Resources Bureau Information
41 Edmund Wright House
49 Tandanya
53 Town Hall
54 Old Treasury Building
57 General Post Office
55 St Mary's Convent
60 Central Bus Station
62 St Francis Xavier Cathedral
63 Central Market
73 Earl of Aberdeen Hotel
75 YHA office
79 Disability Information Centre

Museums

On North Terrace, the **South Australian Museum** is an Adelaide landmark with huge whale skeletons in the front window. Primarily a natural history museum, it also has a fine collection of Aboriginal artefacts, as well as a permanent Aboriginal Dreamtime exhibition, Ngurenderi. It's open between 10 am and 5 pm daily, and admission is free.

The excellent **Migration Museum**, at 82 Kintore Ave, next to the State Library, tells the story of groups from over 100 nationalities who've migrated to SA. It's open weekdays from 10 am to 5 pm, and weekends and public holidays from 1 to 5 pm; admission is free.

As you're leaving this museum, turn left and walk along the lane, then turn right into the double-storey building. The free **Police Museum** can be found here on the 1st floor. It's open on weekends and public holidays from 1 to 5 pm.

The free **Museum of Classical Archaeology** on the 1st floor of the Mitchell Building (in the university grounds on North Terrace) has a fascinating collection of antiquities dating from the third millennium BC. One of its prize exhibits is a Greek hoplite's helmet. It's open from noon to 3 pm during semester.

On the corner of King William and Flinders Sts, in the Old Treasury Building, there's the **Museum of Exploration, Surveying & Land Heritage**. For $3 you can do an interesting two-hour tour of this grand old building (it dates from 1839), taking in the museum, Cabinet Room and underground tunnels. It's open on weekdays from 10 am to 3 pm. Coffee is included in the price.

The **Maritime Museum**, at 126 Lipson St in Port Adelaide, has several vintage ships including the *Nelcebee*, the third-oldest ship on Lloyd's shipping register. There's also an historic lighthouse and a computer register of early migrants. It's open daily from 10 am to 5 pm; admission is $7. Bus Nos 151 or 153 will get you there from North Terrace, or you can take the train.

Next door is the **Port Dock Station Museum**, which features an extensive collection of railway memorabilia. It's open daily from 10 am to 5 pm weekdays and Saturday from noon to 5 pm; admission is $6.

The fascinating **Investigator Science & Technology Museum** is close to the city, at the Wayville Showgrounds off Goodwood Rd. It takes an entertaining look at science and is open daily between 10 am and 5 pm (9 am and 6 pm during school holidays); admission is $9. The museum can be closed while exhibitions are being changed, so check first on ☎ 8410 1115. To get there, take bus Nos 216, 218 or 296 from King William St.

Another interesting museum is the **Old Adelaide Gaol** on Gaol Rd, Thebarton; it's open Sunday and public holidays, when guided tours ($6) are conducted between 11.30 am and 3.30 pm. Features include the hanging tower (45 people were executed here) and various depressing gaol artefacts.

Tandanya

Tandanya at 253 Grenfell St is an Aboriginal cultural institute containing galleries, arts and crafts workshops, performance spaces, a cafe and a good gift shop. It's open weekdays from 10.30 am to 5 pm and weekends and public holidays from noon to 5 pm. Admission is $4.

State Library

Displays at the State Library on North Terrace include Colonel Light's surveying equipment, an 1865 photographic panorama of Adelaide and, in the Mortlock Library in the same complex, memorabilia of cricket star Sir Donald Bradman. The library is open weekdays from 9.30 am to 8 pm (5 pm Thursday) and weekends from noon to 5 pm. It's closed on public holidays.

Art Galleries

On North Terrace, next to the museum, the free **Art Gallery of SA** contains one of the nation's most comprehensive collections of Australian, Asian and European art. It boasts the largest display of Australian art, including a fine selection of paintings by great colonial and contemporary Australian artists. Works by overseas masters include a 375-year-old painting of a seated couple by Sir Anthony Van Dyck, purchased for $1 million in 1994. There's also a magnificent collection of South-East Asian ceramics, and an art bookshop.

In March 1996 the gallery unveiled its splendid new West Wing, part of a $26 million extension and restoration project that has doubled the size of the facility.

The gallery is open daily from 10 am to 5 pm, and there are daily tours from 10 am to 1 pm on weekdays and 10 am to 3 pm on weekends. Activities (such as free lunchtime talks) and highlights are publicised in the gallery's free *News*.

The gallery of the **Royal South Australian Society of Arts**, in the Institute Building on the corner of North Terrace and Kintore Ave, is open weekdays from 11 am to 5 pm and weekends from 2 to 5 pm; admission is free. Other major galleries include the free **Union Gallery** on level 6, Union House, at Adelaide University (open weekdays from 10 am to 5 pm) and the **Festival Centre Gallery** near the Playhouse in the Festival Centre.

Grand City Buildings

Ayers Historic House is at 288 North Terrace, close to the city centre. This stately mansion was originally constructed in 1846 for Sir Henry Ayers (an early premier after whom Ayers Rock in the NT was named) but was added to over the next 30 years. Now completely restored, it houses a restaurant and is open to visitors Tuesday to Friday between 10 am and 4 pm and on weekends and public holidays between 1 and 4 pm. Admission is $2 and there are tours ($4). The elegant bluestone building serves as the headquarters of the South Australian branch of the National Trust (☎ 8223 1655).

At 59 King William St, **Edmund Wright House**, built in 1876, was originally constructed in an elaborate Renaissance style with intricate decoration for the Bank of South Australia. The foyer and reception

The Six Million Dollar Man
The Three Shades (1880) is one of 20 bronze sculptures by master French sculptor Auguste Rodin acquired in March 1996 by the Art Gallery of South Australia.

Coming from the private gallery of New South Wales collector Mr William Bowman, the gallery's acquisition is the largest public collection of Rodin works in the southern hemisphere.

The Rodin coup, which cost $6 million, together with the $26 million renovation to the art gallery, is part of the South Australian Government's cultural tourism push.

Paris-born Rodin (1840-1917) is considered by many to be the world's best-known and most important sculptor after the great Michelangelo. ■

area are open daily from 10 am to 5 pm and admission is free.

The imposing **Adelaide Town Hall**, built between 1863 and 1866 in 16th century Renaissance style, looks out on to King William St between Flinders and Pirie Sts. The faces of Queen Victoria and Prince Albert are carved into the facade. There are free tours on Tuesday and Thursday, but you have to book (☎ 8203 7442).

Opposite the Town Hall, the impressive **General Post Office** (GPO) was commenced in 1867 and altered in 1891. Both these wonderful buildings were designed by architect Edmund Wright, who would turn in his grave if he could see the glass-fronted office blocks that crowd around today.

On North Terrace, **Government House** was built between 1838 and 1840, with further additions in 1855. Its earliest section is one of the oldest buildings in Adelaide, and you can tour the magnificent garden in autumn and spring (contact SATC for details).

Just across King William St, **Parliament House** has an elegant facade featuring 10 marble Corinthian columns. It was built in two stages: the west wing was completed in 1889 and the east wing in 1939. There are tours (☎ 8237 9100) on weekdays at 10 am and 2 pm when parliament isn't sitting – when it is, you're allowed inside at 2 pm to watch the action.

Holy Trinity Church, also on North Terrace, was the first Anglican church in the state; it was built in 1838. Other impressive early churches are **St Francis Xavier Cathedral** on Wakefield St (1856) and **St Peter's Cathedral** on Pennington Terrace, North Adelaide (1869-76).

St Francis Xavier Cathedral is beside Victoria Square, where you'll find a number of other important early buildings: the **Magistrate's Court** (1847-50); the **Supreme Court** (1869); and the Old **Treasury Building** (1839), where you can do tours – see the Museums section for details.

Other Historic Buildings

In Jetty St, Grange (west of the city centre), is **Sturt's Cottage**, home of the famous early Australian explorer. It's open Wednesday to Sunday and public holidays from noon to 5 pm (4 pm in winter); admission is $2.50. Take bus Nos 130 or 137 from Grenfell St and get off at stop 29A.

In Semaphore (north-west of the city), there's **Fort Glanville**, at 359 Military Rd, Semaphore Park. The fort was built in 1878, when Australia was going through a phase of Russophobia as a result of the Crimean War. It's open from 1 to 5 pm on the third Sunday of each month between September and May; admission is $3.

In Springfield (south-east of the city), magnificent **Carrick Hill**, at 46 Carrick Hill Drive, is built in the style of an Elizabethan manor house. All around are 40 hectares of bushland and manicured English-style gardens. The house is open from Wednesday to Sunday and public holidays from 10 am to 5 pm; admission is $8 and includes guided tours at 11 am, noon, 2 pm and 3 pm. Catch bus No 171 from King William St and get off at stop 16.

Festival Centre

The Adelaide Festival Centre (☎ 8216 8600), is close to the Torrens River. Looking vaguely like a squared-off version of the Sydney Opera House, it performs a similar function with its variety of auditoriums and theatres. However, it provides a venue for a much greater range of entertainment.

While the centre is visually uninspiring – let's face it, it's damned ugly – it does have a marvellous riverside setting; you can picnic on the grass in front of the theatre and there are several places to eat. You can also hire pedal boats nearby, or enjoy free concerts (see the Entertainment section in this chapter) and exhibitions.

Botanic Gardens & Other Parks

The city and North Adelaide are both surrounded by green parkland, gardens and large trees. They're separated by the Torrens River, which is itself bordered by public gardens and lawn. Native waterbirds such as swans and pelicans are often seen here looking for a free feed.

At the eastern end of North Terrace, the 20-hectare **Adelaide Botanic Garden** is only a short stroll from the city centre. Its highlights include a unique palm house (1877) and the Museum of Economic Botany (check out its stencilled ceiling). Its wonderful Bicentennial Conservatory (1988) recreates a tropical rainforest environment.

The gardens are open weekdays from 7 am to sunset, and on weekends and public holidays from 9 am to sunset. Free 1½ hour guided tours of the gardens leave from the kiosk every Tuesday and Friday at 10.30 am; they're also held at the same time on Sunday in autumn and spring. The Bicentennial Conservatory is open between 10 am and 4 pm; admission is $2.50.

Rymill Park in the East Parkland has a boating lake and a 600-metre-long jogging track. The South Parkland contains **Veale Gardens**, with streams and flower beds. To the west are a number of sporting grounds, while the **North Parkland** borders the Torrens and surrounds North Adelaide. The **Adelaide Oval**, the site of interstate and international cricket matches, is in the North Parklands on the northern bank of the Torrens River.

The restful **Himeji Gardens** off South Terrace blends two styles of Japanese garden: the *senzui* (lake and mountain) and *kare senzui* (dry garden). Adelaide and Himeji are sister cities. You can get details of guided tours from the ranger on ☎ 8203 7483 between 12 noon and 2 pm weekdays.

Walks & Rides There's an extensive network of walking and bicycle paths through Adelaide's parklands, including the sealed paths that take you from the coast to the Adelaide Hills along the Torrens River Linear Park and O-Bahn Busway. Jim Daly's excellent *Walks in the Adelaide Parklands* and *Cycling in the Adelaide Parklands* describe a number of routes of varying length, each with their own attractions.

Light's Vision

On Montefiore Hill, north of the city centre across the Torrens River, stands the statue of Colonel William Light, Adelaide's founder – he's said to have stood here and mapped out his visionary plan. In the afternoon there's a nice view of the city's gleaming office towers rising above the trees, with the Adelaide Hills making a scenic backdrop.

Adelaide Zoo

On Frome Rd, the zoo exhibits around 1500 exotic and native mammals, birds and reptiles, and also has a children's zoo. It's open daily (including Christmas Day) from 9.30 am to 5 pm; admission is $9. A different way of getting there is to take a cruise on the *Popeye* ($5), which departs daily every 20 minutes (weekends only in winter, except the school holidays) from Elder Park in front of the Festival Centre. You can also catch bus Nos 272 or 273 from Currie St, or take a pleasant walk along the Torrens from Elder Park.

Markets

Close to the centre of town, the **Central Market** (☎ 8203 7345), off Victoria Square between Grote and Gouger Sts, is a great place for self-catering travellers. It sells a vast range of fresh produce – you buy direct from the producer, so things are generally quite a bit cheaper than in the shops. It's open Tuesday (7 am to 5.30 pm), Thursday (11 am to 5.30 pm), Friday (7 am to 9 pm) and Saturday (7 am to 1 pm). Many stalls shut down around lunchtime, so get there late in the morning for real bargains.

The very popular and trendy **East End Markets** (☎ 8232 5606) off the east end of Rundle St are open Monday, Friday, weekends and public holidays from 9 am to 6 pm. There's a huge market bazaar with around 200 variety stalls and a food court selling everything from Asian fare to French bread to Italian gelati. You can also buy your week's fresh groceries here. There's a number of good cafes and restaurants nearby.

The much smaller **Orange Lane Market**, in Norwood, is more casual and will appeal to alternative lifestyles – it's the place to go for Indian fabrics, second-hand clothing, massage, tarot readings, palmistry, remedies, bric-a-brac and junk. You'll find it on the corner of Edward St and Orange Lane (off Norwood Parade) on weekends and public holidays from 10 am to 6 pm. A few steps away on the Parade are a couple of coffee shops and cafes.

Mother Mary MacKillop Sites

Mary MacKillop, who will become Australia's first saint, lived in Adelaide for 16 years and there are a number of sites associated with her. They include **St Mary's Convent** at 253 Franklin St, Adelaide, where she was excommunicated, and **St Ignatius Church** on Queen St, Norwood, where she assisted at mass during her excommunication period.

Another is **St Joseph's Convent** at 286 Portrush Rd, Kensington, where you'll find the **Mary MacKillop Centre** (☎ 8364 5311). The centre has displays of historic photos and various artefacts, as well as a leaflet describing significant pilgrimage sites. It's open weekdays from 10 am to 4 pm and Sunday from 1 pm to 4 pm.

Ice Skating

Adelaide's ice-skating rink (☎ 8352 7977), at 23 East Terrace in Thebarton, is open daily. It has an artificial indoor snow-skiing centre, with a 150-metre-long slope, and you can also do tobogganing. Take bus Nos 151 or 153 from North Terrace and get off at stop 2.

Adelaide Beaches

There are a number of good beaches stretching from Maslins Beach in the far south to Grange in the north. The beaches beyond Grange often have too much seaweed for real enjoyment.

Maslins Beach South, on the Fleurieu Peninsula about 50 km from the city centre, is Adelaide's only metropolitan nudist beach. It's backed by colourful cliffs, and to get to the sand you have to walk down a steep path from the Tuitt Rd carpark.

Heading north, **Seaford** and adjoining **Moana** have a small beach that's popular with novice surfers. You can drive onto the sand from the beach ramp at Moana.

Christies Beach is much larger and has a jetty and reef popular with scuba divers. For

a generally quieter time you can visit nearby **O'Sullivans Beach**, where there's a concrete ramp leading off Galloway Rd.

The first of the 'old-time' metropolitan beaches is **Seacliff**, about 16 km from the city centre. This beach – which includes **Brighton** – is very popular for swimming, windsurfing and sailing. There's a clifftop monument to the Aboriginal Dreamtime ancestor *Tjilbruke* at Kingston Park, just south of Seacliff.

Glenelg has a magnificent white sandy beach, the most popular in Adelaide. You can hire sailboards here. Nearby Jetty Rd is lined with cafes and restaurants, and the popular front bar of the Ramada Grand Hotel is virtually right on the waterfront. This is an easy beach to get to from the city – you simply catch the tram in Victoria Square and get off on the waterfront.

There's another lovely stretch of sand at nearby **West Beach**, the closest (10 km) beach to the city. Continuing north there are more good beaches and eateries at **Henley Beach** and **Grange**, then you're at the last remnants of Adelaide's original dune system at **West Lakes**. The beach here isn't wonderful, but you can swim and windsurf in the nearby lake; if it's been raining heavily, give the lake a couple of days to rid itself of rubbish.

North from here are the last of Adelaide's metropolitan beaches at **Semaphore** and **Largs Bay**. The water at both is shallow, making them good for swimming when there's no weed about. Semaphore is another popular windsurfing spot.

Organised Tours

You can take a huge variety of tours in and around Adelaide including gardens, historic buildings, art galleries and the usual sightseeing tours by various means of transport. SATC can supply details of all tours – and don't forget that the YHA and most backpacker hostels have tour or travel agencies specialising in budget deals. The following will give you an idea of what's available.

Market Adventures (mobile ☎ 018 842 242) does a 90-minute gastronomic discovery of the Central Market for $15. Alternatively, you can do a gourmet edition including breakfast at the Hilton for $30. The tours are said to be very entertaining (and filling). Tours are on Tuesday and Thursday at 10.30 am and 1.30 pm, and Friday at 10 am.

Premier (☎ 8415 5555) has a range of half-day tours including the city sights ($27), Hahndorf in the Adelaide Hills ($28), or Mt Lofty and the Cleland Wildlife Park ($28). They also have reasonably priced day tours. Adelaide Sightseeing (☎ 8231 4144) does much the same thing for much the same prices.

Tour Delights (mobile ☎ 018 845 432) has an excellent Barossa winery tour ($43), including lunch and a visit to six wineries. E&K Mini-Tours (☎ 8337 8739) has a Barossa day tour for $30, including lunch, and a two-hour Adelaide-by-Night tour for $15.

Festival Tours (☎ 8374 1270) offers a range of tours from half-day to two-day. Their day tour of the Adelaide Hills, which includes lunch at the wonderful German Arms Hotel in Hahndorf, costs $50. A three-hour introduction to the city sights is $22.

For $20 you can get a day pass on the Adelaide Explorer (☎ 8364 1933), a road-registered tram replica that completes a continuous circuit of a number of attractions, including Glenelg and the Botanic Gardens. The tour takes 2½ hours and you can get on and off en route; daily departures are at 9 am, 12.20 and 3 pm, and leave from 14 King William St.

Freewheelin' Cycle Tours (☎ 8232 6860) offers a variety of rides, including the McLaren Vale and Barossa wineries (both $39).

Alternatively, there are several Harley Davidson tour operators including Aces High (☎ 8266 1169) and Adelaide Harley Tours (☎ 8276 5456). Both charge around $50 for the first hour and $30 per hour thereafter.

Boat Cruises MV *Foxy Lady* (☎ 8341 1194; mobile 015 395 124) does cruises on the Port River from the Fishermans Wharf at Port Adelaide. Scheduled public cruises are on Sunday, public holidays and school holidays (Wednesday to Saturday) for $7 (one hour) and $12 (two hours).

Falie Charters (☎ 8341 2004) has full-day ($80) and half-day ($65) cruises on St Vincent Gulf in the tall ship *Falie*, leaving from Port Adelaide.

Festivals

The three-week Adelaide Festival of Arts takes place in February and/or March of even-numbered years. It attracts people from all over Australia to drama, dance, music and other live performances, and includes a writers' week, art exhibitions, poetry readings and other activities with guest speakers and international performers. For information phone the Festival Centre on ☎ 8216 8600.

The Fringe Festival, which takes place at the same time, features alternative contemporary performance art and music; phone ☎ 8231 7760 for details.

Places to Stay

Prices for many caravan parks, motels and some hotels rise between Christmas and the end of January, when accommodation is extremely scarce. Some places also put their prices up on weekends and during other school holiday periods. Unless otherwise stated, all prices given here are off-peak.

Places to Stay – bottom end

Camping There are quite a few caravan parks around Adelaide. The following are within 10 km of the city centre – check the tourist office for others. All prices given are for two people.

Adelaide Caravan Park (☎ 8363 1566), two km north-east of the city centre at 8 Bruton St, Hackney; camp sites $18, on-site vans from $36 and cabins $55.

Windsor Gardens Caravan Park (☎ 8261 1091), seven km north-east at 78 Windsor Grove, Windsor Gardens; camp sites $10 and single/double cabins $35/50.

West Beach Caravan Park (☎ 8356 7654), eight km west of the city at Military Rd, West Beach; camp sites $12, on-site vans $32 and cabins $49. This park is close to the beach and only a couple of km from Glenelg.

Marine Land Holiday Village (☎ 8353 2655), also on Military Rd, West Beach; self-contained cabins for $53, two-bedroom holiday units for $58 and two-bedroom villas for $80 (it gets cheaper after two nights). There are no camp sites.

Colleges At the University of Adelaide, *St Ann's College* (☎ 8267 1478) operates as a hostel from the second week in December through to the end of January; beds are $15 ($18 if you need linen). At other colleges, accommodation generally includes meals and is much more expensive.

Hostels There are a couple of hostels near the bus station. When you leave the terminal, turn left onto Franklin St and on the next corner you'll find the rather run-down *Sunny's Backpackers Hostel* (☎ 8231 2430). Dorm beds are priced from $12 and twin share/doubles are $14; mountain bikes are for hire for $15 per day, and off-street parking is available. There's a licensed travel agent on the premises (open at 6 am).

At 11 Cannon St, a lane running off Franklin St opposite the bus station, the *Cannon St Lodge* (☎ 8410 1218) has bunk beds for $11 and singles/doubles for $21/28. It has cheerful murals and friendly staff, but is otherwise on the shabby side. It has a travel agency, and you can hire bicycles here for $12 a day. Cheap meals are available.

Backpack Australia (☎ 8231 0639) is at 128 Grote St, near the Central Market. Beds cost from $10 to $15 and it has a bar, cheap meals, a tiny camping space on the roof, and a travel agency. However, its facilities (particularly the kitchen) are cramped and it could do with some paint and other repairs. By all accounts it has some memorable parties.

New World International Hostel (☎ 8212 6888; toll-free 1800 807 367), at 29-31 Compton St, is handy to the Central Market. This place is very clean (there are even boxes provided under the bunks to put your smelly shoes in) as well as being light and airy, with ducted heating and cooling. Dorm beds cost $12, and someone will pick you up from the airport, bus station or railway station if you ring. It also has a travel agency.

Most of the other hostels are clustered in the south-eastern corner of the city centre. You can get there on bus Nos 191 or 192 from Pulteney St or take any bus going to the South Terrace area (Nos 171 and 172 to Hutt St; 201 to 203 to the King William St and South Terrace corner), although it's not really that far to walk.

The very pleasant *Adelaide YHA hostel* (☎ 8223 6007) is at 290 Gilles St. Beds for members cost $11, and there's a travel agency on the premises. The reception is closed between 11.30 am and 4 pm daily. It's one of the best – if not *the* best – of Adelaide's hostels.

Nearby is the *Adelaide Backpackers Hostel* (☎ 8223 5680) at 263 Gilles St; its 'other' house at 253 is much nicer than the main one at 263, which is run down. Dorm beds cost from $11, and double-bed rooms are $25. Bicycle hire is available at $8 for half a day, and there's a travel agency here as well.

Next door, at 257 Gilles St, *Rucksackers Riders International* (☎ 8232 0823) is very popular with motor bike and bicycle travellers. This lovely 80-year-old house is clean and comfortable, has a reasonably spacious kitchen and its rooms are heated day and night in winter. Dorm beds cost $10, and a twin room with en suite is $12 per person. It doesn't have a travel agency, but tours can be arranged.

Two streets closer to the city centre, at 118 Carrington St, is the small, but clean and friendly *Adelaide Traveller's Inn* (☎ 8232 5330). Dorm beds are $8 and doubles are $20 in reasonable-sized bedrooms, but other facilities are cramped. There's some off-street parking.

Next door at 112 Carrington St, the *Adelaide Backpacker's Inn* (☎ 8223 6635) is a converted pub with dorm beds from $13 and doubles from $32. Its facilities are rather weary and somewhat cramped, but the management is dedicated, which makes up for a lot. In contrast, their annexe across the road at 109 is very pleasant; it has a good kitchen and small but comfortable single/double rooms for $20/36. There's a travel agency on the premises.

Close to the attractive East Parkland at the eastern end of Angas St, *East Park Lodge* (☎ 8223 1228) at No 341 is in a grand old building – it was built 80 years ago as a Salvation Army hostel for young country ladies. It's labyrinthian, but clean and well run, and the management is very friendly; if they spent some money on the place it could be great. Dorm beds cost $12, single rooms $17, twin bunk-bed rooms $13.50 per person, and double-bed rooms $14 per person.

The large *YMCA* (☎ 8223 1611) at 76 Flinders St is central and takes guests of either sex. Dorms cost $11 and singles/twins are $18/30, with a 10 per cent discount for members. Office hours are 8.30 am to 8.30 pm daily.

Hotels Unless otherwise stated, the following provide basic pub-style accommodation with share facilities.

At 205 Waymouth St, the *Cumberland Arms Hotel* (☎ 8231 3577) is more of a backpackers hostel than a pub. It has dorms with five or more beds for $11, rooms with four or less beds for $12, and twin/double rooms for $16. It also has cheap meals and there's a tour office on the premises.

The *Metropolitan Hotel* (☎ 8231 5471), at 46 Grote St, is opposite the Central Market and next to Her Majesty's Theatre. It has singles/doubles for $20/28 plus a $10 key deposit.

If you want to be handy to Hindley St, you won't get any closer than *West's Private Hotel* (☎ 8231 7575), smack in the middle of the mayhem at 110B Hindley St. It's shabby and basic, but cheap: dorm beds are priced from $15 ($10 for subsequent nights), and singles/doubles are $20/30.

At 205 Rundle St the *Austral Hotel*

(☎ 8223 4660) has singles/doubles for $25/35. There's a trendy bar downstairs.

The *Brecknock Hotel* (☎ 8231 5467), at 401 King William St, has singles/doubles for $30/45, including a light breakfast. This is a popular Irish pub, with Irish folk groups on Friday night.

At 44 Flinders St, the *Earl of Zetland Hotel* (☎ 8223 5500) has self-contained rooms for $49/65/75.

Places to Stay – middle
The *City Central Motel* (☎ 8231 4049), at 23 Hindley St, has small rooms, but they're clean and comfortable. Singles/doubles cost $49/54.

At 262-266 Hindley St, the *Princes Arcade Motel* (☎ 8231 9524) has motel rooms from $45/50, and off-street parking is available.

The *Clarice Motel* (☎ 8223 3560) is at 220 Hutt St, around the corner from the youth hostel. There are budget single rooms with shared facilities for $25, doubles/triples with private toilets for $45/55, and a motel-style double for $59. All tariffs include a light breakfast.

Festival Lodge (☎ 8212 7877), 140 North Terrace, is opposite the casino and has rooms from $69/80. There's no on-site parking, but the motel negotiates reduced rates with a nearby car park.

In North Adelaide, the *Princes Lodge Motel* (☎ 8267 5566) is in a grand old mansion at 73 Lefevre Terrace and has budget singles/doubles with a light breakfast from $30/55. It's within walking distance of the city, and handy to the restaurants and cafes on O'Connell and Melbourne Sts.

Although there are motels all over Adelaide, it's worth noting that there's a 'motel alley' along Glen Osmond Rd, the road that leads into the city centre from the south-east. This is quite a busy road so some places are a bit noisy. Worth checking is *Powell's Court* (☎ 8271 7033), two km south-east of the city centre at 2 Glen Osmond Rd, Parkside. Units cost $45/48/55/60 (extra persons are $15 each up to a total of nine) and all have kitchens.

Places to Stay – top end

If it's up-market accommodation you're after, the following are right in the city centre. Most offer package deals on weekends.

Hindley Parkroyal Hotel
65 Hindley St (☎ 8231 5552); from $130 for a standard room and $170 for a suite
Grosvenor Hotel
125 North Terrace (☎ 8407 8888); from $125/140 for business category, guestrooms are relatively cheap at $75/95
Terrace Inter-Continental Adelaide Hotel
150 North Terrace (☎ 8217 7552); from $140 for a standard room and $330 for a suite
Hyatt Regency Adelaide
North Terrace (☎ 8231 1234); from $195 for a standard room
Hilton International Adelaide
233 Victoria Square (☎ 8217 0177); from $130 for a standard room and $400 for a suite

Places to Eat

Adelaide supposedly has more restaurants – there's around 700 in total – per head of population than any other city in Australia, and its huge variety of cuisine makes dining here a culinary adventure. Licensing laws are liberal in SA, so a high proportion of restaurants are licensed.

If it's still being printed, the *Advertiser Good Food Guide* ($12.95) is a useful reference to the constantly changing food scene. It's available from larger newsagencies where you should also find *The Restaurateur's Own Guide* ($6), which covers dozens of the 'better' places to eat.

Rundle St At the eastern extension of the Rundle Mall, Rundle St is Adelaide's Bohemian quarter, with shops specialising in Art Deco artefacts and alternative clothing, and a swag of restaurants and cafes.

The *Terrace Eatery* is a large, casual dining area in the basement of the Myer Centre, between Rundle Mall and North Terrace. Its numerous eateries include Asian, English, Italian and Mexican and there's access through to the evocative *London Tavern* at the North Terrace end. The City Cross Arcade, between Rundle Mall and Grenfell St, also has a variety of European and Asian eateries.

Amalfi, at 29 Frome St, just off Rundle St, has excellent Italian cuisine and a great menu. It can be difficult to get into on Friday night, but is worth the wait.

Tapas Café at No 242 is a wonderful Spanish bar and restaurant. Imagine tucking into treats such as 'kid goat braised in Moroccan spices with an apricot and walnut infused couscous'. Alternatively, you can enjoy the delicious snacks they bring to your table.

Just up the street is 'little Italy'. The *Alfresco Gelateria* at 260 Rundle St is a good place for a gelati, cappuccino or a variety of sweets. *Scoozi*, at No 272, is a huge, cosmopolitan cafe that's popular on Friday and Saturday nights – it's noted for its wood-oven pizzas – while in between is *Marconi's*, which sells pasta and pizza. On balmy nights the tables at the front of these three places merge and it's difficult to tell who's eating where.

At 286 is the *Boltze Café*, another indoors and alfresco place. It specialises in modern Australian fare with a Mediterranean influence – favourites are its Caesar salad, and fish and chips in beer batter with a sweet chilli and lemongrass sauce. There's a bar upstairs which has stand-up comics on Thursday night and live bands on Friday and Sunday nights.

Hindley St Hindley St has become a tad passé, with its glittery bars and discos; however, if you're feeling nostalgic, the old favourites persevere and the quality and variety of food is still good.

On Gilbert Place, which dog-legs between Hindley St and King William St, the *Pancake Kitchen* is open 24 hours a day and has main-course specials for under $5. Next door the *Penang Chinese Restaurant* is open Monday to Saturday from 11 am until 10 pm and is reasonably priced.

Cafe Boulevard at 15 Hindley St is a pleasant coffee lounge with hot meals for under $7 and cheap and delicious sweets on display.

The *Ceylon Hut*, just off Hindley St at 27 Bank St, has tasty curries from $11.

There are two restaurants at the Hindley Parkroyal, 65 Hindley St: *Cafe Mo* with lunch-time buffets for $23 (evenings are

$26); and *Oliphants*, with imaginative main courses from $17.

Abdul and Jamil's friendly *Quiet Waters* downstairs at No 75 is a pleasant Lebanese coffee lounge serving predominantly vegetarian dishes. Takeaways are also available. Garlic is a favourite ingredient, and there's a belly dancer on Wednesday night.

Upstairs at No 79, *Food for Life*, a Hare Krishna restaurant, has vegetarian smorgasbord for $4, including dessert. It's open for lunch on weekdays from noon to 3 pm, and evenings from 5 to 8 pm.

Tung Sing, at No 147, is open every day except Monday from 6 pm to 2 am. Traditional Chinese dishes are between $8 and $13.

At No 157 is the *Hog's Breath Café*, with plenty of corrugated iron creating an outback atmosphere. It has a varied menu, including delicious salads from $8.

Still on Hindley St but across Morphett St, *Blossoms Vegetarian Restaurant* at No 167 serves healthy Asian dishes from $4.50. Walk up Morphett St a little way and you come to *Taj Tandoor* at 76 Light Square. This is one of Adelaide's best Indian restaurants.

At 273 Hindley St *Marcellina* is a favourite with people from the restaurant trade. This place comes alive after 2 am. It has Italian food and all-you-can-eat pizza and pasta for $7.90, but only until 9 pm.

North Terrace The *Pullman Adelaide Casino Restaurant* has a smorgasbord, with lunch at $22 ($24 on weekends) and dinner from $27 ($29 on weekends). *Parlimento*, at No 140 on the corner with Bank St, has chef's specials for under $9 and great coffee. Nearby, at No 150, *Spices Restaurant* in the Terrace Hotel has just about every Oriental cuisine represented. Wonderfully aromatic main courses start at around $15.

Food Affair at the Gallerie Shopping Centre, which runs from North Terrace through to Gawler Place and John Martins on Rundle Mall, has numerous international eateries.

Billy Baxters, at No 224 on the corner with Austin St, is said to have the best pancakes in town – mind you, the same is said about the Pancake Kitchen, but they *are* delicious.

Gouger St Another street of restaurants with many local institutions, Gouger St is to be upgraded with wider footpaths for alfresco dining, reduced traffic speeds, trees and urban art.

The *Central Market* between Gouger and Grote Sts near Victoria Square is good value for all types of food, fruit, vegetables and bread. Tacked on at the market's western end is *Chinatown*, which has a large collection of mainly Asian-style eateries; one group of kitchens shares a communal eating area, providing a cheap and popular option.

At No 55, the very popular *Mamma Getta Restaurant* is an authentic Italian place with most dishes around $7. Just down the street, the award-winning *Star of Siam* at No 67 serves delicious Thai food; a seven-course luncheon banquet costs $16, and evening banquets start at $20. *Paul's*, at 79, is one of the best fish & chip places in town, while the *Rock Lobster Café*, at 108, is a great place for fresh rock lobster (in season) and oysters.

The *Red Ochre Grill*, at No 129, is Australian bush tucker gone gourmet. It's open for lunch and dinner, and the menu reads like an internal memo at the NPWS. Its meals are superb, and you may never again get to sample emu or wallaby, followed by wattle-seed pavlova. It's not cheap – an average of $17 for a main course – but is worth the splurge.

Ming's Palace is an unpretentious Chinese restaurant serving good food at No 201. It's open daily and is renowned for its Peking duck.

Around Town *Goodies Grub* at 108 Franklin St is directly opposite the central bus station. It's open from 7 am to 6 pm Monday to Friday for eat-in and takeaway, and does a good cooked breakfast from $3.50.

The trendy *Equinox Bistro* at Adelaide University is in the Union Complex above the Cloisters off Victoria Drive, close to the city. It's open Monday to Friday from 10 am to 10 pm (8 pm in university holiday periods) and has main courses from just $5. Believe it or not, the *Union Cafeteria* on the ground floor is cheaper.

Also good is *Hawker's Corner*, on the corner of West Terrace and Wright St. It's open for lunch and dinner daily except Monday and has Chinese, Vietnamese, Thai and Indian food. *Hawkers Too*, next door, is a cafe-style eatery with a similar flavour, but main courses start at $6 – it's popular with overseas students.

The *Volga*, upstairs at 116 Flinders St, is Adelaide's only Russian restaurant. It's a friendly place, with gypsy violinists (Friday and Saturday nights) and beluga caviar for those with expensive palates. Main meals (without the caviar) range from $10 to $20.

Around the corner at 63 Hyde St, *Seoul* is a Korean and Japanese restaurant open for lunch and dinner, with mains from $9. Keep heading north a short distance to *Venezia*, a good Italian tavern and restaurant at 121 Pirie St, which has pastas from $9 and steaks from $13. There are a couple of other good Italian restaurants next door.

Adelaide is very well supplied with hotels offering counter meals, particularly at lunch time. Just look for those telltale blackboards standing outside. You won't have to search for long to find one with meals under $5, particularly now that most hotels have poker machines – many offer meals at ridiculous prices to get people through the door.

The *Festival Bistro*, in the Festival Centre on King William St, overlooks the Torrens River. It has sandwiches and snacks and is open late into the evening (it's closed on Sunday unless there's a performance on).

North Adelaide There are a number of good restaurants and cafes on O'Connell St in North Adelaide. *Café Paesano*, on the corner with Tynte St, is a wonderful Italian place with large pasta dishes from $7. It's chaotic, but light and airy, and there's alfresco dining on the pavement. Also popular is *Scuzzi*, another Italian cafe across the road. It's a little more expensive and generally attracts an older clientele.

Himeiji, at No 61, is an authentic Japanese restaurant with one of the best sushi bars in town. It's rather expensive, but the experience is said to be worth it.

At No 43, the *Blue & White Café* is an Adelaide institution for takeaways – the

taxidrivers eat here, so you know it's good. It opens at 11.30 am daily and closes at 2.30 am Sunday to Thursday and 4.30 am other nights.

Kwik Stix is right across the road at No 42. This popular Asian place has a good variety of cheap meals (nothing over $10) and a great kid's menu. It's good for takeaways.

A few steps towards the city from the Blue & White Café, the *Rakuba Restaurant* is pretty basic, but it's Adelaide's only authentic African restaurant. It's open for dinner between Tuesday and Saturday.

There's also a string of cafes and restaurants along Melbourne St, a main thoroughfare into the city. You might find the traffic noise a bit much during peak periods, but there's no denying the quality and variety of the eateries on offer.

The *Old Lion Hotel*, an old favourite at No 163 on the corner with Jerningham St, is a good place to start – or finish. It has a pleasant beer-garden, a couple of nice bars and the *Grapevine Bar & Café*, where you can get an excellent meal from $7.

Diagonally opposite is *Café Flash*, a very busy eatery with a strong Italian influence. Opposite again is *Bacalls* at No 149. It's known for its grills and New Orleans Creole Cajun dishes. Once you've checked these there are many more continuing along the street.

The *British*, at 58 Finniss St, has a pleasant beer garden where you can grill the food yourself at the barbecue. Main courses are about $11 ($2 to $3 less if you cook your own).

Pie Floaters

If you're after a new experience in late-night eating, look for the pie carts that appear every night on city streets from 6 pm till the early hours; they're an institution. The carts sell 'pie floaters', a chunky meat pie doused in tomato sauce and floating in thick pea soup. Judging by the number of people tucking in with obvious enjoyment, the floaters don't taste as bad as they look. You'll find pie carts on North Terrace near the railway station and on the corner by the GPO. If you can't face a pie floater, they sell more conventional pies as well as tea and coffee. ∎

Entertainment

Bookings for music and the performing arts at the various Adelaide venues can be made through BASS (Best Available Seating Service) on ☎ 13 12 46. There are numerous BASS outlets around town, including one at the Festival Centre (open 9 am to 8.30 pm Monday to Saturday) and another on the 5th floor of the Myer department store in Rundle Mall.

SATC and BASS outlets have copies of *BASS Adelaide's Entertainment Update*. Otherwise check The *Advertiser* or get hold of the free newspaper *Arts Monthly*.

For theatre and gallery reviews check the free monthly paper *Adelaide Review*.

Cinemas Adelaide has several commercial cinema complexes, with the wonderful Piccadilly Cinema at 181 O'Connell St in North Adelaide getting the votes for atmosphere. Check the entertainment pages in The *Advertiser* for what's on around town, otherwise phone ☎ 0055 14632 for a recorded listing of current showings.

The *Mercury Cinema* (☎ 8410 1934), in the Lion Arts Centre at 13 Morphett St, is Adelaide's major alternative cinema. It shows a variety of films such as classic, cult, animation and art-house, and is the home of the biennial Frames Festival of Film & Video – this features recent short Australian films and videos and is usually held in September of even-numbered years. The cinema publishes a quarterly calendar.

Other cinemas showing alternative films are the *Piccadilly* (☎ 8267 1500) in North Adelaide, the Trak (8332 8020) at 375 Greenhill Road and the *Capri Theatre* (☎ 8272 1177) at 141 Goodwood Rd, Goodwood. The latter occasionally shows foreign-language films; it often has live performances before a showing, including an organist on Tuesday, Friday and Saturday evenings.

Adelaide still has a few drive-in cinemas, all out in the suburbs.

Theatre Adelaide has a thriving performing arts scene, with the *Adelaide Festival Centre* at its hub; based here are the State Theatre Company and the Magpie Theatre Company, which aims mainly at the youth market.

Among the more popular venues are *Her Majesty's Theatre* (☎ 8212 6833) at 58 Grote St, and the *Lion Theatre & Bar* (☎ 8231 7760) in the Lion Arts Centre on the corner of North Terrace and Morphett St, and Theatre 62 (☎ 8234 0838) at 145 Burbridge Rd in Hillton. The latter is a favourite venue for progressive theatre companies lacking a home base.

Apart from the major companies, there are a number of smaller ones worth checking. Probably the most progressive company in town is *The Red Shed* (☎ 8232 2075) at 255 Angas St. It presents all new local and inter-state material and is a good place to see the work of upcoming playwrights.

Another is *La Mama Theatre* (☎ 8346 4212) at 4 Crawford Lane, Hindmarsh, a straighter but still progressive company. The *Not So Straight Theatre* mainly has shows for gays and lesbians, while *Vital Statistix* (☎ 8447 6211) at 11 Nile St in Port Adelaide specialises in feminist works.

At the Lion Arts Centre, *Doppio Teatro* (☎ 8231 0070) produces works aimed at bridging the gap between Australians and migrant groups. *Junction Theatre* (☎ 8443 6200), on the corner of South Rd and George St in Thebarton, performs exclusively local plays; much of their work involves union-orientated workplace and lifestyle themes.

Rock Adelaide has the usual pub rock circuit, and only a sample is listed here. To find out who's playing around town either check under Gigs at the back of *The Guide* in Thursday's The *Advertiser* newspaper, or phone the radio station SA-FM (☎ 8272 1990) for a recorded run-down.

As well, the free music paper *Rip it Up* is worth checking for its listings – you'll find it at most record shops, hotels, cafes and night spots around town.

In North Adelaide, and handy to the restaurants, there's the *Oxford Hotel* at 101 O'Connell St. It has a DJ on Friday night and is 'in' with the yuppie set.

The *Earl of Aberdeen*, on Carrington St at Hurtle Square, is a very nice, very trendy place with lots of timber and usually a rock band on Wednesday, Friday and Saturday nights. It's handy to the backpackers' hostels in the south-east of the city centre.

On Rundle St, the *Austral* and the *Exeter* at Nos 205 and 246, respectively, often have bands and DJs. They're popular with business folk and office workers during the day (both pubs have interesting lunchtime menus), while at night they're university students' hang-outs. Try them if you're looking for a place to go for a drink before heading out to dinner.

Also good for a predinner drink is the *Universal Wine Bar* at 285 Rundle St. It's got a pleasant atmosphere, with lots of iron filigree, and the doors fold back on summer nights so you can catch the breeze.

In the old Commercial Hotel on the corner of Morphett and Hindley Sts is *Rave on Hindley*, reputedly the most upcoming of the street's nightclubs. A couple of huge bouncers (they're twins) keep the riffraff outside where they belong. It's open between Wednesday and Sunday from 8 pm until late.

Most popular of Adelaide's clubs is the *Heaven 1*, in the grand old Newmarket Hotel on the corner of West and North Terraces. It has DJs between Wednesday and Saturday nights and often has bands on Sunday; it also has *Joplins Nightclub*, which is more appealing to the older set. Another very popular one is *The Planet*, Adelaide's newest nightclub at 73 Pirie St.

The *UniBar* (☎ 8303 5401) in the Union Complex at Adelaide University often features big-name and up-coming rock bands during lunchtime, afternoons and evenings – usually Friday. The bar is also an excellent venue for social, cultural and avant-garde performances and activities. There's always something interesting taking place, and visitors are welcome – the complex is off Victoria Drive and above the Cloisters.

There are often free concerts in the amphitheatre at the *Adelaide Festival Centre* on alternate Sundays during summer, and in the centre's foyer every Sunday during winter.

Jazz The Adelaide jazz scene always has something happening on weekends. To find out about it, either ring the Jazz Line on ☎ 8303 3755, or get hold of the free street newspaper *Adelaide Jazz News* – it's available at universities, clubs and music shops.

Jazz has a loyal following and there are a number of regular venues. At the forefront is the *Governor Hindmarsh Hotel* at 59 Port Rd in Hindmarsh, which has weekly trad sessions put on by the Southern Jazz Club. The Jazz coordinator holds two or three concerts here each month as well.

In the city centre, the *Green Dragon Hotel* at 471 Pulteney St and the *Hindley Parkroyal Hotel* at 65 Hindley St have bands most weeks. At 242 Rundle St, *Tapas* is a great wine bar with jazz on Friday night.

The *Fez Bah*, in the Festival Centre, is a popular jazz and rock venue on Saturday night between 10 pm and 1 am; admission is $7. The Jazz Action Society puts on monthly concerts here.

Folk For information on folk and bluegrass music or dancing contact the Folk Federation of SA (☎ 8340 1069), or get hold of their very informative newspaper *Infolkus*, available from selected outlets around town.

Adelaide has numerous folk clubs and bands of various persuasions to be heard around town. Regular session venues include the *Governor Hindmarsh Hotel* (for bluegrass and folk) and the *Cumberland Arms Hotel*, at 205 Waymouth St.

The Acoustic Music Club plays on Thursday night in the *Flagstaff Hotel*, at 23 Franklin St, while the Songwriters, Composers and Lyricists Association is at the *Jolly Miller Tavern* at 14 Adam St in Hindmarsh on Wednesday night.

Every Friday night the *Irish Club* at 11 Carrington St has live music and dancing from eight until late. Another good Irish venue is the *Brecknock Hotel*, at 401 King William St, which usually has a band on Friday night.

Gay & Lesbian Places There are number of places around town and out in the suburbs.

You'll find them advertised in *Adelaide gt* (☎ 8232 1544), which is available from selected outlets.

Venues include the very popular *Mars Bar*, a dance club for the younger set at 120 Gouger St. It's open seven nights a week from 10 pm until late. *Beans Bar*, another dance club at 258 Hindley St, is also open nightly; Friday night from 5 pm to 9 pm is 'women only'.

The *Edinburgh Castle Hotel* at 233 Currie St, is another very popular one. It's open seven days and has DJs on Thursday, Friday and Saturday nights. You can also get good counter meals here.

Pubs Several pubs brewed their own beer until fairly recently, but it seems the only survivor is the *Port Dock Brewery Hotel*, at 10 Todd St in Port Adelaide. It produces four distinctive beers, the process overseen by a German brew specialist.

The bar at the *Earl of Zetland* pub on Flinders St near the YMCA claims to have the world's largest collection of malt whiskies, with over 275 varieties available by the nip.

Gambling The *Adelaide Casino* is housed in the impressive old railway station on North Terrace. Apart from a wide range of gambling facilities (including a two-up game, of course) there are three bars and two restaurants; informed sources reckon that the best odds are offered by craps and baccarat. Opening times are Monday to Thursday from 10 am to 4 am, and 24 hours a day from Friday to Sunday and on public holidays. Smart casual dress is required.

Most of the pubs around town have poker machines, or 'pokies' as they're more commonly called.

Things to Buy

There's great shopping in Adelaide, with Rundle Mall at the heart of the action. The Myer Centre has 150 speciality shops as well as the huge Myer department store on five levels. Off the mall are several arcades and side-streets crammed with interesting shops selling all manner of wares. Out at Tea Tree Gully, a north-eastern suburb, the Westfield Tea Tree Plaza is the largest shopping complex in SA. You can get there in no time on the O-Bahn Busway from the city.

For clothing there's a swag of places. Rundle St is recommended for retro clothes and boutiques, while the East End and Orange Lane markets are worth checking for second-hand and alternative clothing (see the earlier Markets section for details). There are good bargains in designer label seconds on Glen Osmond Rd in Parkside; several shops on King William Rd in Hyde Park and Unley Rd in Unley feature name and up-coming Australian designer labels.

Unley Road in Unley also has some wonderful antique shops. You can combine antique shopping with a visit to the Adelaide Hills, where there are some good shops in Nairne and Strathalbyn.

Tandanya, the large centre run by the Aboriginal Cultural Institute at 253 Grenfell St, includes a crafts and souvenir shop. A range of high-quality craftwork is produced and sold at the Jam Factory Craft & Design Centre, in the Lion Arts Centre on the corner of Morphett St and North Terrace. They also have a shop at 74 Gawler Place, in the city centre.

If you're after bushwalking, climbing and outdoor gear generally, there are several good shops conveniently grouped on Rundle St: Flinders Camping at No 187, the Scout Outdoor Centre at No 192, Mountain Designs at No 203, the Annapurna Outdoor Shop at No 210, and Paddy Pallin at No 228.

Getting There & Away

All international and interstate flights go via the Adelaide airport, while interstate train services leave from the Keswick terminal. The bus terminal for Greyhound Pioneer, McCafferty's, Stateliner and minor regional bus lines is at 101-111 Franklin St; the Firefly Express is opposite at 110 Franklin Street.

For details of travel to and from Adelaide see the introductory Getting There & Away chapter.

Getting Around

The Airport Adelaide's modern international and domestic airport is conveniently located seven km west of the city centre. An airport bus service (☎ 8381 5311) operates between city hotels at least half-hourly from around 7 am to 9 pm on weekdays and hourly on weekends and public holidays for $6.

The trip from Victoria Square to the domestic terminal takes about 30 minutes and a little less to the international terminal. If you're catching a flight on one of the smaller airlines (eg to Kangaroo Island) let the driver know, as the drop-off point is different. A taxi to the airport costs about $14. You can travel between the city and the airport entrance on bus Nos 276, 277 and 278 leaving from Grenfell and Currie Sts.

Budget, Hertz, Avis and Thrifty have desks at the airport.

Some of the hostels will pick you up and drop you off if you're staying with them.

Public Transport Adelaide has an extensive integrated transport system operated by TransAdelaide (TA) (☎ 8210 1000). The TA Information Bureau, where you can get timetables and buy a transport map for $2, is on the corner of King William and Currie Sts.

The system covers metropolitan buses and trains, as well as the vintage tram service to Glenelg. Tickets purchased on board buses are $2.70 before 9 am, after 3 pm and on weekends and $1.60 between 9 am and 3 pm weekdays. They are valid for two hours from the commencement of the first journey. (Tickets cannot be purchased on board trains.) For travellers, the best deal is the day-trip ticket, which permits unlimited travel for the whole day and costs $4.60.

The free Bee Line bus service (No 99B) runs down King William St from the Glenelg tram terminus at Victoria Square and round the corner to the railway station. It operates every five to eight minutes weekdays from 8 am to 6 pm, and every 15 minutes to 7 pm on Friday and from 8 am to 5 pm on Saturday.

The airport to city bus service calls into the interstate train station (Keswick) on its regular run between the airport and the city ($3) from the station to the city centre.

Taxis Adelaide has around 1000 licensed taxis, and you can either flag one down, find a rank or phone one. Friday and Saturday nights are particularly busy, so if you want to book a cab do it early.

Car & Motorbike Rental The Yellow Pages lists over 20 vehicle rental companies in Adelaide, including all the major national companies. Those with cheaper rates include Access Rent-a-Car (☎ 8223 7466), Action Rent-a-Car (☎ 8352 7044), Airport Rent-a-Car (☎ 8443 8855; toll-free 1800 631 637), Delta (☎ 13 13 90), Rent-a-Bug (☎ 8234 0911) and Smile Rent-a-Car (☎ 8234 0655). Access and Smile allow its cars to be taken over to Kangaroo Island, but few others do.

Show & Go (☎ 8376 0333), at 236 Brighton Rd, Brighton, has motor scooters for $49 per day (car licence required) and motorcycles from 250 cc ($59) to 1000 cc (from $89). A full motorcycle licence is required for all bikes.

Bicycle Adelaide is a relatively cyclist-friendly city, with good cycling tracks through the parks and bicycle lanes on many city streets.

Linear Park Mountain Bike Hire (☎ 8223 6953) is at Elder Park, next to the Festival Theatre; it's right on the Torrens River Linear Park, which wends its way along the Torrens from the beach to the foot of the Adelaide Hills. Bicycles are $8 per hour or $20 for the day.

Velodrome Cycles (☎ 8223 6678) at 43 Rundle Mall rents mountain bikes from $15 per day or $70 for a week.

Freewheelin' (☎ 8232 6860), at 237 Hutt St, in the city has bicycles from $15 to $20 per day, and offers a pick-up and drop-off service. It also has entire touring outfits, including panniers etc. Tours from one day to three weeks are available.

Around Adelaide

GLENELG

The first South Australian Governor, Captain John Hindmarsh, landed on the beach here on 28 December 1836 and proclaimed SA a Province later that same day. Glenelg quickly became a busy seaport and a favoured spot for wealthy squatters, who built their grand townhouses near the beach. It was also one of the first of Adelaide's seaside resorts.

The tourist information centre (☎ 8294 5833) is next to the Town Hall. It's open from 9 am to 5 pm daily, and there's a travel agency on the premises.

Things to See & Do

Glenelg is at its best in warm weather, when you can dine alfresco, laze on the lawns and beach in front of Moseley Square, or go for a swim. In summer, there's daily entertainment on the foreshore including bands, folk dancing and singing. The shops on Jetty Rd are open seven days from 9 am to 5 pm.

PLACES TO STAY

8 Colley Motel Apartments
12 Ensenada Moter Inn
13 Glenelg Seaway Apartments
16 Ramada Grand Hotel
18 St Vincent Hotel
19 Glenelg Beach Headquarters
22 Seafront Holiday Flats
23 Albert Hall

PLACES TO EAT

4 HMS Buffalo
7 Rock Lobster Café
16 Ramada Grand Hotel
17 Alfresco Cafés
18 St Vincent Hotel
20 New Zealand Natural

OTHER

1 Old Gum Tree
2 Glenelg Marine & Scuba Diving
3 Patawalonga Boat Haven
4 HMS Buffalo
5 Wind Surfing Glenelg
6 Holdfast Cycles
9 Side Show Alley
10 Bayside Bowl
11 Magic Mountain
14 Tourist Information Centre
15 Town Hall
21 St Andrews Church
24 Partridge House

The blue-stone **Town Hall** on Moseley Square, the Gothic-style **St Andrews Church** on Jetty Rd, and numerous fine Victorian mansions and stately homes are imposing reminders of Glenelg's prosperous past. The Tudor-style **Partridge House**, at 38 Partridge St, is owned by the town council and is open to visitors. It's not a museum, unfortunately, but you can enjoy the grounds and admire the architecture.

You can see these and other historic places around Glenelg on several **self-guided walks** from Moseley Square; maps are available from the tourist information centre.

Open daily on the foreshore near the town hall is **Magic Mountain**, an amusement parlour with a water-slide, bumper boats, arcade games and other activities. Right next door, **Side Show Alley** has a ferris wheel, side shows and rides – it's open daily in summer and otherwise on weekends.

The foully polluted Patawalonga Boat Haven (now being cleaned up, thank goodness) has Glenelg's premier attraction: a splendid replica of **HMS Buffalo**, one of the ships that brought the original settlers out from England. On board there's a seafood restaurant as well as a museum, which is open for $2.50 from 10 am to 5 pm daily.

About 15 minute's walk away, on McFarlane St, the **Old Gum Tree** was the spot chosen by Governor Hindmarsh to read the proclamation that established the colony. Each year, on Proclamation Day, there's a full-costume re-enactment on the site.

Glenelg's 215-metre-long **jetty** is a popular fishing spot where you can usually catch tommy ruff, whiting and garfish.

For 10-pin bowling there's Bayside Bowl at 18 Colley Terrace. It's open from 9 am to midnight Monday to Saturday, and 1 pm to midnight on Sunday.

Beach Gear & Bike Hire Next door to the tourist information office, Beach Hire (☎ 8294 1477) hires deckchairs, umbrellas, wave skis and body boards. It's open from September to April only; the opening times vary, but if it's sunny, it'll be open.

Wind Surfing Glenelg (☎ 8294 3866) on the corner of Anzac Highway and Colley Terrace has sailboards for $15/50 per hour/ day; a deposit of $200 is required on sailboards and $25 on wet suits. It's open from 9 am to 5.30 pm weekdays and Saturday, and 11 am to 5 pm on Sunday and public holidays.

Holdfast Cycles (☎ 8294 4537), at 768 Anzac Highway, hires well-maintained mountain bikes for the serious touring cyclist. It provides maps for self-guided tours to points of interest, and helmets are included in the rates ($7.50 an hour; $30 a day). The shop is open from 9 am to 5.30 pm weekdays and 10 am to 3 pm on weekends.

Glenelg Marine & Scuba Diving (☎ 8294 7744), on Patawalonga Frontage, hires snorkelling and scuba gear and also does dive charters.

Places to Stay

There is a swag of places to stay in Glenelg. Many are covered in the accommodation directory *Seaside Holidays – Glenelg*, available from SATC and the Glenelg tourist information centre. The following small sample is close to the action in Jetty Rd.

Places to Stay

Hostels Both backpacker hostels in Glenelg are a big improvement on most in the city. They're in grand old buildings and are noted for clean, reasonably spacious facilities and excellent service.

At 7 Moseley St, around the corner from the tram terminus, *Glenelg Beach Headquarters* (☎ 8376 0007) has a pool room, games room and an inexpensive dining room. Comfortable beds (not bunks) are $13 in dorms and $16 per person in smaller shared rooms. There's a book exchange opposite the hostel.

A little further south of the tram line but on the seafront is the wonderful *Albert Hall* (☎ 8376 0488; toll-free 1800 060 488), a beautifully restored mansion at 16 South Esplanade. It has marble bathrooms and a spectacular ballroom. Dorm beds cost from $13; private rooms from $20/30.

Hotels & Motels The *St Vincent Hotel* (☎ 8294 4377) at 28 Jetty Rd has single/twin rooms for $30/52, or self-contained singles/doubles for $40/60 – all with a light breakfast.

Somewhat more luxurious are the units offered by the *Ensenada Motor Inn* (☎ 8294 5822), at 13 Colley Terrace, which has standard rooms for $73/77 and executive suites for $78/82.

Right at the top of the comfort scale, the towering *Ramada Grand Hotel* (☎ 8376 1222) on Moseley Square overlooks Gulf St Vincent from right opposite the tram stop. Rooms with ocean views start at $195, and if you really want to splurge, the Royal Rooms on the 12th floor are $245.

Holiday Flats & Serviced Apartments
There are many holiday flats and serviced apartments in Glenelg; most quote weekly rather than daily rates.

Cheapest of all is the plain but friendly *Glenelg Seaway Apartments* (☎ 8295 8503) at 18 Durham St, about a minute's walk from the tram stop. It has backpacker accommodation at $15 year round, and self-contained apartments for $50 off-peak ($60 peak) for doubles.

Also good value is the *Colley Motel Apartments* (☎ 8295 7535), in a grand old house at 22 Colley Terrace. Its spacious, well-appointed rooms cost $48 doubles off-peak ($58 peak) and $10/20 for extra children/adults. The same people run the more luxurious *Seafront Holiday Flats* (☎ 8295 1728), on South Esplanade near the Ramada Grand Hotel. This beautiful old home was the summer residence of Sir Henry Ayers, an early premier.

Places to Eat
Jetty Rd has a swag of eateries of all styles and ethnic origins. In sunny weather the alfresco cafes between the Grand Hotel and St Vincents Hotel are crowded. If you can't get a seat here, the benches under the date palms in Moseley Square, or the lawns along the beachfront, are nice spots to enjoy a takeaway meal.

You'll find a good variety of eateries in the *Ramada Grand Hotel*. They include inexpensive cafes, where a light lunch costs $5, to silver service in *The Quarterdeck* restaurant. The front bar looks onto the foreshore and is extremely popular on hot days.

For a cold treat on a hot day you won't be able to go past *New Zealand Natural*, at 64 Jetty Rd. It boasts 20 varieties of icecream and frozen yoghurt, and they're all delicious.

On the 12th floor of the Atlantic Tower Motel Inn, at 760 Anzac Highway, the revolving *Rock Lobster Café* has stunning panoramas, although you may find its meals to be over-priced. About 300 metres north across the park, the *Buffalo* is also expensive, but its meals and atmosphere are superb – this is one of Adelaide's finest seafood places.

Getting There & Away
The best way to get from the city to the heart of Glenelg is by TransAdelaide's vintage tram service. Trams leave Victoria Square every 15 minutes from 5.57 am on weekdays, 7.32 am on Saturday and 8.50 am on Sunday, and arrive at Moseley Square about 25 minutes later. The last tram leaves Glenelg at 11.20 pm daily.

Alternatively, you can take bus Nos 263, 266, 275 and 278 from the city to the last stop on Anzac Highway, about five minutes walk from Jetty Rd.

Adelaide Hills

Only 30 minutes drive from the city centre, the scenic Adelaide Hills, which form part of the Mt Lofty Ranges, encompass the region bordered by the towns of Clarendon and Strathalbyn to the south, Mt Barker and Nairne to the east, and Mt Pleasant to the north.

Not surprisingly, the hills are a popular day-trip destination from Adelaide. Apart from the beauty of the landscape, there are numerous attractions such as conservation parks, botanic gardens, wineries and historic villages. There are also plenty of bushwalking options: the region is crisscrossed by hundreds of km of trails, including the Heysen Trail.

European History
German settlers escaping religious persecution were on the scene early, establishing Hahndorf in 1839, and several other villages, including Lobethal, Grunthal (now Verdun) and Blumberg (now Birdwood), within a decade. Mixed in with these are typically British places such as Strathalbyn (established by the Scots), Stirling (by the English) and Callington (by the Cornish).

Copper and gold were mined at several locations from the 1840s – the major goldfields were at Echunga and Woodside. The colony's first highway, from Adelaide to Mt Barker, opened in 1845. By the 1850s, Adelaide's colonial gentry were beginning to build grand summer houses, many with stunning gardens, at higher places like Crafers and Stirling.

The Adelaide Hills are a lush contrast to the rest of the state owing to their relatively high rainfall. Huge eucalypts are a magnificent feature of the landscape, which varies from high steep ridges to gentle hills and valleys. Many buildings of the initial boom period from 1837 to the 1860s have survived, giving the hills a distinctive European heritage. In autumn this is reinforced by the glorious colours of introduced deciduous trees, particularly in the wetter central area

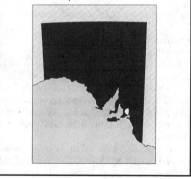

around Mt Lofty. Hahndorf these days is very touristy and many travellers – no doubt shackled by day-trip itineraries – only go there and to the more popular parks, such as Belair and Cleland. This is a pity as there are many more interesting places to visit once you get off the main tourist routes. However, the demand is mainly on weekends so many places, particularly the restaurants, are closed from Monday to Wednesday or Thursday.

Information
The Adelaide Hills Information Centre (☎ 8388 1185), at 41 Main St in Hahndorf, is open daily from 10 am to 4 pm. They have

the useful brochure *Your Guide to the Beautiful Adelaide Hills*, put out by the Adelaide Hills Regional Association.

The RAA produces a travel guide to the Adelaide Hills region ($4 for members and $8 for nonmembers). If you're self-driving, its *Central* touring map will get you around the region without too much fuss.

Also useful, although only for the southern hills, is the informative *Scenic Drives of the Mt Barker District*. This takes you to several towns including Hahndorf, Mt Barker, Clarendon and Strathalbyn.

Communications Throughout this book we use the new statewide STD code (08) and eight-digit phone numbers. The new numbers will be in use in the Adelaide Hills area from February 1997. Should you need to use the old number, simply take off the first two digits and use them in the area code: eg (08) 8526 1000 becomes (085) 26 1000.

Organised Tours

A number of Adelaide operators offer half-day and day sightseeing tours to the Adelaide Hills, and SATC will have details. Generally

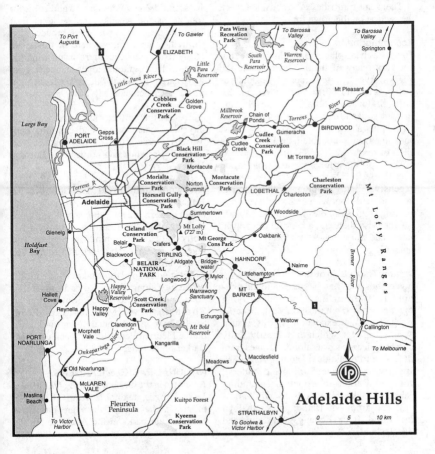

Adelaide Hills

you can expect to pay from $25 for a half-day and from $35 for a day tour.

Gecko Tours (☎ 8339 3800) has an interesting day tour ($75) that takes you on a discovery of the Aboriginal heritage of the Eden Valley area, with some wine tasting thrown in.

Tony's Taxis (☎ 8370 8333) is hills-based and does half-day tours from $17.50 per person for a group of four. If you're by yourself it'll cost $50. Hills Classic Cars (☎ 8370 8832) will get you around in style in their restored Ford LTDs – they do mini, half-day, day and night tours.

There are trail rides at Woodside (check the section on this town for details).

Accommodation

There are cheap places to stay in the hills, but not very many of them. They include the YHA's five 'limited access' hostels for members at Para Wirra, Norton Summit, Mt Lofty, Mylor and Kuitpo. These are all on the Heysen Trail and cost between $4 and $7 per night, plus a key deposit ($10). You must book in advance and obtain the key from the YHA office (☎ 8231 5583) in Adelaide.

The most common style available in the hills is B&B. These places are generally expensive, being popular with escapists from Adelaide, but with luck you'll find one offering singles/doubles for around $50/60.

Otherwise there are a handful of caravan parks, and a few relatively cheap pubs and generally pricey motels.

Getting There & Around

Several bus lines have services into the Adelaide Hills from the city and outlying regional centres, but most only nibble at the edges. The main exception is Hills Transit (☎ 8339 1191), which has mostly daily return services to towns along its routes from Mt Barker to Adelaide (including Hahndorf, Bridgewater, Aldgate, Stirling and Crafers); from Mt Barker to Lobethal (including Hahndorf, Oakbank, Woodside and Charleston); and from Mt Barker to Strathalbyn (including Mylor, Echunga, Meadows and Macclesfield).

In the extreme south of the hills, Premier Roadlines (☎ 8415 5555) does one return trip daily (weekdays only) through Clarendon and Meadows on its run between Adelaide and Victor Harbor.

On weekdays, ABM Coachlines (☎ 8347 3336) runs through Birdwood and Mt Pleasant on its Adelaide to Mannum service. The Murray Bridge Passenger Service (☎ 8415 5555) can drop you off at Nairne on weekdays coming from either Murray Bridge or Adelaide.

Scenic Drives There are plenty of options for scenic drives. Winter isn't a good time for touring as the weather can close in fast; road-weather alerts, which are broadcast on the radio, are common here at this time. Many roads are steep, narrow and winding, often with precipitous slopes on one side, so drive carefully. Watch out for koalas at night in the area between Mt Lofty and Blackwood.

To visit the northern hills area, leave the city via Payneham Rd and continue onto Torrens Gorge Rd. This route takes you through Birdwood and north to the Barossa Valley.

Alternatively, you can head south from Birdwood and travel via Lobethal to Hahndorf before returning to Adelaide on the South Eastern Freeway. For something more exciting than the freeway, return via Mt Lofty and Norton Summit, from where you take the spectacular Norton Summit Rd down to Magill Rd.

Yet another good route takes you south out of the city along Unley Rd and past Belair National Park to Clarendon, then to Strathalbyn via Macclesfield. From Strathalbyn you can head down to Goolwa on the Fleurieu Peninsula, or back up to Mt Barker in the hills.

NATIONAL PARKS & GARDENS

As shown in the brochure *Parks of the Mount Lofty Ranges*, available from all NPWS offices in the region, there are numerous conservation parks in the Adelaide Hills – the following three mentioned are the most

GREG HERRIMAN

DENIS O'BYRNE

DENIS O'BYRNE

DENIS O'BYRNE

DENIS O'BYRNE

A	B
C	D
E	

A: Nora Creina, between Beachport and Robe
B: Historic obelisk, Robe
C: Free vehicle ferry, Murray River

D: Coastal banksia of the South-East
E: Fishing at Ninety-Mile Beach, Coorong National Park

DENIS O'BYRNE

SOUTH AUSTRALIAN TOURISM COMMISSION

MICHELLE COXALL

Top: Classic Australian architecture, Bordertown Hotel, Bordertown
Bottom Left: Ballooning over the vineyards, Barossa Valley
Bottom Right: Owners of historic Carn Brae, Port Pirie

popular. All may be closed on Total Fire Ban days.

You can also visit several excellent botanic gardens; enquire at the Adelaide Botanic Garden (☎ 8228 2311) on North Terrace. A number of outstanding private gardens in the central hills area participate in the seasonal 'Open Garden Scheme'.

Belair National Park (840 hectares)
Only nine km south of the city centre, Belair National Park has some lovely walking trails as well as an ornamental lake, picnic facilities and tennis courts. The grand lifestyle of SA's colonial gentry is on display on Sunday afternoons at **Old Government House**, built in 1859 as the governor's summer residence. The park was declared in 1891, making it Australia's second oldest. It's open daily from 8.30 am to sunset and entry costs $3 per car.

You can get to Belair from Adelaide either by heading south out of the city on Unley Rd, which becomes Belair Rd, or by taking the train – the Belair station is near the park's main entrance.

Morialta Conservation Park (532 hectares)
This rugged park is on the western escarpment 10 km east of the city centre. It has picnic facilities, some spectacular views, and a testing 2.5-hour return walk past a series of **waterfalls** on Fourth Creek – it generally flows from late autumn to early summer. The most impressive falls are the second set, about 45 minutes from the car park.

The park opens at 8 am daily and closes at 5 pm on weekdays and two hours later on weekends. To get there from the city, take bus No 105 from Grenfell and Currie Sts to the main entrance on Stradbroke Rd. If you're driving, head north-east on Payneham Rd, veer right onto Montacute Rd and turn right on Stradbroke Rd.

Cleland Wildlife Park (993 hectares)
This steep park, only 7.5 km south-east of the city centre, stretches from the western foothills up to Mt Lofty. It has many excellent bushwalks winding through its tall eucalypt forests and moist gullies, as well as picnic areas and a decent restaurant at **Waterfall Gully**.

Cleland's major attraction is a 35-hectare wildlife park, which has numerous species of Australian fauna and is open from 9.30 am to 5 pm daily. Admission costs $7 and you can have your photograph taken cuddling a koala for $8 between 2 pm and 4 pm daily; guided night walks ($11.50) leave at 7 pm from 1 May to 30 October and at 8 pm for the rest of the year. There's a good restaurant here as well. To get there from Adelaide take bus No 822 from outside Harris Scarfe on Grenfell St. Otherwise you can visit with one of the day tours that operate from the city.

A short detour south along Summit Rd from the turn-off to the wildlife park takes you to **Mt Lofty Summit**, 727 metres above sea level (it's a 30-minute walk from the wildlife park). The lookout offers impressive views back over the city, particularly at night. Nearby are the impressive remains of **St Michael's Monastery**, destroyed in the 1983 bushfires.

TransAdelaide buses go daily to the Cleland Wildlife Park.

Other Parks
Other good parks to visit for bushwalks and wildlife include: Charleston Conservation Park (63 hectares), eight km east of Lobethal; Black Hill Conservation Park (701 hectares), 10 km north-east of the city centre; Kenneth Stirling Conservation Park (253 hectares), five km west of Oakbank; Loftia Recreation Reserve (145 hectares), four km south of Stirling; and Scott Creek Conservation Park (900 hectares), between Mylor and Clarendon.

Mt Lofty Botanic Garden
From Mt Lofty you continue south for about 1.5 km to the large and scenic Mt Lofty Botanic Garden, which has its main entrances off Summit Rd and off Piccadilly Rd. Here you find stunning views, nature trails, a lake system, exotic temperate plants and native stringybark forest. Its seasonal

camellia, magnolia and rhododendron displays are spectacular.

The garden is open weekdays from 8.30 am to 4 pm, and weekends from 10 am to 5 pm. Admission is free.

Wittunga Botanic Garden
On Shepherds Hill Rd in Blackwood, a southern suburb of Adelaide, this garden has fine displays of Australian and South African plants as well as different habitats such as lakes and a sandplain garden. It opens daily at 10 am and closes at 4 pm on weekdays and 5 pm on weekends. You can get there on a No 728 or 729 bus from Flinders St in the city.

Beechwood
This marvellous heritage garden is on Snows Rd in Stirling. Surrounding one of the early summer residences of Adelaide's colonial gentry, it features the state's oldest conservatory, an old-fashioned rose garden, a Victorian rock garden and beautiful rhododendron hybrids. Beechwood is open for a limited season in spring and autumn only.

National Trust Reserves
The National Trust has a number of small nature reserves in the Adelaide Hills, several of which are dedicated to preserving rare remnants of native forest. For information, ring the Friends of the Mt Lofty Reserves on ☎ 8223 1655.

MARKETS
The monthly markets held on weekends at towns throughout the hills are good places for such things as art, crafts, trash and treasure, second-hand clothing and local produce. They include:

Blackwood
    Blackwood Memorial Hall on Coromandel Ave, 11 am to 4 pm first Sunday of every month; ☎ 8296 6740

Clarendon
    Community Hall, 10 am to 4 pm third Sunday excluding January; ☎ 8383 6385

Echunga
    Echunga Hall, 6.30 am to noon first Saturday of every month; ☎ 8388 6457 or 8388 8137

Littlehampton
    Institute Hall, 8 am to 1 pm second Saturday of every month; ☎ 8391 1259

Macclesfield
    Hall or Town Square, 9 am to 1 pm fourth Sunday of every month; ☎ 8388 9438 or 8388 9378

Meadows
    Community Hall, early am to 1 pm second Sunday of every month; ☎ 8388 3213 or 8388 3122

Mylor
    Mylor Oval, 9 am to 3 pm first Sunday of every month; ☎ 8388 5242 or 8388 5334

Stirling
    Council office lawns, 8 am to 2 pm fourth Saturday of every month; ☎ 8398 3460

Woodside
    Woodside Institute, 7 am to noon third Saturday of every month; ☎ 8388 4207

WINERIES
The Adelaide Hills wine region stretches for about 70 km through the southern Mt Lofty Ranges from Williamstown in the north to Mt Compass in the south.

Although it's virtually unknown today, the region had a thriving wine industry between 1840 and 1900. In fact, the Echunga hock sent to Queen Victoria in 1845 was the first wine ever exported from Australia. What killed it off was fashion; most Australians drank beer, and those who drank wine preferred big reds – as did imbibers overseas.

The industry was reborn in the early 1980s following the growth in popularity of table and sparkling wines. Now there are about 30 local wineries with more on the way. Among the best known labels are **Petaluma** and **Bridgewater Mill**, which you can taste at the historic flour mill (1860) in Bridgewater. The mill has a huge waterwheel and there's a very popular up-market restaurant on the premises.

Other wineries are listed in the leaflet *The Adelaide Hills Wine Region*, available from SATC and tourist offices in the area. Most are too small to have their own tastings, but you can sample all the local produce at the **Adelaide Hills Wine Centre** at 41 Avenue

Rd in Stirling. It's open daily during normal business hours.

STIRLING AREA

The attractive and rather intimate townships of **Crafers**, **Stirling** and **Aldgate** are excellent for autumn colours thanks to their extensive plantings of exotic deciduous trees. Aldgate even has an **Autumn Leaves Festival**, held irregularly in May on even-numbered years.

You'll find some glorious old English-style gardens in all three towns, including **Stangate House** at Aldgate and **Beechwood** at Stirling. The **Mt Lofty Botanic Garden** is near tiny Piccadilly (for details of Beechwood and the botanic garden see National Parks & Gardens earlier in this chapter).

There are self-guided **historic walks** through Crafers and Aldgate, both of which were established around 1840. Crafers has a huge **oak tree** said to have been planted in 1838. The main information outlet for this area is in Crafers at Shop 2, Crafers Court at 2 Main St.

Places to Stay & Eat

The famous *Eagle on the Hill Hotel* (☎ 8339 2211) is on the Mt Barker Rd about three km before Crafers. It burned down in the 1983 bushfire, but has now been resurrected and offers self-contained rooms for $55/60/65, including a continental breakfast. The pub has an award-winning bistro with great views of the city lights.

Overlooking the Mt Lofty Botanic Garden from its eyrie at 74 Summit Rd, Crafers, the baronial *Mt Lofty House* (☎ 8339 6777) was built as a family home in the 1850s. It now offers rooms and meals for equally impressive prices: from $275 for a dinner, bed and breakfast package for two.

Somewhat more affordable is the friendly *Aldgate Village Inn* (☎ 8370 8144), which has backpacker rooms for $15 and B&B for $60 for two people, including a lavish continental breakfast.

The *Aldgate Café*, almost next door to the Aldgate Village Inn, has pasta meals from

$6, while the *Aldgate Pump Hotel* opposite does huge counter meals for similar prices. Up the street towards Stirling, the pleasant *Café Foljambes* does light meals from $4.50.

There are some good, reasonably priced places to eat in Stirling. *Goodies Café* on Mt Barker Rd does truly excellent meals from $7, while the *Organic Market Café* on Druid Ave (walk behind the National Bank on Mt Barker Rd) specialises in vegetarian food and has great coffee. The *Konditorei & Coffee Lounge* in the Stirling Arcade does light meals – you can eat them alfresco in a lovely courtyard setting.

Getting There & Away

The region is serviced by a Hills Transit bus – see Getting There & Around at the start of the chapter for details. If you've cycled up the Mt Barker Rd from Adelaide you have to get off the South Eastern Freeway at the Crafers exit.

MYLOR (pop 100)

The main attraction here is the **Warrawong Sanctuary** (☎ 8370 9422), about three km from town. Covering 14 hectares, it was a treeless dairy farm in 1969. Now the bush has been re-established and 15 native mammal species, several of them endangered, have been introduced behind a vermin-proof fence. You can see them on guided bushwalks at dawn ($15), sunset ($15) and at 1.30 pm ($8); dawn is the best time for wildlife watching.

The usual way to reach the sanctuary from Adelaide is to turn off the freeway at Stirling and follow the signs from the Stirling roundabout. The entrance is on Stock Rd 300 metres from Longwood Rd, or 2.7 km from Strathalbyn Rd if you're coming from Mylor. Be careful, because you won't see the turn-off until you're right on it.

The highlight of the small restaurant here is the large windows which give you a close-up view of the many native birds that congregate for a feed right outside. Most obvious are the rainbow lorikeets; they're beautiful, but their screeching and squabbling are unbelievable. To the delight of the birds – and the horror of cat lovers – a rug made from the skins of 50 feral cats hangs like a trophy above the fireplace.

For $85 you can spend the night in a luxury tent, complete with reverse-cycle air-conditioning. The price includes dinner, guided sunset and dawn walks, and breakfast. Bookings are essential for all walks and accommodation.

HAHNDORF (pop 1660)

The oldest surviving German settlement in Australia, Hahndorf was established in 1839 by about 50 Lutheran families who emigrated to Adelaide on the *Zebra*. They named their new home in honour of the ship's captain, Hahn, who helped them obtain land on arrival; *dorf* is German for 'village'.

The town was placed under martial law in WWI; its Lutheran school was closed and, in 1917, its name was changed to Ambleside. It was renamed Hahndorf in 1935, when the contribution made by those early pioneers to SA's development was officially recognised. Hahndorf still has an honorary Burgermeister, who acts as the town's goodwill ambassador.

The Adelaide Hills Information Centre (☎ 8388 1185) at 41 Main St is open daily from 10 am to 4 pm.

Things to See & Do

Hahndorf's commercial heart is on Main St between English St and Hereford Ave. On weekends and holiday periods it buzzes with activity with its art galleries, craft shops, gift shops, Bavarian-style restaurants and cafes all open.

A strong sense of history still pervades the town. On both sides of Main St is abundant evidence of the first settlers in the form of old buildings that show distinctive German architecture. These include the first **butcher's shop** (1839), **Thiele Cottage** (1842), the former **Australian Arms Hotel** (1854) and the still-licenced **German Arms Hotel** (1862). Seventeen historic sites are described in the self-guided walk brochure *Hahndorf – State Heritage Area*, which you can get from the information centre.

Right next door to the information centre, the **Hahndorf Academy** was established in 1857. It houses an art gallery, craft shop and museum – it had a valuable collection of the works of landscape artist Sir Hans Heysen until early 1995, when thieves made off with it. Guided tours through Sir Hans's studio and house, **The Cedars**, cost $5 and are conducted every Tuesday and Thursday at 11.30 am and 2.30 pm.

The **Antique Clock Museum** at 91 Main St has a fine collection of some 650 timepieces dating from 1680, including what's claimed to be the largest cuckoo clock in the southern hemisphere; admission is $3.

Also worth a look is **German Model Train Land**, in the historic butcher's shop at 47 Main St. It presents a fascinating world of model trains – there are hundreds of replicas – complete with button-faced people and a hand-made miniature working carousel. Admission is $6 per adult or $12 per family.

Hahndorf has several German festivals including **Founders Day**. Held annually on a weekend in January, it features street parades and wine tastings, with the local eateries peddling their wares from tables outside their premises.

Organised Tours

A pleasant way to amble around the town is in the horse-drawn carriage that leaves regularly from in front of the Old Mill Motel at 98 Main St. If that's a little too sedate for you, Original Motorbike Tours (☎ 8212 5588) has Harley rides starting from $10.

Hahndorf Tours (mobile ☎ 018 088 225) does two to four-hour minibus tours of the town costing from $15.

Places to Stay & Eat

Höchstens Convention & Tourist Centre (☎ 8388 7921) has a motel, caravan park and camp sites. It's 1.5 km out of town at 145A Main St. Camp sites start at $10, cabins cost $46 and motel rooms are $79 for singles & doubles.

There are two good motels: the *Old Mill Motel* (☎ 8388 7888) at 98 Main St (from $55/65); and the *Hahndorf Inn Motor Lodge*

(☎ 8388 1000) at 35 Main St (from $60/70). Otherwise there are several B&Bs.

Hahndorf has many good restaurants and several feature German food. They include the *German Arms Hotel* (this place has a wonderful reputation), the *German Cake Shop* and the *Cottage Kitchen*, all on Main St. *Karl's German Coffee House*, at 17 Main St, is recommended by locals for authentic German cuisine.

If you want to purchase home-made German and continental smallgoods, try *Gourmet Foods* at 37 Main St.

The *Beerenberg Strawberry Farm*, at the east end of Main St, allows you to pick your own strawberries between October and May. Their popular Beerenberg-brand preserves are available all year round.

Getting There & Away
You can get to/from Hahndorf by bus from Adelaide, Mt Barker and other local destinations – see the Getting There & Around section at the start of the chapter for details.

Hills Transit (☎ 8339 1191) runs several times daily from the central bus station in Adelaide ($4.10).

NAIRNE (pop 1400)
If you find Hahndorf a little too commercialised, the quiet charm of Nairne will appeal. Only 10 minutes down the South Eastern Freeway and the old Princes Highway from its busy neighbour, Nairne was founded by a Scottish sheep farmer in 1839. It was originally a wheat-growing centre – SA's first flour mill was built nearby on the Woodside road in 1841 – and grew rapidly after the railway arrived in 1883.

As at neighbouring Littlehampton and Mt Barker, the near surrounds of Nairne's historic centre are being gobbled up by brick-and-tile suburbs as city workers build their dream homes on 800 sq metre allotments.

The town information outlet is in the Albert Mill, on Junction St. It's open between 11 am and 5.30 pm from Thursday to Sunday.

There's a weekday bus service connecting Nairne to Adelaide and Murray Bridge – see the Getting There & Around section at the start of the chapter for details.

Things to See & Do
Many stone buildings remain from Nairne's formative years and you can explore them on a **self-guided walk** with the brochure *Nairne – An Historic Walking Tour*. It lists 28 sites including the impressive **District Hotel** (1850), and several cottages from the early 1850s.

The **Albert Mill** was built as a steam-driven flour mill in 1857 and was used for this purpose until 1906. Today it has a craft and antique shop upstairs and a restaurant downstairs. From here it's a short walk to another good antique shop at **Upstairs Downstairs**, on Main Rd.

The summit of **Mt Barker**, about four km from town, offers a superb panorama to the west and down towards Lake Alexandrina. To get there, turn off Main Rd opposite Chapman's smallgoods factory and follow the signs to the communications towers – it's a five-minute walk from there to the lookout. The hill was named after the explorer Captain Collett Barker, who was killed by Aborigines at the mouth of the Murray in 1831.

Callington Continue west along the Murray Bridge road from Nairne and you pass through the tiny township of **Kanmantoo** at 15 km and Callington five km further on. Having been bypassed by commercialism, this quietly decaying little town (established in 1850) has loads of character. If you're an artist or photographer, don't miss it!

Places to Eat
Both pubs in Nairne do counter meals, and for something more stylish there's the *Albert Mill*. It has beautiful atmosphere – all wood and huge beams – and does reasonably priced lunches and dinners from Wednesday to Sunday and public holidays.

On Main Rd, the tiny *Nairne Bakery* has delicious products all baked on the premises. *Elizabeth Nairne's Kitchen*, across the street, does wonderful home-made pies and cakes.

MT BARKER (pop 6200)

The largest town in the Adelaide Hills, and only 25 minutes from Adelaide along the South Eastern Freeway, Mt Barker is the fast-growing commercial centre for this part of the region. It was the first town in the hills, being established in 1839 by the pastoralist Duncan McFarlane.

There's an information outlet in the district council office (☎ 8391 1633) at 23 Mann St, open from 9 am to 5 pm weekdays. See the Getting There & Around section at the start of this chapter for information about bus services to Mt Barker.

Things to See & Do

Mt Barker isn't a tourist town. However, the **Southern Encounter** steam train, which will run to Victor Harbor when its Mt Barker depot is completed, is sure to increase interest on weekends.

The tourist office has three good brochures on self-guided walks and drives in and around town. *Country Walks in the Mt Barker District* details 11 pleasant outings from three to 9.5 km, while *Mt Barker – An Historic Walking Tour* takes you around 37 sites in the town area. *Scenic Drives of the Mt Barker District* guides you as far afield as Callington, Strathalbyn and Clarendon.

The oldest buildings in town are **Dunn's Steam Flour Mill** and the **Miller's Cottage**, both built in 1844. The mill was one of the first in SA, and operated until 1894. It's now a coffee shop, restaurant and B&B.

Places to Stay & Eat

The *Mt Barker Caravan Park* (☎ 8391 0384), at 40 Cameron Rd, has tent/caravan sites for $9/13 and on-site vans from $25 for the first night and $20 for subsequent nights. Cabins are also available.

At the friendly *Hotel Barker* (☎ 8391 1003), at 22 Gawler St, clean rooms with share facilities cost from $30/40 for singles/doubles. The publican's name is Brew – don't bother, he's heard all the jokes!

Otherwise there's B&B for $90 at *The Flour Mill* (☎ 8352 9224), at 14 Cameron Rd. As well as having a coffee shop, the mill

does dinners from Thursday to Sunday. *Millies Bakery*, at 5 Gawler St, and *Giovanni*, a pizza and pasta place at 15 Morphett St, are good for takeaways.

MT BARKER TO STRATHALBYN

If you're in a hurry you can drive straight down to Strathalbyn via **Wistow**, but otherwise it's more interesting to go via **Echunga**, **Meadows** and **Macclesfield**. (There are also buses to these towns – see the Getting There & Around section at the start of this chapter for details.)

At Echunga (population 450) there's the **Jupiter Creek Gold Field**, about five km out of town on the Meadows road. Gold was discovered in 1852 and the field was worked at various times until 1930. To explore the overgrown diggings there are walking trails, interpretive signs and the brochure *Gold at Jupiter Creek*.

Meadows and Macclesfield are both quiet, pretty little places with some interesting heritage buildings. The willows by the **Angas River** at Macclesfield are said to have grown from cuttings brought from Napoleon's grave. There are magnificent views from here to Strathalbyn as the road winds down to the foothills.

Meadows is handy to the 3600-hectare **Kuitpo Forest**, where there are walking tracks, picnic areas and pleasant bush camp sites. For camping permits and a brochure, call in to the forest headquarters (☎ 8388 3267) on the Willunga road. Nearby is *Meadows Lakeside Resort* (☎ (08) 8388 3082), which has bunkhouse beds for $12 and a share kitchen.

All three towns have takeaway outlets and pubs where you can buy meals. Meadows has a great bakery. The old (1841) Tudor-style *Three Brothers Arms* in Macclesfield has a wonderful ambience, and the meals aren't bad either.

STRATHALBYN (pop 2600)

On the Angas River, this picturesque town was established in 1839 by Scottish immigrants. Much of its historic centre has been preserved – Strathalbyn is a classified 'heritage town' – and as a result there are some wonderful old streetscapes and impressive buildings.

The tourist office (☎ 8536 3212) is on South Terrace. It's open from 9.30 am to 4 pm Monday to Friday and 11 am to 4 pm on weekends.

A walking-tour pamphlet ($1.20) lists historic buildings and other sites of interest in the township. The old courthouse and police station are now a National Trust **museum**;

entry costs $2 and it's open from 2 to 5 pm weekends and school and public holidays.

Strathalbyn is well-known for its **antique shops**. Probably the best place if you're on a budget is Isabel Jeans on Rankine St, a good place for bric-a-brac. Jacki's Antiques on Swale St isn't for the budget-minded, but it's worth a visit for its stunning displays of period furniture. You could easily spend a couple of hours browsing in the antique shops and art/craft galleries clustered on

ADELAIDE HILLS

PLACES TO STAY		PLACES TO EAT		OTHER	
1	Studio Gallery	4	Café Ruffino	2	London House Antiques
3	Robin Hood Hotel	6	Commercial Hotel	5	Jacki's Antiques
8	Watervilla House	11	Angas Deli Takeaway	7	Swimming Pool
9	Strathalbyn Council	12	Albyn Riverside	10	Post Office
	Caravan Park	13	Pestka's Bakery	14	Isabel Jeans
12	Victoria Hotel	18	BJ & Sews	16	Hospital
15	Terminus Hotel	21	Gasworks Café	17	National Trust Museum
20	Railway Cottages			19	Tourist Information Office

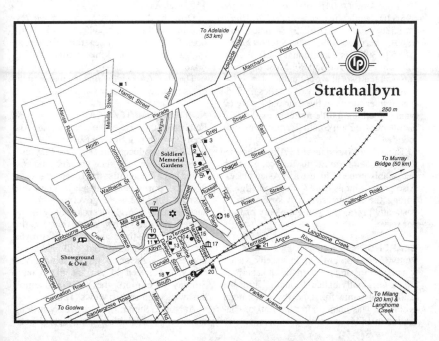

High St; London House is a long-established antique shop here.

Strathalbyn is about 12 minutes drive from the wineries at **Langhorne Creek** (see the chapter on the Fleurieu Peninsula).

Hills Transit (☎ 8339 1191) runs from Adelaide (changing at Mt Barker) to Strathalbyn on weekdays for $6.

Places to Stay & Eat

The modest *Strathalbyn Council Caravan Park* (☎ 8536 3681), in the showgrounds off Coronation Rd, has lawn camp sites for $8 and on-site vans from $20.

The *Terminus Hotel* (☎ 8536 2026) on Rankine St has singles/doubles for $25/45, including a light breakfast. Alternatively, the *Robin Hood Hotel* (☎ 8536 2608) on High St charges $29/45, also with breakfast. The *Victoria Hotel* (☎ 8536 2202), on Albyn Terrace, also has motel units in 1996.

There are several good B&Bs in town. The cosy, self-contained *Railway Cottages* on Parker Ave (☎ 015 601 692) charges $95/110, while historic *Watervilla House* (☎ 8536 4099), off Mill St (it dates from 1849), charges $80/95. The *Studio Gallery* (☎ 8536 3069) is a traditional B&B place in a lovely setting for $50/80. Most days you can watch artists at work there.

Strathalbyn has plenty of eateries, including counter meals at the four pubs – if you want something a little more up-market, the *Gasworks Café* on South Terrace is recommended.

The *Albyn Riverside*, at 18 Albyn Terrace, and *BJ & Sews*, on South Terrace, are both reasonably priced Chinese and Asian places. Also good value is *Café Ruffino*, on High St among the antique shops; it specialises in pasta and pizza, and you get plenty of food per serve.

CLARENDON (pop 300)

Pretty Clarendon grew up in a scenic valley at a major crossing point on the Onkaparinga River. Originally called Toondilla, after the Aboriginal name for a nearby ceremonial ground, it was named after the Earl of Clarendon in 1846.

There are a number of interesting historic buildings, including the **Royal Oak Hotel** (1844). Dominating the town is the **Old Clarendon Winery Complex**, which formed part of the original Clarendon Vineyard Estate, established with vines brought from Spain in the late 1840s. Today it has cellar-door sales and tastings, as well as two craft shops.

There's a weekday bus between Adelaide and Victor Harbor that stops at Clarendon – see the Getting There & Around section at the start of the chapter for details.

Places to Stay & Eat

The *Old Clarendon Winery Complex* (☎ 8383 6166) has a good restaurant with a five-course buffet Sunday lunch for $20. You can also stay there – its comfortable rooms have nice views over the township and cost $65/70/85, including a light breakfast. Alternatively, the *Royal Oak Hotel* (☎ 8383 6113) has counter lunches from $4 and rooms for $50 single/double.

Down by the river, the *Stone Cottage Restaurant* is said to be excellent, but it's only open for lunch and dinner from Wednesday to Sunday. For bookings phone ☎ 8383 6038.

The tiny *Clarendon Bakery* makes delicious pastries, pies, bread and cakes.

NORTON SUMMIT AREA

Perched on the edge of the western scarp, the pretty township of **Norton Summit** (population 250) produced Sir Thomas Playford, SA's longest serving state premier. The post office has a small **museum** (open weekdays 9 am to 2 pm) featuring displays on historic **Marble Hill**, the state governor's former summer residence, about six km away off the Lobethal road. Now classified by the National Trust, the mansion was destroyed in the 1955 bushfire, but still makes an impressive sight on its hilltop setting. You can visit between 11 am and 5 pm on a Sunday to explore the ruins and enjoy bushwalks and superb views ($2).

At Norton Summit you're in easy striking distance of Adelaide's main apple, pear, cherry and salad-vegetable growing area around **Ashton**, **Summertown** and **Basket Range**. There are also several vineyards and wineries.

Places to Stay & Eat

The *Scenic Hotel* in the centre of Norton Summit has a cosy restaurant. In warm weather it's nice to eat on the back verandah and enjoy the views over Adelaide.

For something different there's the 17-hectare *Fuzzies Farm* (☎ 8390 1111) on Colonial Drive about a km from Norton Summit. Set in a scenic valley next to Morialta Conservation Park, this friendly 'eco-village' offers a unique hands-on experience in sharing a cooperative lifestyle. Guests are encouraged to help in activities such as building construction, furniture making, crafts, tending the chooks and shearing the flock of angora goats.

A one-night introduction to Fuzzies costs $20 with dinner or $15 without – the self-contained cottage accommodation is truly superb – and there are special rates for long stays. There's also a package of around $90 for two days and two nights including all meals (meat and vegetarian), accommodation and guided walks of Marble Hill and Morialta Falls. Bookings are essential.

At Summertown, the *Pink Geranium Restaurant* on Greenhill Rd is highly recommended. It's open for lunch on weekends and dinner from Wednesday to Sunday.

There are a number of 'pick your own' farms and roadside stalls selling fruit and salad vegetables in the main agricultural area.

LOBETHAL AREA

Lobethal (pop 1500)

Established by Lutheran settlers in 1842, attractive **Lobethal** has many interesting old buildings including German-style cottages and houses from the 1840s. These are described in the brochure *Lobethal – Valley of Praise*, available from the town's information centre at 2 Woodside Rd.

Lobethal's more modern attractions include **Bushland Park**, a 60-hectare

council reserve with a picnic area, two reservoirs, nice views and bushwalks about 600 metres out on the Gumeracha road. The kids will love **Fairyland Village**, which features life-size German fairy tales, tame deer and native animals.

Hills Transit buses run to Lobethal, Woodside and Oakbank – see the Getting There & Around section at the start of the chapter for details.

Woodside (pop 1000)

Here you find the excellent **Melba's Chocolate Factory**, where chocoholics can watch their favourite sweet being prepared in a converted cheese factory. There's a large variety of confectionery for sale, most of which is made on the premises. As well, various craftspersons including a leatherworker and wood-turner have their workshops and sales areas on the premises.

Almost next door, the **Woodside Horse & Trail Riding Centre** (☎ 8389 7794) has escorted rides from one hour ($15) to full day ($55); half and full day rides include a barbecue lunch and drinks. To find the entrance, look for the big white horse out on the main road.

Oakbank (pop 340)

Each year at Easter, this small village is swamped by visitors who've come to enjoy the hugely popular **Oakbank Easter Racing Carnival**. It's said to be the greatest picnic race meeting in the world, and if dust and crowds have appeal, you'll love it.

Oakbank has several good craft shops including the **Oakbank Weaver** in the old Dorset Brewery, at 9 Elizabeth St. You can visit this and 39 other historic sites with the brochure *Oakbank Heritage Walk*.

BIRDWOOD AREA

Birdwood (pop 580)

Originally called Blumberg (meaning 'the hill of flowers'), this pretty town was established by German settlers in 1848. During WWI it was renamed after the commander of the Australian forces, Field Marshall Lord Birdwood.

In the 1850s Birdwood was a busy gold-mining and agricultural centre, and its old flour mill (1852) is an impressive reminder of those times. The town has a number of buildings classified by the National Trust, including several German-style cottages. These days the mill houses the **National Motor Museum**, which contains Australia's largest collection of vintage and classic cars and motorbikes. It's open daily from 9 am to 5 pm and admission is $8.

Birdwood Cottage next door to the Birdwood Mill is a long-established craft shop with beautiful pottery and ceramics.

Each year in March, Birdwood hosts the fascinating **Medieval Festival**, a celebration of Middle Ages culture with a full weekend of feasting, jousting, games, music, plays, dancing, crafts and many other activities. The **Rock 'n' Roll Rendezvous**, every November, is a good one for ageing rockers, and features cars of the era.

Between Birdwood and Williamstown, the 12,000 hectare **Mt Crawford Forest** has native forests and plantations of eucalypts and *Pinus radiata*. Here you'll find several picnic areas and bush camp sites, and plenty of opportunity for bushwalks – the Heysen Trail passes through the forest.

You can get camping permits and a brochure from the forest headquarters (☎ 8524 6004 or 018 807 824), 13 km from Birdwood on the Williamstown road.

ABM Coachlines (☎ 8347 3336) runs from Adelaide to Birdwood on weekdays for $7.30.

Places to Stay & Eat

At Gumeracha, the *Gumeracha Hotel* (☎ 8389 1001) has rooms for $25/40/60 including a light breakfast. The pub also serves meals.

There are several B&B places in Birdwood including *Birdwood B&B Cottages* (☎ 8568 5444), at 38 Olivedale Rd, which charges from $50/65 on weekdays and $60/75 on weekends.

You can get delicious Devonshire teas and light lunches at the *Birdwood Mill Tearooms*, and there are takeaways across the road. The

nearby *Blumberg Tavern* does lunches and dinners seven days.

At Mt Pleasant, 10 km beyond Birdwood towards Springton, there's the basic *Talunga Caravan Park* (☎ 8569 3048), which has tent and caravan sites. Alternatively, the friendly *Talunga Hotel/Motel* (☎ 8568 2015) has motel-style units for $45/60/70 including a light breakfast. You can get meals here and at the *Totness Inn Hotel*.

Gumeracha (pop 400)

From Adelaide you can drive up through the scenic **Torrens River Gorge** to Gumeracha, seven km from Birdwood, where you find **Gumeracha Cellars** – a good winery with tastings. There's also **The Toy Factory** with its giant rocking horse. The horse doesn't rock (fortunately) but if you want to buy wooden toys this is a good spot to do so.

EDEN VALLEY

This scenic area, which lies between the Adelaide Hills and the Barossa Valley, is noted for its massive gum trees and high-altitude riesling wines. Coming from Adelaide, the valley starts between Mt Pleasant and Springton and includes the attractive hamlets of Springton, Eden Valley and Kyneton.

Johann Menge named it the Rhine Valley in 1838 because he recognised its potential for producing fine wines. He knew what he was talking about, as you'll discover when you visit the cellars of well-known wineries such as **Grand Cru** (near Springton), **Mountadam** (near Eden Valley) and **Henschke** (near Kyneton).

Springton (pop 240)

The main attraction in this lovely old place is the **Herbig Tree**, a gnarled river red gum on the Mt Pleasant side of town. Friedrich and Caroline Herbig used its hollow trunk as a temporary home for two years in the late 1850s before moving to their new pug-and-pine cottage. The first two of their 16 children were born here.

It's definitely worth stopping to browse in the **Springton Gallery**, which has a range of quality crafts. This is the place to get tourist information on the area, but it's only open from Wednesday to Sunday between 11 am and 5 pm.

About three km before Springton you pass the **Merindah Mohair Farm**, where you can buy knitted and woven wool products.

The *Springton Gallery Loft* (☎ 8568 2001) is one of several B&B places in the valley – it's cheaper than most at $80 for two people, including full breakfast provisions. Next door in the Craneford Cellars, *Cafe C* has an interesting menu with light lunches from $12 and main courses from $15; it's open for lunch on weekdays and dinner on weekends.

Other places serving meals in the valley include the old pubs in Springton and Eden Valley, and the *Eden Valley Winery & Restaurant* in Eden Valley.

The basic *Eden Valley Caravan Park* (☎ 8564 1102), 500 metres from Eden Valley on the Springton road, has tent and caravan sites.

Fleurieu Peninsula

The rolling Fleurieu Peninsula, south of Adelaide, is bounded by the Adelaide Hills to the north, Lake Alexandrina to the east and, to the west and south, the coastline from Hallett Cove (on Gulf St Vincent) around to the mouth of the Murray River. The peninsula has many attractions and, because most of it is within an hour's drive of Adelaide, it's popular with day-trippers.

Much of the coastline is extremely beautiful. In the south are booming surf and rugged cliffs, while Gulf St Vincent has quieter beaches. There are several coastal resort towns, all of which tend to overflow during the summer school holidays. A few small conservation parks provide some good opportunities for camping and bushwalking, with the Heysen Trail meandering through en route to the Adelaide Hills. On a more relaxed note, you can explore historic villages such as Old Noarlunga, Yankalilla and Willunga or taste fine wines around McLaren Vale and Langhorne Creek.

History

The peninsula was named in 1802 by the French explorer Nicholas Baudin after Napoleon's minister for the navy. He met up with Matthew Flinders at Encounter Bay where, 35 years later, two whaling stations were established.

The Foundation Inn was built at Encounter Bay in 1838 and quickly became a rendezvous for desperadoes, such as the escaped convicts from Tasmania who lived in the rugged central ranges. Within seven or eight years settlements had sprung up all the way along the Adelaide road.

By then the Aborigines were already in serious decline. Today, just about all that remains of their culture apart from canoe trees and museum exhibits are musical place-names such as Yankalilla, Noarlunga, Carrickalinga, Tunkalilla and Willunga.

Agricultural development of the penin-

HIGHLIGHTS

- Chance the booming breakers at one of the region's popular southern surfing spots
- Enjoy superb views from Mt Magnificent, on the Heysen Trail
- Go whale-watching on The Bluff near Victor Harbour
- Escape the heat of summer at any of the Peninsula's picturesque coastal resorts
- Spend a day or three sampling the fine wines produced by the region's 50 or more wineries

sula was rapid. Goolwa was a busy river port by the 1850s, when other ports were springing up around the coast. Big flour mills were built at places like Yilki (on Encounter Bay), Second Valley and Normanville, although these were soon suffering as soils became exhausted through overcropping. Grand summer retreats started appearing at Port Elliot and Victor Harbor from the 1850s.

Information

There is no single tourist office for the Fleurieu Peninsula, although a major interpretive centre and information office is scheduled to open on Main Rd in McLaren Vale in late 1996 or early 1997.

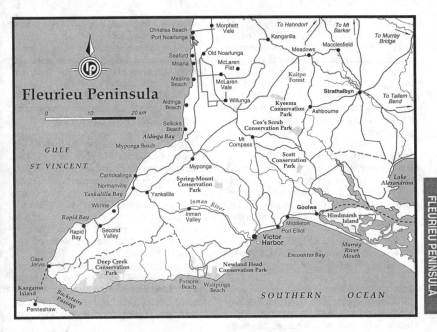

There are well-stocked information outlets staffed by volunteers in McLaren Vale, Victor Harbor and Goolwa.

Communications Throughout this book we use the new statewide STD code (08) and eight-digit phone numbers. For those places on the Fleurieu Peninsula with 085 area codes, the new numbers will take effect in February 1997. Should you need to use the old number, simply take the first two digits (85) and use as the area code (085).

National Parks For information on conservation areas in the southern half contact the National Parks & Wildlife Service office (☎ 8552 3677 at 57 Ocean St in Victor Harbor. Parks in the north are administered from the Belair National Park (☎ 8278 5477).

Maps The Royal Automobile Association's *Central* road map provides good coverage of the area. Also worth getting is the Department of Recreation & Sports's cycle-touring map.

Organised Tours
Several operators offer day and two-day tours from Adelaide; the South Australian Tourism Commission will have details. As a sample, Adelaide Sightseeing (☎ 8231 4144), Festival Tours (☎ 8374 1270) and Wildlife Experience (☎ 018 803 565) all do day trips for around $40. Premier Roadlines (☎ 8415 5555) has two-day tours to McLaren Vale for $69 and Victor Harbor for $99 – both prices are twin share.

Gecko Tours (☎ (08) 8339 3800) has an excellent day tour ($75) which takes you on a discovery of the region's Aboriginal heritage. You visit an 8400-year-old camp site, canoe trees, cave paintings and coastal middens, and learn about the local people's Dreamtime ancestors.

For scenic flights try the South Coast Air

Centre (☎ 8556 5404) at Aldinga or Air Goolwa (☎ 8555 4075) at Goolwa. You can expect to pay around $45 per seat (minimum two passengers) for a half-hour flight.

There aren't many local tour operators, but you can do camel and Harley rides at McLaren Vale, short and extended horse rides at Normanville, sunset penguin walks at Victor Harbor, and boat cruises at Goolwa (see the sections on these towns for details).

Getting There & Around

Bus Premier Roadlines (☎ (08) 8415 5555) has up to three return services daily on its two-hour run from Adelaide through McLaren Vale ($4.70), Willunga ($5), Port Elliot ($11), Goolwa ($11) and Victor Harbor ($11).

Coachlines of Australia (☎ (08) 8332 2644) runs once daily from Adelaide through Yankalilla ($8.90) to Cape Jervis ($13).

Train The depot for the *Southern Encounter* steam train is being relocated from Adelaide to Mt Barker, and the service to Victor Harbor will then recommence, hopefully. For an update contact the Victor Harbor tourist office or SteamRanger (☎ (08) 8231 1707).

The little Cockle Train runs between Victor Harbor and Goolwa (see the Victor Harbor section for details).

Ferry Vehicle and passenger ferries provide a daily service between Cape Jervis and Penneshaw, on Kangaroo Island (see the chapter on Kangaroo Island for details).

Southern Vales

Apart from beaches and coastal resorts, the Fleurieu Peninsula is best known for its Southern Vales wineries. The first winery in the region was established in 1838 by John Reynell at **Reynella**, just 21 km down Main South Rd from Adelaide. The industry went through boom and bust cycles until the 1920s, when the export market collapsed.

Following a renaissance in the 1960s it now seems on a secure footing.

Most of the peninsula's 50 or so wineries are concentrated around **McLaren Vale** and nearby **McLaren Flat**. While the Southern Vales district is particularly well suited to red wines – cabernet sauvignon is the foremost variety – a trend towards white wine consumption in the 1970s prompted growers to diversify.

Adelaide has sprawled so far that the old villages of Reynella, Morphett Vale and Old Noarlunga are now basically outer suburbs. However, their historic precincts are largely intact and include numerous interesting buildings. **Morphett Vale** has St Mary's (1846), the first Roman Catholic church in the state. Some wineries still survive near Reynella, including **Hardys**, one of the largest in the district.

For the history buff, Heritage Research & Walks (☎ (08) 8384 7918) of Port Noarlunga does **guided walks** in the Southern Vales at various places such as Reynella and Old Noarlunga. These take up to two hours and cost $9.

The 1587-hectare **Onkaparinga River Recreation Park** extends down the river from near Clarendon to the sea. There are good walks through the gorge (you need to be fit), and you can canoe all year round between Old Noarlunga and the sea – the return paddle is a leisurely day outing.

The **Lakeside Leisure Park**, on Main South Rd just north of Old Noarlunga, has a variety of activities for the kids, including a water slide, toboggan track and minigolf course.

McLAREN VALE (pop 1470)

Only 37 km from Adelaide and just off busy Main South Rd, this picturesque town is the district's tourist centre. Most of its wineries are within five minutes drive of town.

Until the new facility on Main Road opens in late '96 or early '97, the main information outlet for the district is at the coffee shop in the magnificent Hardy's Tintara winery complex, in the centre of McLaren Vale. It's open daily from 10 am to 4 pm.

Wineries

Most local wineries are open for tastings seven days a week. Each has its own appeal, and it's not always the house product – it may be a superb setting or a particularly interesting cellar. The following are suggestions.

Chapel Hill, Chapel Hill Rd, McLaren Vale south, has a magnificent hill-top location with views over Gulf St Vincent. This is a small vineyard producing sophisticated whites and reds.

d'Arenberg, Osborne Rd, McLaren Vale, has produced consistently good wines since 1928.

Kay Brothers, Kay Rd, McLaren Vale, has a beautiful rural view overlooking its vineyard.

Maxwell, Kangarilla Rd, McLaren Vale, is the only place in SA to specialise in mead, a great drop made from fermented honey. They do good table wines too!

Noon's, Rifle Range Rd, McLaren Vale, specialises in full-bodied reds. This winery is in a pleasant rural setting beside a small creek, and has barbecue facilities.

Seaview, Chaffeys Rd, McLaren Vale, is a large and historic winery with a great atmosphere. It's worth visiting just to see the wonderful old Vat Gallery.

Woodstock, Douglas Gully Rd, McLaren Flat, is a small, friendly winery in a tranquil garden setting. It's well known for its tawny port and botrytis sweet wines.

There's a walking/bicycle track along the old railway line from McLaren Vale to **Willunga**, six km to the south. A number of wineries are within easy walking distance of the town centre.

Festivals

Best known is the **Wine Bushing Festival**, which takes place annually over a week in late October and/or early November. It's a busy time of wine tastings and tours, and the whole thing is topped by a grand feast. You can get around on a free bus service, which wanders from winery to winery picking up and dropping off imbibers.

From the Sea and the Vines is a celebration of wine and seafood over a May weekend, while the **Continuous Picnic** takes place on the first weekend in October – the Labour Day long weekend.

Organised Tours

A great way to visit a few wineries is on a camel with the Outback Camel Co (☎ 8543 2280). Various tours are available, including a one-day trek for $80. Alternatively, you can see the area from a motorbike with SA Harley Tours (☎ (08) 8378 1415); a half-hour jaunt costs $30 and a half-day tour $120.

Places to Stay

The friendly *McLaren Vale Lakeside Caravan Park* (☎ 8323 9255), set amidst vineyards on Field St, has camp sites ($12), on-site vans (from $31) and luxury cabins ($47).

Another nice place is the *Southern Vales B&B* (☎ 8323 8144), on Chalk Hill Rd. It has a colonial authors' theme and charges $75 for doubles. The rustic *Wirilda Creek Winery* (☎ 8323 9688), on McMurtrie Rd, offers B&B from $70 for doubles, and attractive packages for weekends and longer stays.

Alternatively, the up-market and very pleasant *McLarens on the Lake* (☎ 8323 8911) on Kangarilla Rd has singles/doubles/triples for $75/90/105 – it's right beside Andrew Garret Wines. In town, the *McLaren Vale Motel* (☎ 8323 8265), off Main Rd at the Adelaide end of town, has units from $62/72/82.

Places to Eat

There are several excellent restaurants in McLaren Vale. *Magnum's* in the *Hotel McLaren* is recommended for superb cuisine, as is *The Barn* bistro. Both are on Main Rd. Perhaps best of all is the historic *Salopian Inn*, just out of town on the Willunga Rd; it has a fascinating menu – imagine seared soy-basted squid, or roasted Tilbaroo calves' kidneys – but it's fairly expensive (main courses start at $16). You'll need to book (☎ 8323 8769) as it's small and popular.

The wine-tasters' lunches can be good value. *Brook's Restaurant* in the Middlebrook Winery on Sand Rd is open daily, with main courses from $11 (this place has a magnificent craft shop). *Haselgrove Wines*, on the corner of Kangarilla and Foggo Rds, has similar prices and is open from Wednesday to Sunday. You can get a decent 'picker's platter' for $10 at the *Wirilda Creek Winery*, on McMurtrie Rd.

Fortunately for those on a strict budget there are several inexpensive eateries and takeaways in town, including a good bakery. *Yum Wong* on Main Rd does very filling, three-course takeaway packs for two people for $14.

WILLUNGA (pop 1200)

First established as a staging post on the Encounter Bay road, Willunga really took off in 1840 when the mining of high-quality slate commenced nearby. The slate was carted to Port Willunga and exported all around Australia. Today, this quiet, pretty little town is the centre of almond growing in SA and hosts the **Almond Blossom Festival** in July.

The fact that there hasn't been much development in Willunga since its boom years has preserved numerous heritage buildings dating from the 1850s. You can visit them with the booklet *Willunga Walks* ($2), which is widely available around town.

On High St, the old Court House and Police Station (1855) is now a small **National Trust museum**. It's open on weekends and public holidays from 1 to 5 pm.

Willunga is central to the **Kuitpo Forest** (see the section on Meadows in the Adelaide Hills chapter) to the north-east and small conservation parks to the south-east.

These include the 90-hectare **Mt Magnificent Conservation Park**, 13 km from Willunga. An access point for the Heysen Trail, it has outstanding views from the summit of Mt Magnificent – a dirt road goes right past it – as well as beautiful forest and plenty of wildlife. From here it's about an hour's walk down to the 103-hectare **Finniss River Conservation Park**.

On Main South Rd nine km south of Willunga, tiny **Mt Compass** is best known for the annual Compass Cup, a fun day of cow racing and other activities in February. About eight km away on Cleland Gully Rd

is the **Tooperang Trout Farm**, where even the most incompetent angler should be able to catch a fish. If you've never tried smoked trout this is the place to start. It's open between 10 am and 4 pm from Wednesday to Sunday.

Places to Stay

The *Willunga Hotel* (☎ 8556 2135) on High St has rooms from $20/25 for singles/ doubles.

There are a couple of good B&Bs in town. For heritage accommodation there's the stunning *Willunga House* (☎ 8556 2467), on St Peters Terrace behind the council chambers. Singles/doubles cost $90/100. Out of town off St Johns Terrace, *Almond Views* (☎ 8556 2625) has a self-contained guest wing with B&B at much the same price.

About three km south-east of Mt Compass, *Compass Country Cabins* (☎ 8556 8425) has comfortable, fully self-contained units for $65 (they sleep two to four people). The cabins are in a rural setting on Cleland Gully Rd, 1.5 km east of Main South Rd.

Places to Eat

Willunga has several restaurants, cafes and other eateries, and you'll generally find the prices more attractive than at McLaren Vale.

The town's three pubs all do meals. Probably the best in terms of atmosphere and value is the *Willunga Hotel*, which has daily counter meals for $5 and main courses in the dining room for $9.

Friendly *Mt Magnificent Farm*, about a km south of Mt Magnificent summit, serves light lunches and Devonshire teas from Thursday to Sunday and public holidays.

Gulf St Vincent Coast

Popular swimming beaches line the coast from Adelaide to Sellicks Beach, 50 km from the city, with conditions generally quiet unless there's a strong westerly blowing. Past here the coast is rocky virtually all the way to Cape Jervis, although there's a good stretch of sand at Carrickalinga and Norman-ville. The suburbs have gobbled up all the old coastal resorts as far as Maslins Beach.

NORTHERN BEACHES

The first swimming beach on Gulf St Vincent south of Adelaide is **O'Sullivans Beach**, about 35 minutes drive from the city centre. From here a string of sandy beaches stretches south for 13 km past the outer suburbs of **Christies Beach**, **Seaford** and **Moana** to **Maslins Beach South**, where you can legally go skinny dipping. For further details on these places see Adelaide Beaches in the Adelaide chapter.

Outposts of suburbia have developed south of Maslins Beach around the old coastal resorts of **Port Willunga** and **Aldinga Beach**. Both have potential for skin-diving. A lovely white ribbon of sand stretches for the entire six km from Aldinga Beach to **Sellicks Beach**, a popular sailboarding spot 50 km from Adelaide.

Places to Stay

Between Christies Beach and Maslins Beach are the *Christies Beach Tourist Park* (☎ 8326 0311) at Sydney Crescent, the *Moana Beach Tourist Park* (☎ 8327 0677) at 44 Nashwauk Crescent, and the *Maslins Beach Caravan & Camping Ground* (☎ 8556 6113) at 2 Tuart Rd. All are close to the beach and have tent and caravan sites and air-conditioned cabins.

South of Maslins Beach you can stay at the *Port Willunga Caravan Park* (☎ 8556 5430), the *Aldinga Bay Holiday Village* (☎ 8556 5019), and the *Aldinga Caravan & Holiday Park* (☎ 8556 3444).

Getting There & Around

There are suburban trains daily from Adelaide to Noarlunga centre . At the station you can catch TransAdelaide buses as far as Maslins Beach.

SOUTHERN TOWNS

Past Sellicks Beach the road leaves the coast and passes through some beautiful rural scenery to Yankalilla. It touches the sea again

at nearby Normanville, then it's back into scenic hill country to Cape Jervis. From here you can look across the narrow Backstairs Passage to Kangaroo Island, 13 km away.

Yankalilla (pop 550)

This pretty valley town is at the junction of the Cape Jervis road and the 32-km scenic drive via the town of **Inman Valley** to Victor Harbor. If you're heading to Victor Harbor and you're interested in geology, check out the 250-million-year-old gouge marks left by a glacier at **Glacier Rock**, 19 km from Yankallila. The site is in the creek behind the restaurant.

At 48 Main St, the **old schoolhouse** is reputed to have been the first established by the Sisters of St Joseph, the teaching order founded by Mary MacKillop. It's not open to the public, but you can ask about it at the Swiss Cheesecake Shop at No 72.

The **historical museum** on the Normanville road is open from 1 to 4 pm Sunday and more frequently during school holidays. The *Yankalilla Hotel* (☎ 8558 2011) has a cottage sleeping six for a flat rate of $50, linen supplied. The pub is recommended by locals as having the best and cheapest meals of any pub in the area, while the nearby *Yankalilla Bakery* and *Swiss Cheesecake Shop* both sell mouth-watering goodies.

At picturesque Inman Valley, 13 km from Yankalilla, there's a *YHA hostel* (☎ 8558 8277) where beds are $9 for YHA members and $11 for nonmembers. This is an access point for the Heysen Trail; maps are available from the hostel manager.

Normanville & Carrickalinga

Just past Yankalilla, these twin coastal resorts are only three km apart and have the only decent stretch of sand between Sellicks Beach and Cape Jervis. They're both good swimming beaches.

High Country Trails (☎ 8558 2507) at Normanville has a range of short and extended **trail rides**. These cost from $18 for an hour to $100 per day (all-inclusive) for two to four-day packhorse expeditions in the

FLEURIEU PENINSULA

hills. Longer rides are only available between April and October.

The **Wirrina Cove Paradise Resort** (☎ 8598 4001), 12 km south of Normanville, has a range of guided activities at reasonable prices including open sea kayaking ($40 for three hours), horse riding ($75 full day), scuba diving ($80 for three hours) and abseiling.

Places to Stay & Eat The pleasant *Norman-ville Beach Caravan Park* (☎ 8558 2038) is right on the beachfront and has tent/caravan sites for $12/14, on-site vans for $35 and self-contained cabins for $50. About two km down the road towards Cape Jervis, the *Beachside Caravan Park* (☎ 8558 2458) has similar prices – their cabins have excellent shade, but the camp sites are exposed.

A little beyond Normanville, The *Wirrina Cove Paradise Resort* (☎ 8598 4001) has a caravan park with tent/caravan sites for $12/14 and self-contained cabins sleeping four for $75. Its resort rooms cost from $160. The well-shaded and friendly *Second Valley Caravan Park* (☎ 8598 4054) is by the sea 16 km from Normanville and 21 km from Cape Jervis. It has tent/caravan sites for $11/13, on-site vans from $25 and cabins with share facilities from $35. Out on the main road, *Leonards Mill* (☎ 8598 4184) has more up-market accommodation.

There are several places to eat, including the *Normanville Hotel* and the *kiosk* down by the jetty – its fish & chips are said to be quite reasonable. *Min Palace*, the town's only restaurant, has good-value Chinese and Thai meals.

Cape Jervis (pop 100)

At the end of the road and 107 km from Adelaide, this small fishing and holiday centre has the terminal for ferry services to Kangaroo Island. It's also the starting point for the Heysen Trail.

From Cape Jervis you can visit the 4180-hectare **Deep Creek Conservation Park** for spectacular coastal views, good fishing, bush camping and some testing bushwalks.

Contact the ranger's office (☎ 8598 0263) near Delamere for information.

A short detour from the Adelaide road leads you to the 210-hectare **Talisker Conservation Park**. It has attractive bush, views to Kangaroo Island and the interesting remains of an historic (1862) silver-lead mine.

Cape Jervis Charter Services (☎ 8598 0222) takes parties of up to six people for snapper and whiting fishing. They also do dive charters.

Places to Stay On the main road about two km from Cape Jervis, the friendly *Old Cape Jervis Station Homestead* (☎ 8598 0233) has a range of accommodation starting at $12. This gets you a bed in the historic shearers' quarters, with use of the kitchen.

Alternatively, the *Cape Jervis Tavern* (☎ 8598 0276) has rooms for $45/55 and serves reasonable counter meals from $6.50. You can buy light meals next door at the general store.

Deep Creek Conservation Park has five basic but attractive bush camping areas ($2 per site plus $2 per person) and several self-contained cottages. Ring ☎ 8598 4169 for cottage information and bookings.

Surf Coast

Some of SA's most popular resort towns and surfing beaches are on the peninsula's south coast. Port Elliot has the most powerful waves, with swells often holding at three metres; other good breaks for experienced riders are at Waitpinga Beach and Parsons Beach west of Victor Harbor. The best months for surfing are March to June inclusive, when northerly winds prevail.

VICTOR HARBOR (pop 5900)

The main town on the peninsula, and 84 km south of Adelaide, Victor Harbor has so many retired residents that irreverent types refer to it as 'God's Waiting Room'. It looks out onto Encounter Bay where Flinders and

Baudin had their historic meeting in 1802. There's a memorial to the event up on the steep headland known as **The Bluff**, about four km south of town.

Victor Harbor was founded as a whaling centre, and you'll find interesting reminders of those days at **Rosetta Bay**, below The Bluff. The first whaling station was established in 1837 with another following soon after on **Granite Island**. Unrestrained slaughter of southern right whales, on which the industry was based, eventually made operations unfeasible, and they ceased in 1864.

Information
The tourist office (☎ 8552 5738) is at 10 Railway Terrace, diagonally opposite the railway station. It's open daily from 10 am to 4 pm. Big Surf Australia (☎ 8552 5466) at 15 Albert Place will be happy to give you advice on local surfing conditions and locations.

Things to See & Do
Victor Harbor has a number of historic buildings, including **St Augustine's Church of England** (1869) on Burke St, the **Telegraph Station** (1869) on Coral St and the **Fountain Inn** (1838) at Yilki, on the way to The Bluff. The **Old Station Master's Residence** (1866) on Flinders Pde is a National Trust museum, open Sunday and public and school holidays from 11 am to 4 pm. The leaflet *A Historic Walk Around Old Port Victor* takes you on a self-guided walk to several heritage sites.

The Telegraph Station houses a very nice **art gallery** where you can often see exhibitions of the works of well-known Australian artists.

Victor Harbor is protected from the angry Southern Ocean by **Granite Island**, now in the process of being developed (many would say ruined!) as a major tourist drawcard. The 26-hectare island is connected to the mainland by a causeway and you can ride out there on a double-decker tram pulled by Clydesdale draught horses for $3 return.

From the top of the hill there are good views across the bay; it's an easy climb, but if you're feeling lazy you can take the chair lift.

The NPWS operates **Little Penguin Sunset Walks** nightly on Granite Island during school holidays and on Wednesday, Friday and Saturday at other times; phone ☎ 8552 3677 for starting times and bookings. Walks cost $5 and commence at the end of the causeway on Granite Island.

Between June and October you might be lucky enough to see a southern right whale swimming near the causeway. Victor Harbor is on the migratory path of these splendid animals and you can observe them from several lookout points around the bay – The Bluff is a good one.

If you want to learn more about whales, the **South Australian Whale Centre**, at the causeway end of Railway Terrace, is the place to go. It has interesting displays, a theatrette, and a 'whale information network' (for more details see Watching Marine Mammals in the Outdoor Activities chapter). The centre is open daily (times vary depending on demand) and entry costs $5.

Another good spot to see native Australian fauna is the 16-hectare **Urimbirra Wildlife Park**, on the Adelaide road five km from town. It doesn't look much from the road, but first impressions are very misleading – you could easily spend a couple of hours here. The park is open daily from 10 am to 5 pm and entry costs $5.

Greenhills Adventure Park on Waggon Rd is an ideal spot to lose the kids for a day. It's also good for adults, with such activities as canoeing on the Hindmarsh River.

Waitpinga Beach and **Parsons Beach** are in the 1036-hectare **Newland Head Conservation Park**, about 12 km west of town. Both are popular surfing spots, but strong, changeable currents make them suitable only for experienced surfers. They're also good for **surf fishing**, with salmon, mullet, mulloway, tailor and flathead the common catches. The park is on the Heysen Trail.

The **Victor Theatre**, on Ocean St in Victor Harbor, screens daily during school holidays and four or five days a week at other times.

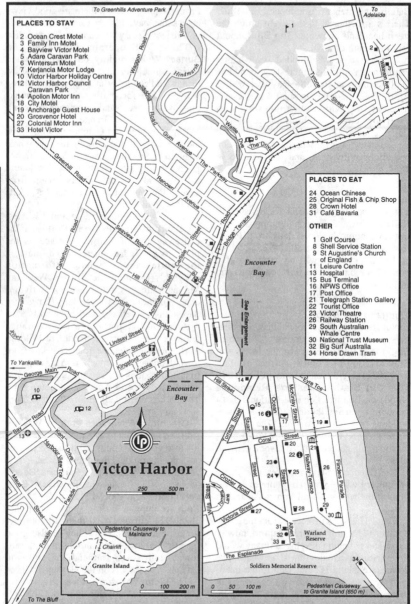

FLEURIEU PENINSULA

PLACES TO STAY

2 Ocean Crest Motel
3 Family Inn Motel
4 Bayview Victor Motel
5 Adare Caravan Park
6 Wintersun Motel
7 Kerjancia Motor Lodge
10 Victor Harbor Holiday Centre
12 Victor Harbor Council
   Caravan Park
14 Apollon Motor Inn
18 City Motel
19 Anchorage Guest House
20 Grosvenor Hotel
27 Colonial Motor Inn
33 Hotel Victor

PLACES TO EAT

24 Ocean Chinese
25 Original Fish & Chip Shop
28 Crown Hotel
31 Café Bavaria

OTHER

1 Golf Course
8 Shell Service Station
9 St Augustine's Church
   of England
11 Leisure Centre
13 Hospital
15 Bus Terminal
16 NPWS Office
17 Post Office
21 Telegraph Station Gallery
22 Tourist Office
23 Victor Theatre
26 Railway Station
29 South Australian
   Whale Centre
30 National Trust Museum
32 Big Surf Australia
34 Horse Drawn Tram

Victor Harbor

0   250   500 m

Encounter Bay

Granite Island

Pedestrian Causeway to Mainland

Chairlift

0   100   200 m

To The Bluff

Warland Reserve

Soldiers Memorial Reserve

Pedestrian Causeway to Granite Island (650 m)

0   50   100 m

Fishing & Dive Charters Victor Harbor Boat Charters (mobile ☎ 0414 52 7474 and 0414 52 7474) offer fishing charters from $55 for a half-day and $90 for a full-day trip, including tackle and bait. They also do dive charters for $25 per dive.

One of Victor Harbor's major attractions for divers is its diversity of marine life including sea lions (in winter), dolphins and an endemic species of leafy sea dragon.

Places to Stay

There are a number of caravan parks, hotels, motels, holiday flats and B&Bs in and around Victor Harbor; you can get details from the tourist office.

Camping Grounds & Caravan Parks

There's an attractive bush camping ground near Waitpinga Beach in *Newland Head Conservation Park*. Sites cost $2 plus $1.50 per adult and you can get your permit from the NPWS office on Ocean St.

I had nothing but good reports on the friendly *Victor Harbor Council Caravan Park* (☎ 8552 1142), on the foreshore at 114 Victoria St. It has tent/caravan sites from $10/12, basic cabins for $35, self-contained cabins for $45 and villas for $55.

Other caravan parks in town are the small *Adare Caravan Park* (☎ 8552 1657) on Wattle Drive and the *Victor Harbor Holiday Centre* (☎ 8552 1949) on Bay Rd.

Hostels The *Warringa Hostel* (☎ 8552 5970) is part of the Anchorage Guest House complex, at 21 Flinders Parade near the railway station. Beds in very basic dorms are $10 for YHA members and $15 for nonmembers, while guesthouse rooms start from $35/60.

There's a *YHA hostel* at Inman Valley, 19 km from town towards Yankalilla (see the Yankalilla section earlier in this chapter).

Hotels, Motels & Flats The *Grosvenor Hotel* (☎ 8552 1011) in the town centre on Ocean St has basic rooms for $25/35/40/45. For something more luxurious, try the tastefully renovated *Hotel Victor* (☎ 8552 1288)

on The Esplanade, where self-contained rooms cost from $65/75/85.

Most central of the town's 11 motels is the *City Motel* (☎ 8552 2455), next to the post office at 51 Ocean St. It has singles/doubles from $45/55 off-peak and $50/60 in peak periods, with $10 for extra adults.

Also close, but charging around $60/70 off-peak, are the *Apollon Motor Inn* (☎ 8552 2777) at 15 Torrens St and the *Colonial Motor Inn* (☎ 8552 1822) at 2 Victoria St. The Colonial has units with a kitchenette for $66/74.

For holiday flats and houses contact the local real estate agents: LJ Hooker (☎ 8552 1944); The Professionals (☎ 8552 2733); Weeks & Macklin/Holms (☎ 8552 2677); and Weston Properties (☎ 8552 3744).

Places to Eat

There are plenty of takeaways, cafes and restaurants in Victor Harbor, but not too many are noted for excellence. If you're buying a takeaway meal and it's a sunny day, eat it among the large Norfolk Island pines on the grassy foreshore.

The *Original Fish & Chip Shop* in the town centre on Ocean St is popular, but the best of all the local seafood takeaways is *Pa's Place*, on Franklin Pde next to the Yilki Store. Both have sit-down meals.

Current champion of the pubs for value meals is the *Grosvenor*, where you can get a decent feed for $5; for more formal dining the *Hotel Victor* is best. The *Crown Hotel* has a bistro and counter meals. Locals recommend *Ocean Chinese*, on Ocean St, for good-value Chinese cuisine. It's open from 1 pm daily except Wednesday.

For a different eating experience, *Klaus's Wurst Haus*, run by the ebullient Klaus himself, claims to sell the best German hot dogs in Australia. You'll find his tiny van on weekends only in the small park at the causeway end of Railway Terrace. Across at the *Café Bavaria*, at 11 Albert Place, you can get delicious German-style pastries and cakes as well as light lunches. This would have to be the nicest small eatery in town, and one of the friendliest.

Also worth mentioning is the *Anchorage Café* in the Anchorage Guest House, which is a good place to go for cosmopolitan meals (light meals start from $4.50 and mains from $9). It has a fascinating bar made from a nine-metre-long river boat, and the room is heated by the boiler from a pilot boat. You can dine alfresco in sunny weather.

Getting There & Around
Premier (☎ (08) 8415 5555) has two to three services daily from Adelaide for $11.

The Cockle Train travels daily along the scenic Encounter Coast between Goolwa and Victor Harbor over Easter and during school holidays, with selected Sunday trips at other times. The return fare is $12, and tickets can be purchased at the station in Victor Harbor.

The Victor Harbor Taxi Service (☎ 8552 2622) operates 24 hours. Approximate fares to outlying areas from the centre of town are: Port Elliot $10, Goolwa $20 and Inman Valley $15.

Motor scooters can be hired for $20 per hour from the Shell service station (☎ 8552 1875) at 165 Hindmarsh Rd, and Victor Leisure (☎ 8552 5772) at 105 Victor St. You may be able to negotiate a day rate in quiet times.

PORT ELLIOT (pop 1200)
On Encounter Bay just eight km east of Victor Harbor on the Goolwa road, Port Elliot was established in 1854 as the seaport for the Murray River trade. It soon became a popular place for Adelaideans to escape the summer heat.

The town has many old buildings and several great beaches, and even in peak periods is a quiet contrast to the bustle and traffic of Victor Harbor. You can explore its interesting heritage with the brochure *Walk into History at Port Elliot*, available from the historical centre in the old railway station.

Picturesque **Horseshoe Bay** has a sheltered swimming beach and a pleasant clifftop walk; Commodore Point at the eastern end is a good surf spot for experienced surfers, but better ones are nearby at **Boomer Beach** and

Knights Beach. The Southern Surf Shop, a few doors west of the Royal Family Hotel, hires surfing gear and can provide information on prevailing conditions.

The **Cockle Train** passes through town on its run between Victor Harbor and Goolwa (see the earlier Victor Harbor section for details).

Places to Stay & Eat
The *Port Elliot Caravan & Tourist Park* (☎ 8554 2134) on Horseshoe Bay has lawn tent/caravan sites from $11/13, on-site vans from $33 and cabins from $45.

At 32 North Terrace (the main road to Goolwa) the *Royal Family Hotel* (☎ 8554 2219) has singles/doubles for $20/25; counter meals start at $7, and there's an excellent bakery across the road. The *Hotel Elliot* at 35 The Strand also serves meals.

Only about 100 metres from Horseshoe Bay, the *Cavalier Inn Motel* (☎ 8554 2067) at 7 The Strand has ground-floor units for $63/68 and first-floor rooms for $68/78 off-peak.

Trafalgar House (☎ 8554 2483), at 25 The Strand, and *Thomas Henry B&B* (☎ 8554 2003), at 8 Charteris St, are both lovely old guesthouses offering B&B for $35 and $45 per person, respectively.

Across from Trafalgar House, *Sitar* is the only Indian restaurant on the south coast. It's open daily from 5.30 pm between August and May inclusive, and most days in winter, and has simple meals from $8.

MIDDLETON (pop 400)
The main attraction at this pleasant little holidayville is **Middleton Beach**, a good spot for novice surfers. Big Surf Australia (☎ 8554 2399), on the Goolwa road near the Strathalbyn turn-off, has up-to-date advice on local conditions. It also hires surfboards and wet suits, and can arrange surfing lessons: $20 per hour if you're in a group (maximum six persons) or $30 per hour for private lessons.

The *Middleton Caravan Park* (☎ 8554 2383) is a short walk from the beach and has tent/caravan sites ($10/11), on-site vans (from $25) and cabins (from $30) – all prices are off-peak. Alternatively, the turn-of-the-century guesthouse *Mindacowie*, on the main road opposite the *Middleton Tavern* (where you can get meals), does B&B from $75 per person.

GOOLWA (pop 3000)

On Lake Alexandrina near the mouth of the Murray River, Goolwa became the second most productive river port after Echuca, in Victoria. As large sea-going vessels were unable to get through the sandbars at the Murray mouth, the state's first railway line was built in 1854 to nearby Port Elliot, which became Goolwa's sea port. In the 1880s a new railway linking Adelaide and Melbourne via Murray Bridge spelt the end for Goolwa as a major port.

Information

The tourist office (☎ 8555 1144), open from 10 am to 4 pm daily, is in the centre of town at the corner of Caddell St and Goolwa Terrace.

Nearby on the waterfront is the **Signal Point River Murray Interpretive Centre**, which contains interesting exhibits on various aspects of river life both past and present. It's open from 10 am to 5 pm daily and entry costs $5.

Things to See & Do

Goolwa has a number of **heritage buildings** dating from the 1850s and '60s and you can visit them on a self-guided walking tour – the tourist office has a brochure. They include the **Goolwa Hotel** (1853), the **Corio Hotel** (1857), and the former **Customs House** (1859). The town **museum** on Porter St ($1 entry) is open between 2 and 5 pm every afternoon except Monday and Friday. It's well worth a visit.

Two km away at the **Malleebaa Woolshed**, you can see 18 breeds of sheep and other sheep-related activities such as shearing and hand-spinning. It's only open by appointment (☎ 8555 3638); entry costs from $4 depending on what you want to do.

Between them, the MV *Aroona* and PS *Mundoo* – a replica paddle-steamer – offer a variety of **cruises**, including the Murray mouth, Lake Alexandrina and (provided the channel is deep enough) the Coorong. Both do coffee cruises for $12 and lunch cruises for $18. A pelican-feeding cruise on the *Aroona* costs $10.

Much more personalised is a trip with the hearty Coorong Pirate (☎ 8552 1221), a large and irredeemably ocker gentleman who runs fun trips from $6. His tours leave on the hour between 10 am and 3 pm.

Goolwa is a very popular centre for water sports. You can hire jet skis, catamarans and sailboards on the waterfront.

A free vehicle ferry from Goolwa over to **Hindmarsh Island** operates 24 hours a day, but this may soon become a thing of the past. Private developers plan to build a controversial bridge to the island. Because of Aboriginal claims that sacred Aboriginal female sites will be damaged, the issue has become a political football in both state and federal parliament.

The **Sir Richard Peninsula**, which separates the sea from the Murray, has a long stretch of firm sandy beach leading from Goolwa to the river mouth. You can drive along it (4WD only) and enjoy good fishing and surfing en route – the trip takes about 20 minutes one way. The beach continues all the way to Kingston from the opposite side of the mouth, but unfortunately there's no way across in a vehicle.

Milang (population 350), on Lake Alexandrina about 33 km from Goolwa, also has an interesting history. It was established in 1853 as a river port, with bullock wagons carrying goods overland to and from Adelaide. In its heyday Milang handled more than half the total Murray River exports from SA. It's a sleepy little place these days, although it comes alive in late January when up to 1000 yachts contest the **Freshwater Yachting Classic** between here and Goolwa.

Further south, tiny **Clayton** is noted for yabby fishing. It's a popular spot for waterskiing and sailing.

FLEURIEU PENINSULA

Places to Stay

Goolwa has several caravan parks, hotels, motels and B&Bs; the tourist office has details.

Caravan Parks The closest caravan park to town is the modest *Goolwa Camping & Tourist Park* (☎ 8555 2144), at 40 Kessell Rd. It has tent/caravan sites ($8/12) and on-site vans ($20 to $30).

On Noble Ave beside the Murray, about four km from town, the *Goolwa Caravan Park* (☎ 8555 2737) has tent and caravan sites, on-site vans and two-bedroom units. It hires canoes and bicycles, and there's boat access to the river.

The *Hindmarsh Island Caravan Park* (☎ 8555 2234) is about 100 metres from the river and has tent and caravan sites and two-bedroom cabins. There's also a bottle shop and scooter hire.

Hostels, Hotels & Motels On Castle St about two km from the town centre and 500 metres from the beach is *Graham's Castle* (☎ 8555 2182), a rambling Georgian mansion built in 1868 for the managing director of the local shipyards and foundry. Dormitory accommodation is available for $12 (linen hire extra). There's a pool and games room, and the owners will pick you up from the town centre if you give them a ring on arrival. They also run ecologically oriented boat expeditions from $22 into the Coorong National Park.

Right in the centre of town, on Railway Terrace, the *Corio Hotel* (☎ 8555 1136) has rooms for $25, including a cooked breakfast.

The modern *Goolwa Central Motel* (☎ 8555 1155) at 30 Cadell St (the main street) has singles/doubles from $54/66 and spa units for $105. Other motels are the *Goolwa South Lakes Motel* (☎ 8555 2194) on Barrage Rd, which charges from $44/48 with kitchenette, and the *Rivers End Resort Motel* (☎ 8555 5033), next to the Goolwa Caravan Park on Noble Ave, which charges from $55/60.

Cottages The several cottages in Goolwa

include the two-bedroom *Goolwa Cottage B&B* (☎ 8555 1021), only 100 metres from the post office at 3 Hays St. It charges $100 for doubles, including breakfast ingredients.

On Hindmarsh Island, *Narnu Farm* (☎ 8555 2002) has cottages from $64 singles & doubles and $8 for extra adults. This is a pioneer-style farm where many things are done the old way. Guests are encouraged to take part in farm activities, such as feeding the animals and hand-milking the cows.

Places to Eat

There are several eateries in the centre of town including some good takeaways. Across from the tourist office, *Charcoal Chicken* receives accolades for its fish & chips (from $3) and roast chickens ($6.50). The nearby *Goolwa Fish Café* has a range of fast food and is also popular.

The most interesting place to eat is the *Goolwa Hotel*, at 7 Caddell St, which has the figurehead from the *Mozambique*, wrecked at the Murray mouth in 1864, on its roof. The tables and chairs in its dining room were also salvaged from the wreck – some of the chair backs show the marks where sailors and passengers held them in their teeth while running races up and down the deck. Talk about being desperate for entertainment! You can get counter meals here and at the *Corio Hotel* from around $4.

Off the Strathalbyn road 10 km from town, the *Currency Creek Winery* serves lunch and dinner every day except Tuesday. This family winery has won numerous awards, particularly for its whites.

Getting There & Around

Daily buses to Adelaide cost $11. See the earlier Victor Harbor section for details of steam trains which pass through Goolwa – the railway station is next to Signal Point and the wharf.

Coastal Cabs (☎ 8555 5333) has a 24-hour service, with approximate fares to outlying centres being $38 to Strathalbyn, $13 to Port Elliot and $35 to Milang.

You can hire a 4WD and drive along the beach to the Murray mouth for $50 for half a day or $90 for a full day; ring ☎ 8555 2211 for details. Alternatively, Goolwa Cycles, at the corner of Oliver and Hutchinson Sts, has rather ordinary bicycles for $5 per hour.

Marine Charters (☎ 8555 3206) on Hindmarsh Island hires a variety of fully-equipped yachts and cruisers. Daily rates start at $100 and weekly rates at $700.

LANGHORNE CREEK WINERIES

Established in 1850, the hamlet of Langhorne Creek, 16 km east of Strathalbyn, is one of Australia's oldest wine growing regions. After a long period of stagnation, things started to happen in the late 1980s. There are now several wineries producing mainly shiraz, cabernet sauvignon and chardonnay varieties, and at least four have tastings.

Worth visiting is **Bleasdale's**, the district's first winery, about two km from Langhorne Creek on the Wellington road. Apart from its large range of wines, the main attraction is its historic cellars, which are classified by the National Trust. The old lever press, made from red gum, is awesome.

There's also the **Lake Breeze Winery**, a small concern that has produced some prize-winning reds. It's in magnificent red gum country by the Bremer River, off Step Rd about three km south of the township. You may notice Aboriginal canoe trees in this area – the most recent one apparently dates from the 1930s.

FLEURIEU PENINSULA

Kangaroo Island

A deeply dissected plateau nearly 150 km long, up to 55 km wide and reaching 307 metres at its highest point, Kangaroo Island is the third-largest island in Australia (after Tasmania, and Melville Island near Darwin). It was cut off from the mainland by rising sea levels about 9500 years ago; Backstairs Passage, the intervening stretch of water, is 13 km across at its narrowest point.

Until fairly recent times Kangaroo Island was a tourism backwater. However, greater awareness of its magnificent coastline, conservation areas, plentiful native wildlife and genuinely friendly residents has brought increasing numbers of visitors. It is now linked to the mainland by a number of airline and ferry services, and there are many organised tours on offer.

History

The island was uninhabited in 1802, when Matthew Flinders made the first recorded visit; to the Aborigines of the Encounter Bay area it was Karta, 'the island of the dead'. Only in 1903 was evidence found of previous Aboriginal habitation, and prehistoric stone implements have since been discovered scattered across the entire island. Archaeologists are uncertain what caused the demise of those early inhabitants, but it's thought they disappeared about 2250 years ago. The evidence for this is contained in charcoal deposits that indicate a dramatic decrease in the frequency of bushfires on the island around that time.

The first thorough survey of the island's coast was carried out by the French explorer Nicholas Baudin on two visits in 1802 and 1803, which explains the numerous French place names. The island itself was named by Matthew Flinders after he and his crew landed at Kangaroo Head near Penneshaw, slaughtered a number of the marsupials and enjoyed a welcome feast of fresh meat.

White settlement took place soon after when a motley collection of whalers, sealers,

HIGHLIGHTS

- Scuba dive around the island's coral reefs and shipwrecks, and observe the marine life
- Surf the waves at Vivonne Bay and savour a freshly caught lobster as the sun goes down
- Explore the spectacular coastal scenery and eucalypt forests at Flinders Chase National Park
- Watch the sea lions sunning themselves at Seal Bay, meet a kangaroo at Rocky River and visit the penguins of Penneshaw

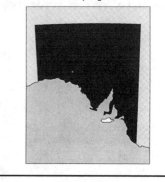

escaped convicts and ship deserters began to make their homes on the island. They brought Aboriginal women from Tasmania with them, and abducted others from tribes on the nearby mainland. Before long, Kangaroo Island had a reputation as one of the most lawless and vicious places in the British Empire. The worst scoundrels were rounded up in 1827, and after that a rough sort of respectability was achieved.

The first official settlement in the new colony of South Australia was established on Kangaroo Island at Reeves Point (near Kingscote) in July 1836. It struggled on for two years, but the lack of fresh water was a major handicap and most of the colonists then moved to Adelaide. Those who were left

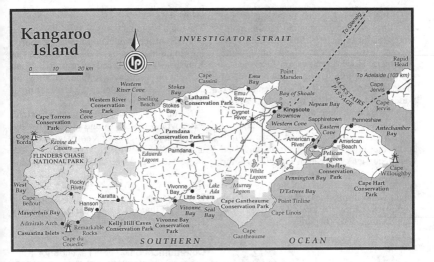

embarked on a semi-subsistence lifestyle which typified the island until the 1940s.

Since then, superphosphate and trace elements have made the mineral-deficient soils suitable for large-scale farming. As a result, most of the native vegetation has been cleared for cereal crops and grazing, and Kangaroo Island has become one of the state's most productive agricultural districts.

Climate
Kangaroo Island has a Mediterranean-type climate, with cool wet winters and warm dry summers. Its small size and the surrounding ocean means the island has a milder climate than most other parts of the state – winter frosts and summer days above 35°C are rare. On average, daily sunshine varies from 8.4 hours in summer to 3.9 hours in winter.

Flora
Kangaroo Island was originally covered by mallee and tea-tree scrub, with large trees generally being confined to the wetter western end. Although most of the island is farmed, there's quite a bit of native bush remaining in road reserves and conservation areas. From July through to November it's

fairly obvious why Kangaroo Island is referred to as a wildflower garden.

One of the island's most common eucalypts, the narrow-leafed mallee, is an excellent source of eucalyptus oil and once supported a thriving industry. Distilleries still operate on the island and you can visit one on a tour.

Fauna
Dingoes, foxes and rabbits are absent, so wildlife tends to be more of a feature here than it is on the mainland. Grey kangaroos, wallabies, bandicoots and possums are fairly common, as you'll be able to tell from the number of road kills. Fortunately, live animals abound in wilderness areas, particularly the Rocky River area of Flinders Chase.

Koalas and the platypus were introduced to Flinders Chase many years ago when it was feared they might become extinct on the mainland. The best place to see koalas is around Rocky River. Echidnas are native to the island but, like the platypus, are shy and rarely seen. Around the southern coast are colonies of New Zealand fur seals and Australian sea lions, while dolphins and southern right whales are often seen offshore.

KANGAROO ISLAND

Of the 243 bird species recorded, several are either rare or endangered on the mainland. One bird species – the dwarf emu – has become extinct on the island since white settlement. However, the glossy black cockatoo may soon join it; only a few hundred of these large, noisy birds are left thanks to the widespread destruction of coastal she-oak woodlands both here and on the mainland (she-oak seeds are their exclusive diet).

There are plenty of good birdwatching spots including Murray Lagoon, in Cape Gantheaume Conservation Park. This is the island's largest wetland and you'll usually see hundreds of swans, ducks, waders and other water birds there. Ospreys and sea eagles nest along the coastal cliffs of Cape Gantheaume and other areas.

Western grey kangaroo –
Matthew Flinders named Kangaroo Island after the roos he saw (and ate) when he first landed on the island in 1802.

KANGAROO ISLAND

Information

The main National Parks & Wildlife Service (NPWS) office, which doubles as the tourist information centre, is at 37 Dauncey St in Kingscote (☎ 2 2381) and opens from 8.45 am to 5 pm on weekdays. Another information centre is due to open near the ferry terminal in Penneshaw during 1996.

If you want to save money get an Island Pass, which costs $15 and is valid for the financial year – it covers entry, guided tour and camping fees for all national parks and conservation parks on the island (but not the penguin walks). Passes are available only from NPWS offices at Kingscote, Cape Borda, Cape Gantheaume, Cape Willoughby, Flinders Chase, Seal Bay and Kelly Hill.

Communications The STD code for Kangaroo Island is 0848 until February 1997, when it becomes 08 like the rest of the state. Local numbers will then change as follows (see also directory opposite): basically all numbers beginning between 22 and 29 have the first digit (2) deleted and 8553 placed in front (ie 2 2XXX becomes 8553 2XXX). All numbers beginning between 31 and 35 simply have 855 placed in front (ie 3 1XXX becomes 8553 1XXX). Those beginning with 36 have the first two digits (36) deleted and 8559 2 placed in front (ie 3 6XXX becomes 8559 2XXX), while those beginning with 37 just have the first digit (3) deleted and 8559 inserted (ie 3 7XXX becomes 8559 7XXX). Finally, numbers beginning between 93 and 96 have 855 put in front of them.

Books & Maps The *Natural History of Kangaroo Island* (Royal Society of SA) gives a comprehensive coverage, although to the layperson much of it will be scientific mumbo jumbo. Much easier to read is *Kangaroo Island Shipwrecks*, by Gifford Chapman, which gives accounts of the 48 wrecks around the coast.

The RAA does a small touring map of the island, while the Department of Environment

& Natural Resources puts out *A Tourist's Map of Kangaroo Island*. This one has plenty of information, good artwork and a map at 1:200,000, but is meant more as a souvenir than a road map.

Water Sports

Swimming The safest swimming is found along the north coast, where the water is warmer and the rips generally less savage than in the south. There are a number of good

---

Kangaroo Island Telephone Directory

Throughout this chapter we use the old telephone numbers, which will be phased out beginning February 1997. For those who can't crack the convoluted new system, here are the new numbers for all places mentioned in the Kangaroo Island chapter. The STD area code for Kangaroo Island will change from 0848 to 08 in February 1997.

Access Rent-a-Car	8223 7466
Adventure Charters of Kangaroo Island	8553 9119
Adventureland Diving	8553 1072
Air & Adventure Tours	8281 0530
Albatross Airlines	8553 2296
American River Rendezvous	8553 3150
Australian Odysseys	8553 1294
Budget	8553 3133
Camp & Drive	8553 2340
Cape Gantheaume Conservation Park ranger's office (Murray Lagoon)	8553 8233
Casuarina Holiday Units	8553 3020
Cooinda Charter Services	8553 3063
Coranda Farm	8553 1019
Country Cottage Shop	8553 2148
Cut-Price Auto Rental	8553 2787
Ellson's Seaview Guesthouse	8553 2030
Emu Air	toll-free 1800 182 353
Emu Bay Caravan Park (ring the Kingscote Caravan Park)	8553 2325
Excel	8553 3255
Flinders Chase Farm Hostel	8559 7223
Flinders Chase National Park Headquarters	8559 7235
Gilgandra Trail Rides	8553 9009
Island Resort Motel	8553 2100
Kangaroo Island 4WD	8553 1163
Kangaroo Island Aquatic Charters	8553 2896
Kangaroo Island B&B Association (Kathy Gloyme)	8559 3267
Kangaroo Island Central Backpackers Hostel	8553 2787
Kangaroo Island Diving Safaris	8559 3225
Kangaroo Island Fast Ferries	8295 2688
	toll-free 1800 626 242
Kangaroo Island Ferry Connections	8553 1233
	toll-free 1800 018 484
Kangaroo Island Holiday Tours	8553 2722

Kangaroo Island Rental Cars	8553 2390
Kangaroo Island Sports Fishing Safaris	8553 2325
Kangaroo Island Wilderness Flights	8559 4254
Kangaroo Island Wilderness Tours	8559 6043
Kelly Hill Caves Conservation Park	8559 7231
Kings	8553 3003
Kingscote Caravan Park	8553 2394
Koala Lodge Car Rentals	8553 9006
Linnetts Island Club	8553 3053
Matthew Flinders Terraces	8553 3100
National Parks & Wildlife Service (NPWS)	8553 2381
Nepean Bay Caravan Park	8553 2394
NPWS cottages for hire at Rocky River, Capedu Couedic and Cape Borda	8559 7235
NPWS office at Flinders Chase National Park	8559 7235
Ozone Hotel	8553 2011
Penguin Walk Hostel	8553 1233
Penneshaw Caravan Park	8553 1075
Penneshaw Hotel	8553 1042
Penneshaw Youth Hostel	8553 1284
Queenscliffe Family Hotel	8553 2254
Rock Pool Cafe	8559 2277
Sealink ferries	13 13 01
Seaview Lodge	8553 1132
Servo Plus	8553 2787
Smile Rent-a-Car	8234 0655
Sorrento Resort Motel	8553 1028
Southern Freedom Charters	8553 2349
Stanton, Kate (nature walks)	8559 2251
Vivonne Bay camping ground	8559 4287
Western KI Caravan Park	8559 7201
Wisteria Motel	8553 2707

beaches, but access can be a problem; those you can get to include Emu Bay near Kingscote, Stokes Bay, Snelling Beach and Western River Cove.

Surfing For surfing you go to the south coast, where the strongest, most reliable waves are at Pennington Bay. Vivonne Bay and Hanson Bay in the south-west can also be good, but you need to be careful of rips – Hanson Bay is only for experienced surfers. A popular break near Point Tinline in D'Estrees Bay in the south-east is called the Sewer.

Scuba Diving There's a huge number and variety of marine creatures and plantlife around the coast, including soft and hard corals such as you might expect to see on the Great Barrier Reef. There are something like 230 species of fish here, including colourful blue groper and blue devil fish. A number of the island's 60 known shipwrecks have been located and these make interesting, but not spectacular, dive sites.

The best diving is off the east and north coasts, which are well sheltered and hence the water is clearer – visibility is 10 to 20 metres on average. The east coast has sheer drop-offs (underwater cliffs) covered in invertebrates and corals – some of the caves have rare black tree corals; waters of the north coast are shallower and have numerous rocky reefs, with drop-offs and chasms. You can expect to meet seals, sea lions or dolphins on most dives.

Fishing There's plenty of good fishing around the island, which has jetties at Kingscote, Penneshaw, Emu Bay and Vivonne Bay. Emu Bay is a poor spot, but the others – particularly Kingscote – can be good. Common catches are garfish, tommy ruffs and squid, while the Kingscote jetty also has gummy shark and snook.

Rock fishing right around the coast can yield trevally and sweep, but you have to be very careful of king waves, particularly on the south coast.

Good surf beaches that you can get to easily are Pennington Bay, the mouth of

South West River at Hanson Bay, and West Bay in Flinders Chase. Salmon, flathead, tommies and whiting are common catches here.

In March and April, most beaches around the coast yield good catches of mullet. The best beaches for King George whiting include the southern end of D'Estrees Bay near Point Tinline, and King George Beach, between Snelling Beach and Stokes Bay on the north coast.

Organised Tours
Ranger-Guided Tours The NPWS operates guided tours and walks at the sea lion colony at Seal Bay, the show cave at Kelly Hill Caves Conservation Park, and the historic lighthouses at Cape Borda and Cape Willoughby. Visits to the penguin rookeries at Kingscote and Penneshaw are also available, but the cost of these is not covered by your Island Pass. Details about all the above tours are given under Things to See & Do headings later in this chapter. Various other ranger-guided activities such as birdwatching and nocturnal walks may be on offer during school holidays at various parks; check with NPWS offices for details.

Package Tours The island's three ferry companies (see Getting There & Away heading in this chapter) and many tour operators on the island offer packages ex-Adelaide; competition is fierce, so if you shop around you should pick up a good deal. Don't forget to check the hostels in Adelaide, many of which sell packages to the island.

As an example of prices, Kangaroo Island Holiday Tours (☎ 2 2722) were offering a day tour including ferry and air fares, lunch and all entry fees for $168. Alternatively, you could arrange much the same thing with Kendell Airlines (☎ 13 13 00) for $159.

Bus Tours Tours designed for backpackers and other budget travellers are run by the Penneshaw Youth Hostel (☎ 3 1284), Sealink (☎ 13 13 01), Kangaroo Island Holiday Tours (☎ 2 2722) and Air & Adventure Tours (☎ 8281 0530). They cost between $65 and $70. for a full day tour (including lunch and entry fees) taking in Seal Bay, Kelly Hills Caves and Flinders Chase National Park.

If money is no object, there are more personalised, luxury 4WD tours in small groups. These are offered by Kangaroo Island Wilderness Tours (☎ 9 6043), Australian Odysseys (☎ 3 1294) and Adventure Charters of Kangaroo Island (☎ 2 9119). You can expect to pay upwards of $160 a day per person, inclusive of lunch and entry fees, and the operators will tailor the tour to suit your requirements.

Walking Tours Andy Gilfillan of Kangaroo Island 4WD (☎ 3 1163) specialises in natural-history walking tours into remote parts of the island. These cost $80 per person for a full day, lunch included; a minimum of six people applies.

At the Penneshaw Youth Hostel, Will Thomas will take you on a three-hour walk into the hills behind town for $5 (yes, $5). You can expect fine views and may even see some rare glossy black cockatoos; there's a minimum of three people per group on this one.

You can do shorter nature walks near Stokes Bay with Kate Stanton (☎ 3 6251); the fee is $7 including morning or afternoon tea.

Horse Rides Gilgandra Trail Rides at Cygnet River (☎ 2 9009) has rides from one hour ($20) to half-day ($70), gourmet lunch included.

Fishing Charters & Safaris You can go fishing from Kingscote with Kangaroo Island Aquatic Charters (☎ 2 2896) and Southern Freedom Charters (☎ 2 2349). Cooinda Charter Services (☎ 3 3063) and the Kings (☎ 3 3003) leave from American River.

The usual charge is around $30 for three hours fishing and $60 for a day trip, although these rates may depend on numbers; the price includes all gear, bait and drinks, and you can keep your catch. Lunch is usually an extra on day trips.

Kangaroo Island Sports Fishing Safaris (☎ 2 2325) has tailor-made one to four-day safaris with shore and/or boat fishing, while Kangaroo Island Aquatic Charters will also do overnight trips; rates are available on request.

Scuba Diving Tours Both of the island's operators cater for new and experienced divers, and offer courses leading to internationally recognised dive certificates.

Adventureland Diving (☎ 3 1072), 10 km from Penneshaw on the Kingscote road, does dive courses, tours and charters. They have a full-day tour for $85, a two-day advanced course for $320, a three-day course for $386 and a five-day tour for $820, among others – these prices include meals, accommodation and equipment, but not ferry fares to and from the island.

Near Western River Conservation Park, on North Coast Rd about 75 km from Kingscote, Kangaroo Island Diving Safaris (☎ 9 3225) offers similar options. Their all-inclusive day tour (ferry excepted) is $135 and the five-day beginners' course is $600 – this includes a minimum of five ocean dives.

Other Tours You can also visit a sheep-milk dairy and cheese factory, a honey farm, a eucalyptus-oil distillery and an oyster farm, and see sheep-shearing demonstrations. The South Australian Tourism Commission (SATC) in Adelaide or the tourist office can provide details.

Scenic Flights Helicopter joy flights are available from the Tandanya Kitchen, one km east of the Flinders Chase National Park near Rocky River (☎ 3 7275). Flights range from five minutes for $29 per person to one hour for $210 per person; a minimum of two people per flight applies. Kangaroo Island Wilderness Flights (☎ 9 4254) does scenic flights from Dingo Creek Farm, near Parndarna, or you can depart from somewhere more convenient if you prefer. Half-hour flights cost $55 per seat and hour flights cost $100, assuming there are two passengers (the plane will take four).

Accommodation

As in other popular holiday areas, rates for most places – particularly flats – rise during the summer school holidays.

There's a good range of accommodation in Kingscote and Penneshaw, including relatively large caravan parks, hostels, hotels, motels and guesthouses. American River has a couple of motels. A growing number of homes (around 20 at last count) are offering B&B; Kathy Gloyme of the Kangaroo Island B&B Association (☎ 9 3267) can tell you all about them.

Holiday flats and cottages are all over the island, with the cheapest being around $50 a night; the main booking agent is Kangaroo Island Ferry Connections (☎ 3 1233; toll-free 1800 018 484), otherwise contact SATC. In addition, the NPWS has a number of remote historic cottages, including the lightkeepers' cottages at Cape Willoughby, Cape Borda and Cape du Couedic, and the old homestead at Rocky River. Rates at these start at $10 per adult. Contact the NPWS office at Flinders Chase (☎ 3 7235) for details.

Getting There & Away

Air Air Kangaroo Island (☎ 13 13 13) has at least twice daily services from Adelaide to Kingscote ($60); 14-day advance-purchase return fares cost $50. Kendell Airlines (bookings ☎ 13 13 00) services Kingscote from Adelaide. Fares are $78 but there's an advance-purchase Saver fare for $45 if you book 14 days ahead.

Albatross Airlines (☎ 2 2296) flies from Adelaide to Kingscote three times daily ($60). Its free courtesy bus transfers passengers between the airport and the town.

Emu Air (☎ toll-free 1800 182 353) has a twice-daily service to Penneshaw and Kingscote from Adelaide; the fare is $63 one way.

Ferry Kangaroo Island Fast Ferries (☎ 8295 2688; toll-free 1800 626 242) runs the passenger ferry MV *Super Flyte* from Glenelg to Kingscote, leaving Glenelg at 8 am daily and 7.30 pm Friday. It carries 500 passengers

and does the trip in just over two hours, charging $35 one way (backpackers $30) and $65 ($55) return.

For a quicker crossing, Kangaroo Island Ferry Connections (☎ 3 1233; toll-free 1800 018 484) runs the passenger ferry MV *Valerie Jane* from Cape Jervis, on the end of the Fleurieu Peninsula, to Penneshaw. It leaves twice daily for $28, taking 30 minutes – during either July or August the service takes a break. For an extra $10, you can travel by bus from Adelaide to Cape Jervis to connect with the ferry. Contact the *Valerie Jane* booking office for details.

Also departing from Cape Jervis, Kangaroo Island Sealink (☎ 13 13 01) operates two vehicle ferries which run all year, taking an hour to Penneshaw. There are at least a couple of sailings each day, with up to 10 in December and January. Return fares are $60 for passengers, $10 for bicycles, $40 for motorcycles and $120 for cars.

If you're making a ferry crossing in rough weather, ask when booking about contingency arrangements (and who pays for them) should bad weather leave you stranded on Kangaroo Island.

A bus service from Adelaide to Port Jervis connects with Sealink ferry departures for $13. It departs from the central bus station and bookings are essential; phone ☎ 13 13 01.

Getting Around

It's important to realise that first, Kangaroo Island is a big place, and second, that there is no public transport. Unless you're taking a tour, the only feasible way to get around is to bring or hire your own transport.

Kingscote and Penneshaw are linked by a good bitumen road which continues on past Parndana to the western end of the island, and there's another stretch from Kingscote to near Seal Bay.

Apart from that, the island's roads are unsealed, often rough and have a terrible reputation for accidents. The danger lies in their loose surface of pea gravel and the inexperience of most visiting motorists; they drive too fast and come to grief, usually by overturning or 'going bush'.

Top: Barrel racing, Barossa Vintage Festival
Bottom Left: Entertaining the crowd, Barossa Vintage Festival
Bottom Right: Preparing for a big feed at the Barossa Vintage Festival

Top: Roman Catholic Church, Laura
Bottom: Butcher shopfront, Terowie

To/From the Airport There's an airport bus running from the Kangaroo Island Airport to Kingscote for $10. The airport is 14 km from the town centre.

To/From the Ferry Landings The Sealink Shuttle (☎ 13 13 01) connects with most ferries and links Penneshaw with Kingscote ($11) and American River ($6.50). You have to book.

Car Rental There are five car-hire companies operating on the island, all based at Kingscote, and more are threatening to open there.

The cheapest starting price is offered by Cut-Price Auto Rental (☎ 2 2787), which has five-seater cars for $45 a day including unlimited km. Next is Koala Lodge Car Rentals (☎ 2 9006) at $58 with unlimited km, and then comes Excel (☎ 2 3255) with $65 – their stand-by rate is $55. Kangaroo Island Rental Cars (☎ 2 2390) has rates starting at $69 with 200 free km, while Budget (☎ 2 3133) charges $70.

Alternatively, you can hire a small 4WD and camper trailer for $165 a day from Island Camp & Drive (☎ 2 2340), including insurance and 250 km.

Very few of Adelaide's car-rental outlets will allow their vehicles to be taken across to Kangaroo Island. Two exceptions are Smile Rent-a-Car (☎ 8234 0655) and Access Rent-a-Car (☎ 8223 7466) – the latter charges a $10 per day Kangaroo Island surcharge.

Motorcycle Rental Kingscote is the only place you can hire scooters and motorcycles.

The Country Cottage Shop (☎ 2 2148), at 6 Centenary Ave, has 50cc scooters for $25/35 per half-day/full day and 185cc trail bikes for $30/50. Servo Plus (☎ 2 2787), at 21 Murray St (next to the backpackers hostel), also has scooters for $30/50.

The Kingscote Caravan Park (☎ 2 2325), at 9 The Esplanade, has scooters for $20/30; it's the only outlet that'll let you take scooters on unsealed roads.

Bicycle Hire Servo Plus has mountain bikes for $5/15 per half-day/full-day and tandems for $6.50/30.

Boat Hire Both American River Rendezvous (☎ 3 3150) and the Kingscote Caravan Park (☎ 2 2325) have dinghies with outboard motors, but you need a boat licence. Their half-day rates are $45 to $50.

PENNESHAW (pop 300)

Looking across Backstairs Passage to the Fleurieu Peninsula, Penneshaw is the arrival point for ferries from Cape Jervis. It's a quiet little resort town nestling under scenic hills. There's no bank in town, but Sharpys has an ANZ agency, Servwel has the BankSA agency and the post office is an agent for the Commonwealth Bank. There are EFTPOS cash-withdrawal facilities at Sharpys and Servwel.

Things to See & Do

Right by the vehicle ferry terminal is **Hog Bay**, which has a beautiful sandy beach – the small white dome at the far end protects the replica of **Frenchman's Rock**, a rock carved by a member of Captain Nicholas Baudin's expedition in 1802.

In the evenings rangers take visitors on **Discovering Penguins** walks – I'm reliably informed that you'll generally see more penguins here than at Kingscote. In summer the tours depart at 8.30 and 9.30 pm, in winter at 7 and 8 pm, and the price is $5. They leave from the CWA hall next to Condon's Takeaway; take sturdy shoes and leave the camera flash behind.

The **Penneshaw Maritime & Folk Museum** has some interesting memorabilia, including artefacts from local shipwrecks. It's open Monday, Wednesday and Saturday between 3 and 5 pm ($2).

If folk music is your thing, be in town on the Australia Day long weekend in January, when Adelaide musos descend for the three-day **Penneshaw Folk Festival**. It kicks off with a jam session at the pub on Friday night.

KANGAROO ISLAND

There are guided tours for $5 at the **Cape Willoughby Lighthouse**, 28 km from town. First operated in 1852, this is the oldest lighthouse in the state; half-hour tours leave every 30 minutes between 10 am and 4 pm daily, but they'll only do the 4 pm tour if there are sufficient numbers.

As well, there are scuba diving, coach and walking tours in the area; see under Organised Tours at the beginning of this chapter. Adventureland Diving (☎ 3 1072), 10 km out on the Kingscote road, does dive tours and also offers abseiling, canoeing and rock climbing for beginners.

About 24 km out towards Kingscote you come to **Mt Thisby**, a large sandhill offering panoramic views north towards American River and south over **Pennington Bay**, one of the island's best surfing and surf-fishing spots. A steep staircase leads up to the summit, where there's a table you can collapse on for heart massage.

Places to Stay

Caravan Parks & Hostels Down by Hog Bay is the very pleasant, if cramped, *Penneshaw Caravan Park* (☎ 3 1075). It has tent/caravan sites for $12/14 and on-site vans for $32; extra adults are $4.

Alternatively there's the *Penneshaw Youth Hostel* (☎ 3 1284), on North Terrace, where beds in dorm rooms are $10 and in twin rooms $12. The friendly *Penguin Walk Hostel* (☎ 3 1233), operated by Kangaroo Island Ferry Connections, has beds in self-contained units for $12/28.

B&Bs, Hotels & Motels At the top of North Terrace, the *Penneshaw Hotel* (☎ 3 1042) has rooms for $30. Also on North Terrace, the *Sorrento Resort Motel* (☎ 3 1028) has very comfortable rooms from $59/78. They also have chalets for $67 and cottages for $78 if you're staying a few days, otherwise there's an overnight surcharge of $25 and $35 respectively.

The most gracious accommodation in town, if not on the entire island, would have to be the *Seaview Lodge* (☎ 3 1132), on the edge of town towards Kingscote (it's just up the Cape Willoughby road). Built as a homestead in 1860, it was first used as a guesthouse in 1890 and has now been beautifully restored. Rates start from $35/70 for twin beds with share facilities to $95 for four-poster queen-size bed, private lounge and bathroom; prices include a full cooked breakfast. The owners are very friendly and will bend over backwards to see that you enjoy yourself.

Out of Town The council offices on Middle Terrace issue camping permits ($2.50) for bush sites at *Chapmans River* (on Antechamber Bay) and *Browns Beach* (12 km from town on the Kingscote road); you can get them from Sharpys Store outside business

Cape Willoughby Lighthouse

hours. Both have sites tucked away among trees by the water, but facilities are rudimentary.

Coranda Farm (☎ 3 1019), seven km from Penneshaw on the Cape Willoughby road, has a self-contained 'tent city' and charges $6 per person in two-person tents – it's only $4 if you have your own tent or campervan.

At Cape Willoughby, *Seymour and Thomas Cottages* (the old lighthouse keeper's quarters) are for hire at $25 per person; enquire at the NPWS office at Flinders Chase (☎ 3 7235).

Places to Eat

If you want an interesting eating experience, the *Old Post Office Restaurant* on North Terrace is not to be sneezed at. It's open for dinner from Thursday to Monday and main courses start at $9. I can heartily recommend their garlic prawns (your partner may not be so impressed) and I saw others drooling over their kangaroo vindaloo. There's often live entertainment, usually provided by the musical chef.

You can also get meals at the pub and *Sorrento Resort Motel*, and there are takeaways in town.

AMERICAN RIVER (pop 300)

On the coast between Kingscote and Penneshaw, this attractive holiday settlement takes its name from the American sealers who built a trading schooner on the site in 1804. The town is on a small peninsula and shelters a calm inner bay named **Pelican Lagoon** by Flinders. Perhaps 'Swan Lagoon' might have been a better name!

At 4.30 pm daily you can watch or take part in the **pelican feeding** down on the wharf (you are provided with a free bucket of fish, and the pelicans provide the feeding frenzy). At night you'll often see wallabies hopping around in the town.

Places to Stay & Eat

A pleasant restaurant with a superb view over Eastern Cove is the highlight of *Matthew Flinders Terraces* (☎ 3 3100), which is

perched on a steep hillside with lovely gardens and lots of greenery. Main courses cost from $12 and motel units are $86/98/113.

Sprawling *Linnetts Island Club* (☎ 3 3053) has a bistro bar, a restaurant and a wide range of accommodation including hostel-style beds ($12), self-contained flats ($47) and spacious spa units ($146). Their motel units start at $79/86.

The same people manage the small and rather ordinary *American River Caravan Park*, which is next door. It has tent/caravan sites for $14/18.

There are several holiday units in town, the cheapest of which is *Casuarina Holiday Units* (☎ 3 3020). This friendly place is next to the post office and has basic self-contained units from $38.

There's a nice bush camping area among gums down on the water's edge by the wharf – you can get camping permits ($2.50) from the American River Rendezvous (on the wharf) or the council offices in Penneshaw. There are no showers, and the nearest toilet is 200 metres away at the wharf.

The Crafty Fisherman across from the wharf does good fish & chips for $5.

KINGSCOTE (pop 1440)

Kingscote, the main town on the island, dates from 1836 when it became the first official white settlement in South Australia. It's a pleasant little town with a great seaside atmosphere, and makes a good base from which to explore the island. There are supermarkets and branches of the ANZ and BankSA in town; EFTPOS cash-withdrawal facilities are available at various shops including Servo Plus at 21 Murray St, next to the backpacker hostel.

The district council office in Dauncey St issues camping permits for Western River Cove in the north-west of the island.

Things to See & Do

The site of the first settlement is at **Reeves Point**, within walking distance of the town centre. It's very picturesque, with lawns and shady trees, but there's not much left apart from the cemetery, a well and a few bits and pieces. The point itself has shallows and sandbars, making it a good spot to observe water birds.

Hope Cottage overlooks Reeves Point from the top of the hill on Centenary Ave. Built in 1857, it's now a National Trust museum furnished in the style of the period; there's a reconstructed lighthouse and a eucalyptus-oil distillery in the grounds. Opening hours are 2 to 4 pm daily and admission is $2.

Kingscote doesn't have a good swimming beach, so most locals head out to **Emu Bay**, 18 km away. The **tidal pool** about 500 metres south of the jetty is the best place in town to swim.

At 4 pm daily there's **bird-feeding** at the wharf near the town centre. Around 40 of those majestic (if somewhat comical) beaked battleships, pelicans, as well as a Pacific gull or two, usually turn up for the free tucker. A 'donation' of $2 is requested.

Each evening at 7.30 and 8.30 pm (8.30 and 9.30 pm during daylight saving) rangers take visitors on a **Discovering Penguins** walk. The walk starts at the reception area of the Ozone Hotel on Kingscote Terrace and costs $5 – wear sturdy footwear and leave your camera flash behind.

If you're interested in crafts, the **Gallery** on Murray St has an excellent selection of local arts and crafts; it's open daily between 10 am and 5 pm. On the wharf, and open at the same times, is **Jenny Clapson's Gallery**. It has contemporary paintings that 'depict the relationship between man and the natural environment of Kangaroo Island'.

The **Cygnet River Oyster Farm**, about five km south of town, allows you to view an oyster nursery and learn how oysters are grown. It's open from 9 am to 5 pm daily (except Sunday) and has tours for $2; fresh oysters cost $6 a dozen, unopened.

Places to Stay
Caravan Parks On the Esplanade a short walk from the town centre, the modest *Kingscote Caravan Park* (☎ 2 2394) has tent/caravan sites for $10/14, on-site vans for $30, self-contained cabins for $45 and flats for $50.

About three km south-west of town at Brownlow, the *Nepean Bay Caravan Park* (☎ 2 2394) has tent/caravan sites for $10/13, on-site vans from $26, cabins with kitchens for $30 and holiday units for $45.

Hostels The spacious and comfortable *Kangaroo Island Central Backpackers Hostel* (☎ 2 2787) is at 19 Murray St. It has dorm beds for $13, twin rooms for $34 and doubles for $36 – it also has a family room sleeping four for $65. Next door, at Servo Plus (it's owned by the same people), you can rent bicycles, scooters and cars (see the Getting Around section at the start of this chapter). There's also an EFTPOS facility where you can withdraw up to $100 without a surcharge.

Hotels & Motels The lovely old *Queenscliffe Family Hotel* (☎ 2 2254), on Dauncey St, has comfortable singles/doubles (some with four-poster beds) for $48/55. Reasonably priced meals are available in the hotel's restaurant.

Down on the foreshore by the jetty, the more up-market *Ozone Hotel* (☎ 2 2011) on Kingscote Tce has singles/doubles for $52/66 ($67/80/85 with sea views). Their family rooms sleep four for $85.

Also on the foreshore, *Ellson's Seaview Guesthouse* (☎ 2 2030), on the corner of Chapman Tce and Drew St, has pleasant rooms with shared facilities for $32/40. Its motel units at the back are an ugly contrast to the gracious old building, but they're popular at $68/80.

On Telegraph Rd, just up from the jetty, the impressive *Island Resort Motel* (☎ 2 2100) has standard units for $65/75, spa units for $85 and executive units for $105. They also have a family unit sleeping five for $85.

The *Wisteria Motel* (☎ 2 2707) on Brownlow Road overlooks the sea about one km south of town and is the newest motel in Kingscote. It has luxurious standard units for $93/105/118 and deluxe units with spa for $121/139/157.

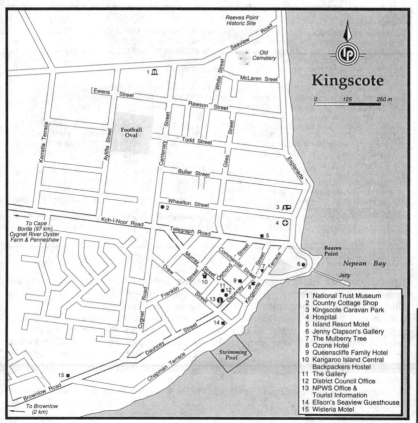

Kingscote

0   125   250 m

1 National Trust Museum
2 Country Cottage Shop
3 Kingscote Caravan Park
4 Hospital
5 Island Resort Motel
6 Jenny Clapson's Gallery
7 The Mulberry Tree
8 Ozone Hotel
9 Queenscliffe Family Hotel
10 Kangaroo Island Central
   Backpackers Hostel
11 The Gallery
12 District Council Office
13 NPWS Office &
   Tourist Information
14 Ellson's Seaview Guesthouse
15 Wisteria Motel

KANGAROO ISLAND

Places to Eat

The pubs and motels have restaurants – the bistro at the *Ozone Hotel* has $5 nights, otherwise you can usually get a feed there for $8.50.

The title of best restaurant is being fought over by the *Mulberry Tree*, opposite the jetty, and *Ellson's Seaview Guesthouse*, but there's not much in it as they both have excellent tucker. The Mulberry Tree has an interesting menu and a relaxed atmosphere, while Ellson's is noted for its air of quiet gentility and magnificent ornamental ceilings.

For breakfast you won't be able to beat the *Blue Gum Café*, next to the Queenscliffe Hotel. It's also popular for coffee, cakes and light lunches, including vegetarian. If he's not too busy, Rugby Wilson, the proprietor, is a good source of information on outdoor activities on the island.

Other than that there's a bakery and several takeaways in town; the shop next to the Mulberry Tree restaurant does a good pizza.

THE NORTH COAST ROAD

The North Coast Rd runs from Kingscote along the coast to meet the Playford

Henry Wallen
One of South Australia's first European settlers was Henry Wallen, who left the brig *Sophia* in 1820 and took up permanent residence on Kangaroo Island. At that time the island was inhabited by an unsavoury bunch of ship deserters, escaped convicts and other desperados. There were also a number of Aboriginal women, whom the men kept in virtual slavery. A Captain Sutherland visited the island in 1819 and described the men as being little better than pirates:

They are complete savages, living in bark huts ... not cultivating anything, but living entirely on kangaroos, emus and small porcupines, and getting spirits and tobacco in barter ... They dress in kangaroo skins without linen, and wear sandals made of seal skins. They smell like foxes.

Wallen proved to be a man of strong character and a good leader. When the worst scoundrels were forcibly removed in 1827 he soon dominated the community, becoming known as the island's unofficial governor. He established a successful farm at Cygnet River and lived in a comfortable home made from wattle-and-daub. In 1834 he was reported to have seven men and five women all living peacefully as his subjects.
  Two years later the South Australia Company's ship *Duke of York* arrived off Reeves Point with the first colonists. Wallen was on the beach to meet them, and after an altercation with the company's manager, Samuel Stephens, he agreed to give up his governorship in favour of Stephens. Unfortunately Wallen had no legal title to his farm, and when Stephens saw what had been achieved he was so impressed that he took that as well.
  Wallen received virtually no compensation for the loss of all his property and eventually moved to the mainland. He died penniless and alone in Adelaide and was buried in the Kingscote cemetery. ■

Highway about 85 km from town. There's some stunning scenery (beaches, cliffs, bush, rolling farmland) en route, particularly in the west, as well as detours into several fine, sheltered beaches. Apart from small shops at Emu Bay and Stokes Bay there are no facilities along this road.

Things to See & Do
The bitumen stops at **Emu Bay**, 18 km from town, where there's one of the best swimming beaches on the island. This is a beautiful sweep of sand about five km long – it's very popular in summer and is one of the few that you can drive a car onto.

About 36 km further west there's **Stokes Bay**, which has a penguin rookery and a large rock pool suitable for swimming. The beach is attractive, but there's a dangerous rip outside the pool. To get there you walk through a natural tunnel among huge boulders just east of the car park.

From here it's 22 km inland to the small farming community of **Parndana**, in the centre of the island. The township has good services including a hotel, supermarket, fuel sales and a seven-day laundrette. There's also the **Kangaroo Island Wool & Wilderness Centre**, which has local crafts and displays on the island's flora, fauna and farming history; it's open daily.

Probably the most attractive beach on the north coast is **Snelling Beach**, which looks absolutely magnificent from the North Coast Rd , especially as the road climbs onto the plateau to the west.

Continue on for seven km and you come to the turn-off to **Western River Cove**. The detour is extremely scenic as it winds about on the ridge tops, with big gums, deep gullies and fine views most of the way. However, it's not suitable for caravans due to steep slopes – the same applies to the southern access, which turns off the North Coast Rd six km further on.

At Western River Cove there is another nice beach crowded by sombre cliffs at either end. The mouth of the river is quite pretty, with jagged grey rocks decorated by vivid splashes of green algae and orange lichen.

About three km west as the crow flies, but 26 km by road, is the 2400-hectare **Western River Conservation Park**. Its major scenic highlight (in winter and early spring) is a picturesque little waterfall that tumbles into a deep, dark gully. Don't try to get to the bottom of the hill in a conventional vehicle if the track is anything but dry.

Places to Stay & Eat

The *Emu Bay Caravan Park* (ring the Kangaroo Island Caravan Park on ☎ 2 2325) is close to the beach. It has tent/caravan sites for $8/10 and self-contained cabins for $60 for up to five people, but no showers. There's a reasonable takeaway nearby.

The *Rock Pool Café* (☎ 3 6277) at Stokes Bay has a small grassed area where you can camp for $3 per person. There's rainwater for drinking, and toilets, but no showers. The café is not your usual greasy spoon – it sells interesting meals served alfresco, and basic provisions.

The uninspiring camping ground at *Western River Cove* is only a short walk from a nice beach. It's in an open grassed area with toilets and a picnic shelter beside the river (really just a rivulet), but no showers; permits are $3.50 per site and you can get one from the council office on Dauncey St in Kingscote.

THE SOUTH COAST ROAD

The South Coast Rd turns off the Kingscote to Penneshaw road about 15 km from Kingscote and terminates at West Bay, in Flinders Chase National Park, 105 km further on. En route there are detours to the coast and major attractions such as Seal Bay and Kelly Hill Caves (there are ranger-guided tours at both). Apart from the coast, and the wildflowers in spring, the scenery along the road itself is nothing startling until you get to the tall timber at Kelly Hill Caves.

Kangaroo Island's south coast, being exposed to the Southern Ocean, is a wild contrast to the sheltered north. Given any sort of blow from the south you'll have booming breakers and great clouds of spray; in fact, exploring the coast under these conditions can be a drenching experience. It's easy to see why some of the island's worst shipwrecks occurred here.

Things to See & Do

The turn-off to the 21,300-hectare **Cape**

Gantheaume Conservation Park is 24 km from Kingscote, then it's a rough 16 km to the ranger's office (☎ 2 8233) at **Murray Lagoon**. This is the island's largest wetland, where you'll normally see hundreds of water birds, particularly swans.

From here it's 23 km to **Point Tinline**, a good surfing and surf-fishing spot on **D'Estrees Bay**. If you're feeling fit you can walk around the coast to Seal Bay, seeing colonies of New Zealand fur seals and Australian sea lions, and spectacular cliffs en route. It's mostly an easy and enjoyable walk, but it'll take two days and there's no drinking water; check with the ranger at Murray Lagoon before setting out.

Seal Bay, with its large colony of Australian sea lions on the beach, is one of the island's major tourist attractions. Ranger-guided tours cost $7.50 and leave from the information centre (open 8.30 am to 5 pm) at 45-minute intervals between 9 am and 4.15 pm daily.

About 500 sea lions live here, but you won't see that many. If it's cold, there may only be four or five on the beach – the rest will be sheltering up in the sandhills – while on a warm day there might be 200 or more

Australian sea lions: beware of getting too close during the breeding season, when they can be quite aggressive.

KANGAROO ISLAND

basking along the water's edge. Although you'll get close-up photos, don't expect exciting action unless it's the breeding season. Most times they lay about having the occasional scratch but otherwise showing no interest in anyone or anything.

The information centre has some interesting displays, including a disturbing one on the effects of plastic rubbish on sea birds and mammals. Nearby is a **lookout** offering a nice view over the beach.

Back on South Coast Rd, the next turn-off on your left (it's just before the Eleanor River about seven km from the Seal Bay road) takes you to **Little Sahara**, a vast expanse of huge white sandhills rising above the surrounding mallee scrub.

Further west, **Vivonne Bay** has a long and beautiful sweep of beach, and the sea looks most inviting on a hot day. However, there are some fierce undertows, so get local advice before plunging in. It's another good surfing spot, with some of the strongest waves on the coast.

Getting close to Flinders Chase is the 7,400-hectare **Kelly Hill Caves Conservation Park** (☎ 3 7231), where the main attraction is a series of limestone caves. Apparently, these were 'discovered' in the 1880s by a horse named Kelly, which fell into them through a hole.

Guided tours of the attractive show cave cost $5 and leave on the hour between 10 am and 4 pm daily (3 pm in winter); adventure caving in small groups is also offered. There's a pleasant picnic area among tall gums and some interesting short walks. The nine-km walk from the cave to the mouth of South West River at Hanson Bay takes you through mallee scrub and past freshwater wetlands, with fine coastal views at the end.

Places to Stay & Eat

The historic *Kaiwarra Cottage* on the south coast road near the Seal Bay turn-off is a good spot for light meals and Devonshire teas. The *Vivonne Bay Store* does the usual takeaways, like pies and sandwiches, and you can buy fresh lobster in season.

There are bush camping areas at *Murray*

Lagoon and *Point Tinline* in Cape Gantheaume Conservation Park; permits cost $2 per adult.

The small camping ground at *Vivonne Bay* (☎ 9 4287) is pleasantly situated in the bush off the road to the jetty. It has toilets but no showers.

FLINDERS CHASE NATIONAL PARK

Occupying the western end of the island, 73,800-hectare Flinders Chase is one of South Australia's most significant national parks. Much of the park is mallee scrub, but there are some beautiful, tall sugar-gum forests, particularly around Rocky River and the Ravine des Casoars, five km south of Cape Borda. There's wild, often spectacular scenery right around the coast, which you can reach in several places from roads and walking tracks (a map is available from the park headquarters).

Information

The park headquarters (☎ 3 7235) is at Rocky River. There's usually someone in the office between 8 am and 5 pm daily – it's over the hill past the information centre, which opens from 9 am to 5 pm in summer (10 am in winter).

Things to See & Do

Once a farm, **Rocky River** is an excellent spot to see wildlife. As I pulled up in the car, a koala, pursued by a small excited boy, galloped across the road and scrambled up a gum tree. It sat there and stared down as if wondering what all the fuss was about, while its pursuer danced and squealed below.

You can't help but see kangaroos at Rocky River; they've become so brazen that they'll badger you for food and won't take no for an answer. This is amusing at first, but not for long. Fortunately, the picnic and barbecue areas are fenced off to protect visitors from the unwelcome demands of the roos.

From here a road leads south to wild and remote **Cape du Couedic**, where there are dramatic cliffs and a lighthouse which was built in 1906. A pathway leads down to **Admirals Arch**, a spectacular archway formed by pounding seas; the walkway within the arch passes through a colony of New Zealand fur seals.

At Kirkpatrick Point, a couple of km east of Cape du Couedic, the **Remarkable Rocks** are a cluster of huge, weather-sculpted granite boulders perched on a dome that swoops 75 metres down to the sea. En route you pass **Weirs Cove**, where a flying fox once brought supplies up the cliffs from the small landing far below.

Another road takes you from Rocky River to picturesque **West Bay**, a good surf-fishing spot. Behind the beach, a wooden cross marks the grave of an unknown sailor from the windjammer *Loch Vennachar*, lost nearby with all hands in 1905.

This road passes the starting points of three short walking tracks that lead down to the sea; longest (and arguably the most interesting) is the six-km return walk to **Breakneck River**. It features beautiful gums, chuckling tea-coloured water and spectacular coastal scenery.

To get to **Cape Borda**, which features a lighthouse (1858) atop soaring cliffs, you have to go the long way around via the West End Highway. There are guided tours of the lighthouse on weekdays between 10 am and 3.15 pm (2 pm in winter and 4.15 pm during summer, autumn and spring school holidays) for $5.

Nearby, at **Harvey's Return**, a poignant cemetery tells a sad story of isolation in the early days. It's a long scramble down to the stony beach, which has unusual striped rocks and the remains of a haulage way. This is where supplies for the lighthouse staff were landed. Standing here you have to wonder how they managed to get the cargo out of the boat without losing half of it, let alone the work involved in getting it up the hill.

From Harvey's Return you can drive to **Ravine des Casoars** (literally 'Ravine of the Cassowaries', referring to the now-extinct dwarf emus seen here by Baudin's expedition in 1803). There's a beautiful walk down to the coast from here, with tall gums

---

A Watery Grave

Since 1847, when the cutter *William* went down in Hog Bay, the rugged storm-swept coast of Kangaroo Island has claimed around 60 ships and dozens of lives. The shipwrecks range in size from the eight-tonne oyster cutter *Atlanta* (1860) to the 5865-tonne Japanese steamer *Portland Maru* (1935).

The hazards of navigating between the island and the mainland were recognised early. To this end, lighthouses were built at Cape Willoughby (1852) and Cape Borda (1858), but it wasn't until a string of disasters occurred on the wild west coast that a lighthouse was constructed on Cape du Couedic, in 1906.

News of Kangaroo Island's worst shipwreck was first heard on 19 May 1877, when three ragged, foot-sore seamen appeared out of the bush at the Cape Borda lighthouse. They were the sole survivors of the 39 passengers and crew of the wooden brigantine *Emily Smith*, which had been wrecked on rocks in heavy seas near Cape du Couedic five days earlier. Although five people had made it to shore, two – a male passenger and a female crew member – soon became exhausted and were left behind. Their skeletal remains were eventually found near West Bay.

In 1899, the three-masted iron barque *Loch Sloy* ran onto rocks close to the wreck of the *Emily Smith*. Only four of the 35 people on board managed to get through the breakers to shore, where an exhausted passenger was left while the others sought help. Fifteen days later, one of the survivors stumbled into the isolated Rocky River homestead and raised the alarm. A search party found his two companions almost dead two days later; the passenger left on the beach had already died and was buried on the clifftop.

Yet another tragedy involved the iron barque *Lock Vennachar*, last sighted 250 km west of Kangaroo Island on 6 September 1905 while en route from London to Port Adelaide. Although reported overdue, it wasn't until wreckage from the ship began turning up along the island's south coast that its fate was confirmed. A single body was washed up on the beach at West Bay, but no trace of the other 26 people on board was ever found. In fact, the wreck's whereabouts remained a mystery until 1976 when it was discovered by a diver. It appeared that the ship had sailed straight into the cliffs at Point Vennachar, near West Bay. ■

beside a gurgling stream. It's a great spot for birdwatching and listening to the sounds of nature.

Places to Stay & Eat
In Flinders Chase you can camp at the Rocky River park headquarters and in other designated areas with a permit ($2 per site plus $2 per adult). Don't leave any food exposed in your tent, even if you've closed it up: kangaroos and possums will rip their way in and cause a lot of damage, quite apart from the fact that they'll ruin your tucker.

There are limited hot showers in the park, but facilities are better at the friendly *Western KI Caravan Park* (☎ 3 7201), on a farm beside South Coast Rd a few minutes drive east from Rocky River. They have tent/caravan sites for $10/15, on-site vans for $35

and a double-decker bus for $45. There are plenty of wild koalas here as well.

The NPWS has a number of cottages for hire at Rocky River, Cape du Couedic and Cape Borda costing from $10 to $27.50 per adult; enquire at their office at Rocky River (☎ 3 7235) for details and bookings.

On West Coast Highway a few minutes drive from Rocky River, *Flinders Chase Farm Hostel* (☎ 3 7223) has beds from $12. Nearby, and just outside the park boundary on South Coast Rd, is *Tandanya Kitchen*, which has reasonable takeaways and sit-down meals – they also have a barbecue where you can cook your own. You can eat alfresco under the trees or in their attractive pine-log courtyard, where there's a bar. It's open daily for lunch, and they'll do you up a picnic basket.

Murray River

Australia's greatest river rises in the Australian Alps and for most of its length forms the boundary between NSW and Victoria. It meanders for 650 km through SA, first heading west to Morgan then turning south for the coast, which it meets at Lake Alexandrina. For virtually its entire course through the state it forms a wide valley often lined with high yellow cliffs. In this semi-arid landscape the cool ribbon of water and lush vegetation is a welcome contrast to the mallee scrub and wheat paddocks on either side.

Thanks to irrigation and its dry sunny climate, the Murray is a major agricultural producer; there's dairying at Murray Bridge, vegetable-growing at Mannum, and an extremely productive fruit and wine area between Waikerie and Renmark. It's also a holiday playground for South Australians, particularly the area closest to Adelaide. Watersports (such as canoeing and skiing), camping and fishing are popular activities, as is houseboating.

The Murray is lined almost throughout with huge river red gums, while its backwaters are important habitats for water birds and aquatic creatures. Although the thousands of trees killed by stream regulation are a depressing sight, the timeless mystique of this big river still makes it one of the greatest places in Australia to spend a holiday.

Blossom of the majestic river red gum

European History

In 1838, only eight years after Charles Sturt's epic journey to the mouth, Joseph Hawdon brought the first herd of cattle to SA from the eastern colonies. He travelled along the Murray from the Goulburn River to Adelaide, so pioneering one of the first of Australia's major overland stock routes. On more than one occasion he was confronted by armed Aborigines in groups up to 100 strong; 'The men stood threatening us with their spears, and motioning us to go away. Not being in a humour to hold conversation with them we passed on...'

A flood of cattle followed in Hawdon's footsteps, and soon a state of open warfare existed between the drovers and the Aborigines. Hostilities reached a peak in 1841, when police parties were sent to the Murray to 'restore order'. A detachment of the 96th

MURRAY RIVER

Regiment was stationed five km south of Blanchetown at Moorundie, established by the explorer Edward John Eyre in 1841. This was the first European settlement on the Murray, and within a decade virtually the entire river frontage in SA was included in vast grazing properties.

The first paddle-steamers appeared on the scene soon after. In 1853 William Randell in the *Mary Ann*, and Francis Cadell in the *Lady Augusta*, steamed from the lower reaches all the way into NSW, their journeys proving that the Murray was a viable transport route.

This stimulated the development of a massive river trade that stretched from Goolwa (the 'New Orleans of Australia') into NSW along the Murrumbidgee and Darling rivers. Busy ports sprang up, with dozens of steamers and barges queueing to off-load their cargoes of wool, wheat, timber and other goods.

Railways sounded the death knell for the river trade, but in the 1890s, when it was already in decline, another industry appeared to take its place. In 1887, brothers and Canadian irrigation experts George and William Chaffey established an irrigation colony at

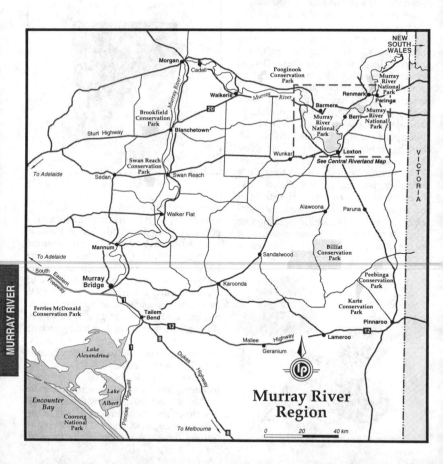

Murray River Region

Renmark and this proved a huge success. Within a few years a thriving export trade had developed in oranges and dried fruits, particularly sultanas and currants. More irrigation schemes followed, as well as swamp reclamation to allow dairying along the lower Murray flats.

Both navigators and irrigators experienced problems with the river's variable flow; there were floods in some years and no flow at all in others. In 1914, under the River Murray Agreement with NSW, Victoria and the Commonwealth, SA commenced work on a series of locks and weirs along the river to regulate its flow and maintain a constant water level. Dams were constructed closer to the Murray's source to allow controlled release of water during times of low rainfall.

These works have made the Murray lands one of Australia's, if not the world's, most productive irrigation areas. It's certainly a river of life for South Australians, most of whom rely wholly or partly on it either for their livelihood or their domestic water supplies. However, there's an unfortunate tendency to take it for granted. As a result, deteriorating water quality has become a major conservation issue in the '90s.

Information

There are major tourist information centres at Murray Bridge and Barmera, and smaller ones at Mannum, Waikerie, Loxton, Berri and Renmark. Useful free regional guides to the Murray River and Murray Mallee are published annually; you can get them from the South Australian Tourism Commission and local centres.

Communications Throughout this book we use the new statewide STD code (08) and eight-digit telephone numbers which take effect in February 1997. Should you need to use the old number, simply take the first two digits (85 for all towns on the Murray) and use as the STD code (085).

National Parks The National Parks and Wildlife Service office (☎ 8595 2111) on

Vaughan Terrace in Berri administers all conservation areas along the river and in the Murray Mallee.

Books & Maps The *River Murray Pilot*, by R & M Baker and W Reschke ($15.95), is an interesting book with useful maps for those on the water. If you're keen on history, the Department of Environment and Natural Resources has the excellent *River Boat Trail – South Australia* ($5). It takes you on a tour of relics associated with shipping on the Murray.

The Royal Automobile Association's touring map *Riverland & Central Murray* is the best one for the river between Mannum and Renmark, and includes the northern half of the Murray Mallee. The river's lower reaches are covered by their *Central* touring map, while their *Upper South-East* map includes the southern Murray Mallee.

The Department of Recreation & Sport has a series of five canoeing guides ($7.30) to the Murray and associated wetlands. One covers the section between Morgan and Swan Reach, while the remainder cover most of the river between Overland Corner and the Victorian border. Also useful are the department's cycle-touring maps, which cover the lower Murray and Riverland.

Fishing

This is a popular activity along the Murray and there are several species you can catch. Minimum legal lengths and bag limits apply to golden perch (or callop), catfish, Murray cod and silver perch, all of which are natives. However, you can haul in as many introduced European perch (or redfin) and European carp as you like. Yabbies (freshwater crayfish) can be caught in summer and at times of high river flow. Backwaters are the best places and stale mutton makes excellent bait.

The Fisheries Division office in Loxton (☎ 8584 7241) can tell you about the rules and regulations attached to fishing in the Murray. For general information, mud maps and equipment try Hook Line & Sinker at 17 William St in Berri; it's open seven days.

Organised Tours

Stateliner (☎ 8415 5555) has several tours from Adelaide to the Murray from $99 per person twin share. Riverland Safaris (☎ 8588 2859; 8588 3270) of Barmera has three-day (from $195), four-day (from $260) and five-day (from $320) 'adventure' tours of the Riverland leaving from Adelaide. They include activities such as canoeing, horse-riding and sailing.

One of the highlights of any trip to the Murray is a cruise on an old paddle-steamer. Several of these shallow-draught vessels have been restored and you can relive the past on cruises that last from a few hours to several days. They include the huge stern-wheeler PS *River Murray Princess*, which regularly makes its stately passage up and down the river from Mannum. Other paddle-steamers are based at Murray Bridge and Renmark.

There are a number of other tours on offer. You'll find trail rides and camel treks near Morgan, eco-tours at Swan Reach, Morgan and Renmark, and boat cruises other than paddle-steamers at Murray Bridge, Mannum, Berri and Renmark. Check the respective sections on these towns for details.

Accommodation

The Murray is a popular holiday destination, so there's plenty of accommodation, including basic riverfront camp sites on public land. Even small towns have at least one caravan park or a hotel or motel, and there's a hostel in Berri.

Houseboats can be hired in most centres. However, they're very popular from October to April inclusive, when it's wise to book well ahead. The houseboat scene is constantly changing but you can get the latest details from SATC or any local tourist office.

The Riverland Holiday Booking Centre at Harvey World Travel (☎ 8586 4444; bookings toll-free 1800 651 166) at 151 Murray Ave in Renmark is a major agent for houseboat hire. Alternatively, the Houseboat Hirers Association has an information and booking centre (24-hour hotline ☎ 8395 0999) with access to over 100 houseboats from Murray Bridge to Renmark.

Getting There & Away

Air Southern Australia Airlines flies twice daily from Adelaide to Renmark on weekdays and once daily on weekends.

Bus Stateliner (☎ 8415 5555) has daily services from Adelaide to the Riverland towns, with their fare to Berri, Loxton and Renmark being $26.50. Other country services go to Mannum and Murray Bridge (see the sections on these towns for details).

Greyhound Pioneer runs through the Riverland en route to Sydney. The fare to Sydney from Renmark is $79. Coming the other way, however, you can't get off until you're past Renmark.

There is no public transport to the towns between Mannum and Waikerie.

MURRAY BRIDGE (pop 13,500)

South Australia's largest river town, only 82 km from Adelaide and connected to it by the South Eastern Freeway, is named for its original bridge. Built in 1879, it was the first to span the Murray. To the detriment of Goolwa and Mannum, the town became a major port after the railway from Adelaide arrived in 1884.

While the river trade is a thing of the past, the town is still an important agricultural and tourism centre. Dairying is a major industry, with cows being grazed on irrigated pastures sown on reclaimed swamp right along the river. Milk factories at Murray Bridge and nearby Jervois process 85% of SA's dairy products.

The friendly and efficient tourist information centre (☎ 8532 6660) is at 3 South Terrace. It opens at 8.30 am on weekdays, closing at 4.30 pm on Monday, 5.15 pm on Friday and 4 pm on other days; on weekends it opens at 10 am, closing at 3.45 pm on Saturday and 2 pm on Sunday and public holidays.

Things to See & Do

The tourist office has details of self-guided walks and drives you can do in the area. Attractions include the **Anglican Cathedral** (built in 1887, it's Australia's smallest) and the **Round House** (1873). The first solid building in town, it was built to accommodate the engineer responsible for constructing the original bridge.

The **Captain's Cottage Museum**, on Thomas St, has some interesting exhibits on the town's early farming and riverboat days. It's open on weekends only between 10 am and 4 pm, and entry costs $3.

Chocoholics will enjoy viewing **chocolate making** – and munching on the end result – Cottage Box Chocolates on Wharf St. It's in the old pump house between the vehicle and railway bridges, on the town side of the river.

Also of interest is **Butterfly House**, four km out on the road to Wellington. Its tropical hothouse contains species of gorgeous butterflies which flutter about your ears while you observe and photograph them. There are also some vivid displays of marine organisms, plus walk-through aviaries and other things. The doors open daily from 10 am to 5 pm, and entry costs $7.

Good for kids is **Puzzle Park**, right next door, which has among its attractions a maze, minigolf and paddleboats. It's open the same hours.

The **Cameo Cinema** at 2 First St in the town centre screens films daily from 9.30 am to 9 pm during school holidays, and usually in the evenings (closed Monday) at other times.

Around Murray Bridge The town that never was – **Monarto** – is 20 km to the west. In the early 1970s an ambitious plan was drawn up to build a second major city for SA by the turn of the century. This site was chosen and land purchased, but nothing further happened and the project was finally abandoned.

The 1000-hectare **Monarto Zoological Park** has a range of Australian and international exhibits, including rare species and herds of grassland animals such as zebras and giraffes. The park is open on Sunday, public and school holidays from 9.30 am to 5 pm, and entry costs $10. Bus tours travel through the Asian and African habitat areas on the hour.

About 14 km south of the zoo, the 845-hectare **Ferries-McDonald Conservation Park** preserves a rare remnant of the mallee that covered this area prior to the arrival of wheat farmers last century. There are some interesting walks, plenty of grey kangaroos and good birdwatching. If you're lucky you'll see a mallee fowl.

Ten km out on the road to Mannum, emus are raised for their meat, oil, leather and feathers at **Talyala Emu Farm**. It's open from 10 am to 4 pm daily and tours run on the hour; admission costs $4.

River Cruises

The MV *Barrangul* operates irregular day cruises and there's a restaurant on board – check at the tourist information centre for times. The PS *Proud Mary* departs from Murray Bridge – two-night cruises start at $345 (triple share), and five-night cruises start at $875. For details contact Proud Australia Holidays (☎ 8231 9472) in Adelaide.

Places to Stay

Murray Bridge has plenty of accommodation including several caravan parks and motels. The tourist information centre will have details of its numerous houseboats.

Caravan Parks At the Adelaide end of town, the *Princes Highway Caravan Park* (☎ 8532 2860) is an attractive spot with tent/caravan sites for $10/12 and self-contained cabins for $38. Rather less inspiring, but closest to the centre of town, is the *Oval Motel & Caravan Park* (☎ 8532 2388), on the corner of Le Messurier St and Alice Terrace.

The *Long Island Caravan Park & Marina* (☎ 8532 6900), on Roper Rd off the road to Wellington, enjoys a good reputation. It has caravan sites from $14, on-site vans for $30 and cabins from $35. Further out on the same road, the *White Sands Resort* (☎ 8532 1421) has a great location but is run-down.

The friendly *Avoca Dell Caravan Park* (☎ 8532 2095) is pleasantly situated next to the river on Loddon Rd, on the east bank. It has tent/caravan sites for $12/14, on-site vans for $28 and self-contained cabins for $38.

About 16 km upstream from town (you get there off the road to Karoonda), the *Willow Banks Resort* (☎ 8535 4203) has camp sites and cabins, as well as jet ski and ski boat hire.

Hotels & Motels The *Murray Bridge Hotel* (☎ 8532 2024), at 6 Sixth St, charges from $16/26 for basic single/double pub rooms. It's marginally cheaper than the *Eureka Bridgeport Hotel*, at 2 Bridge St, which charges from $15 per person.

Also good value is the *Balcony Guest House* (☎ 8532 3830), right in the centre of

town at 12 Sixth St. It has single rooms from $17 and doubles/twins from $38, including a light breakfast.

There are several motels around town. *Motel Greenacres* (☎ 8532 1090) on the Princes Highway, about five km east of the town centre, has rooms from $40/46. *Murray Bridge Motor Inn* (☎ 8532 1144) at 212 Princes Highway, about three km west of town, charges $60/68. *Oval Motel* (☎ 8532 2388), about a km south-west of the town centre at the corner of Le Messurier St and Alice Terrace, has rooms starting from

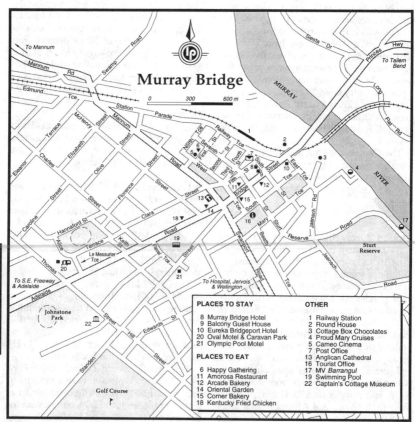

PLACES TO STAY

8 Murray Bridge Hotel
9 Balcony Guest House
10 Eureka Bridgeport Hotel
20 Oval Motel & Caravan Park
21 Olympic Pool Motel

PLACES TO EAT

6 Happy Gathering
11 Amorosa Restaurant
12 Arcade Bakery
14 Oriental Garden
15 Corner Bakery
18 Kentucky Fried Chicken

OTHER

1 Railway Station
2 Round House
3 Cottage Box Chocolates
4 Proud Mary Cruises
5 Cameo Cinema
7 Post Office
13 Anglican Cathedral
16 Tourist Office
17 MV *Barrangul*
19 Swimming Pool
22 Captain's Cottage Museum

MURRAY RIVER

$50/56. *Olympic Pool Motel* (☎ 8532 2358) at 34 Standen St, about one km west of the town centre, charges $40/48.

For a dash of romance, *Treetops Cottage* (☎ 8532 6483) at 117 Murray Drive is a self-contained, one-bedroom retreat overlooking a wetland with lots of birds. There's no phone, but there is a canoe and a complimentary book of original poems. It costs $184 for two persons for two nights.

Places to Eat

The leaflet *Eating Out in Murray Bridge* lists 45 eateries ranging from fast food to the local ultimate in fine dining: the *Amorosa Restaurant*, at 55 Bridge St. It offers international cuisine, with Italian the speciality, and is open for dinner daily except Monday.

If you're starving, but on a budget, the town's pubs have the usual good-value counter meals; the *Eureka Bridgeport Hotel* is most popular. Alternatively, the *Happy Gathering* at 6 First St and the *Oriental Garden* at 18 Adelaide Rd are Chinese places offering large serves for reasonable prices. The *Italian Club* on Lincoln Rd serves dinner from Thursday to Sunday. Thursday is pasta night – all you can eat for $6.

A couple of good bakeries on Bridge St are the *Corner Bakery*, at the intersection with West Terrace, and the *Arcade Bakery*, which has wonderful sticky buns. Both sell coffee, light lunches and fresh-baked goodies.

Also worth trying is the *Cockatoo Haven Diner* out at the Butterfly House. It specialises in all-you-can-eat deals, with lunch from $4 and dinner from $7.

Getting There & Away

Australian National Railways passes through Murray Bridge each night on its way from Adelaide to Melbourne. The fare is $50 economy, leaving at 9.11 pm.

Buses to Adelaide cost $10.50 with the Murray Bridge Passenger Service (☎ 8532 6660); they leave four times daily from outside the tourist office, where tickets can be purchased. If you're travelling from Ade-laide, bookings need to be made with Premier on ☎ 8415 5555.

Tickets to Mt Gambier ($36.90) with Bonds Mt Gambier Motor Service (☎ 8231 9090) must be booked at the Central Bus Station in Adelaide. You can pick up a Greyhound Pioneer bus to Melbourne for $50 or a McCafferty's bus for $45. Both have services at least once daily.

Getting Around

Murray Bridge Taxis (☎ 8531 0555) operates 24 hours, charging around $35 to Mannum and Wellington, and $25 to Old Tailem Town at Tailem Bend. It also has a solitary hire car.

The Riverside Bus Service (☎ 8532 1081) operates a regular two-route town service with buses running weekdays only between 8 am and 5.45 pm.

TAILEM BEND (pop 1600)

The main attraction in this otherwise uninspiring railway town is **Old Tailem Town**, the fascinating recreation of an 1880s pioneer settlement complete with period furnishings. Its collection of 70 buildings (most have been brought from other places) include a cow-dung house and a fisherman's hut made from flattened tar drums. Entry costs $7.50 and it's open from 10 am to 5 pm daily.

For places to stay there are the *River Bend Motel* (☎ 8572 3633), the *Riverside Hotel* (☎ 8572 3655) and the *Rivers Edge Caravan Park* (☎ 8572 3307). All are on the busy Princes Highway.

Down by the river and off the highway six km north-west of town, the attractive and friendly *Westbrook Park River Resort* (☎ 8572 3794) has tent/caravan sites for $12/14, on-site vans from $28 and self-contained two-storey cabins from $40.

WELLINGTON (pop 20)

This tiny hamlet is on the Murray 12 km from Tailem Bend and 11 km from Lake Alexandrina. First settled in the 1840s, it was the main river crossing on the overland route to Victoria. Today there's a **ferry** across the river on the road from Tailem Bend and only one of its four old pubs is still trading.

The *Wellington Hotel* sells counter meals and boasts a nice view of the river from its shaded front lawns – this is a great place to relax with a cold drink on a hot day. Next door, the historic *Old Wellington Court House* (☎ 8572 7330) has a good reputation for its B&B ($45/60) and licensed restaurant.

The small, basic but attractive *Wellington Caravan Park* (☎ 8572 7302) across from the hotel has tent and caravan sites and cabins.

MANNUM (pop 2030)

A thriving port until Murray Bridge took all its trade, picturesque Mannum has many relics of its early boom times, including the boiler from the original *Mary Ann*, in **Mary Ann Park** down by the river. The old paddle-steamer commenced its historic journey nearby in 1853.

A leaflet details three scenic and historical **walks** you can do around town. The attractions listed include the 1898 paddle-steamer *Marion*, now moored alongside the tourist information centre (☎ 8569 1303) as a floating museum. Both are open daily from 10 am to 4 pm; entry to the *Marion* costs $2.50.

Mannum Old Wares, is an old butter factory on Randell St, is worth an hour's browse through its huge selection of antiques, reproductions and bric-a-brac.

You can see numerous water birds in the **Purnong Road Bird Sanctuary**, which starts at the Mannum Caravan Park and runs for several km along the road. Pelicans are a feature; the roosts in the water beside the caravan park are a good spot to see these ungainly birds, especially late in the afternoon. Otherwise, go down to Mary Ann Park and start eating lunch – at least one pelican will soon appear and stand eyeing you hopefully.

The **Cascade Waterfalls**, nine km from town off the main road to Murray Bridge, are worth a visit for their picturesque and rugged scenery. Although the falls only flow during winter, the beautiful river red gums in the creek downstream of the gorge can be enjoyed at any time.

There's a ferry crossing at **Purnong**, 33

km north of Mannum. You can hire canoes and kayaks at the Ferryman's Cottage (☎ 8570 4323) for extended periods; rates are negotiable.

Organised Tours

The grand paddle-steamer *River Murray Princess* operates from Mannum, offering weekend (from $210), three-night (from $334) and five-night ($560) cruises. For more details contact Captain Cook Cruises (☎ toll-free 1800 804 843).

Mannum Big River Cruises (☎ 8569 2606) runs morning and afternoon 'coffee' cruises on MV *Wallamba* on weekends and public holidays. Prices start at $10 for one hour. The MV *Lady Mannum* also does cruises; check the times with the Lady Mannum Cruises office (☎ 8569 1438) on Randell St.

The old PS *Marion* has been recommissioned and there are plans to run cruises; check at the tourist centre for an update.

They may not sound too inviting, but Scruffs Tours (☎ 8569 1554) are actually very good. These are tag-along tours (where you follow the tour guide's vehicle in your own car) and they'll take you to plenty of interesting places you otherwise won't get to.

Places to Stay

The *Mannum Caravan Park* (☎ 8569 1402) on the town side of the ferry crossing, has tent/caravan sites from $10/12 and cabins for $42. Alternatively, you can camp for free on the other side of the river near the ferry and use the shower facilities ($2.50) at the caravan park.

Just out of town on the eastern tourist drive to Purnong, the crowded little *Mannum Holiday Village* (☎ 8561 1179) has cabins for $35. About 15 km further out on the same road, the *Grulunga Caravan Park* (☎ 8569 1820) has tent sites, powered sites and cabins.

The *Mannum Motel* (☎ 8569 1808), on Cliff St above the ferry landing, has comfortable, well-appointed units for $50/60/70.

Matilda's B&B (☎ 8569 1324) on River Lane has a good reputation for friendliness and service; its double rooms cost $80 with a cooked breakfast. Alternatively, *Mannaroo Farm* (☎ 8569 1646) has B&B for $50/70 and full board for $90, including farm tours, boating, fishing and water-skiing. It's 11 km from Mannum on East Front Rd.

Between Mannum and Swan Reach are small camping grounds by the river at Walkers Flat (where there's a store), Caurnamont and 2.4 km south of Caurnamont (ask at the shed opposite the turn-off).

Places to Eat

Best value in town are the regular specials put on by the *Pretoria Hotel* and the *Mannum Club* (meals on Tuesday to Saturday only), both on Randell St. The *Mannum Motel* has a good a la carte restaurant; it does nightly three-course specials for $12.50 and has an all-you-can-eat menu for the same price on Friday night.

Mannum's most exclusive eatery is *SJ's Brasserie*, on Randell St, which does breakfast, lunch and dinner. Otherwise there's a choice of takeaways, bakeries and coffee shops. Locals recommend *The Bakershop* for delicious home-baked products and the *Mannum Takeaway* for quality and value. Both are on Randell St.

Getting There & Around

ABM Coachlines (☎ 8347 3336) has a daily return service on weekdays from Adelaide ($11.20).

Mannum Taxis (☎ 018 834 861) operates weekdays from 6 am to 6 pm and Saturday morning, charging around $30 to Murray Bridge.

SWAN REACH (pop 230)

This sleepy old town has picturesque river scenery thanks to the high yellow cliffs that crowd the eastern bank. The **Swan Reach Hotel** (1905) is perched on the clifftop above the ferry and commands a great view – it's surprising that someone hasn't knocked it down and built a flash resort in its place! Despite the town's name there aren't many swans around, although pelicans are common.

Verminproof fencing encloses over 1000 hectares of virgin mallee at the **Yookamurra Sanctuary** (☎ 8562 5011), 17 km to the north-west. Following the removal of foxes, cats and rabbits, several locally extinct mammals, such as the numbat, were introduced and are now breeding. The complex is open from Wednesday night to Sunday night and offers cabin-style accommodation, meals, habitat walks and day and evening wildlife walks. A one-night package costs $50 and bookings are essential for all activities.

Between Swan Reach and Sedan, to the west, the 2017-hectare **Swan Reach Conservation Park** has diverse vegetation and plenty of wildlife, including wombats, emus and kangaroos. About 15 km south-west (more by road) there are magnificent red gums along the Marne River in the 105-hectare **Marne Valley Conservation Park**. This is a great spot for picnics and walks.

Just downstream from Swan Reach, the Murray makes a tight meander known as **Big Bend**; the lookout beside the road to Walker Flat nine km from town gives you a dramatic view of sweeping curves and towering ochre-coloured cliffs. This is one of the best vantage points for photography you'll find anywhere along the river.

River Murray Educational Nature Tours (☎ 018 085 184) has a range of interesting options including flat-bottom boat sunset tours, gourmet bush lunches, night walks at Yookamurra Sanctuary and a visit to an Aboriginal art site. Rates are available on application.

Places to Stay & Eat

The *Swan Reach Hotel* (☎ 8570 2003) has three bars, daily counter meals, basic twin-share rooms for $28/40 and renovated 'old world' double rooms for $50. Down below by the ferry landing, the *bakery* sells takeaways.

The *Swan Reach Caravan Park* near the ferry is small and unkempt, but will tempt you if you're desperate. A far better proposition is the *Punyelroo Caravan Park* (☎ 8570 2021), which has tent/caravan sites for $11/13 and on-site vans from $25. It's beside the river about five km downstream from Swan Reach and on the opposite bank.

The Riverland

The section between Blanchetown and Renmark is usually known as the Riverland. It has the Murray's only national park (Murray River National Park, between Loxton and Renmark) and the flourishing fruit-growing and wine-making centres of Waikerie, Barmera, Loxton, Berri and Renmark.

BLANCHETOWN (pop 250)

The historic pub (1856) is a reminder of the days when this was a stagecoach stopover on the 'Sydney Road'. Lock One is the start of the system of locks and weirs that keeps the river at a fairly constant level between Blanchetown and Wentworth, in NSW. Completed in 1922, it's a good spot to observe pelicans, and there's a licensed floating restaurant nearby.

Brookfield Conservation Park (5500 hectares) is about nine km west of town on the Sturt Highway. The park was originally purchased by the Chicago Zoological Society as a wombat reserve, and they still support research into the animal's needs. A 10-km 'nature drive' takes you through the haunts of wombats, emus and kangaroos, and there's some good bushwalking.

Australia has three species of wombat. The common wombat (above) is the one you are likely to bump into – sometimes literally!

Places to Stay

The small and friendly *Riverside Caravan Park* (☎ 8540 5070) has tent/caravan sites for $10/12 and six-berth cabins from $34. It hires canoes for $4 per hour and $20 per day, and has a pontoon to fish from.

About three km south of town off the road to Swan Reach, the *Blanchetown Caravan Park* (☎ 8540 5073) is also by the river and has lots of trees. It has tent/caravan sites for $8/10 and basic cabins for $18.

Five km north of town, the *River Palms Holiday Park* (☎ 8540 5035) is uninspiring but does have access to the river. You can camp on the rather desolate bank here for $8 per site.

MORGAN (pop 1350)

Established in 1878, when a railway was built from Adelaide to tap into the river trade, the Morgan of the 1880s was one of the busiest river ports in Australia. Its wharves towered 12 metres high and stretched 170 metres along the bank, and gangs of 40 wharfies worked continuous shifts to unload the cargoes of the barges and paddle-steamers that queued alongside. Not much happens in Morgan these days, however. In fact, the town's commercial life had quietened down so much by 1969 that the railway was closed.

A leaflet details a **historical walk** which includes the PS *Mayflower*. Built in 1884, it's the oldest operating paddle-wheeler in SA. There's also the old **customs house** (1879) and the **Post Office Row** streetscape (1889).

The **Port of Morgan Historic Museum** in the old railway station, next to the wharf, has interesting exhibits on the paddle-steamer days. It opens from 2 pm to 4 pm on weekends.

Also worth visiting is the museum (enquiries ☎ 8540 3329) at historic **Nor-west Bend** homestead (1856), eight km from town on the road to Renmark. The property once covered 5000 sq km, but has had so many bits carved off that it's now less than 10% of that.

If you're after antiques, bric-a-brac or arts and crafts, **Carmine's Antiques** at 212 Railway Terrace is one of the best on the river.

A **ferry** crosses the Murray on the Waikerie road just outside Morgan. There's another at Cadell.

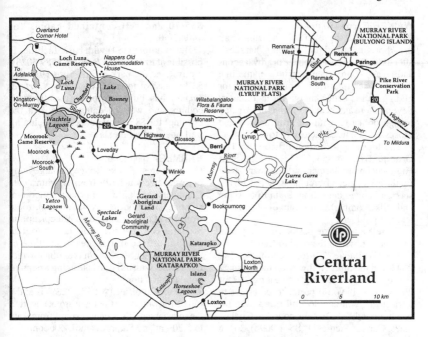

Central Riverland

0   5   10 km

Organised Tours

On the road to Waikerie, the **emu farm** at Molo Estate (☎ 8540 3342) has interesting tours for $5; appointments are necessary.

The Outback Camel Company (☎ 8543 2280) has **camel treks** along the river and through semi-arid station country from its base 20 km east of Morgan on the road to Renmark. Their trips range from one and a half hours ($25) to three days ($385).

Morgan Eco-Tours (☎ 8540 4035) does tours with a biological emphasis to places such as river wetlands, red gum forests, mallee bushland, orchards and the Molo Estate emu farm. A half-day trip costs from $10 and a full day including lunch is $25.

Places to Stay & Eat

The large *Morgan Riverside Caravan Park* (☎ 8540 2207) is next to the ferry and has tent/caravan sites for $9/12, on-site vans for $27 and cabins from $32. It hires tandem bicycles ($4 per hour) and canoes ($6 per hour or $20 per day).

The *Commercial Hotel* (☎ 8540 2107) on Railway Terrace has basic rooms for $15 a person. Across the road, the *Terminus Hotel/Motel* (☎ 8540 2006) has pub rooms for $20/34, including a light breakfast, and motel units for $38/43. Both do good counter and dining room meals.

In Federal St off the road to Burra, the *Colonial Motel* (☎ 8540 2277) has units for $46/54/62.

There are good bush camp sites with no facilities among beautiful big red gums in the *Morgan Conservation Park*, across the river from town. To get there, turn left about 500 metres from the ferry landing. You can also camp by the river at *Nor-west Bend* station (☎ 8540 3237) for $10 per car.

There are magnificent bush camp sites among huge red gums beside the water at *Hogwash Bend*, 7.7 km past Cadell on the road to Waikerie.

MURRAY RIVER

WAIKERIE (pop 1800)

It's thought that the town takes its name from the Aboriginal word for 'anything that flies', after the teeming birdlife on the nearby lagoons and river. Appropriately (with a name like that) it's one of Australia's major centres for gliding, but is better known for its oranges. Several thousand hectares thrive in irrigated orange orchards, with the fruit packed and processed at a huge factory in town.

The tourist information office is in **The Orange Tree** (☎ 8541 2332), on the Sturt Highway on the Barmera side of town – look for the large, green fibreglass sphere with red spots. It's open daily from 9 am to 5.30 pm and sells a comprehensive range of local fruit and nut products.

There's a bird hide beside **Hart Lagoon**, just out of town on the road to Cadell.

The Waikerie Gliding Club (☎ 8541 2644), on the Sturt Highway on the Barmera side of town, has **joy flights** costing $50 for 20 minutes. If you'd prefer to be closer to terra firma, you can do **trail rides** ($15 for one hour and $45 for four hours) at Clydesdales, Carts & Picnics (☎ 8541 9096), 26 km from town off the road to Cadell (see Places to Stay & Eat, below).

On the northern side of the river 12 km from town, the 2850-hectare **Pooginook Conservation Park** consists of rolling sand ridges covered in mallee. Early spring is the best time to visit for wildflowers and birdlife. The park has two bush camping areas.

Places to Stay & Eat

Down by the river on the Cadell side of town, the *Waikerie Caravan Park* (☎ 8541 2651) has tent/caravan sites for $9.50/13 and cabins from $30.

The *Waikerie Hotel/Motel* (☎ 8541 2999), on McCoy St, has self-contained pub rooms with air-con for $35/45 and motel rooms for $40/50, as well as counter meals and a bistro. The *Waikerie Club* on Crush Terrace does evening meals on Wednesday, Friday and Saturday nights, with specials from $5.

On the Sturt Highway on the eastern outskirts of town, *Kirriemuir Motel & Cabins* (☎ 8541 2488) has modern motel units from

$55/70 and self-contained cabins for $40/45/50.

Bush camping ($4) with basic facilities is possible at *Eremophila Park* (☎ 8589 3023), a private nature park off the Sturt Highway 33 km east of town. *Clydesdales, Carts & Picnics* has bush camping (usually with country and western entertainment in the evening) for $85 a day per person including trail rides and all meals.

BARMERA (pop 1900)

On the shores of Lake Bonney, a large body of freshwater which fills from the Murray via Chambers Creek, Barmera was an important stopping point on the overland stock route from NSW to SA. The name is a corruption of Barmeedji, the name of the Aboriginal group that lived in this area at the time of white settlement. The town is another irrigation centre, with its large lake being a popular holiday attraction.

The tourist office (☎ 8588 2289) is at the top of Barwell Ave (the main street), next to the roundabout. It's open weekdays from 9 am to 5.30 pm and Saturday until 12 noon.

Things to See & Do

About nine km from town on the road to Morgan, the stone ruins of **Napper's Accommodation House**, built in 1850 at the mouth of Chambers Creek, are a reminder of the droving era.

So too is the evocative **Overland Corner Hotel**, 11 km further out, which is still trading. The pub takes its name from a bend in the Murray River where drovers and travellers once camped. Built in 1859, it's now owned by the National Trust, which has a small **museum** on-site. The Trust also has a brochure detailing the fascinating geology of the cliffs at nearby **Herons Bend**. There's an interesting, eight-km self-guided **nature trail** down to the river from the pub; pick up a leaflet at the bar.

Lake Bonney is very popular for swimming and water sports. There's a nudist beach at **Pelican Point**, on the lake's western shore – for details contact the caravan park there on ☎ 8588 7366. The lake has numerous dead red gums, all killed by flooding; these are often festooned with cormorants hung out like washing on the stark branches.

On Dean Drive, the **Lake Bonney Aquatic Centre** hires windsurfers, canoes and catamarans. It's open from 12 noon all school holidays and weekends between September and May.

The **Cobdogla Irrigation Museum**, at nearby Cobdogla, features steam engines including the Humphrey Pump, an awesome affair which is fired up on four days each year. The museum only opens on scheduled operating days; these take place on all South Australian long weekends and some Sundays during school holidays.

On the Sturt Highway on the Waikerie side of town, the friendly **Bonneyview Winery** has tastings daily. It's one of the last survivors of the Riverland's small wineries, most of the others having crashed during the last recession.

There's a game reserve at **Moorook** (on the road to Loxton) and another at **Loch Luna** across the river from the small irrigation centre of **Kingston-on-Murray**. Both reserves have nature trails and are good spots for birdwatching and canoeing; the Kingston-on-Murray Caravan Park hires canoes for $5 an hour or $25 per day, and you can paddle across to the reserve.

Riverland Safaris (☎ 8588 3270) offers various **guided tours** including winery visits ($10) and fishing and yabbying trips (from $12), as well as tours further afield to the Barossa and Flinders ranges.

The Barmera Taxi Service (☎ 8588 2869 or 018 839 387) operates 24 hours daily. It costs about $20 to go to Berri and $35 to Renmark.

Places to Stay

On the lake shore within walking distance of town, the large *Lake Bonney Holiday Park* (☎ 8588 2234) has tent sites for $10, on-site vans for $26, cabins from $28 and cottages from $44.

Alternatively, the comfortable *Barmera Hotel/Motel* (☎ 8588 2111) on Barwell Ave has basic rooms from $20/30, self-contained hotel rooms from $35 for singles & doubles

and motel units for $48/50/58. On Lakeside Drive, the *Lake Resort Motel* (☎ 8588 2555) charges $50/55 for its units.

Most exclusive of all is the *Barmera Country Club* (☎ 8588 2888), on Hawdon St, which has 'standard' rooms for $74/80 and spa rooms for $90 singles & doubles.

Out of Town The *Greenwood Park Caravan Park* (☎ 8588 7070) on Lake Bonney is small, quiet, remote (five km from Barmera) and an ideal place for bird watchers. It has camp sites by the water for $9, powered sites for $10.50 and cabins for $33. They also have a bunkhouse where beds are $4, but ring first.

Also on Lake Bonney, the *Pelican Point Nudist Resort Caravan Park* (☎ 8588 7366) off the road to Morgan has tent/caravan sites for $15/18 and kitchen facilities.

There's an attractive *caravan park* at Cobdogla (☎ 8588 7164) and another beside the water at Kingston-on-Murray (☎ 8583 0209). The *Motel Kingston Bridge* (☎ 8583 0206), on the Barmera side of Kingston-on-Murray, boasts nice views over the river.

At Moorook there's *Moorook B&B* (☎ 8583 9355), which charges $25/40 with a light breakfast. You can camp for $3 on the riverfront across from the Moorook General Store; the area has good shade and lawn areas, but little in the way of facilities.

There's no shortage of good bush camp sites ($2 per adult per night) in the Moorook and Loch Luna Game Reserves – ask the rangers in Berri (☎ 8595 2177) for a permit.

The *Overland Corner Hotel* (☎ 8588 7021) has rooms for $35/50 including breakfast.

Places to Eat

The best-value meals in town are served at the *Barmera Hotel/Motel*, which offers counter and dining room meals, and the *Cobdogla Club* (Thursday to Sunday nights only). Both have specials from $5. The *Pagoda Chinese Restaurant* on Barwell Ave is consistently good and reasonably priced.

For more elegant dining, however, you'll have to go to the *Barmera Country Club*, on Hawdon St, and pay accordingly.

The *Barmera Bakery* enjoys a good reputation for its home-baked products, as does *D&I'S Coffee Lounge* for light lunches and coffee. Both are on Barwell Ave. *Jordan's Pizza Bar* on Lakeside Drive and the *Moonlite Café* on Bice St do nice pizzas.

For atmosphere and fine food the *Bonneyview Winery* has a lot going for it. The meals are a little pricey ($12 for a ploughman's lunch) but the wines are reasonably priced and you get appetisers thrown in.

The *Overland Corner Hotel* sells hearty home-cooked meals in the tiny front bar. It also has a dining room, but you have to book in advance.

LOXTON (pop 3320)

From Berri the Murray makes a large loop south of the Sturt Highway, with Loxton at its base. The town was established in 1907, although settlers (mainly of German descent) had been successfully growing wheat in the area for 10 years prior to that. Today it's an important service centre for surrounding farms and irrigation areas.

The tourist office (☎ 8584 7919) is in front of the Loxton Hotel on East Terrace. It's open from 9 am to 5 pm on weekdays and to 12 noon on Saturday – ask at the pub outside these times.

Things to See & Do

The beautiful **Katarapko** section of the Murray River National Park occupies much of the area within the loop; there's great canoeing in the backwaters here, as well as walks along the timbered banks. The park is on the opposite side of the river to Loxton, but you can easily canoe across from town.

If you're not a canoeist, the main attraction here is the **Loxton Historical Village**, which has over 30 buildings furnished from days gone by. It's open from 10 am to 4 pm on weekdays and to 5 pm on weekends; admission is $4. Ask at the tourist office about working days.

Down by the caravan park is a large gum tree with markers showing **flood levels** and dates. With the notable exception of the mighty 1956 flood at five metres – the highest since white settlement – most are around the one-metre mark.

The **Australian Vintage winery** on Bookpurnong Rd is open daily except Sunday from 10 am to 5 pm for tastings and cellar-door sales.

Places to Stay & Eat

Right on the Murray and with beautiful red gums, the *Loxton Riverfront Caravan Park* (☎ 8584 7862) is two km from town. It has backpacker beds in a self-contained lodge for $12 – if there's four of you the rate drops to $8 – as well as camp sites for $9.50, on-site vans for $25 and cabins from $32.

The *Loxton Hotel/Motel* (☎ 8584 7266) on East Terrace has basic pub rooms from $16/24 and motel units from $50/55. Across the road is *Loxton B&B* (☎ 8583 0209), which charges $30 per person including a cooked breakfast.

The hotel has a very good bistro plus counter meals, and you can get a hearty feed for a reasonable price at the *Loxton Community Club*, on Bookpurnong Terrace. Otherwise there are coffee shops, takeaways and bakeries; locals reckon the *Country Bakehouse* on East Terrace is one of the best on the Murray. The Aussie whopper burgers at the *Spring Leaf* takeaway almost next door to the pub are just that – whopping.

You can camp on *Katarapko Island* with a permit for $2 per adult per night; contact the NPWS office (☎ 8595 2177) in Berri.

Getting There & Around

A Stateliner bus calls in daily from Adelaide. Book at the tourist office.

East Terrace Taxis (☎ 018 839 289) offers a 24-hour service around Loxton and further afield; approximate fares from Loxton are $40 to Renmark, $40 to Barmera and $25 to Berri.

Riverland Canoeing Adventures (☎ 8584 1494 after hours) on Alamein Ave, off the road to Renmark, rents one-person kayaks for $12 per day and double kayaks and canoes for $20 a day. Concession rates apply after five days. Transport (allow 50 c/km for drop-off and pick-up), touring maps and camping equipment can be arranged for an extra fee.

BERRI (pop 3700)

Proclaimed in 1911, Berri was another irrigation town (along with Waikerie, Barmera and Loxton) established after the success of Renmark, and today is a major wine-making, fruit-growing and processing centre.

The tourist office (☎ 8582 1655), on Vaughan Terrace, is open from 9 am to 5 pm on weekdays and to 11.30 am on Saturday.

Things to See & Do

There are several wineries in the area. **Berri Estates winery** at Glossop, 13 km west of Berri, is the largest winery and distillery complex in Australia. It's open for tastings and cellar-door sales from Monday to Saturday between 9 am and 5 pm. On Nixon Rd at Monash, about seven km north-west of town, **Norman Wines** is open for tastings and sales on weekdays only from 9 am to 4.30 pm.

Near the ferry landing in town there's a **monument** to Jimmy James, a famous Aboriginal tracker who, in 30 years service with the police, contributed to the arrest of around 40 criminals and the rescue of 10 lost persons.

Managed by the National Trust, **Wilabalangaloo** on the way to Renmark is a 100-hectare flora and fauna reserve with spectacular scenery, walking trails, a tiny historic paddle-steamer and a historic homestead. It's open Thursday to Monday from 10 am to 4 pm (daily during school holidays); entry is $4 for adults and $1 for children.

A **ferry** crosses the river to Loxton from near the Berri Hotel/Motel on Riverside Ave.

Places to Stay & Eat

The *Berri Riverside Caravan Park* (☎ 8582 3723), on Riverview Drive, has camp sites for $9, on-site vans from $29 and six-berth cabins from $34 for singles & doubles. Extra adults are $4.

Berri Backpackers (☎ 8582 3144), on the Sturt Highway at the Barmera end of town, is one of the best equipped hostels you'll find anywhere – but it's only for internationals. Guests have free use of the pool, sauna,

games room, volleyball court, bicycles and canoes, and the manager has excellent contacts if you want seasonal work in local orchards and vineyards. Beds are $12 ($80 per week).

At the *Berri Hotel/Motel* (☎ 8582 1411), on Riverview Drive, singles/doubles cost from $34/38 in the pub, and from $62/70 in the motel. It has counter meals, a bistro, restaurant, coffee lounge and one of the best gaming rooms in country South Australia.

The *Berri Country Club* (☎ 8582 2688), on the Sturt Highway on the Renmark side of town, has units for $62/67. In Zante Worman St (the town part of the Sturt Highway), rooms at the modest *Berri Lodge Motel* (☎ 8582 1011) cost $42/52.

About 300 metres from the Wilabalangaloo Reserve, luxurious *Riverbush* (☎ toll-free 1800 088 191) has eight-berth cabins costing $130 for two persons for two nights; it costs $280 for eight persons for two nights.

The *Berri Club* across the road from Berri Backpackers has great-value meals from Thursday to Sunday nights; it's open every night for drinks, which are cheaper than in town. Not quite in the same league, but still good value, are the specials at the *Berri Country Club* and the *Big River Tavern*, on Shiell Rd.

RENMARK (pop 4300)

This prosperous town was the first of the great irrigation projects that revolutionised the Riverland. Established in 1887 by the Chaffey brothers, who were bankrupted by the bank crash of the early 1890s, Renmark is a flourishing service and processing centre for the surrounding orchards. It's also more organised for tourism than its neighbours, with a better choice of accommodation and tours.

The tourist office (☎ 8586 6704) is on Murray Ave, beside the river. It's open from 9 am to 5 pm weekdays, 9 am to 4 pm on Saturday and noon to 4 pm Sunday. Attached is an interpretive centre ($3) which includes an inspection of the recommissioned 1911 paddle-steamer *Industry*. Ask at the tourist office about cruise times.

Things to See & Do

The **Olivewood Homestead**, a Canadian-style log cabin with wide Australian-style verandahs, was designed by Charles Chaffey and was his home while administering the Renmark estates. It has an interesting museum – check out the mountain lion trap, which was brought here to catch dingoes – and beautiful gardens where you can enjoy lunch and teas. Admission costs $3.50 and it's open from 10 am to 4 pm daily except Tuesday, when it opens at 2 pm, and Wednesday, when it's closed.

Goat Island, also known as Paringa Paddock, is on the Sturt Highway between the Paringa Bridge and Renmark. There are walking tracks among the gums, where you may see koalas – although they're more likely to be near the caravan park on the other side of the road.

The **Angoves winery**, on Bookmark Rd, and **Renmano Wines**, on Industry Rd, have cellar-door sales and tastings on weekdays between 9 am and 5 pm; Renmano is also open on Saturday between 9 am and 4 pm.

The **Chaffey Theatre**, on 18th St, has top-quality films or live theatre every week.

Organised Tours

Bush & Backwaters 4WD Tours (☎ 8586 5344) do half-day ($40) and full-day ($60) tours to conservation areas, wineries, orchards and historic sites around Renmark. They also have a fishing tour, and overnight trips can be arranged.

Renmark River Cruises (☎ 8595 1862) has day and night cruises from $10 on the MV *River Rambler*, departing from the town wharf. Their 1.5-hour backwater dinghy trips are $18 per person (four passengers maximum).

Places to Stay & Eat

Idyllically situated on the river a km east of town, the *Renmark Caravan Park* (☎ 8586

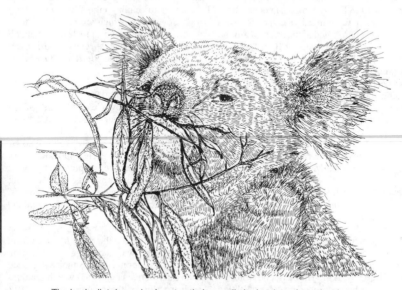

The koala diet depends almost entirely on a limited variety of eucalypt leaves. Although they look cuddly, keep away from a koala on the ground, as it may mistake you for a tree if frightened, and use its powerful claws to attempt to climb you!

MURRAY RIVER

6315) has tent/caravan sites for $10/12, on-site vans for $27 and cabins from $43. It hires canoes for $15 for two hours.

Further along the river beside the Paringa Bridge, the *Riverbend Caravan Park* (☎ 8595 5131) has tent/caravan sites for $9/12, on-site vans for $24, basic cabins for $30 and self-contained cabins from $36. It also hires canoes ($5 per hour).

Grays Caravan Park (☎ 8586 6522) at 27 Pyap St is not very inspiring and mainly caters to permanent residents. The tastefully renovated *Renmark Hotel/Motel* (☎ 8586 6755) on Murray Ave has hotel rooms for $35/40 for singles/doubles and motel units from $60/66/71; it's 100 years old, but doesn't look its age. You can get good meals in the front bar, bistro and dining room.

Citrus Valley Motel (☎ 8586 6717), at 210 Renmark Ave, has singles/doubles from $50/58. *Fountain Gardens Motel* (☎ 8586 6899) on Renmark Ave charges $48/56. *Ventura Motel* (☎ 8586 6481) at 234 Renmark Ave charges $48/55. *Renmark Country Club Motel* (☎ 8595 1401) on the Sturt Highway, about eight km west of the town centre, has standard units for $55/70 and suites for $84.

There are several restaurants and take-aways in town. *Sophia's Restaurant*, in the Southern Cross Roadhouse on the Sturt Highway, has good Greek food and a takeaway service downstairs. For value it's hard to beat the *Renmark Club*, across from the hotel, which has huge specials on Tuesday and Thursday nights.

A good spot for light lunches is *Gran's Coffee Shop*, also opposite the hotel. Try their submarines, or hot chicken and mayo rolls.

Getting There & Around

Southern Australia Airlines (call Qantas on ☎ 13 13 13) flies to Renmark from Adelaide ($104) twice daily on weekdays and once daily on weekends. There is no bus service to the airport, but you can phone Renmark Taxis (☎ 8586 6257) from there – the fare is about $11 to the centre of town.

Stateliner (☎ 8415 5555) has daily bus services from Adelaide to Renmark ($26.50), stopping on Renmark Ave a block

from the central business district. Greyhound Pioneer goes daily through Renmark on its Adelaide to Sydney run, stopping on the corner of 18th St and the Sturt Highway, a short walk from the town centre; the fare from Renmark to Sydney is $79.

You can hire a car from Budget (☎ 8586 5011) depending on availability. Renmark Taxis (☎ 8586 6257) operates a 24-hour service, charging about $25 to Berri and $50 to Loxton. Both the Renmark and River-bend Caravan Parks hire canoes. Rivermate (☎ 018 839 426) has aluminium dinghies on trailers, with a minimum hire time of half a day.

PARINGA (pop 600)

Just four km from Renmark and 19 km from the Victorian border, Paringa is the last town in SA. There's a magnificent view over the river and its high ochre-coloured cliffs from the lookout tower on **Heading Cliffs** – to get there, head north of town for 12 km and turn off on Murtho Rd. Afternoon is the best time for photos of the cliffs.

You can swim at the **Lock Five Sandbar**. However, there have been numerous drownings here because of deep holes, so if you're not a strong swimmer it's smart to wear a lifejacket. To get there, turn off the Sturt Highway between Paringa and the Paringa Bridge, near Renmark, and drive past **Lock Five**, which is open to the public. En route to the river there's a **Houseboat Marina**. Several operators are based here, making it one of the best places to hire a houseboat anywhere on the Murray.

Places to stay are limited. The *Paringa Caravan Park* (☎ 8595 5178) and the *Paringa Hotel/Motel* (☎ 8595 5005) are both in the centre of town. *Woodvale Holiday Cottages* (☎ 8595 5240) are out at the Lock Five Sandbar.

MURRAY RIVER NATIONAL PARK

The park is broken into three sections: **Katarapko** (8905 hectares) between Loxton and Berri; **Lyrup Flats** (2000 hectares) on the southern side of Renmark; and **Bulyong Island** (2380 hectares). All are popular spots

MURRAY RIVER

The Dying Murray

Depending on whether it's a good or a bad rainfall year in SA, the Murray River provides between 40% and 90% of Adelaide's water supply. It's also a vital factor in the state's economic survival; water taken from it irrigates crops worth $3 billion annually in SA, Victoria and NSW. Yet the river is often treated as a convenient drain for effluent, and water is being sucked out at such a rate that experts believe the river is dying.

There are three major problems: insufficient river flow; too many nutrients in the water (particularly phosphates); and increasing salinity. The river is being overused to the extent that, based on current trends, average use will equal average river flow by 2020. Predictions are that the Murray in SA will soon be experiencing drought-like flows in six out of 10 years, and that the mouth will dry up in three of every four years.

In recent years the reduction in flow, which leads to increasing pollution from nutrients, has encouraged the growth of noxious blooms of blue-green algae. The nutrients come from farm run-off and, unbelievably, from effluent that's pumped into the river system from towns in NSW.

Reduced river flow has also had catastrophic consequences for other aspects of the environment. Over the past century the flood-plain wetlands have declined by 70%, with a subsequent reduction in animal life. Murray cod must swim onto the flood plains to breed, but the loss of breeding habitat saw the annual SA catch of this species drop from 100,000 kg in the 1950s to a mere 10,000 kg in the '80s. The introduced European carp doesn't need the flood-plains to breed, and so now accounts for over 80% of the river's fish stocks.

With an eye to future calamity the SA Government is proposing a dramatic plan of action to clean up the river before it's too late. Among the proposals: all urban effluent would be directed away from the river, or at least treated to a high standard before being allowed to enter it; and catchment areas would be improved to reduce the amount of nutrients entering the river from farm run-off. Improved irrigation techniques are also required to reduce both salinity and the amount of water used.

It's a bold plan and a necessary one, but it requires the cooperation of the Commonwealth, NSW and Victoria, not to mention funding. Unfortunately, however, examples of all four working together on matters related to the Murray are rare. All politicians are aware that it is a precious national resource, but many cynics in SA feel nothing much will happen until the Mannum-Adelaide pipeline is redirected to Canberra. ■

for bush camping, fishing, canoeing and birdwatching. Locals descend on the river in droves over Easter, so this is a good time to avoid the place.

Lyrup Flats is one of the most devastated areas on the Murray, with many trees killed by high water levels and salt intrusion. It looks like a bomb has hit the place, but all is not lost. The salty pools are ideal habitats for brine shrimp, a rich food for ducks and other water birds, while the dead trees provide nesting sites.

You can get to Katarapko and Lyrup Flats by road off the Sturt Highway and to Bulyong Island from Renmark North. Alternatively, it's easy to canoe across to both these areas from the opposite bank.

Danggali Conservation Park

This 253,230-hectare park is 90 km north of Renmark and, together with the Murray River National Park and other parks and reserves in the area, forms part of the enormous Bookmark Biosphere Reserve. The park, an amalgamation of four sheep stations, is dominated by mallee and black oak woodlands.

Things to do include nature drives (there's a 100-km 4WD route), walks, wildlife watching and spotting beautiful wildflowers in spring. There is no food or fuel in this remote area, and water is extremely limited. In other words, take your own everything.

Bush camping is permitted and you can stay in the old shearer's quarters – contact the ranger at Canopus on ☎ 8595 8010 or the regional office in Berri.

Murray Mallee

Forming part of the Murraylands region, the Murray Mallee is bordered by the Murray River to the north and west, the Victorian border to the east, and the Mallee Highway to the south. To the first settlers, this rolling sea of mallee scrub was considered 'unfit for any purpose', and the overlanders took pains to avoid its waterless sandhills. Eventually, shallow ground water was found, enabling wells and soaks to be dug. From the 1860s most of the region was taken up for low-intensity grazing.

By the early 1900s, improved wheat varieties and more efficient farming methods had made the Mallee an attractive proposition. Huge areas were cleared for cropping, particularly after 1906 when a development railway opened between Tailem Bend and Pinnaroo. More railways were constructed and 36 townships were surveyed, but the realities of drought and poor soils eventually brought decline.

These days the Mallee is still an important wheat-growing area. However, the farms are much larger and the population much smaller than in those early boom years. Many of the early townships no longer exist, and there are numerous abandoned homes and empty schools throughout the region. Only the towns of **Lameroo** (population 560) and **Pinnaroo** (population 650) on the Mallee Highway have retained any significance as service centres.

MALLEE HIGHWAY

You'd take the Mallee Highway, which runs east from Tailem Bend to Pinnaroo, if you were in a hurry to get from Adelaide to north-western Victoria or Sydney. This good sealed road passes through several small towns, all with basic facilities.

Apart from a couple of major conservation parks, which require long detours, there's not much to see en route. In Pinnaroo, the **Printers Museum** is probably worth a visit if you've got printer's ink in your veins, while the interesting **Gum Family Collection** (☎ 8577 5322) comprises 80 antique stationary engines and other memorabilia. It's off the road to Loxton about 30 km from Pinnaroo.

The 59,148-hectare **Billiatt Conservation Park** is 37 km north of Lameroo, or 54 km south of Loxton via Alawoona. An undulating sea of mallee and sand dunes, the park is home to rare western whipbirds and red-lored whistlers – mallee fowls also live here. The only access is off the unsealed road from Lameroo to Alawoona, which runs through the centre of the park. There are no facilities or drinking water.

South of the Mallee Highway and adjoining the Victorian border is the huge **Ngarkat Conservation Park**, which you can reach from Lameroo, Pinnaroo and towns on the Dukes Highway. For details see the chapter on the South-East.

The Murray Bridge Passenger Service (☎ 8415 5555) runs from Adelaide to Pinnaroo ($31) daily except Saturday.

Places to Stay

At Lameroo there's the *Lameroo Community Hotel/Motel* (☎ 8576 3006), which has units for $40/50/55.

Pinnaroo has the *Pinnaroo Motel* (☎ 8577 8261), with units for $42/52. Alternatively, there's the *Pinnaroo Caravan Park* (☎ 8577 8224), which has tent and caravan sites and basic cabins right on the highway.

The *Meranwyney Host Farm* (☎ 8576 5215), 17 km south of the Mallee Highway (turn off at Wilkawatt), borders the north-west corner of Ngarkat Conservation Park. It offers full board for $90 including farm tours, visits to heritage sites, bush walks and other activities.

MURRAY RIVER

The South-East

Bordered by the Murray Mallee to the north, Victoria to the east and the Southern Ocean to the west and south, the South-East is one of SA's most diverse and productive agricultural regions. Kingston is the dividing point between the drier Upper South-East, north of the town, and the more lush Lower South-East, to the south.

Although it makes up only 3.5% of the state's area, the South-East accounts for nearly 20% of its farm output; softwood timber, beef cattle, sheep for wool and meat, cereals, hay, vegetables and grapes are all important contributors to the local economy. Australia's largest concentration of *Pinus radiata* (Monterey pine) plantations is in the Lower South-East. All its ports have rock lobster fishing fleets, with the state's largest at Port MacDonnell. Crow-eaters generally refer to rock lobsters as 'crayfish' or simply 'crays'.

There are a number of extinct volcanic vents around Mt Gambier and Millicent, with the most recent activity having occurred about 4000 years ago. Otherwise the region is mostly flat to undulating; in the south, vast swampy areas lie between ancient coastal sand dunes which now form low ranges running parallel to the coast. Many seasonal swamps have been drained since 1863, creating rich agricultural land.

The South-East has a number of attractions apart from its long coastline of surf beaches, sheltered bays and rugged cliffs. These include wineries and Mother Mary MacKillop sites around Penola, water birds at the Coorong and Bool Lagoon, and significant limestone caves near Millicent and Naracoorte. There are also the historic ports of Robe, Beachport and Port MacDonnell, whose brief boom times left many interesting buildings for today's heritage hunters to admire.

Information

The major information outlet for the Lower South-East is the Lady Nelson Tourist Information & Interpretive Centre (☎ 8724 1730)

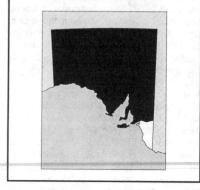

in Mt Gambier. The National Parks & Wildlife Service (NPWS) regional office (☎ 8735 1177) is at 11 Helen St, Mt Gambier.

Communications Throughout this book we use the new statewide STD code (08) and eight-digit telephone numbers, which take effect in February 1997. Should you need to use the old number, simply take the first two digits (either 85 or 87 in the South-East) and use as the STD code (085 or 087).

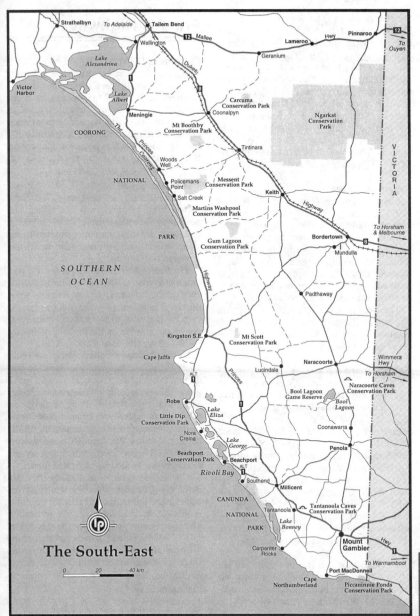

The South-East

0   20   40 km

Books & Maps The Royal Automobile Association of SA (RAA) has the best touring maps; there's one for the Upper South-East and another for the Lower South-East. Also worth getting is the Department of Recreation & Sport's cycle-touring map, which covers most of the Lower South-East.

Apart from the free booklet published by Tourism South-East, the only comprehensive regional guide is the RAA's 136-page *South East*. The Royal Society of SA's *Natural History of the South-East*, edited by MJ Tyler, is a useful reference.

Organised Tours

Although Coorong Nature Tours (☎ 8574 0037) of Meningie specialises in the Coorong area, they have an excellent range of tours to conservation areas all over the South-East. These include three-day trips to the Lower South-East ($360), two days in the Upper South-East ($240), tag-along tours, overnight bushwalks and special trips for birdwatchers or other nature study enthusiasts.

There are fishing charters at Robe, diving charters at Kingston and local tours at Mt Gambier – see the respective sections on these towns for more details.

Getting There & Away

Air Kendell Airlines and O'Connors Air Services fly daily from Mt Gambier to Adelaide and Melbourne. Both fares cost $147).

Bus Bonds Mt Gambier Motor Service (☎ 8231 9090 in Adelaide; 8725 5037 in Mt Gambier) runs from the central bus station in Adelaide to Mt Gambier daily (except Saturday) for $36.90. You can travel along the coast via the Coorong, stopping at Meningie ($17.90), Kingston SE ($28.70), Robe ($32.30) and Beachport ($35.10), or go inland via Bordertown ($27.50), Naracoorte ($35.10) and Penola ($34.30).

Train Victoria's V/Line bus-train service (☎ 13 22 32) runs to Melbourne from Mt Gambier daily (six hours, $46.20) – you take the bus to Warrnambool, then hop on the train to Melbourne.

Princes Highway

The Princes Highway (Highway 1) follows the coast southwards to Kingston, where it veers inland to Millicent, then on through Mt Gambier to Portland in Victoria. A more interesting route from Kingston is to take Alternative Highway 1, which continues along the coast through the picturesque fishing and holiday ports of Robe and Beachport; it rejoins Highway 1 at Millicent.

MENINGIE (pop 800)

On Lake Albert, an appendage of Lake Alexandrina, Meningie was established as a port in 1866 but has never been anything other than small. It's a popular windsurfing spot, which isn't surprising as it always seems to be blowing.

The main **information outlet** for this part of the world is the Melaleuca Centre, a craft shop on the Princes Highway. Rangers from the NPWS office (☎ 8575 1200), on the Princes Highway in town, manage several conservation areas in the district, including the **Coorong National Park**.

Messent Conservation Park, covering 12,250 hectares, has plenty of wildlife and diverse vegetation, including large pink gums and spectacular wildflowers in spring. There's also good bushwalking, and you can camp. The park is only six km from **Salt Creek** on the Coorong. En route you pass the 1880-hectare **Martins Washpool Conservation Park** (4WD access only), which has winter wetlands surrounded by vegetated dunes.

The mallee habitats in 4050-hectare **Mt Boothby Conservation Park** also offer walks and wildlife; the fact that Mt Boothby is only 129 metres high gives you some idea of the surrounding terrain. This park is 40 km east of Meningie and is best reached from **Woods Well** on the Coorong, or from Dukes Highway to the north.

Places to Stay

The attractive *Lake Albert Caravan Park* (☎ 8575 1411) is beside the lake about one

GREG HERRIMAN

DENIS O'BYRNE

DENIS O'BYRNE

DENIS O'BYRNE

Top Left: Secluded beach huts, Chinaman's Wells
Top Right: Tourist train, Moonta mine, Yorke Peninsula
Bottom Left: Mine chimney and enginehouse ruins, Moonta mine, Yorke Peninsula
Bottom Right: Wallaroo Town Hall, Yorke Peninsula

MICHELLE COXALL

MICHELLE COXALL

RICHARD I'ANSON

Top Left: Abandoned farm dray, Yorke Peninsula
Top Right: 'I'm not flipping Cornish', Moonta, Yorke Peninsula
Bottom: Stunning Wilpena Pound, Flinders Ranges

km out on the Narrung road. It has tent/caravan sites for $10/13, on-site vans from $22 and cabins from $33.

There's also the *Meningie Hotel* (☎ 8575 1007), which has pub-style rooms from $25/30/45, and the much more expensive *Lake Albert Motel* (☎ 8575 1077) and *Meningie Waterfront Motel* (☎ 8575 1152). All are on the Princes Highway.

THE COORONG

A wetland of international significance, the Coorong is a slender saltwater lagoon that curves along the coast for about 145 km from the mouth of the Murray River. It's the main attraction in the 46,750-hectare **Coorong National Park**. The park also includes the Younghusband Peninsula, a narrow line of massive white dunes separating the Coorong from the sea.

You can get information on the park from the NPWS office in Meningie, or by picking up a copy of the *Coorong Tattler* newspaper, available at most outlets in the district.

In 1836 the rich resources of the Coorong supported a large Ngarrindjeri Aboriginal population, but by 1860 their numbers had dwindled alarmingly. Today many of their descendants still live in the district, and stone fish traps and middens in the sandhills remain as evidence of a vanished way of life. You can learn more about the Ngarrindjeri at

Pelicans are large and greedy birds. A group will often form a hunting cooperative – rounding up a school of fish by forming a tight circle in shallow water, preventing escape, then gobbling up the fish with their large pouchlike bills.

their **cultural centre** at Camp Coorong, 10 km south of Meningie on the Princes Highway. It's run by the Ngarrindjeri Lands & Progress Association.

The Coorong is home to huge numbers of **water birds**, particularly waders, ducks, swans and pelicans – there's a major pelican rookery in the lagoon. *Storm Boy*, a film about a young boy's friendship with a pelican, and based on the novel by Colin Thiele, was shot here. Among the best places to birdwatch are the freshwater soaks on the coastal side of the lagoon. There's plenty of other wildlife including kangaroos and wombats – be careful driving at night.

There is road access across the Coorong at **Tea Tree Crossing** (summer only) near Salt Creek and the **42-Mile Crossing** further south. With a 4WD you can continue on from both crossings to **Ninety Mile Beach**, a popular surf-fishing spot (mulloway, flathead, salmon and shark). The endangered hooded plover nests on the beach, so if you're going to drive along the beach make sure to keep below the high-water mark.

At Salt Creek there's a full-scale **replica** of the rig used to drill SA's first oil exploration hole, in 1866. This was brought about by the discovery of a rubbery substance called coorongite, which was thought to have originated from oil seepages. It turned out to be a hydrocarbon produced by vast algae blooms in the lagoon.

Organised Tours

Check with the rangers or in the *Coorong Tattler* for holiday programmes of ranger-guided activities.

Coorong Nature Tours (☎ 8574 0037; mobile 015 714 793) does half-day ($40) and full-day ($70) 4WD tours of the Coorong, as well as 4WD tag-along tours ($50 per vehicle) to the ocean beach. They also have a range of bushwalking trips including drop-off and pick-up options.

Places to Stay

The park has dozens of bush camp sites, most with no facilities. A permit costs $3 for up to five people; you can purchase one from numerous outlets in the area including both roadhouses at Salt Creek and the NPWS office in Meningie. The large *42-Mile Crossing* camping ground has long-drop dunnies, drinking water and good shelter, and it's a 20-minute walk over the sandhills to the ocean beach.

Camp Coorong (☎ 8575 1557) has self-contained units and bunk-house beds, but you have to book; rates are available on application.

The *Coorong Hotel/Motel* (☎ 8575 7064) at Policeman's Point, 51 km from Meningie, offers comfortable rooms for $40/45/55 including a very light breakfast. Don't be misled by their advertising – the 'whale' referred to is the burly gentleman behind the bar, not a pet cetacean.

Six km past Policemans Point, the pleasantly situated *Gemini Downs Holiday Village* (☎ 8575 7013) at Gemini Downs homestead has tent/caravan sites from $10/11 and self-contained cabins from $35. It also has canoes for hire.

The *Shell Roadhouse* (☎ 8575 7021) at Salt Creek has spartan huts which sleep six for a $25 flat rate.

There are basic and rather desolate *caravan parks* at Woods Well (☎ 8575 7063), 43 km from Meningie, and at Policemans Point (☎ 8575 7045). Both have tent sites, on-site vans and cabins.

KINGSTON SE (pop 1400)

Established in the mid-1850s as the port for the Upper South-East, Kingston SE (as opposed to Kingston OM – on the Murray) is a small fishing and holiday town near the southern end of the Coorong. It's a centre for rock lobster fishing, and the annual Lobsterfest, held in the second week of January, is celebrated with live bands and exhibitions. The Australian obsession with gigantic fauna and flora is apparent in Larry the Big Lobster, which looms over the highway on the Adelaide approach to town. Larry fronts a tourist information outlet and cafe.

Things to See & Do

Registered by the National Trust, the **Cape Jaffa Lighthouse** was erected at nearby Cape Jaffa in 1869 but is now in Kingston. You get a nice view from the top – except for the water tank it's the highest point for quite a distance. In school holiday periods it's usually open daily, otherwise ask next door at the Kingston Caravan Park.

Mike Davey (☎ 8767 2877) offers **dive charters** centering on Cape Jaffa's spectacular Margaret Brock Reef, which has caves and deep holes. This is a marine sanctuary so you will see plenty of crays and other life forms. You can do one dive for $25 (minimum four divers) or two for $40.

From Kingston, conventional vehicles can drive 16 km north along **Ninety Mile Beach** to an access point at **the Granites** car park. With 4WD you can – depending on conditions – continue to the mouth of the Murray River. Late in January each year the Lions Club holds a hugely popular **surf-fishing** competition on this beach; prizes total $10,000 and there are usually around 1200 entrants.

A small winery offers tastings daily from 10 am to 4 pm at the **Mt Benson Vineyards**, about 30 km from town off Alternative Highway 1. This district has seen great interest from wine makers in recent times, with large areas being converted to vineyards.

Bonds Mt Gambier Motor Service operates a daily bus service to Adelaide ($28.70) and Mt Gambier ($19.40). The booking office is at the Big Lobster.

Places to Stay & Eat

The *Backpackers Hostel* (☎ 8767 2185) at 21 Holland St has basic dorm rooms for $10 including use of the kitchen and lounge, which has an open fire. There's a seven-day laundrette across the road.

Almost right on the waterfront, the *Kingston Caravan Park* (☎ 8767 2050) has tent/caravan sites for $10/12, on-site vans for $24 and cabins from $30. Out at Cape Jaffa, 20 km from Kingston, the *Cape Jaffa Caravan Park* (☎ 8768 5056) charges $10/13 for tent/caravan sites and from $33 for cabins.

Standard pub rooms are available at the *Crown Inn Hotel* (☎ 8767 2005), on Agnes

St, for $16/28 and at the *Royal Mail Hotel*, on Hansen St, for $15/25. Alternatively there are several more expensive motels.

The *Crown Inn Hotel* has large counter meals from $4, while the *Shanghai Chinese Takeaway*, opposite the caravan park, produces consistently good food. Kingston has several other takeaways, of which the three *service stations* on the Princes Highway at the Adelaide end of town are generally best. There's a good *bakery* on Agnes St.

In the lobster season you can buy cooked lobster and fresh fish daily from *Lacapede Seafoods* by the jetty and from *Barry Zadow* on Marine Pde, near the caravan park. Lacapede Seafoods generally has the better range.

ROBE (pop 750)

A small fishing port and holiday town established in 1845, this was once the third most important port in SA. It was the main outlet for South-East wool until its trade was diverted through Port MacDonnell and Kingston in the 1860s.

Robe made a fortune in the late 1850s as a result of the Victorian gold rush. The Victorian government placed a substantial entry tax on Chinese gold miners, and many avoided it by landing at Robe or ports further west and walking overland to the goldfields; 10,000 arrived in 1857 alone. However, the flood stopped as quickly as it started when the SA government slapped its own tax on the Chinese. The Chinamen's Wells in the region (there's one on the Coorong) are a reminder of that time.

Robe is an extremely popular summer holiday destination. To the delight of local businesses, and the despair of anyone wanting quiet and solitude, the population leaps from 750 to 7000 the day after Christmas.

The tourist information office (☎ 8768 2465) is in the public library at the intersection of Smillie and Victoria Sts. If you don't have any luck there, which is quite likely unless the management has changed, the Robe Gallery on Victoria St is a helpful alternative.

Things to See & Do

There are numerous heritage-listed buildings dating from the late 1840s to '70s, and you can find them with the leaflet *Robe Walking Tours*. They include the **Customs House** (1863), on Royal Circus, which is now a nautical museum; it's open from 2 pm to 4 pm on Tuesday, Saturday and public holidays, and daily in January. Nearby is a **memorial** to the 16,500 Chinese diggers who landed at the port from 1856 to 1858.

The town has a sandy **swimming beach** enclosed by a reef. **Long Beach**, two km north off the Kingston road, is good for windsurfing and boardsurfing. There's plenty of potential for **fishing** around the coast and in the freshwater lakes near town. The Robe Charter Service (☎ 8768 2264; mobile 018 854 733) offers reef fishing charters and bay cruises.

Little Dip Conservation Park (2000 hectares) runs along the coast for about 13 km south of town. It features a variety of habitats including wetlands and dunes, and the popular fishing spots of **Bishops Pate**, **Long Gully** and **Little Dip** – these are accessible off the corrugated Nora Creina road and the 4WD coast track. There are several bush camp sites in the park; for permits and information contact the ranger in Robe on ☎ 8768 2543.

The **Narraburra Woolshed**, 14 km from town on the Millicent road, has demonstrations of working sheep dogs, shearing, wool classing and baling; it's open Monday, Wednesday, Friday and Saturday between 9.30 am and noon ($5). If you've never seen a shearing shed in action, this is the place to start.

Places to Stay

There are over 30 accommodation venues in Robe, including caravan parks, hotels, motels, flats, cottages and B&B places. The following is a small selection.

Caravan Parks Friendly *Bushland Cabins* (☎ 8768 2386) is about 1.5 km from town on the Nora Creina road. It has backpacker beds for $10, tent/caravan sites for $10/12, cabins for $34 and plenty of wildlife including wombats, echidnas and possums. The complex is on 11 hectares of eucalypt woodland adjoining Little Dip Conservation Park and pretty Lake Fellmongery.

On the town side of Lake Fellmongery, the *Lakeside Tourist Park* (☎ 8768 2193) has a beautiful setting with excellent shade. Tent/caravan sites are $12/14, on-site vans start from $28 and cabins from $30/40; the cabins sleep up to 10 and extra adults cost $4.

Otherwise there's the much more formal *Long Beach Tourist & Caravan Park* (☎ 8768 2237), about three km from town near Long Beach, and the *Sea-Vu Caravan Park* (☎ 8768 2273) at 1 Squire Drive in town. Both have tent and caravan sites, on-site vans and self-contained cabins.

Hotels & Motels The historic *Caledonian Inn* (☎ 8768 2029), on Victoria St, has basic but tasteful rooms for $30/50, and cottages within a stone's throw of the beach for $70/90. Its restaurant is one of the best in Robe.

Overlooking Guichen Bay from Mundy Terrace, the *Robe Hotel* (☎ 8768 2077) has basic rooms for $35/50 and self-contained rooms for $50/70.

The cheapest of Robe's six motels is the *Guichen Bay Motel* (☎ 8768 2001), on Victoria St, with units from $35/60. One of the most highly regarded is the *Melaleuca Motel* (☎ 8768 2599), on Smillie St, which has well-appointed units from $60/65.

Guesthouses & Cottages Out at Lake Fellmongery, the historic *Lakeside Country House* (☎ 8768 2042) has an excellent reputation and B&B doubles for $120.

The *Grey Masts Guesthouse* (☎ 8768 2203), at 1 Smillie St, has heritage-style B&B rooms for $65/85 . Also well regarded is *Wilsons at Robe* (☎ 8768 2459), on Victoria St, with two charming historic cottages at $105 for doubles, including breakfast provisions.

On Smillie St, the popular *Bowman & Campbell Holiday Units* (☎ 8768 2236) has units with one, two and three bedrooms from $50 per night and $320 per week.

Places to Eat
Robe is not a cheap place to eat. The best value in town are the winter specials at the *Caledonian Inn* – this place has a great old-world atmosphere and a very cosy bar – and the counter meals at the *Robe Hotel*. Sadly, there are no specials at the Inn in summer.

Locals recommend *Wilsons at Robe* for delicious lunches, while the *Country Kitchen* across the road is pretty good too. Of the takeaways, the *Country Kitchen* and the *Mobil service station*, on the main road out of town, get the highest marks.

BEACHPORT (pop 440)
If you have a yen for peace and solitude, you'll love this quiet little seaside town with its aquamarine bay and historic buildings. The **Old Wool & Grain Store Museum** ($2) is housed in a National Trust building. There's also an interesting **Aboriginal Artefacts Museum** ($2) in the former primary school on McCourt St; it's open from 2 to 4 pm daily in January, or by appointment (ask at the council office).

There's good surfing at the local **surf beach**, and windsurfing is popular at **Lake George**, five km north of the township. The town **jetty**, 800 metres long, provides memorable fishing (whiting, school shark, mullet, squid and many more), while Lake George mullet are considered excellent tucker.

Penguin Island, a rookery for little penguins, is in Rivoli Bay about 200 metres off shore. Each summer the parent birds take their young on swimming lessons between the island and the groyne opposite the Beachport Caravan Park.

The 700-hectare **Beachport Conservation Park** is sandwiched between the coast and Lake George two km north of town. Its attractions include Aboriginal shell middens, sheltered coves and bush camping; the ranger (☎ 8735 6053) at Southend can provide permits and details.

The little fishing town of **Southend** (population 300) is at the southern end of Rivoli Bay, 22 km from Beachport. It has a quiet swimming beach, a small caravan park

(☎ 8735 6035) and **Canunda National Park** on its doorstep (see the section on Millicent for details).

On the Robe road, the impressive **Woakwine Cutting** through the Woakwine Range gives you an appreciation of the lengths a determined farmer will go to drain a swamp.

Places to Stay & Eat
The former YHA hostel, which closed down in 1995, has reopened as *Beachport Backpackers* (☎ 8735 8197).

The *Beachport Caravan Park* (☎ 8735 8128) is very ordinary but has a great location near the surf beach. Much more attractive is the *Southern Ocean Tourist Park* (☎ 8735 8153), which has tent/caravan sites for $11 and cabins from $40.

Pub-style accommodation is available at the *Beachport Hotel* (☎ 8735 8003) for $22/40/45 (singles/doubles/triples).

Bompa's (☎ 8735 8333), near the jetty, has a licensed restaurant and bistro. It also has backpacker beds for $12 (the room is above the bar, so it can be noisy) and spacious, heritage-style rooms from $48 (singles & doubles), including a light breakfast.

Out at the *Lake George Holiday Resort* (☎ 8735 7260), at the northern end of Lake George 27 km from town and 10 minutes walk from the beach, powered sites are $15 and self-contained cabins are $55.

MILLICENT (pop 5120)
Finding they were virtually cut off by seasonal swamps for much of the year, Millicent's first settlers threatened to secede from the colony unless something was done to improve communications. Out of this protest came the South-East's first drainage scheme, in 1863. More followed soon after to create some of the region's richest agricultural land.

At the Mt Gambier end of George St, the tourist information centre (☎ 8733 3205) has a good craft shop. Also on the premises is an excellent National Trust **museum** with exhibits on the district's early years. It's open from 9.30 am to 4.30 pm daily and entry costs $2.50. Allow at least two hours to have a good look through it.

The **art gallery** in the civic centre on George St hosts some excellent travelling exhibitions.

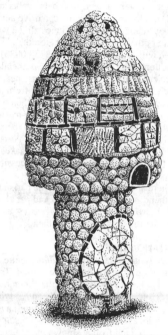

A tribute to kitsch, the Millicent Shell Garden (open mid-August to mid-June) is well worth a visit.

Places to Stay & Eat
About two km from Millicent's post office, the pleasant *Lakeside Caravan Park* (☎ 8733 3947) is beside a small swimming lake on Park Terrace. It has tent/caravan sites for $8/12, on-site vans for $25 and cabins from $35.

In the centre of town on George St, the *Somerset Hotel/Motel* (☎ 8733 2888) is the cheapest of the town's three motels, with units from $28/45 for singles/doubles.

There are three hotels on George St and all have counter meals; there's the usual cutthroat competition because of pokies.

CANUNDA NATIONAL PARK

Covering 9300 hectares, and only 13 km west of town, this is Millicent's main tourist attraction. The elongated park has a number of attractions, including giant sand dunes, rugged coastal scenery, wombats, walks and 4WD tracks. In summer you can drive along the beach and through the dunes all the way from Southend to **Carpenter Rocks**, a boat haven with a caravan park (☎ 8738 0035).

Cullens Bay Blowhole near Southend is spectacular in the right conditions; nearby there's a great view along the coast from the **Boozy Gully Lookout**. It was off the coast near here that the 1056-tonne, three-masted barque *Geltwood* was wrecked in 1876 with the loss of all 31 persons aboard. Now a declared historic site, the wreck makes a spectacular dive but is generally inaccessible because of the swells.

There are bush camp sites in the park near Southend; you can get permits and park brochures from the ranger's office (☎ 8735 6053) on the jetty road in Southend.

TANTANOOLA

In tiny Tantanoola, a *Pinus radiata* centre 15 km south-east of Millicent, the stuffed 'Tantanoola Tiger' is on display at the Tantanoola Tiger Hotel. This beast, actually an Assyrian wolf, was shot in 1895 after creating havoc among local sheep flocks. It was presumed to have escaped from a shipwreck, although why a ship would have a wolf on board isn't clear!

Formed as coastal caves in dolomite, and part of a 2000-hectare conservation park, the highly decorated **Tantanoola Caves** are on the Princes Highway another six km to the south-east. The visitor centre (☎ 8734 4153) runs tours ($5) of the show cave every hour from 9.15 am to 4 pm daily (more frequently over Easter and the summer school holidays). It's the only cave in SA with wheelchair access.

MT GAMBIER (pop 21,150)

Built on the lower slopes of the extinct volcano from which it takes its name, Mt Gambier, 486 km from Adelaide, is the region's major town and commercial centre. It was one of the earliest parts of SA to be settled; Stephen Henty, the first squatter in the Mt Gambier district, built his home on the mount in 1839. However, a settlement wasn't established until 15 years later.

The volcano itself is a striking feature, rising 152 metres above the plain. It was named Gambier's Mountain by Lieutenant James Grant, commander of the tiny brig HMS *Lady Nelson*, who saw it while sailing along the coast en route to Sydney from England in 1800.

The large and well-organised Lady Nelson Tourist Information & Interpretive Centre (☎ 8724 1730), on Jubilee Highway East, is open from 9 am to 5 pm daily. Allow an hour to look through the interpretive centre ($5), which features a replica of the *Lady Nelson*, complete with sound effects and taped commentary. It also has interesting natural-history displays including a walk-through cave and swamp habitat.

Things to See & Do

The **Old Courthouse Museum** on Bay Rd next to the police station is open daily ($2.50) between noon and 4 pm. Built in 1865, it still has the original courtroom furniture.

For culture vultures, the free **Riddoch Art Gallery** on Commercial St East, next to the **Cave Garden**, is SA's only government-funded regional gallery. It's open daily, except Monday, from 10 am (noon Sunday) to 4 pm (2 pm on Saturday and 3 pm on Sunday). Next door, **Studio One** has some fine work by local artists.

Mt Gambier has three volcanic craters, each with its own lake; the beautiful **Blue Lake** is the best known and most spectacular, although from about March to November the water is more grey than blue. In November it mysteriously changes back to blue just in time for the **Blue Lake Festival**, which is celebrated with exhibitions and concerts.

Blue Lake averages 77 metres in depth and there's a five-km scenic drive around it. The lakes are a popular recreation spot and have been developed with boardwalks (over

SOUTH-EAST

Valley Lake), a wildlife park, picnic areas, barbecues, lookouts and walking trails. A fourth lake (Leg of Mutton) dried up when the water table dropped; its former bed is now covered in trees.

The Mount Gambier district is well known for its numerous caves. Two you can visit easily are **Umpherston Cave**, on Jubilee Highway East, which has been attractively landscaped with terraced gardens, and **Engelbrecht Cave**, on Jubilee Highway West. The latter is popular with cave divers, but you can also take guided tours; check with the tourist centre for tour times.

At **Glencoe**, 23 km north-west of town, the 36-stand Glencoe Woolshed (1863) is an impressive reminder of the South-East's early pastoral wealth. It's owned by the National Trust and is open on Sunday between 1 and 3.30 pm.

Local tours, including scenic flights, can be booked at the tourist office. There are tours of Glenelg National Park (in Victoria), Cape Northumberland, sinkholes, timber mills and pine forests. Lake City Taxis (☎ 8723 0000) has a range of town tours from $10 to $35.

Places to Stay
Mt Gambier has numerous caravan parks, hotels, motels, guesthouses and B&B places. You can get full listings from the tourist office.

Caravan Parks The *Central Caravan Park* (☎ 8725 4427) is at 6 Krummel St, about 600 metres east of the post office. It charges $9/12 for tent/caravan sites, $25 for on-site vans and from $28 for cabins. The town's five other parks are further out.

Blue Lake City Caravan Park (☎ 8725 9856), near the lakes two km south of the post office on Bay Rd, has tent/caravan sites for $9/12, on-site vans from $26 and cabins from $40.

Jubilee Holiday Park (☎ 8723 2469), 3.5 km east of the post office on Jubilee Highway East, has powered sites with private facilities for $13 and cabins from $29.

Kalganyi Caravan Park (☎ 8723 0220),

three km north of the post office on the Penola road, has tent/caravan sites for $10/13, on-site vans for $29 and cabins from $32.

Pine Country Caravan Park (☎ 8725 1899), four km south of the post office on Bay Rd, has tent/caravan sites for $8/12, powered sites with private facilities for $15, on-site vans from $27 (some with private facilities) and cabins from $37.

Willow Vale Caravan Park (☎ 8725 3631), five km east of the post office on the Princes Highway, has tent/caravan sites for $8/10, on-site vans for $23 and cabins from $23.

Hotels A number of grand old hotels in the town's busy centre all offer good-value accommodation and meals. The cheapest (at least for singles) is the *Federal Hotel/Motel* (☎ 8723 1099), at 112 Commercial St East, with basic pub rooms for $15/28 and motel units for $40/48.

Also on Commercial St East, at No 78, the *South Australia Hotel* (☎ 8725 2404) charges $17/25, while the *Commercial Hotel* (☎ 8725 3006) on Commercial St West charges $17/28. *Macs Hotel* (☎ 8725 2402) at 21 Bay Rd is a smidgen more expensive at $20/30.

At 6 Ferrers St, the *Globe Hotel* (☎ 8725 1671) has rooms for $25/35 (add $6 for a cooked breakfast), while the *Jens Hotel* (☎ 8725 0188), at 40 Commercial St East, has a range of self-contained rooms from $30/40.

Most sophisticated of the pubs is the *Mt Gambier Hotel* (☎ 8725 0611), at 2 Commercial St West, which has large rooms with spa for $55/65.

Motels The *Blue Lake Motel* (☎ 8725 5211), at 1 Kennedy Ave, just off the highway, has dorm rooms and good facilities, including a kitchen, for $12 per person. Its standard rooms cost from $43/50 for singles/doubles.

The *Mount View Motel* (☎ 8725 8478), at 14 Davison St, charges $33/38/45 for its standard units; those with kitchens are $3 more. Few of the other motels in town come near this price.

SOUTH-EAST

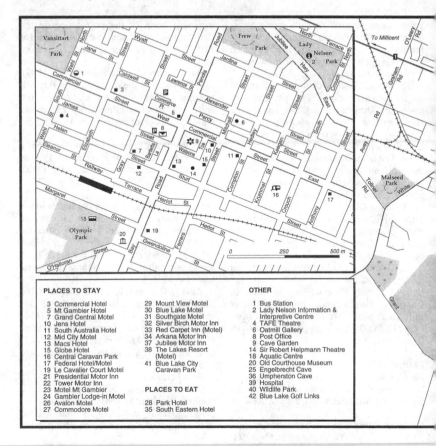

PLACES TO STAY

3 Commercial Hotel
5 Mt Gambier Hotel
7 Grand Central Motel
10 Jens Hotel
11 South Australia Hotel
12 Mid City Motel
13 Macs Hotel
15 Globe Hotel
16 Central Caravan Park
17 Federal Hotel/Motel
19 Le Cavalier Court Motel
21 Presidential Motor Inn
22 Tower Motor Inn
23 Motel Mt Gambier
24 Gambier Lodge-in Motel
26 Avalon Motel
27 Commodore Motel

29 Mount View Motel
30 Blue Lake Motel
31 Southgate Motel
32 Silver Birch Motor Inn
33 Red Carpet Inn (Motel)
34 Arkana Motor Inn
37 Jubilee Motor Inn
38 The Lakes Resort
   (Motel)
41 Blue Lake City
   Caravan Park

PLACES TO EAT

28 Park Hotel
35 South Eastern Hotel

OTHER

1 Bus Station
2 Lady Nelson Information &
   Interpretive Centre
4 TAFE Theatre
6 Oatmill Gallery
8 Post Office
9 Cave Garden
14 Sir Robert Helpmann Theatre
18 Aquatic Centre
20 Old Courthouse Museum
25 Engelbrecht Cave
36 Umpherston Cave
39 Hospital
40 Wildlife Park
42 Blue Lake Golf Links

Places to Eat

The tourist office has a brochure listing over 30 eateries, not including takeaways.

Other than pub meals, the best value in town is said to be the *Barn Steakhouse*, about two km out of town on Nelson Rd, which serves huge meals and often has live entertainment.

The *RSL Club & Bistro*, at 16 Sturt St, and the *Café Bar* bistro in the Mt Gambier Hotel are also recommended.

Worth mentioning is *Squiggles*, a licensed bistro and coffee shop in the old town hall complex on Commercial St. It's a great place to blow your diet with delicious offerings such as Mississippi mud cake.

Among the best of the local takeaways is the *Australian Fish Market* opposite the Commercial Hotel, while the *Colonial Court Coffee Shoppe*, at 10 Helen St near K-Mart, is recommended for its gourmet sandwiches. If you're buying takeaway, the Cave Garden on Commercial St East is one of the nicest places in town to eat it.

Entertainment

There's quite a bit of entertainment in Mt Gambier. For details on what's happening

SOUTH-EAST

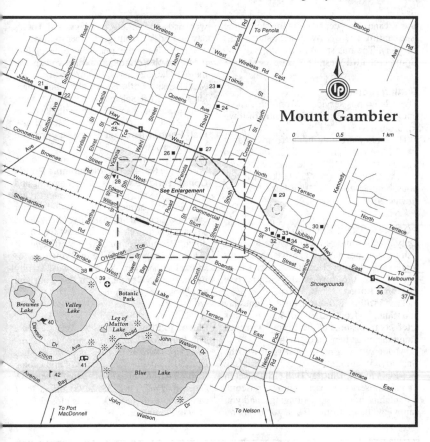

Mount Gambier

where, ask at the tourist centre or get hold of the local newspaper, *The Border Watch*.

On Thursday, Friday and Saturday nights you'll find live bands and DJs in the town's many pubs. There are several regular venues, with the *Commercial Hotel* and *Mt Gambier Hotel* among the most popular. The city centre also has two nightclubs: *Ripples*, in the Ripley Arcade off Commercial St West, and *Javed's* in Compton St.

For movies there's the *TAFE Theatre*, on Helen St, with shows every evening except Monday and Thursday (daily during school holidays). It also occasionally puts on local theatre productions. The excellent *Sir Robert Helpmann Theatre* is in the Civic Centre on Watson Terrace. It's the South-East's major entertainment venue and has something on every week whether it be live theatre, variety concerts, music, ballet or movies.

Getting There & Away

Kendell Airlines (bookings ☎ 13 13 00) and O'Connors Air Services (☎ 8723 0666) have daily flights to Adelaide and Melbourne, with return fares costing $147 to both cities.

Bonds Mt Gambier Motor Service buses depart daily, except Saturday, for Adelaide,

SOUTH-EAST

and V/Line buses depart daily for Melbourne (see Getting There & Away at the start of this chapter). The bus station for both is at 100 Commercial Rd West.

Getting Around
There is no bus service to/from the airport, but you can get a taxi to the centre of town for around $15.

Hire cars are available from Budget (☎ 8725 4340), Hertz (☎ 8723 0870) and Thrifty (☎ 8723 2488). The main taxi service is Lake City Taxis (☎ 8723 0000); it'll cost you about $5 to go to Blue Lake from the town centre.

PORT MACDONNELL (pop 680)
Only 28 km south of Mt Gambier, this quiet fishing and holiday village has the state's largest rock lobster fleet. It was once a busy port, hence the surprisingly impressive **customs house** (1863).

The **Maritime Museum**, open Wednesday and Sunday from 12.30 to 4.30 pm, has artefacts from some of the 25 ships wrecked along the coast here since 1844.

About two km north-west of town, the flamboyant colonial poet Adam Lindsay Gordon's home, **Dingley Dell** (1860), set in a small conservation park, is now a museum. It contains some of his belongings, and you can view them from 10 am to 4 pm on weekends and school holidays, and Thursday and Friday from September to May.

Fine walks in the area include the path to the top of **Mt Schank**, an extinct volcano on the Mt Gambier road 13 km north of Port MacDonnell. **Little Blue Lake**, about three km west of Mt Schank, is a popular swimming place, but its water is freezing even on the hottest day. Nearby is the **Mt Schank Fish Farm**, where you can catch your own rainbow trout.

On the coast adjacent to the Victorian border, the 660-hectare **Piccaninnie Ponds Conservation Park** has walks, camping and reputedly the world's best freshwater diving feature: **the Cathedral** – a large underwater cavern with 40-metre visibility. The water is so clear that flowering plants grow six metres down! Permits from the NPWS office in Mt Gambier are required before you dive or snorkel either here or further west at tiny **Ewen Ponds Conservation Park**, but you can book over the phone.

Places to Stay & Eat
The *Port MacDonnell Harbour View Caravan Park* (☎ 8738 2085) has powered sites from $13, on-site vans from $24 and cabins from $40. Alternatively, the *Woolwash Caravan Park* (☎ 8738 2095) offers tent/caravan sites for $8/10, but is closed from May to December.

The Earth Trembled
The 16 extinct volcanoes in the South-East fall into two distinct groups: those at Mt Gambier and those at Mt Burr, about 40 km to the north-west. The largest is Mt Burr itself, which rises 240 metres above sea level and 158 metres above the plain.

Mt Burr has 15 major eruption centres. Its volcanic structures were formed by varying styles of activity, from fissure flows to explosions, which took place between 20,000 and two million years ago. The ejected material was laid down on limestone then covered with beach sand up to 50 metres thick.

The much smaller Mt Gambier group comprises Mt Gambier, with three volcanic centres, and Mt Schank, with one. These were formed by violent explosions caused by ground water mixing with molten rock at depth, with the Mt Schank event occurring around 7000 years ago and Mt Gambier 3000 years later. Mt Gambier is one of the youngest volcanic features on the Australian mainland.

There is no doubt that the Aborigines saw all these events. The Booandik people had a legend of the giant Craitbul, who dug ovens at Mt Muirhead (near Mt Burr) and Mt Gambier, although at the latter the water kept rising to put his fire out.

Since European settlement there have been several earth tremors to show that the region is still unstable. Two of the state's most powerful earthquakes rocked Kingston in 1897 and Robe in 1948. ■

Starks Bakery in the *Malibu Café* in Port MacDonnell has fresh-baked goodies daily, including the ultimate in Australian cuisine: crayfish pies.

Eastern Wine District

Consisting of a vast system of swamps, most of which have been drained, the red-gum country between Mt Gambier and Bordertown has some of the richest fodder-growing and sheep and cattle grazing in SA. There's also a fast-growing wine industry centred on Coonawarra and Padthaway. Other points of interest in the area include historic Penola (a Mary MacKillop pilgrimage centre), Bool Lagoon and the Naracoorte Caves.

PENOLA (pop 1200)
A quiet little town, Penola has won recent fame for its association with the Sisters of St Joseph of the Sacred Heart, co-founded by Mary MacKillop in 1866. There's a MacKillop Park, a MacKillop School, a MacKillop Tourist Drive and many tacky MacKillop souvenirs on sale. The town has been named as a significant MacKillop pilgrimage site, but aren't they in danger of overdoing it?

The efficient tourist information centre (☎ 8737 2855), on Arthur St, opens between 10 am and 4 pm daily. It's in the **John Riddoch Interpretive Centre**, which has displays telling the history of the district.

Things to See & Do
The tourist office has a leaflet describing a **heritage walk** which takes in Penola's many interesting old buildings. A number of these are owned by the National Trust, including the old **post office** and the **Cobb & Co office** (now housing a BYO restaurant).

The **Woods-MacKillop Schoolhouse** (1867), on the corner of Petticoat Lane and Church St, houses memorabilia associated with Mother Mary MacKillop and Father

Julian Tenison Woods, who founded it; touch the designated keys and the computer displays details of MacKillop's life. The building is open from 10 am to 4 pm daily and admission is a 'gold coin' ($1 or $2) donation.

Mother Mary MacKillop

You'll love **Petticoat Lane** and its quaint old slab cottages – several are open to the public, including Sharam's Cottage (1850), the first dwelling in Penola; watch out the lintel doesn't take your head off as you walk in! On Arthur St, the magnificent little **St Mary's Church of England** (1873) was designed by an accountant (who said they have no soul?).

In dramatic contrast to the cottages is the opulent two-storey mansion **Yallum Park** (1880), built in the Italianate style by the district's first pastoralist, John Riddoch. It's on the Millicent road about eight km west of town, and you can inspect it for $3 (bookings ☎ 8737 2435).

About 20 km north of Penola on the Naracoorte road you pass **Father Woods Tree**. This huge, rather sick-looking red gum was used as an outdoor church by Father Woods, who held services here for the first settlers.

Bonds Mt Gambier Motor Service buses depart daily (except Saturday) for Adelaide ($35.10) and Mt Gambier ($7.50) from the tourist information centre.

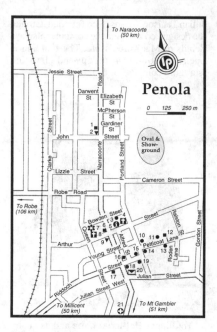

To Naracoorte
(50 km)

Jessie Street

Darwent St

Elizabeth St

McPherson St

Gardiner St

Penola

0   125   250 m

Oval & Show-ground

John Street

Lizzie Street

Cameron Street

Robe Road

To Robe
(106 km)

Bowden Street

Arthur

Young Street

Petticoat Lane

Roden Lane

Gordon Street

Julian Street

To Millicent
(50 km)

Julian Street West

To Mt Gambier
(51 km)

PLACES TO STAY

1   Coonawarra Motor Lodge
6   Log Cabin Hotel/Motel
12   Rectory
16   Royal Oak Hotel
17   Old Kindergarten

PLACES TO EAT

2   Bushman's Inn
9   The Sweet Grape

OTHER

3   Ulva Cottage
4   Presbyterian Church
5   Tourist Office
7   Mother Mary MacKillop Gardens
8   St Mary's Church of England
10   Gammon Cottage
11   Wilson's Cottage
13   Sharam's Cottage
14   Woods-MacKillop Schoolhouse
15   Old Hospital
18   Old Post Office
19   Cobb & Co
20   Post Office
21   War Memorial Hospital &
       Hostel Ambulance Station

Places to Stay & Eat

Backpacker beds are available for $10 at *Whiskas Woolshed* (☎ 8737 2428; mobile 018 854 505), 12 km south-west of town and off the Millicent road. Rooms in the old woolshed sleep up to nine. Each room has oil heating, and there's a large recreation room, kitchen and laundry.

The friendly *Old Kindergarten* (☎ 8737 2250), on Riddoch St, offers cooking facilities and futon beds for $14; although there's no laundry on the premises, the owners run the laundrette just down the road.

At the Millicent end of town, the *Penola Caravan Park* (☎ 8737 2381) has powered sites with en suite facilities for $10 and cabins for $25. It's popular with seasonal workers, so always ring first.

The *Royal Oak Hotel* (☎ 8737 2322), on Church St, has spacious upstairs rooms ($25/50) with four-poster beds and direct access to a huge verandah. Just down the road at the more popular *Log Cabin*

Hotel/Motel (☎ 8737 2402), self-contained units are $42/50. Both have excellent counter meals, although you wouldn't call them cheap.

Also on Church St, the *Coonawarra Motor Lodge* (☎ 8737 2364) has very well-appointed units for $70/80, and there's a heated swimming pool on the premises. You'll find a good restaurant right next door in the historic *Bushman's Inn*.

Alternatively, over 20 mainly historic cottages in and around town – including the *Rectory* (1860s) on Petticoat Lane – offer accommodation, with prices starting at $50 for twin share. For details and bookings contact the tourist office.

The Sweet Grape, a cosy cafe in the commercial centre on Church St, is good for morning and afternoon teas and lunches.

COONAWARRA WINERIES

The compact (24 sq km) wine-producing area of Coonawarra, which is renowned for

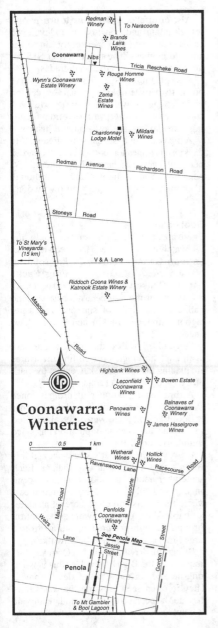

Redman Winery
To Naracoorte
Brands Laira Wines
Coonawarra
Nibs
Tricia Rescheke Road
Wynn's Coonawarra Estate Winery
Rouge Homme Wines
Zema Estate Wines
Chardonnay Lodge Motel
Mildara Wines
Redman Avenue
Richardson Road
Stoneys Road
To St Mary's Vineyards (15 km)
V & A Lane
Riddoch Coona Wines & Katnook Estate Winery
Maaoupe
Road
Highbank Wines
Leconfield Coonawarra Wines
Bowen Estate

Coonawarra Wineries

0   0.5   1 km

Penowarra Wines
Balnaves of Coonawarra Winery
James Haselgrove Wines
Wetheral Wines
Hollick Wines
Ravenswood Lane
Racecourse Road
Naracoorte Road
Penfolds Coonawarra Winery
See Penola Map
Jessie Street
Gordon Street
Penola
Marks Road
Weirs Lane
To Mt Gambier & Bool Lagoon

its reds, starts at Penola's northern outskirts and straddles the road to Naracoorte for the next 14 km. The district attracts wine lovers from all over Australia. **Wynn's Estate** is the best-known winery, but there are 21 others offering cellar-door sales, mostly on a daily basis. If you don't have time to try them all, at least check out the following – they're listed in order from Penola:

Hollick Wines is a very friendly place where you can taste good, reasonably priced reds and whites in a historic miner's cottage.

James Haselgrove Wines has produced some excellent wines, such as its 1992 Reserve Cabernet Sauvignon. They also have a very nice, full-bodied grenache shiraz.

Balnaves of Coonawarra has a friendly, if pretentious, tasting area with a small art gallery and trout pond. Balnaves produces some of the best reds and whites in the district; I wanted to try their cabernet sauvignon but found it difficult to get past the chardonnay.

Leconfield Coonawarra is noted for its big reds.

Katnook Estate has a good variety of styles and prices. Its Riddoch wines are reasonably cheap, while those under the Katnook brand are more expensive but delicious.

Wynns Coonawarra Estate is at Coonawarra township, nine km from Penola. As the district's first winery, it is worth visiting just to see the historic stone complex (1891) and the large wooden kegs in its cellar. On a cold day the tasting area is frigid.

Redman Winery produces classic Coonawarra reds at reasonable prices.

Places to Stay & Eat

The modern *Chardonnay Lodge Motel* (☎ 8736 3309), eight km from Penola, has huge units for $80/95 including a light breakfast, and a restaurant with excellent but pricey meals. *Nibs*, in Coonawarra, is a popular BYO bistro grill with a salad bar where you can fill up for $7.

You can also stay at numerous cottages in the area; contact the Penola tourist office (☎ 8737 2855) for details and bookings.

NARACOORTE (pop 4710)

Established by Scottish settlers in 1845, this attractive town is the service centre for a rich grazing and agricultural district. Naracoorte is a corruption of the Aboriginal name for a waterhole in the area.

The tourist office (☎ 8762 1518) is at the award-winning **Sheep's Back Museum** on MacDonnell St. Open from 10 am to 4 pm daily, the museum ($3) is housed in a three-storey flour mill (1870) and has interesting displays on the wool industry.

On Jenkins Terrace, the **Home of a Hundred Collections** ($5) is well worth a visit for its displays of everything from fossils to cameras to live reptiles. It's closed from mid-July to the end of August, but otherwise is open daily from 10 am to 5 pm (2 to 5 pm Sunday).

At **Padthaway**, 47 km north of town on the Keith road, the **Padthaway Estate winery** has tastings in an old stone shearing shed; the original settler's cottage (1847) is next door, as is an elaborate chateau-style homestead (1882) which has B&B for $130/180 (☎ 8765 5039). The nearby **Padthaway Conservation Park** (1000 hectares) is set on a former coastal sand dune.

Naracoorte Caves

The 600-hectare **Naracoorte Caves Conservation Park** (☎ 8762 2340) is 12 km south-east of town and off the Penola road. Its limestone caves featured in David Attenborough's *Life on Earth* series, and have earned World Heritage listing thanks to the significance of the Pleistocene mammal fossil deposits in the **Victoria Fossil Cave**.

There are four show caves: **Alexandra Cave** (the main attraction), **Blanche Cave**, the Victoria Fossil Cave and the **Wet Cave**. The Wet Cave can be seen without a guide. For the others, guided tours run daily from 9.30 am to 4 pm, with prices starting at $4.

The **Bat Cave**, from which around 250,000 common bent-wing bats make a spectacular departure on summer evenings, isn't open to the public because of its importance as a maternity cave – it's the only one left in this part of the world.

However, infra-red TV cameras allow you to view the cavern and the fascinating goings-on inside it ($6).

Also on offer are **adventure tours** involving climbing and crawling in undeveloped caves in the area (wear sneakers or sandshoes and old clothes). The tours start at $15 for novices and $30 for advanced grades.

Apart from caves the park has attractive bush, so between caving trips you can go birdwatching and walking. There's also a kiosk and an attached **interpretive centre** featuring a display on the caves' natural history.

A pleasant but basic camping area next to the kiosk has sites for tents ($2 per site and $2 per adult) and caravans ($7 per site and $2 per adult). You can light a fire here, although it's not a bad idea to bring your own wood.

Bool Lagoon

There are around 155 bird species, including 79 water birds, at the 3100-hectare **Bool Lagoon Game Reserve**, 24 km south of Naracoorte. With the adjoining **Hacks Lagoon Conservation Park** (2000 hectares), this is one of the South-East's best wetland habitats. The chain of shallow freshwater lagoons stretches 14 km and covers 3000 hectares.

Self-guided walks and guided tours are available, although cost-cutting measures are placing the tours at risk. Contact the park office (☎ 8764 7541) for an update.

A diminishing number of brolgas, once widespread in the region, spend the summer at Bool Lagoon; there were several hundred a few years ago but the population has since shrunk to around 100.

However, the district's straw-necked ibis doesn't appear to be in any danger. Each September about 200,000 of them descend on the wetland to breed in tea tree areas, where the adults and chicks create an indescribable din. You can watch the action through medium-powered binoculars from a large hide on the Tea Tree boardwalk.

Be careful driving around in October, particularly on the Big Hill road, as this is when long-necked tortoises come out to breed. They're often seen crossing the roads, and they don't speed up to accommodate anyone in a hurry.

Places to Stay

The attractive *Naracoorte Caravan Park* (☎ 8792 2128) at 81 Park Terrace charges $10/14 for tent/caravan sites, $30 for on-site vans and from $36 for cabins.

In the centre of town, the classic *Naracoorte Hotel/Motel* (☎ 8762 2400), at 73 Ormerod St, has motel units for $47/65 and pub-style rooms for $24/43. It also offers backpackers beds for $10 to holders of YHA or VIP cards.

The *Kincraig Hotel* (☎ 8762 2200), at 158 Smith St, has standard pub rooms for $20/30, while the *Commercial Hotel* (☎ 8762 2100), at 20 Robertson St, has self-contained rooms for $30/40.

At 32 Robertson St, next to the Woolworths supermarket, *La Eurana House* (☎ 8762 2054) has very pleasant upstairs rooms for $19 per person (linen $5 extra). This lovely two-storey home was built as a convent in 1903. No, Mary MacKillop didn't stay here, but one of her relatives did!

Naracoorte has four motels and the tourist office can provide details.

At Bool Lagoon there are two grassy camping areas with shade near the park office. Sites cost $6 for two people and wood fires are not permitted at any time. Alternatively, you can stay at friendly *Tintagel* (8764 7491), a farm on the Penola road offering B&B for $50/70. It's about 8.5 km from Bool Lagoon and there's excellent birdwatching on the property.

Places to Eat

The *Old Aussie Eatery*, at 190 Smith St, has an interesting menu, including drover's delight ($11) and a swaggy's dream ($12.50). If you haven't yet tried roo, camel or crocodile, this is a good place to start.

Right next door to the Sheep's Back Museum, the *Family Mill Restaurant* does tasty pizzas and has a steak and salad bar. The town's pubs all have reasonably priced meals. Alternatively there are several takeaways; the *Showgrounds Café,* on Smith St next to the showgrounds, is popular for fish & chips.

Dukes Highway

The busy Dukes Highway, from Tailem Bend through Bordertown, provides the most direct route between Adelaide and Melbourne (729 km). You wouldn't take it if you want to see interesting country, although there are some worthwhile detours to conservation areas and wineries.

The highway follows fairly closely the **gold escort route** that was blazed through the waterless mallee from Wellington, on Lake Alexandrina, to the Bendigo diggings in central Victoria in 1852. Concerned at the way the Victorian gold rush was draining its finances, the SA government established a monthly gold escort as part of a short-lived and ambitious scheme to make Adelaide a financial centre for the goldfields.

Thanks to its mineral-deficient soils, much of the Upper South-East was once known as the **Ninety Mile Desert** – a good place to avoid. Development of the district was mainly confined to low-intensity grazing until after WWII, when improved farming practices, including the use of superphosphate and trace elements, brought closer crop farmers. These days, the 'desert' is a productive mixed farming area.

There are several service towns with good facilities along the highway: **Coonalpyn** (64 km from Tailem Bend), **Tintinara** (90 km), **Keith** (128 km) and **Bordertown** (177 km).

TINTINARA (pop 320)

The name of this small railway town is said to come from *tin-tin-yara*, the Aboriginal name for the stars of Orion's Belt. Tintinara is an access point for **Mt Boothby Conservation Park**, 22 km to the west, as is the tiny township of **Coonalpyn** back towards Tailem Bend.

Historic *Tintinara Homestead* (☎ 8757 2146) has bush camping and shearer's quarters where you can stay. The 930-hectare property is six km west of town towards Mt Boothby.

In town, *Tintinara Caravan Park* (☎ 8757 2095) has tent/caravan sites for $7/11 and on-site vans from $20; it also has a motel where units with air-con are $35/40. Alternatively, the *Tintinara Hotel* (☎ 8757 2008) has basic rooms for $25/35.

Near Coonalpyn, *Bayree Farm* (☎ 8571 1054) offers bush camping, homestead rooms with private bathroom and lounge, self-contained cabins, bushwalks and farm activities – you can milk a cow if you want.

Ngarkat Conservation Park

A vast sea of mallee and jumbled sandhills, the 262,700-hectare Ngarkat group of conservation parks is 19 km east of Tintinara. It's a magnet for 4WD enthusiasts looking for a big place to drive around. In the west, a network of 4WD tracks between Tintinara and Lameroo takes you through the park for 81 km via **Gosse Hill** and **Mt Rescue**. In the east, you can leave the Pinnaroo road at **Pertendi Bore**, 85 km north of Bordertown, and detour to Pinnaroo on the 4WD track via **Pine Hut Soak** in the extreme north-east of the park.

The park's other attractions include solitude, wildflowers (the banksias are stunning in early spring), walks, relics of the pastoral era, birdwatching (particularly when the mallee and banksia are in flower) and bush camping. Several camping areas are at soakages where emus and kangaroos come to drink.

For camping permits and park information contact the ranger at Tintinara on ☎ 8562 3412.

KEITH (pop 1180)

Another access point for the Ngarkat Conservation Park, Keith is at the highway's junction with the Naracoorte road. You can detour to the Padthaway Estate winery, 63 km south of Keith towards Naracoorte, then head north-east to Bordertown. Eleven km from Keith, the 93-hectare **Mt Monster Conservation Park** is a prime birdwatching spot in a sea of lucerne paddocks and scattered red gums.

The pleasant *Keith Caravan Park* (☎ 8755 1630) is removed from the highway and has tent/caravan sites for $10/14, on-site vans for $25 and cabins for $30. Pub rooms with air-con cost $40/46 in the *Keith Hotel/Motel* (☎ 8755 1122), while units are $48/53. Alternatively, the *Keith Motor Inn* (☎ 8755 1500) charges $55/61.

BORDERTOWN (pop 2230)

The last town in SA, at the junction of the highway and the main road from Mt Gambier to the Riverland, Bordertown is the largest service centre in the Upper South-East. Former Australian prime minister RJ (Bob) Hawke was born here; there's a bust of Bob outside the town hall, and photos of him in **Hawke House Museum**, on the corner of Farquhar and Binnie Sts.

On the right as you leave town for Victoria is a **wildlife park** with various Australian species, including rare white kangaroos. Somewhat more inspiring is historic **Clayton Farm**, three km south of town on the Kingston SE road. Classified by the National Trust, it has many old-style farming exhibits in and around its original 1870s outbuildings. It's open daily, except Saturday, from 2 to 5 pm and entry costs $5.

The *Bordertown Caravan Park* (☎ 8752 1752), on Penny Terrace near the town centre, has tent/caravan sites for $12/14 and on-site vans from $25.

On East Terrace, the grand *Bordertown Hotel* (☎ 8752 1016) has air-conditioned rooms for $20/30. Bordertown has several motels, by far the cheapest of which is the *Parklands Motel* (☎ 8752 1622), on Park Terrace, where modest but adequate units cost $33/40.

Built in 1859, the *Wheatsheaf Inn* in the town centre has counter meals and a bistro. Most of the town's roadhouses sell fast food.

Barossa Valley

Only 65 km from Adelaide, the Barossa Valley is renowned for its excellent wines and German heritage. Colonel William Light named the range on the valley's eastern side the 'Barrosa' after a Peninsula War battle-site in Spain (Barrosa is close to where Spanish sherry comes from). However, a later misspelling changed it to Barossa.

Running north-east for about 25 km from Lyndoch to Stockwell, and up to 11 km wide, the valley was colonised in 1842 by 25 German families who established the settlement of Bethany. The following year more families settled at Langmeil (now Tanunda). Small groups continued to arrive over the next 20 years, creating a Lutheran heartland where German traditions persisted well into this century. The signs of this are everywhere. The valley is dotted with the steeples of distinctive little churches, while German-style farmhouses and cottages are common. Other legacies of the early settlers include brass bands and singing societies (*Liedertafel*).

As is so often the case, you must get off the main roads to begin to appreciate the Barossa Valley's true character. Take the scenic drive between Angaston and Tanunda, the palm-fringed road to Seppeltsfield and Marananga, and wander through sleepy Bethany, and you'll be halfway there.

Although the Barossa is promoted as a day-trip destination from Adelaide, you could easily spend several days enjoying the many attractions on offer.

Information

The very efficient and helpful Barossa Valley Visitors Centre (☎ toll-free 1800 812 662) is at 66-68 Murray St, Tanunda. It's open from 9 am to 5 pm Monday to Friday and 10 am to 4 pm on weekends and holidays. The complex includes a new wine interpretation centre designed to educate visitors in the various processes involved in wine making.

Ask for the informative regional guide put

HIGHLIGHTS

- Hop on a bicycle and discover vine-lined valleys, historic Lutheran churches and old German farmhouses
- Look down from the basket of a hot-air balloon over Australia's most famous wine region
- Learn how to nose a pinot noir, swirl a shiraz and savour a semillon at the Barossa wineries
- Eat Bavarian brezel, pastries baked in a wood-fired oven and quaff quandong mead – if you dare

out by the Barossa Wine & Tourism Association. It has details on most of the valley's wineries, accommodation venues, eateries and attractions.

The valley has numerous heritage buildings and many can be visited using the various historic walk brochures. There's also the interesting booklet *Barossa Valley Scenic Heritage Drive* ($4.95), which takes you on a looped tour from Tanunda, and includes town walks at Angaston and Tanunda.

Communications Throughout this book we use the standard new statewide STD code (08) and eight-digit telephone numbers, which take effect in February 1997. Should

BAROSSA VALLEY

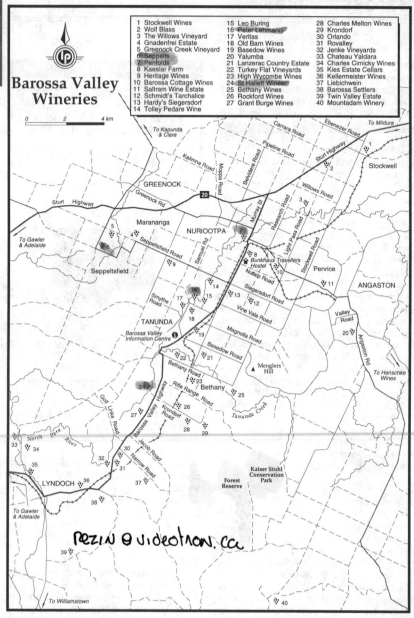

Barossa Valley Wineries

1 Stockwell Wines	15 Leo Buring	28 Charles Melton Wines
2 Wolf Blass	16 Peter Lehmann	29 Krondorf
3 The Willows Vineyard	17 Veritas	30 Orlando
4 Gnadenfrei Estate	18 Old Barn Wines	31 Rovalley
5 Greenock Creek Vineyard	19 Basedow Wines	32 Jenke Vineyards
6 Seppelts	20 Yalumba	33 Chateau Yaldara
7 Penfolds	21 Lanzerac Country Estate	34 Charles Cimicky Wines
8 Kaestar Farm	22 Turkey Flat Vineyards	35 Kies Estate Cellars
9 Heritage Wines	23 High Wycombe Wines	36 Kellermeister Wines
10 Barossa Cottage Wines	24 St Hallett Wines	37 Liebichwein
11 Saltram Wine Estate	25 Bethany Wines	38 Barossa Settlers
12 Schmidt's Tarchalice	26 Rockford Wines	39 Twin Valley Estate
13 Hardy's Siegersdorf	27 Grant Burge Wines	40 Mountadam Winery
14 Tolley Pedare Wine		

rezin @ videotron.ccu

you need to use an old number, simply take the first two digits (85 in the Barossa Valley) and use as the STD code (085).

Books & Maps The tourist centre issues free road maps which show most of the wineries. Alternatively, the Royal Automobile Association's *Central* regional map includes the Barossa and access routes from Adelaide, but its scale is too small to be useful around the valley. A much better one is the Department of Recreation & Sport's cycle-touring map *Barossa Valley*, which encompasses the valley and out as far as Springton, Gawler and Kapunda.

If you want a souvenir map, the Department of Environment & Natural Resources has a colourful sheet with plenty of illustrations and information for $6.95.

Explore the Barossa, by the Royal Geographical Society of Australia (SA) is an excellent guidebook. Its 160 pages have a swag of general information, including natural and social history, and descriptions of town and country walks and drives.

Wineries

In 1847 Johann Gramp planted the valley's first grapes on his property at Jacobs Creek, and produced the first wine three years later. However, the industry saw only slow growth until the 1890s, when phylloxera disease devastated vineyards in the eastern colonies. As a result, plantings in the Barossa increased dramatically; it became Australia's major wine producer after tariffs were removed following Federation in 1901.

Today, local wineries, with their many varieties of reds and whites produced from pure Barossa fruit, dominate Australian wine shows. The valley is best known for shiraz, with riesling the most important of its whites. There are over 50 wineries ranging from boutiques to huge complexes – the latter are mostly owned by multinationals. Almost all are open to the public for free wine tastings; the tourist centre has a leaflet giving locations and opening hours.

Following are some well-known (and some not so well-known) wineries:

Chateau Yaldara, at Lyndoch, was established in 1947 in the ruins of a 19th century winery and flour mill. It has a notable antique collection which can be seen on conducted tours ($2).

St Hallett, at Tanunda, is a small winery well known for its top-quality wines. There is a keg factory opposite where you can watch kegs being made.

Orlando, at Rowland Flat, between Lyndoch and Tanunda, was established in 1847 and is one of the oldest wineries in the valley.

Saltram Wine Estate, in Angaston, is another old winery. Established in 1859, it has friendly and informative staff, and is set in beautiful gardens.

Seppeltsfield, at Seppeltsfield, was founded in 1852. Its magnificent old bluestone buildings are surrounded by gardens and date palms, and there's a Grecian mausoleum on the road in. This extensive complex includes a picnic area with gas barbecues. Daily tours cost $3.

Wolf Blass, out beyond Nuriootpa on the Sturt Highway, was only founded in 1973, but quickly became one of the better known wine makers in Australia. There's an interesting heritage museum behind the tasting room.

Yalumba, in Angaston, was founded way back in 1849. The blue-marble winery, topped by a clocktower and surrounded by gardens, is the largest family-owned wine company in Australia – in the Barossa it's the only major winery still in family ownership.

Bethany Wines, on Bethany Rd, Bethany, is a small family-operated winery in a scenic location – its white port is highly recommended. The Schrapel family is descended from the original settlers.

Grant Burge Wines, Jacobs Creek, Barossa Valley Highway, Tanunda, is a relative newcomer but has earned a reputation for consistently good wines. The winery boasts a beautifully restored tasting room.

Rockford Wines, on Krondorf Rd near Tanunda, is another small, family-owned winery noted for its full-bodied wines. Its intimate tasting room is in a historic stable.

Unfortunately, few wineries have restaurants, mainly because there are too many others in opposition. Those that do all have a high standard and include Kaeslers and Chateau Dorrien (both near Nuriootpa), Chateau Yaldara (Lyndoch), Saltrams (Angaston) and Gnadenfrei (Marananga).

Festivals

The colourful, seven-day **Vintage Festival** is the Barossa's big event, starting on Easter Monday in odd-numbered years. The festival features processions, music (including brass bands), tug-of-war contests between the wineries, maypole dancing and, of course, a lot of wine tasting.

Even more fun – according to locals – is the **Classic Gourmet Weekend** held in August or September. It has a carnival atmosphere with stalls, fine food, wine and music. There are also cheap shuttle buses to whiz you safely between the different venues (remember the 0.05 blood-alcohol limit).

Other events include the **Oom Pah Fest** in January; the **Essenfest** in March; the **Hot Air Balloon Regatta** in May; and the **Barossa International Music Festival**, which features jazz and classical music over two weeks in September-October.

The main events in the Barossa move with the grape-growing seasons. It takes four to five years for grapevines to reach maturity after they are first planted in September and October. Their useful life is usually around 40 years. The vines are pruned back heavily during the winter months (July to August) and grow and produce fruit over the summer. The busiest months in the valley are from March to early May, when the grapes are harvested.

Wine Tasting

There are a few terms and practices in wine tasting that are worth knowing if you don't want to act like a complete ignoramus. For starters, perhaps the most important principle is be true to your own impressions. Trust yourself: you at least know whether you like it or not.

Whether seriously appraising or simply tasting a wine, consider these three elements: colour and appearance, nose, and palate.

Colour & Appearance Use a clean, clear glass in good light and examine the wine's colour and appearance by holding it against a white background.

White wines vary in colour from water white to intense gold depending on age, grape variety and wine making techniques. It should not be brown. A red wine will generally progress from crimson through brick red to tawny as it ages. In all but aged wines and especially with white wines, the colour should be brilliant and clear with no deposit.

Nose When nosing a wine, preferably use a glass with a tapered mouth. This assists in concentrating the volatile aromas rising from the wine. Your nose is a particularly potent sensory organ – accordingly it is essential to remember that we smell much of what we would describe as 'tastes'. Characteristics such as 'berries', 'spicy' or 'wood' are not tasted in the mouth, but registered through the nose. (You only have to hold your nose to prove it, or remember how things have no taste when you have a cold.) The wine's nose should have several pleasant smells and be free of any obvious rank odours.

Palate Your tongue and mouth can basically only detect four taste sensations. These are salt, sweetness, bitterness and acid, and they are apparent on different areas of the tongue. Your palate is used to qualify the expectations of the wine's colour and nose. When ideally 'savouring' a wine in your mouth, consider the wine's balance. The amount of fruit must be in balance with the acids and tannins.

Persistence of flavour is a major virtue of any wine. The longer it lasts, the greater the pleasure. A very easy test of how 'good' a wine is is its persistence of flavour.

One important lesson: a wine that is not good to begin with will not 'come good in a couple of years'. Good wine gets better. Poor wine gets worse.

Finally, if you want to purchase a bottle of wine to accompany your meal, it is usually best to select one that matches the cuisine. For example a fresh, herbaceous sauvignon blanc or semillon with warm salads, more robust white wines such as wood-aged chardonnay with pasta, lighter red styles such as pinot noir with rich chicken dishes, rich opulent reds such as shiraz and cabernet sauvignon with hearty roasts and barbecued foods. Desserts are complemented by luscious botrytised rieslings and semillons.

Adam Marks

Organised Tours

There are several day tours on offer from Adelaide; the South Australian Tourism Commission (SATC) has details. Premier Roadlines (☎ 8415 5555) has day tours in luxury coaches for $39 including lunch and winery visits.

Among the smaller operators, Tour Delights (mobile ☎ 018 845 432) does a well-regarded day tour for $43, while E&K Mini-Tours (☎ 8337 8739) charges $30. Festival Tours (☎ 8374 1270) is more expensive at $54, but has a good reputation – you get lunch at one of the better restaurants. The Wayward Bus Touring Company (☎ 8232 6646) has a full-day tour on Tuesday and Friday for $32, including the St Kilda Mangrove Trail (see the chapter on the Mid-North).

Also from Adelaide, Freewheelin' Cycle Tours (☎ 8232 6860) has rides around the wineries for $39.

A handful of local operators offer tours of the Barossa. Valley Tours (☎ 8562 1524) of Tanunda charges $34 for the day, including a three-course lunch. If cost is no object, Fruits of Inheritance (☎ 8563 3483), also of Tanunda, is excellent value from $150 per person; their down-to-earth, tailor-made tours can include private wine tastings, bush walks and church tours conducted by Lutheran pastors.

You can also take helicopter flights (☎ 8524 4209) from $12 for 10 minutes to $60 for an hour (three passengers on board). A hot-air balloon flight with Balloon Adventures (☎ 8389 3195) costs $195.

Sadly, health and safety regulations have killed off the winery tours that were once so popular; Seppeltsfield and Chateau Yaldara do have tours, but these have a heritage bias and are not working wineries. The interpretive centre at Tanunda has been designed to take the place of the real thing.

Accommodation

The Barossa Valley has plenty of accommodation, including youth and backpacker hostels, several caravan parks, hotels, generally pricey motels, and a large and growing number of B&B places. The latter are mainly around $100 for doubles, including breakfast ingredients; hardly any have you eating with the owners.

If all the accommodation in the valley is booked out you may be able to find something at Gawler or Kapunda, although neither have a great choice. Both towns are only a short drive from the action.

Getting There & Away

There are several routes from Adelaide to the valley. The most direct is via Main North Rd through Elizabeth and Gawler, but if you're in no hurry, try the more interesting and picturesque routes through the Torrens Gorge and Williamstown, or via Birdwood and Springton.

If you're coming from the east and want to tour the wineries before hitting Adelaide, the scenic drive from Mannum via Springton and Eden Valley to Angaston is recommended.

The Barossa Adelaide Passenger Service (☎ 8564 3022) has three services daily on weekdays and one daily on weekends between the valley and Adelaide via Williamstown and Gawler. Fares from Adelaide are: Lyndoch $7.60, Tanunda $9.30, Nuriootpa $10.10 and Angaston $11. There are no services on public holidays.

Getting Around

The Barossa Taxi Service (☎ 8563 3600) has a 24-hour service throughout the valley from Tanunda. It costs around $12 to Angaston and $10 to Nuriootpa. Alternatively, you can rent a medium-sized sedan from the Caltex service station (☎ 8563 2677), on Murray St in Tanunda, for $65 per day for up to 150 km.

The Zinfandel Tea Rooms in Tanunda and the Bunkhaus Travellers Hostel in Nuriootpa rent bicycles. There's plenty of potential for cyclists, with many interesting routes, and gradients varying from easy to challenging; a cycle path runs between Nuriootpa and Tanunda, passing the Bunkhaus Travellers Hostel en route.

LYNDOCH (pop 960)

Coming up from Adelaide via Gawler, you arrive in the valley at Lyndoch, at the foot of the scenic Barossa Range. The fine old **Pewsey Vale Homestead** is near Lyndoch. About one km west of town on the road to Gawler, the **Museum of Mechanical Music** (☎ 8524 4014) has some fascinating old pieces and an entertaining owner. Admission is $5 – less if you're in a group.

Off Yettie Rd, about seven km south-east of Lyndoch, the Barossa Reservoir has the famous **Whispering Wall**. The acoustics of this massive curved structure are such that you can stand at one end and listen to a conversation in normal voices at the other end, 150 metres away.

Places to Stay

The friendly *Barossa Caravan Park* (☎ 8524 4262), two km before town on the Barossa Valley Highway from Gawler, has tent/caravan sites for $10/13, on-site vans from $25 and cabins from $40.

On the edge of Sandy Creek Conservation Park, about 3.5 km south of town on the Cockatoo Valley road, *The Vale* is a YHA hostel in a restored stone farmhouse with views of vineyards and bush. Beds are $7 for members and you can book through YHA in Adelaide on ☎ 8231 5583.

The *Chateau Yaldara Motor Inn* (☎ 8524 4268), on the Gawler side of Lyndoch, has well-appointed units for $75/83.

In town, the *Lyndoch Bakery & Restaurant* has a great atmosphere and is reputed to be the valley's only true German-style bakery, with Bavarian *brezel* fresh daily; you can get a pot of good coffee and a pastry for $5, and a main meal from $9. Across the road, *Errigo's Italian Restaurant* does tasty pizzas, while the nearby *Lyndoch Hotel* has good-value counter meals.

TANUNDA (pop 3100)

In the centre of the valley, this is the most Germanic of the valley's towns and the acknowledged tourist centre. Many of its highlights are on Murray St, the main road through town. Tanunda has numerous historic buildings including the early cottages around Goat Square, which is the site of the original marketplace of Langmeil and called Ziegenmarkt.

Things to See & Do

There are also some interesting Lutheran churches. The **Tabor Church** on Murray St dates from 1849, but was rebuilt in 1871. On Jane Place, the 1868 **St John's Church** has life-size wooden statues of Christ, Moses, and the apostles Peter, Paul and John, that were donated in 1892. Most significant of all, however, is the **Langmeil Lutheran Church** on Maria St. It's associated with Pastor Kavel, who arrived in SA in 1838 and was its first Lutheran minister.

At 47 Murray St the **Barossa Valley Historical Museum**, in the old telegraph station (1866), has exhibits on the valley's early days. These include a 'church room' complete with a beautiful marble altar from the Immanuel Lutheran Church at Bower. It's open Wednesday to Sunday between 11 am and 5 pm, closing for lunch between 1 and 2 pm.

Brauer Biotherapies, at 1 Para Rd, produce homeopathic medicines and remedies for local consumption and export throughout the world. Free tours (30 to 45 minutes) are conducted at 11 am on weekdays.

On the Barossa Valley Highway about halfway between Tanunda and Nuriootpa, the excellent **Technology & Heritage Centre** features Kev Rohrlach's amazing collection of everything from postcards to stationary engines to military vehicles. It's open from 10 am to 5 pm daily; allow a couple of hours to do it justice. Admission costs $5.

Three km out on the Gomersal road, trained sheepdogs go through their paces at **Breezy Gully farm** at 2 pm on Monday, Wednesday and Saturday. Admission costs $6.

For children, **Storybook Cottage**, off the highway on the outskirts of town towards Lyndoch, has hands-on models and a rabbit warren where they can play at being Peter the Rabbit. **Kiddy Park**, on the corner of Menge Rd and Magnolia St, has a minizoo, train rides, a playground and other amusements.

Norm's Coolies travel in style to their shows at Breezy Gully Farm.

Murray St has several **arts and crafts** outlets catering for all tastes and budgets. Eve's Apple at No 38 is considered one of the best in the valley, with stunning exhibits. Even if you can't afford to buy, it's nice just to look.

From Tanunda, take the scenic route to Angaston through Bethany and via **Mengler Hill**. It runs through beautiful rural country featuring huge gums; the view over the valley from Mengler Hill is superb if you can ignore the unfortunate 'sculpture park' in the foreground. Do it in the reverse direction if you're cycling.

En route you can visit the 390-hectare **Kaiser Stuhl Conservation Park**, which has walking tracks and attractive bush on top of the Barossa Range. The turn-off is about a km towards Angaston from Menglers Hill, and the tiny car park is four km farther on. You can get a brochure with map from the Tanunda tourist office.

Places to Stay

The *Tanunda Caravan Park* (☎ 8563 2784) is an attractive place one km out of town towards Lyndoch on the Barossa Valley Highway. It has tent/caravan sites for $11/13, on-site vans from $27, basic cabins for $33 and self-contained cabins for $45.

Alternatively, the small and basic *Langmeil Road Caravan Park* (☎ 8563 0095) has powered sites for $8. It's two km

north of the town centre by the North Para River.

At 51 Murray St, the *Tanunda Hotel* (☎ 8563 2030) has singles/doubles from $38/44. Towards Nuriootpa, at No 182, the *Barossa Motor Lodge* (☎ 8563 2988) charges $75/83; they often have more attractive package deals. The *Weintal Hotel/Motel* (toll-free ☎ 1800 648 269), on the Barossa Valley Highway towards Nuriootpa, has standard units for $73/79 and units with queen-size beds for $83/89.

Halfway between Tanunda and Nuriootpa, the *Barossa Junction Motel* (☎ 8563 3400) has a railway theme; its rooms are converted carriages and cost from $72/86/104. About 100 metres away is the friendly *Barossa House B&B* (☎ 8562 4022), the valley's cheapest B&B place at $65 for couples, including a cooked breakfast.

Seppeltsfield About a km before the Seppelts winery on the Marananga road, *Seppeltsfield Holiday Cabins* (☎ 8562 8240) has self-contained cabins with wood fires and air-con from $50 (singles & doubles) for one night and $40 for two. Deluxe cabins cost $95/85 for one/two nights.

Right at Seppeltsfield, *The Lodge Country House* (☎ 8562 8277) is a licensed guest-house with luxury accommodation. B&B for couples is $250, with dinner $100 extra.

Places to Eat

Connoisseurs of country bakeries should head straight to the *Apex Bakery*, on Elizabeth St. This traditional bakery with a German bias produces a variety of breads, pastries and cakes in a wood-fired oven.

There are plenty of good places to eat on Murray St. *Crackers Restaurant* at No 36 specialises in French cuisine and has a good selection of local boutique wines. At No 47, the BYO *Fortune Garden* has a very good reputation. It specialises in Chinese dishes with mains starting from $7. The *Tanunda Hotel* at No 51 has huge counter meals for around $8.

In an 1870s cottage at 58 Murray St, the popular *Zinfandel Tea Rooms* specialises in German lunches and cakes. It's a great coffee house and the meals are excellent value. Opposite the tourist centre, at No 89, *La Buona Vita* has pasta dishes from $7, as well as Australian-style meals. The place to be seen is the *1918 Bistro & Grill* at No 94, which has a trendy atmosphere and prices to match.

Lange's Wurst Haus, at 117 Murray St, has

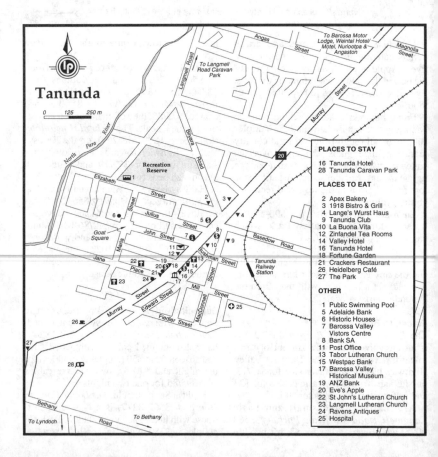

Tanunda

0   125   250 m

PLACES TO STAY
16 Tanunda Hotel
28 Tanunda Caravan Park

PLACES TO EAT
2   Apex Bakery
3   1918 Bistro & Grill
4   Lange's Wurst Haus
9   Tanunda Club
10 La Buona Vita
12 Zinfandel Tea Rooms
14 Valley Hotel
16 Tanunda Hotel
18 Fortune Garden
21 Crackers Restaurant
26 Heidelberg Café
27 The Park

OTHER
1   Public Swimming Pool
5   Adelaide Bank
6   Historic Houses
7   Barossa Valley
    Vistors Centre
8   Bank SA
11 Post Office
13 Tabor Lutheran Church
15 Westpac Bank
17 Barossa Valley
    Historical Museum
19 ANZ Bank
20 Eve's Apple
22 St John's Lutheran Church
23 Langmeil Lutheran Church
24 Ravens Antiques
25 Hospital

a mouth-watering selection of locally made German smallgoods as well as eat-in and takeaway meals; their very filling wurst platter (sausage, potato salad and sauerkraut) costs $8.50.

For real value, however, it's hard to beat the *Tanunda Club* at 45 MacDonnell St, which sells hearty meals for $5.50. It's open for lunch and dinner seven days.

NURIOOTPA (pop 3300)

At the northern end of the valley, Nuriootpa is the commercial centre of the Barossa Valley. There are several pleasant picnic areas along the Para River, as well as nice river walks close to the town centre.

Luhrs Cottage is a delightful little dwelling in the hamlet of **Lights Pass**, about three km east of Nuriootpa. Built in 1846 of mud and straw, and now a museum, it's open weekdays from 9.30 am to 4.30 pm and weekends from 1 pm to 4.30 pm. There's a school museum and ancient farm implements out the back.

The **Barossa Quilt Centre**, on the Angaston road, is the place to go if you're into quilting.

Places to Stay & Eat

The attractive *Barossa Valley Tourist Park* (☎ 8562 1404), on Penrice Rd, has tent/caravan sites for $11/13, basic cabins for $30 and self-contained cabins from $40.

On Kalimna Rd, just before the Sturt Highway 1.5 km north of town, the basic *Barossa Gateway Motel & Hostel* (☎ 8563 2571) has beds in self-contained rooms for $10 and motel units for $30/34. There's a small kitchen you can use.

Much nicer is the *Bunkhaus Travellers Hostel* (☎ 8562 2260), on Nuraip Rd, which is set on a family vineyard one km outside Nuriootpa on the highway to Tanunda (look for the keg on the corner). It's a very pleasant and welcoming place with dorm beds for $11, plus a comfortable cottage for four people for $30. Mountain bikes can be hired for $8 per day. Jane Matthew, the proprietor, will help you plan your day if you want.

The *Angas Park Hotel* (☎ 8562 1050), at 22 Murray St, has basic rooms for $15 and counter lunches from $5.

At 14 Murray St, the *Vine Inn Hotel/Motel* (☎ 8562 2133) has standard units for $45 (singles & doubles) and deluxe units for $60/75/90. Its restaurant has good-value meals that start from $7 for main courses, or you can eat for $4 in the bar. Units cost from $52/63/77 at the *Top of the Valley Motel* (☎ 8562 2111) at 49 Murray St.

On the outskirts of town towards Tanunda, the *Kaesler Winery Restaurant* has great food and you can eat outside in a lovely garden setting. If you're on a tight budget you'll find the German platter excellent value.

Closer to Tanunda, the *Chateau Dorrien Bistro* is set up as a *bierhaus* and has an emphasis on German-style meals. You can get a good meal here for $6, and there are wine, cider and mead tastings – I heard their quandong mead is a knockout.

ANGASTON (pop 2000)

On the eastern side of the Barossa Valley, this picturesque town was named after George Fife Angas, one of the area's pioneers. Unlike its two neighbours it's managed to retain a strong rural flavour. There are tourist information outlets in the **Angaston Galleria** at 18 Murray St, and in **Saltrams winery** on the road to Nuriootpa.

About seven km from town towards Springton, the magnificent **Collingrove Homestead** shows how the other half once lived. Built by George Angas' son, John, in 1856, it's now owned by the National Trust and has a house museum; you can visit from 1 to 4.30 pm weekdays and from 11 am to 4.30 pm on weekends and during festivals. Admission costs $3.

Bethany Arts & Crafts, in the old police station at the corner of Fife and Washington Sts, is one of the best **arts and crafts** outlets in the valley, if not country SA. Its excellent wares includes paintings, pottery and ceramics, and it often holds exhibitions. The Angaston Galleria also has arts and crafts.

At 3 Murray St, the **Angas Park Fruit Company** has a promotion centre where you can purchase an amazing variety of dried and glacé fruits, nuts, chocolates and other confectionery. The products aren't necessarily cheaper than in the shops, but they are fresher.

Places to Stay & Eat

Angaston is normally much quieter than Tanunda, so in busy times check here for accommodation before going further afield.

The *Barossa Brauhaus* (☎ 8564 2014) at 41 Murray St is a reasonable hotel with B&B rates of $18 per person. Just down the street at No 59, the *Angaston Hotel* (☎ 8564 2428) has B&B for $25 per person. Both do counter meals from $5.

Two km out of town on Stockwell Rd, the friendly *Vineyards Motel* (☎ 8564 2404) has standard units for $45/49 (singles/doubles) and deluxe units for $54/59; its family rooms sleep four for $69. Across the road, *Vintners Restaurant* has a good reputation for elegant meals, which start at $17. It's open from Tuesday to Sunday for lunch and Friday and Saturday for dinner.

For something cheaper in the food line, the *Roaring Fordies* on Murray St is a bakery, cafe and licensed steakhouse where mains cost from $9. It's very popular with locals. The *Saltram Estate Bistro*, at Saltram's winery, has an interesting lunch menu including Italian, South-East Asian and Moroccan dishes from $6.50.

If you really want to pamper yourself, the acclaimed *Collingrove Homestead* (☎ 8564 2061) has B&B accommodation in the old servants' quarters for $93/135.

OTHER BAROSSA TOWNS
Bethany

Site of the first German settlement in the Barossa, this sleepy hamlet is about five km from Tanunda on Bethany Rd. You can stroll along the tree-lined avenue admiring its historic dwellings, which include the tiny **Landhaus**. Built of stone, mud and straw in the 1840s, it's now a licensed restaurant (☎ 8563 2191); the first resident was a shepherd and, judging by the height of the lintels, not a very tall one.

Also worth a visit is the little **cemetery**, which has headstones in Gothic script dating from the 1860s. The depressing number of children's' graves illustrate the hardships faced by the early settlers.

Stockwell

This quiet English-like village (population 400) is at the northern end of the Barossa Valley about nine km from Nuriootpa. It has numerous old stone buildings, including the very photogenic **St Thomas Lutheran Church**. On a cold wet day, the Stockwell Hotel is the cosiest pub in the valley.

Williamstown

In the Barossa Range eight km south of Lyndoch, picturesque Williamstown is on an alternative scenic drive between Adelaide and the Barossa Valley.

The 1410-hectare **Para Wirra Recreation Park**, which has good walking trails, views, picnic areas and tennis courts, is five km east of town. At the park's northern end, the **Barossa Gold Field** was the scene of a frantic rush in the late 1860s when 4000 diggers descended on the scene. The frenzy soon fizzled out although gold continued to be mined into the 1930s. There's a walking trail around the diggings.

Three km south-east of Williamstown, the hilly 191-hectare **Hale Conservation Park** is good for walks and birdwatching. You can walk from here to the nearby **Warren Conservation Park** (363 hectares), which is traversed by the **Heysen Trail**.

Places to Stay In Williamstown you can stay at *Queen Victoria Jubilee Park* (☎ 8524 6363), a small caravan park with tent/caravan sites for $8/12, on-site vans for $26 and self-contained cabins for $40.

About five km north of Kersbrook, on the road from Torrens Gorge to Williamstown, the *Kersbrook YHA Hostel* (☎ 8389 3185) has beds for $7 for YHA members. It's in the grounds of a National Trust property called **Roachdale**, which has an interesting nature walk through a rare patch of pristine native forest.

Gawler

On Main North Rd, 43 km from Adelaide and 33 km south-west of Nuriootpa, this fast-growing dormitory and service centre was SA's second country town. There are a number of **heritage sites**, including some 1840s cottages, and you can visit them using the brochure *Gawler Walking Tours*.

The tourist office (☎ 8522 6814) is on the Lyndoch road and opens at 9.30 am daily, closing at 3.30 pm on weekdays and 2 pm on weekends and public holidays.

Gawler is a jumping-off point for the Barossa Valley and may have accommodation available when the valley is full. The town has three caravan parks, of which the *Gawler Caravan Park* (☎ 8522 3805), on Main North Rd, is recommended. The *South End Hotel*, at 23 Murray St, has basic pub rooms for $20/35.

The Mid-North

Stretching from the Barossa Valley in the south to Port Pirie and Jamestown in the north, the Mid-North is a region of rolling hills and plains almost entirely covered by a patchwork of farms. To the west it butts onto Yorke Peninsula, while to the east of Burra and Eudunda it fades into the more arid Murraylands. There are a some beautiful timbered areas in the hills, but often the landscape is entirely treeless. Much of the Mid-North was open grassland at the time of European settlement, and the farmers and miners cleared more.

Tourism, an important (if localised) industry, is centred on the region's old copper-mining towns and Clare Valley wineries. There are also many wonderful colonial buildings at places like Auburn, Bungaree and Mintaro. Apart from that, the region has numerous small, friendly towns which don't appear to have changed much since their heyday of last century.

European History

The explorer Edward John Eyre crossed the northern part of the region in 1839 and was suitably impressed by the rich grazing land he saw there. His glowing reports attracted squatters, and by the mid-1840s almost the entire Mid-North was taken up by huge runs. One of the first on the scene was George Hawker, who established Bungaree station in 1841 with 2000 ewes. By the early '50s the station covered nearly 700 sq km and had a flock of 100,000 sheep.

The second major development was the discovery of rich copper lodes at Kapunda (1842) and Burra (1845). Miners and their families – mostly Cornish but also Welsh and German – flocked to the area in their thousands. It was Australia's first mining rush and put the infant colony of SA on its feet.

Railways followed the miners, and by the '60s the great runs were being broken up into farms. The resulting wheat boom brought a wave of prosperity during which many

towns were established. Today the Mid-North is the heartland of South Australian agriculture, with wool, beef and cereal grains being its major products.

Information

The main tourist information offices are at Burra, Clare and Port Pirie. The free brochure *Visitor's Guide to South Australia's Far North* covers the region town by town and is reasonably comprehensive. It's available from SATC and tourist offices throughout the region.

Communications Throughout this book we use the new statewide STD code (08) and eight-digit telephone numbers, which take effect in February 1997. Should you need to use the old number, simply take the first two

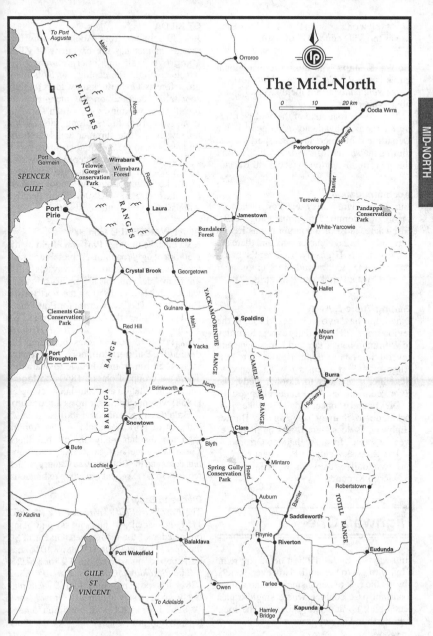

MID-NORTH

digits (either 85 or 86 in the Mid-North) and use as the STD code (085 or 086).

Books & Maps The most useful regional guide is the RAA's 216-page *Mid North & Yorke Peninsula* ($4 for members and $8 for nonmembers).

The RAA's road map of the Mid-North is by far the best available. Also good is the Department of Recreation & Sport's cycle touring map *Lower Mid-North*, which covers the area from Riverton to Clare and Burra.

Accommodation

Burra, the Clare Valley and Port Pirie have plenty of accommodation, including B&Bs. Elsewhere, most of the larger towns have a caravan park and a pub or two, and there are motels along Highway 1. There's back-packer-style accommodation in or near Clare, Crystal Brook and Port Pirie.

Getting There & Away

Stateliner has two services through the region from Adelaide: daily except Saturday to Wilmington via Clare and Jamestown; and several times daily along Highway 1 to Port Augusta. At Port Augusta you can connect to Stateliner's services to Coober Pedy, the Eyre Peninsula and the Flinders Ranges.

Greyhound Pioneer's daily service from Adelaide to Sydney runs up the Barrier Highway, as does Bute Buses on its thrice-weekly service from Adelaide to Orroroo.

The Barossa Adelaide Passenger Service has two daily buses on weekdays from Gawler to Kapunda.

Highway One

Highway 1 is by far the best bet if you're in a hurry to get to the north. However, there's always the risk of being stuck behind a slow roadtrain past Lochiel, where single-trailer semis pick up an extra trailer for the long haul north to Darwin or west to Perth.

ST KILDA

Just 30 minutes from Adelaide, this tiny seaside hamlet has the excellent **St Kilda Mangrove Trail** and interpretive centre, which highlight the ecology of SA's mangrove forests. Great flocks of waders (mainly spoonbills) descend on the mangroves to breed in early summer – you can view the goings-on from hides along the 1.7-km boardwalk. In late summer and March the birds leave and the mosquitoes take over.

The trail opens daily except Monday from 10 am to 4 pm; guided walks are conducted on weekends and public and school holidays (call the centre on ☎ 8280 8172 for details). Admission to the centre costs $6.

PORT WAKEFIELD (pop 500)

It's a mistake to judge Port Wakefield by the plethora of ugly roadhouses, motels and fast-food joints on the nearby highway. Only 100 km from Adelaide, this sleepy historic town was established in 1850 as the port for the Burra mine. The boom times for Port Wakefield ended when the mine closed in 1877.

The brochure *Port Wakefield Historic Walk* takes you to 34 sites including the diminutive **Bubners Inn**, once a stop on the stagecoach run from Adelaide to Wallaroo. There's a group of classic 1860s **cottages**, and a police station and courthouse complex (1858) which is being set up as a **museum**.

Balaklava (population 1300) is about 25 km east of Port Wakefield on the Auburn road and also has many fine old buildings. There are three historic walks, two good museums and the **Courthouse Gallery**, which receives some excellent travelling exhibitions.

Places to Stay

The *Port Wakefield Caravan Park* (☎ 8867 1151) is shaded and pleasant despite being on the edge of the mangroves. On Burra St, the *Port Wakefield Hotel* (☎ 8867 1016) has basic pub rooms with colour TV for $17/25.

The *Balaklava Caravan Park* (☎ 8862 1261) has powered sites for $9. Alternatively, you can stay at either the *Royal Hotel* (☎ 8862 1607) – it has air-conditioned heritage-style rooms for $25/38 – or the more basic *Terminus Hotel* (☎ 8862 1006) for $18/30. Both are in the town centre.

CRYSTAL BROOK (pop 2000)

In 1839 the explorer Edward John Eyre stopped for a drink at a gurgling stream, and was so impressed by the clarity of the water that he gave it this lovely name. Maybe the water isn't so clean today, but many of the huge river red gums that Eyre saw along the creek are still there.

The National Trust **museum** has displays devoted to local industry and lifestyles; it's open from 2 to 4 pm on Sundays and public holidays, and admission is $2.

Site of one of the district's earliest homesteads, **Bowman Park** is Crystal Brook's main tourist attraction. The complex, which includes a fauna park, is in a beautiful valley five km north-east of town at the southern tip of the Flinders Ranges. It's an access point for the Heysen Trail.

Places to Stay

Near town on the Port Pirie road, the basic *Crystal Brook Caravan Park* (☎ 8636 2640) has ancient gum trees and good shade. Alternatively, the *Crystal Brook Hotel* (8636 2023) on Railway Terrace has pub rooms for $18/30.

At *Bowman Park* (☎ 8636 2116) you can camp among huge gums at the bush camping area for $3 per person. There's also a spartan bunkhouse in the old stables for $7.50, and the very basic Heysen Hut – beds are free in the latter if you're hiking the trail, and $4.50 if you're not.

PORT PIRIE (pop 15,100)

Port Pirie, 231 km north of Adelaide, is an industrial centre with a huge silver, lead and zinc smelting complex which processes ore from Broken Hill. Established on mudflats as an unofficial loading point for nearby sheep stations in 1847, it became a focus for new railways that tapped the farms in its hinterland in the '70s. The settlement really took off when the first smelting works started up in 1888.

Unfortunately, your first impression of Port Pirie isn't likely to be favourable.

Driving into town from Highway 1, the skyline is an ugly jumble of power pylons, belching chimneys and banks of huge grain silos. Over everything towers the whopping 205-metre-high 'Big Stack'.

Information

The tourist office (☎ 8633 0439) is in the Tourism & Arts Centre in the former railway station on Mary Ellie St, opposite the silos. It's open from 9 am to 5 pm weekdays, 9 am to 4 pm on Saturday and 10 am to 3 pm on Sunday.

Things to See & Do

The **Art Centre**, which is open the same hours as the tourist office, receives some excellent touring exhibitions. Ask to see the exquisite silver tree fern.

You can take a 45 to 60-minute **self-guided walk** of interesting sites in and around the town centre with the brochure *National Trust Walking Tour*.

In the town centre on Ellen St, the National Trust **museum complex** features diprotodon bones, a marine exhibition, old shopfronts and a steam shunting engine. It includes Port Pirie's first railway station, with its amazingly ornate Victorian facade, together with the old customs house and police station. It's open from 10 am to 4 pm Monday to Saturday and 1 pm to 4 pm on Sunday; admission is $2.

Gracious **Carn Brae**, a magnificent house at 32 Florence St, has many features including stunning stained glass windows, beautiful antiques and large collections of all sorts of things. The courtly Mr Young, who lives there, will take you on a tour and describe the function and history of the exhibits; the $5 admission is well worth it. Opening hours are 10 am to 4 pm daily.

One-hour tours of the **smelting works** leave from the tourist office on Monday, Wednesday and Friday – 24-hours notice is required so they can organise a guide. You can take the guide in your own car ($2.50 per person) or go in the council bus ($5) if there's a minimum of six people. Ring the tourist office for details.

MID-NORTH

Places to Stay
Caravan Parks Most highly recommended of the town's four caravan parks is the very formal *Port Pirie Caravan Park* (☎ 8632 4275), on Beach Rd. It has tent/caravan sites for $8/12, on-site vans for $25 and cabins from $28.

Hotels & Motels Beds are $15 in both the *Family Hotel* (☎ 8632 1382), on Ellen St, and the *Central Hotel* (☎ 8632 1031), on Florence St.

The *Newcastle Hotel* (☎ 8632 2365), at 18 Main Rd, has rooms with air-con for $20/35. At the more luxurious *International Hotel/Motel* (☎ 8632 2422), on Ellen St, air-conditioned, self-contained hotel rooms with TV are also $20/35; motel units are $45/50.

Cheapest and most basic of the town's seven motels is the centrally located *Abaccy Motel* (☎ 8632 3701), on Florence St, which charges $40/45/50. The tourist office has details on others.

Places to Eat
There's no fine dining in Port Pirie, although there are good restaurants in the *John Pirie Motel*, on Main Rd outside town, and the *Flinders Ranges Motor Inn* at 151 Main Rd. For value, you can't beat the pubs – only the Newcastle doesn't do meals.

Locals recommend *Annie's Coffee Shop* at 15 Jubilee Place for home-made lunches; *Spud's Chicken & Bread Barn*, at 92 Main Rd, has delicious takeaway chicken and salad. Alternatively, you can try the very popular *Port Pirie Chinese Restaurant* at 34 Main Rd. A *pie cart* is often parked near the post office at night.

Getting There & Around
Stateliner calls in to Port Pirie ($21.80) several times daily on its service between Adelaide and Port Augusta. The bus station is in the former railway station next to the tourist office on Mary Ellie St, opposite the silos.

The Port Pirie Taxi Service (☎ 8633 0439) operates 24 hours.

Main North Road

At Tarlee, on the Barrier Highway 89 km from Adelaide, you continue heading north for six km then veer left on Main North Rd to Clare and Gladstone. If you're making for the Flinders you can easily cut across to Burra on the Barrier Highway, then head back to Main North Rd and continue on through Gladstone to Melrose.

The Clare Valley, which starts at Auburn (30 km from Tarlee), is described later in this chapter.

GLADSTONE (pop 1000)
Once an important railroad junction, Gladstone prospered because it had three railway gauges all coming together at the one siding. The resulting chaos was great for employment as on-going freight had to be transferred from one train to another.

With the demise of SA's country railways, Gladstone now relies almost entirely on farming; its grain silos, which hold a total 82,800 tonnes, are the state's largest inland grain storage facility.

Built in 1881, the impressive 125-cell **Gladstone Gaol** closed in 1975 and is now quietly decaying through lack of maintenance funds. It's well worth visiting simply to roam its eerie, echoing halls, and to wonder what it must have been like to be incarcerated there. The gaol is open Friday to Tuesday from 1 to 4 pm; admission is by donation.

Places to Stay
The *Gladstone Caravan Park* (☎ 8662 2036), off Main North Rd at the Laura end of town, has plenty of trees but no lawn. It has tent/caravan sites for $8/10 and the town swimming pool is right next door.

Alternatively, there are basic rooms with air-con and colour TV at the *Commercial Hotel* (☎ 8662 2148), in the town centre, for $20/25/35 singles/twins/doubles.

DENIS O'BYRNE

MICHELLE COXALL

MICHELLE COXALL

MICHELLE COXALL

RICHARD NEBESKY

A	C
	D
B	E

A: River red gum, Flinders Ranges
B: Aboriginal art, Arkaroo rock
   shelter, Flinders Ranges

C: Elbow Hill Inn, Eyre Peninsula
D: Old truck, Elbow Hill
E: Church at Poonindie,
   Eyre Peninsula

DENIS O'BYRNE

DENIS O'BYRNE

DENIS O'BYRNE

Top Left: Purnie Bore, Simpson Desert, Witjira National Park
Top Right: Sturt's Desert Pea, South Australia's floral emblem
Bottom: Lonely graves in the abandoned cemetery at Farina

JAMESTOWN (pop 1300)

This prosperous service town has one of the widest main streets (about 60 metres) in the state. Like its neighbours, Jamestown was established during the wheat boom of the 1870s, and there are a number of attractive stone buildings dating from those heady days. These include the town's four pubs and its court house; I assume the former provided customers for the latter.

The brochure *A Tour of Jamestown* takes you on a self-guided **walking tour** which includes the National Trust **museum**, in the old railway station. It has some interesting displays on local history including industry, the railways and lifestyles. Opening hours are 10 am to 5 pm Monday to Saturday, and 2 to 4 pm on Sunday; admission is $2.

Ten km out on the Spalding road is the **Bundaleer Forest** headquarters. Turn west to a pleasant bush picnic area, from where you can do scenic walks up to five km.

Places to Stay & Eat

On Bute St at the southern end of town, the *Jamestown Country Retreat Caravan Park* (☎ 8664 0077) has tent/caravan sites for $8/10, on-site vans for $25 and cabins for $45/50/55. The town swimming pool is next door.

Right in the town centre, the *Belalie Hotel/Motel* (☎ 8664 1065), at 36 Ayre St, has air-conditioned pub rooms for $20/32 and basic motel units for $32/40.

Across the street is the *Commercial Hotel* (☎ 8664 1013), which has just had its upstairs rooms renovated. They're air-conditioned and cost $25/35 with share facilities and $30/40 with private facilities, including a light breakfast.

Also on Ayre St, at number 79, the *Jamestown Hotel* (☎ 8664 1387) has very basic rooms for $20/30 including a light breakfast.

The *Railway Hotel/Motel* (☎ 8664 1035), at 32 Alexandra Ave, charges $39/49 for its motel units.

LAURA (pop 800)

This pleasant little town dines out on the fact that CJ Dennis lived here for a time during his early years; he had his first poem published by the now defunct *Laura Standard* when he was in his late teens. There's a four-metre-high copper **statue** of Dennis in front of the Dick Biles Art Gallery, on Main North Rd.

The town sees itself as the craft centre of the Mid-North, which explains all the antique, arts and crafts shops in the broad main street. One of the most interesting is **Possum Park Crafts**, in the old *Laura Standard* office. It doubles as the local tourist information outlet.

The **Laura Folk Fair** is a fun time of buskers, dancing, music, craft stalls and so on held on the first or second weekend in April (it doesn't clash with Easter).

Places to Stay

There's plenty of shade and space at the *Laura Caravan Park* (☎ 8663 2389), on Main North Rd, which has tent/caravan sites for $8/10.

Otherwise there's the *North Laura Hotel* (☎ 8663 2421), on Main North Rd at the northern end of town, which has basic rooms for $23/40. A cooked breakfast here costs $6.

Clare Valley

This narrow valley, which stretches 30 km from Auburn in the south to just north of Clare, is the state's second most important wine-growing area. It's also very scenic thanks to its hilly topography and mosaic of small villages, vineyards, farmland and native bush, including big gums. Amongst its major attractions are numerous historic buildings dating from the 1840s, particularly around Auburn, Mintaro (a declared heritage town), Watervale and Clare.

Information

Open daily from 10 am to 4 pm, the main tourist office (☎ 8842 2131) is in the Clare town hall on Main St. It's very friendly and efficient, and has an excellent stock of leaflets and brochures.

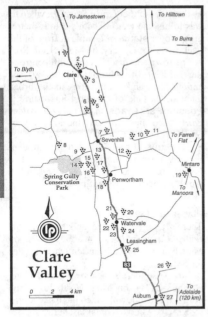

Clare Valley

0   2   4 km

WINERIES

1   Jim Barry Wines
2   Tim Knappstein Wines
3   Leasingham Wines
4   Wendouree Cellars
5   Tim Adam Wines
6   Duncan Estate
7   Sevenhill Cellars
8   Eldredge Wines
9   Stringybrae Wines
10 The Wilson Vineyard
11 Pike's PolishHill River Estate
12 Paulett Wines
13 Waninga Wines
14 Jeanneret Wines
15 Skillogalee Wines
16 Mitchell Winery
17 Pearson Wines
18 Penwortham Wines
19 Mintaro Cellars
20 Black Opal Quelltaler Vineyards
21 Crabtree of Watervale
22 Stephen John Wines
23 Rosenberg Cellars
24 Clos Clare
25 Horrocks Winery
26 Taylors Wines
27 Grosset Wines

Wineries

The first winery in the Clare Valley was established by Jesuit priests at their **Sevenhill College** in 1851. They wanted to produce altar wine for their Catholic brethren in the colony and overseas, and did so with great success. In fact, a Jesuit brother still oversees the making of altar wine there.

Today the valley is noted for its rieslings, but it also produces other good whites as well as reds, particularly shiraz. There are some big-name wineries here, such as Leasingham and Taylors, and several good boutiques. All up there are 28 wineries – the number is growing all the time.

The following shouldn't be missed:

Black Opal Quelltaler Vineyards, near Watervale, has a large winery complex that includes an interesting little museum of early wine-making equipment.

Crabtree of Watervale, also near Watervale, is a boutique winery that does a very nice shiraz-cabernet.

Skillogalee Wines, off to the west between Penwortham and Sevenhill, has a delightful tasting room in a historic cottage. There's an excellent restaurant here as well – it's the only winery restaurant in the valley that's open daily. They're noted for their shiraz, and also make a decent port.

Paulett Wines, between Penwortham and Mintaro, is perched high on the ridge dividing the Clare and Polish valleys; there's a magnificent view over the Polish Valley from the verandah. Their sparkling riesling isn't a bad drop.

Sevenhill Cellars just east of Sevenhill township has several large and marvellous old stone buildings, including a church, in lovely grounds. Their fortified verdelho (a Portuguese-style white port) is excellent. There are no tastings on Sundays, of course.

Leasingham Wines on the southern outskirts of Clare produces the award-winning Classic Clare range of wines, featuring cabernet and shiraz. The winery is in an old jam factory.

Tim Knappstein Wines, in an old brewery and soft-drink factory in central Clare, has a very nice if cavernous tasting area. Try their fumé blanc.

Jim Barry Wines is just north of Clare. Although the tasting area is rather ordinary, the staff are friendly and their shiraz is very popular. They do lunches, but only on weekends.

Organised Tours

Stateliner (☎ 8415 5555) has three-day tours from Adelaide to the valley from $99 per person twin share.

Clare Valley Scenic Tours (book at the

Clare tourist office) does good-value minibus tours including a two-hour breakfast tour to Spring Hill Conservation Park ($10), a two-hour look at Clare township ($10) and a four-hour winery tour ($15).

Festivals

The major local cultural event is the **Clare Valley Gourmet Weekend**, a festival of fine wine and food put on by about 20 local wineries over the Adelaide Cup weekend in May. It's like a huge, all-day progressive dinner. Several venues put on good live music ranging from jazz to classical.

Another event not to be missed is **Music in the Vines**, held on the first weekend in December. On Saturday there's a picnic and live music at the Black Opal winery near Watervale. The following day, Martindale Hall at Mintaro puts on a carnival with craft stalls, music, wine and food.

Accommodation

There's a very large choice of places to stay and the Clare tourist office can provide details. Included are two caravan parks, 13 hotels and motels, and around 50 B&Bs ranging from mansions to cottages. Only a selection are mentioned here.

Getting There & Around

Stateliner has a service daily except Saturday from Adelaide to Wilmington via Auburn ($12) and Clare ($14.30).

Clare Valley Taxis (☎ 018 847 000) operates throughout the valley. It'll cost around $9 to get from Clare to the Sevenhill winery and $25 to Auburn.

AUBURN (pop 330)

There are many beautiful heritage buildings in this historic township, 24 km south of Clare, which was established in 1849. In its infancy Auburn serviced the bullockies and South American muleteers whose wagons, up to 100 a day, trundled to and fro between the Burra copper mines and Port Wakefield.

Auburn grew to become an important commercial centre in the 1870s, when it boasted a flour mill, gas works and two breweries. Sadly, there are no beers brewed here today, but the Clare Valley's largest winery, **Taylor's Wines**, is nearby.

You can get local information from the post office on St Vincent St on week days, and on weekends and public holidays from Petherick's Antiques, across from the Rising Sun Hotel on Main North Rd.

Twenty-four of Auburn's historic places, including the birthplace of famous colonial author and poet CJ Dennis, are featured on a three-km **heritage walk** described in the leaflet *Walk with History at Auburn*. Some of SA's finest stonework can be seen here, particularly in the buildings grouped near the intersection of Main North Rd and St Vincent St.

Places to Stay & Eat

Several cottages offer B&B accommodation. They include historic *Petherick's* (☎ 8849 2282), on Main North Rd, which enjoys an enviable reputation. It has antique brass-and-iron beds, and to set the mood you're greeted with flowers and a complimentary bottle of local wine. They charge $95 for one couple, $170 for two and $210 for three, including breakfast provisions.

The *Rising Sun Hotel* (☎ 8849 2015) recently won an award for being the 'best small hotel in Australia'. You'll see why as soon as you walk in the door! The dining room is charming and the food is excellent – as is the wine cellar – yet meals are reasonably priced (main courses are from $11). Its modern, self-contained bedrooms cost $40/65 for singles/doubles.

Next door, the historic *Rising Sun Mews* (same phone number) has tastefully restored heritage-style rooms for $60/80 including a decent breakfast. It's considered among the best of the valley's so-called 'catered alternative accommodation'.

Next door again, and also with heritage-style rooms, *Tatehams* (☎ 8849 2030) has B&B for $100/130. Its gourmet restaurant produces magnificent meals; imagine local undercut beef fillet served with chipped parsnips and a glaze of red wine and caramelised onion, followed by a chocolate soufflé with home-made chocolate icecream. Drool!

MID-NORTH

MID-NORTH

If you don't want to splurge, the closest thing to budget accommodation here is the modest *Auburn Motel* (☎ 8849 2125), on Main North Rd. It has a decent restaurant and motel units for $30/40/48/56.

LEASINGHAM TO SEVENHILL

The main concentration of wineries is between Leasingham and Sevenhill. Leasingham and Watervale grew from camping places along the Burra to Port Wakefield road; turn off at Leasingham if you're going to Mintaro.

Watervale has several heritage-listed buildings, including the impressive **Stanley Grammar School**, and you can explore them with the aid of a historic walks brochure.

Penwortham was laid out by pastoralist John Horrocks in 1840, making it the first town in SA north of Gawler. Horrocks lies in the local cemetery; he died in 1846, aged 28 years, after accidentally shooting himself during an exploring expedition in the north.

The main attraction at Sevenhill is the nearby **winery** established by the Jesuits in 1851. They arrived on the site from Vienna in 1848, calling it Sevenhill after the seven hills of Rome. Of interest are its solid old winery buildings as well as **St Aloysius Church**, which they completed in 1875.

About three km south-west of Sevenhill, the 400-hectare **Spring Gully Conservation Park** features blue gum forest and SA's only stand of red stringybarks. There are 18-metre-high cascades here in winter, as well as kangaroos, birdlife (50 species) and 4WD and walking tracks. You can get a park brochure from the Clare tourist office.

Places to Stay

Pub-style rooms are offered by the grand old *Watervale Hotel* (☎ 8843 0109) for $30/40 including a country breakfast. There's also *Leasingham Cabins* (☎ 8843 0136), which has comfortable cabins from $35. Dinner B&B packages are available.

Bryvon Homestay (☎ 8843 4331), on Horrocks Rd near Penwortham, sleeps six from $80 a couple for B&B; it boasts beautiful views of the surrounding countryside and is within walking distance of Spring Gully Conservation Park.

Just north of Sevenhill, on the Quarry Hill Rd, *Miss Nobel's B&B* (☎ 8843 0020) is a delightful historic cottage in a rural setting. There are country walks, open fires and farm-style breakfasts for $70 for singles & doubles – the cottage sleeps seven and extra persons are $15. It's recommended as one of the best-value B&Bs in the valley.

MINTARO (pop 80)

Off the main tourist route and 19 km south-east of Clare, this historic village was established in 1848. Its main industry is slate mining; Mintaro slate is of such high quality that it's used internationally in billiard tables. Like a little piece of England plonked down in the Australian countryside, Mintaro is so well preserved that the whole town is a declared heritage site. Call in to the tourist office at Clare or Auburn for a historic walk brochure.

Among Mintaro's more interesting relics is the **Magpie & Stump Hotel** (1851), which acts as the information outlet. There's also **Martindale Hall**, a gracious 1880 Georgian mansion with period furnishings, a magnificent blackwood staircase, Italian marble fireplaces and lovely grounds. It's three km from town and opens daily from 11 am to 4 pm except weekends, when it opens at noon; admission is $5.

Places to Stay & Eat

In and around town are a number of old houses and quaint cottages offering B&B.

If you've saved up you can pamper yourself at *Martindale Hall* (☎ 8843 9088), which charges $60 per person B&B, and $115 for dinner B&B; dinner on weekends is served formally by a butler and maid. They'll also make up delicious picnic hampers for $18 per person, but require 24 hours notice.

The *Magpie & Stump Hotel* does counter lunches and teas daily.

CLARE (pop 2600)
This attractive and prosperous town, 135 km from Adelaide, was settled in 1842 and named after County Clare in Ireland. Although tourism is a growth industry, so far it's managed to avoid many of the trappings characteristic of the Barossa Valley.

The town has a number of heritage-listed buildings, many of which are covered by the brochure *Clare Historic Walk*. They include the impressive **St Michael's Church** (1849), which was the valley's first substantial building.

The former police station and courthouse (1850) is now an interesting National Trust **museum**; it's open 2 to 4 pm on Sundays and from 10 am to noon and 2 to 4 pm on Saturdays and public and school holidays.

Clarevale, on Lennon St, is another good museum with displays of wine-making equipment used during the valley's early years. Check at the tourist office for opening hours.

Also of interest is the splendid **Wolta Wolta Homestead** (1864), home to four generations of the Hope family. However, it only opens on Sundays (and then not always) from 10 am to 1 pm. It was gutted by a bushfire in 1983, but has since been almost completely restored.

Just outside the northern end of the valley, 12 km from Clare, **Bungaree Station** covers 2200 hectares and is a mere shadow of its former vast self. At one time the homestead was like a small town and boasted its own council chambers, police station and Anglican church; the church is still in use. It's listed with the National Trust and visitors are welcome. You can do a self-conducted cassette tour of the old buildings (they date from 1842) for $8, including morning or afternoon tea.

Geralka Farm, 25 km north of Clare on the Spalding road, also caters for visitors. It features the fascinating Wheal Sarah mine (you'd never know it was a fake) and you can do wagon rides and guided walks. The farm closes during February, but otherwise it's open Friday, Saturday, public holidays and school holidays (except summer); admission is $6.

Arts & Crafts
For something different, the **Warenda Creek Gallery** on Warenda Rd features the acclaimed work of local artist Russell Pick, as well as contemporary art from Japan and Indonesia. It's open between 10 am and 6 pm from Wednesday to Sunday.

Also worthwhile is **Springfarm Galleries**, a collection of old stone buildings in a vineyard setting on Spring Farm Rd, about two km south-east of town. It has several artists and craftspeople in residence, including a silversmith and blacksmith, and opens from 10 am to 5 pm daily.

At Blyth, a small township 11 km west of Clare, is the **Medika Gallery** of artist Ian Roberts. Ian is well known for his stunning watercolours of birds and plants. The gallery, in the photogenic 1886 **St Petrie Kirche Lutheran Church**, opens from 10 am to 5 pm weekdays and 2 to 5 pm weekends.

Places to Stay
Caravan Parks & Cabins The very friendly and attractive *Christison Park Caravan Park* (☎ 8842 2724) is on Main North Rd three km south of the town centre. It has tent sites for $10 ($5 if you're travelling solo), powered sites for $14, on-site vans for $30, and self-contained cabins from $40.

Clare Valley Cabins (☎ 8842 3917) are in a peaceful bush setting with lots of birds about three km north-east of town. The cabins have fans and pot-belly stoves, and sleep up to six; they cost $44 for singles & doubles on weekdays and $49 on weekends.

At *Geralka Farm* (☎ 8845 8081), on the Spalding road, you can camp for $11 or stay in on-site vans from $25. There's also a self-contained unit for $40.

Hotels & Motels On Main St, the basic *Taminga Hotel* (☎ 8842 2808) has rooms for $15/30, while the more popular *Clare Hotel* (☎ 8842 2816) has single pub rooms for $18 and motel units for $35/40.

The relatively luxurious *Bentley's Hotel/Motel* (☎ 8842 2815), also on Main St, has air-conditioned hotel rooms with private facilities for $35/45/55, and motel units for

$45/55/65. A separate and rather spartan backpacker section has beds for $15 (very expensive for what you get).

The *Clare Valley Motel* (☎ 8842 2799), on Main North Rd south of town, looks expensive but its large, well appointed units are reasonably priced at $50/55/63. On Main St, the more luxurious *Clare Central Motel* (☎ 8842 2277) charges $59/62 for its standard rooms.

B&B There are many B&B establishments in and around Clare and all are considered worthwhile. Recommended as being excellent value is *Green Gables* (☎ 8842 2576), set in a beautiful garden on Mill St. It has a range of luxurious rooms for $75/100 including an excellent breakfast.

Six km north of town, *Wuthering Heights* (☎ 8842 3196) gets rave reviews for its three romantic cottages on 30 hectares of trees and farmland. They include Heathcliff's Cabin, a small timber structure sleeping five for $55 singles & doubles and $10 for extra adults. The price includes full breakfast provisions.

Bungaree Station (☎ 8842 2677) has accommodation in the shearers' quarters for $15 a bed, but groups have precedence. There are also several heritage cottages sleeping from two to eight for $40 per person.

Places to Eat

All the hotels and motels have meals. The bistro at *Bentleys Hotel/Motel* is very airy and pleasant, and represents the best dining on the hotel scene.

For Chinese food there's the *Clare Dragon Restaurant*, on Main St, which does dine-in or takeaway meals for reasonable prices. Also on Main St, the *Chaff Mill Country Kitchen* has a very pleasant atmosphere and is noted for its country-style meals. Steaks are a specialty.

Also worth trying is the *Clarevale Restaurant*, which adjoins the wine museum on Lennon St. It's open for lunches daily and dinner from Thursday to Sunday; main courses start at $9.

Barrier Highway

Running mainly through open sheep and wheat country, the Barrier Highway is the most direct route from Adelaide to Burra, the old copper-mining town. You can go this way to the Flinders Ranges by turning off at Terowie, or continue north-east from Terowie to Sydney via Broken Hill.

KAPUNDA (pop 2000)

Sleepy Kapunda, which is just outside the Barossa Valley, is on the most direct route from Nuriootpa to the Barrier Highway. A rich copper deposit was found here in 1842 and two years later Cornish miners were hard at work.

Kapunda became the first mining town in Australia. At its peak, in 1861, it had 11 hotels and was the colony's major commercial centre outside Adelaide. Large-scale operations ceased in 1878 and the mines closed altogether in 1912. Thanks to the lack of development since then, many of the solid stone buildings erected during the boom years have survived intact.

The tourist office on Hill St, just off Main St, opens depending on the availability of volunteers.

Things to See & Do

Right at the entrance to town on the Adelaide side, you're greeted by an impressive eight-metre-high bronze statue of 'Map Kernow' (the 'Son of Cornwall' in old Cornish). The town's Cornish heritage is celebrated by the annual **Celtic Folk Festival**, held over three days on the weekend before Easter and featuring traditional Celtic music, singing and dancing.

You can learn more about the boom times at the **mining interpretive centre** (admission $2), at the rear of the tourist office, where there's a half-hour video of the town and its history, as well as mining displays. It's open 1 pm to 4 pm Saturday to Thursday except winter, when it's only open weekends and public holidays.

Open the same hours, and almost next door in the heritage-listed Baptist Church (1866), the **Kapunda Historical Museum** has a very large and fascinating collection of memorabilia. This is definitely one of the best museums in country SA; admission is $3.

Many of Kapunda's fine old buildings can be viewed on a 10-km **heritage trail** around the streets and mine site, and on a much shorter walk through the town centre. Both are described in the booklet *Discovering Historic Kapunda* ($5.95), which gives historical background and describes over 60 heritage sites. You can get one from the newsagent.

Places to Stay & Eat
The historic *Sir John Franklin Hotel* (☎ 8566 3233) on Main St dates from 1849; it has solid counter meals from $4 and rooms costing $25/50 for singles/doubles (its family room sleeps five for $55).

Across the street, the friendly owners of *Ford House B&B* (☎ 8566 2280) charge from $80 for couples.

There's also the *Dutton Park Caravan Park* (☎ 8566 2094), at the end of Baker St, with limited facilities but plenty of trees and birdlife. It has tent/caravan sites for $8.50/10 and cabins for $40.

Probably the nicest place to eat in town is *Fresh Fields* on Main St. It has a cosy atmosphere, friendly service and good-value meals – lunches average $5 and evening meals (à la carte) average $10. It's BYO.

Getting There & Away
The Barossa Adelaide Passenger Service (☎ 8564 3022) has two daily buses on weekdays from Gawler to Kapunda ($5.70).

TARLEE (pop 100)
Halfway between the Barossa and Clare valleys, the main attraction here is **Tarlee Antiques**. Reputed to be one of the best such shops in SA, its seven rooms are crammed with a fascinating selection of antiques, collectables and bric-a-brac.

The shop has a cosy licensed *restaurant* with open fire where you can buy delicious lunches and dinners. There's also a pine-log *motel* (☎ 8528 5328) with comfortable, well-appointed rooms for $55/65.

RIVERTON (pop 750)
Originally a camping place for the wagon teams that carted copper ore from Burra to Port Adelaide in the 1840s, Riverton was the scene of a dramatic shoot-out in 1921. It happened at the railway station, when a crazed passenger on the Broken Hill Express fired numerous shots into the crowded dining room. Several people were wounded and Broken Hill MP Percy Brookfield was killed when he tried to disarm the gunman. Apparently you can still see one of the bullet holes in the wall.

Scholz Park Museum, in the main street, has a fully furnished house, coach-building shop and blacksmiths shop, set up as they would have been late last century. It's open by appointment only – contact the district council office on ☎ 8847 2305.

Eighteen km further north, at **Saddleworth**, there's a historical folk museum with an extensive collection of various memorabilia. It's open from 2 to 5 pm on Sundays; admission is $2.

In Riverton you can stay at the little *Riverton Caravan Park* (☎ 8847 2419), while the *Central Hotel* (☎ 8847 2314) has pub rooms. Saddleworth has a basic camping at the town oval. There's also the *Saddleworth Hotel* (☎ 8847 4013), where a hearty cooked breakfast is $5 and rooms are $15 per person.

BURRA (pop 1200)
Only 42 km north-east of Clare, this pretty little town is literally bursting at the seams with historic sites dating from the 1840s to '70s. The district, Burra Burra, takes its name from the Hindi word for 'great' by one account, and from the Aboriginal name of the creek by another.

Thomas Pickett, a shepherd, discovered copper at Burra in 1845. The deposit proved to be phenomenally rich, and by 1850 it was supporting the largest metalliferous mine in Australia. In 1851 the township had a population of 5000, which made it the country's seventh largest. By then Pickett was dead; he'd fallen into his lonely campfire while drunk and burned to death.

Burra originally consisted of several villages. The mining company had set up Kooringa, which is now the township's central part, but most people preferred to live outside company control. As a result, the Cornish (who were the most numerous) established Redruth, the Scots Aberdeen, the Welsh (who ran the smelter) Llwchwr, and the English Hampton.

By 1860 the mine was produced 5% of the world's copper; over 1000 men and boys, most of them Cornish, were employed there at that time. It closed 17 years later, mainly because of flooding problems and falling ore grades, but reopened for 10 years from 1971.

Information

The tourist office (☎ 8892 2154) in Market Square is open from 9 am to 4 pm daily. It can provide a comprehensive listing of attractions and accommodation, as well as good advice on just about everything of interest in town.

They can also sell you *Discovering Historic Burra* ($5.95), which gives historical background and describes around 60 heritage sites. You can see them all by doing the 11-km heritage trail (you can drive or walk) and a short walking tour around Market Square.

The booklet is included with the Burra Passport, which costs $20 for a car containing up to five people. The passport includes a key which allows access to several sites, as well as half-price entry to the Enginehouse and Bon Accord museums.

Things to See & Do

Burra has many evocative relics of the mining days. Most are made of stone and include tall chimneys, enginehouses, grand hotels, massive churches and tiny cottages. You'll also notice the lack of trees on the grassy hills around town. Their original cover of she-oaks and gums was stripped to feed the smelter furnaces.

Right in Burra's commercial centre, the **Market Square Museum** (admission $2) is across from the tourist office; it features a shop, post office and house as they might have looked between 1880 and 1930. Opening hours are from 2 to 4 pm on Saturday and 1 to 3 pm on Sunday.

The 33 attached cottages at **Paxton Square** were built for Cornish miners in the 1850s. One of them, **Malowen Lowarth**, has been furnished in 1850s style, and provides a fascinating glimpse of how a mine captain lived. It's open Saturday from 1 to 3 pm and Sunday and public holidays from 10.30 am to 12.30 pm; admission is $3. The others are available for accommodation (see Places to Stay).

In Burra's early days about 1800 people lived in **dugouts** along the creek, but a flood in 1851 drove most of them out. Since then floods have destroyed all but two of the dugouts.

More substantial relics include the **Redruth Gaol** (1856) which featured in the film *Breaker Morant*, **St Mary's Anglican Church** (1849) and **Peacocks Chimney**, which provided up-draught for the boilers at a now-demolished enginehouse.

The open-air **Burra Mine Museum** has numerous sights including tall stone chimneys, a powder magazine, ore-dressing floors and a deep open-cut mine – there are lookouts and excellent information signs with historic photos. Included is the **Enginehouse Museum**, which features a model of the mine workings; it's open from 11 am to 2 pm Monday to Friday, but you can wander elsewhere around the mine site at any time.

The **Bon Accord Mine** was a Scottish enterprise that ended in failure; instead of rich copper ore, the miners discovered plentiful underground water. Not to be deterred, the canny Scots sold their lease to the town, and the mine shaft supplied Burra's water until the 1960s. Now an interpretive centre, Bon Accord opens weekdays from 12.30 to 2.30 pm; admission is $3.

Organised Tours

Minibus heritage tours leave the tourist office at 10 am daily for $15; they take two hours and visit six major sites.

Impressive Tourist Services (8892 2636) does an informative 1½ hour guided walking tour of heritage sites in and around the town centre for $6. It's a great way to explore the early social scene of Burra.

Their 1½ hour 'tombstones by torchlight' tour through Burra cemetery is proving popular – they're not particularly creepy, even though you visit the grave of a murdered sailor. Tours start around 7 pm, usually on a moonlit night, and cost $6. Bring your own torch.

Three km from town off the Morgan road, Burra Trail Rides (☎ 8688 92 2627), on Basin Farm, does escorted horse rides through the scenic Burra Hills. These vary from one hour ($15) to all day ($60 including a picnic lunch).

Places to Stay

Caravan Park The town's only *caravan park* (☎ 8892 2442) is down by peaceful

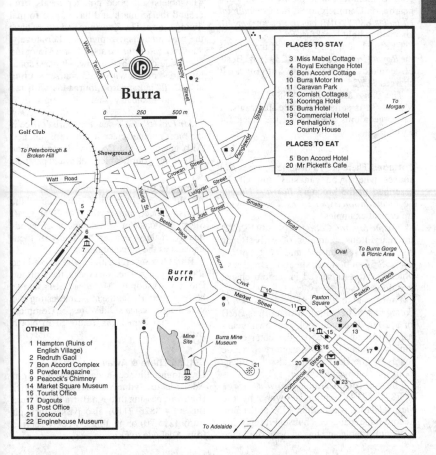

PLACES TO STAY

3 Miss Mabel Cottage
4 Royal Exchange Hotel
6 Bon Accord Cottage
10 Burra Motor Inn
11 Caravan Park
12 Cornish Cottages
13 Kooringa Hotel
15 Burra Hotel
19 Commercial Hotel
23 Penhaligon's Country House

PLACES TO EAT

5 Bon Accord Hotel
20 Mr Pickett's Cafe

OTHER

1 Hampton (Ruins of English Village)
2 Redruth Gaol
7 Bon Accord Complex
8 Powder Magazine
9 Peacock's Chimney
14 Market Square Museum
16 Tourist Office
17 Dugouts
18 Post Office
21 Lookout
22 Enginehouse Museum

MID-NORTH

Burra Creek, near the centre of town. It's basic but pleasant, and has good shade; tent/caravan sites are $10/12.

Hotels & Motels There are four historic hotels offering much the same standard of basic pub-style accommodation, and one motel.

On Market Square in the middle of town, the *Burra Hotel* (☎ 8892 2389) has rooms with ceiling fans for $26/50, including a cooked breakfast. The nearby *Kooringa Hotel* (☎ 8892 2013), on Kitchen St, charges $35/50 including a light breakfast. Also nearby, on Commercial St, the *Commercial Hotel* (☎ 8892 2010) has rooms for $25/40, also with a light breakfast.

Cheapest (and most basic) of the pubs is the *Royal Exchange* (☎ 8892 2392), on Bests Place in old Aberdeen (now North Burra). It charges $15/25.

The *Burra Motor Inn* (☎ 8892 2777), on Market St, is somewhat more luxurious; it has large rooms overlooking the creek for $50/55.

Cottages There are 15 historic cottages and houses where you can stay and all are described in the brochure *Burra – Unique Accommodation Experiences*. The following are typical examples.

Paxton Square Cottages (☎ 8892 2622) are marvellous examples of early Burra; they're self-contained and cost $40/50 ($45/55 if you need sheets). Breakfast, which is extra, is served in the old chapel next door.

There's also the 1850s *Miss Mabel Cottage* (☎ 8362 3306), which offers B&B for $120 for two (you cook your own breakfast). Built in the 1850s, the cottage has homely touches like 19th-century romantic novels by the bed! There's also a garden-room spa and open fireplace.

The secluded *Bon Accord Cottage* (☎ 8892 2519), which is owned by the National Trust, was built in 1959 as the Bon Accord mine manager's house. Fittingly, it's very comfortable and has an open fire in the

lounge. It charges $75 for doubles, including breakfast provisions.

Yet another fine place is the gracious *Penhaligon's Country House* (☎ 8892 2259), which once accommodated the directors of the Burra mine. Dating from the 1840s, and tastefully furnished with antiques and original paintings, it's considered one of the loveliest of Burra's early homes. It's the only fully hosted B&B in town, and charges $65 per person.

Places to Eat

The hotels sell good counter meals from around the $5 mark and have more formal dining rooms. The *Kooringa* and *Burra* have the most imaginative menus. Alternatively, *Jumbuck's Restaurant* at the Burra Motor Inn is considered the best in town. It has a small but varied menu, with main courses starting at $12; their kangaroo tournados with red wine and cranberry sauce is simply delicious.

Mr Pickett's Café near the tourist office is the most popular place in town for lunches. Also nearby is the *Country Pantry*, which has yummy gourmet pies, cakes and pastries.

Things to Buy

An old stone barn in Drew Lane, behind the tourist office, houses the Off-Beat Craft Shop. It boasts a wide variety of good-quality, mainly local crafts, many of them unusual as the name suggests.

Burra has several antique and bric-a-brac shops. If you're keen on clocks, the Antique Clock Workshop on Morehead St is said to be very good. By far the most interesting and varied of the rest are Old Wares, on Commercial St, and Sara's, on Young St in North Burra.

Getting There & Away

Greyhound Pioneer's daily service from Adelaide to Sydney runs up the Barrier Highway, passing through Burra ($17). Bute Buses (☎ 8826 2110) also passes through Burra ($15.70) on its thrice-weekly service from Adelaide to Orroroo.

HALLETT (pop 100)

Noted for fine Merino wool, the most interesting thing about Hallett is the 91-km **Dares Hill Scenic Drive**, which takes you the round-about way to Terowie. You can get a route map and notes from Hallett Country Corner, a friendly craftshop on the Barrier Highway in town.

The unsealed road takes you via the abandoned settlement of **Mt Bryan East**, an accommodation point on the Heysen Trail. There's good variety in the landscapes along the way, including a spectacular outlook towards the Murray River from Dares Hill, 27 km from Hallett. About 43 km further on, in the Woma Range, the 1056-hectare **Pandappa Conservation Park** has attractive hill scenery and plenty of wildlife including euros and red and grey kangaroos.

Places to Stay

Seven km from town is *Tooralie Homestead* (☎ 8894 2067), which offers B&B in the homestead ($40 per person) and renovated shearers' quarters ($30). All-inclusive accommodation is $80 and $60 respectively.

The *Wildongoleechie Hotel* (☎ 8894 2014) in Hallett has basic rooms, as does the interesting old *Whyte-Yarcowie Hotel* (☎ 8659 1131), 21 km farther north on the highway at tiny Whyte-Yarcowie.

TEROWIE (pop 200)

Almost but not quite a ghost town, Terowie is definitely worth the short detour off the Barrier Highway. The town was originally linked by broad-gauge railway to Adelaide and narrow-gauge to Peterborough. Because goods had to be transferred between carriages from one line to the other, the sprawling railway yards – they stretched for three km – provided hundreds of jobs. At its peak, during WWII, the population exceeded 2000 people.

But in 1969, when the broad-gauge line was extended to Peterborough, the death knell sounded for Terowie as a major centre. Today, this gutsy town is worth a visit as much for its lingering air of a bygone age as for its wonderful, though sadly deteriorating, historic streetscapes.

If you're a photographer or artist, and keen on old buildings, you'll easily spend an enjoyable day capturing the character of Terowie. Professional photographer John Ogle, of Munjibbie Crafts (☎ 8659 1092) on Main St, can arrange photographic weekends. Ask him for the brochure *A Tour of Terowie*, which will take you on a walk around 30 points of interest.

Places to Stay

On Main St, the *Terowie Hotel* (☎ 8659 1012) has basic rooms for $20/30, including a cooked breakfast. There's also the *Old Terowie Hospital* (☎ 8659 1061), on Mitchell St, where B&B is $30/48.

Out on the Barrier Highway, the *Terowie Motel* (☎ 8659 1082) has units from $28/30.

TEROWIE TO BROKEN HILL

From Terowie you can either head northwest to Peterborough (24 km) and Orroroo (61 km), or north-east along the sealed Barrier Highway to Broken Hill (296 km).

The Barrier Highway passes through semiarid station country, with small service centres at **Oodla Wirra** (35 km), **Yunta** (97 km), **Mannahill** (137 km), **Olary** (178 km) and **Cockburn** (246 km and right on the border). Each has a pub and fuel sales. Oodla Wirra has a fruit-fly check point for travellers coming from NSW.

Yorke Peninsula

Explorer Matthew Flinders described Yorke Peninsula as an 'ill-shaped leg', with its heel in Gulf St Vincent, the sole of its foot in Investigator Strait and its knee in Spencer Gulf. The peninsula is mainly flat to undulating and there are no watercourses to speak of, but much of its coastline is very attractive – you can fish, dive or swim almost all the way around it. In the south there's the spectacular Innes National Park and some of SA's best surfing. At the northern end, the towns of Wallaroo, Moonta and Kadina preserve a rich copper-mining heritage from the last century.

European History

White settlement on Yorke Peninsula began in 1846 when a sheep station was established at Stansbury, on the east coast. Others soon followed, but those first settlers had a hard time of it; the Aborigines were hostile, the thick mallee scrub made poor pasture and there was little fresh water.

The peninsula was looking distinctly unpromising until major copper deposits were discovered at Kadina and Moonta around 1860. Worked mainly by Cornish miners, the largest mines remained open until the early 1920s and made a massive contribution to the state economy.

By 1880 most of the big stations had been subdivided into farms. Scrub rollers pulled by horses were busily flattening the mallee, and since then almost all the native bush has been cleared to make way for cereal crops. Today, thanks largely to superphosphate and a relatively cool moist climate, the peninsula is Australia's richest barley-growing district. Most of the harvest is exported through the shipping terminals at Ardrossan, Port Giles and Wallaroo.

Information

The Yorke Peninsula Visitor Information Centre (☎ 8821 2093) is in the Kadina town hall.

> ### HIGHLIGHTS
>
> - Discover the copper-mining heritage of Moonta, Kadina and Wallaroo
> - Catch the waves at Pondalowie and other surf beaches around Innes National Park
> - Feast, folk dance, drink lots of 'swanky' and chase sprites at the Kernewek Lowender Festival
> - Scuba dive amongst the shipwrecks around Wardang Island
> - Survey Australia's thickest wheat belt from a gypsy wagon pulled by Clydesdales

The free pamphlet *Yorke Peninsula* is a reasonably informative guide covering most aspects of interest to visitors. It's available from SATC and the Kadina tourist office.

Communications The STD code for Yorke Peninsula is 08.

Books & Maps The RAA has a good road map, as does the Department of Recreation & Sport with its cycle touring map. The most informative map is published by Westprint.

The RAA's 216-page *Mid North & Yorke Peninsula* ($4 for members and $8 for non-members) is a comprehensive general guide to the region.

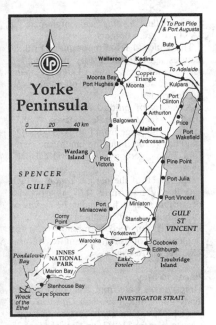

Yorke Peninsula

To Port Pirie & Port Augusta

Bute

Wallaroo Kadina

To Adelaide

Moonta Bay Copper
Port Hughes Triangle
  Moonta Kulpara

Port
Clinton

Arthurton

Balgowan Price

Maitland Port
Wakefield

Ardrossan

Wardang
Island Port
  Victoria Pine Point

SPENCER
GULF Port Julia

Port Minlaton Port Vincent
Minlacowie
Corny Stansbury GULF
Point ST
  VINCENT
Yorketown

Warooka Coobowie
  Edithburgh
Pondalowie INNES Lake Troubridge
Bay NATIONAL Fowler Island
  PARK
  Marion Bay

Stenhouse Bay
Wreck Cape Spencer INVESTIGATOR STRAIT
of the
Ethel

0   20   40 km

you can often catch a feed simply by wading
around at night with a dab net and torch.

Organised Tours
There are diving and/or fishing charters at
Edithburgh, Foul Bay, Port Broughton, Port
Hughes, Port Victoria and Wallaroo.

You can do camel treks at Corny Point,
nature walks at Ardrossan, 4WD tours from
Warooka, boat cruises at Edithburgh and
Wallaroo, scenic flights from Edithburgh,
and a variety of other tours in the Copper
Triangle. See the sections on these places for
details.

Also of interest is the innovative Creative
Activities Network, which operates throughout the peninsula and incorporates activities
such as arts and crafts workshops, bush
walks, heritage tours and farm visits. A range
of 'personalised learning experiences' are
available, from spending a day on a sheep
farm to attending a bush painting workshop
with a local artist. For more details, contact
SATC or the Kadina tourist office.

Accommodation
There are numerous caravan parks, hotels,
motels and holiday flats throughout the peninsula, particularly near the sea. However,
the coast is an extremely popular destination
during Easter and the October and January
school holiday periods. As a result, coastal
caravan parks and any form of self-contained
accommodation are usually booked out at
these times.

For something different, you can hire a
horse-drawn gipsy caravan in Stansbury.

There's bunkhouse-style accommodation
at Innes National Park and Port Vincent, and
bush camp sites in the national park. Apart
from a number of places on the 'foot', the
peninsula has few opportunities for bush
camping. Contact the district council offices
for details on where you can camp on public
land outside conservation areas.

Getting There & Away
Premier (☎ 8415 5555) has a daily bus from
Adelaide to the copper towns of Kadina,
Wallaroo and Moonta as well as Port Hughes

National Parks The National Parks & Wildlife Service office (☎ 8854 4040 or 8854 4084)
in Innes National Park administers all parks
on the peninsula and its off-shore islands.

Fishing
Several towns have jetties which make
worthwhile fishing spots if you don't have a
boat. The best is the deep-water jetty at Port
Giles, where you can catch a variety of species
including snapper, salmon, squid, garfish
and tommies. Wallaroo has a similar variety.

Garfish, squid and tommies are the main
catches at most other jetties, the best of
which are at Ardrossan, Edithburgh, Moonta
Bay, Port Hughes, Port Victoria and Port
Vincent. Unfortunately, you need a boat at
most places to get amongst the King George
whiting.

Blue-swimmer crabs are plentiful in the
open season (September to April) at beaches
and jetties north of Port Vincent and Port Victoria. Shallow mud flats are the best places –

and Moonta Bay. It costs $14.50 to all three copper towns. Stateliner (☎ 8415 5555) charges $19.80 to Port Broughton on its daily service from Adelaide to Whyalla.

The Yorke Peninsula Passenger Service (☎ 8391 2977) has a daily service from Adelaide to Yorketown, alternating between the east coast and down the centre of the peninsula. Fares from Adelaide are: Ardrossan $18, Port Vincent $23.20, and Edithburgh and Warooka both $24.40.

East Coast

The sealed road from the top of Gulf St Vincent down to Stenhouse Bay near Cape Spencer is generally within a km or two of the sea. En route, tracks and roads lead in to sandy beaches and secluded coves. Small fishing and holiday towns dot the coast.

PORT WAKEFIELD TO ARDROSSAN

Turning off Highway 1 just north of Port Wakefield, the road passes the 1960-hectare **Clinton Conservation Park**. The park, which has tidal shallows and mangroves, is noted for its migratory wading birds and breeding colonies of cormorants.

Price, 18 km further on, has the friendly *Price Progress Association Caravan Park* (☎ 8837 6311), with tent/caravan sites for $7/8 and on-site vans for $25. Between Price and Ardrossan, dirt roads turn off to **Macs Beach** and **Tiddy Widdy Beach**. Both are good crabbing spots.

ARDROSSAN (pop 1000)

This attractive grain-exporting port is dominated by its huge silos. The town of today is a far cry from the early 1870s, when it was called Clay Gully and its residents lived in dugouts. You get a nice view of the town from the **lookout** at BHP's dolomite mine on the Port Vincent road.

Ardrossan was the home of the famous **'stump-jump' plough**. This ingenious invention, developed at nearby Arthurton, could jump over the mallee stumps and rocks

that made land development a nightmare for SA's early grain farmers.

The **National Trust museum** on Fifth St features agricultural history including, of course, the stump-jump plough. It opens between 2.30 pm and 4 pm on Sunday and public holidays.

A variety of **guided nature walks** are offered by local farmer Peter Davey (☎ 8837 3116). These range from four hours ($50) to a full day ($100 including lunch) and cover flora, fauna, geology and Aboriginal heritage.

The wreck of the barque *Zanoni*, which sank during a storm in 1867, is a popular local **dive site**. It lies under 20 metres of water about 16 km south-east of town; to dive on it you need permission from the Department of Environment & Natural Resources in Adelaide.

Places to Stay

Almost on the waterfront, and with plenty of shady gums, the *Ardrossan Caravan Park* (☎ 8837 3262) on Park Terrace has tent/caravan sites for $10/11, on-site vans for $25 and cabins from $30. On the northern side of town, the very formal *High View Holiday Village* (☎ 8837 3399) has powered sites with private facilities for $13 and cabins from $40.

The *Ardrossan Hotel Motel* (☎ 8837 3008) on First St has motel units for $35/45. Nearby, on Fifth St, the attractive *Royal House Hotel Motel* (☎ 8837 3007) has air-conditioned pub rooms for $20/25 and motel units for $40/50.

ARDROSSAN TO EDITHBURGH

South from Ardrossan the main road passes the tiny coastal resort of **Pine Point**, where there's a basic caravan park (☎ 8838 2239). From here you can drive to **Black Point** for bush camping, passing a beautiful long sandy beach and many ugly holiday shacks along the shore of Port Alfred.

Further south is **Port Julia**, another holiday spot with a good beach. It's reputed to be one of the best crabbing spots on the coast.

Port Vincent (pop 500)
This quiet, picturesque resort town is set on a sweeping bay with a safe swimming beach. It has many beautiful old stone buildings, an interesting two-km **nature trail** along the coast and reasonable **fishing** off the jetty.

At the entrance to town, the *Tuckerway Youth Hostel* (☎ 8853 7285) has dorm beds from $8, grassy camp sites for $4 per person and powered sites for $6 per person.

In town there's the *Port Vincent Caravan Park* (☎ 8853 7073) and *Port Vincent Seaside Flats & Caravan Park* (☎ 8853 7011). On the waterfront, the *Hotel Ventnor* (☎ 8853 7036) has basic rooms for $18/28, while *Gulf View Holiday Units* (☎ 8853 7302) has self-contained flats without bedding from $30.

Stansbury (pop 500)
This was the site of the **Oyster Bay** homestead, the first White settlement on Yorke Peninsula. Proclaimed in 1873, Stansbury was originally called Oyster Bay after the molluscs that were harvested here until the 1880s.

There's a jetty and a swimming beach both here and further south at **Wool Bay**, which has an old lime kiln on the clifftop. Many local farmers eked out a living in the early days by burning limestone to extract lime for use in cement manufacture.

A **lookout** at the lime kiln gives you a beautiful view along the coast to the grain silos at **Port Giles**.

Places to Stay The friendly *Stansbury Foreshore Caravan Park* (☎ 8852 4171) has plenty of lawn and trees and is handy to town. It charges from $9.50 for powered sites. Alternatively, the *Oyster Point Drive Park* (☎ 8852 4171), about two km south of town, has tent/caravan sites for $7.50/9.

The *Dalrymple Hotel* (☎ 8852 4188), on the waterfront, has rooms with ceiling fans and electric blankets for $30/50 including a light breakfast. There's also the *Stansbury Holiday Motel* (☎ 8852 4455), on the Adelaide road. It has lovely ocean views and comfortable units with cooking facilities from $59/69.

The motel handles the bookings for *Gypsy Waggons*, which has horse-drawn caravans carrying up to five persons; you can hire them for three to seven nights and the minimum rate is $399. The owners have set up camp sites and established an interesting route along tracks and quiet back roads.

The budget-oriented *Oyster Court Motel* (☎ 8852 4136), on the corner of South Terrace and West Terrace, charges $36/48 and also has cooking facilities.

Stansbury has several holiday flats and there are more at Wool Bay.

Coobowie (pop 200)
There's a safe swimming beach here and some interesting old buildings left over from busier times when it was a shipping point. Nearby **Salt Creek** inlet is a good spot for birdwatching.

The attractive *Coobowie Caravan Park* (☎ 8852 8132) has tent/caravan sites for $8.50/10, on-site vans from $22 and self-contained cabins for $40. Alternatively, *The Shores Holiday Units* (☎ 248 1531) has three self-contained units sleeping up to six from $40.

EDITHBURGH (pop 500)
Once a thriving port exporting salt, grains and wool, this attractive service town has a great seaside atmosphere and many lovely old buildings. There's usually a cool sea breeze in summer.

The **museum** on Fifth St has a large and fascinating collection of memorabilia, including displays on local shipwrecks. Featured is a large, red 1942 fire engine – the sort that small boys once dreamed of driving. It's open from 2 to 4 pm on Sunday, public holidays and school holidays; entry costs $2.

From the clifftop above the town jetty there's a view across to **Troubridge Island**, about six km off shore. The island is a conservation park and has important rookeries of little penguins, black-faced shags and crested terns.

There's good **scuba diving** on wrecks and reefs near Edithburgh, with visibility usually from five to eight metres. Its reefs have soft corals, fish life, drop-offs and caves. The most popular wreck dive is the 3600-tonne cargo steamer *Clan Ranald*. It went down in 1909 with the loss of 40 lives and lies in 23 metres about a km off **Troubridge Point**. The drowned seamen are buried in a mass grave in the town cemetery.

There are some nice nature walks in the pretty 17-hectare **Edithburgh Flora Park** and along the coast to **Sultana Point** (four km) and **Coobowie** (six km). The coast walks feature geology, marine biology, bird life and native plants; Joan Koch at the Anchorage Motel (☎ 8852 6262) will be happy to give you details.

Diving & Fishing Charters

Troubridge Island Charters (☎ 8852 6290) does fishing and diving trips for two to five people. Fishing costs $50 a day per person, while diving trips to the *Clan Ranald* are $40 per person; a one-tank dive on a reef costs from $25.

There's also Edithburgh Charter & Boat Hire (☎ 8852 6288). Their nine-metre powered catamaran takes up to 10 people and has a toilet on board; a full day charter costs $550. If you want to do your own thing you can hire their six-metre runabout for $150 a day (it takes four people).

Organised Tours

Edithburgh Charter & Boat Hire's sunset cruises cost from $25 per person, while Troubridge Island Charters have an interesting two-hour guided tour out to Troubridge Island. Here you'll see the tall cast-iron lighthouse (1856) and keepers houses (all of which were prefabricated in England), and learn about local shipwrecks.

Apache Air (☎ 8852 6186) does scenic flights over the southern Yorke Peninsula coast and islands. Prices range from $15 per person for 10 minutes (minimum two passengers) and $90 for 60 minutes (minimum three).

Places to Stay & Eat

The attractive *Edithburgh Caravan Park* (☎ 8852 6056) is right on the waterfront and has tent/caravan sites ($9/10), on-site vans and cabins.

The town has two pubs of which the *Edithburgh Seaside Hotel/Motel* (☎ 8852 6172) is the classiest. It's right in the centre of town on Edith St and has motel units from $38/48 for singles/doubles. Diagonally opposite, the *Troubridge Hotel/Motel* (☎ 8852 6013) has pub rooms for $18/30 and motel units for $40/48.

Edithburgh House (☎ 8852 6373), also on Edith St, has very nice guesthouse accommodation for $70 per person for dinner B&B. They have *Rose Cottage*, which sleeps four for $65.

Ocean View Holiday Units (☎ 8852 6029) on the foreshore has self-contained two bedroom units sleeping up to six from $35.

Both pubs serve huge inexpensive meals. For the best wining and dining, however, visit the tasteful *Faversham's Restaurant* in Edithburgh House.

EDITHBURGH TO MARION BAY

As an alternative to the main road through Yorketown and Warooka, you can drive to Marion Bay via the 82-km unsealed coast road from Edithburgh. There's a tall lighthouse and rugged cliffs at **Troubridge Point**, 18 km from Edithburgh. The point is a good spot for whale-watching between June and October.

Fifty km further on, *Hillocks Drive* (☎ 8854 4002) is a large farm with visitor facilities and a seven-km coastal frontage. The friendly Butler family offer wonderful scenery, safe swimming beaches, surfing, salmon fishing, bushwalks, native wildlife and wildflowers (August to November). Bush camping is $5 per car, and on-site vans are $22 to $25; there's a $3 entry fee for day visitors. Every year the farm closes on 18 June for two months.

Five km past Hillocks Drive, **Mehan Hill Lookout** gives a nice view across Investigator Strait to Kangaroo Island. To the east are dramatic cliffs, while westwards a long white surf beach stretches all the way to Marion Bay.

Yorketown (pop 750)
Established in 1872, Yorketown is the region's business and administrative centre. Although it's an attractive town there's not much here for visitors unless coastal accommodation is booked out. About 200 small **salt lakes** in the immediate area once supported a thriving salt-mining industry.

The district council office on Edithburgh Rd has a good range of brochures on the southern Yorke Peninsula.

Places to Stay The peaceful *Yorketown Caravan Park* (☎ 8852 1563) on Memorial Drive has tent/caravan sites for $9/10 and on-site vans with TV for $25.

In the centre of town, on Warooka Rd, the *Melville Hotel/Motel* (☎ 8852 1019) has hotel rooms for $18/24 and motel units for $40/48. The modest *Yorke Hotel* (☎ 8852 1221) is across the road and has rooms for $20/35 including a cooked breakfast. Both have counter meals daily.

Warooka (pop 250)
This pleasant little town has some nice old buildings including the original police station (1879), which now houses a **folk museum**. Its elevated position – a rarity on Yorke Peninsula – affords good views of the surrounding farmland. The down side is the weather; Warooka is a local Aboriginal word meaning 'windy hill'.

Shorecatch Fishing Safaris (☎ 8854 5311) has **4WD tours** ranging from a full day ($40) to four days ($395). Everything is provided except rods, reels and swags.

About 36 km from town on the Marion Bay road is the entrance to the 4000-hectare **Warrenben Conservation Park**. There's bush camping here and plenty of good birdwatching in the mallee.

The *Warooka Hotel/Motel* (☎ 8854 5001) has motel units for $35/45/53.

Marion Bay (pop 20)
Originally the port for nearby gypsum mines, Marion Bay was almost abandoned when the present shipping facility was developed at Stenhouse Bay. The Marion Bay Store

(☎ 8854 4008) is a good spot to get information on fishing, diving and surfing in the area. It also sells provisions, takeaways and ice, fills scuba tanks and can arrange boat hire.

The friendly *Marion Bay Caravan Park* (☎ 8854 4094) has tent/caravan sites for $8/10, on-site vans from $25 and cabins from $45. The *Marion Bay Seaside Apartments* (☎ 8854 4066) has elevated, self-contained units sleeping five from $60.

INNES NATIONAL PARK
At the south-west tip of Yorke Peninsula, the popular 9140-hectare Innes National Park mainly comprises coastal heath and rolling mallee country bounded by a spectacular coastline. All roads within the park are unsealed and can be rough. There are plenty of blind corners and inexperienced drivers, so be careful.

Information
Either phone the park office on ☎ 8854 4040 or write to Innes National Park, Stenhouse Bay, SA 5577.

Entry permits cost $3 per car and you pay at the entry station, which has useful guides to the park's heritage sites, walks, fishing and surfing. If it's closed, try the Stenhouse Bay Trading Post across the road. The general store here also sells fishing tackle, bait, ice and food.

Things to See & Do
There's plenty of **wildlife** including the endangered mallee fowl – the park is one of its last refuges on the peninsula. While you're unlikely to meet a mallee fowl, you should see plenty of other birds, including emus. Western grey kangaroos are fairly common.

The coastline boasts impressive grey-and-orange limestone cliffs, particularly at **Cape Spencer**, **The Gap** and **West Cape**. There's a beautiful view from Cape Spencer across to the rugged **Althorpe Islands** and beyond to Kangaroo Island.

Just past The Gap you can look down on **Ethel Beach**, where waves crash in over the rusting remnants of the Norwegian barque

Ethel. Amazingly, only one person was drowned when it blew ashore in 1904.

Apparently people actually **surf** off Ethel Beach, but you'd have to know what you were doing. Fortunately there's plenty of other surfing breaks, of which **Pondalowie Bay** is the most popular and consistent. It's suitable for beginners, but not so **Chinaman's Hat**. This is the park's most powerful break and is definitely only for experienced surfers; national competitions are sometimes held here.

There's also good **fishing**. Among the most popular spots are **Browns Beach** (salmon), the southern end of Pondalowie Bay (garfish, King George whiting, flathead, squid and salmon, among others), **West Cape** (sweep, tommy ruff, salmon) and **Stenhouse Bay** (tommies and King George whiting).

The park's most interesting historical site is the abandoned gypsum-mining settlement of **Inneston**. Established in 1913 and closed in 1930, it housed 130 people and even had its own plaster factory. A walk with information signs (allow one hour) takes you around the old stone buildings and ruins.

Wildflowers are a highlight in July to November, when the normally drab heath and mallee communities burst into colourful blooms.

Places to Stay & Eat

There are a number of sheltered bush camp sites close to nice beaches. The surfers' camp at Pondalowie Bay is the best appointed – it has solar-heated showers, but don't expect hot water in winter. Permits cost between $3 and $6 depending on the location of the camp site and its facilities. Drinking water is limited (bring your own in summer), and you can purchase firewood at the store.

Alternatively, you can stay in rudimentary but comfortable houses at *Inneston* ($40 for four persons), a bunkhouse at *Stenhouse Bay* ($8), and a shepherd's hut at *Shell Beach* ($22 for four persons). Contact the park office for details.

The *Stenhouse Bay Trading Post* has a general store and adjoining tavern which sell meals (dine-in and takeaway), liquor and basic provisions.

West Coast

The west coast is more sparsely settled than the east, with fewer and smaller towns. Unlike the east it tends to miss out on the sea breezes in summer (these prevail from the south-east), so as a result is generally hotter. There are plenty of good fishing and surfing beaches in the south-west.

MARION BAY TO POINT TURTON

Heading north from Marion Bay, a dirt road with many loose corners runs through mallee and farmland to meet the bitumen near **Corny Point** at 42 km. Tracks en route lead off to remote surfing, fishing and bush-camping spots along the wild stretch of coast between Innes National Park and the Corny Point lighthouse.

One of the strongest surfing breaks is at **Trespassers** on Formby Bay, the turn-off to which is 17 km from Marion Bay. A lookout on the clifftop gives you a stunning view along a white sandy beach backed by enormous dunes. Further north, **Daly Heads** has the area's largest surfable waves (up to four metres high).

At rugged Corny Point there's another beautiful view of sweeping empty beach, dunes and cliffs. You can visit this area on a **camel ride** with Coastline Camel Safaris (☎ 8855 3400), based near the Corny Point store. They have a range of tours lasting from one hour ($19) to two days ($180).

The coast road from Corny Point to the tiny resort of **Point Turton**, right on the peninsula's 'instep' about 30 km eastwards, passes a number of quiet beaches. En route there's the 490-hectare **Leven Beach Conservation Park**, which conserves dunes and native bush.

Places to Stay & Eat

As shown on the RAA touring map, there's a string of bush camping areas along the coast between Formby Bay and Point Turton. All are managed by the Warooka district council (☎ 8854 5055), whose ranger comes around to collect fees ($3 per site) and dispense local knowledge and rubbish bags.

The most popular are at Gleesons Landing in the west and Burners Beach in the north. Both are very basic, but have good shelter and are sufficiently large that you can usually find a spot to yourself.

There are caravan parks at Corny Point (☎ 8855 3368) and Point Turton (☎ 8854 5222), while the *Point Turton Motel* (☎ 8854 5005) has units with cooking facilities. Both these areas have general stores where you can get provisions and takeaway meals.

POINT TURTON TO PORT VICTORIA

Dirt roads and tracks take you along the coast from Point Turton to Port Victoria, with more remote fishing spots and small resorts en route. Alternatively, you can take the sealed road through Minlaton in the centre of the peninsula.

An old grain port, tiny **Port Rickaby** has the nicest beach and the best swimming on this stretch of coast; there's also a caravan park (☎ 8853 1177) with caravan sites and on-site vans. The 22-km coastal track from here to Port Victoria is suitable only for 4WD.

Minlaton (pop 750)

This attractive service town, which refers to itself as the 'barley capital of the world', makes an ideal base for exploring the central peninsula.

The town has an impressive **memorial** to local pioneer aviator and WWI ace Captain Harry Butler. Open daily, it has displays on Butler's exploits as well as the Bristol fighter he flew in France during the war. There's also a National Trust **museum** (open Thursday, Friday and school holidays from 10.30 am to 4.30 pm) and two good **art galleries**.

You can stay at the attractive *Minlaton Caravan Park* (☎ 8853 2345) and the *Minlaton Hotel/Motel* (☎ 8853 2014).

PORT VICTORIA (pop 500)

At one time this was the state's fourth largest export shipping terminal, with huge windjammers calling in as late as 1949 to load wheat bound for England. Nowadays,

however, it slumbers undisturbed except in the tourist season.

At the jetty there's a small but interesting **nautical museum** with displays featuring the windjammer era. It's open from 2 pm to 4 pm Sunday; ask at the kiosk outside these times.

There are two fine swimming beaches south of town at **Rifle Butts Beach** and **Second Beach**.

Port Victoria has good scuba diving potential. You can dive with sea lions around **White Rock** and the **Goose Islands**, and there are a number of shipwrecks dating from 1871 in the shallow waters off **Wardang Island**. The wrecks are described in the booklet *Wardang Island Maritime Heritage Trail* ($5).

Wardang Island Charters (☎ 8834 2155) does **fishing and diving charters** for $360 a day, lunch not included. Port Victoria Boat Hire (☎ 8834 2247) has four-metre aluminium boats powered by outboard motors for $80 a day. They'll launch and retrieve them for you if required.

Places to Stay & Eat

Above the jetty, the friendly *Port Victoria Progress Association Caravan Park* (☎ 8834 2001) has tent/caravan sites for $8/10 and on-site vans for $27. If you get tired of fishing you can hire a TV for $2 a day.

Right next door is the much larger and better appointed *Gulfhaven Caravan Park* (☎ 8834 2012). It has tent/caravan sites for $7.50/9.50, basic cabins for $30 and self-contained cabins for $40.

At the *Port Victoria Hotel/Motel* (☎ 8834 2069), on Main St near the jetty, comfortable units sleep up to seven for $40/55/65/75. It has quite a nice restaurant, and there are pictures of windjammers in the bar.

The *Bay View Holiday Flats* (☎ 8834 2082) in Davis Terrace has self-contained family units starting at $25 for two adults and two children.

If the fish aren't biting you can get *fresh seafood* daily at the two local fisheries, both in the centre of town.

MAITLAND (pop 1100)

Established in 1872, attractive Maitland is the commercial centre for this part of the peninsula. The National Trust **museum** in the old state school on Gardiner Terrace has displays of local German and Aboriginal history. It's open Sunday and public and school holidays from 2 to 4 pm. There's a good local **craft shop** in the main street.

There's a free camping area with toilets beside the Maitland sportsground at the northern end of town. Alternatively, the *Maitland Hotel* (☎ 8832 2431) on Robert St has basic but comfortable rooms for $25/$35/$40. It serves counter and dining room meals Monday to Saturday.

The self-contained *Eothen Farmhouse* (☎ 8836 3210) is 13 km from town on the Balgowan road. It sleeps eight people and costs are on a sliding scale of $70 for two and $450 for eight. The price includes escorted tours of the 1000-hectare property, which has sheep, cattle, cereal crops and about 120 hectares of native bush.

PORT BROUGHTON (pop 1400)

North of the Copper Triangle, this quiet holiday and fishing town is home to a large prawn fleet. The best swimming in town is off the jetty.

Port Broughton Charter Boats (☎ 8635 2030) takes groups of four to seven people on **fishing trips** of four to six hours. Prices are $40 per person for whiting and $65 for snapper.

The town has two caravan parks, with the most inspiring being the *Port Broughton Caravan Park* (☎ 8635 2188) on the foreshore south of the jetty. It has tent/caravan sites for $11/12.50, on-site vans for $25 and cabins from $30.

Otherwise there's the magnificent old *Hotel Broughton* (☎ 8635 2004), on Bay St overlooking the water, which has counter meals daily and basic pub rooms for $20/25. The *Sunnyside Hotel/Motel* (☎ 8635 2100) further up the street has an average restaurant and motel units for $45/50/55.

The Copper Triangle

In 1859 a shepherd working on Wallaroo station found traces of copper in the bush. The station owner staked a claim and brought four Cornish miners down from Burra to sink a trial shaft. They hit a mother lode of copper, and so began nearly two decades of Croesus-like prosperity that saved SA from bankruptcy.

The new Wallaroo mine was in full swing a year later when news came of another strike only 16 km away. From this came the even richer Moonta mine. Cornish miners and their families flocked to the area, and the towns of Kadina and Moonta sprang up to service the mines. The Cornish influence was so strong that even today the area is referred to as 'Little Cornwall'.

In 1861 a port and a copper smelter were developed at nearby Wallaroo, which joined with Kadina and Moonta to form the so-called 'Copper Triangle'. By 1875 the district had a population of 20,000, about 60% of whom lived in and around Moonta. However, the lack of clean drinking water was a huge health problem. Hundreds of children died in the typhoid epidemics that raged unabated until 1890, when a safe water supply was developed.

Falling copper prices, dwindling ore reserves and industrial problems saw the mines close in 1923. By this time the underground workings extended for 150 km and had produced 334,000 tonnes of copper.

Sixty years of prosperity gave the Copper Triangle many fine public and commercial buildings, churches and homes. A large number of these have survived thanks to the lack of development since then, and this is one of the major drawcards for today's visitors.

Festivals

Held on odd-numbered years over four days, usually in May, the Kernewek Lowender Festival is a celebration of the Copper Triangle's Cornish heritage. The festivities are held in all three towns and include Celtic games, a Cornish fair, feasting, folk dancing and town walks. Meanwhile, the tables groan under the weight of traditional Cornish pasties and a special Cornish beer called 'swanky'.

You might even meet a piskey – a mischievous sprite which superstitious Cornish people believe brings good luck. If no piskeys come your way, it's probably a sign that you haven't drunk enough swanky.

Sample a famous Cornish pastie – their unique shape was designed so that grime-covered miners could grab the handle and eat their lunch, then throw the dirty handle away.

Getting Around
Copper Triangle Cabs (☎ 8821 3444) of Kadina provides a 24-hour taxi service to the entire area.

A tourist train consisting of a 1960s diesel locomotive and three 100-year-old carriages runs between Wallaroo and Kadina on the second Sunday of every month and also on weekends over Easter and Kernewek Lowender. Return tickets cost $5 and you can book by phoning ☎ 8823 2860.

MOONTA (pop 2300)
In 1861, an illiterate alcoholic shepherd, Patrick Ryan, found copper at the entrance to a wombat burrow. So began the richest mine that SA has ever seen. Not that this did

Paddy much good; he'd drunk himself to death within a year of his great discovery.

Numerous mines were developed around Paddy's find, but by far the most successful was the Moonta Mine. By 1870, when over 5000 people depended on it for their livelihood, it was producing over 20,000 tonnes of dressed ore annually. Although profits declined after the 1870s, the Moonta Mine was so rich that large-scale operations continued for another 40 years.

In the boom years, Moonta's population was exceeded in the state only by Adelaide's. However, only 1350 residents remained soon after the mines closed in 1923.

Information
The main local outlet is in the town hall (☎ 8825 2622) in George St. It's open from 9 am to 5 pm weekdays; if they're closed, try the Moonta Bakery, also on George St.

The excellent booklet *Discovering Historic Moonta* ($5.95) includes self-guided tours which will take you to over 60 places of interest around the mines and township.

Things to See & Do
The best place to discover Moonta's mining heritage is out at **Moonta Mines**, the site of an early mining village on the Arthurton road about one km from town. Its relics include stone chimneys and enginehouses – these massive structures housed the engines that provided power for pumping and crushing operations.

Now a National Trust museum, the impressive **Moonta Mines School** (1877) once had 1100 students on its roll. Now its cavernous rooms are filled with interesting displays including the story of Elizabeth Woodcock, the only woman in SA ever to be executed. Entry costs $2.50 and it's open from 1.30 to 4 pm Tuesday to Sunday (11 am to 4.30 pm on school and public holidays).

Every weekend and all public and school holidays, a tiny **tourist train** takes passengers on a 50-minute ride ($2) from the museum to Moonta's photogenic railway station (1908). Check at the tourist office for times.

Nearby is the **Methodist Church** (1865), an austere building which can seat 1250 people. The nearby **Miners Cottage** (1870) is a romantic Cornish cottage filled with period furnishings. It's open Wednesday and weekends from 1.30 to 4 pm (11 am to 4 pm school and public holidays).

Many of Moonta's finest historic buildings are features of the **Moonta Heritage Walk**, which is covered in the booklet *Discovering Historic Moonta*. Outstanding examples are the Gothic-style Methodist Church (1873) and the contrasting Italian-style Bible Christian Church (also 1873). They're almost side by side in Robert St.

Nearby **Port Hughes** and **Moonta Bay** are both quiet seaside resorts with sandy beaches. The area's best swimming beach is just south of the jetty at Port Hughes.

Organised Tours

Port Hughes Fishing Charters (☎ 8825 3388) takes between four and ten people for $70 each per day, lunch not included. Charging the same rate is Blue Fin Fishing Charters (☎ 8825 2880), also of Port Hughes, who'll take between two and four people.

Two-hour guided walks of Moonta cost $4 and leave from the rotunda in Queen Square at 2 pm every Saturday – also Wednesday during school holidays. For details contact the Pug 'n' Dabble Gift Gallery (☎ 8825 3003) in George St.

The very professional and friendly Copper Coast Heritage Tours (☎ 8825 3496) has minibus tours of the Copper Triangle. A half day around Moonta costs $25 and a full day to all three towns is $35.

The heritage tours ($3) of Moonta and Moonta Mines offered by Moonta Tramways (☎ 8825 3654) are also worthwhile. Their 'Thomas the Tank Engine'type road vehicle pulls carriages taking seven passengers each. It departs from the railway station at 11 am, 12.30 pm, 2 pm and 3 pm on weekends and school holidays.

Places to Stay

The *Cornwall Hotel* (☎ 8825 2304) on Ryan St in Moonta has rooms for $27.50/40; at the nearby *Royal* (☎ 8825 2108) they're $25/40, including a light breakfast.

The *Moonta Bay Caravan Park* (☎ 8825 2406) is above the jetty and has tent/caravan sites for $11/13 and cabins for $46. Alternatively, there's the nearby *Patio Motel* (☎ 8825 2473), with comfortable rooms for $55/64. Its family room sleeps five for $75.

Overlooking the jetty at Port Hughes, the *Port Hughes Caravan Park* and nearby *Port Hughes Tourist Village* (both ☎ 8825 2106) have tent/caravan sites for $11/13 and cabins for $52.

The nearby *Blue Fin Apartments* (☎ 8825 2880) has well-appointed holiday flats sleeping six. They cost $100 for singles & doubles and $10 for extra adults, and stays are two nights minimum.

Places to Eat

Locals are divided as to whether *Prices Bakery* of Kadina or the *Cornish Kitchen* on Ellen St in Moonta produces the best Cornish pasties in the Copper Triangle. I became fat doing research on this, but in the end decided in favour of the Cornish Kitchen by a long shot. Their home-made soup and pastie for $3.70 is a very satisfying lunch on a cold day.

On one side of the Copper Kitchen, the *Shaft Steakhouse* is the most upmarket restaurant in town. It's correspondingly rather pricey, although you can't say that about its Friday night, three-course specials for $10. On the other side, the *Fish 'n' Grill* has dine-in and takeaway. It's reputed to sell the best fish & chips in the Copper Triangle.

The *Moonta Bakery* on George St is an outlet for Price's products. It's open at 7 am daily and does a good breakfast. Further down the street, the *Moonta Pizza Cafe* is also recommended.

Tony's Chinese Takeaways next to the BP service station on George St, has tempting lunch specials for $4 and $5.

For home-made light lunches and teas, try the *Australian Heritage Giftshop & Cafe* on Blanche Terrace. You can browse through their interesting shop while you're waiting.

KADINA (pop 4500)

The capital of Yorke Peninsula was laid out in 1860 to service the Wallaroo Mine, which had been established earlier in the year. Kadina is from the Aboriginal words *kaddy-yeena*, meaning 'lizard plain', while Wallaroo is from *wadla-waru*, meaning 'wallaby's urine'.

The Wallaroo Mine reached its peak in the early 1870s, when it employed up to 1000 men and boys. Kadina's population plummeted after the mine closed in 1923, but while Moonta stagnated, it managed to prosper as an agricultural, commercial and administrative centre.

Information

The visitors information centre (☎ 8821 2093) is in the town hall. It's open between 10 am and 2 pm on weekdays and 9.30 am to 1.30 pm on Saturday.

If you're keen to explore the many heritage sites in and around town, the booklet *Discovering Historic Kadina* ($5.95) will be your best guide – it takes you to about 50 sites of interest.

Things to See & Do

Just off the Moonta road on the southern side of town is an interesting National Trust museum in **Matta House** (1863). This was originally the Matta Matta mine manager's residence, the Matta Matta mine being one of several early small mines in this area. Opening hours are from 2 to 4.30 pm on Wednesday, weekends and public and school holidays. Entry costs $3.

The **Wallaroo Mine** is about one km west of town off the Wallaroo road. It takes half an hour to stroll around the site, which includes numerous deep shafts. It features the tall stone ruin of **Harvey's Engine-house**, now a home for pigeons.

If you're interested in money (and who isn't?), the **Banking & Currency Museum** in the old Bank of SA building (1873) on Graves St has comprehensive displays. It's open from 10 am to 5 pm daily except Thursday, and entry costs $3. Guided tours are optional, and you can buy and sell coins there.

Kadina's Banking & Currency Museum

While not as rich in heritage as Moonta, the town still has many interesting old buildings. You can see them by strolling around the **Kadina Heritage Walk**, described in *Discovering Historic Kadina*. Included is the imposing **Royal Exchange Hotel** (1874) on Digby St; the prefix Royal was added after the Duke of Clarence stayed there in 1880.

Places to Stay

The attractive *Kadina Caravan Park* (☎ 8821 2259), on Lindsay St, is mainly residential. It has a few lawned camp sites for $11 and on-site vans for $30.

The *Wombat Hotel* (☎ 8821 1108), on Taylor St, charges $19 per person. Alternatively there's the *Kadina Hotel* (☎ 8821 1008), a block away and also on Taylor St, which has rooms with private bathrooms for $30/47/56.

There are two motels on the outskirts of town: the *Kadina Village Motel* (☎ 8821 1920) on Port Rd, which charges $44/54/66 including a light breakfast; and the more luxurious *Kadina Gateway Motor Inn* (☎ 8821 2777) on the Adelaide road, which charges $69/72.

On Datson Rd near the Wallaroo Mine is

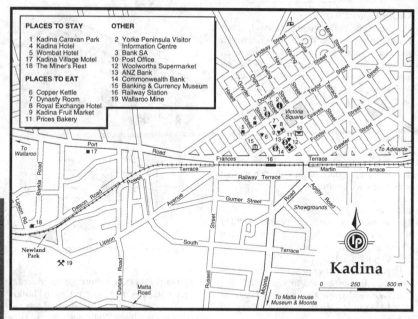

PLACES TO STAY
1 Kadina Caravan Park
4 Kadina Hotel
5 Wombat Hotel
17 Kadina Village Motel
18 The Miner's Rest

PLACES TO EAT
6 Copper Kettle
7 Dynasty Room
8 Royal Exchange Hotel
9 Kadina Fruit Market
11 Prices Bakery

OTHER
2 Yorke Peninsula Visitor
Information Centre
3 Bank SA
10 Post Office
12 Woolworths Supermarket
13 ANZ Bank
14 Commonwealth Bank
15 Banking & Currency Museum
16 Railway Station
19 Wallaroo Mine

Kadina

The Miner's Rest (☎ 8821 3422). Built in 1870, it's a delightful three-bedroom cottage furnished in heritage style and offering beds for $80 for two people, including generous breakfast provisions.

Places to Eat

The three local pubs do excellent cheap meals; they all have pokies, so competition for business is fierce. The *Royal Exchange Hotel* has the largest gaming room and the most imaginative menu.

Prices Bakery is on Graves St. *Sarah's Place* on Goyder St specialises in pancake and crepes while the *Dynasty Room*, also on Goyder, is a Chinese and Thai dine-in and takeaway. The *Copper Kettle*, another dine-in and take away on Hallett St, is one of the very few places in Kadina that's open for a feed on Sunday night.

The *Kadina Fruit Market* on Graves St is the best place in town for fresh fruit and vegetables.

WALLAROO (pop 2250)

This was the port for Moonta and Kadina. It also had a huge copper smelter, said to be the largest in the southern hemisphere at that time. Unlike the mines, most of its employees were Welsh – although still Celtic.

The town's population had reached 5000 by the early 1920s, but crashed after the mines closed. Soon after this the smelting works were demolished, leaving a single tall chimney which remains as a local landmark. It's dwarfed by the banks of huge white silos that advertise Wallaroo's modern role as a grain port.

Information

The tourist information desk (☎ 8823 2020) in the post office, on the corner of Irwin St and Owen Terrace, has an extensive range of brochures on the Copper Triangle. It's open from 9 am to 5 pm on weekdays and 9 to 11.30 am on Saturday; ask at the Sonbern Lodge on John Terrace outside these hours.

The interesting booklet *Discovering Historic Wallaroo* ($5.95) features two self-guided tours which will take you to numerous places of interest around the township.

Things to See & Do

In the old post office, on Jetty Rd, there's the fascinating **Heritage & Nautical Museum**, which has comprehensive displays on various facets of life in early Wallaroo. It's open between 2 and 4 pm on Wednesday, weekends and public and school holidays; admission is $2.50.

The museum is the starting point for a nine-km **heritage trail** and a much shorter **walking trail** through the town's commercial centre. Both are described in the booklet *Discovering Historic Wallaroo*.

Organised Tours

Alicia's Tours (☎ 8823 2682) offers a range of personalised tours in their 1957 'Silver Shadow' Rolls Royce and military jeep. Their three-hour heritage and sunset tours in the Rolls costs $75 per person, including chicken and champagne. Alternatively, you can take a one to three-hour jeep tour to remote beaches for $15 and $30 respectively.

Wallaroo Yacht Charters (☎ 8825 6235; mobile ☎ 018 859 531) does day sailing, fishing and diving trips for $80 per person (maximum six) including lunch. They also offer adventure cruises in the gulf for two persons from two to eight days.

Places to Stay

Caravan Parks Near the jetty, the cramped *Office Beach Holiday Cabins & Caravan Park* (☎ 8823 2722) has powered sites ($10), on-site vans ($25) and cabins (from $40).

A km from town, the large *North Beach Caravan Park* (☎ 8823 2521) is by a good swimming beach. It has tent/caravan sites for $10/13 and well-appointed motel-style units almost on the beach from $55.

Hotels, Motels & Holiday Flats The grand old guesthouse *Sonbern Lodge* (☎ 8825 6235), on John Terrace, has a marvellous old-world atmosphere right down to stained glass windows in the foyer and a richly chiming grandfather clock in the hall. For value this is among the best in the state. Its standard rooms are $24/38/47, rooms with private bathroom are $31/50/58 and motel units (very tasteful) are $52/66/74.

A block away on John Terrace, the *Weerona Hotel* (☎ 8823 2008) has singles/doubles for $22/32.

Dwarfed by huge silos, the visually uninspiring *Esquire Motor Inn* (☎ toll-free 1800 81 4299) on Lydia Terrace has a decent restaurant and rooms from $40/50. It offers 'lost weekends' for $88 per person including two nights' accommodation, two light breakfasts and a dinner.

Alicia's Lodge (☎ 8823 2682) on Ireland St is a nicely restored 1864 villa which sleeps seven. It charges $60 for singles & doubles and $15 for each extra adult. Their two-night off-season special of $150 (one couple) and $250 (two couples) includes full breakfast ingredients and a one-hour tour in a Rolls Royce.

At 9 Jetty Rd, virtually on the water's edge, *The Mac's Beachfront Villas* (☎ 8823 2137) include several fully self-contained two-bedroom units sleeping four to six people for around $100 a night. For romantics, there's a special one-bedroom unit with a spa.

Places to Eat

Although only one of the town's five pubs offers accommodation, they all have hearty counter meals for a good price.

There are several takeaways, including Price's *Wallaroo Bakery* on Owen Terrace. The *Wallaroo Café* on Hughes St has a varied menu and a good reputation. *Best Pizza* on Irwin St is aptly named – their small pizzas from $5.50 are a substantial meal. Down at the jetty, *Wallaroo Fisheries* sell fresh seafood as well as fish & chips.

Locals recommend *The Collection & Fine Craft Tea Rooms* on Irwin St for home-made Devonshire teas and lunches.

YORKE PENINSULA

Flinders Ranges

A continuation of the spine of hills that forms the Mt Lofty Ranges, the Flinders Ranges begin near Crystal Brook and run north for 400 km to Mt Hopeless, where they peter out on the southern fringe of the Strzelecki Desert. There are no towering mountains here; the highest point, St Mary Peak, rises 1170 metres above sea level. Even so, the often stark, semi-arid scenery of rugged purple ridges, dramatic bluffs and gum creeks is a spectacular contrast to the surrounding plains.

As well as bushwalks and great views, there are numerous sites of cultural interest such as abandoned mines and settlements, and Aboriginal art galleries. The latter include rock paintings (at Yourambulla and Arkaroo) and petroglyphs, or rock carvings (eg Sacred Canyon and Chambers Gorge).

As in many other dry mountain regions of Australia, the vegetation is surprisingly diverse and colourful; tall river red gums are a feature throughout, while dark stands of native pine are more obvious in the north. The western flanks are in a rain shadow, so the vegetation here is much sparser than the eastern side. In the south the hills are covered with large gums, while beyond Quorn the vegetation generally becomes scrubbier.

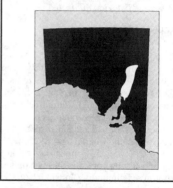

History

The Adnyamathanha, or 'hill people', have inhabited the Flinders Ranges for many thousands of years. The ranges and the people who lived there were an integral part of the long-distance trade routes that crossed the continent. Dotted amongst the hills and gullies are a number of archaeological sites, including ochre and stone quarries.

The first white people to visit the Flinders Ranges were members of the crew of HMS *Investigator*, who climbed Mt Brown (near Quorn) in 1802.

Next on the scene was Edward John Eyre. On two expeditions in 1839 and 1841 he travelled the length of the ranges from Crystal Brook to Mt Hopeless, which he named while in a despairing mood. After climbing it he became convinced that his way north was blocked by an impenetrable barrier of salt lakes.

A combination of remoteness and Eyre's unfavourable reports on the far north meant there was no land rush as in the south. Even so, sheep runs were established around Wilpena in 1851 and farther north at Mt Serle later in the decade. But overstocking, and the resulting destruction of pasture combined with drought in the early 1860s, caused many runs to be abandoned.

Better rainfall years lured wheat farmers, who reached Hawker by 1880. For a time

FLINDERS RANGES

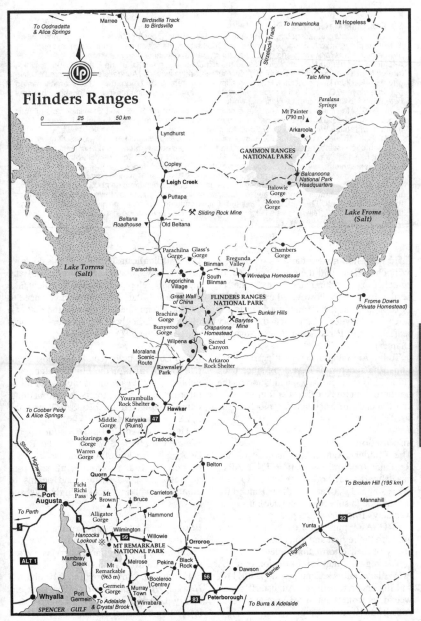

Flinders Ranges

0   25   50 km

Sir Douglas Mawson

One of Australia's greatest geologists, scientists and explorers, Douglas Mawson was born in Yorkshire in 1882 and migrated to Sydney as a child. In 1905 he became a lecturer in mineralogy and petrology at Adelaide University, where he developed an interest in glacial geology.

During this period Mawson investigated the mineralogical potential of the Barrier Ranges, which stretch from the northern Flinders through Broken Hill, and discovered Australia's first major radioactive deposit – Radium Hill near Olary. His explorations of this remote and rugged area were largely carried out on a bicycle. Observing the huge amount of ancient glacial sediments in the ranges, he became determined to see first-hand a glacier at work.

In 1907, Mawson was appointed as a scientific assistant on Sir Ernest Shackleton's Antarctic expedition. The following year he and a companion became the first people to climb Mt Erebus (3960 metres) and reach the vicinity of the South Magnetic Pole.

Mawson returned as leader of the Australasian Antarctic Expedition (1911-14), which mapped over 1500 km of coastline, penetrated 500 km inland and collected a large amount of scientific data. His account of a 1912 trip, *Home of the Blizzard*, which told of his 160 km solo trek following the death of his two companions, became a classic in the annals of polar exploration.

Mawson led two further polar expeditions between 1929 and 1931, which confirmed the existence of a land mass below the ice cap. Although the Antarctic earned him fame he never lost his fascination for the northern Flinders Ranges, returning often with his students to study the geological diversity of the Arkaroola area. Described as having 'infinite resource, splendid physique and astonishing indifference to frost', Mawson was knighted in 1914 and died in Adelaide in 1958. ■

---

there were rich golden harvests on the vast Willochra Plain, and there was wild talk of cereal crops stretching all the way to the NT border. Eventually, however, the grim reality of drought sent the farmers packing to the safety of Goyder's Line (see the History section in the Facts about South Australia chapter).

Today, a number of early settlements lie in ruins; the sheep runs have long since been cut up into smaller blocks, and Quorn is the northern limit for cereal crops. Tourism is the chief means of survival for most of the smaller towns.

Information

The Flinders Ranges & Outback of SA Regional Tourism Association (FROSART) has its main tourist office (☎ 373 3430; toll-free 1800 633 060) at 56B Glen Osmond Rd in Parkside (a suburb of Adelaide); it's open weekdays from 9 am to 5 pm.

FROSART puts out a useful free visitor guide to the region and you can pick one up at any of their information outlets.

The region's major information outlet is in Wadlata Outback Centre (☎ 8642 4511) at 41 Flinders Terrace in Port Augusta. It's open weekdays from 9 am to 5.30 pm and weekends from 10 am to 4 pm.

Communications Throughout this book we use the new statewide STD code (08) and eight-digit telephone numbers which take effect in February 1997. Should you need to use the old number simply take the first two digits (86 throughout the Flinders Ranges) and use as the STD code (086).

Maps Local experts reckon the most accurate touring map of the Flinders Ranges is published by Westprint; it includes a lot of information on local towns and attractions. Others published by FROSART and the RAA are also good.

The excellent 200-page *Guide to the Flinders Ranges* ($17.50), by the Royal Geographic Society of Australia (RGSA) SA branch, includes general information, natural and social history and details of numerous walking tracks, highways and byways.

Books The RAA's comprehensive 130-page touring guide *Flinders Ranges* ($4 for members and $8 for nonmembers) is packed with useful information.

For history buffs, Hans Mincham's *Hawker, Hub of the Flinders* (Hawker Centenary Committee, 1980, $12) gives an interesting historical account of Hawker and several now-vanished towns in the central part of the Flinders.

If you're keen to identify the local flora get hold of the pocket-sized *Wildflowers of the Southern Flinders* and *Wildflowers of the Northern Flinders* – both cost $7 and are widely available.

The modest brochure *Interpreting Rock Art of the Flinders Ranges* (available from most information outlets) explains the meanings of various symbols and so will give you a better understanding of Aboriginal art sites.

National Parks The National Parks & Wildlife Service (NPWS) has its Far North regional headquarters at Hawker (☎ 8648 4244), in the same building as the post office; contact them for details of parks in the northern Flinders. They also have an office at Wilpena (☎ 8648 0048) – see the section on the Flinders Ranges National Park later in this chapter.

Parks in the southern ranges are administered by the NPWS' office (☎ 8648 5310) in Port Augusta, at 9 Mackay St (in the SGIC building).

Organised Tours

Coach/4WD Tours SATC and FROSART can provide details of all tour companies operating to and within the ranges. A number of tours start from Adelaide.

You can tour in luxury coaches or look at more adventurous options with operators such as: Trekabout Australia (☎ 8396 2833) and Gawler Outback Tours (☎ 8278 4467), based in Adelaide; Intrepid Tours (☎ 8648 6277) in Quorn; and Ridge Tours (☎ 8648 4874) in Blinman.

Stateliner (☎ 8415 5555) does backpackers specials to the Wilpena area for three days ($120), four days ($135) and five days ($150). These prices include coach trips and accommodation, but not meals.

Horse & Camel Rides Horse rides are available at Gammon Ranges National Park, Wilpena Pound, Pichi Richi Holiday Camp (near Quorn), Wilmington and Bangor (near Port Germein). These are mostly short rides.

Camel rides and treks are on offer at Blinman. See the sections on these places for details.

Bushwalks The Adelaide-based companies Adventure SA (☎ 8223 5544; mobile 014 098 372), Ecotrek (☎ 8383 7198) and Osprey Wildlife Expeditions (☎ 8388 2552) have guided bushwalks in the Flinders Ranges during the cooler months.

Accommodation

Hotels, motels, caravan parks, cottages, farms and stations offer a wide range of accommodation, particularly south of Blinman. There's plenty of budget accommodation as well as bush camp sites; the usual camping fee for bush sites in conservation areas is $2 for the site and $2 per person per night.

Quornucopia in Quorn and the Wilmington Deli in Wilmington are agents for various alternative accommodation venues in their areas and farther afield. Otherwise check with SATC or the Wadlata Outback Centre.

The busiest times in the Flinders Ranges are September, October and Easter, when you should book in advance. Generally, rates increase during school and public holidays from spring to Easter.

Getting There & Away

Port Augusta is the main transport hub for travel to and from the Flinders Ranges. See the Port Augusta section later this chapter for details on air, bus and train services.

Bus Stateliner has four services a week from Adelaide to Wilpena Pound ($49) via Quorn ($34.90) and Hawker ($45.80) – two of these go on to Copley ($61) via Blinman ($50.60) and Parachilna ($52.50). Stateliner also has a daily service through Clare and Gladstone to Wirrabara ($24.50) and on to Wilmington ($27.20), while another service runs up Highway 1 to Port Augusta ($27.20).

Bute Buses (☎ 8826 2110) has a thrice-weekly service from Adelaide to Peterborough ($20.70) and Orroroo ($25) via the Barrier Highway.

Car The Flinders Ranges are reached by sealed roads leading off Highway 1 and Main North Rd, both from Adelaide, and the Barrier Highway from NSW.

As an alternative if you're coming from NSW, you can turn off the Barrier Highway at Yunta and take gravel-surfaced back roads to Wilpena Pound, the Gammon Ranges National Park and Arkaroola.

Getting Around

Anyone planning to travel off the main roads, particularly in the north, should always be prepared for the shortage of water, shops and service stations.

Most points of interest in the south are accessible from good sealed roads. Heading north, there are sealed roads from Port Augusta and Melrose to Wilpena Pound via Quorn and Hawker, but farther on the roads are gravel or dirt. While these unsealed roads are usually quite reasonable when dry, they can be closed by heavy rain.

For recorded information on road conditions in the region phone ☎ 11 633. Otherwise contact the various NPWS offices and hotels for a local update.

Southern Ranges

The southern Flinders Ranges extend from just north of Crystal Brook to Hawker. They include the Mt Remarkable National Park and several conservation parks, most of which are south of Quorn. We include in this section the areas around Peterborough and Orroroo.

PETERBOROUGH (pop 2300)

Established in the 1870s, Peterborough was first called Petersburg after the German settler Peter Doecke, who owned the land it was built on. The name was anglicised during the anti-German hysteria of WWI.

Although its beginnings were agricultural, Peterborough became an important railway junction – three gauges met here – and at one time over 100 trains passed through each day. Unfortunately for locals, the interstate gauges were recently standardised and, as a result, prospects for future employment are not good.

The tourist office (☎ 8651 2708) is in the old railway carriage near the imposing town hall, on Main St. It's open from 9 am to 4 pm daily.

Things to See & Do

There are a couple of ghost towns near Peterborough, the most interesting of which is **Dawson**, about 25 km to the north-east.

Steamtown is a working railway museum with four steam locomotives, numerous freight and passenger vehicles, and an enormous railway roundhouse with turntable. Ask at the tourist office if you want to check it out.

On holiday weekends between April and October, narrow-gauge **steam trains** run between Peterborough and Orroroo ($22 return) or Euralia ($29 return); phone ☎ 8651 2106 for details (bookings are sometimes necessary).

Peterborough has the state's only operating government **gold battery**; it's used to treat ore brought in by small producers from goldfields to the north-east. Built in 1897, it's a 10-head gravity stamp battery powered by a diesel engine, and when the stampers are pounding up and down the din is terrific. Contact the tourist office for access details.

Eric Rann's Museum, on Moscow St, has an amazing collection of well-polished stationary engines, while **Ivan Ley's Museum**, on Queen St, has everything from dolls to butter churns. Ask at the tourist office for information about opening times of both museums.

You can also visit **St Cecilia's** (1912), a magnificent 20-room mansion on Callary St. Originally a bishop's residence, it became a convent and boarding school for the Sisters of St Joseph of the Sacred Heart. Richly furnished with antiques, the building, is full of Roman Catholic history and memorabilia. There are daily tours from 10 am to noon, and 2 to 5 pm; admission is $5.

Places to Stay & Eat
Caravan Parks & Hostels On Grove St, the friendly *Peterborough Caravan Park* (☎ 8651 2545) has tent/caravan sites for $9/12, on-site vans for $22, basic cabins for $30 and self-contained cabins for $35.

Also good value is the *Budget Travellers' Hostel* (☎ 8651 2711), on Railway Terrace behind the railway station, which has beds from $12. Its clean, homely facilities and dedicated manager make it one of the best of SA's country hostels.

Hotels & Motels The town's oldest pub, the *Peterborough Hotel* (☎ 8651 2006) on Main St, has very basic rooms with share facilities for $16/26 and motel units for $29/39.

Somewhat more sophisticated is the *Railway Hotel/Motel* (☎ 8651 2427), also on Main St. It has pub rooms with ceiling fans for $20/30/45 singles/doubles/triples and pleasant motel units for $49/56/60. The most popular of the town's four pubs with younger people, it also has an imaginative menu and a large gaming lounge.

Units at the friendly *Peterborough Motor Inn* (☎ 51 2078), on Queen St, cost $49/56/70. Their restaurant enjoys a good reputation – it's a 'Sizzler' style eatery where main courses (as much as you can eat) are $10.

St Cecilia's (☎ 8651 2654), on Callary St, has spacious, tasteful rooms for $48/78 with breakfast. It's famous locally for its 'murder mystery' banquets.

ORROROO (pop 600)
This attractive little town began in 1864 as an eating house on the stage-coach route from Burra to Blinman and Port Augusta. From here you can continue north to Hawker via Carrieton, where the sealed road ends, or head west to Wilmington.

The **Yesteryear Costume Gallery** on Main St is a real surprise. Its fascinating collection of period costumes and accessories, dating from 1830 to 1930, can be viewed most days; admission is $3.

Cellar Antiques, also on Main St, has several rooms filled with a wide range of antiques and bric-a-brac. It also sells unrestored furniture. It's open Thursday to Sunday from 10 am to 5 pm .

On the way up to **Tank Hill Lookout**, which has a great view over the town and surrounding farmland, you pass the **Early Settler's Cottage**, on Fourth St. This evocative little dwelling of slab, pug and stone has been expertly restored. It's definitely worth a visit, and you can arrange one by phoning ☎ 8658 1219.

The **Lion's Park** on Pekina Creek features a pleasant picnic area with a lawn and shady gums. From here you can walk upstream past Aboriginal **rock carvings** and return via a rock with a rather sad poem which was etched into it by an early settler.

Just out of town and north of the Wilmington road, there's a huge **river red gum** on the western bank of Pekina Creek. This magnificent specimen has a trunk three metres in diameter and a canopy 20 metres across. It's not the biggest tree in the world, but it's not bad for up this way.

Late in December each year at **Carrieton** (population 200), 37 km north of Ororoo, a rodeo on the national circuit usually attracts a good crowd.

Places to Stay
The little *Ororoo Caravan Park* (☎ 8658 1235), at the Wilmington end of town, has tent/caravan sites for $9/12, on-site vans for $22 and basic cabins for $25. The attractive *Commercial Hotel* (☎ 8658 1272) on Main St has basic rooms for $30/50.

In Carrieton, the *Carrieton Hotel* (☎ 8658 9007) has single/twin rooms for $30/50 including a cooked breakfast.

PORT GERMEIN (pop 220)
Founded after a road was built through nearby **Germein Gorge** in the 1870s, Port Germein became an important outlet for the golden wheat fields farther east. The great windjammers called in here to load grain for England as late as the 1940s, but these days this quaint place survives mainly on holidaymakers. Each New Year's Day the town has the **Festival of the Crab**, which honours the

FLINDERS RANGES

blue swimmer crabs caught in abundance along the coast here.

On the Germein Gorge road, 14 km off Highway 1, is Placid Place Trail Rides (☎ 8666 5210), where **horse rides** are $15 (30 minutes) to $65 (all day). The country through here is beautiful, and on the longer rides you end up in the Wirrabara Forest.

Euros and yellow-footed rock-wallabies inhabit the steep hills and crags of the 2000-hectare **Telowie Gorge Conservation Park**, 10 km east of town. The access road from the highway ends at a car park, from which a 20-minute stroll takes you up an attractive rocky creek to a semipermanent water hole in the gorge.

Places to Stay & Eat

The basic *Progress Association Caravan Park* (☎ 8634 5266) on the Esplanade has tent/caravan sites for $8/10 and on-site vans for $20.

Otherwise there's *Casual Affair* (☎ 8634 5242), a coffee shop, gallery and craft centre with backpacker accommodation. Dorm beds in a tranquil Japanese-style room cost $9. Meals are also available.

There are a couple of secluded bush camp sites without facilities on the road to Telowie Gorge, about one km before the carpark.

MT REMARKABLE NATIONAL PARK

This steep, rugged park covers 15,600 hectares and straddles the ranges between Melrose and Wilmington. Dramatic scenery, secluded gorges, a variety of plant and animal habitats, and some good bushwalks, including part of the Heysen Trail, are among its attractions.

The park's main access points are at Wilmington to the north, Melrose to the east (walkers only) and Mambray Creek to the west.

Information

The park headquarters at Mambray Creek (☎ 8634 7068) is usually open daily between 8.30 am and 4.30 pm. The ranger station on top of the main ridge between Wilmington

and Alligator Gorge is where you pay the entry fee of $3 per vehicle.

There are numerous walking trails and these are shown on the park brochure. For the longer walks you'll need the Melrose and Wilmington 1:50,000 topographical maps produced by Auslig.

Things to See & Do

Wilmington Area Turning off Main North Rd just south of town, a gravel road, which offers tremendous views, takes you 11 km up and over the main range to car parks near the colourful **Alligator Gorge**. There's a short but rather testing walk to this picturesque feature, where grey-and-red sandstone walls close in to just two metres apart.

From here you can also walk to places such as **Teal Dam** (20 minutes), **Kingfisher Flat** (two hours), **Hidden Gorge** (four hours) and **Mambray Creek** (seven hours).

Melrose Area A walking track climbs up from a car park about three km north of the township to the summit of 960-metre-high **Mt Remarkable**. You'll probably see euros, and there are stunning views on top; allow four hours for the return walk. The Heysen Trail descends along the Mt Remarkable Range from the summit to Wilmington.

Mambray Creek The road into Mambray Creek turns off Highway 1 about 21 km north of Port Germein. Majestic red gums and tall native pines line the creek, and farther in is a quiet scenic gorge where you might see euros and yellow-footed rock wallabies. Red kangaroos are reasonably common on the plains, while noisy birdlife (particularly kookaburras and corellas) is a feature along the creek.

A number of **walking tracks** head off into the ranges from Mambray Creek. If you're really fit and well-prepared you can walk to Alligator Gorge, then across to the Mt Remarkable Range and on to Melrose via Mt Remarkable.

About 15 km north of the Mambray Creek turn-off, the 7800-hectare **Winninowie Conservation Park** is another good spot to see kangaroos and many bird species including emus; its mangroves support breeding colonies of waders. Access is by dirt road leading in to Miranda and Chinamans Creek.

Places to Stay & Eat

The bottom car park near Alligator Gorge is usually the best place to go for a quiet picnic in this area. From here it's a 20-minute walk to the *Teal Dam* camp site; there are a number of similar places in the park where you can camp for $1.

The only vehicle-based camping is at *Mambray Creek*, where permits ($2 for the site and $2 per adult) can be obtained from the ranger's office. The camping area is by the creek and has many magnificent gums. You can also stay in a cabin with a kitchen and four bunk beds for $25 per person.

Just north of the Mambray Creek turn-off, the little *Mambray Creek Roadhouse* does good-value meals and takeaways.

PORT AUGUSTA (pop 15,200)

Matthew Flinders, who came ashore here and sent an exploring party into the nearby ranges, was the first European to set foot in the area. Called *kurdnatta* (heaps of sand) by the Aborigines, initial discouraging reports on the surrounding country kept settlers away. However, the need for an outlet for the new agricultural districts to the east and north-east resulted in the port being established at the head of Spencer Gulf in 1854. Shipping boomed until the early 1880s, after which it declined as the new railways took trade elsewhere. Port Augusta was ultimately saved from extinction when it became the headquarters for the Transcontinental Railway to Perth.

Today, this busy modern town is a major crossroads for travellers. From here, sealed roads and highways head west across the Nullarbor to WA, north to Alice Springs and Darwin, south to Adelaide and east to Broken Hill and Sydney. The main railway lines between the east and west coasts, and between Adelaide and Alice Springs, pass through Port Augusta.

Information

The tourist centre (☎ 8641 0793) is in the Wadlata Outback Centre at 41 Flinders Terrace. It's the major outlet for information on the Flinders Ranges and outback regions, and also has a good selection of material on the Eyre Peninsula. The office is open weekdays from 9 am to 5.30 pm and weekends from 10 am to 4 pm.

There are seven-day laundrettes behind Ian's Chicken Hut (on Highway 1) and at 74 Stirling Rd (about a km from the town centre). Locals warn against walking by yourself at night near any of the town's hotels.

Things to See & Do

The acclaimed **Wadlata Outback Centre** (entry $6) has many excellent interpretive exhibits tracing the Aboriginal and European history of the Flinders Ranges and outback. The place is under-utilised, probably because most travellers are in a hurry to get somewhere else. This is a pity as it really is worth a visit. It is open the same hours as the tourist centre.

Brochures at the tourist office detail a two-hour **heritage walk**. It takes in numerous historic sites such as **AD Tassie's house** (1864), the **Troopers Barracks** (1860) and the Corinthian frontage of the **Town Hall** (1887).

There are tours ($2) of the **School of the Air**, at 59 Power Crescent, at 10 am on weekdays. Tours also operate at the **Royal Flying Doctor Service** base, 4 Vincent St, on weekdays between 10 am and noon, and 1 and 3 pm; admission is by donation.

Another educational tour (free) takes you around the **Northern Power Station** (☎ 8642 0737), by the gulf just south of town. Tours depart at 10 am, 11 am and 1 pm, and closed footwear, long trousers and long-sleeved shirts are essential. Built in 1985, this huge complex generates about 40% of SA's electricity by burning brown coal mined at Leigh Creek in the northern Flinders Ranges.

Other attractions include the **Curdnatta Art & Pottery Gallery**, in Port Augusta's

FLINDERS RANGES

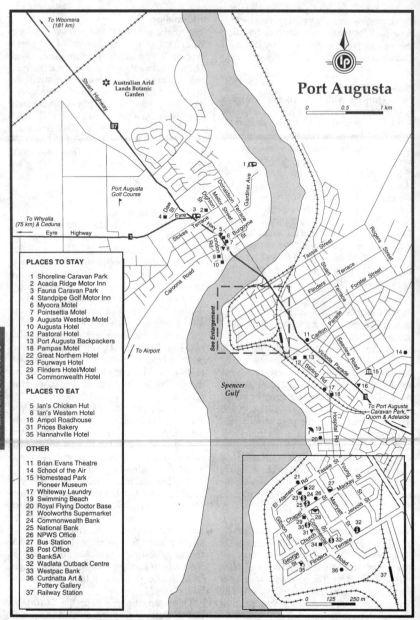

Port Augusta

0   0.5   1 km

To Woomera (181 km)

Australian Arid Lands Botanic Garden

Port Augusta Golf Course

To Whyalla (75 km) & Ceduna

Eyre   Highway

To Airport

Spencer Gulf

To Port Augusta Caravan Park, Quorn & Adelaide

See Enlargement

PLACES TO STAY

1   Shoreline Caravan Park
2   Acacia Ridge Motor Inn
3   Fauna Caravan Park
4   Standpipe Golf Motor Inn
6   Myoora Motel
7   Pointsettia Motel
8   Augusta Westside Motel
10 Augusta Hotel
12 Pastoral Hotel
13 Port Augusta Backpackers
18 Pampas Motel
22 Great Northern Hotel
23 Fourways Hotel
29 Flinders Hotel/Motel
34 Commonwealth Hotel

PLACES TO EAT

5   Ian's Chicken Hut
8   Ian's Western Hotel
16 Ampol Roadhouse
31 Prices Bakery
35 Hannahville Hotel

OTHER

11 Brian Evans Theatre
14 School of the Air
15 Homestead Park
    Pioneer Museum
17 Whiteway Laundry
19 Swimming Beach
20 Royal Flying Doctor Base
21 Woolworths Supermarket
24 Commonwealth Bank
25 National Bank
26 NPWS Office
27 Bus Station
28 Post Office
30 BankSA
32 Wadlata Outback Centre
33 Westpac Bank
36 Curdnatta Art &
    Pottery Gallery
37 Railway Station

0   125   250 m

FLINDERS RANGES

first railway station (1887) at 105 Commercial Rd, which has some beautiful work and hosts travelling exhibitions. The **Homestead Park Pioneer Museum**, on Elsie St, features an original pine-log homestead (1850s) furnished in period style. It's open daily from 10 am to 5 pm ($2.50).

On the Stuart Highway just north of town, is the **Australian Arid Lands Botanic Garden**, with walkways and an interpretive centre on 200 hectares of sandhills and clay flats. Check with the tourist centre for opening times.

Places to Stay

Caravan Parks & Hostels At Stirling North, on the Quorn road about nine km east of town, the friendly *Port Augusta Caravan Park* (☎ 8643 6357) charges $10 for its backpacker beds provided you're in a group of six or more. It also has camp sites ($10), caravan sites $12), on-site vans ($26), converted railway carriages ($32) and cabins (from $30)

On Highway 1, the modern *Fauna Caravan Park* (☎ 8642 2974) has tent/caravan sites for $14/16, on-site vans for $33 and cabins from $38. It also has a four-bed bunkhouse ($10) with an adjacent campers' kitchen.

The *Shoreline Caravan Park* (☎ 8642 2965) is in an attractive setting down near the water on Gardiner Ave. It charges $12/14 for tent/caravan sites, $23 for on-site vans, $25 for basic cabins and $38 for self-contained cabins.

Port Augusta Backpackers (☎ 8641 1063) at 17 Trent Rd is a friendly place with beds for $12. They also do Flinders Ranges 4WD tours ($70 for a day trip to Wilpena). The hostel is just off Highway 1, and if you ask the long-distance bus drivers they'll drop you off nearby.

Hotels The only other cheap accommodation in town is offered by the *Flinders Hotel/Motel* (☎ 8642 2544), at 39 Commercial Rd, where backpackers beds cost $14; self-contained rooms are $39/50. Other hotels are:

Augusta Hotel (☎ 8642 2701), at 11 Loudon Rd, has pub rooms for $25/40 and dinner, bed and breakfast deals for $35/50.

Commonwealth Hotel (☎ 8642 2844), at 73 Commercial Rd (right on the mall), has pub rooms for $25 per person. It doesn't do meals.

Fourways Hotel (☎ 8642 2522), also on Commercial Rd, has rooms being renovated and new prices not available.

Pastoral Hotel (☎ 8642 2818), corner Stirling Rd and Carlton Pde, has comfortable rooms with continental quilts for $30/40.

Great Northern Hotel (☎ 8642 3906), 4 Tassie St, has rooms for $25/35.

Motels There are a number of motels, most being of the uninspiring transit variety. They include:

Acacia Ridge Motor Inn (☎ 8642 3377), 33 Stokes Terrace, about four km north-west of the town centre, has units for $44/49.

Augusta Westside Motel (☎ 8642 2488), 3 Loudon Rd, has well-appointed units for $62/68 (double bed) and $66/72 (queen-size bed). It also has a playground and swimming pool.

Myoora Motel (☎ 8642 3622), on the Eyre Highway at the Whyalla end of town, has units for $49/56.

Pampas Motel (☎ 8642 3795), 76 Stirling Rd, about two km from the post office, has units for $40/50.

Pointsettia Motel (☎ 8642 2856), at 24 Burgoyne St, about three km north of the post office, has units for $40/45.

Port Augusta East Motel (☎ 8642 4033), first on the left on Highway 1 coming from Adelaide, has units for $40/45.

Highway One Motel (☎ 8642 2755), second on the left coming from Adelaide, has spacious units from $55/61 and a swimming pool.

Standpipe Golf Motor Inn (☎ 8642 4033), on Daw St at the intersection of the Eyre and Stuart highways, has very pleasant units for $64/69 and a sauna.

Places to Eat

There are plenty of places to eat, including most of the hotels, motels and roadhouses. Locals recommend the *Hannahville Hotel*, on Gibson St, and the *Flinders Hotel/Motel* as being consistently good value – both are in the town centre. The *Highway One Motel*, *Myoora Motel* and *Standpipe Golf Motel* are all reasonable, if not for the budget-minded.

Most of the takeaway places on the highway are pretty ordinary. However, the

FLINDERS RANGES

Ampol Roadhouse near the railway bridge is popular for breakfast, and *Ian's Chicken Hut*, just east of the Stuart Highway intersection, has an excellent reputation.

On Commercial Rd, in the centre of town, *Prices Bakery* and the bakery in *Woolworths* supermarket are both good. The Tuckerbox in the Wadlata Outback Centre is popular for lunches and coffee. There are several other coffee shops and cafes in the town centre.

Entertainment

The tourist office can tell you what's happening in town, or check the local weekly newspaper *The Transcontinental*.

For films there's the *Brian Evans Theatre* on Carlton Pde in the town centre. It's open daily except Thursday, and screens films mainly in the evenings from 8 pm.

There's usually a rock band at one of the football clubs on Friday night, while the *Augusta Hotel* usually has a DJ, also on Friday night. For video clips of your favourite star, try *Pete's Bar* in the Pastoral Hotel on Wednesday, Friday and Saturday nights.

Getting There & Away

Air Augusta Airways (☎ 8642 3100; bookings ☎ 13 1300) flies weekdays to Adelaide ($105) and Leigh Creek ($94).

On Saturday you can take the mail plane to Boulia ($310) in outback Queensland, stopping at Innamincka ($175) and Birdsville ($255) on the way; for details check with Augusta Airways.

Bus The Stateliner bus station (☎ 8642 5055) is at 23 Mackay St. Buses run to Adelaide ($27.20), Coober Pedy ($59), Wilpena Pound ($23.90), Whyalla ($11), Port Lincoln ($38.50), Ceduna ($50.60) and other places on the Eyre Peninsula. All but the trip to Wilpena Pound (which runs four times a week) are daily services.

Greyhound Pioneer (bookings ☎ 13 2030) travels daily to Perth ($189), Alice Springs ($141) and Sydney ($114), also from 23 Mackay St.

Train By train, Sydney is 32 hours away and

a standard economy/economy sleeper/1st-class sleeper ticket costs $149/287/453. It's 33 hours to Perth; a standard economy/economy sleeper/1st-class sleeper ticket is $197/382/596. It's four hours to Adelaide ($29).

In Port Augusta, phone ☎ 8641 8111 for enquiries and bookings.

Getting Around

There is no bus service to the airport, but you can ring Augusta Taxis (☎ 8642 4466) from the phone box there – it costs about $9 to town.

Hire cars are available from Budget (☎ 8642 6040) and Handy (☎ 8642 4466).

LAURA TO MELROSE

Heading north along Main North Rd you officially enter the Flinders Ranges region at **Stone Hut**, 10 km north of Laura.

Nine km further on is **Wirrabara** (population 250), a friendly town showing the faded prosperity of former times. It has the lovely old *Wirrabara Hotel* (☎ 8668 4162), where you can stay for $15, and the *Wirrabara Takeaway*, one of the best takeaway shops in the Flinders. You can camp at the sports oval for $5 – a key is available from the Horseshoe Cafe.

There's another basic camping ground in the nearby **Wirrabara Forest** (headquarters ☎ 8668 4163), as well as a YHA hostel (☎ 8668 4158) with beds costing $7 for members and $9 for nonmembers. The forest was noted for its huge river red gums – once a valuable source of jetty timbers and railway sleepers – and the majestic **King Tree** has been preserved as an example. The forest also has some nice walks, including the Heysen Trail.

About 10 km north of Wirrabara you can turn left and travel through the scenic **Germein Gorge** towards Port Germein. Just before tiny **Murraytown**, where there's a pub, is the turn-off to *Vondon Homestead* (☎ 8666 4209). This friendly place offers a package of $190 for two people for two nights, including all meals.

MELROSE (pop 200)

Established in 1853 when a copper mine was opened nearby, this pretty little town is the oldest settlement in the Flinders Ranges. It's in a great setting right at the foot of lofty **Mt Remarkable** (960 metres), on the southern edge of the Mt Remarkable National Park. If Melrose has a down side it's being woken early in the morning by the screeching clouds of corellas that feed on fallen grain in the wheat paddocks close to town.

Things to See & Do

The town has a number of fine old buildings including the police station and courthouse, which today houses a National Trust **museum**; it's open daily from 2 pm to 5 pm and admission costs $2. The photogenic **Mt Remarkable Hotel** was built in 1859 and its exterior looks like it has scarcely changed since. Just down the road, the **North Star Hotel** was licensed in 1854.

Also of interest is the **old cemetery** in Paradise Square, used between 1858 and 1880.

You can explore Mt Remarkable's lower slopes on a pleasant three-km marked trail from the caravan park. This takes you up to a **war memorial**, where there's a nice view, then back via the abandoned **copper mine** that marked the beginning of Melrose.

About 15 km to the south-east, the township of **Booleroo Centre** (population 300) has a museum with the largest collection of stationary engines in SA (☎ 8667 2193 for enquiries). Held in March every year, the rally of the Booleroo Steam & Traction Engine Society is worth attending if you're in the area.

Heading north from Melrose on Main North Rd, you'll notice many magnificent gnarled gums, some with large hollows at the base of their trunks. Apparently the hollows were used as shelters by Aboriginal people, who created them with the clever use of fire. Such trees are common throughout the ranges.

About 14 km north of Melrose, a turn-off on the left takes you to the old **Spring Creek Mine**. Copper was discovered here in 1860 and the deposit was worked off and on until 1916. All that's left today are some crumbling stone ruins in a lovely valley.

Places to Stay & Eat

Down by a pretty creek with huge river red gums, the *Melrose Caravan Park* (☎ 8666 2060) has bush camp sites ($8), powered sites ($11), on-site vans ($24) and cabins ($35). A backpacker unit has 16 beds for $10.

You can also stay at the *showgrounds* (caretaker ☎ 8666 2154) off the Wilmington road, which has good camp sites scattered among gum trees. Facilities are very basic, which is reflected in the rate of $2 per person (it's $5 extra with power).

The *Mt Remarkable Hotel* (☎ 8666 2119) does good meals but its transportable units are overpriced at $30/40/50 for singles/doubles/triples.

There are several holiday cottages and flats in the area; you can get details from SATC or local information outlets. They include *Elders Holiday Flat* (☎ 8666 2174), about six km north of Melrose. For $30 you can have the air-conditioned flat which sleeps four people. The friendly owner is German-speaking. From here it's an easy walk along the back fence to connect with the Mt Remarkable walking trail.

WILMINGTON (pop 250)

Originally called Beautiful Valley, Wilmington is a stark and somewhat dusty contrast to its near neighbour, Melrose. It grew around a pub and Cobb & Co staging post in the 1860s and soon became an important agricultural centre. Although the town is pretty quiet these days, the **Wilmington Hotel** (1879) is an imposing reminder of more prosperous times.

The Wilmington Deli (☎ 8667 5017) is the best place to go for information on local walks and other attractions around town.

Things to See & Do

Stan Dawes' Museum features a huge collection of minerals, fossils and shells; it's on the corner of Second St and Naria Terrace, and opens most days from 1 to 5 pm . **Aussie**

Relics on Main North Rd has everything from military rockets to vintage engines and mineral specimens. It's open on Sunday only from 2 to 4 pm.

On the road to Port Augusta, the five-km detour to **Hancocks Lookout** turns off three km from town. The views en route, and the expansive panorama over the western foothills to Spencer Gulf, make it worthwhile. Continuing on over scenic **Horrocks Pass** towards Port Augusta, the barren western scarp is a dramatic contrast to the steep gullies and big trees on the eastern side.

If you're heading for Quorn, the **Gunyah Rd scenic route** is an excellent if winding and dusty alternative to the bitumen farther east. It takes you through the eastern foothills of **Mt Brown**, with many beautiful views along the way.

Another alternative route goes via the ghost town of **Hammond**, on the vast Willochra Plain 23 km north-east of Wilmington. Surprisingly, there's an excellent restaurant here, and a museum in an old store.

Coonatto homestead (☎ 8659 0013) has three-hour trail rides for $35 per person which feature great views and billy tea. The homestead was once the headquarters of a vast station and even had its own church. It's about six km past Hammond on the Carrieton road.

Places to Stay & Eat

The well-shaded *Beautiful Valley Caravan Park* (☎ 8667 5197) is just south of town on Main North Rd. It has camp sites (the ground is hard and dusty) for $10, powered sites for $13, on-site vans for $25 and cabins from $30.

About four km to the east off Amyton Rd, *Nobes Tourist Park* (☎ 8667 5002) has tent/caravan sites for $12/14, on-site vans from $25 and cabins from $30. It's in a very pleasant bush setting on the banks of a creek.

In the centre of town, the *Wilmington Hotel* (☎ 8667 5154) has basic rooms (some with air-con) for $20/35/50. A cooked breakfast costs $7.50 and you can get a two-course lunch in the long front bar for $4.

There's quite a bit of alternative accommodation in and around town, and you can get details from the Wilmington Deli. Included is the very comfortable, two-bedroom *My-Ora Holiday Home* (☎ 8667 5017), on First St, which costs $85. Adjacent is an air-conditioned bunkhouse sleeping 10 for a total of $20, bedding included, although you have to be renting the house to use it.

Out of Town   Off Gunyah Rd 14 km from town is *The Gunyah* (☎ 8667 5199), a remote, five-bedroom stone farmhouse set by a creek in the scenic foothills of Mt Brown. During the week it costs $30 for the first two people and $5 for extras, and on weekends and school holidays it's $50 and $5. The Heysen Trail is nearby and there's plenty of potential for other walks.

Molly Brown's Kitchen (☎ 8659 0051), in the Bank of Adelaide building in Hammond, has an excellent reputation; its 'old times' menu includes kangaroo tail soup, rabbit schnitzels and bread-and-butter pudding. You can also stay here: B&B costs $70 for doubles.

QUORN (pop 1400)

A picturesque town on the edge of the outback, Quorn is about 330 km north of Adelaide and 50 km north-east of Port Augusta. Wheat farming began in the area in 1875, and the town was surveyed three years later with the arrival of the Great Northern Railway from Port Augusta.

The railhead moved north in 1880 and soon after the town was linked to the main line from Adelaide to the eastern states. Quorn thus became an important railroad junction and service town for the surrounding farms and stations. Although the railroads have long since closed, it retains a strong flavour of its early boom days.

Quorn is within 50 km of a number of attractions such as Mt Remarkable National Park and the Kanyaka ruins.

Information

The tourist information centre (☎ 8648 6031), next to the council chambers in Seventh St, is open weekdays from 9 am to

2 pm and on weekends and public holidays from 9 am to 4 pm. Outside these times you can ask at Quornucopia, on Railway Terrace.

Things to See & Do

One of Quorn's most appealing features is the evocative **Railway Terrace** streetscape across from the railway station. The almost unbroken line of two-storey hotels and shops, which dates from late last century, is an impressive reminder of busier times. You don't need much imagination to picture the horde of thirsty passengers erupting from the train to slake their thirst in the four pubs across the road.

In the same street there's a solid old **flour mill** (now a motel and restaurant), built in 1878, and an elaborate stone **town hall** (1891). The brochure *Quorn Historic Buildings Walk* takes you on a self-guided walk past these and other sites.

Part of the old Great Northern Railway line has reopened as the **Pichi Richi Railway**, which runs from Quorn to Woolshed Flat, in the scenic Pichi Richi Pass, about 16 km towards Port Augusta. The train is often pulled by a vintage steam engine, and makes the three-hour round trip for $17. It runs fairly frequently during school holidays, but at other times only operates every second weekend and on public holidays between early April and mid-November; phone the tourist centre or ☎ 8276 6232 for details.

Ask at the railway station about tours ($4) of the large **railway workshop**, which normally run on days when the train is running. Here you'll find a mind-boggling collection of around 20 steam-and-diesel-powered locomotives as well as numerous carriages, freight wagons, brake vans and sundry items. Most of the rolling stock is in working condition.

The town has a couple of **art galleries**: Quornucopia on Railway Terrace is worth a visit just to see an old-style emporium (it also offers a range of crafts and gifts); and the Studio Gallery, on First St, has an interesting collection of fine arts, leadlighting, batik, antiques and bric-a-brac.

Out of Town For $15, the Quorn Mill Motel will hire you a key to gain access to private **4WD tracks** around Devils Peak and Mt Brown East. You'll find great spots for picnics, bush camping and bushwalks at both; it's a tough two-hour return trek to the top of Devils Peak, but the views are terrific.

The rugged **Mt Brown Conservation Park** is reached by a walking track from the end of the road near **Olive Grove** homestead, about 14 km south of Burra. Allow five hours for the 12-km return walk to the top of the mountain (970 metres) via **Waukarie Falls**. It's described by an excellent brochure, available at the tourist office.

Starting at Woolshed Flat in Pichi Richi Pass, the **Waukarie Creek Trail** follows the attractive Waukarie Creek to meet the **Heysen Trail** near Olive Grove homestead; there's plenty to see, so allow at least five hours for the return walk of about nine km.

The unsealed **scenic route** heading north from Quorn along the eastern foothills has plenty of interest, including the 3500-hectare **Dutchman's Stern Conservation Park**. It's dominated by the Dutchman's Stern (820 metres), a bold bluff shaped like the rear end of an 18th century Dutch sailing ship. The Heysen Trail runs through the park. You can get to the top of the bluff via an eight-km walking track, described in a separate brochure. The park turn-off is seven km from Quorn.

Another nine km farther on is the turn-off to the **Junction Art Gallery** (☎ 8648 6470), where artist Val Francis displays many marvellous paintings featuring wildlife and landscapes. There's a nice walk from the homestead to the top of the **Ragless Range**, where you get good views.

Continuing on you pass tracks leading into **Warren Gorge**, **Buckaringa Gorge** and **Middle Gorge**, all of which are small but picturesque; there's a nice camping ground among gums at the entrance to Warren Gorge. I was delighted to see three **yellow-footed rock-wallabies** drinking from the creek here. Apparently, the area has the healthiest colony of these beautiful animals in the entire ranges.

Meet Petrogale Xanthopus

Found in the rocky hills of the Barrier, Flinders and Gawler ranges of SA, the large yellow-footed rock-wallaby (Petrogale xanthopus) is easily identified by its brown-and-orange banded tail. This is one of the prettiest of Australia's marsupials, its coat being richly ornamented with reddish-brown, black, grey and white. At one time it was hunted so enthusiastically for its skin that extinction was feared. It was protected in SA in 1912, but hunting for the fur trade continued for some time after that.

The total population of yellow-footed rock-wallabies was estimated at 10,000 in 1981 and significantly less than that in 1995. It is now classified as 'vulnerable' to extinction. There are around 200 known colonies, with most consisting of six to 12 animals but some being as large as 40. The main threat comes from foxes, which seem to prevent the recovery of local populations after drought. Another major threat is competition from intoduced grazing animals, particularly sheep, goats and rabbits.

All is not lost, however. Since the early 1990s the Department of Environment & Natural Resources has been baiting foxes in selected areas, including the Flinders Ranges National Park and adjoining stations, and local wallaby populations appear to have doubled as a result. Also, goats are no longer present in the ranges in such huge numbers as previously, while rabbits have sharply declined thanks to the calicivirus.

The wallabies' preferred habitat is steep rocky slopes with overhangs and boulders where their young can shelter from wedge-tailed eagles. There are a number of places in the Flinders Ranges where yellow-footed rock-wallabies can often be seen. Probably the best are the gorges around Warren Gorge north of Quorn, and Brachina and Wilkawillana gorges in the Flinders Ranges National Park. Early morning and late afternoon are the best times to see them. ■

Buckaringa Sanctuary, which encompasses the Buckaringa and Middle Gorges, lies 30 km north of Quorn. An ecotourism venture in the style of Warrawong Sanctuary in the Adelaide Hills is planned for the area, and it may happen soon – contact SATC for details.

The scenic route eventually comes onto the main road to Hawker about 34 km from Quorn.

Organised Tours

Specialising in 4WD natural history trips, Intrepid Tours (☎ 8648 6277) of Quorn is excellent value and very entertaining. They depart Port Augusta and Quorn daily; from Quorn it costs $40 for a half-day to places like **Mt Arden** or **Depot Creek**, and $75 for a full day to the Wilpena area or **Blinman** (add $5 if you're getting on at Port Augusta). They also do weekend and extended tours.

The Quorn Mill Motel (☎ 8648 6016) can arrange half-day 4WD trips to Dutchmans Stern for $38.

The Pichi Richi Holiday Camp (☎ 8648 6075), 14 km south of Quorn in Pichi Richi Pass, has horse rides for $40 (two hours), $65 (half-day) and $90 (full day including a barbecue lunch). It also does a seven-day trek in the Wilpena area.

Places to Stay

Shaded by huge gums populated by kookaburras, parrots, galahs and little corellas, the *Quorn Caravan Park* (☎ 8648 6206) is one of the nicest parks in the Flinders. It has tent/caravan sites for $9/13, on-site vans for $26 and self-contained cabins for $42.

The *Transcontinental Hotel* (☎ 8648 6076) on Railway Terrace is the pick of the town's four hotels for accommodation. It's a friendly place with backpackers' beds costing $12 and standard rooms at $25/35 for singles/doubles.

Second on the list is the *Austral Hotel* (☎ 8648 6017), which has motel units for $40/50/60. Also with rooms are the *Criterion Hotel* (☎ 8648 6018) and the *Grand Junction Hotel* (☎ 8648 6205), both of which are very ordinary. All are on Railway Terrace.

At the east end of Railway Terrace, *Quorn Mill Motel* (☎ 8648 6016) has pleasant, airy units for $50/60/70.

Out of Town Quornucopia (☎ 8648 6282) is the agent for a dozen or so alternative accommodation venues in the area.

At the bottom end of the range is the isolated and very basic *Moxam Hut*, where costs vary from $19 for two people (off-peak) to $29 (peak). It's in a very scenic setting but you need a 4WD to get there. At the top is the well-appointed *Waukarie Cottage* in Pichi Richi Pass, which can sleep six in three bedrooms; it costs from $59 for the first two people and $12 for extras (off-peak) to $69 and $12 (peak).

The *Pichi Richi Holiday Camp* (☎ 8648 6075) in Pichi Pass has a self-contained cottage for $80 per night for up to six people.

Places to Eat

Quorn's four hotels all offer counter and dining room meals, usually starting around $6. For something more up-market there's a very good restaurant in the *Quorn Mill Motel*, where main courses start at $13.

Alternatively, there's the cosy *Quandong Café* on the corner of First and Sixth Sts. It's open daily from 9.30 am to 5 pm for coffee, snacks and lunches, and sells excellent gourmet pies (such as kangaroo and claret).

The *Old Willows Brewery Restaurant*, about 10 km out on the Port Augusta road, has a menu which will really get the juices working. Specialising in gourmet-style bush tucker, it offers such things as Kangaroo Wellington, damper with acacia seeds, and quandong pie.

Getting There & Away

Stateliner (☎ 8415 5555) visits daily except Tuesday and Saturday from Adelaide via Port Augusta ($34.90). It's $5.90 to Port Augusta and $12.20 to Wilpena.

KANYAKA

The ruins of several early settlements are scattered along the road between Quorn and Hawker, with the most impressive being those at Kanyaka, 41 km from Quorn. Here, by a gum-lined creek about 500 metres off the road, are the substantial remains of the 16-room **Kanyaka homestead** and various stone outbuildings. Founded in 1851, the station ran 50,000 sheep and employed 70 families before it was devastated by drought and overstocking in the 1860s. The homestead was finally abandoned in 1888, after which the property was subdivided.

Kanyaka's founder, Hugh Proby (third son of the Scottish Earl of Carysfort), is buried under an imported granite tablet beside the Quorn scenic route 12 km northeast of the Brachina Gorge turn-off. He drowned in a flash flood in Willochra Creek in 1852, aged a mere 24 years.

From the homestead ruins you can take a 10-minute walk to the old woolshed. The track continues about 1.5 km to a beautiful permanent water hole, overlooked by a massive boulder known locally as **Death Rock**. According to one story, local Aborigines once placed their dying kinfolk here to see out their last hours.

If you're coming from Wilpena Pound, don't be confused by the sign which indicates the old Kanyaka town site (surveyed 1863); the clearly marked turn-off to the homestead ruins is four km farther on.

Northern Ranges

Much more remote and undeveloped than the southern ranges, the sparsely populated area between Hawker and the Strzelecki Desert contains three of the state's finest conservation areas: the Flinders Ranges and

FLINDERS RANGES

Gammon Ranges national parks, and the privately owned Arkaroola Wildlife Sanctuary.

The road from Hawker to Marree is sealed as far as Lyndhurst. To get to the Gammon Ranges National Park and Arkaroola from this direction you take the gravel road from Copley, just north of Leigh Creek. Alternatively, you can go from Wilpena Pound via Wirrealpa station and Chambers Gorge.

HAWKER (pop 450)

Hawker is 55 km south of Wilpena Pound and, like Quorn, owes it existence to the now-defunct Great Northern Railway. It was established in 1880, by which time the surrounding Willochra Plain was gaining a reputation as one of the colony's finest wheat-growing areas. Optimism was high, but the uncertain seasons eventually brought a decline that culminated in the last significant harvest, which took place in 1947.

The main information outlet is in the Mobil service station (☎ 8648 4014) on the corner of Wilpena and Cradock Rds. They have the pamphlet *Hawker's Heritage Walk* ($1.50), which takes you on a **self-guided walk** around the town's oldest buildings.

The **Jarvis Hill Lookout** is about six km south-west of Hawker and gives nice views over the Willochra Plain to Hawker and north to Wilpena Pound.

There are Aboriginal rock paintings 12 km south of Hawker at **Yourambulla**, where three sites are open to visitors. They're among overhangs and cliffs high up on Yourambulla Peak, a half-hour walk from the car park. The name means 'two men' and refers to the twin peaks just east of the art sites.

Places to Stay

Hawker Caravan Park (☎ 8648 4006) at the Wilpena end of town has tent/caravan sites at $9/13 ($3 extra for private facilities) for singles/doubles, on-site vans for $25/28, and deluxe cabins for $50.

About one km out on the Leigh Creek road, the friendly but rather exposed *Flinders Ranges Caravan Park* (☎ 8648 4266) has tent sites, powered sites and on-site vans

for almost identical prices as Hawker Caravan Park.

Hawker Hotel/Motel (☎ 8648 4102), on Elder Terrace, charges $25/35 for basic hotel rooms (most are air-conditioned) and $50/60 for motel units. The *Outback Motel* (☎ 8648 4100) on Wilpena Rd charges $50/60.

Also in town is the *Chapmanton Holiday Village* (☎ 8648 4140), on Arkaba St, which has fully equipped holiday flats sleeping up to six people for $45/55/65.

There are a number of alternative accommodation venues on farms around town; details are available from SATC or the Mobil service station. They include *Merna Morna Station* (☎ 8648 4717), 46 km north of Hawker on the Leigh Creek road, where you can stay in self-contained flats for $40 singles & doubles and $5 each extra adult (the flats take from four to six persons). The property has beautiful scenery and plenty of wildlife.

Places to Eat

Sight-Seers Cafe, on Elder Terrace opposite the information bay, has reasonably priced sit-down meals and takeaways, as does the *Hawker Shopping Centre*, on Wilpena Rd, where there's a well-stocked grocery section. *Hawker Hotel/Motel* and *Outback Motel* also do meals.

The classiest place to eat in town is the reasonably priced *Old Ghan Restaurant*, in the old railway station. Its atmosphere and food are marvellous, but unless the management has changed you may find the service rather brusque. It's open from 11.30 am to 8.30 pm Wednesday to Sunday.

HAWKER TO WILPENA

There are increasingly compelling views of the rugged **Elder Range** and **Rawnsley Bluff** as you head towards Wilpena Pound. **Rawnsley Lookout**, about 41 km from Hawker, has magnificent views of bold bluffs and soaring cliffs to the north-west and the rugged **Chase Range** to the south. Rawnsley Bluff marks the southern end of the **Flinders Ranges National Park**.

Arkaba Station, 21 km north of Hawker, offers 4WD tours into the spectacular Elder Range. These include sweeping panoramas from high ridgetops and cost $60 for a full day; you can book through the Wilpena Pound Motel (☎ 8648 0004).

A little farther north, the 28-km **Moralana Scenic Route** runs between the Wilpena and Leigh Creek roads and takes in magnificent scenery between the Elder and Wilpena ranges. The turn-off is 24 km from Hawker on the Wilpena road, and 43 km on the Leigh Creek road.

Friendly **Rawnsley Park**, 35 km from Hawker, offers a range of activities such as sheep shearing demonstrations ($6), trail rides ($35 for two hours and $90 for a full day), and half and full-day 4WD tours ($45 and $75 respectively). There's also good bushwalking on the property. The Stateliner bus passes four days a week from Adelaide and will drop you at the homestead. See the following Places to Stay section for the telephone numbers.

Arkaroo Rock, 40 km from Hawker, is another Aboriginal art site. Here you find reptile and human figures executed in yellow and red ochre, charcoal and bird lime on the underside of a huge fallen boulder. This is one of the Flinders' most important Aboriginal cultural sites, and was used for initiation ceremonies as late as 1940.

The return walk from the car park, where there's a nice picnic area among native pines, has views of towering cliffs and takes about one hour.

Places to Stay

Graham Dunn's Bush Retreat on Arkaba Station (bookings ☎ 8648 0004) has twin-share huts in a marvellous bush setting. They cost $360 per person for three nights and $440 for four nights, including all meals as well as guided bushwalks and 4WD tours.

Rawnsley Park (☎ 8648 0030 or 8648 0008) has tent/caravan sites for $8.50/15.50, on-site vans for $15/32 and self-contained cabins for $52. The views to nearby Rawnsley Bluff are stunning.

FLINDERS RANGES NATIONAL PARK

The park's attractions include quiet gorges, rugged ranges, gum-lined creeks, abandoned homesteads, Aboriginal sites, abundant wildlife and carpets of wildflowers in early spring. Most areas of interest are readily accessible from the park's network of dirt roads and walking tracks.

The rangers' office (☎ 8648 0048) on the entrance road just before the Wilpena Tourist Village has information on display 24 hours a day and is usually staffed daily from 8 am to 5.30 pm.

Things to See & Do

The best-known feature in the ranges, and main attraction in the 94,500-hectare Flinders Ranges National Park, is the large natural basin known as **Wilpena Pound**. Covering about 90 sq km and ringed by steep ridges, it's accessible only through a narrow gorge near the tourist village. On the outside, the Wilpena Wall soars 500 metres; inside, the basin slopes relatively gently away from the peaks.

Standing up on the rim, you can see why the Adnyamathanha people considered it to be the joined bodies of two snakes *(akurra)*, with the head of one being St Mary Peak. *(Wilpena* is their word for 'bent fingers'.)

You could easily spend two or three days at Wilpena doing tours and walks, or longer if you wanted to explore further afield.

For natural-history enthusiasts there's the 20-km **Brachina Gorge Geological Trail**, which you can follow in your car. It features an outstanding geological sequence of exposed sedimentary rock, covering 120 million years of Earth history. An excellent brochure ($1) and information signs along the way explain it all.

You can make the trail part of a full-day, 110-km round trip from Wilpena, taking in the scenic **Bunyeroo Valley**, Brachina Gorge, **Aroona Valley** and **Stokes Hill Lookout**. All are worth visiting. Take the time to do some short walks and make sure to stop at **Bunyeroo Valley Lookout** for its spectacular views. The geology trail starts at the junction of the Brachina Gorge and

FLINDERS RANGES

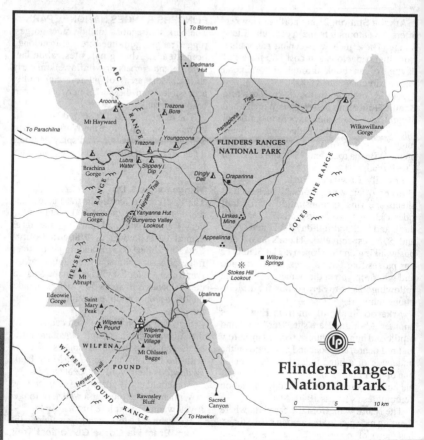

Flinders Ranges National Park

Blinman roads, so if you want to follow it logically you'll have to do the round trip in an anticlockwise direction.

Wildlife is plentiful. Red kangaroos are often seen and yellow-footed rock-wallabies are reasonably common in Brachina Gorge, although you have to be there early or late in the day. Their numbers are on the increase, now that poison baiting has reduced the fox population.

Just outside the park's south-east corner, Sacred Canyon has galleries of **Aboriginal rock carvings**, which feature abstract designs and animal tracks.

Bushwalks

If you're planning to walk for more than three hours, fill in the logbook at the ranger's office – and don't forget to 'sign off' when you return. Searches are no longer initiated by the rangers, so make sure someone responsible knows the details of your walk. Remember that this is arid country – carry plenty of drinking water.

There are numerous walking tracks marked (sometimes not very clearly) by blue triangles; sections which incorporate parts of the Heysen Trail are indicated by red markers. The leaflet *Bushwalking in the*

Flinders Ranges National Park ($1) will whet your appetite with its brief descriptions of around 20 walks. In addition, the RGSA (SA) has excellent pamphlets on several walks. Topographical maps (scale 1:50,000) are available for $7.50 from the ranger's office and the Wilpena store.

Most of the walks around Wilpena start from the camping ground. They vary from short walks suitable for those with small children, to longer ones taking more than a day. The walking times indicated are for a reasonably easy pace.

The best option, in terms of interest, challenge and rewarding views, is the full-day return walk from the Wilpena camping ground to **St Mary Peak** – you can do it either as an up-and-back walk or a round trip. If you go for the first option, it's faster and more interesting to take the route outside Wilpena Pound and then up to the **Tanderra Saddle**, just below St Mary Peak.

The final climb up to the saddle is fairly steep and the stretch to the top of the peak is a real scramble. However, the views are superb from both the saddle and the peak; the white glimmer of Lake Torrens is visible off to the west and the Aroona Valley stretches away to the north.

Descending back to the saddle you can return to the tourist village by the same direct route or take the longer, but very pleasant walk through the native pines and mallee on the pound floor. The Pound was a wheat farm between 1902 and 1914, and you pass the old **homestead** near the end; ironically, it was a flood not drought that brought its demise. A detour takes you to spectacular **Edeowie Gorge** in the Pound's north-west corner. If you're going there as well you'll need to be prepared for an overnight stay at the **Cooinda** bush camping ground.

If you don't have all day, but want to enjoy a challenge and some views, the track up **Mt Ohlssen Bagge** might suit. The walk – steep, rocky and tough going in parts – takes about three hours return from the Wilpena camping ground. A stunning panorama awaits at the summit.

A good short walk is the one-hour return trip to the old homestead inside the pound. En route you walk through scenic **Sliding Rock Gorge**, the only break in the pound rim, and if you go in early morning or late afternoon you should see euros.

Organised Tours

Adnyamathanha stockman Ron Coulthard takes **trail rides** in the Wilpena area and can go as far as the ABC Range. Ron doesn't have a set programme, but he'll certainly teach you something about the bush and Aboriginal culture. You can book through the Wilpena Pound Motel (toll-free ☎ 1800 805 802); prices range from $20 for one hour to $50 for four hours.

The Pichi Richi Holiday Camp (☎ 8648 6075) has six and seven-day horse treks on Willow Springs station, outside the park, costing from $100 per person per day.

You can do a half-day **4WD tour** to rugged Brachina Gorge for $50 and another on Arkaba station, which takes you along a high ridgetop with spectacular views; the cost is $60 including lunch. Book at the Wilpena Pound Motel (see the following Places to Stay & Eat section).

Scenic flights over the pound and surrounding ranges cost $40 (for 20 minutes) or $55 (30 minutes); prices are based on three passengers – if there are less it'll cost more. Book through the Wilpena Pound Motel.

Places to Stay & Eat

Unless you have a tent there is no cheap accommodation at Wilpena Pound. A camping ground in the Wilpena Tourist Village ($9 for an unpowered site and $14 for powered) has facilities including a well-stocked store, which sells groceries. Camping permits can be purchased at the store.

Also in the Wilpena Tourist Village is the *Wilpena Pound Motel* (☎ toll-free bookings 1800 805 802), with all mod cons, including a swimming pool. Its budget rooms cost $35/45 while more luxurious rooms are $79/83, including a light breakfast (during December and January rates are $69/74). Counter lunches (from $5) are available in the bar, and there's also a good restaurant.

Elsewhere in the park are scattered bush camping grounds with very basic facilities for $2 per person; you can purchase a permit from roadside stands along the way. The nicest grounds are *Trezona*, *Aroona*, and the east end of *Brachina Gorge*, all of which have tranquil creek-bank sites among big gum trees; remote *Wilkawillana Gorge* in the north-east is the quietest.

You can also stay in the bunkhouse at the old *Oraparinna* homestead; book at the NPWS office in Hawker for this one.

BLINMAN (pop 50)

This quaint hamlet owes its existence to the shepherd 'Peg Leg' Blinman, who discovered copper here in 1859. A mine was soon operating, but things didn't really get moving until 1903, when a smelter was built on site. Four years later the town had a population of 2000, but soon after went into decline with falling copper prices and dwindling reserves. The mine closed in 1918, having produced 10,000 tonnes of copper.

Today, Blinman's main distinction is that it's the state's highest town: 610 metres above sea level. The mine is on a hilltop about a km to the north. Most of the original mine structures have long been demolished, but you can view the surface workings through the safety fence. The site is being developed as a tourist attraction with lookouts, walks and information signs.

Range Tours (☎ 8648 4874), at the Blinman Deli, offers interesting **4WD tours** with a local expert, who will show you Aboriginal rock carvings, historic ruins, fossicking spots and other out-of-the-way places.

From Blinman, the Outback Camel Co (☎ 8648 4874 or ☎ 8543 2280) does 1½-hour camel rides for $25 and treks lasting from two days ($275) to eight days ($875).

Places to Stay

The delightful *Blinman Hotel* (☎ 8648 4867) has a real outback pub flavour. Its timber panelled rooms cost $20 per person, or $25 with private facilities.

Next door, the dusty little *Blinman*

Caravan Park (ask at the pub) has camp sites for $5 and powered sites for $8.

At the mine is the heritage-style *Captain's Cottage* (☎ 8648 4895), a tastefully restored stone house dating from the 1860s; originally it was the mine captain's quarters. It can sleep six for $180, or doubles for $80, including full breakfast provisions.

AROUND BLINMAN

There are several day trips you can do from Blinman on the network of generally good dirt roads around town. These include a loop through the Flinders Ranges National Park via Aroona Valley and Brachina Gorge.

About 12 km south of Blinman on the Wilpena road is the **Great Wall of China**, a low ridge with a wall-like layer of sandstone on top, and not a patch on the real thing. Three km further down the road, Gum Creek station (☎ 8648 4883) has a range of **guided tours and walks**.

Chambers Gorge

On the road towards Arkaroola, Chambers Gorge features huge gum trees, dramatic tan-coloured dolomite cliffs and galleries of **Aboriginal rock carvings**. It's accessible by a rough track off the Arkaroola road, about 64 km from Blinman.

To reach the carvings, park your car and walk up the little gorge on your left 8.3 km from the main road; the first major gallery is 350 metres upstream and on your left just before a small waterfall. Most of the carvings were produced by 'pecking' at the surface with a hard, hand-held rock.

You can get as far as the carvings in a conventional vehicle, while a 4WD with good clearance will take you into the main gorge. It's a scramble to the top of **Mt Chambers**, the highest point on the right just inside the gorge, but the view is worth it. You can see over **Lake Frome** to the east and all the way along the ranges to **Mt Painter** in the north and Wilpena in the south.

The SA Museum's *A Field Guide to Chambers Gorge*, by Graham Medlin, is a very useful reference which describes numerous walks.

Parachilna

There's some really inspiring scenery on the 31-km drive from Blinman down through **Parachilna Gorge** to tiny Parachilna, on the saltbush plain to the west. As well as beautiful views most of the way down, there are good picnic spots along the creek, and there's a great old pub in Parachilna. The northern end of the Heysen Trail is two km past the **Angorichina Tourist Village**, 15 km from Blinman.

Having reached Parachilna, you can head south to Brachina Gorge or north on the Marree road to the Beltana Roadhouse. From here a bush road heads east for eight km to historic Old Beltana.

Old Beltana

This was once a busy centre on the Great Northern Railway. Home to over 400 people in the 1880s and 90s, when it had 70 houses as well as a railway station, telegraph station and hotels, these days Old Beltana is only saved from being a ghost town by a handful of people seeking to escape the rat race. It's a fascinating spot with a number of ruins and old stone buildings surrounded by saltbush; ask at the Beltana Roadhouse about the booklet *Beltana Trails* ($5), which gives a **self-guided tour** of the old township.

Continue east from Old Beltana for about 23 km and you come to the abandoned **Sliding Rock copper mine**, by beautiful Sliding Rock Creek in the western foothills. Opened with feverish optimism in the early 1870s, it produced about 1000 tonnes of copper before it was closed by flooding in 1877. There are some interesting ruins, including the Rock Hotel, a couple of tall stone chimneys and the inevitable graveyard. It's hard to believe today, but the mine supported a population of 400 in its heyday.

Places to Stay & Eat

You'll find excellent bush camp sites with shady gum trees along the creeks in Parachilna and Chambers gorges.

Angorichina Tourist Village (☎ 8648 4842) in Parachilna Gorge boasts a magnificent setting with steep hills all around. It has

camp sites ($8), on-site vans ($20/30 for singles/doubles), backpacker beds ($13) and self-contained units (from $42). Stateliner buses will drop passengers at the front door.

At Parachilna there's the *Prairie Hotel* (☎ 8648 4895), which has powered sites for $15, basic cabins from $40 and tasteful hotel rooms for $35/55. Its imaginative menu features gourmet Australian bush tucker – the emu pate on damper is delicious.

Almost next door, the *Old Schoolhouse* (☎ 8648 4676) has bunks and cooking facilities for $12 per person. Ask here about camel rides to Lake Torrens.

Station Accommodation *Gum Creek Station* on the Wilpena road (☎ 8648 4883) has shearers' quarters for $10, but there's a minimum charge of $50 per night.

Angorichina Station (☎ 8648 4863), nine km east of Blinman, is the booking agent for several station properties near town. All have beds for $15, with a minimum booking of $60. Angorichina in particular has excellent walks near the homestead.

Historic *Beltana Station* (☎ 8675 2256), between Beltana Roadhouse and Old Beltana, has beds in old shearers' quarters.

LEIGH CREEK (pop 1400)

Coal was discovered on Leigh Creek in 1888, but mining operations didn't get under way until 1943. Since then the field has produced 50 million tonnes of hard brown coal for use in power stations at Port Augusta; the current annual production is about 2.5 million tonnes. All operations are controlled by the Electricity Trust of South Australia (ETSA).

The present township of Leigh Creek was developed in 1980 when the original town was demolished to make way for mining. Landscaping and tree planting have created a pleasant, leafy environment in dramatic contrast to the stark surroundings.

ETSA offers a range of free **guided tours** of its mining operations. These are very informative and last up to 2½ hours. For an update on schedules contact either the ETSA office (☎ 8675 4214) at the shopping centre or ring the tour guide on ☎ 8675 4216 between 7.30 am and 4.15 pm Monday to Friday. Tours generally leave from the parking bay 200 metres south of the town turn-off on the Marree road.

Leigh Creek's water supply comes from scenic **Aroona Dam**, 10 km to the south-west, where there's a pleasant picnic spot and a small camping ground operated by the ETSA.

ETSA runs a motel in the town centre costing $49/59 for singles/doubles, and a caravan park with camp sites ($6) – the amenities at the latter are very good but the ground is like concrete. The ETSA canteen is next door to the motel and offers reasonably priced meals as well as bar facilities.

Copley

Just five km north of Leigh Creek, this little township (population 100) is at the turn-off to the Gammon Ranges National Park (99 km) and the Arkaroola Wildlife Sanctuary (129 km); see the following sections for details. The drive into these areas is extremely scenic, but the road winds and it's easy to come to grief if you're not careful.

At first glance Copley doesn't have much going for it. However, hidden away on the main street is *Tulloch's Bush Bakery*, the home of the gourmet pies I raved about back at Quorn. Always expect the unexpected!

You can stay at the pleasant old *Leigh Creek Hotel* (☎ 8675 2281) for $30/46, including a light breakfast.

GAMMON RANGES NATIONAL PARK

Covering 128,200 hectares, this remote park has deep gorges, rugged ranges and beautiful gum-lined creeks – you'll see many kangaroos in the late afternoon and (sadly) even more feral goats. Most of the park is difficult to get to. It's certainly not the place for anyone who isn't prepared for the isolation and lack of facilities.

The ranger's office (☎ 8648 4829) is at the old **Balcanoona** homestead, 99 km from Copley, but there's rarely anyone there until after hours. There's a rather useless map in

the park brochure; a much better one is in Westprint's map of the Flinders Ranges.

Things to See & Do

On the drive in from Copley you pass through **Nepabunna** Aboriginal community in the park's south-west corner, after which it's 22 km to scenic **Italowie Gorge**; RM Williams, the famous designer of bush clothing and footwear, made his first pair of riding boots while camped here in the 1920s.

At Balcanoona, the faded but interesting information signs in the big old shearing shed give you some details of the park's cultural and natural history. Included is the story of a murder at **Grindells Hut**, an outcamp in the park's central pound.

Grindells Hut is in a very pretty area with commanding views and stark ridges all around. You can reach it on a 4WD track off the Arkaroola road, or by walking through **Balcanoona Gorge** and **Weetootla Gorge**. The hike is worthwhile, but it's 13 km return; if you leave early in the morning you've a good chance of seeing yellow-footed rock-wallabies in the gorges. Check with the ranger before attempting to drive or walk in to this area.

The RGSA (SA) has informative brochures detailing several walks you can do from Grindells hut.

There's also an interesting 4WD round trip of about 160 km from Balcanoona, passing Grindells Hut, **Idnina** outstation, **Yankaninna** homestead, **Owieandana** homestead and Nepabunna Aboriginal community. En route you can make a five-km detour to climb **Arcoona Bluff** in the park's extreme west. It's not a hard climb if you're fit, and the views are fantastic.

Aboriginal ranger Gil Coulthard leads two-hour to whole day **trail rides**, with a cultural emphasis, from Balcanoona.

Places to Stay

There are bush camping areas at Italowie Gorge, Grindells Hut, Weetootla Gorge and Arcoona Bluff; camping permits are available at Balcanoona.

Grindells Hut is available for hire, but if you're going during the winter or spring school holidays you'll need to book at least a year in advance.

ARKAROOLA WILDLIFE SANCTUARY

Once a sheep station, and now a privately operated wildlife sanctuary complete with a self-contained tourist village, Arkaroola is in a remote and scenically spectacular part of the Flinders Ranges. The sanctuary was established in 1968 by Reg and Griselda Sprigg. They introduced strict conservation measures – 80,000 feral goats have been shot or trapped since 1974 – and the previously degraded 61,000-hectare property is now well on the way to recovery.

For information and bookings contact either the Arkaroola Travel Centre (☎ 8212 1366) at 50 Pirie St in Adelaide, or ring the resort direct on ☎ 8648 4848.

Things to See & Do

The resort has an interesting **interpretive centre** with displays on the area's natural history, including a scientific explanation of the earth tremors; there's a seismological recording station in the centre.

You can take guided or tag-along **tours**, or do your own thing on over 100 km of graded, generally single-lane tracks. Most places of interest are accessible to conventional vehicles, with some hiking involved. For something more active there are a number of excellent **bushwalks**. The RGSA (SA) has detailed brochures covering four walks ranging from six to 15 km; all leave from the tourist village.

One of Arkaroola's highlights is the four-hour, 4WD **Ridgetop Tour**, along a rough mineral-exploration road through wild mountain country. It's not for the faint-hearted as there are some adrenaline-pumping climbs

---

Local Legends

The 'spirit of place', almost palpable in the Flinders Ranges, has inspired a rich heritage of Dreaming stories. Many of these legends – many secret, but some related by Adnyamathanha ('hill people') elders – explain creation, the extraordinary geological features of Wilpena Pound, and the native birds and animals which inhabit it.

Arkaroola comes from Arkaroo, the name of a Dreamtime serpent ancestor. Suffering from a powerful thirst, Arkaroo drank Lake Frome dry, then carved out the sinuous Arkaroola Creek as he dragged his bloated body back into the ranges. Arkaroo went underground to sleep it off, but all that salty water had given him a belly ache. Today, his constant moving about to relieve the pain explains the 30 to 40 small earth tremors that occur in the area each year.

Another story relates that the walls of the pound are the bodies of two Akurra (giant snakes), who coiled around Ikara (Wilpena Pound) during an initiation ceremony, creating a whirlwind during which they devoured most of the participants.

In another story, the bossy eagle Wildu sought revenge on his nephews, who had tried to kill him, by building a great fire. All birds were caught in the flames, and, originally white, they emerged blackened and burnt. The magpies and willie wagtails were partially blackened, but the crows were entirely blackened, and have remained so until this day. ■

and descents. Apart from the sweeping panoramas you may see wild goats (there are 3000 left on the property), wedge-tailed eagles, euros and yellow-footed rock-wallabies. The tour costs $50 and is well worth it.

Another excellent tour, which has the entertaining Doug Sprigg as your guide, allows you to view the heavens through a high-powered telescope at the **Arkaroola Astronomical Observatory**. This one costs $15 and lasts 1½ hours.

Other attractions include scenic gorges and waterholes with euphonic Aboriginal

Bolla Bollana copper smelter

names such as **Nooldoonooldoona** and **Barraranna**. The area has received plenty of attention from prospectors and miners; relics include the ruins of the **Bolla Bollana** copper smelter.

Paralana Hot Springs, about 28 km from the tourist village, is the 'last hurrah' of Australia's geyser activity. A small hot pool – the water is heated by the radioactive decay of underlying granite – was used as a health spa for a short time in the 1920s. Ironically, those who came to be cured of their aches and pains probably overdosed on radon. It's not worth a special trip unless you're particularly interested in geology.

You can do 40-minute **scenic flights** (with a geological and botanical emphasis) over the ranges from $50 per seat, provided there's at least three passengers. Charters of two hours or more cost $250 per hour.

Places to Stay & Eat

The resort has a caravan park and three motel complexes, which offer differing standards. Camp sites in the dusty hilltop caravan park and along the creek (much more enticing) cost $10, as do beds in spartan huts. Comfortable cabins (share facilities) are $29 twin share, while motel units cost from $39 for singles & doubles.

There's a small shop where you can buy basic supplies, and a good restaurant with main courses from $11.

Eyre Peninsula & West Coast

The vast, triangular Eyre Peninsula is bounded by Spencer Gulf to the east, the Great Australian Bight to the west, and the Gawler Ranges to the north. It takes its name from Edward John Eyre who, in 1841, made the first overland crossing between Port Augusta and Albany, WA.

Apart from low ranges in the east, and some scattered hills and granite outcrops elsewhere, the peninsula is mainly flat to gently undulating. Superphosphate and trace elements have made its infertile soils suitable for cereal crops, and as a result it now produces about 40% of the state's wheat crop. There's a large gypsum mine near Penong, and deposits of iron ore are mined in the Middleback Ranges; the ore is railed to Whyalla for processing and export.

Fishing and tourism are other important industries. The coastline is dotted with small ports and resort towns, with the sheltered bays between Cowell on the central east coast and Coffin Bay in the south being most popular with summer holiday-makers. Port Lincoln is home to the state's tuna fleet, and there are lucrative rock lobster, abalone and prawn fisheries. Oyster farming is practised at several places on the east and west coasts.

The coastline from Port Lincoln to the WA border is exposed to the full fury of the Southern Ocean; the Great Australian Bight is one of the roughest stretches of water anywhere in the world. Here you find surf beaches, spectacular coastal scenery and breeding grounds for southern right whales, Australian sea lions and great white sharks (some scenes for *Jaws* were filmed here).

Information

There are efficient and well-stocked tourist information centres at Whyalla, Port Lincoln and Ceduna; the Wadlata Outback Centre in Port Augusta also has quite a bit of information on the peninsula. See the sections on these towns for details.

The Eyre Peninsula Tourism Association

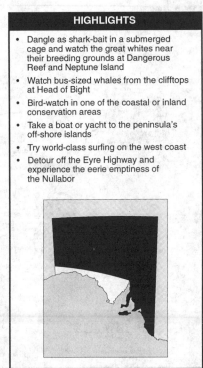

HIGHLIGHTS

- Dangle as shark-bait in a submerged cage and watch the great whites near their breeding grounds at Dangerous Reef and Neptune Island
- Watch bus-sized whales from the clifftops at Head of Bight
- Bird-watch in one of the coastal or inland conservation areas
- Take a boat or yacht to the peninsula's off-shore islands
- Try world-class surfing on the west coast
- Detour off the Eyre Highway and experience the eerie emptiness of the Nullabor

has a comprehensive regional guide available free from most outlets.

Communications Throughout this book we use the new statewide STD code (08) and eight-digit telephone numbers, which take effect in February 1997. Should you need to use the old number, simply take the first two digits (86 for Eyre Peninsula) and use as the STD code (086).

Books & Maps About the only decent reference book to the region is the Royal Society of South Australia's 230-page *Natural*

Eyre Peninsula

0   40   80 km

History of Eyre Peninsula, which gives an excellent coverage of its natural and social history.

The RAA has two good touring maps: *Lower Eyre Peninsula* and *Upper Eyre Peninsula & Far West Coast. A Tourist Map of the Nullarbor Plain (Perth to Adelaide)* by Cartographic is an attractive souvenir and guide.

National Parks Most conservation areas south of the Eyre Highway between Port Augusta and Ceduna are administered by the National Parks & Wildlife Service office at 75 Liverpool St, in Port Lincoln (☎ 8688 3111). The NPWS office at 9 Mackay St, Port Augusta (☎ 8648 5301) looks after areas north of the highway.

For the far west of the state, including the Streaky Bay area, you should contact the NPWS office at 11 McKenzie St in Ceduna (☎ 8625 3144).

Organised Tours
Bus/4WD Tours Stateliner (☎ 8415 5555) has several options available. Their four-day tour to Streaky Bay departing from Adelaide costs $155, while five days to Port Lincoln

costs $235 – all prices are based on twin share. They have other tours down the Spencer Gulf coast.

Great Australian Bight Safaris (☎ 8682 2750) offers tours and safaris from Port Lincoln including local sightseeing, bush camping and fishing, and visits to Head of Bight for whale-watching. Operating from Ceduna, Nullarbor Adventure Tours (☎ 8625 3447; toll-free 1800 65 0477) has local 4WD tours, and will also take you to Head of Bight and caves in the Nullarbor National Park.

There are 4WD minibus and tag-along tours to the Coffin Bay National Park from Coffin Bay township. At Wudinna, on the Eyre Highway between Port Augusta and Ceduna, you can do horse treks as well as 4WD tailor-made tours into the scenic Gawler Ranges.

Boat Charters/Cruises There's a good choice at Port Lincoln, where several operators offer diving, fishing and sightseeing charters to nearby places such as the Sir Joseph Banks Group of Islands, Thistle Island and the Dangerous Reef seal colony. For more details see Organised Tours in the section on Port Lincoln.

Accommodation

Eyre Peninsula has a good range of accommodation, particularly on the Spencer Gulf coast. Most towns south of Cowell have holiday flats if you want to spend a few days, but book early if you're heading that way over January or Easter.

West of Coffin Bay there are fewer places to stay, although all towns along the coast have at least one caravan park and there are plenty of spots where you can camp without facilities. Most townships along the Eyre Highway between Port Augusta and Ceduna have transit-style motels and caravan parks, as do the roadhouses west of Penong.

Several privately owned islands, such as Boston Island off Port Lincoln, offer accommodation mainly for extended stays.

There's backpacker accommodation at Whyalla, Streaky Bay and, on the Eyre Highway, at Kimba and Pandurra Station (between Port Augusta and Iron Knob).

Getting There & Away

Air Kendell Airlines flies daily from Adelaide to Port Lincoln ($116) and Whyalla ($114), and daily except Saturday to Ceduna ($194). Lincoln Airlines (☎ toll-free 1800 018 234) flies between Port Lincoln and Adelaide for $90 four times daily. Whyalla Airlines (☎ toll-free 1800 088 858) has daily services from Adelaide to Cleve ($85), Wudinna ($135) and Whyalla ($90).

Bus Stateliner (☎ 8415 5555) has daily services from Adelaide to Port Augusta ($27.20), Whyalla ($31.10), Port Lincoln ($54.70), Ceduna ($64) and Streaky Bay ($57.30).

Boat There are plans for a ferry service between Wallaroo, on Yorke Peninsula, and Cowell. Check with the South Australian Tourism Commission for an update.

Getting Around

The Eyre Highway from Port Augusta to WA cuts across the northern part of the peninsula to Ceduna, then generally follows the coast to the border. It's 468 km from Port Augusta to Ceduna and another 482 km to the WA border.

The coast road around the peninsula is in two parts: the 344-km Lincoln Highway runs south-west from Port Augusta to Port Lincoln; and the 402-km Flinders Highway runs north-west from Port Lincoln to Ceduna.

Stateliner buses from Adelaide run to Whyalla, Port Lincoln and Ceduna with many stops along the way.

East Coast

Between Whyalla and Port Lincoln are the popular resort towns of Cowell and Tumby Bay; these and other small ports were busy shipping points in the days before heavy motor transport, and retain the character of those times.

WHYALLA (pop 25,000)

The largest city in the state after Adelaide, industrial Whyalla was born in 1901 when mining giant BHP constructed a 55-km tramway from Hummock Hill on the coast to its new iron ore mine at Iron Knob. Just a shipping point at first, the town grew slowly until 1938, when the threat of war caused a dramatic expansion in industrial activity. A deep-water port was dredged and a blast furnace and five-berth shipbuilding facility were built. A pipeline bringing water from Morgan on the Murray River was completed in 1944, resulting in further development in steel-making and shipbuilding.

Economic difficulties and loss of markets to overseas competition caused the shipyards to close in 1978. The population reached a peak of 33,400 in 1976, but steadily declined throughout the '80s due to continuing recession in the SA manufacturing sector. In 1994, Whyalla produced 1.2 million tonnes of raw steel and 1.5 million tonnes of pellets from ore mined at Iron Knob, Iron Monarch, Iron Princess and Iron Duke.

Information

The helpful Whyalla Tourist Centre (☎ 8645 7900), on the Lincoln Highway at the northern entrance to town, is open from 8.45 am to 5.10 pm weekdays, 9 am to 4 pm on Saturday and 10 am to 4 pm on Sunday. You can't miss it – it's beside a large naval vessel sitting high and dry beside the road.

Things to See & Do

On the highway 10 km north of town, the 1100-hectare **Whyalla Conservation Park** has myall and saltbush communities; euros, grey and red kangaroos and over 70 species of birds can be seen here. There's a walking trail from the car park to the top of **Wild Dog Hill**, a prominent sandstone outcrop in the park's north-west corner.

Next to the tourist centre, the **Maritime Museum** features the 650-tonne, WWII corvette HMAS *Whyalla*. It's open daily from 10 am to 4 pm and guided tours leave on the hour between 11 am and 3 pm; admission is $5.

Tours of the **BHP steel works** cost $6 and start from the tourist centre at 9.30 am on Monday, Wednesday and Saturday. They take 2½ hours and cover everything from where the ore comes in, to where the steel goes out. Long trousers, long-sleeved shirts and closed footwear are essential.

Hummock Hill Lookout gives a good view of the town, BHP complex and Spencer Gulf. The concrete fortifications housed a WWII anti-aircraft battery which was supposed to protect the shipyards from Japanese attack; as there were only four guns (one is still there) it's a good job nothing eventuated. The distant jetty to the east is at **Lowly Point**. Ships are loaded here with natural gas piped from Moomba, in the state's north-east.

The historic **Mt Laura Homestead**, on Ekblom St, has been overtaken by the town and is now a museum. It's open Sunday, Monday and Wednesday from 2 to 4 pm and Friday from 10 am to noon; admission is $2.

Set in attractive bushland on the Lincoln Highway seven km south of town, the informal **Whyalla Wildlife & Reptile Sanctuary** is the state's largest wildlife park outside the Adelaide area. It has a good collection of native reptiles, over 50 species of native mammals and a huge walk-through aviary. It's open daily from 10 am to dusk and admission is $5. Allow at least two hours for a visit.

The town's major entertainment venue is the **Middleback Theatre** on Nicholson Ave. There's usually something happening here, whether it be films, an art exhibition, live theatre or variety entertainment. The tourist centre has programmes.

Places to Stay

Caravan Parks & Hostels Two km from the town centre, and with a beach frontage, the *Whyalla Foreshore Caravan Park* (☎ 8645 7474) on Broadbent Terrace has tent/caravan sites for $10/13, on-site vans for $24 and cabins from $28.

A friendly Finnish couple own the *Hillview Caravan Park* (☎ 8645 9357), off the Lincoln Highway five km south of town. Their rates are similar except cabins cost from $35.

Backpackers' accommodation is available at the *Bushman's Rest* (☎ 8644 0620), 46 Aikman Crescent. Beds in a shared room are $13 for a one- to three-night stay, or you can have a private room for $14.

Hotels & Motels Rooms in the town's four hotels all have private facilities. The cheapest rate for singles/twin share is $25/30 offered by both the *Hotel Spencer* (☎ 8645 8411), on Playford Ave, and the *Lord Gowrie Hotel* (☎ 8645 1611), on Gowrie Ave.

Other hotels are the *Hotel Bayview* (☎ 8645 8544) on Forsyth St ($25/45) and the *Hotel Eyre* (☎ 8645 7188) on Playford Ave ($25/35).

Cheapest of the six motels is the *Sundowner Motor Inn* (☎ 8645 7688) at $42/46; it's on the Lincoln Highway near the airport, five km from town. The tourist office has details of other motels.

Places to Eat
There are plenty of places to eat in Whyalla. The pubs are good, as always; the *Eyre* has a smorgasbord and is considered the best value in town. *Vega's Bar & Bistro*, in the Westland Hotel/Motel on MacDouall Stuart Ave, has a salad bar and specials from $5. Also in the Westland, the *Bottle & Bird* is very popular with locals; you line up on one side for your booze, then on the other for takeaway chicken.

The *Oriental Inn* Chinese restaurant, at 83 Essington Lewis Ave, is considered the best of the Asian places. There are several Italian eateries including *Spaggs*, a BYO restaurant, also at 83 Essington Lewis Ave. It has dine-in and takeaway meals (including vegetarian) from $6, and they do a three-course special for $15.

Almost next door to the Oriental Inn, at No 89, the popular *Bogart's Caffé* has a stylish black-and-white decor and mouth-watering cakes. There's a comfortable lounge area upstairs where you can relax with coffee.

Getting There & Away
Kendell Airlines and Whyalla Airlines both fly daily from Adelaide for $114 and $90 respectively.

Stateliner has daily buses from Adelaide ($31.10) to the bus station at 23 Darling Terrace.

Getting Around
There is no bus service to the airport, but you can use the public phone there to ring Des's Cabs (☎ 8645 7711) – they charge around $8 to the town centre.

Hire cars are available from Avis (☎ 8645 9331), Budget (☎ 8645 5333) or Hertz (☎ 8645 3354). Whyalla City Transport (☎ 8645 7257) operates a town bus service – the tourist centre has details.

COWELL (pop 700)
Once an important port, this pleasant little town on mangrove-fringed **Franklin Harbor** was settled in the 1850s when the brothers McKechnie emigrated from Scotland and established Wangaraleednie Station.

In the nearby Minbrie Range is a large **jade deposit** with several mines, all of which have closed due to marketing difficulties. Local jade products are sold at the Jade Motel, on the highway at the northern end of town.

There's a small **folk museum** in the old post office (next door to the 'new' one) and an **agricultural museum** on the Lincoln Highway. Oysters are farmed locally, and you can buy them from several outlets for as little as $5 a dozen.

Cleve (population 750) is 42 km inland from Cowell in the scenic Minbrie Range. It has an interesting National Trust agricultural and folk museum in the old council chambers – ask at the council office for a key. The *Cleve Hotel/Motel* (☎ 8628 2011), on Fourth St, has pub rooms for $20/30 and motel units for $45/55.

Places to Stay
Two km north of town, the basic *Harbour View Caravan Park* (☎ 8629 2216) has camp sites for $8, on-site vans for $20 and cabins from $26.

Close to the town centre, the *Cowell Foreshore Caravan Park* (☎ 8629 2307) charges

$10/12 for tent/caravan sites, $27 for on-site vans and from $32 for cabins. It also has dinghies you can hire for $60 a day.

There are two lovely old pubs in the main street: the *Franklin Harbour Hotel* (☎ 8629 2015) has rooms for $15/25/33/41, while the nearby *Commercial Hotel* (☎ 8629 2181) charges $20/30. Otherwise there's the *Jade Motel* (☎ 8629 2002), which charges $50/55.

For something more homely there's *Schultz Farm* (☎ 8629 2194), where spacious rooms cost $25 per person including a cooked breakfast. It's on Smith Rd about one km south-west of town.

SOUTH OF COWELL
Elbow Hill

The first township heading south from Cowell on the Lincoln Highway is tiny Elbow Hill, at 15 km. From here you can drive to **Point Gibbon** (six km), which has cliffs and beautiful beaches; en route you pass four concrete **bunkers**, the remains of a WWII communications facility.

The very hospitable *Elbow Hill Inn* (☎ 8628 5012), in the old telegraph office, has light lunches daily and gourmet dinners on Friday and Saturday nights. There's a double room with en suite ($60 B&B for two persons), or you can stay in a renovated church ($75 B&B for two).

Arno Bay & Port Neill

Forty-three km from Cowell, **Arno Bay** (population 300) has a nice swimming beach and a fishing jetty. You can stay at the basic *Arno Bay Caravan Park* (☎ 8628 0085) or in the town's grandest building, the *Hotel Arno* (☎ 8628 0001).

Turn left 33 km past Arno Bay to picturesque **Port Neill** (population 200), which boasts two good swimming beaches. There are some interesting exhibits including vintage engines and vehicles at **Vic & Jill's Living Museum**, opposite the caravan park; it's open daily (just knock on the house door, or get a key from the caravan park).

Port Neill has a caravan park (☎ 8688 9067) and pub (☎ 8688 9006) where you can stay.

Tumby Bay (pop 1100)

Named by Matthew Flinders in 1802, the bay is now graced by a very attractive town with a wonderful seaside atmosphere; its long, curving white-sand beach is one of the peninsula's nicest. The best swimming is west of the jetty.

Hales Mini Mart (☎ 8688 2584) on North Terrace (the Port Lincoln road) has tourist information and also hires tandem bicycles ($3 per hour).

Tumby Bay has a number of interesting old buildings including the original school house, on Lipson St. This now houses the **CL Alexander National Trust Museum**, open Friday and Saturday from 2.30 to 4.30 pm.

On Thurunna Rd, about 10 km south of town, the **Shoalmarra Quandong Farm** claims to be the largest quandong orchard and nursery in Australia. Tours run on Tuesday at 9.30 am and 2.30 pm, when you can try and buy quandong products.

About five km south-east of town, **Ski Beach** is a popular swimming and picnic spot. From here you can wade out to **Tumby Island Conservation Park** – the water is knee-deep at low tide. This is a rookery for several bird species, including Cape Barren geese, and there's good fishing on the Gulf side.

The **Sir Joseph Banks Group of Islands**, 25 km south-east of town, form a marine conservation park, with bird rookeries, sea lion colonies and excellent scuba diving. An old homestead and scattered implements are evidence of past farming activity. LEP Boat Charters and Yachtaway, both based in Port Lincoln, offer diving, fishing and sightseeing charters to the islands (see the following section on Port Lincoln).

At **Koppio**, a farming centre in picturesque hills 25 km south-west of Tumby Bay, there's the National Trust's excellent **Koppio Smithy Museum**, open daily except Monday from 10 am to 5 pm. It has an extensive and varied collection of memorabilia, including numerous restored vintage tractors and engines.

Across the road, **Kurrabi Lodge Cottage**

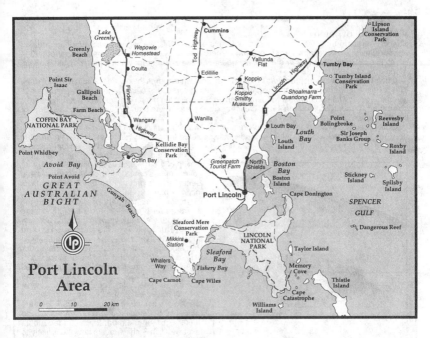

Port Lincoln Area

0   10   20 km

Crafts serves Devonshire teas in a wonderful home-garden setting. The friendly proprietor's dried-flower and gum-nut arrangements really are amazing; her scones aren't bad either.

Places to Stay & Eat On the foreshore, the large and attractive *Tumby Bay Caravan Park* (☎ 8688 2208) has tent/caravan sites for $12/14, on-site vans for $26 and self-contained cabins for $38.

The *Sea Breeze Hotel* (☎ 8688 2362) on Tumby Terrace has pub rooms for $19/27, while the grand *Tumby Bay Hotel* (☎ 8688 2005), on North Terrace, charges $19/29. On Berryman Terrace, the basic *Tumby Bay Motel* (☎ 8688 2311) has units from $50/60.

Both the pubs do counter and dining room meals, or there's *Tumberlinas* on Lipson Rd for a more intimate atmosphere and home-style cooking. Otherwise there are several takeaways and a good bakery.

At **Louth Bay**, 31 km south of Tumby Bay, there's a camping area with toilets close to a sandy beach.

PORT LINCOLN (pop 13,000)

Port Lincoln, at the southern end of the Eyre Peninsula, is 662 km from Adelaide by road but only 250 km as the crow flies. It was named by Matthew Flinders after his home county of Lincolnshire and is considered the finest natural harbour in SA. It's certainly the most attractive, with hills all around and Boston Island protecting the entrance.

Governor Gawler wanted to make Port Lincoln the site for the capital, but Colonel Light rejected it because of its lack of fresh water. The first settlers arrived in 1839 and made a good start. Yet within three years the settlement was in danger of being abandoned due to economic problems and the fear of Aboriginal attack. A number of whites were killed, and at least as many blacks shot or hung in reprisal. By 1845 the local Aborigines had been 'pacified', although violence continued

A Mouthful of Teeth

Sharks were around 150 million years before the dinosaurs, having evolved from a group of armour-plated animals known as Placoderms. There are 375 known species worldwide, about 90 of which live in South Australian waters. The largest of these is the great white shark, or white pointer, which grows to eight metres.

One of the most efficient predators on Earth, the great white roams the oceans of both hemispheres. The primitive fear and loathing that we have for anything capable of biting large chunks out of us has given the great white an undeserved reputation. In SA, only nine persons have been taken by sharks since the first recorded attack in 1926. Over the same period more than 1200 people have drowned, but that doesn't put us off swimming.

Until recently the popular attitude to great whites was 'the only good shark is a dead one', and decades of unrestrained slaughter have seriously depleted their numbers. Today, there is a growing awareness that these are magnificent creatures with an essential role to play in their environment.

With some estimates placing the global population of great whites as low as 2000, the state government is considering joining California and South Africa in protecting them. Their proposals include: banning game-fishing of the species; extension of marine park boundaries; and the development of a limited-entry licensing scheme for the shark-viewing industry. Observing great white sharks from boats and submerged cages is growing in popularity in Port Lincoln, which is close to global 'hot spots' at Dangerous Reef and the Neptune Islands.

Although commercial fishing of great whites was banned in SA in 1994, many juveniles drown each year after becoming entangled in nets. Two species of shark – gummy and school shark – are commercially fished in SA, with the annual catch being around 1000 tonnes. Called 'flake', this shark meat once ended up in takeaway fish & chips, but is now more likely to be found in restaurants. With Asian diners prepared to pay up to $20 for a bowl of shark-fin soup there seems little likelihood that shark-netting will end in the near future. ■

---

elsewhere on the peninsula until at least the 1860s as settlement spread outwards.

Since these unpromising beginnings, Port Lincoln has grown into a thriving and prosperous town. It has the state's largest grain-exporting terminal and most of its tuna fleet is based here. Fishing is big business; there are over 40 tuna farms in Boston Bay and the town has several seafood-processing factories.

Information

The tourist office (☎ 8682 6666) is at the Eyre Travel Centre on Tasman Terrace. It's open from 9 am to 5.30 pm weekdays, 9 am to noon on Saturday and (during school holidays only) 10 am to noon on Sunday.

The NPWS office (☎ 8688 3111) has the annual Eyre Parks Pass, which costs $30 per car and entitles you to unlimited entry and camping at all Eyre Peninsula's conservation areas, excluding the far west. Otherwise, the entry fees to Lincoln National Park (see Around Port Lincoln) and Coffin Bay National Park (see Port Lincoln to Streaky Bay) are $3 per vehicle ($5 Memory Cove) and camping fees are $4 per vehicle per night ($10 Memory Cove).

Things to See & Do

On Dorset Place is the **Old Mill** (1846), built as the tower for a flour mill which was never completed; you can climb up to the lookout for nice views out over the bay. The **Lincoln**

Hotel dates from 1840, making it the oldest hotel on the peninsula.

On the Flinders Highway, **Mill Cottage** is a historic homestead built in 1866. It houses many artefacts from the Bishop family, who came to Port Lincoln in 1839, and is open daily except Monday from 2 to 4.30 pm. Nearby, at the Eyre Peninsula Old Folk's Home, the **Rose-Wal Memorial Shell Museum** ($2) has a huge collection of seashells. It opens daily between 2 and 4.30 pm.

The **Axel Stenross Museum** ($3), on the coast by the Lincoln Highway, doesn't look too promising, but its relics and photographs of the windjammer days are said to be quite interesting. You can visit the museum most days from 1 to 5 pm.

Winters Hill Lookout, five km from town off the Flinders Highway, gives a beautiful view over the town and surrounding bay and countryside. Go in the afternoon for the best photographs.

Organised Tours

Port Lincoln has a variety of land and sea tours and all can be booked through Eyre Travel.

Great Australian Bight Safaris (☎ 8682 2750) has an excellent range, including a town tour ($20), a town tour plus Whalers Way ($55), 4WD day tours to Memory Cove ($55) and the Coffin Bay Peninsula ($65), a five-day sail-and-4WD safari ($650) and fishing trips (from $70).

Operating out of Adelaide, Great Bight Tours (☎ 8369 2773) has an excellent range of water-related tours, including a day's diving ($360), a weekend's sailing ($490) and two days game fishing (from $530) and diving ($570). All prices include return air fares from Adelaide but you can join at Port Lincoln if you want.

Yacht Away (☎ 8684 4240; mobile 018 083 529) has a very good reputation thanks to its personable skippers and comfortable

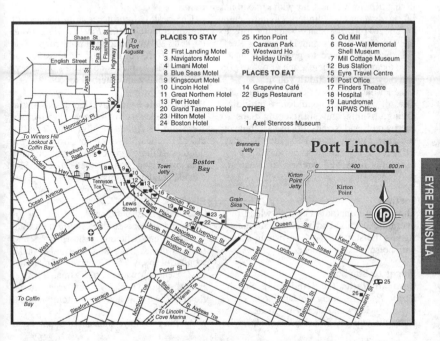

PLACES TO STAY

2 First Landing Motel
3 Navigators Motel
4 Limani Motel
8 Blue Seas Motel
9 Kingscourt Motel
10 Lincoln Hotel
11 Great Northern Hotel
13 Pier Hotel
20 Grand Tasman Hotel
23 Hilton Motel
24 Boston Hotel
25 Kirton Point Caravan Park
26 Westward Ho Holiday Units

PLACES TO EAT

14 Grapevine Café
22 Bugs Restaurant

OTHER

1 Axel Stenross Museum
5 Old Mill
6 Rose-Wal Memorial Shell Museum
7 Mill Cottage Museum
12 Bus Station
15 Eyre Travel Centre
16 Post Office
17 Flinders Theatre
18 Hospital
19 Laundromat
21 NPWS Office

Port Lincoln

EYRE PENINSULA

yachts. They do twilight, half-day, day and extended cruises to off-shore islands, with their yachts sleeping up to nine passengers. Costs are very reasonable: $85 per person for 24 hours all-up (except liquor) for a minimum of four passengers.

Thirty-one km offshore is Dangerous Reef, an important breeding area for the white pointer or great white shark. Sightings of sharks are rare, but you'll normally see plenty of Australian sea lions from the resident colony. Cruises to the reef can be arranged through Westward Ho Holiday Units (☎ 8682 2425). Prices start at $50 and include a visit to an underwater viewing area at a tuna farm moored near Boston Island. Trips to the tuna cost $27.

For a real adrenalin rush you can hang out over the side of a boat in a suspended cage to view white pointer sharks which (hopefully) are attracted by burleying – I'm told the success rate is around 65% to 70%. Westward Ho has four and five-day live-aboard diving trips for $2400 a day with a maximum of six divers. The Flinders Diving Centre (☎ 8682 4140) has shark-watching trips to the Neptune Islands and Dangerous Reef, but specialises more in group bookings – give them a ring if there's one or two of you and they may be able to fit you in.

LEP Boat Charters (☎ 8688 2311) do half-day, day and extended tours including diving, fishing and sightseeing trips to nearby reefs and islands. Prices vary, but you can expect to pay around $55 for a half-day, $100 for a day and $180 per day for over-nighters, provided there's at least six passengers.

Festival
The annual Tunarama Festival, which runs over the Australia Day weekend in January, signals the start of the tuna-fishing season with boisterous merriment.

Places to Stay
Caravan Parks On Hindmarsh St, the *Kirton Point Caravan Park* (☎ 8682 2537) has nice views and plenty of shade. For a camp site you pay $5 per person, otherwise

it's $14 for powered sites, $22 for basic cabins, $43 for deluxe cabins and $35 for on-site vans. You'll pay more for cabins and vans in peak periods, but considerably less for a week's stay in the off-season.

Hotels & Motels The cheapest of Port Lincoln's five hotels is the *Boston Hotel* (☎ 8682 1311) on King St, which has pub rooms for $20/30/38 and self-contained rooms from $30/40/48.

Close behind is the venerable *Lincoln Hotel* (☎ 8682 1277), on Tasman Terrace, which charges $20/35 for rooms with shared facilities and $25/40 with private bathroom. The *Great Northern Hotel* (☎ 8682 3350) on Hallett Place charges $20/38/48.

On Tasman Terrace, the *Pier Hotel* (☎ 8682 1322) has self-contained rooms for $40/45. Also on Tasman Terrace, the *Grand Tasman Hotel* (☎ 8682 2133) has the best standard of the town's pubs – it charges $48/60 for its renovated self-contained rooms.

Cheapest, but not necessarily nastiest, of the seven motels is the *First Landing Motel* (☎ 8682 2919), about two km from town on Shaen St. Its units cost $44/48/56 for singles/twins/triples, and there's a honeymoon special with waterbed for $81.

Holiday Flats Eyre Travel has details on the several holiday flats in the area. They include *Westward Ho Holiday Units* (☎ 8682 2425), at 112 London St, which cost from $50 for doubles. If there's six of you, and you have your own linen, you can get a flat for $58 outside holiday periods.

Places to Eat
One of the most popular places in town for lunch and dinner is *Bugs Restaurant* on Eyre St, which has delicious pasta from $8 and seafood dishes from $13. They also make wonderful soups. *The Grapevine Café* in the Civic Centre Arcade, at 60 Tasman Terrace, is another good spot for lunch – they do pie floaters for $2.50 and large, home-cooked takeaways for $5.

All the pubs have substantial counter and

dining room meals; probably the best is the *Great Northern*, which is noted for seafood. The *Grand Tasman* has a reasonably priced a la carte restaurant, where you can also get good-value takeaways.

Entertainment

For films there's the Flinders Theatre, at 3 Hallett Place, with shows daily (usually afternoon and evening) except Monday and Tuesday. There's invariably a live rock band at one of the pubs on Friday and Saturday nights, while the Tasman Hotel has a regular disco on Friday night.

Getting There & Away

Kendell Airlines flies daily from Adelaide for $116 while Lincoln Airlines has four daily flights for $90.

Stateliner buses run daily from Adelaide via Cummins or Tumby Bay for $54.70; there is no public transport between Port Lincoln and Streaky Bay. The bus station is at 24 Lewis St in the city centre.

Getting Around

There is no bus service from town to the airport, but Lincoln City Taxis (☎ 8682 1222) have a 24-hour service and will do the trip for around $15. They charge around $50 for a ride to Coffin Bay.

The Port Lincoln City Bus Service (☎ 8682 2167) runs weekdays on five routes around town, although on most you'll be waiting a long time between buses.

The local hire-car agencies are Avis (☎ 8682 1072), Budget (☎ 8684 3668) and Hertz (☎ 8682 1933).

AROUND PORT LINCOLN

At the entrance to Boston Bay, **Boston Island** is a sheep-grazing property. You can have the entire island to yourself by renting it for $750 per week – the homestead accommodates 12. Contact Eyre Travel for details.

You can also stay at a holiday lodge on 400-hectare **Spilsby Island**, in the Sir Joseph Banks Group, for $100 for two people ($160 for four) plus $50 per person return flight from Port Lincoln; ring ☎ 8684

5013 for details and bookings. The island has lovely beaches and good swimming and snorkelling.

There are several **surfing and diving** spots elsewhere around town. For information about the best areas, contact the Port Lincoln Skin-Diving & Surfing Centre (☎ 8682 4428), at 73 Mortlock Terrace. You can also hire scuba diving equipment, provided you're a licensed diver.

Cape Carnot, better known as Whalers Way, is 32 km south of Port Lincoln. It features rugged coastal scenery with 120-metre-high cliffs and lookouts. At **Fishery Bay** are the remnants of a whaling station, abandoned in 1842. There are fur seals at spectacular **Cape Wiles**, while poignant memorial plaques at Cape Carnot recall the anglers and others who've been swept off the rocks by king waves. The area is privately owned, but you can visit by obtaining a permit ($15 plus key deposit) from most petrol stations or from the Eyre Travel office in Port Lincoln. This is valid for 24 hours and enables you to camp at Redbanks or Groper Bay.

En route to Whalers Way you pass **Sleaford Mere**, a large brackish lake with waterbirds and stromatolites. A little further on is the turn-off to **Sleaford Bay**, with its beautiful beaches. Cabins are available for overnight or weekly stays at the *Sleaford Bay Holiday Park* (☎ 8688 3177).

Continuing on towards Whalers Way is **Mikkira**, the first sheep station on Eyre Peninsula. You can visit its **koala sanctuary** (closed November to February) with a permit ($8) from most petrol stations in Port Lincoln.

Lincoln National Park

South of Port Lincoln, and accessed from the Whalers Way road, this 29,100-hectare park has a magnificent coastline of quiet coves, sheltered beaches and sheer cliffs. Apart from some cleared areas showing past farming activity, most of the park is covered by thick mallee scrub. There are a number of bush camp sites, as well as caravan access to a couple of spots. If you don't have an Eyre

Parks Pass you'll need to obtain camping and/or entry permits from the rangers at the park entry station.

The park has a good network of unsealed roads and tracks, over 60% of which are suitable for conventional vehicles. You will definitely need a 4WD to negotiate the tracks to the huge **Sleaford and Wanna Dunes**, in the south-west, and to tranquil **Memory Cove**, in the south-east about 50 km from Port Lincoln.

At Memory Cove is a **memorial** to the two officers and six crew who drowned off Cape Catastrophe during Matthew Flinders' 1802 expedition. There are a number of tall rugged islands off the coast here – some visible as you drive along the high clifftops towards Memory Cove – and Flinders named eight of them after the missing men.

South-West Coast

The Flinders Highway from Port Lincoln to Ceduna takes you past a number of popular summer holiday destinations, including Coffin Bay, Elliston and Streaky Bay. Scattered between them are smaller resorts and beautiful surf beaches where you can ride the waves or go fishing.

PORT LINCOLN TO STREAKY BAY

The most scenic part of the entire coastal route from Port Augusta to Ceduna is the section from Port Lincoln to past Coffin Bay. For about 75 km you drive through rolling farmland with beautiful gums and occasional freshwater lakes and brooding hills, then it's back to the dreariness of stunted mallee and wheat paddocks.

Coffin Bay

Ominous-sounding Coffin Bay (named by Matthew Flinders to honour Sir Isaac Coffin, a British Lord of the Admiralty) is a large and attractive estuary with many quiet beaches. There's also good fishing, particularly for the revered King George whiting.

Coffin Bay township (usual population 200) literally bursts at the seams in January. From here you can visit wild coastal scenery along the ocean side of Coffin Bay Peninsula, which is entirely taken up by the 28,100-hectare **Coffin Bay National Park**. Entry to the park costs $3 per car, which you pay at the ranger station (☎ 8685 4047) near town.

Access to conventional vehicles is limited within the park; you can get to scenic **Point Avoid** (20 km) and adjoining **Gunyah Beach** quite easily, but otherwise you need a 4WD. If you're experienced in soft sandy conditions try the 50-km track to **Point Sir Isaac**, taking care with tide times on **Seven Mile Beach**. Allow a full day for this trip.

For something less arduous, the 1780-hectare **Kellidie Bay Conservation Park**, east of the township, is good for birdwatching (113 species), with some unusual species such as the buff-banded rail and the wood sandpiper.

If you don't have an off-road vehicle, Riji Dij Safaris (☎ 8685 5005) do half-day ($45), full-day ($90) and two-day ($150) **4WD tours** into the national park from Coffin Bay. They also do tag-along tours.

You can hire dinghies and runabouts at Hire Boat Haven opposite the caravan park; a four-metre runabout costs $65 per day plus fuel.

Places to Stay & Eat The *Coffin Bay Caravan Park* (☎ 8685 4170) is the only place in town where you can camp ($8); it also has on-site vans ($25) and cabins ($35). There are motel units at the *Coffin Bay Hotel* (☎ 8685 4111) from $48/55. It does counter meals from $4, otherwise there are a couple of basic takeaways.

The township has a large number of holiday flats, homes and cottages. The best people to ring about bookings are Myles Pearce Real Estate (☎ 8685 4063) in Coffin Bay.

Bush camping (no drinking water and generally difficult access) is allowed at several places in the national park. Permits cost $4 per car.

Coffin Bay to Elliston
At the fading hamlet of **Wangary**, on the Flinders Highway 14 km past the Coffin Bay turn-off, a gravel road leads to **Farm Beach**. This is a popular boat-launching spot – you'll know it by the old tractors, which are used to pull boats into the sea. You can camp on the beach (4WD only) or by the nearby toilet block.

Further north is the stretch of coastline known as **Gallipoli Beach**, so-called because it was the location for the Peter Weir film *Gallipoli*.

Near **Coulta**, 18 km from Farm Beach, gravel roads lead to **Convention Beach**, **Greenly Beach** and **Coles Beach**, all popular surfing and surf-fishing spots. If you don't want to camp rough near the beach,

Wepowie Ostrich Farm (☎ 8687 2063), on the Edillilie road about five km north of Coulta, has on-site vans and does B&B.

Turning off 67 km past Coulta, the road to **Sheringa Beach** takes you past huge white dunes and **Round Lake**, which has excellent windsurfing and sheltered camp sites. The beach is another good surfing spot – the breaks here are suitable for all classes, including beginners.

You can buy fuel, basic provisions and takeaways at the Sheringa Store on the highway.

Spectacular **Locks Well Beach**, 23 km past the Sheringa turn-off, is a famous salmon-fishing spot. To get to the beach you have to scramble down a steep slope; fortunately there's a chain to hang onto.

Return of the Bettong
At the time of European settlement, the brush-tailed bettong (*Bettongia penicillata*) was widespread in the open forests and woodlands across southern Australia. It's now rare, having vanished in the wild apart from a few scattered populations on islands and the WA mainland.

One of a group generally referred to as 'rat kangaroos', the bettong has an average length, including its tail, of about 65 cm. It appears to mainly eat the fruiting bodies of underground fungi, supplementing this uninspiring diet with roots and insects. Its nest is a domed affair made of grass and shredded bark, which it carries to the site using its tail.

Prior to its extinction in SA the bettong was one of many marsupial species that inhabited the Venus Bay area, on the west coast of Eyre Peninsula. In 1994, the National Parks & Wildlife Service decided to attempt a reintroduction programme. A rabbitproof fence was built across the neck of the peninsula in the Venus Bay Conservation Park, and the numbers of foxes and feral cats were reduced by baiting and trapping. Finally, 67 bettongs were released.

Late in 1995 the bettongs appeared to be doing well, although an 8.5 kg feral cat accounted for a number of them before it was trapped. The exercise is proving the theory that if only foxes and cats can be controlled, the potential to reintroduce native animals to their former range is unlimited. ■

EYRE PENINSULA

Elliston (pop 240)

A nondescript town on tranquil Waterloo Bay, 167 km from Port Lincoln, Elliston was created in the 1860s as a shipping point for wool. It has a beautiful swimming beach and (allegedly) one of the best jetties in SA from which to fish for tommy ruff.

Just north of town, take the rough seven-km loop road to **Salmon Point** and **Anxious Bay** for some dramatic ocean scenery. En route you pass **Blackfellows**, which has some of the best surfing breaks on the west coast. From the clifftop you can see distant **Flinders Island**, where there's a sheep station and tourist accommodation; Flinders Island Holidays (☎ 8626 1132) in Streaky Bay can provide details.

Places to Stay & Eat There are two caravan parks. The basic *Elliston Jetty Caravan Park* (☎ 8687 9061), on the Flinders Highway north of town, has tent/caravan sites for $10/12, on-site vans for $20 and cabins from $22. It's popular with visiting surfers and the manager, John Burtonwood, can tell you all about surfing and fishing on the west coast.

In town, the *Waterloo Bay Caravan Park* (☎ 8687 9076) charges similar prices, but has much better facilities.

Alternatively, the *Elliston Hotel* (☎ 8687 9009) has self-contained rooms for $35 and dinners from $8. The nearby *Ellen Liston Motel & Holiday Flats* (☎ 8687 9028) has motel units with kitchen for $45/50/58/66 and holiday units for $35 for two people (extras are $5).

North of Elliston

The 8400-hectare **Lake Newland Conservation Park** starts about 20 km north of Elliston. Containing huge white dunes, wetlands and yet another long surf beach, it continues a further 20 km up the coast to **Talia Caves**. Here you can explore colourful low cliffs, collapsed crevices and sinkholes.

Seven km beyond the Talia Caves turn-off a road takes you to **Mt Camel Beach**, another good salmon spot. Just to the north on Venus Bay are the small sleepy resorts of

Venus Bay and **Port Kenny**, both with quiet beaches and small caravan parks.

There's 4WD access into the 1650-hectare **Venus Bay Conservation Park** on the northern side of the bay. The park has kangaroos, prolific birdlife (including ospreys, pelicans and migratory waders), breathtaking coastal scenery and a bush camping area.

Baird Bay Area

Between Port Kenny and Streaky Bay, gravel roads take you by various routes to **Point Labatt**, where there's a large colony of Australian sea lions. You can view the animals from the clifftop, 50 metres above.

At **Sceale Bay**, 23 km north of Point Labatt (28 km south of Streaky Bay) there are cliffs and a long sandy beach where you can swim, surf and fish. There's also the new *Sceale Bay Caravan Park* (☎ 8626 5099).

Based at **Baird Bay**, a small fishing village 50 km south of Streaky Bay, Baird Bay Charters (☎ 8626 5017) does sightseeing, fishing and diving **charters** from $20 to $50 (a minimum of five passengers applies). They also have a large house you can rent.

Back on the Flinders Highway, the road to the west 21 km past Port Kenny (39 km from Streaky Bay) takes you to Point Labatt via **Murphy's Haystacks**. These tall, colourful weather-sculpted granite tors stand on a hilltop about two km from the highway.

A further 12 km towards Point Labatt on this road is the south-east corner of **Calpatanna Waterhole Conservation Park** (3600 hectares). You can camp at Wedina Well, in the park's north-east corner.

STREAKY BAY (pop 1000)

This attractive little fishing and agricultural centre gets its name from the 'streaks' of seaweed Matthew Flinders saw in the bay. Established as a wool port in 1865, when it was called Flinders, it soon consisted of a hotel, store, a couple of cottages and an Aboriginal ration station. A small oyster cannery was built in the 1870s. Oysters are farmed here and you can buy them cheap ($5 a dozen) from various outlets including the caravan park.

The main **information outlet** is the Shell Roadhouse on Alfred Terrace.

Across from the roadhouse, the **Restored Engine Centre** features numerous engines dating from 1904. It's open on Tuesday and Friday from 2 to 4 pm and at other times by arrangement. On Montgomery Terrace, and open the same hours, the National Trust's **Old School Museum** has many interesting exhibits, including a restored pioneer hut and mail coach.

The coastline near Streaky Bay has some outstanding scenery as well as surfing and fishing spots. **Cape Bauer**, about five km north-west of town, has high colourful cliffs. To the south, **Back Beach** is good for surfing and salmon fishing, as is **High Cliff** further on. **Yanerbie**, at the northern end of Sceale Bay, has white Sahara-like dunes and a swimming beach.

Streaky Bay Air Charter (☎ 8626 1385) offers **scenic flights**, with 30 minutes along the coast costing between $70/30 for two/five passengers.

Places to Stay & Eat

About a km from town, by a safe swimming beach, the attractive *Foreshore Tourist Park* (☎ 8626 1666) has tent/caravan sites from $11.25/14.50 and cabins from $30. The adjoining kiosk does good takeaways.

Dorm-style beds are $10 in *Labatt House* (☎ 8626 1126), on Alfred Terrace across from the Shell Roadhouse (you'll know it by the aquatic scenes painted on its front wall). It's said to be quite friendly, and its kitchen, dining room and lounge are spacious and clean.

Units at the nearby *Streaky Bay Motel* (☎ 8626 1126) cost $40/48, while just up the road in the centre of town, the comfortable *Streaky Bay Community Hotel/Motel* (☎ 8626 1008) has basic pub rooms for $25/30 and motel units for $44/52/66. Both serve meals.

Alternatively, *Headland House* (☎ 8626 1315) on Flinders Drive has a very good reputation, offering B&B in tastefully furnished rooms from $45/55.

SMOKY BAY (pop 100)

There's not much to do in Smoky Bay but fish, swim or lay on the beach contemplating your navel, and that's what attracts most visitors. There's a gravel road to scenic **Point Brown**, 26 km south-west; a whaling station operated at nearby **Point Collinson** between 1850 and 1860.

Twenty km north of Smoky Bay towards Ceduna, the 267-hectare **Laura Bay Conservation Park** has mallee scrub, rocky headlands, mangroves and tidal flats, making it an excellent spot for birdwatching. There are car parks by the shore.

The friendly *Smoky Bay Caravan Park* (☎ 8625 7030) is right on the foreshore and has tent/caravan sites for $7/10 and cabins from $16. Smoky Bay has a promising oyster-farming industry; you can buy fresh oysters for $5 a dozen at the general store, which has a bottle shop as well as fuel and provisions.

Eyre Highway & West Coast

PORT AUGUSTA TO CEDUNA

The Eyre Highway's first 140 km takes you through semi-arid station country to near Kimba, where the wheat paddocks begin. These keep you company all the way to Ceduna, with a string of small agricultural service centres and grain terminals in between.

There's not a huge amount of interest on this route apart from the Iron Knob mine and some granite outcrops near Wudinna and Minnipa. A more adventurous, if longer and slower, alternative is to leave the highway at Iron Knob and take the gravel roads to Wudinna or Minnipa via the scenic Gawler Ranges.

Iron Knob (pop 275)

Australia's oldest working mine is 62 km south-west of Port Augusta. BHP commenced mining the iron ore deposits here in

1899, and built a tramway to its port at Whyalla two years later. Iron Knob and other open-cut mines in the Middleback Ranges produce 2.8 million tonnes of ore annually for processing at Whyalla.

Guided tours of the huge open cut leave from the Iron Knob tourist centre at 10 am and 2 pm weekdays except public holidays. Tours last about one hour and cost $3. The tourist centre is a mining museum and has an informative video on mining and steel-making.

In Leigh Creek you can stay at the caravan park (☎ 8646 2025), the hotel (☎ 8646 2013), or the basic motel (☎ 8646 2058) on the highway.

On the highway halfway between Port Augusta and Iron Knob, *Pandurra Station* (☎ 8643 8941) has backpacker beds ($15), single/twin rooms ($30/50) and tent/caravan sites for $12/15.

Gawler Ranges

Consisting of steep granite hills and ridges, the Gawler Ranges commence about 30 km north-west of Iron Knob and run west for 200 km. There's plenty of interest here, including picturesque scenery, unusual rock forma-tions, historic ruins, wildlife and, in spring, magnificent wildflowers.

Mt Ive Station, in the central ranges, has fuel sales, a store, tent sites ($12), bunkhouse accommodation ($15, or $30 if you want linen and blankets) and a communal kitchen. Run by the Andrew family, this 32,700-hectare sheep property is 121 km from Iron Knob. It has a number of attractions, includ-ing bushwalks, birdwatching (70 species) and access to **Lake Gairdner National Park**.

Kimba (pop 680)

The local Aboriginal word for 'bushfire', Kimba is the largest of the peninsula's north-ern wheat towns. Apart from grain silos, its most obvious feature is the **Big Galah** (ho hum!). This eight-metre-tall, steel-and-fibreglass likeness of the bird stands in front of a shop selling carved emu eggs and other novelties.

On the highway 18 km east of town, the 45,100-hectare **Lake Gilles Conservation Park** has diverse habitats, including salt lakes, granite outcrops, sandhills and tall mallee. There's 4WD access to Lake Gilles in the north, where you can camp.

Between Kimba and **Koongawa**, 57 km to the west, the highway passes close to the southern boundary of 127,150-hectare **Pinkawillinie Conservation Park**. Consist-ing mainly of jumbled sand dunes covered by mallee scrub, it's accessible off the gravel road from Koongawa to Buckleboo.

There's a caravan park and motel units ($54/62) at the *Kimba Motel* (☎ 8627 2040). The *Kimba Community Hotel/Motel* (☎ 8627 2007) has backpacker beds for $10, air-conditioned pub rooms for $20/35 and motel units from $40/52.

Tod Highway

Turning off the Eyre Highway at **Kyancutta**, a tiny grain terminal 88 km west of Kimba, the Tod Highway south to Port Lincoln passes through **Lock** (population 220) at 55 km.

Named after a local farmer who was killed in action in Belgium in WWI, Lock is central to three large conservation parks: **Hambidge** (38,000 hectares), **Hincks** (66,300 hectares) and **Bascombe Well** (31,300 hectares). The parks preserve tracts of the mallee scrub that originally covered most of Eyre Peninsula. Bascombe Well, which has stone ruins, old wells and stands of beautiful red gums, is probably the most interesting.

For places to stay, Lock has a very basic caravan park (caretaker ☎ 8689 1192), the *Lock Hotel/Motel* (☎ 8689 1181) and the *Boomerang Motel* (☎ 8689 1193).

Wudinna (pop 570)

This little township's main attraction is **Mt Wudinna**, a large granite inselberg. While interesting, it is nowhere near as spectacular as the local tourist industry would have you believe. A **tourist drive** links Mt Wudinna, 10 km north of town, with other granite outcrops in the area.

Gawler Ranges Wilderness Safaris (☎ 8680 2020; toll-free 1800 625 556) can arrange **horse treks** (from $30 for a day-ride) and tailor-made **4WD camping safaris** ($150 per day).

In Wudinna, the *Gawler Ranges Motel & Caravan Park* (☎ 8680 2090) has tent/caravan sites for $10/13, on-site vans from $18, cramped motel units for $45/50 and larger ones from $50/58. There's also the *Wudinna Hotel/Motel* (☎ 8680 2019), which has single pub rooms for $18 and self-contained units for $35/45.

At **Minnipa**, 37 km west, the friendly *Minnipa Hotel/Motel* (☎ 8680 5005) charges $20/32 in the pub and $40/50/55 in the motel.

Tiny **Poochera**, 35 km further on, has a pub (☎ 8626 3025) and adjoining caravan park.

CEDUNA (pop 3600)

Just past the junction of the Flinders and Eyre highways, Ceduna is at the start of the long, lonely drive across the Nullarbor Plain into WA. The town was founded in 1896, although there'd been a whaling station on St Peter Island, off nearby Cape Thevenard, back in 1850.

Ceduna is the service and administrative centre for the west coast, as well as being a major export terminal for cereal grains, salt and gypsum – the deep-water port is at nearby Thevenard. Its fishing fleet keeps three seafood-processing factories in business. A newer industry, oyster farming, is celebrated each October over a long weekend with the frivolous Oysterfest.

There are branches of the ANZ Bank and BankSA (the latter has an ATM), a Commonwealth Bank agency in the post office and an EFTPOS cash-withdrawal facility (maximum $500) in the Foodland Supermarket. All are on McKenzie St.

The tourist office, open Saturday mornings and weekdays from 9 am to 5.30 pm, is in the Ceduna Travel Centre (☎ 8625 2780) at 58 Poynton St.

Things to See & Do

The **Old Schoolhouse Museum** on Park Terrace has pioneer exhibits, but more interesting are the artefacts and newspaper clippings from the British atomic weapons programme at Maralinga. Entry costs $2 and it's open daily except Sunday – check at the tourist office for times.

Off the coast between Ceduna and Smoky Bay, the 18 islands of **Nuyts Archipelago** and the **Isles of St Francis** conservation parks have sea lions, little penguins and endangered greater stick-nest rats, which have vanished from the mainland. Millions of short-tailed shearwaters nest here each year before their winter migration to the northern hemisphere.

Just 28 km north of town, on the edge of the **Great Victoria Desert**, you enter the arid emptiness of the adjoining **Pureba Conservation Park** (144,400 hectares), **Yellabinna Regional Reserve** (2,522,700 hectares) and **Yumbarra Conservation Park** (327,600 hectares).

This vast area is best suited to experienced outback travellers, so seek advice from the NPWS office (☎ 8625 3144) at 11 McKenzie St before going there.

Denial Bay, 14 km west of town, has an oyster farm (☎ 8625 2933) which you can tour. The bay was the site of **McKenzies Landing**, the district's first farming settlement.

Organised Tours

Nullarbor Adventure Tours (☎ 8625 3447; mobile 015 397 360; toll-free 1800 650 477) have a range of options, including half-day ($70) and full-day ($105) tours in and around town. Their two-day whale-watching trip to Head of Bight costs $400, or you can do a four-day trip including whale-watching and the Nullarbor caves for $595.

Ceduna Boat Charter (☎ 8625 2654; mobile 018 859 477) does fishing and diving charters in the area. They also do sightseeing trips out to Nuyts Archipelago and, with Nullarbor Adventure Tours, fully catered surf and/or boat-fishing trips for $120 per day.

Places to Stay

Caravan Parks & Cabins Best of the local caravan parks is the attractive *Foreshore Caravan Park* (☎ 8625 2290), on South Terrace in the town centre. It has tent/caravan sites for $12/14 and cabins from $33.

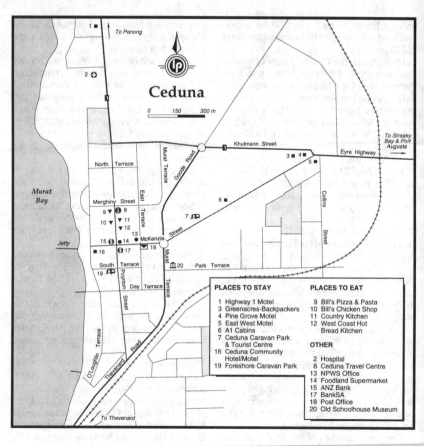

Ceduna

PLACES TO STAY

1 Highway 1 Motel
3 Greenacres-Backpackers
4 Pine Grove Motel
5 East West Motel
6 A1 Cabins
7 Ceduna Caravan Park & Tourist Centre
16 Ceduna Community Hotel/Motel
19 Foreshore Caravan Park

PLACES TO EAT

9 Bill's Pizza & Pasta
10 Bill's Chicken Shop
11 Country Kitchen
12 West Coast Hot Bread Kitchen

OTHER

2 Hospital
8 Ceduna Travel Centre
13 NPWS Office
14 Foodland Supermarket
15 ANZ Bank
17 BankSA
18 Post Office
20 Old Schoolhouse Museum

If the budget is all-important, *A1 Cabins* (☎ 8625 2578) at 41 McKenzie St has basic cabins for $22 singles/doubles; they'll sleep five for $31.

Also cheap is *Greenacres-Backpackers* (☎ 8625 3811), behind the Pine Grove Motel at 12 Kuhlmann St, where beds cost $12, or you can camp.

Hotels & Motels The *Ceduna Community Hotel/Motel* (☎ 8625 2008), on the foreshore on O'Loughlin Terrace, has pleasant pub rooms from $25/29 and motel units from $58/63/71.

On McKenzie St at the intersection with the Eyre Highway, the unpretentious *Pine Grove Motel* (☎ 8678 2201) has basic units with comfortable waterbeds for $44/49. Other motels are the *East West Motel* (☎ 8625 2101), opposite the Pine Grove, which has units from $58/63, and the *Highway 1 Motel* (☎ 8625 2208), which charges from $44/49.

Places to Eat

There are plenty of places to eat in Ceduna. The *Pine Grove Motel* has a small bar and does substantial dinners from $6, while the

EYRE PENINSULA

hotel also has good-value counter and bistro meals.

Poynton St has some good eateries. The *West Coast Hot Bread Kitchen* does great sandwiches and sit-down lunches, while the *Country Kitchen* is popular for coffee and cakes, as well as home-style cooked breakfasts and lunches.

Also on Poynton, *Bill's Pizza & Pasta* is amazing; it specialises in Greek food, but also does Australian, Bosnian, Chinese, French and Italian (a different country each day). It has daily lunch specials from $3, and there's nothing modest about the servings.

Getting There & Away
Kendell Airlines flies daily except Saturday from Adelaide for $194.

Stateliner has daily bus services from Adelaide ($64) to its station at 3 Day Terrace. Greyhound Pioneer buses pass through daily en route to WA ($146 to Norseman and $189 to Perth), calling in at the Pine Grove Motel.

Getting Around
There is no bus service from town to the airport, but A1 Cabs (☎ 8625 2964), which

has a 24-hour service, will run you in or out for around $6. You can rent a car from Budget (☎ 8625 2742) or Ceduna Rent-a-Car (☎ 8625 2085).

CEDUNA TO WA BORDER
Wheat and sheep paddocks line the highway to Nundroo, 150 km from Ceduna, then it's attractive eucalypt woodland until 50 km past Yalata roadhouse. The gums start to thin out before petering out altogether in a flat sea of shrubby bluebush 20 km later. You're now on the true **Nullarbor Plain** (*nullarbor* is Latin for 'no trees'), which is mainly to the north of the highway.

There's quite a bit of interest on this section. You can detour to good surf beaches between Ceduna and Penong, then visit the historic coastal township of Fowlers Bay. Past Yalata, there's whale-watching at Head of Bight and some great lookouts on the Nullarbor Cliffs.

Penong (pop 250)
This fading township has a historic shearing shed (1865), now converted into an interesting **museum and craft shop** (it's open daily

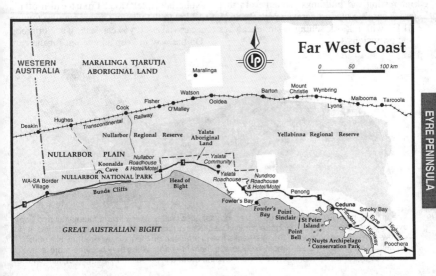

between 10 am and 4 pm). Coming from Ceduna, you turn off at 54 km to popular surfing and surf-fishing spots at **Point Bell** and **Rocky Point**.

Penong is the jumping-off point for **Point Sinclair**, 21 km to the south. On the ocean side of the point, **Cactus Beach** is one of Australia's most famous surfing spots. It has a number of strong breaks including left and right-handers, as well as waves suitable for beginners.

Ron Gates, manager of the *Point Sinclair Camping Ground* (☎ 8625 1036), is a mine of information on local surfing. You can camp here for $5 per person ($30 per week) but there's a 12-week limit. Ron supplies bore water for showers (use it sparingly) and firewood, but you must bring your own drinking water.

In town, the *Penong Hotel* (☎ 8625 1050) has pub rooms for $30/40.

Penong to Head of Bight

The turn-off to **Fowlers Bay** is 34 km west of Penong, and it's another 31 km to this virtual ghost town. Established as a wool port in the 1860s, Fowlers Bay was once the most isolated settlement in SA and several interesting old buildings remain from that era. There's a modest caravan park (☎ 8625 6143) with a kiosk selling basic takeaways and provisions.

Continuing west on the Eyre Highway there's accommodation at the *Nundroo Hotel/Motel* (☎ 8625 6120), 78 km from Penong, and the *Yalata Roadhouse* (☎ 8625 6807) 51 km further on. Nundroo has a 24-hour fuel stop and a restaurant. There's a selection of Aboriginal artefacts for sale at Yalata, which is owned by the nearby Yalata Aboriginal community.

Head of Bight

This is a major breeding area for **southern right whales**. Between 20 and 30 calves are born here each year between June and October, and most times from July to September you'll see up to six adults swimming along the cliffs. There are excellent lookout points but it's best if you have binoculars.

Entry permits for the observation area at Head of Bight (it's Aboriginal land) cost $5 per adult or $10 per vehicle and information can be obtained from the Yalata Roadhouse and the Nullarbor Hotel/Motel. You'll be asked to show the permit at the warden's hut on the way in – if you haven't already got your ticket you can buy one here.

The unmarked turn-off to Head of Bight is 78 km west of Yalata and 16 km east of the Nullarbor Hotel/Motel. From the turn-off it's 12 km to the viewing area; if you're towing a caravan ask if you can leave it at Nullarbor. On the way in keep an eye out for the bare

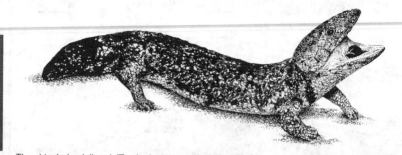

The shingle-back lizard *(Trachydosaurus rugosus)*, also called sleepy lizard, stumpytail and bog eye, is a member of the blue-tongue family. Despite its aggressive display when threatened, it is slow-moving and harmless. Shingle-backs like to sunbake on the road, where they are often squashed by drivers. You are most likely to see them in spring, when they become more active. The males in particular spend a lot of time stumping around in pursuit of the female of their choice.

EYRE PENINSULA

earth mounds beside the road that indicate wombat burrows.

Head of Bight to Border Village

At the Nullarbor tourist complex you enter the 558,300-hectare **Nullarbor National Park**, which follows the coast to the WA border. Although the surface is dry, flat and featureless, several world-class limestone caves open at sinkholes on the plain on both sides of the border. All are off-limits to casual visitors but you can inspect the **Murrawijinie Cave**, an overhang behind the Nullarbor Hotel/Motel. (For details of tours to the Nullarbor caves see the Caving section in the Activities chapter.)

From the motel you can drive north into the **Nullarbor Regional Reserve** (2.3 million hectares) and experience the awesome space, silence and solitude of the treeless plain. It's obvious why the Mirning Aboriginal people call it Undiri ('bare like a bone').

There are several signposted **lookouts** along the spectacular 80-metre-high Bunda Cliffs, where the tabletop plain nosedives into the Bight between Nullarbor and Border Village. Locals recommend the one 70 km west of Nullarbor as having the most extensive views.

The *Nullarbor Hotel/Motel Inn* (☎ 8625 6271) and *Border Village* (☎ (090) 39 3474), on the SA side of the border, both have caravan park, motel and restaurant facilities. Border Village has a 24-hour service station.

Outback

The wide open spaces of SA's arid outback stretch north from Port Augusta to the NT and Queensland borders. This mainly flat to undulating region covers about 80% of the state and has 1% of the population. Thanks to its low rainfall (250 mm to less than 150 mm annually) and high evaporation there is no agriculture here; apart from a few isolated waterholes in various creeks and rivers, the only permanent water is the chain of mound springs that marks the western rim of the Great Artesian Basin. About half the region consists of sandy and stony deserts and dry salt lakes, or is reserved Aboriginal land, with the remainder being used for low-intensity sheep and cattle grazing.

The outback contains most of the state's mineral wealth: the Moomba oil and gas field is a major contributor to state coffers, as is the Roxby Downs copper and uranium mine. Opals are mined at Andamooka, Coober Pedy and Mintabie, and promising gold discoveries were made recently in the Tarcoola area north of Ceduna. Although sparsely populated and often difficult to travel through without a 4WD vehicle (or a camel), the outback has plenty of interest. You can't help but be fascinated by the opal towns, while the natural and social history of the Oodnadatta Track is equally compelling. For an experience in remote touring, the Birdsville Track is unforgettable – as is a 4WD crossing of the Simpson Desert's silent emptiness.

In keeping with its wide horizons, the outback's conservation areas are *big*. Witjira National Park is in the western Simpson Desert, and Lake Eyre National Park includes (yes!) Lake Eyre; other parks cover the dry beds of Lake Torrens and Lake Gairdner. The Simpson Desert, Strzelecki and Innamincka regional reserves all sprawl across the map. Most are best reached in a 4WD, although parts of Witjira and Lake Eyre national parks and Innamincka Reserve are accessible to conventional vehicles.

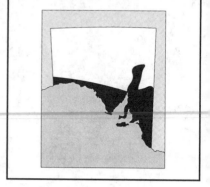

Public entry to most of the outback's western half requires a permit. Virtually the entire area is either Aboriginal land or part of the Woomera Prohibited Area.

Although the outback is a fascinating place, its harsh and uncompromising environment is entirely alien to most visitors.

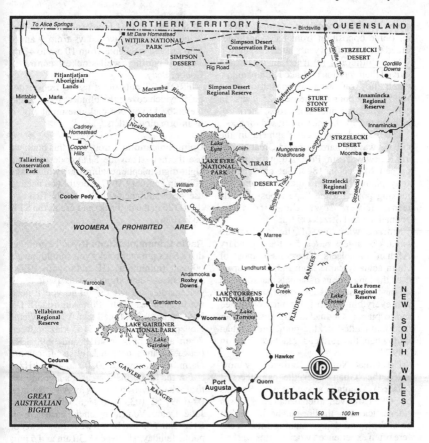

Outback Region

NORTHERN TERRITORY
QUEENSLAND

To Alice Springs
Birdsville
Mt Dare Homestead
WITJIRA NATIONAL PARK
Simpson Desert Conservation Park
STRZELECKI DESERT
SIMPSON DESERT
Rig Road
Cordillo Downs
Pitjantjatjara Aboriginal Lands
Macumba River
Simpson Desert Regional Reserve
Warburton Creek
Birdsville Track
Mintabie
Marla
STURT STONY DESERT
Innamincka Regional Reserve
Oodnadatta
Cadney Homestead
Neales River
Lake Eyre
Copper Creek
Innamincka
Copper Hills
Mungeranie Roadhouse
STRZELECKI DESERT
Moomba
Tallaringa Conservation Park
Stuart Highway
LAKE EYRE NATIONAL PARK
TIRARI
DESERT
Strzelecki Regional Reserve
Strzelecki Track
Coober Pedy
William Creek
Birdsville Track
Oodnadatta Track
WOOMERA PROHIBITED AREA
Marree
Tarcoola
Lyndhurst
FLINDERS RANGES
Lake Frome Regional Reserve
Andamooka
Roxby Downs
Leigh Creek
Lake Frome
Yellabinna Regional Reserve
Glendambo
LAKE TORRENS NATIONAL PARK
Woomera
Lake Torrens
NEW SOUTH WALES
LAKE GAIRDNER NATIONAL PARK
Lake Gairdner
Ceduna
GAWLER RANGES
Hawker
GREAT AUSTRALIAN BIGHT
Port Augusta
Quorn

0   50   100 km

Always be prepared for the fact that there is little drinking water and very few facilities of any kind for travellers away from the few towns and roadhouses.

European History

The first reports on the outback from explorers such as Edward John Eyre (1839) discouraged settlement. Twenty years later, however, John MacDouall Stuart was impressed by the grazing potential he found in the Lake Eyre Basin. His efforts in the region included an epic south-to-north crossing of the continent in 1862.

Following Stuart's success, and his favourable reports on the country he'd travelled through, the SA government decided to construct an overland telegraph line from Port Augusta to Darwin. The line, which took two years to build and was completed in 1872, became a conduit for settlement of the outback; enormous stations were established all the way to the NT border within a year or two of its completion. In the 1870s and '80s, more land was taken up to the north-east as far as the Queensland border.

In 1867, Lutheran and Moravian Brethren missionaries established mission stations among the Dieri people on Cooper Creek, but fierce opposition from the Aborigines forced them out four years later.

The Lutherans returned in 1877 and revived their mission on Lake Killalpaninna, which they ran as a sheep station with Aboriginal labour for the next 25 years. In 1914, when the once numerous Dieri had declined to 150, the mission closed for good.

The second major development in the outback was the narrow-gauge Great Northern Railway from Port Augusta, which reached Marree in 1883. Set on a barren stony plain, the town quickly became the trucking point for the huge mobs of cattle being driven down the Birdsville, Oodnadatta and Strzelecki tracks.

Marree was one of· the Australian outback's largest bases for the legendary 'Afghan' cameleers. These men, most of whom actually came from Pakistan, supervised the long strings of camels that supplied the far-flung stations and other settlements with everything from flour and corrugated iron to pianos. Oodnadatta became another important cattle-trucking point and Afghan base when the railhead reached there in 1889.

The Great Northern Railway (by now called the 'Ghan' after the cameleers it replaced) eventually arrived at Alice Springs in 1929. However, after decades of losses and inefficiency – the line had been built 'on the cheap', and delays running into weeks were often experienced when storms washed out the tracks – the Commonwealth decided to build a new line further to the west. The 'New Ghan' opened for business in 1980, following which the 'Old Ghan' line was closed.

Information

The Flinders Ranges & Outback of SA Regional Tourism Association (FROSART) has its main tourist office (☎ 8373 3430; toll-free 1800 633 060) at 56B Glen Osmond Rd in Parkside (a suburb of Adelaide); it's open weekdays from 9 am to 5 pm.

The region's major tourist information outlet is in the Wadlata Outback Centre

(☎ 8642 4511) at 41 Flinders Terrace in Port Augusta. It's open weekdays from 9 am to 5.30 pm and weekends from 10 am to 4 pm. There's another well-stocked centre in Coober Pedy.

FROSART puts out a useful free visitor guide which covers the Flinders Ranges and the outback; you can pick one up at any of its information outlets.

Communications Throughout this book we use the new statewide STD code (08) and eight-digit telephone numbers, which take effect in February 1997. Should you need to use the old number, simply take the first two digits (86 in the outback) and use as the STD code (086).

Radio Communications If you're going to drive SA's remoter tracks you should have a 50-watt (minimum) HF radio with RFDS frequencies – and know how to use it.

Regardless of where you go you'll need the frequencies of the Port Augusta RFDS base (☎ 8642 2044; call sign VNZ – Victor November Zulu). It uses 8165 kHz between 7 am and 5 pm, or 4010 and 6890 kHz between 7 am and 9 pm daily; its after-hours alarm frequencies are 2020 and 4010 kHz.

For the far northern areas it's a good idea to also have the frequencies for Alice Springs (☎ (089) 52 1033; call sign VJD – Victor Juliet Delta). You can reach the base here on 5410 and 6950 kHz on weekdays (except public holidays) between 8.30 am and 5 pm; for after-hours emergencies use 2020 and 5410 kHz.

Give the radio a long-range test before you leave civilisation, making sure that the emergency alarm button is operational. Telephone the RFDS radio operators (or better still call in personally) for a friendly chat and to familiarise yourself with their services.

Books The Royal Automobile Association of SA publishes *Outback South Australia*, a 312-page guidebook which includes the Alice Springs region and the parts of WA, Queensland and NSW that adjoin SA. If you want to do the Birdsville Track, Oodnadatta

Track, Simpson Desert or Strzelecki Track, Lonely Planet's *Outback Australia* has a detailed rundown on each.

The Natural History of the North East Deserts (Royal Society of SA, 1990) is another useful reference, giving a comprehensive description of the region's natural history.

More localised references are mentioned where applicable.

Maps The best available regional road map is the RAA's *Northern Areas*, while Westprint's *Desert Parks* shows how to get around the parks and reserves in the northeast of the state.

Meant more as a souvenir than a road guide, *Outback Central & South Australia*, published by the South Australian Department of Lands, is still an excellent tourist map with lots of interesting information.

For more localised coverage, Westprint has several popular maps, all with text giving a wealth of information. The *Birdsville & Strzelecki Tracks, Dalhousie & Simpson Desert, Innamincka & Coongie Lakes* and *Oodnadatta Track* maps should be purchased if you're going into those areas.

All Westprint's maps mentioned above come with your Desert Parks Pass (see below).

National Parks The National Parks & Wildlife Service has its Far North regional headquarters at Hawker (☎ 8648 4244), in the same building as the post office; contact them for details of all parks in the outback, including those north of the Nullarbor Plain. There's a ranger based at Innamincka.

National Park Permits

To visit the outback's national parks and conservation reserves you need a Desert Parks Pass, which costs $50 per vehicle. It's valid for a year and includes an excellent information booklet and detailed route and area maps.

If you just want to visit Cooper Creek in the Innamincka Regional Reserve, Lake Eyre in the Lake Eyre National Park or Dalhousie Springs in the Witjira National Park, you need only buy a day/night permit for $15 per vehicle. These are available from Mt Dare Homestead, the Pink Roadhouse in Oodnadatta, the William Creek Hotel, the Oasis Café in Marree and the ranger's office in Innamincka.

Desert Parks Passes are available in many places, including: Adelaide (the RAA and others), Alice Springs (Shell Todd service station), Birdsville Track (Mungeranie Roadhouse), Broken Hill (the RAA), Coober Pedy (Underground Books), Hawker (Hawker Motors), Innamincka (Trading Post), Marree (Ghan General Store, Oasis Café), Mt Dare Homestead, Oodnadatta (Pink Roadhouse), Port Augusta (Wadlata Outback Centre) and William Creek (William Creek Hotel).

For an update on outlets and park information, contact the Desert Parks HQ at PO Box 102, Hawker 5434, or ring them on ☎ 8648 4244.

Organised Tours

You can do town and mine tours at Andamooka, Coober Pedy and Roxby Downs, and visit the rocket-firing ranges at Woomera. If you've got a day to spare, the mail-run tours to remote homesteads from Coober Pedy and Cadney Homestead, a roadhouse on the Stuart Highway, are great value. You can also do three-day 4WD safaris from Coober Pedy to Witjira National Park. For details see the relevant sections later in this chapter.

A number of operators offer tours from Adelaide into the outback; SATC or FROSART can supply details.

Stateliner (☎ 8415 5555) has a three-day tour in a luxury coach to Roxby Downs and Andamooka for $199, meals not included.

If you want to visit the Pitjantjatjara people of north-western SA and learn something of their culture, the Aboriginal-owned Desert Tracks (☎ (089) 56 2144) is your best bet. The well-regarded tours range from two days ($480) to eight days ($1825) ex-Ayers Rock (minimum numbers apply).

Outback n' Coastal Tours (☎ 8250 2911)

has 4WD safaris along the Oodnadatta, Birdsville and Strzelecki tracks for around $130 per day (tours are from seven to 10 days). It also has a five-day opal tour for $695.

On weekends only, Dick Lang's Desert-Air Safaris (☎ 8264 7200) does round trips from Adelaide via Lake Eyre, the Simpson Desert, Birdsville, Innamincka, the Flinders Ranges and Leigh Creek. You stay overnight at Birdsville and land at the 'Dig Tree', Innamincka and Leigh Creek for land tours. The cost is $699 per person all-inclusive, with a minimum five passengers.

Scenic flights over Lake Eyre are available at William Creek and Marree.

Accommodation

The roadhouses scattered along the Stuart Highway all have caravan park and motel facilities. There's an excellent range including backpacker hostels in Coober Pedy, which has more accommodation than the rest of the outback put together.

Otherwise there is very little accommodation, apart from what you find at the few small centres such as Oodnadatta and Innamincka. The July school-holiday period sees heavy booking, so always check ahead if you don't want to camp.

There are countless good bush camp sites near the outback's main routes, although you may need a 4WD to get off the road. In warm weather the bushflies and mosquitoes can be bad; mosquito netting (or a tent with plenty of insect-screened ventilation space) is pretty well essential at such times. Large areas of the outback are devoid of firewood, so either carry some in your car or use a gas stove.

Always carry plenty of drinking water (the bore water on the Oodnadatta and Birdsville tracks is mainly undrinkable), and *never* camp near or pollute stock-watering points.

Getting There & Away

Air Kendell Airlines (bookings ☎ 13 13 00) flies daily from Adelaide to Coober Pedy and most days to Roxby Downs and Woomera (see the sections on these towns for details).

Bus Stateliner runs up the Stuart Highway daily to Coober Pedy, visiting Woomera and Roxby Downs along the way. Greyhound Pioneer and McCafferty's also go to Coober Pedy and continue on to Alice Springs and Darwin. These are the only bus services to the outback.

Stuart Highway

The Stuart Highway was named after the explorer John MacDouall Stuart, whose expeditions in SA and the NT took him through much of the country traversed by the road. You reach the NT border at 930 km from Port Augusta, after which it's 294 km to Alice Springs.

The highway passes through Coober Pedy; if you want to visit the other opal towns you can detour at Pimba through Woomera to Andamooka, and from Marla to Mintabie. There are several minor roads from the highway across to the Oodnadatta Track.

Fuel and accommodation facilities for travellers are scattered along the highway at Pimba (171 km from Port Augusta), Glendambo (285 km), Coober Pedy (535 km), Cadney Homestead (689 km), Marla (771 km) and Kulgera in the NT (949 km). All but Cadney and Kulgera have 24-hour fuel sales.

WOOMERA (population 1000)

Established in 1948, Woomera was used during the '50s and '60s to launch experimental British rockets and conduct tests in an abortive European project to send a satellite into orbit. In its heyday it housed 7500 people, but these days its main role is as a service town for the mostly US personnel working at Nurrungar, a communications facility at nearby Island Lagoon. Rocket launches and defence exercises are still carried out and there are signs that such activities will increase in the future.

A small **heritage centre** in the centre of town has several interesting displays on

---

Missiles & Bombs

Woomera (an Aboriginal term for a spear-throwing tool) was established by Britain and Australia as a base for international space research and the testing of guided missiles. In its heyday in the 1950s and '60s over 3000 rockets were launched, including a major programme of test firings of the 32-metre Europa rocket.

Things have been fairly quiet since, although a resurgence in activity in 1995 could mark the rebirth of the rocket range. The American space agency NASA fired a number of rockets late in 1995, while at the same time Japanese and Russians were showing interest in using the facility.

Further west, on the northern edge of the Nullarbor Plain, the British exploded atom bombs at Emu in 1953 and Maralinga in 1956 and '57; Maralinga is an Aboriginal word for thunder. The largest explosion, equivalent to a 26.6 kilotonne conventional bomb, was detonated on a balloon about 300 metres above ground level.

Between 1960 and '63 the British conducted a number of 'safety tests' with simulated bombs containing plutonium at Maralinga. These were detonated with conventional explosives to discover whether or not nuclear weapons would release nuclear energy in the event of an accident.

Prior to the tests, most of the nomadic Aborigines who lived in the area were moved to Yalata, west of Ceduna. Concerns about the effects of the tests on local Aboriginal people prompted a Commission of Enquiry in the mid-1980s. It found that they had suffered greatly because of the tests and that the bomb sites were still contaminated. The Commission also suggested that it was Britain's responsibility to clean up the mess. Finally, after years of argument and stalling, a $104-million clean-up (40% funded by the British Government) was due to commence in 1996. ■

Woomera's past and present roles, and what may happen in the future. Outside is a collection of old military aircraft, rockets and missiles. The centre is open daily from March to November from 9 am to 5 pm. It's closed during the summer.

Woomera Rocket Range Tours (☎ 8671 0788) takes you to local attractions such as the Koolymilka firing range and the main operational area at Range E. The tours take three hours and cost $26, with a minimum of four passengers.

Fuel at Woomera's two service stations is up to nine cents a litre cheaper than at nearby **Pimba**, on the highway. Pimba is a dramatic contrast to neat, leafy Woomera – stranded on a saltbush-covered plateau, it's one of SA's most unappealing towns.

Places to Stay & Eat

The *Woomera Travellers' Village* (☎ 8673 7800), near the town entrance, has backpacker accommodation for $12/20 singles/doubles, tent/caravan sites for $10/14, on-site vans from $25 and self-contained cabins for $50. There's a camper's kitchen of sorts.

The only alternative is the *Eldo Hotel* (☎ 8673 7867) on Kotara Ave ('Eldo' is the acronym for the European Launcher Development Organisation). It looks rather awful from the outside, but its ugliness is misleading; comfortable rooms with share facilities cost from $33/45/53, while self-contained rooms are $65 singles & doubles (extras $8). You can get good counter meals for around $8 and restaurant meals averaging $14 for a main course.

In Pimba, *Spud's Hotel* (☎ 8673 7473) has self-contained motel units for $20 per person.

Woomera's small shopping centre has a coffee lounge and snack bar with the usual takeaway fare.

Getting There & Away

Air Kendell Airlines (bookings ☎ 13 13 00) flies from Adelaide to Woomera on weekdays for $184.

Bus Woomera is seven km off the Stuart Highway from Pimba, and Stateliner and the long-distance bus lines pass through town daily. With Stateliner it's $45.50 to Adelaide and $39.40 to Coober Pedy.

ANDAMOOKA (pop 470)

Off the Stuart Highway, and 110 km north of Woomera by sealed road via Roxby Downs township, Andamooka is a rough-and-ready opal-mining centre with a strong frontier flavour; if you think Coober Pedy is barren and moonlike, wait until you see this place! Despite its Wild West 'badlands' appearance, however, the local residents are friendly and welcoming, as a rule. Unfortunately for them, the ground generally isn't safe enough to have dugouts in which to escape the searing summer heat, and air-conditioning is a luxury in a place where water often has to be trucked in.

Information

The best place to get information is the Andamooka Opal Showroom in the centre of town. Next door is the historic precinct, which has several fascinating old dugouts in the creek bank (get a key from the Andamooka Opal Showroom). The creek is the main road, so if it rains you don't go anywhere – the soil here is pure clay and all the 'streets' are like skating rinks when wet. It's a time when the residents go a little madder than usual.

Organised Tours

For an educational mine tour call in at the Treasure Chest, by the tall gums at the entrance to town. Tours ($4) leave at 2 pm daily (you drive yourself). Olympic Dam Tours (☎ 8671 0788) has a three-hour tour of the town and mines departing from Roxby Downs ($48) and Andamooka ($24).

Places to Stay & Eat

You can camp for $12 or stay in an on-site van from $27 at the dusty *Andamooka Caravan Park* (☎ 8672 7117). There's not much shade here – not that there is anywhere else in town. If you don't mind really roughing it, the *APOMA camping ground* at the entrance to town (just past the Treasure Chest) has camp sites for $2.

Alternatively, the *Andamooka Opal Hotel/Motel* (☎ 8672 7078) has basic pub-style rooms for $35/45 and motel units for $45/65. *Duke's Guesthouse* (☎ 8672 7007) was being upgraded and rates weren't available at the time of writing, but the management has a good name so check them out.

The best place in town to eat is the *Tuckerbox Restaurant*, which sells hearty meals for reasonable prices. You can also eat at the hotel.

Getting There & Away

Stateliner (☎ 8415 5555) has three buses a week from Adelaide to Andamooka ($88.60).

ROXBY DOWNS (pop 2000)

Just 30 km from Andamooka, but a world away in appearance, the modern Roxby Downs township is the dormitory and service centre for the huge **Olympic Dam** uranium, copper, gold and silver mine. The ore body was discovered in 1976 and the town developed in 1988 after much public soul-searching on the question of uranium mining. Plentiful underground water and better soil than Andamooka have allowed the whole town to be pleasantly landscaped.

There's a National Bank branch with an ATM in the town centre.

Surface tours of the mine and town cost $16.50. They run daily at 9.45 am from the Olympic Dam Tours office (☎ 8671 0788), next to the BP service station.

Places to Stay & Eat

The *Roxby Downs Caravan Park* (☎ 8671 1000) has lawned tent/caravan sites for $10/12 and on-site vans for $32. On Richardson Place in the town centre, the *Roxby Downs Motor Inn* (☎ 8671 0311) charges $88 for rooms and has a reasonably priced restaurant.

You can get good bistro and counter meals at the *Roxby Downs Tavern* across from the motel and, on Wednesday to Saturday nights, counter meals at the *Roxby Downs Club*. Otherwise there's a very good *bakery* in the town centre.

Getting There & Away

Kendell Airlines (bookings ☎ 13 13 00) flies in daily except Saturday to Roxby Downs from Adelaide ($192) and Coober Pedy ($104).

Stateliner (☎ 8415 5555) has three buses a week from Adelaide to Roxby Downs ($69.90).

GLENDAMBO (pop 20)

Glendambo is 114 km north-west of Pimba

and 253 km south of Coober Pedy. It was created in 1982 as a service centre on the new Stuart Highway to replace the township of Kingoonya, which was bypassed. Glendambo has a good pub, a motel, two roadhouses and a caravan park. The Mobil Roadhouse is the RAA agent and offers 24-hour service.

The township howls on the last weekend of November when the annual **Bachelors & Spinsters Ball** is held out at the racetrack. Bring a swag and be prepared to meet some real characters.

From Glendambo you can take the unsealed road west to fast-fading Kingoonya (43 km), then south to the Gawler Ranges and on to the Eyre Peninsula coast. Alternatively, keep going west from Kingoonya for another 80 km to the old gold-mining centre of **Tarcoola**, where the New Ghan to Alice Springs and the Indian-Pacific to Perth part company. There are gold diggings to explore here.

Places to Stay & Eat
The *Glendambo Tourist Centre* (☎ 8672 1030) has bars, a restaurant, a 12-bed bunkhouse and 72 motel units each sleeping up to five people. Beds in the bunkhouse cost $12, while the motel charges from $49/59 for singles/doubles plus $8 for each extra person.

Right next door, the *Caltex Roadhouse & Caravan Park* (☎ 8672 1035) has tent/caravan sites for $7.50/11.50 and on-site vans for $25/30/35.

In Tarcoola you can stay in an air-conditioned room at the *Wilgena Hotel* (☎ 8672 2042) for $25/40.

The roadhouses and hotel all sell meals; generally, Glendambo's Caltex Roadhouse is the best place for a feed.

COOBER PEDY (pop 3000)
On the Stuart Highway, 535 km north of Port Augusta, Coober Pedy is one of Australia's best-known outback towns. The name is Aboriginal and supposedly means 'white fellow's hole in the ground'. This aptly describes the place, as about half the population lives in dugouts to shelter from the extreme climate: summer temperatures can soar to over 50°C and the winter nights are freezing cold. Apart from the dugouts, there are over 250,000 mine shafts in the area. Keep your eyes open!

Coober Pedy is in an extremely harsh area and the town reflects its environment; even in the middle of winter it looks dried out and dusty, with piles of junk everywhere. It's hardly surprising that much of *Mad Max III* was filmed here – the town looks like the end of the world!

Coober Pedy is also very cosmopolitan, with about 40 nationalities represented. Greeks, Serbs, Croats and Italians form the largest groups among the miners, while the gem buyers are usually from Hong Kong.

The town has a reputation for being volatile: since 1987 the police station has been bombed twice, police vehicles have been blown up, the courthouse has been bombed once and the most successful restaurant (the Acropolis) was demolished by a blast. Hundreds of thousands of dollars worth of mining equipment has gone the same way.

To state the obvious, while the town is generally perfectly safe for visitors, it would be unwise for lone females to wander around unaccompanied late at night, or accept invitations from unfamiliar men to visit mines or opal collections.

Information
The tourist office (☎ 8672 5298) is in the council offices, adjacent to the Opal Inn as you enter the town. It's open weekdays between 9 am and 5 pm. Otherwise, Peter Caust at Underground Books (☎ 8672 5558) is very knowledgeable on the local area and the outback in general. If there's any work available for backpackers you can find out about it here.

There are plenty of opal shops, but banking facilities are limited: there's an EFTPOS cash-withdrawal facility at Fast Photo (limit $500), a Westpac branch, and a Commonwealth Bank agency in the post office. All are on the main street (Hutchison St).

There's a seven-day laundrette on Post Office Hill Rd, 600 metres from the main street.

OUTBACK

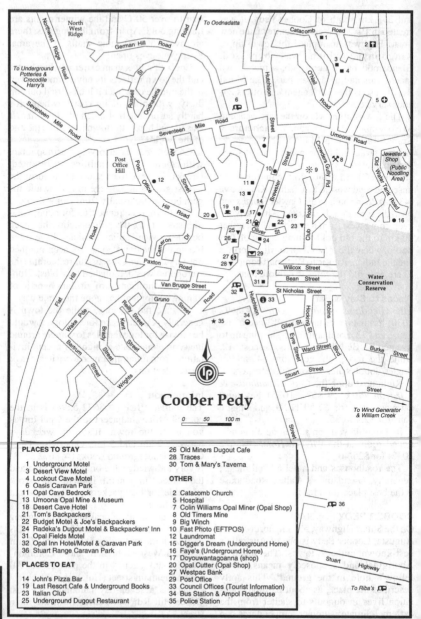

Coober Pedy

0   50   100 m

To Oodnadatta

To Underground Potteries & Crocodile Harry's

North West Ridge

Northwest Ridge Road

German Hill Road

Russell St

Oodnadatta

Seventeen Mile Road

Post Office Hill

Post Office

Alp Street

Hill Road

Cameron Dr

Paxton Road

Van Brugge Street

Gruno Street

Reilly Street

Kent Street

Brady Street

Bartrum Street

Wake Pde

Flint Hill Road

Wrights

Seventeen Mile Road

Hutchison Street

Crowders Gully Rd

Brewster Street

Oliver St

Club Road

Umoona Road

Catacomb Road

O'Neil Road

Old Water Tank Road

Jeweller's Shop (Public Noodling Area)

Water Conservation Reserve

Willcox Street

Bean Street

St Nicholas Street

Hutchison Street

Giles St

Hocking St

Robins Blvd

Eyre St

Ward Street

Stuart Street

Burke Street

Flinders Street

To Wind Generator & William Creek

Stuart Highway

To Riba's

OUTBACK

PLACES TO STAY

1 Underground Motel
3 Desert View Motel
4 Lookout Cave Motel
6 Oasis Caravan Park
11 Opal Cave Bedrock
13 Umoona Opal Mine & Museum
18 Desert Cave Hotel
21 Tom's Backpackers
22 Budget Motel & Joe's Backpackers
24 Radeka's Dugout Motel & Backpackers' Inn
31 Opal Fields Motel
32 Opal Inn Hotel/Motel & Caravan Park
36 Stuart Range Caravan Park

PLACES TO EAT

14 John's Pizza Bar
19 Last Resort Cafe & Underground Books
23 Italian Club
25 Underground Dugout Restaurant

26 Old Miners Dugout Cafe
28 Traces
30 Tom & Mary's Taverna

OTHER

2 Catacomb Church
5 Hospital
7 Colin Williams Opal Miner (Opal Shop)
8 Old Timers Mine
9 Big Winch
10 Fast Photo (EFTPOS)
12 Laundromat
15 Digger's Dream (Underground Home)
16 Faye's (Underground Home)
17 Doyouwantagoanna (shop)
20 Opal Cutter (Opal Shop)
27 Westpac Bank
29 Post Office
33 Council Offices (Tourist Information)
34 Bus Station & Ampol Roadhouse
35 Police Station

Opals

The first opals were discovered by 14-year-old Willie Hutchison in 1915. Today there are literally hundreds of working mines in the various opal fields that lie scattered over the barren saltbush plain around town; coming up the highway you see the first diggings 38 km before town and the last ones 34 km after it.

There are no big operators in opal mining, and the claims, which measure 50 metres by 50 metres, are limited to one per person. This means that when somebody makes a find on new ground, dozens of miners home in like bees around a honeypot. You'll take one look at the large areas of virgin saltbush between the diggings and wonder just how much opal is yet to be found here.

Several specialised items of opal-mining equipment have been developed. They include automatic hoists (these work off a car differential), tunnelling machines and giant truck-mounted vacuum cleaners known as 'blowers'. If you see columns of white dust rising like smoke above the waste dumps you'll know that a blower is at work.

Keen fossickers can have a go themselves, the safest area being the **Jeweller's Shop** opal field in the north-east corner of town – fossicking through the mullock (waste) dumps for opal is called 'noodling'. You can rent or buy sieves from several outlets around town.

There are numerous reputable – and some not so reputable – opal outlets in town; it's best to shop around and be wary of anyone offering discounts over 30% (there's a 30% sales tax on opal, so discounts of much more than this could be a sign that the opal is overpriced). Some of the best buys are found at the **Opal Cutter** on Post Office Hill Rd.

Dugouts

Living and working underground is the way to go in Coober Pedy, as no matter what the mercury is doing outside, the temperature inside remains at a steady 23°C. Apart from dugout homes, there are numerous underground churches, shops, restaurants and places to stay.

Many of the early dugout homes were simply worked-out mines, but these days they're usually cut specifically as residences; the opal found during excavation often pays for the hire of the digging machinery. However, virtually all the suitable ground near town – the dugouts are all excavated into hillsides – has now been taken up.

Several homes are open to visitors for around $2 admittance, including Faye's, Digger's Dream and, the most eccentric of them all, **Crocodile Harry's**. On the Seventeen Mile Rd north-west of town, this off-beat dugout has featured in a number of documentaries, as well as the movies *Mad*

Colour in Opal

It's thought that opal was formed by the hardening of a silica-rich gel which collected in cracks and other spaces, such as those left by the solution of organic material like shells and bones. Look through an electron microscope and you'll see that opal is made up of spheres of silicon dioxide, much like a bag of oranges, with the spaces filled with water.

A piece of opal in which the spheres are regular in size, shape and arrangement acts like a three-dimensional diffraction grate, splitting white light into the different colours of the spectrum. Large spheres produce all the colours (violet, indigo, green, blue, yellow, orange and red), intermediate ones produce violet to yellow and small ones produce violet only. However, in most cases the spheres are irregular in size, shape and arrangement. This scatters the white light and produces milky or white potch.

The patterns seen in precious opal depend on variations in the size, regularity and arrangement of the spheres. Created during the opal's formation, these variations commonly consist of horizontal banding and the bending of those bands; others include concentric disturbances and the irregular presence of trace elements. ■

Max III and *Ground Zero*, and the miniseries *Stark*. Harry, actually a Latvian baron, spent 13 years in far north Queensland and the NT hunting crocodiles.

Breakaways Reserve
The Breakaways Reserve is a starkly attractive area of arid hills and scarps about 30 km by road north of Coober Pedy – the signposted turn-off is on the highway 20 km from town. You can drive to a lookout in a conventional vehicle and see the colourful mesa known as the **Castle**, which featured in the films *Mad Max III* and *Priscilla, Queen of the Desert*. Late afternoon is the best time for photographs.

You can also make an interesting 70-km loop from Coober Pedy which takes in the Breakaways before following the **Dog Fence** back to the barren, table-like **Moon Plain** on the Oodnadatta road. Underground Books has a leaflet and 'mud map' for $1; check road conditions before attempting this route.

Other Attractions
Coober Pedy has a number of other attractions worth a look. The most prominent is the **Big Winch**, which has a lookout over the town and an extensive display of cut and uncut opal. At the lookout is the sculpture of a tree made from the remains of a burnt-out truck – for many years it was the largest 'tree' in town, but the laying-on of a town water supply in recent times means that real trees can now be grown.

The fascinating **Old Timers Mine**, near Crowders Gully Rd, is an early (1916) mine and underground home which is well worth the $3 entry fee. You'll be suitably impressed by its labyrinth of low tunnels and the way the diggers climbed up and down the shafts.

The **Umoona Opal Mine & Museum** is right in the centre of town; opal was still being pulled out of here until mining within the town limits was banned some years ago. Informative tours of the mine ($5) run throughout the day, and there are displays on the mythology and traditions of the local Aboriginal people, as well as exhibitions on the early mining days.

A couple of km out of town to the northwest, **Underground Potteries** has some creative pieces. **Doyouwantagoanna**, on Hutchison St, produces interesting and unique silk-screen designs featuring Australian fauna. Their work appears on the uniforms of Australia's netball team.

Organised Tours
There are several local tours, most taking three hours and costing between $18 and $24. Joe's Tours (book at the Budget Motel – see Places to Stay) is the only one to include Crocodile Harry's, while Desert Cave Tours (book at the Desert Cave Hotel – see Places to Stay) is probably the best value – the tour lasts four hours ($24) and you visit such places as the underground Catacomb Church, the Breakaways and Moon Plain.

Apu Waru Tours (book at Tom's Backpackers – see Places to Stay), which is Aboriginal-owned and operated, has an interesting culture tour ($24). Prospectors Opal Tours (☎ 8672 5338) offer very good local history tours.

On Monday and Thursday you can travel with the mail truck along 600 km of dirt roads as it does the round trip from Coober Pedy to Oodnadatta and William Creek. This is a great way to get off the beaten track and visit remote homesteads and small towns. The backpackers' special price is $60, which doesn't include lunch, while others pay $89. For details, call ☎ toll-free 1800 069 911 or contact Underground Books.

Perentie Outback Tours (☎ 8672 5558) has a very good reputation, and offers tours for small groups. It has three-day 4WD camping safaris ($395) from Coober Pedy to Witjira National Park, including visits to interesting places such as the Painted Desert and Dalhousie Springs.

Places to Stay
Caravan Parks There are four caravan parks in and around town. None are visually inspiring – there's no lawn but plenty of dust, and the ground is as hard as nails. Reasonably central to the action are the *Oasis Caravan*

Park (☎ 8672 5169) – which has the best shade and shelter, as well as camp sites ($5.50 per person), on-site vans ($34) and cabins ($26) – and the brand-new *Opal Inn Caravan Park* (☎ 8672 5054), which only has tent sites ($6) and caravan sites ($12). They're at opposite ends of Hutchison St.

The *Stuart Range Caravan Park* (☎ 8672 5179) is the largest in town and has the best facilities; its self-contained cabins ($50) are more like motel rooms. The park is about one km from town near the main entrance off the Stuart Highway.

The friendliest and most basic of all is *Riba's* (☎ 8672 5614), on the William Creek road five km from town. It's also the cheapest, with camp sites costing $3.50 per person; showers are free, unlike at the other places, and the owners have a 1½-hour mine tour for $5 if you're staying there.

Hostels The underground *Joe's Backpackers* (☎ 8672 5613), attached to the Budget Motel on Oliver St, has beds for $12 including linen and showers, or $11 if you produce your YHA card. Although not brilliant, it's considered to be the best of the local hostel accommodation – it certainly has a very good kitchen.

The *Backpackers' Inn* at Radeka's Dugout Motel (☎ 8672 5223) offers underground dormitories for $12 including linen and showers.

Tom's Backpackers (☎ 8672 5333) on Hutchison St opposite the Desert Cave Hotel has underground accommodation for $12. It also has uninviting above-ground rooms (no air-conditioning) for the same price.

The very basic *Opal Cave Bedrock* (☎ 8672 5028) on Hutchison St has a 52-bed dormitory for $6 a bed and more private, if cell-like, four-bunk rooms for $10 a bed. Showers cost 20 cents for one minute and linen is $6 extra.

Hotels On Hutchison St, the *Opal Inn Hotel/Motel* (☎ 8672 5054) has comfortable above-ground pub rooms for $25/35 and motel rooms for $65/70. The luxurious *Desert Cave Hotel* (☎ 8672 5198) is further

down the street in the centre of town. It has rooms above and below ground for $124 for singles & doubles.

Motels Also on Hutchison St, the underground *Umoona Opal Mine* (☎ 8672 5288) has singles/doubles for $20/25. Bathrooms are communal and there are kitchen facilities.

The *Budget Motel* (☎ 8672 5163) on Oliver St has above-ground rooms with share facilities for $18/30/36 and rooms with private facilities for $35/45. Nearby is *Radeka's Dugout Motel* (☎ 8672 5223), which charges $90 for its underground family room sleeping six. Singles/doubles in its 'budget' above-ground rooms cost $45/55.

One of the friendliest places in town is the *Opal Fields Motel* (☎ 8672 3003), on St Nicholas St, which has rammed-earth units for $60/70/85.

Another nice place, with a beaut panorama towards the Breakaways, is the *Underground Motel* (☎ 8672 5324) on Catacomb Rd, charging $60/80 including a light breakfast.

There's an excellent lookout on the hilltop above the nearby *Lookout Cave Motel* (☎ 8672 5118), which charges $58/75 with a light breakfast. Virtually next door, the underground *Desert View Motel* (☎ 8672 3330) has comfortable, spacious units with kitchen, lounge and laundry facilities for $65/80/100.

About four km from town at Black Point, the *Opal Dreaming Underground Cottage* (☎ 8672 5985) is very well appointed and has stunning views of the wide open spaces. It charges $60 for two people and you can book at the Underground Art Gallery in Hutchison St.

Places to Eat
There are plenty of places to eat in Coober Pedy. The *Last Resort Cafe*, next to Underground Books, has excellent and imaginative food and is easily the best place in town for breakfast; the filling Bircher müesli ($6.20) is very popular with Swiss visitors. It sells

delicious homemade ice creams, cakes and quiches and you can enjoy them either underground or alfresco. Sadly, it's open only during the day, and not at all on Sunday.

There are a couple of Greek places on Hutchison St, *Tom & Mary's Taverna* and *Traces*, and both are popular in the evenings (Traces stays open until 4 am).

If you crave Italian, locals reckon *John's Pizza Bar*, also on Hutchison St, does the best pizzas between Alice Springs and Adelaide. Alternatively, the *Italian Club* has good-value meals on Friday and Saturday.

For Chinese food try the *Opal Inn Chinese* restaurant in the Opal Inn. Main courses here start at $8. You can get a reasonably priced counter meal in the pub's saloon bar.

The *Old Miners Dugout Cafe* is indeed underground and has a pleasant, quiet atmosphere. Its menu is limited but interesting, with dishes like kangaroo tail soup, sauerkraut cabbage rolls and Mexican chicken enchiladas on offer. It's popular for dinner, but isn't what you'd call cheap (the 'backpacker special' is $7).

Alternatively, there's the more expensive *Umberto's* in the Desert Cave Hotel; its prices are quite reasonable given the quality of the food and service. Otherwise, the main street has several takeaways and coffee lounges.

Getting There & Away
Air Kendell Airlines (bookings ☎ 13 13 00) flies from Adelaide to Coober Pedy ($250) most days of the week, and from Coober Pedy to Uluru ($206) on Saturday only. The Desert Cave Hotel handles reservations and operates the airport shuttle bus ($5 one way).

Bus Stateliner charges $82 from Adelaide; with Greyhound Pioneer it's $87 from Adelaide, $70 from Alice Springs and $107 from Uluru. Both companies have their depots in the Ampol Roadhouse at the main entrance to town.

McCafferty's charges $69 from Alice Springs and $99 from Uluru, stopping at John's Pizza Bar.

Getting Around
Coober Pedy Tours (☎ 8672 5333) runs the local taxi service. It also rents out conventional vehicles from $50 to $80 per day and 4WDs from $105 to $125; the rates include 100 km per day and insurance, although there's a hefty excess should you have an accident in a 4WD.

MARLA (pop 150)
Situated in the mulga scrub 159 km south of the NT border, Marla replaced Oodnadatta as the official regional centre when the Ghan railway line was rerouted in 1980. Fuel and provisions are available here 24 hours a day; there's also an EFTPOS cash-withdrawal facility.

The small, frontier-style **Mintabie** opal field is on Aboriginal land 35 km to the west of Marla. It has a general store, restaurant and caravan park. To visit, you need a permit ($5) from the Marla police station.

The *Marla Travellers Rest* (☎ 8670 7001) has camp sites for $5 per person (power $5 extra), backpacker units for $19/28 (in summer you need to check that they're air-conditioned) and basic cabins with air-con for $26.50/38. The comfortable and spacious motel rooms cost $59/65/70/76 – a TV and phone in the room are $10 extra.

CADNEY HOMESTEAD
On the Stuart Highway 82 km south of Marla and 151 km north of Coober Pedy, *Cadney Homestead roadhouse* (☎ 8670 7994) has camp sites for $6 per person, powered sites for $16 and cabins for $35, or there are motel rooms for $70/77/83.

If you're heading for Oodnadatta, turning off the highway at Cadney gives you a shorter run on dirt roads, rather than going via Marla or Coober Pedy. You pass through the aptly named Painted Desert on the way, and there's camping and cabins at *Copper Hills homestead*, about 32 km east of the roadhouse. You can visit this interesting area on the Tuesday mail run from Cadney with local identity and artist Hugh Frahn, who owns Copper Hills. The tour takes all day and costs $55, lunch included.

Outback Tracks

The Birdsville, Oodnadatta and Strzelecki tracks are minor unsealed routes which are tracks in name only these days – unless, of course, it rains. However, they'll appeal to the more adventurous traveller by virtue of their loneliness and lack of facilities, and the fact that they cross some of Australia's most inhospitable country. Most times you can do them in a conventional vehicle provided it's robust and has good ground clearance.

If you want to be even more daring there's the Rig Road (4WD only) across the Simpson Desert from Mt Dare Homestead to Birdsville. Alternatively, you can take the Old Andado Track (also 4WD only) from Mt Dare to Alice Springs via the Old Andado Homestead.

All these tracks are covered in detail in Lonely Planet's *Outback Australia*. They are summarised only briefly in this book.

LYNDHURST (pop 20)
Squatting amongst low, barren hills at the southern end of the Strzelecki Track, Lyndhurst is at the end of the bitumen, 300 km north of Port Augusta. About one km out along the track is the eccentric home and workshop of Cornelius Alferink, otherwise known as Talc Alf, who produces magnificent abstract carvings from lumps of local talc.

The taipan, which grows to 2.5 metres long, is the world's most venomous snake. Found in the state's arid north-east, fortunately they are rarely encountered, preferring like all snakes to give humans a very wide berth.

You can get fuel and meals daily at the local roadhouse, while the *Lyndhurst Hotel* (☎ 8675 7781) has rooms for $25/50/60 and counter meals.

STRZELECKI TRACK
The Strzelecki Track runs for 460 km to the tiny outpost of Innamincka, close to the Queensland border. Once just a two-wheel track meandering through the sandhills of the Strzelecki Desert, the route was substantially upgraded after the discovery of huge oil and gas deposits near **Moomba** in the 1960s. However, the amount of heavy transport travelling on it means the surface is often badly corrugated.

The track skirts the northern Flinders Ranges at first, coming to the ruins of historic **Blanchewater** homestead on MacDonnell Creek, 157 km from Lyndhurst. Established in 1857, it became the largest horse-breeding enterprise in Australia, but was abandoned after a huge flood devastated the homestead in 1940. The station is associated with the exploits of the famous cattle duffer Harry Redford, who pioneered the track with a stolen mob from Queensland in 1870.

There are no facilities of any kind between Lyndhurst and Innamincka. Tourists are only permitted to enter Moomba in the event of an emergency.

INNAMINCKA (pop 10)
At the northern end of the Strzelecki Track, Innamincka is on Cooper Creek – close to where the ill-fated Burke and Wills expedition of 1860 came to its tragic end. One of Innamincka's major attractions is the famous **Dig Tree**, which marks the site of the expedition's base camp – the word 'dig' is no longer visible, but the expedition's camp number can still be made out.

While the Dig Tree is on the Queensland side of the border, the memorials and markers where Burke and Wills died, and where King, the sole survivor, was found are downstream in SA. There is also a memorial where Howitt, who led the rescue party, set up his depot on the creek. For a moving

Robert O'Hara Burke

William John Wills

account of the Burke and Wills expedition, read Alan Moorehead's *Cooper's Creek*.

Cooper Creek flows only rarely – it takes big rains in central-west Queensland to bring it down in flood – but has deep, permanent waterholes and the semipermanent **Coongie Lakes**. These lakes are significant habitats for aquatic fauna and water birds, and are a major reason why the surrounding **Innamincka Regional Reserve** (1.4 million hectares) was created.

The restored **Australian Inland Mission** hospital now has the NPWS ranger's office (☎ 8675 9909) and interpretive displays on the regional reserve. Talk to the ranger before attempting the 4WD track via Walkers Crossing to the Birdsville Track.

You can take a conventional vehicle over the road to Birdsville via **Cordillo Downs** homestead. Built in 1883, the station's huge stone shearing shed, which had stands for 120 shearers, is one of SA's most outstanding pastoral relics.

Places to Stay & Eat

The *Innamincka Hotel* (☎ 8675 9901) has four motel-style rooms with air-con at $40/50/75/85. It does reasonable takeaways and has counter meals in the evenings; its Wednesday night 'Beef-and-Reef' and Sunday night roasts are both good value at $10 for all you can eat. Alternatively, the *Innamincka Trading Post* (☎ 8675 9900) has three very modest two-bedroom cabins for $25 per person. Fuel and provisions are available here.

Otherwise there are plenty of nice places to camp among the coolibahs along the Cooper Creek system – see the ranger about a permit ($15 per vehicle per night).

LYNDHURST TO MARREE

About five km north of Lyndhurst, the **Ochre Cliffs** are exposures of red and yellow ochre in a low breakaway. Be there in the late afternoon to get the best photos of its striking colours.

The ghost town of **Farina** is 25 km from Lyndhurst. Established in 1882 as a farming centre on the Great Northern Railway (the name is Latin for flour), the little township survived well into this century but is now in ruins. The only substantial remains among the scattered chimneys and debris are those

OUTBACK

of the Transcontinental Hotel and post office; nearby is the Farina homestead (☎ 8675 7790), which offers guided tours of the area.

There's a pleasant bush camping area among large red gums down by the creek about 500 metres north of the ruins; sites are $2 per person and you pay at the honesty box. Go through the camp ground to get to the sad old **cemetery**, on a desolate gibber rise two km away. The Afghan section is by itself to the north.

MARREE (pop 80)

At the junction of the Birdsville and Oodnadatta tracks, 380 km north of Port Augusta, sleepy Marree has managed to survive several hard blows: first came the replacement of the camel teams (1930s) and drovers (1960s) by motor transport, then came a knockout punch with the closure of the Great Northern Railway in 1980.

Although it's now a shadow of its former self, there are still signs of the town's former prosperity. By far the grandest building in town is the two-storey Great Northern Hotel, built in the 1880s, and the railway complex complete with old locomotives is still more-or-less intact. A couple of date palms and a large sundial in the shape of a squatting camel (it's made from railway sleepers) recall the camel teams of old.

Thanks to its isolation the town has a good range of facilities, including a small hospital, fuel sales and minisupermarkets. The Commonwealth bank agency and post office are in the Ghan Store, while the Oasis Café has an EFTPOS cash-withdrawal facility.

Marree comes to life during the winter tourist season, but really fires up in July on odd-numbered years when the Marree Camel Cup is held over a weekend. There's an Aboriginal **heritage museum** in the Arabanna Centre.

The Muloorina (pronounced mu-LOO-rinah) **scenic drive** is worth doing, taking you to Lake Eyre and a beautiful deep waterhole in Frome Creek. Allow a day for the round trip; the Oasis Café can give you a mud map.

Book at the Oasis Café for **scenic flights** over Lake Eyre, Cooper Creek, the Flinders Ranges and other fascinating areas. A one-hour flight costs $100 per person.

Places to Stay & Eat

In town, the *Oasis Caravan Park* (via the Oasis Café, ☎ 8675 8352) has little shade but there are lawned camp sites for $5 per person. The somewhat dustier *Marree Tourist Park* (☎ 8675 8371) is at the start of the Birdsville Track about a km south of town. It has camp sites for $6 per person ($2.50 extra per site for power) and on-site vans for $20/30/40.

Alternatively, the *Great Northern Hotel* (☎ 8675 8344) has standard twin rooms for $25 per person, or $35 with a cooked breakfast, and family rooms sleeping five persons for $50. Counter meals cost from $10.

BIRDSVILLE TRACK

For nearly 80 years from the early 1880s, huge mobs of cattle from south-west Queensland were walked down the 520-km Birdsville Track to Marree, where they were loaded onto trains for the last part of their journey to the Adelaide markets. Motor transport took over from the drovers in the 1960s, and these days the cattle are trucked out in road trains.

There are some fascinating books on the Birdsville Track. *Mail for the Back of Beyond* by John Maddock (Kangaroo Press) is an inspiring account of the early motor mail service – if you reckon the track is tough today, read this book. Eric Bonython's *Where the Seasons Come and Go* (Illawong) is an absorbing read covering history, lifestyles and adventure on the Cooper up to the 1950s.

In Australia you won't find country much harsher and drier than the land which lies along the Birdsville Track. The route more or less follows the join between the sand dunes of the Simpson Desert to the west and the desolate gibber wastes of Sturt Stony Desert to the east. At one point it touches the fearsome Tirari Desert, the closest thing Australia has

The Birdsville Track owes its existence to cattlemen, who opened up the outback in search of the quickest overland cattle route between Queensland and the Adelaide stock markets.

to true desert. Despite its unpromising appearance, however, you pass scattered homesteads as well as various scant ruins, while artesian bores gush boiling-hot sulphurous water at several places.

Like most of the Lake Eyre Basin, you don't need to travel across this country to feel thirsty – just looking at a few pictures of it is usually sufficient. Dozens of people have perished of thirst along the track, the last being a family of five in December 1963. Their vehicle broke down and, having failed to take adequate water, they paid the ultimate price for their lack of preparation.

At **Clifton Hills**, about 200 km south of Birdsville, the track splits, with the main route swinging around the eastern side of Goyders Lagoon; the 4WD 'Inner Track' crosses the lagoon (actually a vast seasonal swamp) and is the more interesting way to go, except when it's wet!

Although conventional vehicles can usually manage the main road without difficulty, it's worth bearing in mind that traffic is anything but heavy – particularly in summer, when days can go by without a vehicle passing.

Petrol, diesel, minor mechanical repairs, meals, accommodation and a camp ground are available at the *Mungeranie Roadhouse* (☎ 8675 8317), about 205 km north of Marree and 315 km south of Birdsville. They also sell lovely cold beer. Birdsville, which is just inside Queensland, has an excellent range of facilities, including a police station, small hospital, hotel, vehicle repairs, caravan park and general store.

OODNADATTA TRACK

Reeking with history, the 615-km Oodnadatta Track from Marree to Marla is a fascinating and adventurous alternative to the Stuart Highway. Between Marree and Oodnadatta, the road closely follows the route of the old Overland Telegraph Line and the Great Northern Railway; here you'll find plenty of evocative ruins of fettlers huts, railway sidings and telegraph stations to

OUTBACK

excite the imagination. You can also detour to Lake Eyre (the world's sixth largest lake) and to various mound springs, the natural outlets for the Great Artesian Basin.

There are several routes across to the Stuart Highway. With a conventional vehicle you can normally drive from Lake Eyre South via Roxby Downs to Pimba; from William Creek to Coober Pedy; and from Oodnadatta to Coober Pedy and Cadney Homestead.

Fuel, accommodation and meals are available at Marree, William Creek (204 km from Marree), Oodnadatta (406 km) and Marla.

Coward Springs

The *Coward Springs Camp Ground* (☎ 8675 8336) is 130 km from Marree at the old Coward Springs siding. Shaded camp sites cost $10 a vehicle, and there's a hot pool you can soak in. Nearby, a new **conservation park** includes the Bubbler and Blanche Cup mound springs, and there's a wetland with numerous water birds behind the camp ground. You can also do camel rides and, if you've got more time, a five-day trek to Lake Eyre.

William Creek

The *William Creek Hotel* (☎ 8670 7880) has a camp ground ($4 per person or $10 per family), modest motel-style units with air-con ($30 per person) and a bunkhouse without air-con ($12). The pub can arrange **scenic flights** costing from $30 each with two passengers; you can see Lake Eyre for $75 each with two passengers ($50 with three).

OODNADATTA (pop 200)

The tiny town of Oodnadatta (like Marree, it lost much of its population when the railway closed down) is at the point where the main road and the old railway line diverged. It has an excellent range of services, including a police station, small hospital, vehicle repairs, general store and pub.

For travellers, the gathering place at Oodnadatta is the **Pink Roadhouse**, an excellent place to ask advice about track conditions and attractions in any direction. The owners, Adam and Lynnie Plate, have spent a great deal of time and effort putting in road signs and km pegs all over the district – even in the Simpson Desert you'll come

---

The Birdsville Mail Run

Heading north on the Birdsville Track you cross the broad flood plain of Cooper Creek and enter a world of high yellow dunes which, for the next 20 km, roll away on either side like ocean waves. Known as the Natterannie Sandhills, they mark the convergence of the Strzelecki Desert to the east and the Tirari Desert to the west.

Provided you stay on the road there is little likelihood that you'll become bogged in this frightful country, but it wasn't always so. In the droving days, before the track became a road, the Natterannie Sandhills were a nightmare for anyone travelling in a motor vehicle. Even the famous mail-driver, Tom Kruse, who became an expert in taking heavy vehicles through soft sand on his fortnightly trips up the track, found them tough going.

There was little chance of not getting stuck on this section, and because each bog meant unloading the truck then loading it again, it usually took Kruse eight hours to get through the worst section of 12 km. The tyre-deflation method could rarely be used because the effort involved in pumping up the tyres put the driver at risk of heat exhaustion, or worse.

The innovative Kruse tried various strategies in his efforts to defeat the sandhills. Any truck that was fitted with dual rear wheels carried six-metre lengths of 75-mm-diameter bore casing. These were laid on the sand in the direction of travel so that the rear wheels could grip them and hopefully find traction.

Alternatively, the sand in front was covered with heavy iron sheets to provide a solid surface; great care had to be exercised here as the sheets were liable to fly up and damage the underside of the truck if tackled at speed. Kruse even tried using conveyor belts to create a half-track vehicle, but with limited success. Mostly, it was a case of charge as far as you could, get out, unload the truck and start digging. ■

across signs erected by this dedicated pair! They've also produced a series of mud maps to make it even easier.

Across from the general store, the old railway station (by far the most impressive building in town) has been converted into an interesting little **museum**. You can pick up a key from the pub, store or roadhouse.

From Oodnadatta you can head north-west to Marla (209 km) or north to the 771,000-hectare **Witjira National Park** (245 km), on the western fringes of the Simpson Desert. The park contains **Dalhousie Springs**, a large group of artesian springs which are of great significance as the only permanent surface water in a vast area. Talk to Phil Hellyer at **Mt Dare Homestead**, within the national park, before attempting the 4WD routes to Alice Springs and Birdsville.

If you're heading up to Dalhousie and the Simpson Desert, a couple of very interesting references are *Simpson Desert* by Mark Shephard and *Natural History of Dalhousie Springs* (South Australian Museum).

Places to Stay & Eat

The *Oodnadatta Caravan Park* (☎ 8670 7822), attached to the Pink Roadhouse, has tent/caravan sites for $12.50/16.50, an on-site van for $30, cabins sleeping five for $30/35/40 and a self-contained backpacker unit sleeping seven for $9 each. Alternatively, there's the *Transcontinental Hotel* (☎ 8670 7804), which charges $30/55. You can get meals at both the pub (dinner only) and the roadhouse.

Lonely *Mt Dare Homestead* (☎ 8670 7835) provides the only facilities in Witjira National Park; it's the last place to fuel up before heading for Birdsville or Alice Springs via the Old Andado Track. They have basic accommodation in the old homestead and a camp ground – book ahead if you want a room or casual meals.

Index

MAPS

TEXT

NATIONAL PARKS & RESERVES

Arkaroola Wildlife Sanctuary 273-4
Bascombe Well CP 290
Beachport CP 196
Belair NP 129
Billiatt CP 189
Black Hill CP 129
Bookmark Biosphere Reserve 188
Bool Lagoon Game Reserve 206
Bowman Park 223
Brookfield CP 180
Buckaringa Sanctuary 264
Bushland Park 137
Calpatanna Waterhole CP 288
Canunda NP 198
Cape Gantheaume CP 167
Charleston CP 129
Cleland Wildlife Park 129
Clinton CP 238
Coffin Bay NP 286
Coorong NP 193
Danggali CP 188
Deep Creek CP 146
Dutchman's Stern CP 263
Ewen Ponds CP 202
Ferries-McDonald CP 175
Finniss River CP 144
Flinders Chase NP 29, 168-70
Flinders Ranges NP 267-70, **268**
Gammon Ranges NP 272-3, **272**
Hacks Lagoon CP 206

Hale CP 218
Hambidge CP 290
Hincks CP 290
Innamincka Regional Reserve 310
Innes NP 241-2
Kaiser Stuhl CP 215
Kellidie Bay CP 286
Kelly Hill Caves CP 168
Kenneth Stirling CP 129
Kuitpo Forest 134
Lake Gairdner NP 290
Lake Gilles CP 290
Lake Newland CP 288
Laura Bay CP 289
Leven Beach CP 242
Lincoln NP 285-6
Little Dip CP 195
Loch Luna game reserve 183
Loftia Recreation Reserve 129
Martins Washpool CP 192
Messent CP 192
Monarto Zoological Park 175
Moorook game reserve 183
Morialta CP 129
Mt Boothby CP 192, 207
Mt Brown CP 263
Mt Crawford Forest 138
Mt Magnificent CP 144
Mt Monster CP 208
Mt Remarkable NP 256-7
Murray River NP 184, 187
Naracoorte Caves CP 206
Newland Head CP 147
Ngarkat CP 189, 208

Nullarbor NP 29, 77, 295
Nullarbor Regional Reserve 295
Onkaparinga River Recreation Park 142
Padthaway CP 206
Pandappa CP 235
Piccaninnie Ponds CP 202
Pinkawillinie CP 290
Pooginook CP 182
Pureba CP 291
Purnong Road Bird Sanctuary 178
Scott Creek CP 129
Spring Gully CP 228
Swan Reach CP 179
Talisker CP 146
Telowie Gorge CP 256
Troubridge Island CP 239
Urimbirra Wildlife Park 147
Venus Bay CP 288
Warren CP 218
Warrenben CP 241
Western River CP 167
Whyalla CP 278
Whyalla Wildlife & Reptile Sanctuary 278
Wilabalangaloo flora & fauna reserve 185
Winninowie CP 256
Witjira NP 314
Yellabinna Regional Reserve 291
Yookamurra Sanctuary 179
Yumbarra CP 291

WINERIES

Adelaide Hills Wine Centre 130
Angoves Winery 186
Australian Vintage Winery 184
Balnaves of Coonawarra 205
Bethany Wines 211
Black Opal Quelltaler Vineyards 226
Bleasdale's 153
Bonneyview Winery 183
Bridgewater Mill 130
Chapel Hill 143
Chateau Yaldara 211
Coonawarra Wineries 205
D'arenberg 143
Grand Cru 138
Grant Burge Wines 211

Hardys 142
Henschke 138
Hollick Wines 205
James Haselgrove Wines 205
Jim Barry Wines 226
Katnook Estate 205
Kay Brothers 143
Lake Breeze Winery 153
Leasingham Wines 226
Leconfield Coonawarra 205
Maxwell 143
Moundadam 138
Mt Benson Vineyards 194
Noon's 143
Norman Wines 185
Old Clarendon Winery Complex 136
Orlando 211

Padthaway Estate 206
Paulett Wines 226
Petaluma 130
Redman Winery 205
Rockford Wines 211
Saltram Wine Estate 211
Seaview 143
Seppeltsfield 211
Sevenhill 228
Sevenhill Cellars 226
Skillogalee Wines 226
St Hallett 211
Taylor's Wines 227
Tim Knappstein Wines 226
Wolf Blass 211
Woodstock 143
Wynns Coonawarra Estate 205
Yalumba 211

LONELY PLANET JOURNEYS

JOURNEYS is a unique collection of travellers' tales – published by the company that understands travel better than anyone else. It is a series for anyone who has ever experienced – or dreamed of – the magical moment when they encountered a strange culture or saw a place for the first time. They are tales to read while you're planning a trip, while you're on the road or while you're in an armchair, in front of a fire.

JOURNEYS books will catch the spirit of a place, illuminate a culture, recount a crazy adventure, or introduce a fascinating way of life. They will always entertain, and always enrich the experience of travel.

ISLANDS IN THE CLOUDS
Travels in the Highlands of New Guinea
Isabella Tree

This is the fascinating account of a journey to the remote and beautiful Highlands of Papua New Guinea and Irian Jaya. The author travels with a PNG Highlander who introduces her to his intriguing and complex world. *Islands in the Clouds* is a thoughtful, moving book, full of insights into a region that is rarely noticed by the rest of the world.

'One of the most accomplished travel writers to appear on the horizon for many years ... the dialogue is brilliant' – Eric Newby

LOST JAPAN
Alex Kerr

Lost Japan draws on the author's personal experiences of Japan over a period of 30 years. Alex Kerr takes his readers on a backstage tour: friendships with Kabuki actors, buying and selling art, studying calligraphy, exploring rarely visited temples and shrines ... The Japanese edition of this book was awarded the 1994 Shincho Gakugei Literature Prize for the best work of non-fiction.

'This deeply personal witness to Japan's wilful loss of its traditional culture is at the same time an immensely valuable evaluation of just what that culture was'
– Donald Richie of the Japan Times

THE GATES OF DAMASCUS
Lieve Joris
Translated by Sam Garrett

This best-selling book is a beautifully drawn portrait of day-to-day life in modern Syria. Through her intimate contact with local people, Lieve Joris draws us into the fascinating world that lies behind the gates of Damascus.

'A brilliant book ... Not since Naguib Mahfouz has the everyday life of the modern Arab world been so intimately described' – William Dalrymple

SEAN & DAVID'S LONG DRIVE
Sean Condon

Sean and David are young townies who have rarely strayed beyond city limits. One day, for no good reason, they set out to discover their homeland, and what follows is a wildly entertaining adventure that covers half of Australia. Sean Condon has written a hilarious, offbeat road book that mixes sharp insights with deadpan humour and outright lies.

'Funny, pithy, kitsch and surreal ... This book will do for Australia what Chernobyl did for Kiev, but hey you'll laugh as the stereotypes go boom' – Andrew Tuck, Time Out

LONELY PLANET TRAVEL ATLASES

Lonely Planet has long been famous for the number and quality of its guidebook maps. Now we've gone one step further and in conjunction with Steinhart Katzir Publishers produced a handy companion series: Lonely Planet travel atlases – maps of a country produced in book form.

Unlike other maps, which look good but lead travellers astray, our travel atlases have been researched on the road by Lonely Planet's experienced team of writers. All details are carefully checked to ensure the atlas corresponds with the equivalent Lonely Planet guidebook.

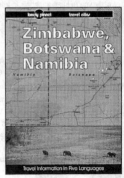

The handy atlas format means no holes, wrinkles, torn sections or constant folding and unfolding. These atlases can survive long periods on the road, unlike cumbersome fold-out maps. The comprehensive index ensures easy reference.

- full-colour throughout
- maps researched and checked by Lonely Planet authors
- place names correspond with Lonely Planet guidebooks
  – no confusing spelling differences
- legend and travelling information in English, French, German, Japanese and Spanish
- size: 230 x 160 mm

Available now:
Thailand; India & Bangladesh; Vietnam; Zimbabwe, Botswana & Namibia

Coming soon:
Chile; Egypt; Israel; Laos; Turkey

LONELY PLANET TV SERIES & VIDEOS

Lonely Planet travel guides have been brought to life on television screens around the world. Like our guides, the programmes are based on the joy of independent travel, and look honestly at some of the most exciting, picturesque and frustrating places in the world. Each show is presented by one of three travellers from Australia, England or the USA and combines an innovative mixture of video, Super-8 film, atmospheric soundscapes and original music.

Videos of each episode – containing additional footage not shown on television – are available from good book and video shops, but the availability of individual videos varies with regional screening schedules.

Video destinations include: Alaska; Australia (Southeast); Brazil; Ecuador & the Galápagos Islands; Indonesia; Israel & the Sinai Desert; Japan; La Ruta Maya (Yucatán, Guatemala & Belize); Morocco; North India (Varanasi to the Himalaya); Pacific Islands; Vietnam; Zimbabwe, Botswana & Namibia.

Coming soon: The Arctic (Norway & Finland); Baja California; Chile & Easter Island; China (Southeast); Costa Rica; East Africa (Tanzania & Zanzibar); Great Barrier Reef (Australia); Jamaica; Papua New Guinea; the Rockies (USA); Syria & Jordan; Turkey.

The Lonely Planet TV series is produced by:
Pilot Productions
Duke of Sussex Studios
44 Uxbridge St
London W8 7TG UK

Lonely Planet videos are distributed by:
IVN Communications Inc
2246 Camino Ramon
California 94583, USA

107 Power Road, Chiswick
London W4 5PL UK

Music from the TV series is available on CD & cassette.
For ordering information contact your nearest Lonely Planet office.

PLANET TALK

Lonely Planet's FREE quarterly newsletter

We love hearing from you and think you'd like to hear from us.

When...is the right time to see reindeer in Finland?
Where...can you hear the best palm-wine music in Ghana?
How...do you get from Asunción to Areguá by steam train?
What...is the best way to see India?

For the answer to these and many other questions read PLANET TALK.

Every issue is packed with up-to-date travel news and advice including:

- a letter from Lonely Planet co-founders Tony and Maureen Wheeler
- go behind the scenes on the road with a Lonely Planet author
- feature article on an important and topical travel issue
- a selection of recent letters from travellers
- details on forthcoming Lonely Planet promotions
- complete list of Lonely Planet products

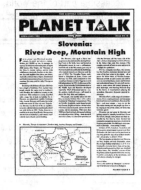

To join our mailing list contact any Lonely Planet office.

Also available: Lonely Planet T-shirts. 100% heavyweight cotton..

LONELY PLANET ONLINE

Get the latest travel information before you leave or while you're on the road

Whether you've just begun planning your next trip, or you're chasing down specific info on currency regulations or visa requirements, check out the Lonely Planet World Wide Web site for up-to-the-minute travel information.

As well as travel profiles of your favourite destinations (including interactive maps and full-colour photos), you'll find current reports from our army of researchers and other travellers, updates on health and visas, travel advisories, and the ecological and political issues you need to be aware of as you travel.

There's an online travellers' forum (the Thorn Tree) where you can share your experiences of life on the road, meet travel companions and ask other travellers for their recommendations and advice. We also have plenty of links to other Web sites useful to independent travellers.

With tens of thousands of visitors a month, the Lonely Planet Web site is one of the most popular on the Internet and has won a number of awards including GNN's Best of the Net travel award.

http://www.lonelyplanet.com

LONELY PLANET PRODUCTS

Lonely Planet is known worldwide for publishing practical, reliable and no-nonsense travel information in our guides and on our web site. The Lonely Planet list covers just about every accessible part of the world. Currently there are eight series: *travel guides, shoestring guides, walking guides, city guides, phrasebooks, audio packs, travel atlases* and *Journeys* – a unique collection of travellers' tales.

EUROPE

Austria • Baltic States & Kaliningrad • Baltic States phrasebook • Britain • Central Europe on a shoestring • Central Europe phrasebook • Czech & Slovak Republics • Denmark • Dublin city guide • Eastern Europe on a shoestring • Eastern Europe phrasebook • Finland • France • Greece • Greek phrasebook • Hungary • Iceland, Greenland & the Faroe Islands • Ireland • Italy • Mediterranean Europe on a shoestring • Mediterranean Europe phrasebook • Poland • Prague city guide • Russia, Ukraine & Belarus • Russian phrasebook • Scandinavian & Baltic Europe on a shoestring • Scandinavian Europe phrasebook • Slovenia • St Petersburg city guide • Switzerland • Trekking in Greece • Trekking in Spain • Ukranian phrasebook • Vienna city guide • Walking in Switzerland • Western Europe on a shoestring • Western Europe phrasebook

NORTH AMERICA

Alaska • Backpacking in Alaska • Baja California• California & Nevada • Canada • Hawaii • Honolulu city guide • Los Angeles city guide • Mexico • Pacific Northwest USA • Rocky Mountain States • San Francisco city guide • Southwest USA • USA phrasebook

CENTRAL AMERICA & THE CARIBBEAN

Central America on a shoestring • Costa Rica • Eastern Caribbean • Guatemala, Belize & Yucatán: La Ruta Maya • Jamaica

SOUTH AMERICA

Argentina, Uruguay & Paraguay • Bolivia • Brazil • Brazilian phrasebook • Buenos Aires city guide • Chile & Easter Island • Colombia • Ecuador & the Galápagos Islands • Latin American Spanish phrasebook • Peru • Quechua phrasebook • Rio de Janeiro city guide • South America on a shoestring • Trekking in the Patagonian Andes • Venezuela

AFRICA

Arabic (Moroccan) phrasebook • Africa on a shoestring • Cape Town city guide • Central Africa • East Africa • Egypt & the Sudan • Ethiopian (Amharic) phrasebook • Kenya • Morocco • North Africa • South Africa, Lesotho & Swaziland • Swahili phrasebook • Trekking in East Africa • West Africa • Zimbabwe, Botswana & Namibia • Zimbabwe, Botswana & Namibia travel atlas

ALSO AVAILABLE:

Travel with Children • Traveller's Tales

MAIL ORDER

Lonely Planet products are distributed worldwide. They are also available by mail order from Lonely Planet, so if you have difficulty finding a title please write to us. North American and South American residents should write to Embarcadero West, 155 Filbert St, Suite 251, Oakland CA 94607, USA; European and African residents should write to 10 Barley Mow Passage, Chiswick, London W4 4PH; and residents of other countries to PO Box 617, Hawthorn, Victoria 3122, Australia.

NORTH-EAST ASIA

Beijing city guide • Cantonese phrasebook • China • Hong Kong, Macau & Canton • Hong Kong city guide • Japan • Japanese phrasebook • Japanese audio pack • Korea • Korean phrasebook • Mandarin phrasebook • Mongolia • Mongolian phrasebook • North-East Asia on a shoestring • Seoul city guide • Taiwan • Tibet • Tibet phrasebook • Tokyo city guide

MIDDLE EAST & CENTRAL ASIA

Arab Gulf States • Arabic (Egyptian) phrasebook • Central Asia • Iran • Israel • Jordan & Syria • Middle East • Turkey • Turkish phrasebook • Trekking in Turkey • Yemen

Travel Literature: The Gates of Damascus

ISLANDS OF THE INDIAN OCEAN

Madagascar & Comoros • Maldives & Islands of the East Indian Ocean • Mauritius, Réunion & Seychelles

INDIAN SUBCONTINENT

Bengali phrasebook • Bangladesh • Delhi city guide • Hindi/Urdu phrasebook • India • India & Bangladesh travel atlas • Karakoram Highway • Kashmir, Ladakh & Zanskar • Nepal • Nepali phrasebook • Pakistan • Sri Lanka • Sri Lanka phrasebook • Trekking in the Indian Himalaya • Trekking in the Nepal Himalaya

SOUTH-EAST ASIA

Bali & Lombok • Bangkok city guide • Burmese phrasebook • Cambodia • Ho Chi Minh city guide • Indonesia • Indonesian phrasebook • Indonesian audio pack • Jakarta city guide • Java • Laos • Lao phrasebook • Malaysia, Singapore & Brunei • Myanmar (Burma) • Philippines • Pilipino phrasebook • Singapore city guide • South-East Asia on a shoestring • Thailand • Thailand travel atlas • Thai phrasebook • Thai audio pack • Thai Hill Tribes phrasebook • Vietnam • Vietnamese phrasebook • Vietnam travel atlas

AUSTRALIA & THE PACIFIC

Australia • Australian phrasebook • Bushwalking in Australia • Bushwalking in Papua New Guinea • Fiji • Fijian phrasebook • Islands of Australia's Great Barrier Reef • Melbourne city guide • Micronesia • New Caledonia • New South Wales & the ACT • New Zealand • Outback Australia • Papua New Guinea • Papua New Guinea phrasebook • Queensland • Rarotonga & the Cook Islands • Samoa • Solomon Islands • South Australia • Sydney city guide • Tahiti & French Polynesia • Tonga • Tramping in New Zealand • Vanuatu • Victoria • Western Australia

Travel Literature: Islands in the Clouds • Sean & David's Long Drive

THE LONELY PLANET STORY

Lonely Planet published its first book in 1973 in response to the numerous 'How did you do it?' questions Maureen and Tony Wheeler were asked after driving, bussing, hitching, sailing and railing their way from England to Australia.

Written at a kitchen table and hand collated, trimmed and stapled, *Across Asia on the Cheap* became an instant local bestseller, inspiring thoughts of another book.

Eighteen months in South-East Asia resulted in their second guide, *South-East Asia on a shoestring*, which they put together in a backstreet Chinese hotel in Singapore in 1975. The 'yellow bible', as it quickly became known to backpackers around the world, soon became *the* guide to the region. It has sold well over half a million copies and is now in its 8th edition, still retaining its familiar yellow cover.

Today there are over 180 titles, including travel guides, walking guides, language kits & phrasebooks, travel atlases and travel literature. The company is one of the largest travel publishers in the world. Although Lonely Planet initially specialised in guides to Asia, we now cover most regions of the world, including the Pacific, North America, South America, Africa, the Middle East and Europe.

The emphasis continues to be on travel for independent travellers. Tony and Maureen still travel for several months of each year and play an active part in the writing, updating and quality control of Lonely Planet's guides.

They have been joined by over 70 authors and 170 staff at our offices in Melbourne (Australia), Oakland (USA), London (UK) and Paris (France). Travellers themselves also make a valuable contribution to the guides through the feedback we receive in thousands of letters each year.

The people at Lonely Planet strongly believe that travellers can make a positive contribution to the countries they visit, both through their appreciation of the countries' culture, wildlife and natural features, and through the money they spend. In addition, the company makes a direct contribution to the countries and regions it covers. Since 1986 a percentage of the income from each book has been donated to ventures such as famine relief in Africa; aid projects in India; agricultural projects in Central America; Greenpeace's efforts to halt French nuclear testing in the Pacific; and Amnesty International.

'I hope we send the people out with the right attitude about travel. You realise when you travel that there are so many different perspectives about the world, so we hope these books will make people more interested in what they see. These are guidebooks, but you can't really guide people. All you can do is point them in the right direction.'
– Tony Wheeler

LONELY PLANET PUBLICATIONS

Australia
PO Box 617, Hawthorn 3122, Victoria
tel: (03) 9819 1877 fax: (03) 9819 6459
e-mail: talk2us@lonelyplanet.com.au

USA
Embarcadero West, 155 Filbert St, Suite 251,
Oakland, CA 94607
tel: (510) 893 8555 TOLL FREE: 800 275-8555
fax: (510) 893 8563
e-mail: info@lonelyplanet.com

UK
10 Barley Mow Passage, Chiswick,
London W4 4PH
tel: (0181) 742 3161 fax: (0181) 742 2772
e-mail: 100413.3551@compuserve.com

France:
71 bis rue du Cardinal Lemoine, 75005 Paris
tel: 1 44 32 06 20 fax: 1 46 34 72 55
e-mail: 100560.415@compuserve.com

World Wide Web: http://www.lonelyplanet.com